Prince William County, Virginia Patriots and Pensioners 1752-1856

Military Records from the
Prince William County, Virginia
Minute and Order Books and
Other Source Records

By
Joan W. Peters, CG

HERITAGE BOOKS
2009

HERITAGE BOOKS
AN IMPRINT OF HERITAGE BOOKS, INC.

Books, CDs, and more—Worldwide

For our listing of thousands of titles see our website
at
www.HeritageBooks.com

Published 2009 by
HERITAGE BOOKS, INC.
Publishing Division
100 Railroad Ave. #104
Westminster, Maryland 21157

Copyright © 2009 Joan W. Peters

All rights reserved. No part of this book may be reproduced or transmitted in any form or by any means, electronic or mechanical, including photocopying, recording or by any information storage and retrieval system without written permission from the author, except for the inclusion of brief quotations in a review.

International Standard Book Numbers
Paperbound: 978-0-7884-4908-6
Clothbound: 978-0-7884-8177-2

Dedicated to the staff at R.E.L.I.C, Beth, Bev, Darlene, Don, and Trish with thanks

ACKNOWLEDGEMENTS

First and foremost, I'd like to give my heart felt thanks to all the staff at the Ruth E. Lloyd Information Center for Local History and Genealogy, better known as R.E.L.I.C, at the Bull Run Regional Library in Manassas, Virginia. Each staff member there made doing long-distance research from Washington State in the genealogy, local history, and microfilm collection in the library a breeze! So, take a collective bow, you deserve it!

Belinda Wisnoski, as in previous projects, was tireless in her effort to run down elusive soldiers who may or may not have been Prince land holders. With her help I was able to pinpoint the whereabouts of several purported veterans of the French and Indian war and the Revolutionary War.

I would be remiss if I did not also add my thanks to Emerson Peters who spent a day working with me on the compilation of the index.

I could not have completed this book without the help of footnote.com. This website made searching the Revolutionary War compiled service records and pension records on file at the National Archives painless, uncomplicated, and straightforward. Especially so, since the North West branch of the Archives is some four hours away in Seattle. It is a website I can recommend without reservation if you have a Revolutionary War ancestor. Added to this commendation is also one touting its ease of operation.

Likewise, Ancestry.com's service records relating to the War of 1812 were also beneficial. Ancestry has placed online the NARA microfilmed publication on M 602, the *Index to compiled service records of Volunteer Soldiers Who served during the War of 1812*. This online publication made it possible to compile a roster of the 36th and 89th Regiments of Virginia Militia, Prince William's two regiments in this war.

The cover illustration and other graphics in this book were copied from images on Dover's *American Historical Illustrations and Emblems*, Electronic Clip Art, Dover Publications, 2001.

Preface

I began this project several years ago with the idea of identifying and expanding the knowledge base of Prince William officers and soldiers in the French and Indian War and Revolutionary War for patrons and staff of R.E.L.I.C. at the Bull Run Regional Library in Manassas, Virginia.

The project then took on a life of its own when records became available on footnote.com and ancestry.com. Footnote has digital images of Revolutionary War service records and Revolutionary War pension files, housed on microfilm at the National Archives and some its branches. Ancestry.com has the War of 1812 service records. These records along with abstracted source records from leading historians have allowed me to identify many of the Prince William veterans and their units.

It is my hope that this survey of Prince William Patriots and Pensioners, drawn from the County Court Minutes and other source records will lead to a greater insight and familiarity with the men and their record base. These records underscore the value in the documentation of Prince William's veterans who took part in the various eighteenth and nineteenth century conflicts.

Joan W. Peters, CG
Coupeville, Washington,
October 2008

ABBREVIATIONS

@	at
Admr	Administrator
Battn	Battalion
bu	bushel
CW	Churchwardens
Capt	Captain
Col	Colonel
C^t	Count
Ct	Court
d	pence
Do, d^o	ditto
DM	Drum Major
d/o	daughter of
dau.	daughter
etc, +c, &c	etcetera
Exor	Executor
Extrx	Executrix
FM	Fife Major or Forage Master
fother	fodder
Gent	Gentleman
Gdn, gdn/o	Guardian, guardian of
grd/o	Grand daughter of
Jr., Jun.	Junior
£	English money in pounds
lb, lbs	pound(s)
Lt, Lieut	Lieutenant
Lt Col	Lieutenant Colonel
p^r	per
OP	Overseers of Poor
Prince Wm.	Prince William
Prvt	Private
PSC	Public Service Claim
PW, PWC	Prince William County
QM,	Quarter Master
Rgt	Regiment
Sgt	Sergeant
Sr., Sen.	Senior
sw^n	Sworn
s/o	son of
w/o	wife of
wid/o	Widow of
/	pence
7/6	7 shilling, 6 pence

TABLE OF CONTENTS

Acknowledgments
Preface
Abbreviations

Introduction

Part I The French and Indian War Period, 1752–1769	1
Chapter 1 Virginia's Militia and the Law: An Overview	3
Chapter 2 Prelude to War	15
Chapter 3 Military Records from the Prince William County Virginia Minute and Order Books, 1752–1759	35
Part II The Revolutionary War Period, 1775–1784	45
Chapter 4 The Transition from a Colonial Militia to A Continental Army	47
Chapter 5 Military Records from the Prince William County, Virginia Minute and Order Books, 1778–1784	63
Part III The War of 1812 Period, 1804–1806, 1812–1814	95
Chapter 6 Historical Introduction	97
Chapter 7 Military Records from the Prince William County, Virginia Minute and Order Books, 1804–1806, 1812–1814, Paymaster Acct, 36th Rgt, Virginia Militia, in Prince William County, Virginia Deed Book, 1804–1806	113
Part IV Prince William Pensioners, 1833–1850, 1853–1856	125
Chapter 8 Historical Introduction and Overview of Pension and Bounty Land Law	127
Chapter 9 Military Records from the Prince William County, Virginia Minute and Order Books, 1833–1850, 1853–1856	151
Appendices	
Appendix 1 A Partial Listing of Prince William Soldiers and Officers, French and Indian War from other Source Records	169
Appendix 2 Elijah Green's Pension File S 37961, 1818–1836	189
Appendix 3 Patrollers, 1804–1806, The 36th and 89th Regiments Virginia Militia, War of 1812, and Major Townsend Dade's Court martial proceedings, November 1806 from the Fauquier County Clerks Loose Papers	195
Index	221
Bibliography	365

INTRODUCTION

HISTORICAL BACKGROUND

1. The Formation of Prince William County

Prince William County was formed in late March 1731 from Stafford and King George Counties. Its formation was recorded in Henings, *Statutes at Large* for March 1731. The legislature created this new county because of the "divers and sundry inconveniences" which the "upper inhabitants" of Stafford and King George, experienced when they had to travel great distances to the courthouse and other places selected for public meetings. The county's new bounds were placed within the headwaters of Stafford and King George above Chappawamsick Creek on the Potomac and then ran in a southwesterly direction from the head waters of Deep Run.

The County Court, the colonial legislators decided, was to meet on the third Wednesday of every month.[1] Next on the agenda was the nomination and oath taking of the new Justices. This was the Governor's responsibility, with advice given him by his Council.

So, a little more than a month later, in late April 1731, Governor Gooch nominated Justices of the Peace for the new County Court. These Justices were Thomas Harrison, Dennis McCarty, William Linton, Francis Awbry, Robert Jones, Burr Harrison, Moses Quarles, Leonard Barker, William Harrison, Valentine Barker, John Wright, John Allen, William Hackney, and Joseph Hudnal. The governor also appointed Robert Jones as High Sheriff.

Once these men were appointed, the next task was to survey the new county. The Governor ordered the Surveyor of the county to run and mark the dividing line from Chappawamsick to Deep Run in order to establish the bounds between the new county and Stafford and King George. The last step in the process was the placement of the new Court, which, it was decided, was to be held on the upper side of the Occoquan near the ferry landing. It was left to the justices to take care of the building of a court house, prison, pillory, and stocks.

At the time the county was formed in 1731, the upper side of the Occoquan near the ferry was the site of the Hamilton Parish church. However, John Warner's Map of the Northern Neck, drawn in 1737, located the new courthouse on the *lower* side of the Occoquan, on land formerly owned by George Mason.[2]

Once all this had been done, the Justices met, took their oaths of office and began to conduct the official business of the County. Court was now, as they say, "in session."

2. The Prince William County Court Minute and Order Books

The court minutes, recorded by the clerk of the court, recounted the daily activities of the county court. These proceedings were varied and diverse. They comprised grand jury presentments and indictments; civil and criminal suits filed as ended causes; notices of land conveyances, like deeds, leases, and trusts; probate records, like the recordation of wills, appraisements, inventories, guardianships, and appointments of administrators and executors of estates; churchwarden apprenticeship indentures, records relating to slaves; road petitions for more convenient ways to travel to mills, to ports like Dumfries or Alexandria, or even to the new county courthouse. The Court normally appointed surveyors and overseers of the roads.

---

[1] William Waller Hening, *Statutes at Large,* May 1730 (http://vagenweb.org/hening/vol04-15.htm), 5:303 (Accessed July 16, 2008). Afterwards, Hening, *Statutes at Large.*

[2] Fairfax Harrison, *Landmarks of Old Prince William (*1924; reprint, Baltimore: Gateway Press, 1987), 314–315.

Unfortunately, the early minute books from 1731–1751 are missing. This means that the earliest minute books for the county begin in 1752. Fortunately, the minute books from 1752–1769 are still extant. So, it is these minute and order books that chronicled the military activities of Prince William's soldiers and officers during the French and Indian War.

3. Military Records in the Prince William Court Order and Minute Books

Indeed, the military records found here made for some of the most interesting reading in these records books. During the French and Indian War, the minute books from 1752–1769 regularly encompassed militia slave patrols, recommendation of the appointment of colonial militia officers, and their oaths.

The minute book for the Revolutionary War period formed an even more assorted record base. Recommendations for militia officers and their oaths of office, county assistance to families whose sons or husbands were in the service, disability pensions, public service records, and other records relating to revolutionary war soldiers in difficulty with the law filled these pages of the 1778–1784 order book. There was even a certification of bounty land to heirs of French and Indian War officers uncovered here. In addition, the Court was responsible for certifying service of soldiers in the Revolutionary war who presented discharges to the court and for the certification of heirs at law of officers and soldiers who had died in the service of their country.

The War of 1812 period was comprised of the two extant minutes books which remain for that time frame: those for 1804–1806, and another set for 1812–1814. Because of the missing court minutes from 1800–1803, 1807–1811, and 1815–1818, researchers must look to other sources for disability pensions of Revolutionary War veterans from Prince William.

However, the military records for these two minute books that *did* survive, allow a glimpse into Prince William's two regiments of Virginia's militia during this time frame. Military records showed increased militia slave patrols as well as military appointments to the two militia regiments in Prince William. The Prince William Deed Book 1805–1807 has been included because it contained a paymaster account for the 36th Regiment of the Virginia Militia. This account named various officers in that regiment.

The Minutes books from 1815–1832 have been lost. This meant that the names of those veterans who applied in Prince William for a need-based pension according to the March 1818 Pension Act have also been lost so researchers must look elsewhere for these pensioners.

Fortunately, the minute books from 1833–1853 and for 1853–1856 have survived. These books are a gold-mine of information for anyone doing Revolutionary War research. Heirs at law, Revolutionary War pensioners, soldiers in Virginia State regiments and Virginia Continental Line regiments, sailing-masters and seamen in Virginia's State Navy, and pension declarations and schedules fill these pages. There was even a Mexican War soldier in these minute books and the notice of the death by drowning of a Brevet Colonel of Artillery whose family resided in Prince William.

ORGANIZATION AND CONTENT

I have divided the minute books into four different time frames, suggested by the dating of the minute book's records. An historical overview of the importance of the law in relation to the militia follows this introduction. This overview provides a backdrop for the transition from a colonial militia in the French and Indian War to the enlistment of men into Virginia Line Regiments on the Continental Establishment and various State Regiments and other Continental units like Colonel William Grayson's Additional Continental Regiment.

Each of the four sections—the French and Indian War Period, the Revolutionary War Period, the War of 1812 period, and the Pensioners— have their own introduction, acquainting the reader with the salient historical context within the time frame being discussed.

Part I has three chapters associated with it. **Chapter 1** begins with an overview of the law in relation to the militia. It is essential to understand this relationship since it was the colonial legislature that wrote the regulations for the militia. The Governor acted as the commander-in-chief. **Chapter 2** deals with the French and Indian War and provides a discussion of the undeclared war in British North America along the Virginia, Maryland, and Pennsylvania frontier. Hostilities here erupted in 1753 as a result of the French presence in the Ohio River Valley. It concludes with the Braddock Expedition and its consequences. All of these events occurred well before the official outbreak of hostilities in May 1755.

With this backdrop in mind, the surviving Prince William Court Minute and Order book, the subject of **Chapter 3**, offer insight into the local Court's responsibilities relating to the militia, Colonel Washington's Virginia Regiment, and veterans whose day-to-day activities sometimes connected with those of the Court. The extant record books cover the period from 1752–1769, found on LVA Microfilm Rolls 25, 25a, and 26.

These books are filled with the names of Prince William militia officers. Wherever possible, these officers have been identified from information in the *Journals of the House of Burgesses*, and Lloyd DeWitt Bockstruck's *Virginia Colonial Soldiers,* along with other derivative sources.

Part II concerns the Revolutionary War. The introductory chapter, **Chapter 4,** discusses the colonial militia and the transition from a local defense force to a Continental Army. It is necessary here to understand the fundamental differences between a local militia organized for local defense, and the formation of a Continental Army, organized as a combat unit.

While the Prince William militia officers were involved from a County Court perspective, the war was fought on a Continental level. Not much is known about the part Prince William's militia played in the larger context of a Continental war. The same rules operated in this war as in the war with the French and Indians. The local militia was used as a defense force. The militia was called out on a state-wide basis only after Cornwallis invaded the state.

Chapter 5 concerns the military establishment during the Revolutionary War in the newly-recovered minute book for the county from 1778–1784, on LVA Microfilm Roll 88.

Many of the officers and men here have also been identified thanks to Revolutionary War service records on footnote.com and the microfilmed records at the National Archives. I used Francis B. Heitman's *Historical Register of the Officers of the Continental Army during the War of the Revolution, 1775–1783*, and E. M. Sanchez-Saavedra, *Guide to Virginia Military Organizations in the American Revolution, 1774–1787* to find Virginia Continental Line, State Regimental, and county militia officers. Hamilton Eckenrode's *Virginia Soldiers of the American Revolution* and J.T. McAllister's *Virginia Militia in the Revolutionary War* were also helpful in pinpointing Virginia Continental and militia veterans.

Part III begins with an introduction to the War of 1812, in **Chapter 6**, and concludes with **Chapter 7** which gives details of the officers and men who fought in this war. The Court minute books confirm the continuing dedication that the generation following the revolution from Prince William had; these young men were just as patriotic and active in the Virginia militia service. They, too, joined the two Prince William Militia units: Colonel Enoch Rennoe's 36th Virginia and Colonels Philip Klipstine and Gerrard Alexander's 89th Virginia Regiment of Militia to fight in the War of 1812.

These minute books provide a glimpse into this little-known period of Prince William military history. There are only two minute books that have survived this time frame, one from 1804–1806 and the other from 1812–1814, both found on LVA's microfilm roll 26.

Many of the officers and militia slave patrols could be identified, thanks to NARA's *Index to Compiled Service Records for volunteers ... for the War of 1812,* M602 found in Ancestry.com's collection of military records. Other local militia records were found in the two volume set from the Rolls of the Auditor's Office in Richmond, *Virginia Militia in the War of 1812.*

Part **IV**'s introductory chapter, **Chapter 8,** presents an overview of pension law from 1778–1856. An understanding of the law in relation to the veteran is critical to understanding the position of the government in relation to paying the soldier well after the war was over as well as to understanding the attitude of the veteran who believed his government had forgotten him. Many of these men simply wished to hold the federal government accountable for promises made them decades before. Most of the pensions applied for in the Court Minutes were for services rendered in the Revolution.

The real worth of the information found in **Chapter 9,** in the 1833–1856 minutes, can not be underestimated. Most of these men have now been identified thanks to either their pension applications or their service records, found as part of the National Archives collection of Revolutionary War records on footnote.com.

These records furnished some of the most valuable information in the minute books as it applied to Revolutionary War and War of 1812 pensions and service records. They were recorded in minute and order books from 1833–1850 and 1853–1856 on LVA's microfilm roll 27.

The men mentioned in these minute books could be easily identified by either their pensions or their service records, many of which were found on footnote.com. Officers were determined by records from E. M. Sanchez-Saavedra's *Guide to Virginia Military Organizations in the American Revolution* or Francis B. Heitman's *Historical Register of the Officers of the Continental Army.*

Sometimes earlier pensions could be found in nearby counties. I discovered at least one Prince William resident who had applied for a pension in Fauquier. Several of the Prince William pensioners served in the 3rd Virginia and were identified in my newly published *History of the Third Virginia Continental Regiment: With Flags Flying and Drums Beating, 1776–1778.* Others served in the 1st Virginia State Regiment, Grayson's Additional Continental Regiment, and various other Virginia Continental Line units; their records were found on footnote.com.

Three Appendices have been included. The first Appendix makes a stab at identifying Prince William men who fought in the French and Indian War. Size rolls kept by commanding officers in Colonel Washington's regiment were extremely helpful in this process. Lloyd Bockstruck's *Virginia's Colonial Soldiers* and his *Bounty and Donation Land Grants in British North America,* Murtie June Clark's *Colonial Soldiers of the South 1732–1774,* and the *Virginia Military Records from the William and Mary Quarterly, the Magazine of History and Biography, and Tyler's Quarterly* all contributed to the process.

The second appendix details the struggle that Elijah Green underwent in his successful and lengthy attempt to obtain a Revolutionary War pension. He first applied in 1818, was initially granted a pension which was taken away a year later because it was determined that his unit was a state regiment and not a continental one. The appendix describes his determined and sustained individual efforts, the county's attempt and his family's endeavors to restore this pension.

The third appendix deals with the men in the 1803-1814 militia's slave patrols who were members of Colonel Enoch Renno's 36th Regiment of Virginia Militia who saw action in the War of 1812. Also included are muster rolls of several Captains for both the 36th and the 89th Regiment, along with the rosters for both regiments. Both the 36th and 89th regiments were recruited from Prince William and other Northern Virginia counties.

Finally, an every name index and a bibliography complete this volume.

THE USE OF PRIMARY AND DERIVATIVE SOURCES

The search for a French and Indian soldier or officer should begin on the local level, with the Court minute and order books for that period, if extant. If that is not possible, then other sources should be consulted. H. R. McIwaine's *Journals of the House of Burgesses* is an excellent place to begin or to add to your knowledge base of French and Indian soldiers. Lloyd Bockstruck has written two excellent books on this period, one on *Virginia's Colonial Soldiers* and the other on *Bounty and Donation Land Grants in British Colonial America*. Two other excellent primary source records for men in the French and Indian War include Murtie June Clark's *Colonial Soldiers of the South 1732–1774* and *Virginia Military Records* from the *Virginia Magazine of History and Biography*, the *William and Mary Quarterly*, and *Tyler's Quarterly*. The latter details muster rolls and County units during the war.

There are a plethora of original record sources available for the Revolutionary War. Heitman's *Historical Register of Officers of the Continental Army 1775–1783* is one such source that comes immediately to mind, especially for those with a Revolutionary War officer who served in the Continental Line. Both Lloyd Bockstruck's *Revolutionary War Bounty Land Grants Awarded by State Governments* and Marcus Gauis Brumbaugh's *Revolutionary War Records: Virginia* are unusually noteworthy for their information on bounty land recipients in the Northwest Territory. Other sources, like W. T. R. Saffell's *Records of the Revolutionary War* feature men in muster and pay rolls and provide other information relating to the record base for this conflict.

Whenever possible, I have used microfilmed Revolutionary War military sources and pension papers found at the National Archives, and digitized on footnote.com, and War of 1812 Records found on Ancestry.com.

Stuart Butler's *Guide to Virginia Militia Units in the War of 1812* is a book everyone should have on their shelves, especially those who had an ancestor who fought in this war. It explains Virginia's militia system in the first decade of the eighteenth century and breaks down by county, the militia units who fought in the war. Another extremely important source for this war is the Auditor's Rolls at Richmond on the Virginia Militia for the war. Muster rolls and pay rolls reveal names of soldiers who took part in this conflict between 1812–1814.

It is essential that researchers interested in these eighteenth and nineteenth century wars understand the niceties of the law—Continental, federal, and state—especially as it related to the appointment of officers, guidelines for relief for families, the award of bounty land for service, and the entire pension system. An overview of Continental and Congressional legislation may be found in Christine Rose's *Military Pension Laws 1775–1858*. This is another book that belongs on everyone's bookshelf, especially if you have an ancestor who applied for a pension.

William Waller Hening's *Statutes at Large* have been transcribed up to 1792 online at vagenweb.org. Samuel Shepard's *Statute at Large of Virginia from October 1792 to December 1806* may be found in the larger genealogical collections on the state and regional level.

While the sources listed here are by no means a listing of the entire primary record base relating to these hostilities it is important to note that there are other original source records that should be examined in researching the men who served in various units in these three important eighteenth and nineteenth century wars. The number and quality of primary and derivative sources a researcher utilizes determines the quality of the profile or snapshot of the soldier. The more, the better, especially in terms of the original record base. Beginning with the local record base and expanding it to include other original sources will only help lend insight into the soldier's "historical present," — how he lived his life in his own time.

CAVEATS

Caveats deal with certain underlying assumptions as well as warnings and cautions relating to the data found in the narrative. They act as a sort of "Be aware that the author has…" Below are several caveats associated with the narrative in this book.

While I have kept the spelling true to its time period, I have used modern punctuation and paragraphing when quoting from historical sources. I have found it easier to understand the writer if words are not capitalized in the middle of a sentence and accounts are broken into paragraphs from page long paragraphs of the original.

I have used footnotes rather than endnotes primarily because the note usually carries an explanation of either a reference or of a further explanation relating to the soldier. The reader then does not have to go to the end of the chapter. He or she merely needs to go to the bottom of the page.

In general, I have followed the format described in *Evidence Explained* by Elizabeth Shown Mills for footnote citations. For online citations, it is my understanding that access dates need not be cited if they are more than two years old. I have followed that policy here. Only online records accessed in the past two years are indicated here.

While many of the Court entries have been given verbatim, others have been summarized. I have not differentiated between the two in the Court record narratives. In any event, I have included all the important information found therein.

Despite my best efforts, I have found that errors sometimes creep into the compilation of narratives dealing with court records, especially in the form of "typos" or in the format of citations. While I have made every effort to escape these pesky little faults, "due diligence" is often not enough to prevent their omission.

A Colonial Militiaman

Part I

The French and Indian War Period
1752–1769

Chapter 1

Virginia's Militia and the Law: An Overview

Chapter 2

Prelude to War

An Undeclared War Begins: Jumonville Glen, May, 1754

Fort Necessity, June 1754

The Braddock Expedition, May to July 1755

Chapter 3

Military Records from the Prince William County Minute and Order Books 1752–1769

A Colonial Militiaman

FRENCH AND INDIAN WAR PERIOD

CHAPTER 1

VIRGINIA'S MILITIA AND THE LAW: AN OVERVIEW

HISTORICAL BACKGROUND

Many of the entries in the Prince William County court minutes dealt with the appointment and oaths of office of militia officers. This was especially true for the court minutes between 1752–1769, and 1804–1806, and 1812–1814. The 1752–1769 minutes fell roughly into the time frame of the French and Indian War while the nineteenth century records alluded to, were found to be in the War of 1812 time period.

In order to understand the importance of the militia in the lives of eighteenth century settlers and nineteenth century inhabitants, it is essential to understand the law, since the legislature was responsible for the militia's regulation. The governor and his council, on the other hand, called out the militia when it was needed to put down civil unrest and to protect the frontier.

It is also vital to understand how the county formation impacted the movement of the frontier and the need to protect those outer-most borders from enemy attacks. Both the legislative acts relating to a military force and a requirement to protect frontier settlements from Indian attacks make a compelling case for a brief review of seventeenth century events and acts. Many of the eighteenth century traditions about the county militia had their precedents set in the preceding century.

It should be kept in mind, too, that the northern-most frontier of seventeenth century Virginia was Stafford County. The county was large and included most of the future Prince William County, Fauquier County, Loudoun County, and Fairfax County. The last three counties had been formed from Prince William by the mid-eighteenth century.

1. A brief history of Virginia County formation to 1700.

The frontier expanded westward as the colony grew from the original northern neck settlements. Colonists moved up the rivers into areas formerly inhabited by Indians. The original counties, Charles City, Henrico, Isle of Wight, James City, Northampton, Warwick River, and York, had all been formed by 1634. Norfolk followed in 1636, Lower Norfolk and Nansemond in 1637.

A period of consolidation followed with another movement north to the Maryland line and westward onto the colony's frontier. Northumberland was formed from the Indian District of Chickacoan in 1648. In the next decade, a flurry of counties had their legislative beginnings—Gloucester, in 1651; Surry, in 1652; Westmoreland, in 1653; and Lancaster and New Kent, in 1654. These counties were all along the major river ways, the James, the Rappahannock, and the Potomac. In 1664, Stafford was formed, the northern most outpost of Virginia's settlements.

Three years before Bacon's unsuccessful rebellion in 1676, Middlesex County was formed. Then eighteen years later, in 1691, King and Queen was created, followed quickly, a year later, by Essex and Richmond. The new century saw the formation of King William in 1700.[1]

2. Setting the stage for legislation: Eighteenth Century Indian and Settler's relations.

To appreciate the value of the militia fully, especially during the French and Indian War and the War of 1812 where militia forces were used extensively, it is necessary to briefly review its legislative roots.

In the seventeenth century, there were two certainties that would push the legislature into action: hostile Indians on the frontier and the fear of invasion from a foreign enemy. These were not idle fears. By the third quarter of the century, settlers on the frontier began to demand that Indians living on treaty-

---
[1] George Everton, *The Handy Book for Genealogists*, 8th Edition (Logan: Everton Publishers, 1991), 263–273.

protected land be driven out or killed. Militia forces raided a settlement there and killed thirty natives. Acting against the Governor's orders, a larger force surrounded and attacked a Susquehannock village, killing chiefs, who on the governor's advice, were going to negotiate with the militia. The Susquehannock retaliated by attacking plantations and killing hundreds of settlers on the frontier.

The Governor opted for a policy of containment, proposing a series of forts along the frontier to keep watch over the Indians. Frontier settlements were not impressed. They thought the plan expensive and inadequate and just another reason to raise taxes.[2]

While all this was occurring along the frontier, there were other problems with the Indians closer to home. In 1675, the Conestoga tribe, driven from their home on the Susquehanna River in Delaware and Maryland, were forced into Virginia where they attacked white settlements along the coast. The Virginia tribes were accused of these attacks and a number of unauthorized expeditions were led against them.

In June 1676, the legislature declared war on the Indians and made provisions for a military force of 1000 men to prosecute the war. Among the provisions in this act was the distribution of forces between horsemen and foot soldiers. One eighth was to be horsemen and dragoons with proportionate amount of troops from the counties of the time. Stafford was to provide twenty-nine men, who were to be paid by the county. Other provisions included authorization to the justices and militia officers in the county to raise the men and provide provisions for the troops. The county had a month to ready and convey the troops to the mustering field appointed by the commander-in-chief, who was to be Nathaniel Bacon Jr.

Foot soldiers were to be paid 1500 pounds of tobacco a year and after that, a proportionate for the time they served. Horsemen were to be paid 2250 pounds of tobacco a year. Any Indians taken prisoner were to be considered slaves for life. As in other acts dealing with military forces, any soldiers maimed and disabled in the service were to be maintained by the public by an annual pension for life, during the time they were disabled.

The legislature also decreed that forts in Henrico, New Kent and Rappahannock were to be discontinued and the soldiers stationed there, to be transferred to the frontier.

The military forces were divided into a southern force and a northern force. New Kent and counties north of it were considered northern forces. Thus Stafford County's troops were in the northern tier.[3]

The war ended quickly. In August 1676, the Indians made a stand at a fort near Richmond and were massacred. The remnants of the Virginia tribes sued for peace which was granted on condition of an annual tribute to the colonial government from each village.[4]

3. Bacon's Rebellion

Meanwhile Bacon had emerged as a rebel leader; he accused Berkeley of corruption, when he failed to be granted a military commission to attack the Indians. So he mustered his own forces, some 400–500 men and attacked the Doeg and Pamunkey tribes. The only problem here was that they had not been involved in the previous confrontations. Berkeley then had Bacon arrested although his men quickly secured his release and forced a new election of the Burgesses.

The newly elected legislature enacted a number of reforms, limiting the power of the governor and granting suffrage to freemen who did not own land. Berkeley, however, refused to authorize any retaliation against the natives. It appeared that he did this because he had investments in the fur trading business with the Indians and these resources would have been jeopardized.

In July 1676, Bacon and his followers issued a document called the *Declaration of the People of Virginia*. Virginia's native Indians were to be either killed or removed. Berkeley's administration as governor was harshly criticized. The governor came under attack on three points: he levied unfair taxes,

---

[2] "Nathaniel Bacon (diplomat)," Wikipedia, the free encyclopedia (http://en.wikipedia.org/wiki/Nataniel_Bacon_%28Diplomat%29). Afterwards, "Nathaniel Bacon (diplomat)."

[3] Hening, *Statutes at Large*, June 1676 (http://vagenweb.org/hening/vol02-17.htm), 2: 342–349.

[4] "Powhatan Indian Tribe History" (http://www.accessgenealogy.com/native/tribes/powhatan/powhatanhist.htm).

he appointed friends to his position, and most damning, he failed to protect farmers on the frontier against Indian attacks. Two months later, Bacon and his followers burned down Jamestown.

Before the English could arrive to restore order, Nathaniel Bacon died, in October 1676, from dysentery. His rebellion, now without a leader, collapsed. Governor Berkeley then seized the property of several of the rebels and hung twenty-three of them. However, upon an investigation of his administration, Charles II relieved him of the governorship and Berkeley returned to England.[5]

4. Legislation to keep watch on Indian movements along the frontier 1679–1684.

The outcome of these events was a November 1679 legislative act, setting up four forts and garrisons of rangers to watch Indian movements on the frontier. One of those garrisons was to be erected at Neabsco, near the Occoquan in Stafford. A long store house, sixty by twenty-two feet, was to be built to store ammunition and paid for by public taxes. Major Isaac Allerton, Colonels St Ledger Codd and George Mason were to provide the building materials and be reimbursed by the residents in the counties where they lived.

The other storehouses were to be located on the head waters of Virginia's major rivers: the Rappahannock, the Mattapony above the Indian towns there, and the James. Every forty Tithables within the colony were assessed to provide one completely armed man for the garrisons. So, depending on the population, the garrisons would provide adequate defense against Indian attacks. The soldiers were to assist in building the forts and garrisons were to be provided with a boat and oars sufficient to carry at least four horses.

Soldiers who were wounded or disabled in actions against the Indians were granted annual pensions at the discretion of the assembly.[6]

In June 1680, the legislature decided to continue the defensive fortifications and garrisons. However, in November 1682, the passed laws to dismantle the forts and disband the soldier serving there because they felt it placed a tax burden on the colony. Instead, the Burgess decreed that twenty men were to be raised from Henrico, New Kent, Rappahannock, and Stafford, to act as rangers along the frontier. These men were to scout and spy out Indian movements and notify the militia on possible threats.[7]

It is interesting to see that this legislation specifically called for rangers, *not* militia, to keep an eye on possible Indian threats along the frontier. The rangers were the first line of defense in the event of a possible Indian attack. The militia was the second and last line of defense.

In April 1684, legislation was passed with two purposes in mind: first, to allow colonists to provide themselves with arms and ammunition, so that if called upon, they could defend themselves. The second purpose provided for the arming of the militia.

Within two years, the Burgesses stated, the mounted troopers in the militia in each county were to furnish themselves with a horse, saddle, and all necessary arms and accoutrements. Foot soldiers were to supply themselves with a sword, musket, and accoutrements needed as a soldier. Both horse and foot soldiers were to be provided with two pounds of powder and eight pounds of shot. They were to keep their arms cleaned and fit for service.

Captain and troop commanders of both the mounted and foot soldiers were to hold musters at least once every three months, or more often if the situation warranted. The colonels in charge of county militia regiments were to hold a general muster each year on the first Thursday in October.[8]

Later that month, the legislature, governor and his council all decided to repeal the previous acts setting up forts and garrison troops. Instead they desired "a standing force for the more sure and safe guarding the frontiers," The hoped, with the establishment of a more permanent military presence, to

---

[5] "Nathaniel Bacon (diplomat) (http://www.wikipedia.org).
[6] Hening, *Statutes at Large,* April 1679 (http://vagenweb.org/hening/vol02-21. htm), 2: 434–439. (Accessed July 16, 2008).
[7] Ibid., November 1682, (http://vagenweb.org/hening/vol02-24htm), 2: 499–501.
[8] Ibid., April 1684, 3: 13–14.

prevent the murders, depredations, and incursions by the Indians. These new troops were *not* considered militia troops. Instead they were horsemen who scouted the area and spied out potential Indian incursions.

To do this, the colonial government decreed that four troops of horsemen, thirty able-bodied men per troop, were to be raised. They were to be well-horsed and armed. Every soldier was to have a good, able horse, a case of pistols, a carbine, a sword and any other accoutrement necessary for a horse soldier.

One of the four troops was to be raised on the upper parts of the James River, one troop from the upper parts of the York River, one troop from the upper parts of the Rappahannock, while the last troop was to be raised from the upper parts of the Potomac. The governor and legislature hoped this could be done by volunteers; however, if not, then the governor was authorized to issue warrants for raising the numbers of men needed to complete the troops.

Chief officers of the militia were given the responsibility to nominate to the governor, men who were the most fit and able to be Captains of each of the four frontier companies. Troops were to be mustered every month. The forces were to range and scout about the heads of the rivers to which they were appointed at least once a week, or more often, if the occasion demanded. In order to do this effectively, the forces were to be quartered near their own frontiers as near together to one another as possible.

At the first discovery of the enemy, the troops were to report back to the militia officer in their area. The militia officer were then to immediately "put the militia under their command, in a posture of defence and readiness ..." As in previous acts, the legislature arranged for annual pensions for soldiers wounded and disabled in the King's service.[9]

5. Interlude I: The frontier expands: January 1686 "Brenton" or "Brent Town" Grant of 30,000 acres in Stafford

Two years later, in January 1686, Lord Culpeper, head of the Fairfax Proprietary, granted a huge slice of territory, some 30,000 acres known as the "Brenton Grant," to Nicholas Hayward, George Brent, Richard Foote, and Robert Bristow. This grant was located in Stafford County between the Rappahannock and the Potomac and the branches of Occoquan, spreading westward towards the mountains.[10] The four proprietors wanted "Brenton," or "Brent Town," as it came to be called, as a religious haven for French Huguenots.[11]

There was one challenge, however, to settlement. The grant was in the middle of Indian territory. The Iroquois were proving difficult to track and a block house had been erected on the grant as early as 1692 to keep an eye out for their movements. In 1695, the Virginia Council had bolstered this military activity when they ordered Rangers to "give particular care to guard Brent Town."[12]

When the Iroquois drove the Susquehannock out of Maryland in the mid seventeenth century, they took over the vanquished tribe's trading path which had been established to trade with the Indians in the Carolinas. Instead of a trade path, the Iroquois used it as a path for their marauding expeditions.. At the time, this path was located western most edge of what was to become the Brent Town grant, the portion issued to Nicholas Hayward. Parts of the path were located above Walnut Creek, and crossed Cedar Run, following the course of Elk Run to the eighteenth century site of Elk Run Church and from there moving southward.[13] Only a small portion of this hunting path traversed the Brent Town Grant, enough, however, to place an observation point to observe the Iroquois's movements.

The Iroquois, not liking their movements being traced, decided to make a detour northward in their route to the south and avoid the persistent eyes of the rangers stationed at the blockhouse at Brenton. After they abandoned this path, white settlers in the region called it the "Shenandoah Hunting Path."

---

[9] Ibid., (http://vagenweb.org/hening/vol03-01htm), 3: 17–22.
[10] Fauquier County Bicentennial Committee, *Fauquier County, Virginia 1759–1959* (Warrenton: Virginia Publishing, 1959), 12. Afterwards, FCBC.
[11] Harrison, 177–178.
[12] Ibid., 181–183.
[13] FCBC, 39.

Unfortunately, these events did not materially affect the settlement of the Brenton Grant as Huguenots were lured by promises of better land elsewhere. Then, too, since the grant had never been surveyed, it proved difficult to attract settlers, especially when they did not know where the bounds of the larger grant were to be located. Eventually the fort was abandoned, since the Iroquois were no longer around, and the rangers at the outpost disbanded, and sent home.

6. Early eighteenth century legislation strengthens the militia and ranger service 1701–1705

In 1700, events in Europe threatened the colonies with involvement in what came to be called Queen Anne's War by the British colonies of North America. It was largely a European War fought between England, Holland, and Austria against France.

Military action in the colonies was limited to New England, the Carolinas, and Florida.[14] While Virginia was not directly involved, their colonial legislature was sufficiently alarmed to pass legislation that would strengthen their frontier against attacks by Indian allies of the French and to set up lookouts along the coast for any possible enemy approaches, meaning the French navy.

In August 1701, the colonial government attempted to do just that. They wanted to encourage settlement of the frontier to offset dangers from that region as well as to discourage Indian incursions. Once the provisions for settlement had been attended to, the Burgesses turned to the protection of the frontier.

A fort, they decreed, was to be set up on every 500 acres of land opened for settlement on the frontier with at least one "able warlike Christian man between sixteen and sixty ..., perfect of limb, able and fit for service." He was to be provided with a musket, pistol, a sharp simeter,[15] tomahawk, and five pounds of good, clean pistol powder and twenty pounds of sizeable leaden bullets. He was to live and have his dwelling there, and be within 200 acres of a palisaded fort that was to be built within the middle of the grant. Within two years after that, Grantees were responsible for providing ten more armed "able warlike Christian men," to man the fort.

While the governor could appoint the fort's commander, the soldiers were to reside within the fort and be responsible for all the military affairs according to orders received either from the royal governor of the colony's commander-in-chief. Fort commanders were also expected to give the colonial government some direction regarding raising the necessary troops and maintaining and keeping the forts in good repair.

Militarily, these forces were expected to see to the further security of the frontier as well as the sea "during these times of danger and for discovering the approaches of an enemy by sea...", especially along the coastal counties. They were to act as rangers, spying out possible enemy threats, especially from Indian allies of the French and Spanish.

Once enemy threats were verified, reports were to be made to the militia forces. If such a situation arose, the chief militia officer in any frontier county was authorized immediately to issue warrants for impressing a horse, man, and boat to carry the message to the governor.

Chief Officers of the militia in the next adjacent frontier county was authorized to "call together such numbers of the militia as he [thought] fitt," and together with the advice of his commissioned officers, march the militia against the enemy, thereby "battling, repelling, subduing, taking, killing, or destroying them."

If the militia were out for more than four days, they were to receive pay for each day after that. Captains, after finding himself a horse, arms, ammunition, provisions and other needed items, ten thousand pounds of tobacco and cask for one year, or in proportion to a shorter or longer time; lieutenants, after providing themselves with the same material, were to receive five thousand pounds of tobacco and cask for a year, in proportion to the time they served. Private soldiers, after outfitting

---

[14] Howard H. Peckham, *The Colonial Wars, 1689–1762* (Chicago: University of Chicago Press, 1964), 59–60.

[15] This may be a seventeenth century spelling for a *scimitar*, which was a short, curved sword with an edge. See *Merriam-Webster's Collegiate Dictionary*, 10th Edition (Springfield: Merriam-Webster's Incorporated, 1994), 1201.

themselves, were to receive three thousand pounds of tobacco and cask for one year in proportion to their tours.[16]

The military provisions in this act have been described in some detail for several reasons. First, they legislature showed that it was well aware of the importance of a quiet frontier, especially in the light of the European War that ensued over the succession crisis caused by the death of Charles II of Spain, without an heir in 1701. It lasted twelve years, with the British emerging as the clear victor and France, as the clear loser. Secondly, the legislature continued its reliance on a fast moving ranging unit, placed on the frontier as a watchdog to seek out potential Indian threats. They were *not* a combat unit, but an observation one. Once a threat had been determined, they notified the militia who then swung into action and acted as a local defense unit to protect the frontier. The militia was short term troops. They were not a combat unit.

During this war, called Queen Anne's war by the colonists, the Virginia legislature took steps to put the militia on a firm footing with an act in October 1705 for the "settling, arming and training" of a militia for Her Majesty's service. The militia was to be ready "on all occasions for the defence and preservation of the colony. The chief officers of the county militia were to list all males from sixteen to sixty within his county. They were required to serve either as mounted horsemen or as foot soldiers. It was up to the chief officer to assign them to either force, taking into consideration their abilities.

There were exemptions, of course, to serving in this local defense force. Members of Her Majesty's council, a speaker or former speaker of the House of Burgesses, Her Majesty's Attorney General, present and former, Justices of the Peace within the colony, ministers, clerks of the court, parish clerks or schoolmasters, overseers with four or more slaves under his care, constables, millers, imported servants, and slaves were all specifically relieved from service in the militia.

So were, surprisingly, men who had a military commission of captain or higher. They were to be relieved "merely for the dignity of the office" they held. However, they *were* required to provide and keep at their homes a trooper's horse, arms, and ammunition and produce these to the chief militia officer at a general muster every year. So it appears that these officers need not appear at the periodic musters held throughout the year; instead their presence was required at yearly musters. Overseers were also exempted if they had responsibility for four or more slaves. If an overseer *did* show up, then he was expected to appear with arms and perform his duty as any other private soldiers in the militia did.

In the event of a rebellion or an insurrection, the militia was obliged to appear under their colonel or chief militia officer in the county in which they resided. They were to serve in "such stations as are suitable for gentlemen." As in the earlier 1701 act, the chief militia officer was responsible for making a list of capable men and enrolling them into troops or companies.

Troopers and foot soldiers were responsible for providing their arms and ammunition. Foot soldiers were to be provided with a firelock, musket or fusee,[17] a good sword and cartouch box,[18] and six charges of powder. He was to bring these with him to the musters. In addition, he was required to keep two pounds of powder and eight pounds of shot at his home, bringing the additional ammunition to the musters when required.

Troopers were to be provided with a good serviceable horse and saddle, holsters, breast plates and crouper, a case of good pistols, a sword, a double cartouch box, and twelve charges of powder. Like the

---

[16] Hening, *Statutes at Large,* August 1701 (http://vagenweb.org/hening/vol03-13.htm), 3: 207–210.

[17] A "fusee, "fuzee" or "fusil" was a light musket designed for artillery or light infantry. British officers and, occasionally non-commissioned officers, carried these weapons. Fuzees were distinguished from artillery muskets by their superior workmanship. The mounting of these muskets were often engraved or decorated in some way. See Harold L. Peterson, *The Book of the Continental Soldier* (Harrisburg: The Stackpole Company, 1968), 29.

[18] A cartouche box was either a paper box for cartridges or individual small thin paper containers holding the ball and powder necessary to load one round of a firearm. See Paul Drake, *What Did They Mean By That? A Dictionary of Historical Terms for Genealogists* (Bowie: Heritage Books, 1994), 36.

foot soldier, he was required to keep at home a well fixed carbine, with belt and swivel,[19] two pounds of powder and eight pounds of shot, bringing them, when required, to the muster field.

Militia men who either failed to appear at musters or reported with their arms and ammunition were fined. Others were fined if they failed to keep the required equipment at home and bring it with them to the muster field. The fine was a severe one: one hundred pounds of tobacco for each warning or failure to report. However, none of the soldiers or horsemen could be fined more than five times in a year for failure to appear.

The men were given eighteen months to procure their arms and could not be fined until that grace period was over. None of their equipment could be impressed or taken by legal action. If this occurred, then the aggrieved party could sue and receive double the damages on recovery.

Musters were to be held once every three months for training and exercise, or more often, if the situation deemed it necessary. A general muster was also held where all the militia troops, foot and horse, could be called upon to exercise together. The men were expected to "observe and obediently perform the commands of their officer relating to their exercising according to the best of their skill."

Mutineers could be or imprisoned. So, too, were men who did not perform their duties as soldiers on muster days. They could be fined up to fifty pounds of tobacco or imprisonment for up to ten days, without bail or mainprise.[20] If militia men failed to appear in the event of an incursion, invasion, insurrection, rebellion, or other alarm or surprise, they also could be fined £10 current money or spend three months in jail, without bail or mainprise.

There evidently had been some difficulties in finding soldiers willing to serve as sergeants, corporals, drummers or trumpeters, which the legislature thought to be "absolutely necessary" in troops and companies. So it was decided to "encourage" the acceptance of these appointments, made by the company commanders. Men who refused to serve in one of those ranks or capacities were fined five hundred pounds of tobacco. However, if he paid his fine and still refused to serve, he could not be fined again.[21]

This Militia Act spelled out, quite explicitly the duties expected of troopers and foot soldiers. Militia service was required of all males sixteen to sixty. The men were expected to equip themselves and to be ready to serve when called out. The reasons for their call-up were also unambiguous: an incursion, invasion, insurrection, rebellion, or other alarm or surprise. The colony's militia was used for defense purposes only. It was not a combat force.

7. Interlude II: The Fairfax Proprietary expands its settlements under Robert Carter and Thomas Lee 1702–1730

In the spring of 1702, Robert Carter of Corotoman took over as agent for the Northern Neck Proprietary, Lord Fairfax's vast domain which included the original Northern Neck counties as well as Stafford and what was to become eighteenth century counties like King George, Prince William, Fauquier, Loudoun, and Fairfax.[22]

Stafford was still the most northernmost outpost and grants were given here that avoided Indian paths, like the Shenandoah Hunting Path along upper most portion of Stafford's frontier. The Deep Run area in northern Stafford, now part of the dividing line between Fauquier and that county, was settled

---

[19] A swivel is a "chain link made in two parts, one piece fitting like a collar below the bolt head of the other and turning freely about it." The swivel portion of the chain has a hook that joins the two chains together. See definition and illustration in *Webster's New World Dictionary of the American Language, College Edition* (New York: World Publishing Company, 1953), 1475.

[20] *Mainprise* is the delivery of a person to someone called a *mainpernor* who acted as security for the appearance of the person under arrest. In this instance, a soldier could be remanded to jail without a security bond and without the right to find someone who could guarantee his future appearance into Court. See Henry Campbell Black, *Black's Law Dictionary* (St Paul: West Publishing Company, 1990), 953.

[21] Hening, *Hening's Statutes at Large*, October 1705 (http://vagenweb.org/hening/vol03-20.htm), 3: 335–340.

[22] FCBC, 14.

between 1704 and 1709. The Great North Marsh, in present-day Fauquier, was settled, along with the Rappahannock Marsh and the Elk Marsh between 1710 and 1715.

The western Elk Run Valley, also in Fauquier, was settled between 1712 and 1718. Dorrill's Run, a tributary of Cedar Run and the Potomac, was settled by grantees beginning in 1710. Elk Run and its tributaries were settled between 1716 and 1726. Thus by 1727, most of the lands in what would become the southern end of Fauquier, then part of Stafford, had been taken up.[23] The land in present-day Fauquier had to undergo a change, first in 1731 when Prince William was formed from Stafford and King George, and then, in 1759, in the midst of the French and Indian War, when it became a county on its own right.

8. The Treaty of Albany effectively opens the Virginia frontier to settlement

This seating of the Stafford frontier was no doubt helped when the Treaty of Albany was signed in 1722. Virginia Governor Spotswood and representatives of northern confederacy known as the Five Nations of the Iroquois Confederacy met in Albany, New York, in late August 1722. The Iroquois agreed

> That the great River of Potowmak & the High Ridge of Mountains which extend all along the Frontiers of Virginia to the Westward of the present Settlements of that Colony shall be forever the established Boundaries between the Indians subject to the Dominion of Virginia & the Indians belonging to and depending on the 5 Nations:
> So that neither our Indians shall, on any pretence whatsoever, pass to the Northward or Westward of [these] boundaries without having to produce a Passport, under the Hand and Seal of the Governor or Command^r in Chief of Virginia nor your Indians pass to the Southward or Eastward of [these] boundaries without a Passport ... from the Governor or Commander in Chief of New York.[24]

This provision, then, effectively ended their attacks on the colony's Powhatan Confederacy, a tribal grouping of Virginian Algonquian tribes, including the Chicahominy, Nansemond, Pamunkey, and Mattapony tribes.[25]

Governor Spotswood warned the Iroquois Confederacy about the penalties involved in the event that this provision was disregarded. If Virginia's Indians disregard this stipulation, he stated, by law they could be put to death, or transported and sold as a slave. While Virginia would not take any action against the Iroquois for taking Virginia Indians on the north side of the Potomac and the west side of the high ridge of mountains, he went on to say, still the Five Nations should not look upon it as a breach if Virginia hangs or transport any of the Iroquois Confederacy taken without a proper passport within the south side of the Potomac and east side of the mountains.[26]

This treaty had a huge impact on the settlement of the frontier and on legislative objectives in strengthening the militia. Now that the Iroquois had been removed as a threat to not only Virginia's native tribes but also to the frontier, new settlements arose there, especially those in northern Stafford. Prince William was created in 1731 from Stafford and King George, with settlements growing along the Rappahannock and Potomac. The latter county had been established by legislative action in 1720.

Other settlements occurred along the James River leading to the formation of Goochland in 1727. Brunswick, established in 1732 on the Carolina-Virginia border, western-most boundary was fixed at the "high mountains" of the Treaty of Albany. Orange County rounded out this mix in 1734. Thus, within twelve years of the Treaty of Albany, Virginia's western frontier was firmly established at the Blue Ridge.[27]

Less than a year after the Treaty of Albany, in May 1723, Virginia's colonial legislature decided to strengthen the militia, perhaps due to their concerns that the Iroquois confederacy might not abide by the

---

[23] FCBC, 25.
[24] *"Great Treaty of 1722"* (http://earlytreaties.unl.edu/treaty.00001.html), 669–670.
[25] "Powhatan Indian Tribe History" (http://www.accessgenealogy.com/native/tribes/powhatan/powhatanhist.htm).
[26] *"Great Treaty of 1722,"* 673.
[27] "Virginia County Formation Maps," (http://www.familyhistory101.com/maps/va_cf.html). Maps 1720, 1728, 1730, 1731, 1732. 1734, 1735 (Accessed July 23, 2008).

Less than a year after the Treaty of Albany, in May 1723, Virginia's colonial legislature decided to strengthen the militia, perhaps due to their concerns that the Iroquois confederacy might not abide by the Treaty of Albany signed the previous year. Then, too, the creation of three new counties King George, Spotsylvania, and Hanover, meant that a militia infrastructure needed to be set up. The Burgesses were also concerned that the previous acts regulating the militia were not doing the job. So, the chief officer of the county militia was authorized to list all free male persons from twenty-one to sixty within the county and place them in the requisite horse or foot company.

Exemptions were expanded to include the president, masters, professors, and students at William an Mary, along with founders, people employed in iron, copper, or lead work or any mines, Free Negroes, Mulattoes, or Indians. However, free people of color who were capable, could be listed and employed as drummers or trumpeters. In an invasion, insurrection, or rebellion, all free Negroes, Mulattoes, and Indians were obliged to attend and march with the militia as pioneers or perform other "servile labour" as required.

The remaining portions of this act basically duplicated the 1705 Act and thus need no further elucidation.[28]

9. The War of Jenkin's Ear, 1739–1742 and King George's War 1740–1748 begins a a long drawn out conflict between England, Spain, and France for control of the North American colonies.

The War of Jenkin's Ear was caused by a British ship captain, whose ear had been cut off by the Spanish for taking part in illegal black market activities in the Caribbean. Trade agreements between England and Spain had allowed the Spanish to board the British merchant ship *Rebecca* and, as claimed by its Captain, Robert Jenkins, cut off his ear. This occurred in 1731. Captain Jenkins did not show his pickled ear to the British House of Commons until 1739. So the British declared war on the Spanish, in part because of a desire to control the entire Atlantic basin of North America, especially as regard to commerce and military affairs.

Spain had thriving colonies in the Caribbean and Latin and South America with trade centering at Havana, and Porta Bello in the Caribbean and in the Latin America at Vera Cruz, in Mexico; and in South America at Cartagena, Columbia.

In the opening salvo, in November 1739, Admiral Edward Vernon captured the Spanish port of Porto Bello in New Granada. While the poorly defended port was easily captured, it was just as quickly recaptured by the Spanish. Then, in March 1741, now in charge of a huge invasion fleet, Vernon attacked Cartagena.[29] He did not meet with success as barely one tenth of the men who had set out to conquer the Spanish Caribbean, Latin, and South American empire returned home. Yellow fever killed more men than the Spaniards. By 1742, the War of Jenkin's Ear "had died of inertia…"[30]

Among his forces was a large contingent of Americans, four battalions worth, under Colonel Gooch, known as Gooch's American Regiment. This war proved to be noteworthy only from the standpoint that it was the first time American troops were deployed outside their borders in a European war.[31]

Unfortunately, the early Prince William minute books, from 1731–1751 which might have identified officers who could have been part of this American Regiment have not survived.

The outset of war was enough to alarm the Virginia assembly who, in May 1740, passed legislation to provide for increased security of the colony. Since the American colonies were not at war, it was necessary to keep the militia under stricter discipline and insure that they were more frequently trained and exercised and armed sufficiently to contend with the regular troops.

---

[28] Hening, *Statutes at Large,* May 1723 (http://vagenweb.org/hening/vol04-06htm), 4: 118–126.
[29] "Battle of Cartagena de Indias," Wikipedia, the free encyclopedia (http://en.wikipedia.org/wiki/Battle_of_Cartagena_de_Indias) (Accessed July 23, 2008).
[30] Walter P. Hall and Albion, Robert G, *A History of England and the British Empire*, 3rd edition (New York: Ginn and Company, 1953), 450,
[31] W. G. Stanard, editor, "The American Regiment in the Carthagena Expedition," *The Virginia Magazine of History and Biography,* XXX, January 1922, 1–20.

in year— March and September— in their counties or more often if the situation warranted it. This act was to remain in effect for three years and no longer. However, if the present war should end before the expiration of this act, then upon the proclamation of peace, this act would become null and void.[32]

While this two year sideshow, demonstrating the greed of the British, had been rapidly turning into a farce, events in Europe presaged a more ominous outcome. Another war was in the offing caused by yet another succession crisis— this time by the Austrians and the Prussians. Both Kings died without male heirs and a wholly German affair widened into a European War. This, in turn, coupled with the Anglo-French colonial rivalry, transformed this conflict into another European war with colonial consequences. The British and Holland supported their traditional ally: the Austrians. The French supported Prussia, hoping to break up Germany into a several weak states under French influence.

Meanwhile, in Virginia, the colonial government grew alarmed again at the possible incursion of Indian allies of the French all along its frontier. Virginians were apprehensive about a possible slave insurrection as well if men were sent out of counties with large slave population to guard the frontier. Then, there was a possible invasion of forces by sea for which the colony's coastal counties would have to deal.

In the midst of these alarms, events were taking place in Lancaster, Pennsylvania which would push the Virginia, Pennsylvania, and Maryland frontier further west. In June 1744, the Lieutenant-Governor of Pennsylvania, George Thomas, and commissioners from Virginia and Maryland met with the Iroquois at the Lancaster Courthouse in Pennsylvania. Virginia was represented by Thomas Lee, of Prince William and Colonel William Beverley. Maryland sent Edmund Jennings, Philip Thomas, Colonel Robert King, and Colonel Thomas Colville to the Pennsylvania Court treaty site. The Iroquois were represented by five tribes—the Onondagas, Senecas, Cayuga, Oneidas, and the Tuscaroras.[33]

The three colonial governments wanted to bring Five Nation attacks along their frontiers to an end. This was accomplished when peace was concluded in early July. The Iroquois ceded the region between the Alleghenies and the Ohio to the English.[34]

The net effect of this treaty was to open up the region around the Ohio River for settlement. This was to occur more rapidly with the formation of the Ohio Company in 1747. This company was composed of a number of influential men who were looking to speculate in the rich lands in the Ohio Country and resell it to immigrants. The proprietors, all Virginians, along with London merchant John Hanbury, wanted to expand push Virginia's frontiers into the Ohio River Valley. They were Thomas Nelson, Thomas Lee, William Thornton, William Nimms, Daniel Cresap, Michael Cresap, Lawrence Washington, George Fairfax, Jacob Giles, Nathaniel Chapman, and James Woodrop.[35] Other members were John Mercer, Augustine Washington, Jr., Virginia Governor Robert Dinwiddie, the Duke of Bedford, and George Mercer, who was the company's agent in England.[36]

Of these original proprietors, two lived or held land in Prince William: Thomas Lee,[37] and Nathaniel Chapman.[38] George Fairfax and Lawrence Washington came from nearby Fairfax County, which had been spun off from Prince William and Loudoun in 1742.

---

[32] Hening, *Statutes at Large,* May 1740 (http://vagenweb.org/hening/vol05-06htm), 5: 90–91.

[33] "Early Recognized Treaties with American Indian Nations," *Ratified treaty # 3 A Treaty Held at the Town of Lancaster, by the Honourable Lieutenant Governor of the Province, and the Honourable Commissioners for the Province of Virginia and Maryland, with the Indians of the Six Nations in June, 1744* (http://early treaties.unl.edu/treaty.00003.html), 41–43 (Accessed July 30, 2008).

[34] —, "Period of Early Exploration [of Fayette County]," (http://www.burgesslegacy.org/fayette/chapter_v.htm), 77. (Accessed July 30, 2008).

[35] Ibid.

[36] "The Ohio Company," Wikipedia, the free encyclopedia (http://enwikipedia.org/wiki/Ohio_Company). (Accessed July 30, 2008). Afterwards, http://enwikipedia.org.

[37] "Thomas Lee (Virginia colonist)" Wikipedia, the free encyclopedia (http://enwikipedia.org/wiki/Thomas_Lee_%28 Virginia_colonist%29) (Accessed July 30, 2008).

[38] "The Ohio Company," Wikipedia, the free encyclopedia (http://enwikipedia.org) (Accessed July 30, 2008)

The Ohio Company looked to the western wilderness rather than lands closer to home primarily because the vast Fairfax Proprietary effectively blocked any settlement between the Potomac and far reaches of the Rappahannock River in Virginia. Thus the broad, well-irrigated land over the Appalachians opened up the prospect of settlement and profits once roads were cut through the mountains.[39]

A year later, in 1748, the British Crown approved a petition from the company for a grant of 200,000 acres near the "forks" of the Ohio. In July 1749, the governor and council of Virginia made the grant with the condition that, within seven years, the company would settle 100 families in the area and build a fort there to protect themselves and enhance England's claim to the territory. The company also wanted to establish regular trade with the local Indians and thereby maintain friendly relations with them.[40]

The push west into the Ohio, it should be remembered, was taking place in the midst of "King George's War" as the War of Austrian Succession was called in the colonies. The colony was beset with fresh fears of attacks by Indians allied with the French along the expanded frontier, a possible slave rebellion if the militia was withdrawn to move westward; coastal communities were worried about an invasion by a sea-borne enemy.

During the last month of this war, the colonial House of Burgesses finally decided to take action. The legislators made provisions for all three of these contingencies. They gave the governor, or the commander-in-chief of Virginia, full authority to levy, raise, arm, and muster the militia need to repel an invasion or suppress an insurrection. The governor or commander-in chief also had the authority to order the militia in any of the counties to anyplace in Virginia to put down the invasion or insurrection. The soldiers would be disbanded only when the danger was over.

Militia officers had the authority and, indeed, were required to raise the militia and sent immediate notice to his county lieutenant on how he and his troops were to proceed. Officers were to keep their troops under arms until ordered differently by their superior officers. The county lieutenants in charge of the militia were to keep the governor informed by dispatches, as best he could, of the strength and movement of the enemy. County lieutenants had full authority to impress boats and hands, along with men and horses to carry these dispatches.

Look-outs were appointed along the coast to watch for enemy ships. If enemy vessels were sighted, look-outs were to notify their field officer who was then directed to transmit his account to the governor, and the county lieutenant or commanding officer of militia of the look-out's county.

While the militia would be paid for out of public accounts, troopers and foot soldiers were expected to provide their own arms and ammunition.

The governor or commander-in-chief, were authorized to appoint and assign militia to assist with coastal defense and protect the batteries erected along the river ways of the colony. This legislation was to continue for seven years and no longer.[41]

While there were other minor provisions in this act, these were the most important ones and signaled a massive change in concept from previous militia acts. There was a real sense of urgency and alarm in the reading of these provisions. Militia from several counties would be working together and could be moved anywhere they were needed in the colony. Only after the danger was over, could they be disbanded. The governor, for the first time, was to be kept apprized of the situation, in as timely a fashion as militia officers could arrange. Militia was sent to guard the batteries along the rivers. The colony was on full alert. Finally, one clause was conspicuous by its absence: There was no provision in this legislation for pensions for wounded or disabled soldiers.

---

[38] "The Ohio Company," Wikipedia, the free encyclopedia (http://enwikipedia.org) (Accessed July 30, 2008)
[39] Fred Anderson, *The War That Made America: A Short History of the French and Indian War* (New York: Penguin Books, 2005), 29.
[40] Ibid.
[41] Hening, *Statutes at Large,* October 1748, (http://vagenweb.org/hening/vol06-06htm), 6: 112-118.

10. Epilogue

King George's War ended in with the signing of the Treaty of Aix-la-Chapelle in mid October 1748. Most of the provisions dealt with a European settlement, which was dictated by the victors, England and their allies. Nothing was settled in the American colonies. Fort Louisbourg, on Cape Breton Island in Canada, although taken by American colonists from New England, was returned to the French. Both the French and Americans continued to hold assiduously to their claims to the Ohio country.[42] This was an ominous portent of events to come.

11. Conclusions

Colonial expansion north and westward placed increasing pressure on Indian settlements as colonists encroached upon their villages, their hunting and their burial grounds. Conversely, as the frontier expanded, more pressure was exerted on the colonial infrastructure to guard their borders from Indian attacks. It was not until the 1722 Treaty of Albany that Virginia's frontier could be expanded to the Blue Ridge and was recognized as such by the Iroquois Confederacy.

In April 1730 Prince William was formed from King George and Stafford, thus pushing the frontier to the Maryland line. The Treaty of Albany made it safe for settlers to move into this area since the Iroquois abandoned the Shenandoah Hunting Path and moved west of the Blue Ridge.

The Treaty of Lancaster in 1744 presaged the opening of a vast frontier beyond the Alleghenies. This brought the Americans into conflict with the French since the Ohio country was at least a nominal part of France's North American empire. The advent of the Ohio Company pushed the stakes higher as confrontation was to become conflict in the struggle to control American expansion beyond the Alleghenies.

The legislative acts of the sixteenth and seventeenth century, laid out in the preceding pages, pointed up several underlying concepts for Virginia's militia.

- Early legislation relating to rangers and militia dealt primarily with the frontier.
- Militia forces were to be used for local defense only. They were not combat forces.
- They could be called out only for specific purposes— slave insurrections or other forms of civil unrest, Indian incursions on the frontier or along the coast, invasion by a foreign enemy, French or their Indian allies or the Spanish, alarms, or dangerous situations.
- Auxiliaries to the militia were the Ranger service. These men were expected to range along the frontier, spying on Indian movements and reporting any threats to the militia officers in the frontier counties.
- Except for the 1748 legislation, annual pensions were given to wounded or disabled soldiers, sometimes for their lives and sometimes for as long as their disability existed.
- Exemptions were given for militia service, usually to those who made up the colony's infrastructure or whose employment was considered necessary to the civilian regime.

---

[42] Ohio Historical Society, "King George's War" (http://www.ohiohistorycentral.org/entry.) (Accessed July 30, 2008).

THE FRENCH AND INDIAN WAR PERIOD

CHAPTER 2

A PRELUDE TO WAR

1. Response and Counter-response

In the last year of "King George's War," it will be remembered, the Ohio Company had been successful in obtaining a large grant of some 200,000 acres near the forks of the Ohio. The colonial government made the grant conditional upon the settlement of at least 100 families within the bounds of the grant. The Company had seven years to make this happen and also agreed to build a fort to protect the new settlers and to augment British control of the territory within the grant.

Since the primary purpose of the company was to settle families within the forks of Ohio and to encourage trade with friendly Indians in the area, the proprietors hired Christopher Gist, a skilled woodsman and surveyor, to explore the Ohio Valley and survey lands for possible settlement. Based on Gist's report, the Ohio Company decided upon settlement in an area in Western Pennsylvania and present-day West Virginia. In 1752, the company pushed forward a path between small fortified posts at present-day Cumberland, Maryland and Brownsville, Pennsylvania.[43]

♦ French claims to the Ohio Valley, 1747–1752

This activity could not help but alarm the French who claimed the Ohio Valley as part of their North American empire. They, too, wanted this land for settlement since the climate and soil were better than that in French Canada, especially during the winter. The Ohio River watershed was also a factor since it provided a critical link between French Canada and French Louisiana.

The French, in order to cement their claim to the Ohio Valley, had in 1747, built thirty some cabins, some with stone chimneys, on a plateau above the original Logstown village. These cabins were handed over to the Indians residing there. The Iroquois sent emissaries to live in Logstown the same year.

In response to this, the colony of Pennsylvania sent out an ambassador to the Six Nations and he held a council with a gathering of chiefs who consented to count their warriors in the region.

Then, the French countered by marking *their* claim to the Allegheny and Ohio River watersheds. The Canadian governor of New France sent out Celeron de Bienville to move down the Allegheny and Ohio, with copper plates to place on trees and leaden plates to bury near the river mouths.

When he arrived at Logstown, he was infuriated to find English traders there. He evicted the traders and wrote a note rebuking the governor of Pennsylvania for allowing this to happen. Celeron then made sure the Indians knew that this region was going to be dominated by the French, not the English. Some of the Iroquois, annoyed by these tactics, left Logstown for their own homeland, tearing down the French copper plates from the trees as they went.[44]

♦ Treaty of Logstown, 1752

In 1752, the colony of Virginia and the Ohio Company upped the stakes when a delegation of Virginians and representatives from the Ohio Company negotiated a treaty, with Ohio Indians at

---

[43] "The Ohio Company," *Wikipedia, the free encyclopedia* (http://en.wikipedia.org) (Accessed July 31, 2008).
[44] "Logstown," *Wikipedia, the free encyclopedia* (http://en.wikipedia.org/wiki/Logstown).

Logstown, in western Pennsylvania.[45] Colonel Joshua Fry and two other commissioners represented the colony while Christopher Gist acted for the Ohio Company.[46]

Both the Delaware and Iroquois acknowledged Virginia's claim to territory south of the Ohio. The English were to be allowed to form settlements on the south and east side of that river. The Iroquois confirmed the land cessions in 1744 and gave the British permission to build a blockhouse at the forks of the Ohio, the site of present-day Pittsburg. The Iroquois signed this treaty and then confirmed their cessions of land in the Treaty of Lancaster in 1744.[47]

Among other things, this agreement between the Indians of the Ohio Valley and Virginia and the Ohio Company, stated that

> Whereas, at the Treaty of Lancaster, in the County of Lancaster & Province of Pennsylvania, held between the Government of Virginia & the six united Nations of Indians, in the Year of our Lord one thousand seven hundred & seventy-four [sic, forty-four is meant], the Honorable Thomas Lee and William Beverly, Esqrs., being Commissioners, a Deed recognizing & acknowledging the Right & title of his Majesty, our sovereign Lord, the King of Great Britain, to all the land within the Colony of Virginia, as it was then or hereafter, might be peopled & bounded by his Majesty, our sovereign Lord, the King, his heirs and successors, was signed, sealed & delivered by the Sachems & chiefs of the six united Nation, then present ...
> ... We, Conogariera, Cheseago, Cownsagret, Enguisara, Togrondoaro, Thonorision, Sachems & Chiefs of the sd united Nations, now met in Council at Loggs Town, do hereby signify our Consent & Confirmation of said Deed in as full & ample a Manner as if the same were here recited.
> And whereas his Majesty has at present a design of making a settlement of Settlements of British Subjects on the Southern or Eastern parts of the River Ohio, called otherwise Allegany. We in Council (Joshua Fry, Lunsford Lomax, and James Patton being commissioners on behalf of his majesty) do give our consent, thereto & do further promise that the said settlement or settlements shall be unmolested by us and that we will, as far in our power assist and Protect the British Subjects there inhabiting.[48]

♦ The French Response: construction of forts in the Ohio Valley, 1753

Their immediate response was to begin constructing a series of forts in the Ohio Valley. This began in 1753. The French envisioned a line of forts protecting their interests in the Ohio Valley from British and colonial encroachment stretching from the forks of the Ohio and Monongahela to Lake Erie.[49]

In 1753 the fort-building in French Ohio Valley commenced. Two forts were constructed during that year. Fort Presque Isle was erected along Presque Isle Bay, at present-day Erie, Pennsylvania. Built by French soldiers, the Fort was part of a line that included Fort Le Boeuf, Fort Machault, and Fort Duquesne.[50]

Fort Le Boeuf was begun in July 1753 and was completed in December of that year. It was located on a fork of French Creek, near present-day Waterford, in northwest Pennsylvania. Located some fifteen miles from Lake Erie, the newly built stronghold allowed the French to portage trade goods, war materiel, and supplies overland from Lake Erie overland to the fort. It proved to be first-class base for travel to the

---

[45] University of Virginia, "The Logstown Treaty" from Papers of Walker and Page Families, 1742–1886, Accession # 3098, Special Collections, University of Virginia Library, University of Virginia, (http://www.vcdh.virginia.edu/lewisand clark/students/projects/adventurers/documents/logstowntreaty). (Accessed July 31, 2008).
[46] "Logstown," *Wikipedia, the free encyclopedia* (http://en.wikipedia.org/wiki/Logstown).
[47] TNGenWeb Project, "Treaty of Logstown, 1752," *Colonial Period Indian Land Cessions in the American Southeast* (http://www.tngenweb.org/cessions/colonial.html) (Accessed July 31, 2008).
[48] "Early Recognized Treaties with American Indian Nations," *Ratified Treaty # 4 The Treaty of Logstown, 1752* (http://early treaties.unl.edu/treaty.00004.html.), 173–174.
[49] Ruth Sheppard, ed., *Empires Collide: The French and Indian War 1754–1763* (Oxford: Osprey Publishing, 2006), 11.
[50] "Fort Presque Isle," Wikipedia, the free encyclopedia (http://en.wikipedia.org/wiki/Fort_Presque_Isle) (Accessed August 1, 2008).

Allegheny, the Ohio, and the Mississippi, whose territory was controlled by the French colonial government in Canada.[51]

In 1754, Fort Machault, the last in this line of forts, was constructed near the forks of the Allegheny and French Creek, in northwestern Pennsylvania. The fort was built on a hill, close to the Allegheny, in the form of a parallelogram. The curtain[52] was constructed of hewn timber that was stacked length-wise. Bastions[53] were found at the four corners, built in the form of polygons, from saplings eight inches thick and thirteen feet high. A gate faced the Allegheny. Inside the fortification, there was a magazine, officer barracks. Soldier's barracks were outside the fort. The fort was completed in April, less than a month before hostilities broke out at Jumonville Glen. It was named for a prominent French politician, Jean Baptiste de Machault D'Arnouville.[54]

In April 1754, the French were the recipients of another fort in the Ohio River Valley when they forced the surrender of a partially-built fort, called Fort Prince George. This fort was located at the junction of the Allegheny and Monongahela rivers in present-day downtown Pittsburgh.

Three months before, in 1755, Governor Dinwiddie had dispatched a Virginia force to build Fort Prince George at the forks of the two rivers. Construction began in February 1754. However, a large French force arrived at the forks of the rivers in mid-April and forced the surrender of the small garrison there. The French razed the British fort and erected another on the site, which they named Fort Duquesne, for Marquis Duquesne, the Governor-General of New France.[55]

♦ The American Response: Governor Dinwiddie orders Major George Washington to the Ohio Country with an ultimatum to the French to leave the territory

Virginia Governor Robert Dinwiddie was worried. He did not like what was happening in the Ohio country. He was not about to let the French disrupt the British claim to Ohio Valley, much less Virginia's and the Ohio Company's claim. He realized that all three had much to lose here. Not only from the commercial ventures associated with possible settlement and Indian trade in the Ohio River Valley but also because of the hard-won treaties with the Iroquois, ceding land there to Virginia, and to a lesser extent, Pennsylvania and Maryland.

If Virginia did nothing and allowed French forts in an area he regarded as British, then the French claim would become legitimate. The Ohio Country would be lost to Britain and more important, from his standpoint, to Virginia and the Ohio Company.

Having communicated his fears to the British, Governor Dinwiddie received orders authorizing him and his fellow governors to remove the French from any intrusions made along the frontier. His instructions were separate and very precise. First, he was to demand a French withdrawal from the forts they had built. Secondly, the governor was given full authority to build and man forts in the Ohio country and repel any French attempt to dislodge them. Finally, if the French refused to leave forts that were within the "undoubted limits of his Majesty's dominions," the Governor was authorized to force their evacuation by sending men and arms against them. The British government would see to it that Dinwiddie had the necessary cannon and ammunition to defend any British fort built on Virginia's frontier.[56] Armed with these instructions, the Governor felt it was up to him to respond to this latest move by the French to

---

[51] "Fort Le Boeuf," Wikipedia, the free encyclopedia (http://en.wikipedia.org/wiki/Fort_Le_Boeuf). Afterwards http://en.wikipedia.org.

[52] This was part of the earthen embankment, or rampart which encircled the fort See *Webster's New World Dictionary*, 2nd College edition (New York: World Publishing, 1972), 348, 1175.

[53] Ibid., 118. Bastions were projections which moved out from the fort, designed to give riflemen within a wider firing range.

[54] "Fort Machault," Wikipedia, the free encyclopedia (http://en.wikipedia.org/wiki/Fort_Machault).

[55] "Fort Duquesne," Wikipedia, the free encyclopedia (http://en.wikipedia/org/wiki/Fort_Duquesne) (Accessed August 3, 2008).

[56] Anderson, 37–38.

claim the territory. It was up to Virginia to insure the French knew they were intruding on the British claim, and not the other way around.

So he sent young Major George Washington into the wilderness to deliver a letter demanding the French abandon their forts and leave British territory. Washington, along with Christopher Gist, an Iroquois chief and some Indians, a translator, and a few men, journeyed into the wilderness to Fort Le Boeuf. In December, 1753, Washington and his forces delivered Governor Dinwiddie's letter to the Commandant of the Fort.[57] Dinwiddie's letter accused the French of encroachment and fort building with British territory:

> The lands upon the River Ohio, in the western parts of the Colony of Virginia, are so notoriously known to be the property of the Crown of Great-Britain, that it is a matter of equal concern and surprise to me, to hear that a body of French forces are erecting fortresses, and making settlements upon that river, within his Majesty's dominions.[58]

The French commandant, Captain Jacques Legardeur de Saint Pierre, took a day to consult with his officers and then drafted a polite but firm rebuttal. He would see that the Governor's letter was sent to Canada for a reply. Until he had further instructions, the French would stay where they were.[59]

Washington put his time to good use while at Fort Le Boeuf. He gathered intelligence about the forces there and the state of the fortifications. He noted that there were 100 men, a large number of officers, some fifty birch canoes and seventy pine canoes, many of which were not yet finished.

He described the fort's location, on the southwest fork of French Creek, near the water. The sides of the fort comprised four houses. Bastions were made of sharpened piles driven into the ground, standing twelve feet in the air. Each bastion mounted eight six-pound cannon while four-pound cannon guarded the gate. Inside the bastion were a guard-house, chapel, doctor's house, and the commandant's private stores. Outside the fort were several log barracks. In addition, there were stables, a blacksmith shop and other buildings.[60] Clearly, the French had come to stay.

His trip home was adventurous, to say the least. He was attacked by hostile Indians. Then, while crossing the ice-flecked Alleghany, he fell overboard into the frigid waters, only to be rescued, thankfully, by Christopher Gist. On his return to Williamsburg, he wrote a report, in the form of a journal, to Dinwiddie in which he described the results of the meeting with the French.[61] He had, he said, visited both Fort Machault and Fort Le Boeuf. Both were well-built and well supplied. Washington took it for granted that the canoes and bateaux on the banks of the river and in the woods near Le Boeuf indicated a fourth French fort at the Forks of the Ohio, was in the offing.

Dinwiddie dispatched a copy of the journal to the British in London, who agreed that the governor should proceed with erecting and manning a British fort at the forks of the Ohio with all due dispatch. Dinwiddie had a much harder time convincing the colonial legislature to go along with his ideas.

2. Virginia prepares to defend the colony against the French along the Ohio River Valley frontier

♦ **The Virginia legislature's response I: An Act for raising £ 20,000 for the protection of his majesty's subjects against the insults and encroachments of the French, October, 1754**

In the end, however, Dinwiddie was successful. In October 1754, the Burgesses passed an "Act for raising the sum of twenty thousand pounds for the protection of his majesty's subjects against the insults

---
[57] Sheppard, 18–20.
[58] Walter R. Borneman, *The French and Indian War: Deciding the Fate of North America* (New York: Harper-Collins, 2006), 23.
[59] Ibid.
[60] "Fort LeBoeuf," *Wikipedia, the free encyclopedia* (http://en.wikipedia.org).
[61] Borneman, 23–24.

and encroachments of the French." Among the more important provisions of this legislation were how the money was to be raised and who was to oversee how the money was spent.

This money was raised by a tax of 2s 6d, or thirty pounds of tobacco, to be paid by every tithable within the colony. The tax was to be collected in April and October of 1754. Fourteen men were appointed as directors to direct and appoint the way the money was to be applied towards the maintenance of the soldiers and forts on the frontier.[62]

- **The Virginia legislature's response II: An Act for raising levies and recruits to serve in the present expedition against the French, on the Ohio, October 1754**

Once the money for forts and troops had been allocated and a way had been found to pay for these expenditures, the colonial legislature turned its attention to more practical matters— the raising of the requisite troops to operate the forts and defend the frontier against the French.

Officers, who were normally empowered to enlist men, were given the authority to raise and levy able-bodied men who are unemployed and had no lawful support and maintenance. These officers were to apply to the Justices of the county for warrants to impress these levies into service as soldiers. Those who could vote, along with indentured servants, slaves, and men under twenty-one and over fifty, were exempted from service.

Soldiers, raised in this manner, were paid from the time they were taken and delivered to the requisite military officer. These levies would receive the same reward as any other enlisted soldier. If any of these new levies were wounded or maimed so they were not capable of maintaining themselves, upon their return home, were to be supported at public expense. This act was to be in effect for one year from its passage and no longer.[63]

- **Dinwiddie appoints George Washington as lieutenant colonel of new regiment authorized by the colony of Virginia**

Now that money and troops had been allocated for frontier duty, the next step was to find a commanding officer. Washington, who knew the Ohio River valley better than any other officer, requested a command within the regiment as a lieutenant colonel. Dinwiddie agreed and gave him the authority to enlist men for the frontier regiment.

Unfortunately, the new lieutenant colonel had a dreadful time persuading men to volunteer. Part of this was due to the wage of a common soldier, which was less than half what a common laborer was paid. Even though a bounty land grant would be given for service, Washington still had a tough time in finding volunteers. Many of the levies were paupers or unemployed drifters who had been coerced into signing up. "The regiment as a whole was poorly clad, poorly shod, poorly supplied, and as yet wholly untrained."[64]

Despite all this, the young lieutenant colonel was not all that worried. What he lacked in experience, he could learn. The regiment's commanding officer, Colonel Joshua Fry had emigrated from England to Essex County, Virginia, in 1737, as a young man. He had served as a member of the House of Burgesses and a justice for Essex County. In 1743, he moved to what was to become Albemarle County. Named chief surveyor of the new county, he and Peter Jefferson mapped the region for the colonial legislature. His military experience was well known since he had commanded the Albemarle militia since its inception in 1745.[65]

---

[62] Hening, *Statutes at Large,* August 1754 (http://vagenweb.org/hening/vol06-20.htm), 6:435–436.
[63] Ibid., 6: 438–440.
[64] Anderson, 45.
[65] "Joshua Fry," *Albemarle Adventurers* (http://www.vcdh.virginia.edu/lewisandclar/students/projects/adventurers/frybio.html) (Accessed August 3, 2008).

♦ The Virginian Encampment at Great Meadows, May 1754

Colonel Fry was going to bring more troops and supplies to Washington at the fort on Wills Creek. Washington felt better too, about his Virginia Regiment because he knew that a company of British regular troops from South Carolina would also be joining him and his men. Once everyone had arrived, training for his inexperienced men would begin in earnest and then they could leave for the Ohio country. The troops were ultimately to be deployed at Fort Prince George, on the forks of the Ohio and Allegheny rivers.[66]

In early April, Washington moved westward with part of a regiment of Virginia backwoodsmen to build a road to Redstone Creek, located on the Monongahela River, at present-day Brownsville, Pennsylvania.[67] By mid-April Washington and the 159 men who made up his command had marched as far as Will's Creek, a tributary of the north branch of the Potomac, located in the westernmost portions of Maryland and Pennsylvania.[68]

Once he and his men had arrived at Wills Creek, the force learned that Fort Prince George was in French hands. He decided to push on to Redstone Creek and await further orders.[69]

They had been at Wills Creek for only a few days when he received the disturbing news that hundreds of French troops had appeared on the Allegheny in canoes carrying men and cannons. He looked his men, forty of whom were short of arms, foot, and ammunition, the rest ill prepared and untrained, and decided discretion was the better of valor. He wrote the necessary reports to Dinwiddie and prepared the men to march to Red Stone fort and await reinforcements before attacking the French.[70]

By May 24th, the regiment had built a crude wagon road over fifty of the eighty miles that separated Redstone from Wills Creek. They made camp in a valley between two mountains, called Great Meadows. It was a quarter-mile wide, marshy grassland about a mile long. The creek wandered through its center. It would make, Washington thought, a useful way station. Both water and fodder were plentiful. So he ordered a delay so his men could clear the brush, cut fodder for the draft animals and build a storehouse.

Three days later, Christopher Gist rode into the encampment to report that a party of French troops had passed his trading post the day before. Gist thought the French detachment was within five days of the Virginian camp. Fearing an attack, Washington sent half his command westward towards the Monongahela to scout out the French.

Later that day a Mingo warrior came into camp with a message from his chief Tanacharison, called "Half King" by the English.[71] The French, the Indian said, were bivouacked only seven miles north of the American camp. Washington, realizing he had sent his men in the wrong direction, gathered up half of his remaining troops and headed to the Mingo's camp. Marching all night, in a heavy rain, the group reached Half King's camp around sunrise.

Half King urged an immediate attack on the French camp, contending that the French meant to ambush Washington's command. Together, the Indians and part of Washington's regiment went off in pursuit of the French. When they arrived at a site overlooking a small glen, the young lieutenant colonel saw that the French were just awaking and getting ready for breakfast. He quickly arranged his men above the hollow while Half King and his warriors moved quietly off below to block any escape route.

---

[66] Anderson, 45.

[67] "Fort Necessity National Battlefield – Prelude to War," National Park Service (http://www.nps.gov/fone/prelude.htm) (Accessed August 3, 2008).

[68] "Will's Creek," *Wikipedia, the free encyclopedia* (http://en.wikipedia.org/wiki/Wills_Creek_%28North_Branch_Potomac_River &29).

[69] "Fort Necessity National Battlefield," National Park Service (http://www.nps.gov).

[70] Anderson, 45–46.

[71] "Tanacharison," *Wikipedia, the free encyclopedia* (http://en.wikipedia.org/wiki/Tanaghrisson) (Accessed August 3, 2008).

An Undeclared War between Virginia and the French in the Ohio Valley Erupts over the Jumonville Affair, May – July 1754

1. The Virginians under Washington and Half King ambush the French at Jumonville Glen

- **Jumonville Glen, May 28, 1754**

Washington maintained afterwards that the shooting began when the French saw men on the rocks above them and seized their muskets and began firing. The French, on the other hand, argued that a group of Washington's men let loose a volley at them without warning. However it began, it ended quickly. The French officer in charge was wounded and called out for a cease-fire. One Virginian was dead, three were wounded.[72] Nine French soldiers were killed, twenty-one were captured and two were wounded.[73]

Ensign Joseph Coulon de Villiers de Jumonville was the officer in command of the French. Through an interpreter, he explained that he had been sent out by the commander at Fort Duquesne, on a diplomatic mission— to deliver a letter to Washington ordering his evacuation from French lands, or to accept the consequences.

As the letter was being translated, Half King suddenly moved up to Jumonville, raised his hatchet and shattered the ensign's skull. Before Washington could intervene, the Indians had scalped one of the two wounded French prisoners.[74]

- **The French Response to attack on the French at Jumonville Glen**

One of the French prisoners, a Canadian militia man named Monceau, managed to escape from Jumonville Glen. He made his way to Fort Duquesne where he informed the garrison there of the events of what became known as the "massacre at Jumonville Glen."[75] It was this version of Jumonville's death that was sent to Governor-General Duquesne:

> In the morning, at seven o'clock, they [the French] found they were surrounded by English on one side and Indians on the other. They received two volleys from the English, and none from the Indians. Through an interpreter M. de Jumonville told them to stop, as he had to speak to them. They [the English] stopped. M.de Jumonville had read to them my summons to retire ... While it was being read, ... Monceau saw all our Frenchmen coming up behind M. de Jumonville, so that they formed a group in the midst of the English and Indians. Meanwhile, Monceau slipped to one side, and went off through the woods.[76]

A gunner at Fort Duquesne also obtained a version of the massacre from Monceau. Monceau, he declared "had heard musket shots and a few moments later, a second volley with cries of the dying," The Canadian had concluded that his party had been ambushed and defeated and decided to return to Fort Duquesne as fast as his legs would carry him. After six days of eluding the British-allied American Indians, Monceau reached the fort.

Another witness was Ensign Pierre-Jacques Drouillion, who was also captured by Washington's men. He wrote Governor Dinwiddie directly of the incident. In his letter, he thought Washington ought to have noticed, when he attacked early in morning that the French detachment did not take up their arms. Washington might have listened to the French interpreter call out, instead of firing on the French forces.

On hearing of these separate versions of the incident, the French commandant of Fort Duquesne, de Contrecoeur, made a note on his copy of the summons that his ensign had been killed while reading it. He

---

[72] Anderson, 47.
[73] "Tanacharison," Wikipedia, the free encyclopedia (http://en.wikipedia.org) (Accessed August 3, 2008).
[74] Anderson, 47.
[75] Alan Axelrod, *Blooding at Great Meadows: Young George Washington and the Battle that Shaped the Man* (Philadelphia: Running Press, 2007), 182. See also Sheppard, 43.
[76] Sheppard, 44.

received other news from Indians allied with the French that confirmed the killing of Jumonville and his forces while the summons was being read to the Americans.

The French were outraged. They said that Washington and his Indian ally, Half King, had ambushed a French officer on a peaceful diplomatic mission, without provocation. In the French eyes, it was murder, pure and simple.

As soon as Commandant de Contrecoeur learned of the ambush, he did two things. First, he wrote to Governor-General Duquesne in Quebec, informing him of the killings. The French commandant then immediately set about organizing a strong force to go after the Virginians. Within days, he had put together a force of 500 French soldiers and Canadian militia men, along with a few Indian allies, and prepared to set out. The force was to be under the command of Captain le Mercier.

Before they set out, Captain Louis Coulon de Villiers, an experienced frontier officer arrived with some 300 Indians in a convoy of canoes and bateaux. This was Jumonville's older brother. Since he was the senior officer present, he requested the command of the expedition.

In late June, the French called for a council of war with their Indian allies. They were aided by the Contrecoeur's reputation among the Indians and the fact that de Villiers was held the position as Commandant of the Indians in the area. The two French officers explained the recent events and the desire of the French to avenge their men. Bolstered by the high regard the Native Americans had for them, and, no doubt, by a few casks of French wine, the American Indian chiefs decided to "take up the tomahawk."[77] The next day, de Villiers left Fort Duquesne with 500 French regulars and Canadian militia, and at least 300 American Indians.

Meanwhile, the French officers taken prisoner at Jumonville Glen also lent their voices to a protest against the Americans. On their way back to Virginian encampment, they insisted that they were officers of the French crown on a diplomatic mission to serve notice on the English that the Virginians were intruding on French territory. The officers demanded to be accorded that respect and be returned to Fort Duquesne.

The French bolstered their claim with written orders. Chief among these was an official summons issued by the commandant of Fort Duquesne, written four days before the massacre. The summons was an order to the English troops to withdraw from the Ohio country or "suffer eviction by force of arms, despite the desire of France to preserve peace between the crowns of the two nations."

There was also another set of orders signed by the French commandant identifying the officers, their force, and an English interpreter, all charged with locating the road which connected to the newly opened wagon road of the Virginians. The force under the young, slain ensign was ordered to investigate Indian claims that the English were preparing to attack the French, despite the peace that then existed between the two nations. If Jumonville were to discover hostile intentions, he was to give the English commander, in this case Washington, the summation, wait for a reply and then return with it to Fort Duquesne.

Washington thought this business of the French claim to be a diplomatic one was nonsense. The French objective, he thought, was to pose as diplomats, and as such, be invited to British headquarters. There they would gather intelligence about the British and Virginia troops and then return with that information to Fort Duquesne. These men were akin to undercover agents, working out of Fort Duquesne; he advised Governor Dinwiddie to hang them as "spies of the worst sort." [78]

These events, this time set into play by an American act and a French counter-response in force, were an ominous portent of measures to take place in the near future. Through Washington's unwitting actions, Great Britain and France were that much closer to war.

---

[77] Ibid., 46.
[78] Axelrod, 182–184.

- **Virginia's Response I: Governor Dinwiddie's letter to London explaining the incident**

In his official report to the Virginia governor, Washington took great pains to blame the French. However, the size of the French force and the fact that the Virginians were the first to fire, contradicted his actions. So, too, did the French survivors. Dinwiddie realized that the events at Jumonville Glen would not make his British masters happy either. He laid the blame squarely on Half King and his Indians. He wrote London that "this little skirmish was by the Half King and the Indians. We were auxiliaries to them, as my order to the commander of our forces was to be on the defensive."[79]

2. Washington builds Fort Necessity at Great Meadows, May 29–June 3, 1754

- **Virginia's Response II: Fortification of Great Meadows, May–June 1754**

After this "skirmish" at Jumonville Glen, Washington was apprehensive that his Virginians "might be attacked by considerable forces." Upon his return to Great Meadows, he began an immediate fortification of the site, with the construction of a circular palisaded fort which he called Fort Necessity.[80] It was begun on May 29 and completed on June 3 1754. A recently discovered deposition by John B. W. Shaw, a member of the Virginia Regiment at Fort Necessity, provided a description of the fort in June 1754:

> There was at this Place a small stocado fort made in a circular form round a small house that stood in the middle of it to keep our provisions and ammunition in. And it was cover'd with bark and some skins, and might be about fourteen feet square ... the walls of the Fort might be eight feet distance from the ... house all round.[81]

Colonel James Burd, who was responsible for a force of 200 Virginians charged with clearing the road from the Chestnut Ridge to Redstone Creek during the French and Indian War, noted in his diary in late September, 1759 that he had seen Colonel Washington's fort. At that time, it was a "small circular stockade, with a small house in the center; on the outside [was] a small ditch that [went] around it about eight yards from the stockade. It is situate in a narrow part of the meadows commanded by three points woods. There is a small run of water just by it."[82]

Fort Necessity then, appeared to have been a round wooden stockade some fifty-three feet in diameter. A storehouse was placed in the center of the fort to protect provisions and powder from the elements. The building could also double as a hospital, if needed. It was small; no more than fifty men could fit into the palisaded settlement. Outside the stockade, Washington laid down a series of trenches and covered sites.[83] His Indian allies under the leadership of Half King were not impressed. The chief called it "that little thing upon the Meadow."[84]

Although crude, the fort was also unique. Frontier stockades normally were shaped as triangles or diamonds. These forts were, in essence, a simplified plan of the more traditional pentagonal layouts, which had been built since the mid seventeenth century. Fort Duquesne, for example, used the traditional pentagonal design. The advantage of this design allowed defenders to create crossfire from the projecting corners of the structure. This made attacks on the fort much more lethal to offensive forces.

A circular design, like Fort Necessity, while simple, made it difficult for defenders to concentrate their fire in any particular direction. However, it was easier to build and required less materiel, and thus would take less time to construct. Washington *did* add two angle-bracket shaped earthwork mounds outside the

---

[79] William M. Fowler, Jr., *Empires at War: The French and Indian War and the Struggle for North America, 1754–1763* (New York: Walker & Company, 2005), 43.
[80] "Fort Necessity National Battlefield," National Park Service (http://www.nps.gov) *(Accessed August 3, 2008).
[81] Ibid., 192.
[82] Axelrod, 193.
[83] Fowler, 44.
[84] Axelrod, 191.

fortification which provided an acute angle for concentrated fire. The earthworks may have acted as the first line of defense, making the stockade the fall-back position. Since Washington intended to do most of his fighting outside the stockade, he did not worry too much about the interior.[85]

While in the midst of construction, the young commander had learned that his Colonel, Joshua Fry, had been killed when he fell from a horse at Wills Creek on the last day of May. As a result, Governor Dinwiddie had promoted him to the colonelcy of the Virginia Regiment. This meant he was now in charge of the defense of the Ohio Valley frontier.

3. Washington's negotiations at Christopher Gist's plantation with the Ohio Indians fail

Then just as the fort was being finished, on June 3, Half King and his Indians returned. On June 9, two Virginia companies, under Captains Robert Stobo and Andrew Lewis, arrived from Alexandria[86] with supplies and nine small cannon, called swivel guns. These two companies, and another one which also reported for duty, were all part of the Virginia Regiment under the command of Major George Muse.[87]

A few days later, the South Carolina contingent under Captain James MacKay arrived. However, MacKay, who held a royal commission as captain would not place his men under Washington's control, since that commission was a colonial one.[88] Further strains developed between the two men when MacKay's men refused to work on the road to the Monongahela without extra pay.[89]

Although concerned about the French, Washington was determined to finish the road to Redstone Creek. Leaving his Virginians to work on the road, he rode to Christopher Gist's plantation to confer with Indian delegations summoned there to talk about joining the English in defending the frontier against the French. Washington had been encouraged by Half King's assertion that the Ohio Indians would join his forces if he remained steadfast and determined. It was on the basis of this claim that the young Colonel decided to attack the French at Fort Duquesne.

Negotiations went on for three days as the Virginian and Half King did their best to persuade the Ohio Indian delegations to join them against the French. It proved to be a hopeless task. The Iroquois Confederation had sent word to "their Ohio brothers that they should stay neutral in the quarrel between the white men."[90] Knowing that the French would retaliate against the Virginia forces for Jumonville Glen, Half King and his warriors also abandoned Washington.

Washington was not deterred. He was still set on attacking Fort Duquesne. With this in mind, he sent Captain Andrew Lewis with a detachment of officers and sixty men to work on the Redstone Road. He and the rest of the men would remain at Gist's plantation awaiting word of the French location.[91]

Washington convened his officers in council of war. They agreed that their forces should be consolidated immediately. Captain Lewis's road detail, MacKay's independent South Carolina Company, and Washington's Virginians should be brought together to defend themselves against an imminent French attack. The best place to convene was undoubtedly Gist's plantation since that was where the South Carolinian swivel guns were. As his men prepared another improvised stockade, MacKay and Lewis returned with their men, ready to fight.[92]

Then an Oneida Indian, Scarouady, who had become the de facto representative of the Iroquois League, arrived in camp to inform him that a large French and Indian force had reached Fort Duquesne and were preparing to attack him.[93] Washington convened another Council of War where it was decided

---

[85] Ibid., 194.
[86] Fowler, 44.
[87] Axelrod, 201.
[88] Fowler, 44.
[89] Sheppard, 47–48.
[90] Fowler, 44.
[91] Axelrod, 215–216.
[92] Ibid.
[93] Anderson, 49–50.

to return to Fort Necessity. No matter how the French approached, they could be spotted more quickly from the fort than from Gist's plantation.[94]

4. The French attack Fort Necessity

A two day forced march brought him and his weary men back to Fort Necessity, on July 1. Washington found conditions at the fort far from satisfactory Nearly 100 men were too sick to continue to work on its defensive structure and to weak to protect the fortifications.[95] Then, on the evening of July 2, it began to rain. The next morning, a visual inspection revealed that the trenches were filled with water. Morning roll call that day disclosed only 300 of the 400 men at Fort Necessity fit for duty.

At dawn, on July 3, the fort defenders heard a single musket shot. A guard had been shot in the heel. Washington ordered his men to arms in the light drizzle that showered down on the fort. The drizzle slowly turned into a steady downpour, drenching his men and trenches. Five hours later, his scouts reported that the French and Indians were on the march. They were about four miles away. Another report estimated the French strength at 900 soldiers, approaching from the Monongahela.

> With water rising and mud churning, there was only one useful command Washington could give: *Keep your powder dry.*
>
> A small circular stockade fifty-three feet in diameter with waterlogged trenches just beyond it. Four hundred men, a third of them too hungry or sick to fight. The rest huddled in the stockade, or crouching in the muddy water of a trench, or kneeling or lying at a distance behind whatever clump of cover Washington himself had failed to clear. They were men who had been living for well over a week on nothing but parched corn and, before that, a little stringy beef. Their commander was twenty-tow year old. The captain of the independent company did not pay him much heed, and the Indians—there never were very many of them to begin with—had all drifted away.
>
> *Keep your powder dry.* It was, at least, something to focus on as the insistent drumming of the rain marked each minute.[96]

At 11:00 that morning, the French appeared—six hundred regulars and Canadian militia with two hundred Indian allies from the Great Lakes region.[97] Captain de Villiers stood at the perimeter of the woods on the southwest side of the fort, in full view of the stockade. They outnumbered the defenders nearly two to one.

> They advanced across the field toward the English position in three columns. Washington and Mackay formed their men in ranks in front of the entrenchments. The French halted, fired a volley, and continued their approach. As they drew nearer, Washington ordered his men to fall back into the prepared trenches. With surprising precision the men followed the colonel's orders. Not wishing to risk a frontal assault against a protected enemy, the French withdrew and set out to invest the fort.[98]

The French troops quickly surrounded the fort. The rain continued to pour down on attacking and defending forces. The French took up positions under cover of the wooded hillside overlooking the fort, firing down on the men crowded together in the saturated trenches. Shielded by the leaves of the overhead trees, the French were able to keep *their* powder dry. The defenders were not as fortunate and those in the soggy trenches quickly became targets. By nightfall, thirty were dead. Another seventy had been severely wounded. The survivors knew what their chances were if the French and Indians renewed their attack the following morning. Rum stores were scavenged at the fort and disorder reigned.[99]

---

[94] Axelrod, 217–218; Anderson, 49–50.
[95] Sheppard, 48.
[96] Axelrod, 224.
[97] Anderson, 50.
[98] Fowler, 45.
[99] Anderson, 50.

Meanwhile, the French commander Captain de Villiers, was looking over his forces with something less than satisfaction. They were tired, having marched and fought in the steady downpour. Ammunition was low. The Indians threatened to leave the next day, fearing British reinforcements. Then, there was his legal position. What was he to do with the prisoners? France and Britain were not at war so de Villiers realized he could not make any of the defenders prisoners of war. Besides, there was no place to hold them at Fort Duquesne and no way to transport them to Canada for trial. He had come to avenge his brother and had done that.[100] Perhaps it was time for a parley.

5. The French terms

The French called out to the fort's garrison that if the two sides wanted to meet, the French would order a cease fire. The Virginia forces accepted and sent an officer out to meet with the French. Captain Le Mercier, the second-in-command of the French forces, offered to allow the garrison, the "honors of war" if they surrendered, adding that it would otherwise be a challenging task to control their Indian allies.

All the Americans needed to do, Le Mercier said, was to sign articles of capitulation and adhere to the conditions stipulated in those articles: the Virginians would return the prisoners taken from Jumonville's detachment, they would leave the Ohio River Valley immediately and not return for at least a year. They would leave two officers as hostages to insure compliance. His soldiers could keep their arms, colors, personal property and one piece of artillery.

Washington and McKay knew their position was hopeless. Fort Necessity had been targeted from all sides. There was no escape. Thirty-one men had already died and seventy had been wounded by the pinpoint musketry of the French forces. The fort was already a sodden mess from the torrential rains. The men were in no condition to continue the battle; many were said to be drunk.

Washington said no to the initial offer. He knew that a meeting would give the French a mush closer look at the Fort, including the entrenchments. The French then asked if he would send an officer to them, under parole. Washington considered. He could see that his powder and cartridges were soaked. His cattle and horses were dead. His supplies were desperately low.[101] He decided to agree.

So, he signed the articles, not knowing that the French version stated that he and his men were responsible for "*L'assassinat de Sr de Jumonville*," that is Jumonville's assassination. Nor did he know that de Villiers described the Jumonville expedition as "our officer carrying a summons ... to prevent any establishment [of the British] on the lands of the King, my master."[102] The French interpreter had translated the phrase "*L'assassinat de Sr de Jumonville,*" as the "death," or "killing" of the Lord Jumonville.[103]

Under eighteenth century law, if a diplomatic envoy was assassinated, it was considered an act of war. The French government published the incriminating surrender document, together with a translation of Washington's personal journal, found in the ruins of Fort Necessity, a few months later. Only then were the English to understand that the young colonel had done much more than fail to expel the French from the forks of the Ohio. The surrender documents he signed had given the French all the justification they would need to declare war on the British.[104]

---

[100] Sheppard, 48; Anderson, 50–51.
[101] Axelrod, 229–230.
[102] Anderson, 50–52; Sheppard, 48–49.
[103] Axelrod, 233; Anderson, 50–52.
[104] Ibid.

6. Aftermath

Washington left one of his captains, Robert Stobo, with the French as a hostage until his exchange could be arranged. The rest of garrison force left hurriedly, early on July 4, before the French arrived to take over the fort. The defenders left behind twenty-five wounded or sick Virginians and the unburied bodies of the twelve men who were killed defending the fort.

The Indian allies of the French had agreed to the capitulation although the booty they were promised was denied them by the American's quick departure. Once the Indians learned this, warriors went after the retreating soldiers and captured ten stragglers, whom they brought back to de Villiers. When the French captain reprimanded the Indians, saying this was contrary to the capitulation agreement, the Indians proceeded to kill and scalp three of the hapless soldiers; the remaining seven were allowed to leave.

While these events were taking place, the French and Canadian militiamen demolished Fort Necessity and broke the swivel guns. Thus, the French, by their actions, had demonstrated their strategic pre-eminence in the frontier region and ensured the allegiance of the Native Americans in the area.[105]

7. The French Response to the capture of Fort Necessity: Propose Ohio as a neutral, demilitarized zone

Surprisingly, the French did not use Washington's blunders at Jumonville Glen as an immediate pretext for war, despite their Governor-General's urging that very course. Instead, the Versailles proposed making the Ohio Country a neutral zone with a permanent ban on military operations within the region.

8. The British Response to the Fall of Fort Necessity: Send in the Regulars

In London, the British reacted to the fall of this fort with alarm. The crown offered Virginia £120,000 to shore up its defenses and contemplated sending regular army officers to the colony to train the provincial troops. With proper training, the British thought, these forces could then remove the French from Fort Duquesne and the Ohio Country.

The king's son, William Augustus, Duke of Cumberland proposed sending Major General Edward Braddock with the 44th and 48th British Regiments to America. Two more regular army regiments, to be raised in the colonies, were to become the 50th and 51st Regiments. The plan was to have Braddock and his British regulars remove the French from the Forks and from the garrisons at Fort Machault, Le Boeuf, and Presque Isle. The 50th and 51st Regiments, made up of colonial soldiers, were to destroy Fort Niagara on the Great Lakes. Finally, provincial forces, recruited for a year, were to demolish Fort Saint Frederic on Lake Champlain while another colonial force, under British command, was to flatten the forts on the Nova Scotia frontier. That was the plan.

Braddock was given extraordinary powers to accomplish these goals. He now had authority over the governors of the colonies and could also dictate to colonial assemblies the way these campaigns were to be paid.[106]

While the British made no attempt to hide Braddock's appointment or the orders sending the two British regiments to the colonies, this set off another wave of response and counter-response among the players.

---

[105] Sheppard, 49.
[106] Anderson, 56–57.

9. The French response to British build-up in their colonies: Send six regiments of French troops to Canada

The French, of course, viewed these developments with apprehension, anxiety, and pronounced unease. Their response was to send *their* regulars to their colonies— seventy-eight companies of regular infantry— the equivalent of six regiments or nearly 3000 men. These troops included some of the best trained soldiers in the French Army. They left France in the spring of 1755.[107]

10. Major General Braddock arrives in Virginia and convenes a conference of governors at Alexandria, April 1755

Major General Edward Braddock appeared in Virginia in February 1755. His two regular infantry regiments, the 44th and 48th were not scheduled to land until mid-March. So, he spent the last weeks of February conferring with Governor Dinwiddie on the recent events in the Ohio Valley frontier; in March, he sent out dispatches and commands for the quartering, provisioning, and enlistment of troops for the upcoming campaign against the French.[108]

In April he convened a conference of colonial governors from Virginia, Maryland, Pennsylvania, New York, and Massachusetts. He didn't ask for advice. He simply read his commission to them and put on the table his campaign plans—at least what he thought they needed to know. He dealt with funds first. All of the colonies, Braddock informed the governors, were to contribute to a common fund for military operations. They were to instruct their legislative bodies of that. It was then up to the governors to insure the execution of their colony's monetary responsibilities.[109]

Braddock then revealed his military plans. Those of concern here dealt with the two infantry units now on their way to the Virginia and Pennsylvania frontier. The 44th and 48th Regiments were already en route to Wills Creek and from there to move on Fort Duquesne. The other two regiments, to be created in the colonies were to proceed with William Shirley of New York and seize the French fort of Niagara. Once the French had been expelled from the forks of the Ohio, Braddock's forces would move north along the Allegheny, destroying the French forts there and join up with Shirley in the fall.[110] At least that was the plan.

The Major General refused to listen to the governors when they told him that the geography of the region would make it difficult if not impossible to move in the manner he desired. Braddock refused to listen, too, to the protests that the colonial legislatures would make about committing funds to a common pool with which to pay for the expected operations.

The governors were dismayed. William Shirley, the son of the New Yorker given the task of subduing Fort Niagara, and assigned as Braddock's secretary, wrote "We have a general most judiciously chosen for being disqualified for the service he is employed in almost every respect."[111]

Meanwhile George Washington was angling for a colonelcy of a unified Virginian command, similar to his position during the Ohio Valley hostilities. Governor Dinwiddie had already increased the Virginia militia to ten companies. Instead of placing these ten companies into a regiment, Dinwiddie ordered them into the field as independent companies under the command of a captain. Washington refused a captaincy in the provincial forces, resigned his commission, and returned to Mount Vernon.

Major General Braddock, meeting with the young commander in Williamsburg, "could offer him no better deal. Washington reacted to the general as he had to the governor: He withdrew to Mount

---

[107] Ibid., 60–61.
[108] Fred Anderson, *Crucible of War* (New York: Vintage Books, 2000), 85. Afterward, Anderson, *Crucible*.
[109] Ibid., 86–87
[110] Ibid., 87.
[111] Borneman, 46.

Vernon."[112] Undeterred by Washington's rebuff, Braddock made a new offer. He instructed his aide, Captain William Orme, to make a new proposal.

> The general, having been informed that you expressed some desire to make the campaign, but that you declined it upon some disagreeableness that you thought might arise from the regulation of command [i.e., rank], has ordered me to acquaint you, that he will be very glad of your company in his family, by which all inconveniences of that kind will be obviated."[113]

Edward Braddock knew that he needed Washington's knowledge of the Ohio County and its terrain. He knew, too, that the former commander of the late Virginia Regiment would be helpful in facilitating relations with the Indians there and was someone local British traders in the area knew and trusted.[114] Somewhat mollified, Washington decided to join Braddock, albeit as a volunteer and aide de camp to the general. In early May, he traveled to Winchester and became part of the expedition.

THE BRADDOCK EXPEDITION, MAY TO JULY, 1755

1. The British set out for the Ohio Country, May 1755

In late May, 1755, the British Army forces gathered at Fort Cumberland in western Maryland to begin their march to the Ohio country. General Braddock had some 1600 men with him—British regulars, Virginia troops, and some Indians— along with artillery, hundreds of wagons, waggoners, and packhorses.

Six hundred men left Fort Cumberland to find a way through the mountains and clear a road for the artillery train through Will's mountain to Little Meadows, about twenty miles to the west. Fortunately the advance force found a pass through a valley and around the mountain. They were able to clear the road in less than three days so the laborious task of moving the heavy guns westward could begin. Their progress was excruciatingly slow—at least that is what Braddock must have thought. By June 11, the British and Americans had gone only twenty-five miles and were still in Maryland.

At this juncture, Braddock determined to lighten their load. He began by asking his officers to send any of their unnecessary baggage back to Fort Cumberland. He decided, too, to return some of the artillery to the fort along with ordnance stores. An escort of fifty men was to accompany the artillery. He sent the more dispensable troops back to Philadelphia and decided to use lighter farm wagons rather than the heavy army wagons.

2. The French watch ... and wait

The British, lighter now by several cannon, wagons, large draft horses, and men, cautiously moved through the wilderness. The road, cut by the advance party, was narrow and forced the army into a narrow, winding column of wagons, horses, teamsters, and soldiers, stretched out over nearly four miles. It was a situation fraught with danger, especially if the French or their Indian allies decided to attack.

The British were right to be cautious. The French *were* watching. They had sent out scouts who watched the column from a safe distance and were rarely seen. The British were worried. They expected "the French Indians to attack ... every day."[115]

---

[112] Fowler, 58.
[113] Ibid.
[114] Ibid.
[115] Sheppard, 67-68.

3. The British reach Little Meadows

The advance party reached their destination—Little Meadows— by June 16, although General Braddock was still unhappy with what he considered to be the slow-moving pace of his forces. So he lightened the army's baggage and men still further. He also received intelligence through a friendly Indian that Fort Duquesne had only 100 French troop and seventy Indians. Since his army was stronger, he determined to push on to the fort before the French could receive reinforcements.

So he took a calculated risk: he split the army, leaving some of the artillery troops, the supply wagons, and waggoners at Little Meadows. He, himself, planned to lead a faster moving detachment of some 1200 men— two British regiments, the 44th and 49th, a New York Independent Company, three companies of Virginia rangers, a company of Virginia artificers and carpenters, a company of light horse, a detachment of sailor, and some gunners. By doing this he would be able to move more rapidly to invest Fort Duquesne before the French could bring in reinforcements. Then, the men left at Little Meadows could join him with the additional artillery, troops, and supplies to lay a successful siege to the French fort.

4. The British and American forces move into the Ohio Country

Braddock and his detachment left Little Meadows on June 18 with provisions for a little more than a month. His forces ran into immediate trouble when the Indian chief who were to scout out the route, was captured by the French. He was left tied to a tree, to be found and released by the British. This unpleasant incident confirmed that the French-allied Indians were indeed prowling the area.

However, they pushed on, reaching Great Meadows on June 25. There were now virtually daily skirmishes with the French and Indians. The French were successful in harrying the British, wounding or killing members who strayed too far from the column. The British were unable to counter these moves since the enemy melted away into the woods before an attack could be organized.

5. The British set out for Fort Duquesne

After a council of war, Braddock decided to push on although he was unsuccessful in his attempts in persuading his Indian allies to scout the French fort for intelligence. Finally Christopher Gist went on the mission with a few of his Indian friends and returned on July 6 with word they had seen just a few men at the fort and no one between the fort and Braddock's forces.

While Gist may not have seen anyone between Braddock and Fort Duquesne, the Indians raided the baggage train on his return, causing nervous soldiers to fire at any moving targets. Unfortunately, one of those targets proved to be the son of the Indian chief who had been captured by the French. The young man was killed, further worsening the relationship between the British and their Indian allies.

Unfortunately for the British, they had to proceed without any verifiable information regarding the location of any reconnoitering French or Indian units or the situation at Fort Duquesne. Sending out scouts would have been wise but time was of an essence, so without further delay to gather intelligence, Braddock sent Lieutenant-Colonel Thomas Gage and a group of men to secure the crossings on the west bank of the Monongahela and then as the river meandered westward, the north bank, near Fort Duquesne. This was done and the British reached the north bank of the Monongahela on July 9.

6. The French plan

Meanwhile, the French were not sitting idly by. In a council of war on July 7, they realized they had only two options open to them since the fort was indefensible against artillery. They could blow up the fort and retreat or they could attack the British. Destroying the fort and retreating would accomplish nothing from their point of view. The French decided instead to leave a small garrison at the Fort and, with a larger force, attack the British somewhere around the north bank of the Monongahela. The Indians were reluctant to do this they decided instead to ambush the British column from both sides once contact had been made.

7. The Ambush and Attack

The British had already crossed the river and reached the north bank of the Monongahela; they were marching west towards the French fort even while the French were holding their council of war.

Their trail was long and narrow and the British forces stretched out along it in a long snake-like column. Scouts and six troopers of light horse were followed by the vanguard of the advanced part, the advance party under Gage, a working party to clear the road, gunners and the rear guard of the advanced party. Then came the rest of the light horse, the sailors, artificers, and more gunners. Finally, General Braddock and his aides de camp, staff and guard, made up the last part of the column along with the main body of troops on each flank of a convoy of packhorses and cattle, and a few gunners with cannon at the rear. Flank guards were posted on each side to guard the column's advance.

At two in the afternoon, the Virginia light horse returned and reported a large body of enemy troops head, primarily Indians. The British formed up, fixed their bayonets and opened up into the woods before them. The initial volleys caused a panic among the Canadian militia who broke and ran. Then the British cannons opened fire and the French commander was killed in the volley.

Braddock and his main force, about 300 yards behind his vanguard, heard the shooting and ordered his men to be ready for action. He fully expected to "mop up" the French, thinking his vanguard would prevail.

Someone forgot to tell the French this as they rallied and opened up a heavy fire, from the cover of the forest, into the British ranks. The detached British flank guards were soon cut off from the main column.

The new French commander, Captain Dumas, saw an opportunity to envelope the enemy, attacking with an enfilading fire on their flank while covered by the forest. So the Indians, Canadian militia and French forces were deployed in the woods on either side of the British and attacked the flanks of the British advanced forces.

Braddock, in the meantime, heard the heavy firing and realized that his men were having more trouble dispersing the French than he thought and ordered more troops forward while halting the march of the rest of his men. He left 400 troops to safeguard the artillery and baggage and he, his staff, and his two aide de camps, Lieutenant Orme and Colonel Washington, set off for the front.

Meanwhile, Gage and his command saw that they were outflanked and ordered a withdrawal some thirty yards behind his original position. In doing this, he ran into the front of the British column moving in to reinforce him. This column was also being fired upon by Indians from a nearby hill. As his men were getting ready to return fire, Gage's column arrived and confusion ensued. Now the British presented a huge target from an enemy hidden from view.

British officers died as they called upon their troops to rally. General Braddock ordered the officers to form small divisions and attack. It did not work. The French and Indians were invisible, for all intents and purposes and with the fog of musket smoke, even the French flash from muskets was hard to see. The British were now enveloped on all sides. Their baggage and ammunition train were attacked from the rear. Cannon fire had little impact on the enemy scattered throughout the woods.

The commander in charge of the rear guard, Sir Peter Halket, was killed when he tried to form a defence and ordered the cannon with the baggage train to open fire into the woods. The French advanced unmolested and capture the cannon.

In the meantime, General Braddock was fully engaged, trying to avert a disaster. He was under fire from all sides, and had four or five horses shot from under him. He quickly ordered a party to advance and support his gunners and this two remaining cannon. He also ordered his men to clear the hill from which the Indians had attacked.

At this point, two of his aide de camps had been wounded. Only Washington was unscathed. His attack on the hill proved fruitless when Lieutenant Colonel Burton was wounded. Then, when Braddock was attempting to rally his troops, he was hit in the shoulder and chest. The wound proved to be mortal.

All of Braddock's senior officers had been wounded in this battle. The enemy's shots were precise and helped when the British soldiers closed ranks to return fire. Even through the smoke and fog caused by discharging muskets, the British offered excellent targets for French, Canadian, and Indian fire.[116]

> Colonel Washington faced a hopeless situation. He was seemingly the only officer of rank who had not been killed or wounded. Four bullets had pierced his coat and two horses had been shot under him, but he had escaped any injury. Nobody knew the true extent of the army's disorder or who was not the commanding officer. The British force was now in chaos and the battle was lost. The cannon fell silent, and the whole body gave way and crossed the river. The few American Indians with the army were determined; bu the rest of the army would not stand.[117]

8. Retreat

General Braddock, just barely alive, ordered Washington to withdraw to Dunbar's camp. While the young officer managed to rally officers and men as a rear guard and retreat in some order to the ford at the Monongahela, the dead and wounded, all the artillery, and baggage were left at the field of battle.[118] One of the British officers said that the French and Indians "pursued [them] butchering as the came, as far as the other side of the river. During [the] crossing, they shot many in the water and dyed the stream with their blood, scalping and cutting them in a most barbarous manner."[119]

Hundreds of bodies lay along the blood filled road. Every fallen British soldier had been scalped and his body stripped. All the British equipment that had been abandoned in the retreat fell to the French. By nightfall, Dumas and the French were back at Fort Duquesne with British survivors, lucky enough to have been spared the attention of the Indians and Canadian militia. The Indians returning with the French continued their own celebrations which included dancing, feasting and torturing their prisoners. Among the loot taken on the field was an unexpected prize: Braddock's dispatch box. It contained secret instructions and plans to attack the French forts on the Ohio.[120]

The British troops, meanwhile, were on the road in full retreat. Braddock, still alive, was carried in an ammunition cart, dying only when he reached British troops near Jumonville Glen. Washington arranged to have him buried along the road so the army could obliterate any trace of the grave and thus prevent the Indians from exhuming him and mutilating his body further.

9. Colonel Dunbar orders a withdrawal to Philadelphia

Colonel Washington brought the remnants of the troops back to camp, reuniting his men with those remaining units under Colonel Thomas Dunbar. The reunited forces numbered more than 1300 men fit for duty, more than sufficient number of troops to head back and capture Fort Duquesne, Ironically, had the British counter attacked, they would have found Fort Duquesne nearly defenseless. The Indians had left and the fort held too few men to withstand a siege. However, Dunbar was thoroughly shaken by the news of the disaster and the death of General Braddock and other senior British staff. He found it impossible to order his men to move out and lay siege to the French fort.

He was more worried about what he thought could be an imminent attack by French and Indians who might be surrounding him than about redeploying troops in the direction of Fort Duquesne and an

---

[116] Sheppard, 72–79. See also Anderson, *Crucible,* 97–103.
[117] Sheppard, 79.
[118] Ibid., 80–81.
[119] Fowler, 72.
[120] Ibid.

uncertain reception there.¹²¹ He and his men reached Fort Cumberland on July 21.¹²² Once safe at the British fort, he ordered "the remnants of the largest military force British America had ever seen to destroy supplies, mortars, and ammunition and march for Philadelphia with all possible speed."¹²³

10. Consequences of the British defeat in the Ohio Country

There were three immediate consequences to this disaster. First, Braddock's defeat and Dunbar's withdrawal from the frontier left western Pennsylvania, Virginia, and Maryland open to attack from the French and their Indian allies. Frontier families living in these areas cursed the two British commanders with the same intensity as they traditionally saved for the French and Indians who terrorized their borders.[124]

Second, the British casualties were horrendous: 1000 men, including at least 450 who were killed. All the leading officers had been slain or wounded. All of the artillery and baggage had been captured by the French. Of the provincial forces, Washington commented that "our poor Virginians behaved like men and died like soldiers." In comparison, the French lost only twenty-three killed, including fifteen Indians, and twenty wounded, including twelve Indians.[125]

Third, those Virginians who survived the Fort Duquesne campaign remained at Fort Cumberland. There Governor Dinwiddie ordered them reconstituted as the Virginia Regiment with Washington in command. His task for the next three years was to oversee the defense of more than 300 miles of backwoods settlements along the whole length of the Shenandoah Valley.

Meanwhile, to the north, Pennsylvania's frontier lay open to raiding parties of Ohio Indians. Western settlers fled for safety in the east. The abandonment of this frontier brought about "the greatest refugee crisis in the history of the colonies and the most widespread war British North America had ever known."[126]

11. The downward slide towards war

It was nearly ten months before war was officially declared—May 17, 1756—between France and England. In the interim, Colonel Washington use his time to recruit men for his Virginia Regiment. Among the men from Prince William who served in the Virginia Regiment were Phillip Askins, who enlisted in Colonel Washington's company in January 1755.[127] Another Askins, Philemon Askins enlisted in Captain George Mercer's Company in September 1755.[128]

Other men from Prince William who served under various captains in Colonel Washington's Regiment were John Askins,[129] Francis Austin,[130] William Bare,[131] Doctor Bowles,[132] and John Cole,[133]

---

[121] Anderson, 72.
[122] Fowler, 73.
[123] Anderson, 72.
[124] Fowler, 73.
[125] Sheppard, 83.
[126] Anderson, 73.
[127] Lloyd Dewitt Bockstruck, *Virginia's Colonial Soldiers*, (Baltimore: Genealogical Publishing Company, 1988), 105. Afterwards, Bockstruck, *VCS*.
[128] Murtie June Clark, *Colonial Soldiers of the South 1732–1774* (Baltimore: Genealogical Publishing Company, 1983), 404.
[129] Ibid., 404. John Askins had enlisted in October 1754 as a private in Captain George Mercer's Company in August 1756.
[130] Bockstruck, *VCS*, 90. Francis Austin was a sergeant in Captain Thomas Waggener's Company in September 1756.
[131] Ibid., 79. William Bear had enlisted in November 1754 in Captain Robert Spotswood's Company.
[132] Ibid., 108. Doctor Bowles was a private in Captain Thomas Waggener's Company at Fort Holland on the South Branch of the Potomac in August 1757.
[133] Clark, 415, 463. John Cole served as a private and corporal in Captain Thomas Waggener's Company. He made his first appearance in this company as a private in July and August 1756.

For a more complete listing of Prince William men who served in the Virginia Regiments, see Appendix 1 at the end of this book.

Neither Britain nor France proposed to begin a war over the Ohio country. However, the British could not accept their eviction for two reasons. The Ohio Company had too much invested in their lands and too many important investors like Robert Dinwiddie and others. Even more importantly, a continued French presence there threatened the security of both Virginia and Pennsylvania. Since provincial forces did not prove adequate to remove the French threat, the British resorted to their regulars. The escalation into a full-scale war had very little to do with European machinations and everything to do with the Ohio Valley campaign.[134]

---

[134] Matthew Ward, *Breaking the Backcountry: The Seven Years War in Virginia and Pennsylvania, 1754–1765* (Pittsburgh: University of Pittsburg Press, 2003), 85–86.

French and Indian War Period

Chapter 3

Military Records from Prince William County Order Books 1752–1769

Prince William County Order Books 1752–1757

Prince William County Order Book 1752–1753

May 30, 1753 Court, pg. 119.
Benjamin Bullet took the Oaths appointed by Act of Parliament to be taken and repeated, and subscribed the Test as a Military Officer.

May 30, 1753 Court, pg. 125.
George Neavill Gent, took the oaths appointed by Act of Parliament to be taken and repeated, and subscribed the Test in respect to his Military commission.

May 31, 1753 Court, pg. 159.
Anthony Seale Gent., took the Oaths appointed by Act of Parliament to be taken and repeated, and subscribed the Test in respect to his Military commission.

June 26, 1753, pg. 168.
Henry Peyton and **John Bell,** Gent., took the Oaths and repeated and subscribed the Test in respect to their Military Commissions.

June 27, 1753, pg. 173.
Howson Kenner, Gent., produced a commission from the hand of his Honour the Governor, appointed him Captain of a Foot Company whereof Gawin Corbin Esqr., is County Lieutenant [and] took the Oaths to the Government, [and] subscribed the Test ...

July 23, 1753 Court, pg. 180.
William Eustace took the oaths appointed by Act of Parliament to be taken and repeated, and subscribed the Test as a Military officer.
Augustine Jennings took the oaths appointed by Act of Parliament to be taken and repeated, and subscribed the Test as a Military officer.
Richard Hampton[1] took the oaths appointed by Act of Parliament to be taken and repeated, and subscribed the Test as a Military officer.

July 24, 1753 Court, pg. 192.
John Crump, Gent., took the oaths appointed by Act of Parliament to be taken and repeated, and subscribed the Test as a Military officer.

---

[1] Richard Hampton's claim was one of several presented to the House of Burgesses on Wednesday, April 21, 1756 for his service as a lieutenant in the militia for twenty-two days at twenty-five pounds of tobacco per day. The entire claim totaled 550 pounds of tobacco and was allowed by the colonial legislature. See H.R. McIlwaine, ed., *Journals of the House of Burgesses of Virginia 1752–1755, 1756–1758,* (1909; reprint, Bowie: Heritage Press, 1995), 378.

August 27, 1753, pg. 226.
  Thomas Harrison, Gent., **took** the oaths appointed by Act of Parliament to be taken and repeated, and subscribed the Test as a Military Officer.

September 26, 1753 Court, pg. 279.
  Cuthbert Harrison, Gent., took the oaths appointed by Act of Parliament to be taken and repeated, and subscribed the Test as a Military officer.

November 22, 1753 Court, pg. 309
  Richard Blackburn took the oaths appointed by Act of Parliament to be taken, repeated, and subscribed the Test as Military officer.

Prince William County Order Book 1754–1755

March 25, 1754, pg. 7.
  William Bronaugh, Gent., produced a commission from under the hand of his Honour the Governor appointing him Ensign [and] took the oaths appointed by Act of Parliament to be taken, and repeated and subscribed the Test as a Military Officer.

April 22, 1754 Court, pg. 42.
  John Bailis took the oaths appointed by the Act of Parliament to be taken and subscribed the Test as a Military officer.

May 28, 1754 Court, pg. 72.
  William Bailis[2] took the oaths appointed to be taken by an Act of Parliament and subscribed the Test as a Military officer.

March 25, 1755 Court, pg. 191.
  Joseph Nevill[3] took the oaths appointed to be taken by an Act of Parliament and subscribed to the Test as a Military Officer.

March 26, 1755 Court, pg. 201.
  Ordered that where Companies of Soldiers are marching through this county or any or any person traveling with an Express on His Majesties service and are supplied at any of the ordinaries within this county with liquors, provisions, then a fifth of the charges against the soldiers and public expresses be deducted by the Ordinary keepers of the price rated by the Court.

July 28, 1755 Court, pg. 263.
  Henry Lee, Gent., **took the oaths** appointed to be taken by an Act of Parliament and subscribed to the Test as a Military officer. [Marginal Note: Lee … sworn [as] County Lieut.]

August 25, 1755 Court, pg. 270.
  John Baylis[4] took the oath, as a Captain of a troop, appointed to be taken by an Act of Parliament and subscribed the Test as a Military officer.

---

[2] Ibid. In early April 1756, the Virginia House of Burgesses refunded twelve shillings to William Bayliss, the amount of money advanced to John Edwards, per his receipt.

[3] Ibid. Joseph Nevill's claim for ninety-three days of service as a trooper was also allowed by the Virginia colonial legislature on April 1, 1756.

Foushee Tebbs[5] Gent., took the oath, as a Captain, appointed to be taken by an Act of Parliament and subscribed the Test as a Military officer.
Francis Stribling Gent., took the oath, as a Lieutenant, appointed to be taken by the Act of Parliament and subscribed the Test as a Military officer.
William Carr Gent., took the oath, as a Lieutenant, appointed to be taken by an Act of Parliament and subscribed the Test as a Military officer.

August 26, 1755 Court, pg. 279.
John James took the oaths as a Militia officer... and subscribed the Test as a Military officer.

September 22, 1755 Court, pg. 312–313
Howson Hooe Gent., **took the oaths as a Captain**... and subscribed the Test as a Military officer.
John Hooe took the oaths as Lieutenant... and subscribed the Test as a Military officer.
William Barr[6] took the oath as an Ensign... and subscribed the Test as a Military officer.

October 3, 1755 Court, pg. 2.
Lynaugh Helm Gent., presented his commission from under the hand of his honor, the Governor appointing a Captain of Foot and took the oaths and subscribed the Test as a Military officer.

November 24, 1755 Court, pg. 15.
From the County Levy to patrollers[7]
To George Calvert the Younger, Bond Veale, George Foster, William Bear, Thomas Hazlerigg, Henry Hampton, Reuben Reeves, John Adams, and John Randolph, patrollers.

March 7, 1756 Court, pg. 45.
John Baylis[8] Gent., and **William Splawn**[9] made oath to an account of the number of days the Militia of this County were on duty on the Frontiers which was ordered to be certified.
John Baylis gent made oath to sundry receipts produced by him for money expended for the use of the Militia which was ordered to be certified.

March 7, 1756 Court, pg. 46.
Henry Lee[10] Esq. made oath to a receipt produced by him for money expended for the use of the Militia which was ordered certified.

---

[4] Captain John Baylis, or Bailis, as his name was sometimes spelled, was allowed his militia claim for 26 days service. See Lloyd DeWitt, Bockstruck, *Virginia Colonial Soldiers* (Baltimore: Genealogical Publishing Company, 1988), 162.

[5] Ibid. Foushee Tebbs's Militia Claim for 13 days service was allowed by the colonial legislature

[6] Ibid. William Barr was allowed his militia claim for 8 days service as a trooper

[7] Patrollers were considered to be quasi-military individuals who regularly patrolled the slave population. The office was militia-based. "If enough men lived in an area for a militia to muster, the law required that patrols be established as well." See Sally E. Hadden, *Slave Patrols: Law and Violence in Virginia and the Carolinas* (Cambridge: Harvard University Press, 2001), 32.

[8] McIlwaine, 377. John Bayliss's claim for service as a Captain in the Prince William County militia was allowed in early April 1756. He submitted a claim for twenty-six days service at thirty pounds of tobacco per day.

[9] Ibid. This is probably William *Splane* in the House of Burgesses records for April 1, 1756. He submitted a claim as a Lieutenant of Horse, for ninety-three days service at thirty pounds of tobacco per day. His pay totaled 2790 pounds of tobacco. The claim was allowed.

[10] Ibid., 378. One of the claims submitted by Henry Lee was not allowed by the House of Burgesses. Lee put in for money paid James Lemen. He also served as a delegate to the House of Burgesses although his election was declared void by the House on March 31, 1756. A new election was held, resulting in the choice of Henry Peyton to replace him. See McIlwaine, x, 352.

    John Baylis Gent., produced sundry receipts for money expended by **Capt. William Baylis**[11] for the use of the Militia commanded by him on the Frontiers. William Baylis was not in Court to swear to these. The court ordered the receipts be certified.

    George Calvert[12] the Younger made oath to an amount of services done by him for his Majesty. The Court ordered these to be certified.

March 23, 1756 Court, pg. 62.
    Clement Norman[13] v. Jonathan Gibson – On a petition
It is considered that the plaintiff ought to recover against the defendant the sum of 3L 4s 3d current money with lawful interest thereon from the first day of April 1754 until paid and his cash expended in his behalf.

April 26, 1756 Court, pg. 65.
    John Frogg, Gent., took the oaths appointed by Act of Parliament to be taken and repeated and subscribed the Test as a Military Officer.
    Bertrand Ewell, Gent., took the oaths appointed by Act of Parliament to be taken and repeated and subscribed the Test as a Military Officer.

May 24, 1756 Court, pg. 72.
    William Grant, Gent., **Edward Blackburn, Nathaniel Overall,**[14] **George Turberville Kenner,**[15] and **Samuel Baylis** took the oaths appointed by an Act of Parliament to be taken, repeated, and subscribed the Test as Military Officers.

June 28, 1756 Court, pgs. 117–118.
    William Blackwell, Gent., produced a commission from the Governor, appointing him as a Lieutenant Colonel of Foote. He took the oaths appointed by an Act of Parliament to be taken and repeated, and subscribed the Test as a Military officer.
    John Bell,[16] Gent., produced a commission from the Governor appointing him Major of Horse of this County, and took the oaths appointed by an Act of Parliament to be taken and repeated, and subscribed the Test as a Military officer.
    John Bailis, Gent., produced a commission from the Governor appointing him a Major of Foote and took the oaths appointed by an Act of Parliament to be taken and repeated, and subscribed the Test as a Military Officer.

August 23, 1756 Court, pg.183.
    William Buchanan[17] took the oaths appointed by Act of Parliament to be taken and repeated, and subscribed the Test as a Military Officer.

---

[11] Ibid. The claims of William Bayliss for money advanced to Lewis Casselman, John Hite, and Enoch Pearson were not allowed by the Virginia legislature. Nor were the payments advanced by John Bayliss to Owen Jenkins, Robert Paris, Enoch Pearson, and James Lemen. The legislature gave as its reason that it was not clear exactly what these expenditures had amounted to.

[12] Ibid. Among the services of George Calvert Junior was that of an express rider. He was allowed six shillings and 8 pence for this service in early April 1756.

[13] Ibid. Clement Norman received payment for sixty-six days as a trooper in the Prince William Militia on his claim submitted to the House of Burgesses, also in early April 1756. This court action detailed above appeared to be for the collection of a debt from Jonathan Gibson.

[14] Ibid., 378. Nathaniel Overall, listed as a "trooper" in the colonial House of Burgesses records for April 1, 1756, was allowed a claim for thirteen days service at twenty pounds of tobacco per day. The claim was allowed.

[15] Ibid., 377. A George Kenner, with no middle name, was listed as a corporal and given credit for sixty-six days service at twenty-two pounds of tobacco per day in April 1756. This obviously was not the same person as the George Turberville Kenner who took the oath and test as an officer in May 1756.

[16] Ibid., x. John Bell and Henry Lee were the delegates elected to the House of Burgesses.

August 23, 1756 Court, pg. 197.
Augustine Jennings took the oaths appointed by an Act of Parliament to be taken and repeated, and subscribed the Test as a Military officer.

August 25, 1756 Court, pg. 211.
Foushee Tebbs, having produced a commission from under the hand of His Honour the Governor appointing him Captain of a Troop of Horse within the County of Prince William took the Oaths appointed by Act of Parliament to be taken and repeated and subscribed the Test as a Military Officer.

September 27, 1756 Court, pg. 214.
Captain Howson Kenner and **Captain William Grant** came into Court and made their excuse on oath for not attending a Council of War last held in this County, which excuse the Court thought reasonable.
Major John Baylis came into Court and made his excuse on oath for not attending a council of War last held in this County, which excuse the Court thought reasonable.

November 22, 1756 Court, pg. 243.
Patrollers in County Levy:
To Gerrard Masters, William Askins, Thomas Homes, Garvan Pierce, William Hill, Thomas Smith, Thomas Matthews, Lewis Pritchett, Valentine Bethel, Joshua Tullos, John Adams, Henry Hampton, William Watkins, Reuben Reeves, John Randolph, George Reeve, **Lewis Reno**, Francis Reno, John Farrow, **Nathaniel Overall,** Israel Folsom, Daniel Stewart, George Harper, John Martin, Isaac Davis, Thomas Dowell, John Calvert, Obed Calvert, and **George Calvert the Younger.**

November 23, 1756 Court, pg. 249.
From County Levy:
Contra: By a fraction in **Captain Anthony Seale's** hand, and in **Colonel John Frogg's**[18] hand.

February 27, 1757 Court, pg. 260.
Edward Blackburn took the oath appointed by Act of Parliament to be taken and repeated and subscribed the Test as a Military Officer.

March 7, 1757 Court, pg. 260.
William Baylis exhibited an Account of Provisions impressed from Peter Peterson and made oath they were received and appraised according to the Account, which was ordered certified to the General Assembly.

---

[17] Ibid., 377. William Buchanan was a corporal in April 1756 when he filed a claim for payment with the House for sixty-six days of service at twenty-two pounds of tobacco. His claim for payment was honored.
[18] Ibid. Colonel John Frogg was *Major* John Frogg in April 1756 when he submitted a claim for twenty-three days service at forty pounds of tobacco per day. His claim was allowed. He later became Sheriff of Prince William. In that capacity, the Burgesses sent for him, and placed him in the custody of the Sergeant-at-Arms, to shew cause why he had not returned the writ for electing a burgess for Prince William. See McIlwaine, 352.

March 28, 1757 Court, pg. 271.
Charles Duncan is appointed surveyor of the road from the **Fort on Thumb Run** to meet a lower road on Carter's Run. It is ordered that he keep the same in good repair with the male laborers of Tithables between Thumb Run and the River and all above Carter's Run, convenient to the said Road. It is also ordered that he erect posts or stones where necessary according to law.

May 23, 1757 Court, pg. 275.
Simon Miller took the oaths appointed by Act of Parliament to be taken and repeated and subscribed the Test as a Military Officer.

May 28, 1757 Court, pg. 284.
William Grant, Gent., is appointed to settle the Tithes working under **Captain John Allan** and Benjamin Crump, surveyors of the road.

May 27, 1757 Court, pg. 308.
Thomas McClanaham took the oaths appointed by an Act of Parliament to be taken and repeated, and subscribed the Test as a Military Officer. [Marginal Note: "McClanaham sworn Capt."]

Military Records from Prince William County Order Books 1759–1761

There were no entries for military officers that could be identified in this order book.[19]

Military Records from Prince William County Order Books 1761–1763, 1766–1769

Prince William County Order Book 1761–1763

November 23, 1761 Court, pg. 36.
Patroller in County Levy
William Moore, paid 250 lbs tobacco.

November 24, 1761 Court, pg. 41.
George Calvert the Younger is **appointed a constable** in the place of Joseph Davis and is to be sworn before some justice of this county before he enters into the execution of this office.

January 25, 1762 Court, pg. 54.
Captain **Scarlett Maddin**, by virtue of the Governor's commission, took the Oaths appointed by Act of Parliament to be taken and repeated and subscribed the Test as a Military Officer.

February 22, 1762 Court, pg. 57.
William Bennett, by virtue of the Governor's commission, took the oaths appointed by Act of Parliament to be taken and repeated, and subscribed the test as a Military officer. [Marginal note: "Bennet sw^n (sworn) Capt."]
James Tebbs, by virtue of the Governor's commission, took the oaths appointed by Act of Parliament to be taken and repeated, and subscribed the test as a Military officer. [Marginal note: "Tebbs sw^n Capt."]

---

[19] This particular order book, Prince William Order Book 1759–1761, LVA microfilm reel 25a was not indexed. There were no identifiable militia officers in this order book.

Thomas Stribling, by virtue of the Governor's commission, took the oaths appointed by Act of Parliament to be taken and repeated, and subscribed the test as a Military Officer. [Marginal note: "**Stribling sw^n Lieut.**"]

Peter Glascock, by virtue of the Governor's commission, took the oaths appointed by Act of Parliament to be taken and repeated, and subscribed the test as a Military Officer. [Marginal note: "**Glascock Sw^n Lieut.**"]

May 3, 1762 Court, pgs. 94–95.

The Grand Jury returned with a presentment against **Nathaniel Overall** of Dettingen Parish for living in adultery with Charity Higgins.

The Grand Jury also returned a presentment against Charity Higgins for living in adultery with Nathaniel Overall.

It was ordered that those persons presented by the Grand Jury be summoned to appear at the next Court to answer the charges against them.

May 4, 1762 Court, pg. 102.

Robert Foster produced a commission from under the hand of his Honour the Governor appointing him Ensign in the Captain Daniel Kincheloe's company and took the Oaths appointed by Act of Parliament to be taken and repeated and subscribed the Test as a Military Officer.

May 6, 1762 Court, pg. 120.

John Tyler Jr[20] produced a commission from the Governor appointing him Lieutenant of a company whereof **James Tebbs is Captain.** Tyler took the oaths appointed by Act of Parliament to be taken and repeated, and subscribed the test as a military officer.

July 6, 1762 Court, pg. 173.

Thomas Blackburn Esquire, by virtue of the Governor's commission, appointing him **Captain of a company whereof William Ellzey Gent., was Captain and resigned**, took the oaths appointed by Act of Parliament to be taken and repeated, and subscribed the test as a Military Officer. [Marginal note: "**Blackburn Sw^n Capt.**"]

July 8, 1762 Court, pg. 206.

William Davis, Gent, produced a commission from the Governor **appointing him ensign** of a company **whereof Howson Hooe**, Gent., **is Captain.** Davis took the oaths appointed by Act of Parliament to be taken and repeated, and subscribed the test as a Military officer. [Marginal note: "**Davis sw^n Ensign.**"]

October 4, 1762 Court, pg. 337.

William Barr, Gent., took the oath appointed by Act of Parliament to be taken and repeated, and subscribed the test as a Military officer. [Marginal note: "**Barr sw^n Lieut.**"]

---

[20] There are two John Tylers in the 3rd Virginia. The first is Lieutenant John Tyler, commissioned on February 9, 1776. He resigned in August of 1776. The second John Tyler may be the John Tyler Jr who was a Lieutenant in Captain James Tebbs's 1762 Prince William Militia Company. A John Tyler Jr served as an Ensign in the 3rd Virginia until his death in January 1777. See Francis B. Heitman, *Historical Register of Officers of the Continental Army during the War of the Revolution, April 1775 to December 1783*, (1914; reprint, Baltimore: Clearfield Publishing Company, 2003), 553. See also NARA, *John Tyler's compiled service records*, M 881 MR 951, *Officers, 3rd Virginia*. These records do not say who his captain was. He was commissioned as an ensign in March 1776 and promoted in October of that year to a 2nd Lieutenant.

November 2, 1762 Court, pg. 385.
Robert Peyton,[21] orphan of Valentine Peyton, Gent, decd, came into Court and chose Benjamin Rush as his guardian, who is to enter into and execute a bond at the next Court with "good & sufficient Securities for his faithfull performance of his… guardianship."

December 6, 1762 Court, pg. 388.
Benjamin Rush, with John Tyler and Benjamin Bridges, his securities, entered into bond for the guardianship of Robert Peyton. The bond is ordered to be recorded.

April 5, 1763 Court, pg. 443.
Reuben Calvert[22] is **appointed constable** in the place of William Calvert. It is ordered that he be sworn before some Justice of this County before he enters into the execution of this office.

April 9, 1763 Court, pg. 497.
John Hancock produced a commission from under the hand of his Honour the Governor appointing him a Lieutenant in Captain Thomas Blackburn's Company; he took the oaths appointed by Act of Parliament to be taken and repeated and subscribed the Test as a Military Officer.

June 6, 1763 Court, pg. 522.
John Simms produced a commission from his Honour the Governor appointing him Lieutenant in Captain Lewis Reno's Company; he took the Oaths appointed by Act of Parliament to be taken and repeated and subscribed the Test, which was ordered to be recorded.

July 4, 1763 Court, pg. 544.
John Macmillion[23] produced a commission from the Governor appointing him an ensign in the company where **Lewis Reno is Captain**. Macmillion took the oaths appointed by Act of Parliament to be taken and repeated, and subscribed the Test as a military officer.

Prince William County Order Book 1766–1769

April 6, 1767 Court, pg. 33.
Bertrand Ewell, Gent., being removed from the office of Surveyor of this County, it is ordered that Cornelius Kincheloe, Richard Graham, William Grayson, and **Captain Thomas Bullitt**, or any two, inspect his books and that these books be lodged with the Clerk of the County, to be kept among the County records.

June 2, 1767 Court, pg. 45.
Ordered that **Major Tebbs, Captain William Tebbs,** and William Carr, or any two of them, allot and divide the tithes to work under Warren and Bland.

---

[21] Robert Peyton went on to serve as an Ensign in Captain John Peyton's 3rd Virginia Regiment, Continental Line from October 1776 until his death at Brandywine on September 11, 1777. See NARA, *Robert Peyton's compiled service records,* M 881 MR 951, *Officers, 3rd Virginia.*

[22] Reuben Calvert also was a 3rd Virginia veteran. He served as a sergeant in Captain John Peyton's Company of the 3rd Virginia Regiment from October 1776 until his death in January 1777. See NARA, *Reuben Calvert's compiled service records,* M 881 MR 952, *3rd Virginia Regiment.*

[23] McIlwaine, 378. In April 1756, John M'Millon had presented a claim for pay as a trooper with fifty-six days service in the Prince William Militia, at twenty pounds of tobacco per day. His claim was allowed.

June 3, 1767 Court, pg. 46.
Stephen Lee is appointed Surveyor of the Road from the Fauquier Line down to the bridge on Slatey Run and **Captain Helm,** William Alexander, and Lewis Reno, Gent., allot the tithes to work on this road.

August 7, 1767 Court, pg. 56.
John Simms took the oaths +c in respect to his military commission.

September 7, 1767 Court, pg. 57.
John Maximillion took the oaths applied and subscribed the Test in respect to his military commission.

June 5, 1769 Court, pg. 194.
The Court ordered the Churchwardens to bind out **Martin Wingate,**[24] son of Betty and Henry Wingate, to Jesse Moor according to law.

---

[24] Martin Wingate served in Captain John Ashby and Captain Valentine Peyton's 3rd Virginia Regiment between February 1777 and his discharge on December 1, 1777. In June 1777, he was selected by Colonel Daniel Morgan to serve in his independent rifle company. He was with Colonel Morgan from June to October 1777 and saw action at Saratoga. See NARA, *Martin Wingate's compiled service records,* M 881 MR 956, *3rd Virginia Regiment.*

A Colonial Militiaman

Part II

The Revolutionary War Period
1775–1784

Chapter 4

The Transition from a Colonial Militia to a Continental Army

Identified Prince William Officers in the Army of the Revolution

Chapter 5

Military Records from the Prince William County Court Order Book 1778–1784

THE REVOLUTIONARY WAR PERIOD

CHAPTER 3

THE TRANSITION FROM A COLONIAL MILITIA TO A CONTINENTAL ARMY

LESSONS LEARNED FROM THE FRENCH AND INDIAN WAR

1. <u>Historical Background</u>

When war came to the Ohio Country and the Virginia frontier in 1755, it was to a region that had seen very little conflict between the British colonists and their Indian neighbors. As a result Virginia was not prepared to wage a war against the French along the frontier. The militia in the previous century had been used primarily as a defensive force to protect the colony against the Indians and the Iroquois Confederacy. The militia also had another important purpose: to put down civil unrest like Bacon's Rebellion.

After 1676, civil unrest died out and the colony oversaw the creation of new counties throughout the northern neck. This period of growth took place as the frontier expanded steadily like spokes of a wheel from its hub. By the mid-eighteenth century, Virginia's Indians had been pacified and treaties with the Iroquois opened up the Shenandoah Valley to settlement.

During this time, the militia had gone from an active defensive force to more of a social institution. Militia musters had become much more of a social gathering rather than as an opportunity to instill discipline in the ranks. Young gentlemen were more likely to seek a rank as an officer that reflected their enhanced status in society. They were much less likely to become an officer so they could prove their military prowess on a battlefield.

2. <u>These Weaknesses in the traditional Militia system were revealed during the French and Indian War</u>

   ♦ **Local Militia captains and companies were reluctant to defend the frontier.**

   Initially, Governor Dinwiddie had anticipated that the militia would form the backbone of the colony's defense against the French. With this concept in mind, the colony passed laws to organize militia units for the protection of the frontier against French or Indian attacks. This tactic revealed a weakness immediately in the militia structure. Militia captains, looking at their post as more social than military, were reluctant to risk their lives during any defense of the frontier.

   In October 1755, during a raid on the Virginia frontier, one militia commander refused to call out his troops. He maintained that his wife, family and crops, as well as those of his soldiers, were at stake. So it was not possible for him to answer the call. When Governor Dinwiddie ordered the Frederick County, Virginia militia out to protect their county from Indian raids, they refused to muster.

   ♦ **Militia terms of service were too short to get the job done and once companies thought their time of service had expired, they went home.**

   Militia companies normally served for a month at time. Since marching to a post could take quite a while, when companies arrived at their post, they felt they had served long enough and would disband immediately.

   In May 1756, the Governor called up the northern Virginia militia to defend Frederick and Hampshire counties against Indian attacks. To his dismay, many of the men deserted before they even reached the two counties. The few who arrived refused to serve for any further time. They had, they said, done *their* duty by marching on the frontier. At other times, whole companies decided on their own that they had served a sufficient time at the frontier post and simply went home, abandoning the fort.

To make matters worse, militia companies sometimes refused to leave their own counties. Frederick County militia, for example, declined to go into neighboring Hampshire County even though Indian raiders were passing through Hampshire to attack the Frederick frontier.

- **Militia companies were untrained in military tactics needed to fight along the frontier.**

Because the militia companies and their officers looked at musters as social gatherings, the men had little idea of how to approach the idea of fighting Indians along the frontier. As a result, frontiersmen did not make good soldiers. Instead of moving quietly through the woods in order to surprise any Indians lurking nearby, the men would thrash through the forest, hooping and hollering, and thus alerting any war parties.

- **Militiamen were poorly armed with out of date equipment.**

Fewer than half the militiamen had guns. Those who did had weapons which were old and out of date, making it impossible to provide ammunition for them. To add to this difficulty, the men were not particularly experience or known as marksmen.

Even George Washington recognized this dilemma. He advised recruiters in the frontier counties to take pains to enlist "active Marksmen," those who were experienced hunters.

- **Militia companies often elected their own captains which meant the most popular received the command, rather than those most experienced in leadership.**

Since militia companies elected their officers, those elected were reluctant to carry out orders that might make them unpopular with their men. In addition, militia officers were especially sensitive to their rank as they looked at it as an indication of their social status rather than a military one. Even the men in the company were aware of their status. Sometimes companies refused to work on forts, believing that such unskilled work was beneath them. They demanded more pay and even when that occurred could refuse to do the work.

- **Militiamen failed to respond in adequate numbers to repel Indian incursions along the frontier.**

In June 1755, the Governor called out the militia to engage the Indians in southwestern Augusta County. Even though the Indian raid was a small one, the militia was in such chaos that it could not ward off the attack. Few militiamen even showed up at the musters. Dinwiddie complained bitterly to militia leaders that the men lacked the "proper spirit" to face down the invaders. The complete failure of the militia here appalled Dinwiddie along with the settlers who found themselves unprotected and were forced to flee their homes. As useless as the militia was proving to be in defending the frontier, still Dinwiddie continued to use them. They had one huge advantage over a provincial army: they did not cost as much.

- **When the Virginia militia and the Virginia Regiment were posted together, problems arose.**

The Governor attempted to circumvent the weaknesses inherent in the Militia infrastructure by deploying them with the Virginia Regiment under the command of Colonel George Washington. Unfortunately, the two forces' dislike of each other was extreme.

By mid-summer 1756, it was apparent that the militia could not be depended upon to protect the frontier against the French or their Indian allies.[1]

---

[1] Ward, 91–95.

THE CREATION OF A PROVINCIAL ARMY: THE VIRGINIA REGIMENT

1. Historical Background.

Governor Dinwiddie attempted to circumvent the challenges associated with the militia command and rank and file by creating a Virginia Regiment under the command of Colonel George Washington. Dinwiddie had hoped that volunteers would enlist from patriotic motives or from a young man's seeking of adventure.[2]

Unfortunately, without an incentive like bounty money, few eligible men joined the regiment. Within three months of the creation of the Virginia Regiment, only half the men needed, joined—some 500 recruits. Officers of the regiment were faced with a quandary since their commissions depended on filling out their companies.

♦ Enrollment problems, desertion, and insubordination plague recruitment in the Virginia Regiment.

While the concept of a unified command under a regimental system ultimately replaced the militia as an effective fighting force in the Ohio Valley campaigns, this structure was not without its own growing pains and problems.

After Braddock's defeat, the Virginia's colonial legislature expanded the regiment and put it on a more regular footing. In March, 1756, the assembly passed legislation to enlist militia voluntarily or draft other able-bodied men by lot for duty for eight months in the Virginia Regiment. The men who were drafted in this fashion were to be entitled to the same pay, immunities, and privileges as other soldiers in the regiment.[3]

Needless to say, this legislation was very unpopular. In counties throughout the colony, there were protests and in some instances, draft riots. Most of the men drafted were poor; some were vagrants. This created more problems, both among the regulars already in the regiment, and within the counties for elected officials responsible for enforcing the draft.

Finally, in 1757, the British promised to pay the burden of the costs for recruiting provincial soldiers. This news prompted the Virginia assembly to increase the tiny amount of bounty-money paid to join the regiment and resulted in more volunteers to fill up the ranks of the Virginia Regiment.[4]

Desertion was most widespread among troops drafted into the regiment from the militia. Each county had been given a quota of men to provide for the regiment. Since the militia had now been opened to a draft from all eligible able-bodied men, their ranks were often filled with the lowest economic and social strata of the county's inhabitants. Many of these men then ended up in the Virginia Regiment. Some were convicted thieves, given a choice between their Court sentence and service in the war.[5]

Another problem was insubordination in relationships between militia men and the officers and men of the Virginia Regiment. A militia contingent from Prince William, who believed they were superior to the privates and officers of the Virginia Regiment, became so abusive that one of their men was seized and locked up overnight for his insolence.

This did not set well with the Prince William militia or their officers so an officer of that county's militia and his men stormed the guard house and released the prisoner. He declared that the officers of the Virginia Regiments "were all scoundrels."

This insult to the Regiment also did not pass unnoticed and the militia officer was properly reprimanded and informed of the consequences of his act under military law. Thus chastised, he

---

[2] Ibid., 97.
[3] Hening, *Statutes at Large,* March 1756, 7: 14–18 (http://vagenweb.org/hening/vol07-01.htm) (Accessed August 22, 2008).
[4] Ward, 97–98.
[5] Ibid., 109–110.

proceeded to headquarters and presented his apology. Washington decided not to court martial the officer since the Regiment had made him sufficiently aware of his impudence.

At the same time, Washington thought it was a good idea to deploy the Prince William militia elsewhere and sent them off to build stockades and storehouses on the Little Cacapon and Patterson Creeks. Originally, he intended Captain Baylis to command the men. However Bayliss's superior officer in the militia, Lieutenant Colonel Henry Peyton, insisted on the command. So Washington issued orders to Peyton to strengthen the garrison at Cocke's and Ashby's' forts and to build another one to secure the pass at the mouth of Little Cacapon.

The next day, fourteen of Lieutenant Colonel Peyton's militiamen deserted. When Washington received news of this, he immediately delivered an order that if any militia ordered to these small forts on the South Branch of the Potomac deserted, they would be immediately drafted into the Virginia Regiment.[6]

♦ **A unified Regiment, used as a combat unit, became the model for Virginia forces during the Revolution as the state shifted from a defensive posture to an offensive force during the Revolutionary War.**

Despite the challenges encountered in the French and Indian War with a unified command, the knowledge and experience gained in those hostilities led the way to the formation of a new model, based on a regimental structure, when hostilities broke out in 1776.

The newly-formed state government realized the need for a combat unit who could take the offensive, both in Virginia and elsewhere. The Governor also realized that the militia were not that dependable and should be used only in the traditional sense—as a local short-term defense force.

So the Commonwealth, along with other states, raised individual state lines, divided into regiments and paid for by the state. They were organized for local defense and distinct from militia troops. Thus there were Virginia Continental line forces and State line forces. The Virginia Continental Line was paid by Congress, the State Line was paid by the General Assembly.

In September 1776, the Continental Congress established the size of the Continental Army at eighty-eight regiments or *battalions*, fifteen of which were assigned as Virginia's quota.[7]

2. Governor Dunmore's actions, culminating in the confiscation of gunpowder from the Williamsburg depot in 1775, bring about a new de facto government in Virginia.

The new governor's reception was initially favorable; however, the response eventually turned chilly due to his arrogance and his attempts to control the colonial legislature. Things came to a head in April 1775 when Dunmore confiscated the powder in the Williamsburg depot. This action and subsequent ones, like the proclamation freeing any slaves who would come over to the British to fight, angered Virginians throughout the colony and made a peaceful rapprochement between the governor and the legislature impossible.

There were two immediate consequences. First, the colony, already alarmed by the Governor's dissolution of the colonial legislature earlier in the year, sent out word for an election of delegates to a Virginia Convention, which would become the new de facto government. The second consequence was much more far-reaching: In March 1775, the second Virginia Convention completely revamped the colony's military establishment.[8]

---

[6] Sandra Mayo, "Fairfax and Prince William Counties in the French and Indian War," *Northern Virginia Heritage*, February 1987 (Vol. IX, No. 1) (http://www.historicprincewilliam.org/fiwar.html), 6 of printout. (Accessed August 4, 2008).

[7] E. M. Sanchez-Saavedra, *A Guide ot Virginia Military Organizations in the American Revolution, 1774–1787* (Richmond, Virginia State Library, 1978), 3.

[8] John Gott and Triplett Russell, *Fauquier in the Revolution* (Warrenton: Warrenton Printing and Publishing Company, 1977), 54.

3. The second Virginia Convention began to revamp the military establishment by establishing the minute service, an independent militia unit.

- **Independent militia companies were established for local defense with each county raising at least one infantry company.**

Patrick Henry proposed the establishment of an independent militia, to serve in the defense of the colonies. The Convention passed a resolution to set up independent militia units and recommended that each county raise at least one infantry company to be trained and ready for any emergency. The infantry company was to be composed of sixty-eight men with a captain, two lieutenants, an ensign, four sergeants, four corporals, and drums and colors. Each soldier was to be provided with a rifle, a bayonet, cartridge box and tomahawk, as well as a pound of gunpowder and four pounds of ball, fitted to the bore of his gun. Men were to be clothed in a hunting shirt and were expected to become acquainted with military exercise appropriate for an infantry company.[9]

Prince William had its own independent company, formed in November 1774. It was comprised of an independent company of cadets, organized among the gentry of the county. The company was commanded by Captains William Grayson and Philip Richard Francis Lee.[10] This company adopted a uniform based on one designed by George Washington in the French and Indian War. Their motto was *Aut Liber, Aut Nullus*. They prevailed upon Washington to act as their commanding officer. In April 1775, they were on the way to Williamsburg to confront Governor Dunmore over his removal of gunpowder from the Williamsburg magazine, when Washington persuaded them to return to Prince William.[11]

In July, 1775, the Continental Congress appointed Washington as the commander-in-chief of continental forces, with orders to go to Boston and take command there. Washington wrote the following letter to the independent companies of which he was the commanding officer:

> I am now about to bid adieu to the companies under your respective commands, at least for a while. I have launched into a wide and extensive field, too boundless for my abilities and far, very far, beyond my experience.
>
> I am called, by the unanimous voice of the colonies, to the command of the continental army; an honour I did not aspire to, an honour I was folicitous *[sic]* to avoid, upon a full conviction of my inadequacy to the importance of the service. The partiality of the Congress, however, assisted by a political motive, rendered my reasons unavailing; and I shall, to-morrow, set out for the camp near Boston.
>
> I have only to beg of you, therefore, before I go (especially as you did me the honour to put your companies under my direction, and know not how soon you may be called upon in Virginia for an exertion of your military skill) by no means to relax in the discipline of your respective companies…"[12]

- **Cavalry units were also established for defensive purposes.**

The convention also recommended the formation of cavalry units, to consist of thirty men, excluding officers; each trooper was to be provided with a good horse, bridle, saddle, and pistols and holsters, a carbine or other short firelock, a saddle pocket for his rifle, a cutting sword, or a tomahawk. He too was to be provided with a pound of gunpowder and four pounds of ball. The cavalry was to use "utmost

---

[9] Ibid., 58. See also Colonial Williamsburg Foundation, "Proceedings of the 2nd Virginia Convention," *Virginia Gazette*, (Pinkney) March 30, 1775, 2, col. 2–3 (http://research.history.org/JDRLibrary?online_Resources/Virginia Gazette). Afterwards, CWF, *Virginia Gazette* (http://research.history.org).

[10] Captain Philip Richard Francis Lee went on to become another captain in the 3rd Virginia Regiment. He was wounded at Brandywine, in September 1777 and died of those wounds in January 1778. See Peters, The *Third Virginia Regiment*, II: 47.

[11] Sanchez-Saavedra, 9.

[12] CWF, "Letter from General Washington, dated the 20th of June, at Philadelphia, to the independent companies of Fairfax, Prince William, Fauquier, Spotsylvania, and Richmond," *Virginia Gazette*, Supplement, July 14, 1775, 2, col. 1(http://research.history.org/DigitalLibrary/VirginiaGazette/VGImagePopup.cfm?ID=5047&Res=HI&CFID =564937&CFTOKEN=88982684) (Accessed August 31, 2008).

diligence in training and accustoming his horse to stand the discharge of Fire-arms and in making himself acquainted with military exercise for cavalry."[13]

4. The situation escalated with the Governor's removal of gunpowder from the Williamsburg magazine.

Then, in April 1775, the Governor responded to what he regarded as an attempt to over ride his own authority as the commander-in-chief of the Virginia militia. Alarmed by the possibility that this new militia might turn out against him, he attempted to defuse the situation by removing the powder from the magazine at Williamsburg with the express purpose of transferring it to a British ship anchored four miles away on the James River. British troops had entered Williamsburg quietly on April 21, 1775 to carry out the Governor's orders. The keeper of the magazine gave up the keys and then warned town authorities that the Governor had ordered the locks removed from the muskets and was about to carry off the powder.[14]

The Governor hoped, that by removing the powder from the capital, he would be able o put an end to any armed resistance to British policies in Virginia. He began looking, instead, for troops to restore royal authority although calls for loyalists to take up arms did not bring the return for which he hoped.[15]

Once the removal of the arms and powder became known, independent militia throughout Virginia, authorized by the second Virginia Convention, prepared to march on Williamsburg. Lord Dunmore, concerned about the extent of the public outcry, attempted to defuse the affair by paying for the gunpowder although this did not measurably end the public concern. The situation remained volatile throughout May.[16]

By the end of the month, Dunmore came to realize that he was in no position to fight without British help while the Virginia patriot leadership recognized that the independent militia service they created at the 2nd Virginia Convention was in no condition to engage the British.[17] Thoroughly alarmed by the fervor of the patriots' response, Dunmore determined it was safer to leave with his family for the safety of the British Navy. In June, he did exactly that.

Since the British forces were currently occupied with the civil unrest in Massachusetts as a result of Concord and Lexington two months previously, the Governor knew that he would receive little aid from that quarter. He was also less than successful in arousing the loyalists to take up arms in his behalf especially after he promised Virginia's slaves freedom if they fought for the British.[18]

THE THIRD VIRGINIA CONVENTION COMPLETELY OVERHAULED THE COLONY'S MILITARY ESTABLISHMENT.

1. The Virginia Assembly authorized two Virginia Regiments and fifteen Minute Battalions for defense against invasion and insurrection.

With Dunmore effectively out of the picture, the de facto government fell to the third Virginia Convention. Delegates met in August and formed a new military establishment for the colony.

---

[13] See note 9.
[14] Gott and Russell, 64.
[15] Michael Cecere, *They Behaved Like Soldiers: Captain John Chilton & the Third Virginia Regiment, 1775–1778* (Bowie: Heritage Books, 2003), 1.
[16] M. Lee Minis, *The First Virginia Regiment of Foot, 1775–1778* (Westminster: Willow Bend, 1998), 3. See also Sanchez-Saavedra, 6–7.
[17] Gott and Russell, 64.
[18] *Journals of Continental Congress*, A Century of Lawmaking for a New Nation: U.S. Congressional Documents and Debates, 1774–1875, 3, image 403 (http://www.loc.gov/ammem/amlaw/lwjclink.html.) Afterwards, *JCC* (http://www.loc.gov/ammem). The circumstances surrounding Lord Dunmore's proclamation, along with the text of the document and Virginia's response can be found on the *Black Loyalist Home Page*, (http://www.collections.ic.gc.ca/blackloyalists/documents/official/dunmore.htm). See also Gott and Russell, 67.

In July 1775, the Virginia Assembly appointed a Committee of Safety, who was charged with putting together a defensive strategy for the colony. They authorized two regiments of regular troops and fifteen battalions of minute men to defend the colony against invasion and civil unrest.

In August, 1775, the third Virginia convention recommended the formation of fifteen companies of sixty-eight men each. Eight of these companies would form the 1st Virginia Regiment. The regiment would be subject to service outside Virginia. The commanding officer of the 1st Virginia would also command all of the Virginia troops. The remaining companies were to be part of the 2nd Virginia Regiment. The four western districts were asked to recruit riflemen only; then each regiment would have two rifle companies for use as light infantry.[19]

2. The Convention delegates formed a new military establishment for the colony—a three-tier system.

- **Two 500-man Regiments replaced the independent militia companies and were raised for service throughout the colony for a term of one year.**

The Convention gave orders to replace the independent militia companies with a three-tier military system. At the top were two 500 man Battalions or Regiments—the 1st and Virginia 2nd Virginia Regiments. These units encompassed full-time soldiers raised throughout the colony to serve for one year. The regiments were a throw-back to the Virginia military establishment utilized during the French and Indian War.[20]

- **Minute Battalions were created within sixteen recruiting districts.**

The second tier was a newly created minute service. The delegates divided Virginia into sixteen recruiting districts, with each district responsible for raising a regiment of 500 minute men.[21] These units were to be ready and able to serve at a minute's notice. The men recruited into the minute service were to be between sixteen and sixty years of age. All in all, they were better trained and prepared than the militia.

  - **The Prince William Minute Battalion.**

Prince William had its own District Battalion, recruited from Prince William, Fairfax, and Loudoun. Colonel William Grayson was the commanding officer of the Minute Battalion. The battalion was formed late in 1775 and took part in action against Dunmore around Norfolk and Hampton in early 1776.[22]

There were eight companies in this minute battalion. Five of these companies were headed by men from Prince William. Captain Andrew Leitch,[23] and Captain William Johnson,[24] who also served as the paymaster of the regiment, were two of the Prince William men who provided experienced officers for Continental Regiments in the Revolution. Captain John Fitzgerald,[25] Captain Cuthbert Harrison,[26] and

---

[19] Gott and Russell, 72. See note 14 on page 72 for the third Virginia Convention's organization of the Virginia military.

[20] Joan W. Peters, *The Tax Man Cometh: Land & Property in Colonial Fauquier County, Virginia 1759–1782* (Westminster: Willow Bend Books, 1999), iii. See also Colonial Williamsburg Foundation, "Proceedings of the 3rd Virginia Convention," *Virginia Gazette*, (Purdie) August 24, 1774: 1–6, (http://research.history.org).

[21] Mary Steven Jones, ed. *An 18th Century Perspective: Culpeper County, Va* (Culpeper: Culpeper Historical Society, 1976), 15.

[22] Sanchez-Saavedra, 22.

[23] Andrew Leitch was another early Captain of the 3rd Virginia. He was promoted out of the regiment to be a Major in the 1st Virginia Regiment. He died of wounds suffered at Harlem Heights in October 1776. See Joan W. Peters, *The Third Virginia Regiment of Foot, Continental Line 1775–1778: With Drums Beating and Flags Flying* (Westminster: Willow Bend Books, 2008), II: 48. Afterwards, Peters, *The Third Virginia Regiment.*

[24] This captain may have been the same man who served as a captain in the 11th Virginia. See Sanchez-Saavedra, 65.

[25] Captain Fitzgerald was another 3rd Virginia officer, commissioned in February 1776. He was promoted to major in September 1776 and to lieutenant-colonel in November. He served as an aide-de-camp to General Washington. He was wounded at Monmouth. He resigned his commission in July 1778. See Peters, *The Third Virginia Regiment*, II: 34.

[26] Cuthbert Harrison went on to serve in the 1st Continental Light Dragoons as a captain of the 4th company of troopers. He received a continental commission in February 1777. See Sanchez-Saavedra, 102.

Captain Henry Lee rounded out the group.[27] Henry Lee began his Continental career as a captain in the 1st Regiment of Continental Light Dragoons in June 1776.[28] As a reward for his service, Captain Lee was promoted by Congress to major-commandant of his own unit, Lee's Legion, and authorized to raise three troops of horse for special missions.[29]

- **Colonel William Grayson was given the command of this Minute Battalion.**

The Prince William minute battalion, comprised of some 350 minute-men, commanded by Colonel William Grayson, arrived in Williamsburg in December 1775.[30] Unfortunately, there was no further mention of their participation in the hostilities against Governor Dunmore in the *Virginia Gazette* so their contribution to that campaign can not be recognized here. It was believed that they took part in the successful campaigns around Norfolk and Hampton in early 1776. Then, in August, 1776, the battalion was ordered to replace the two regular Virginia Regiments, stationed in that area. The 1st and 2nd Virginia Regiments were sent north to Pennsylvania.[31]

In March 1776, Colonel Grayson informed the president of the Committee of Safety, of his resignation as the Colonel of the Prince William minute Battalion.[32] The command of the Minute Battalion was offered to James Hendricks, who refused it. It was then offered to John Quarles, who accepted for a brief time. The command of the battalion finally devolved upon Major Levin Powell who took charge after March 1776.[33]

Colonel Grayson was a well-known a resident of Prince William and very well-known throughout Virginia, whose name has now been forgotten by history. His resignation from the minute battalion had been occasioned by his promotion an assistant secretaryship to General Washington and his continental command. He served in that post until January 1777 when he was given his own regiment, part of the additional continental regiments, authorized by Congress, the previous December. His regiment was recruited at large from Virginia and Maryland and attached to General Charles Scott's brigade in 1777. In June 1778, this unit suffered great losses at Monmouth. Then in April of the following year, the regiment was all but decimated by smallpox. The remaining men were merged with Nathaniel Gist's Additional Continental Regiment and Colonel Grayson was placed in command of the Continental War office.[34]

Colonel Grayson also served as a delegate to the Confederation Congress from 1785–1787. He was an Anti-Federalist and, true to those beliefs, opposed the ratification of the Constitution at Virginia's ratifying convention in 1788. Despite this, Governor Patrick Henry appointed him to the first U. S. Senate where Grayson served until his death on March 12, 1790.[35] His will was probated in Fauquier County in December, 1790.[36]

---

[27] Ibid., 22.
[28] Ibid., 102–103.
[29] Ibid., 95–96.
[30] Colonial Williamsburg Foundation, "Minute Men of Prince William arrive in Williamsburg," *Virginia Gazette*, Purdie, December 29, 1775, 2, col. 2 (http://research.history.org/DigitalLibrary/VirginiaGazette/VGImagePopup.cfm?ID=5186&Res =HI&CFID=564937&CFTOKEN=88982684) (Accessed August 31, 2008).
[31] Sanchez-Saavedra, 22
[32] CWF, "Resignations in Prince William Minute Battalion," *Virginia Gazette,* Purdie, March 22, 1776, 3, col. 2 (http://research.history.org/DigitalLibrary/VirginiaGazette/VGImagePopup. Cfm?ID=5526&Res=HI&CFID=564937&CFTOKEN=88982684) (Accessed August 31, 2008).
[33] Sanchez-Saavedra, 22.
[34] Ibid., 74–75.
[35] Wikipedia, "William Grayson," *Wikipedia, the free encyclopedia* (http://en.wikipedia.org/wiki//William_Grayson) (Accessed September 2, 2008).
[36] Joan W. Peters, *Being of Sound Mind ... An Index to the Probate Records in the Fauquier County, Virginia Loose Papers and Superior and Circuit Court Records, 1759–1919* (Westminster: Willow Bend Books, 2001), 81.

- **The militia service became the third tier of the new military establishment.**

The Virginia militia had a long history in Virginia which has already been recounted in Part I. The deficiencies in the discipline and leadership of militia units led to their demotion during the War of Independence. However, they did provide a pool of men between sixteen and sixty for duty in the state and continental lines.

The county militia units were never really considered an effective or unified fighting force since their officers were elected and the men were never really trained to accept military discipline. However, the system itself did provide a workable method of registering eligible men.

In Virginia, the county militia companies were commanded by a County lieutenant. These men were usually men of education and wealth, gentlemen with other local responsibilities— they were justices, surveyors, planters, lawyers, or delegates to the legislature. As the county lieutenant, the commander of the local militia outranked all other militia officers.

No more than one-tenth of the local militia was on active duty an any given time. Their duty consisted of guarding supplies and hunting suspected tories or felons. There was no evidence in the records to suggest that the Prince William militia played a part in the southern campaign after the British captured the Virginia continental line at Charleston in May 1780.[37] A fuller listing of officers in the Prince William Militia during the Revolutionary War may be found in Chapter 5.

THE TRANSITION FROM COLONIAL "PROVINCIAL" FORCES TO A CONTINENTAL FORCE.

1. The Continental Congress authorized the raising of six continental battalions in Virginia in December 1775.

On December 28, 1776, the Continental Congress, sitting in Philadelphia, authorized six continental battalions to be raised in Virginia. The regiments were to be raised and paid as continental forces "unless the convention ... can raise them on better terms."[38]

- **Identified Prince William men in the 1st Virginia Continental Regiment.**

One of the Prince William pensioners who served in the 1st Virginia Regiment was *Thomas White*, a former sergeant in that unit. His pension may be found in Chapter 9.

- **Identified Prince William veterans in the 2nd Virginia Continental Regiment.**

Richard Bradley was a private in the 2nd Virginia Regiment, in Captain John Peyton Harrison's Company. His service can be found in note 30 in Chapter 5.

- **Identified Prince William officers and men in the 3rd Virginia Continental Regiment.**

In January 1776, the Virginia Convention met to select the field officers of the new battalions. Six of these battalions were to be made up of ten companies of sixty-eight men each. Prince William men have been identified in the 3rd Virginia regiment, commanded by Colonel Hugh Mercer and Colonel George Weedon. *Captain Philip Richard Francis Lee*, of Prince William was an early captain who raised men from Prince William. *Captain Andrew Leitch* was another early 3rd Virginia captain whose men were raised from the county.[39]

A third captain in this illustrious regiment was *Captain John Fitzgerald*, another veteran from the Prince William Minute Battalion. He received a continental commission as a captain in the 3rd Virginia in February 1776. In November, he was promoted out of the regiment as a lieutenant-colonel and aide-de-

---

[37] Sanchez-Saavedra, 137–147.
[38] *Journals of Continental Congress, 1774–1789* (Washington: Government Printing Office, 1906), 3: 463. Afterwards, *JCC*.
[39] Sanchez-Saavedra, 39.

camp to General Washington. He was wounded at Monmouth in June 1778 and resigned his commission in July 1778.[40]

The 3rd Virginia regiment was involved in the New York campaign, at Harlem Heights; and in every major campaign in New Jersey and Pennsylvania from September 1776 until June 1778.[41] *Captain Leitch* died of lockjaw in early October, resulting from wounds suffered at Harlem Heights in September 1776.[42] *Captain Phil Lee* was wounded at Brandywine, in September 1777 and died of his wounds in late January 1778.[43] Prince William residents also served in the rank and file of the 3rd Virginia. More than three dozen men from Prince William enlisted in the 3rd Virginia.

Some served in Captain John Peyton's company while others served in *Captain Philip Richard Francis Lee*'s 3rd Virginia Company. One of the Valentine Peytons in Prince William began as a lieutenant in Captain John Ashby's Company and succeeded to the captaincy when Ashby was forced to resign due to wounds in October 1777. This Valentine Peyton died at Charleston in May 1780.[44]

A close reading of Chapter 5 of the men mentioned in the Court minutes from 1778–1784 uncovered even more men and officers. Among these 3rd Virginia veterans, whose names appear in this minute book, were *Lieutenant Matthew Whiting, Sergeant Willoughby Brent,* who died in the service; *John Randolph, Daniel Holifield, Zachariah Crook* who also died in the war; *John King, John Gunyon, Thomas Hines, Charles Lenox, Corporal John Sidebotham, Ensign George Peyton,* and *Lieutenant Robert Peyton,* who both died in the service; *Benjamin Tennill,* and *Philip* and *William Conner.*

Chapter 9, which related to pension applications and heirs-at-law certification revealed even more Prince William veterans or veterans who lived in Prince William when they applied for a pension. Partial listings of these men were: *John Alvey, Robert Alvey,* and *Spencer Anderson;*[45] *Reuben Calvert,* who died while in the service in the 3rd Virginia; his son Tommy was bound out in Prince William to learn a trade.[46] *Moses Daulton, John Davis, William Davis,* and *John Edwards* also served in the 3rd Virginia, enlisting from Prince William.[47] *Benjamin Hamrick, James Holliday,* and *Cornelius Hurley,* and *Francis Kendall* were other veterans who served in the 3rd Virginia from Prince William.[48]

Unfortunately, space considerations here forbade the inclusion of all the Prince William men who served in the 3rd Virginia.[49]

2. The Continental Congress authorized fifteen Continental Virginia Regiments in September 1776.

The Continental Congress authorized the raising of another fifteen regiments in Virginia in September 1776. Representatives from Prince William served in the 11th, 12th, and 13th Virginia.

♦ Identified Prince William men in the 10th Virginia Continental Regiment.

The 10th Virginia was one of the six new regiments ordered to be raised by the General Assembly in October 1776. This was done to comply with the quota of fifteen Virginia regiments set out by the Continental Congress the month before. The 10th Virginia was raised at large throughout Virginia.

The regiment traveled north in the spring of 1777. The men reach the main army in June and were placed in George Weedon's brigade. The regiment served at Brandywine, Germantown and the remaining campaigns in New Jersey and Pennsylvania.

---

[40] Heitman, 229.
[41] Ibid., 38–41.
[42] Peters, *The Third Virginia Regiment,* I: 80–83.
[43] Ibid., I: 135.
[44] See Chapter 5 and Peters, *The Third Virginia Regiment,* II: iii–vi and 82–83.
[45] Peters, *The Third Virginia Regiment,* II: 125–128.
[46] Ibid., II: 170.
[47] Ibid., II: 189–190, 192, 194–195, and 203–204.
[48] Ibid., II: 234, 241–242, 245. For a full listing of 3rd Virginia men who lived in Prince William either at their enlistment or when they applied for a pension, see Peters, *The Third Virginia Regiment,* volume II: Biographies of the Men and Officers of the 3rd Virginia.
[49] Ibid.

In September 1778, in the reorganization of the Virginia line, the 10th Virginia was designated as the 6th Virginia.[50]

Thomas Bowne of Prince William began his career in the 10th Virginia as a 2nd Lieutenant in April, 1777. He was promoted to 1st Lieutenant and became the Regimental Adjutant of the regiment.[51] In the September 1778 reorganization of the Virginia Line, the 10th Virginia became the 6th Virginia and Thomas Bowne's was a captain of this reconstituted regiment, serving in that capacity from February 1781 to January 1783.[52] Then, later the same year, in another arrangement made at Winchester, Virginia, of the remnants of the Continental troops still in service, Thomas Bowne appeared as a captain of the 9th Company in the 1st Virginia Regiment.[53]

Captain Bowne was mentioned in Chapter 9 in March 1839 as a "Captain in the Virginia Continental service in the revolutionary war." His heirs-at-law were certified during this court session.

- ♦ **Identified Prince William Men in the 11th Virginia Continental Regiment.**

The 11th Virginia was ordered to be raised by the General Assembly in October 1776 in order to meet Virginia's quota of fifteen regiments set by Congress in September 1776. This regiment was commanded by Colonels Daniel Morgan and Christian Febinger and raised in Prince William, Amelia, Loudoun, and Frederick counties.

One of the early captains in this regiment was *Charles Gallahue*, a Prince William resident. He received his continental commission as a captain of the 9th Company in January 1777.[54] He was killed, four months later, on May 23, 1777, in a raid by the American forces on Sag Harbor,[55] near the tip of Long Island.[56]

Chapter 5, which related military information in the minute books from 1778–1784, revealed five veterans from Prince William who served in the 11th Virginia. *George White, Roger McMahon,* and *Leander Murphy* all served under Captain Gallahue. *James Hay* was recruited by Sergeant Hatcher of the 11th Virginia while *Peter McGinnis* was a private in Captain Thomas Willis's 11th Virginia Company.

Chapter 9, which contains information about the Prince William pensioners in the Court Order Books, disclosed two more veterans who served under Captain Gallahue: *John Mattingly* and *John Dickinson*.[57]

William Johnson was another captain in the 11th Virginia—of the 4th Company. He was commissioned by Congress in November 1776.[58]

The brothers and sisters of *Thomas Ransdell*, an early officer in the 11th Virginia, who was promoted from 3rd lieutenant to 1st lieutenant between July 1776 and July 1777, appeared in the Prince William Court in September 1843 to apply for certification as his only heirs.[59]

- ♦ **Identified Prince William veterans in the 12th Virginia Continental Regiment.**

Chapter 5 unearthed just one Prince William resident: *Major Charles Simms*, who served from November 1776 to September 1777. He was then promoted to lieutenant colonel of the 6th Virginia. He served in this capacity from September 1777 to September 1778.[60] In the reorganization of the Virginia line which took place in White Plains on September 14, 1778, Lieutenant-Colonel Simms was transferred to the 2nd Virginia. He remained with the 2nd Virginia until his resignation in December 1778.[61]

---

[50] Sanchez-Saavedra, 50.
[51] Heitman, 113.
[52] Sanchez-Saavedra, 50–51.
[53] Ibid., 33.
[54] Ibid., 65.
[55] Heitman, 241.
[56] Mark M. Boatner, *Encyclopedia of the American Revolution* (Mechanicsburg: Stackpole Books, 1996), 955.
[57] See Chapter 9 for pension information about these Prince William veterans.
[58] Sanchez-Saavedra, 65.
[59] See Chapter 9 and Heitman, 458.
[60] See Sanchez-Saavedra, 67.
[61] Ibid., 35.

♦ **Identified Prince William veterans in the 13th Virginia Continental Regiment.**

Chapter 5's treatment of the minute books from 1778–1784 uncovered two Prince William veterans who served in Captain George McCormick's 13th Virginia Company: *George Purcell* and *Hugh Davis*. Only one pensioner in the County Court Minutes in Chapter 9 was identified as a soldier in the 13th Virginia. *William Dowell* served as a private and corporal in Captain George McCormick's company from January 1777 until September 1778.[62]

♦ **Identified Prince William officers and men in Grayson's Additional Continental Regiment.**

Colonel William Grayson's Additional Continental Regiment of Infantry, was formed as the result of Congressional legislation in December 1776. Colonel Grayson had been promoted to the commandant of the regiment, raised at large in Virginia and Maryland. In 1777, the regiment was attached to General Charles Scott's brigade.

The regiment fought in the Pennsylvania campaigns of 1777 and saw action at Monmouth in 1778. In April 1779, after smallpox had all but decimated the unit, three of its companies were merged with Nathaniel Gist's Additional Continental Regiment. In late 1779, Gist's newly enlarged regiment, with additions from both Grayson and Colonel Thurston's units, was sent south to defend Charleston. When the British captured Charleston in May 1780, Gist's men were made prisoners. In November 1780, a general order disbanded the regiment.[63]

There were Prince William men who served in Grayson's Regiment. *John Linton* and *William Linton*, appeared in Chapter 5, the sole surviving minute book from Prince William for the revolutionary war, with court entries from 1778–1784.

Some more names appear in Chapter 9, dealing with the Court Minute Books for 1833–1850, and 1850–1856. *Edward Williams* and *William Mitchell* were two veterans who served in his regiment. Both men served in Captain Thomas Triplett's Company, of Grayson's Regiment.[64] A full listing of the officers and men in Colonel Grayson's Additional Continental Regiment may be found on http://www.footnote.com. under *Continental Troops, Grayson's Regiment*.[65]

♦ **Identified Prince William officers in Colonel Henry Lee's Partizan Legion.**

Colonel Henry Lee's Partizan Legion was another unit organized by a Prince William officer. Partizan organizations were radical departures from the traditional strategy of battles. These legions were "small, highly mobile units," composed of cavalry, infantry and artillery. On forced marches foot soldiers often rode double with cavalrymen or ran beside the horses holding onto the stirrup. Artillery pieces were small field guns, either one or three-pounder, mounted on grasshopper carriages.

Thus, each legion was, in effect, a miniature army.[66] Henry Lee's Legion was formed in April 1778. Captain Lee had begun his career as a captain in the Prince William Minute Battalion. In May 1776, the fifth Virginia Convention passed legislation creating six troops of horsemen who were to serve for one year.

The Virginia Committee of Safety then issued commissions to captain, lieutenants and cornets of these troops. Captain Henry Lee received his commission as the captain of the 5th troop in June. The horsemen, known as Light Dragoons, were originally commanded by Major-Commandant Theodorick Bland. His dragoon leadership "represented the cream of the state's society, talent, and military leadership. All the officers would rise in rank before the war ended, and Henry Lee would be voted a medal by Congress for gallantry at Paulus Hook."[67]

---

[62] See Chapter 9 and NARA, *William Dowell's compiled service records, 13th Virginia Regiment*, M 881 (http://www.footnote.com), 2–24, Images 23082605 to 23092658.

[63] Sanchez-Saavedra, 73–75.

[64] See Chapter 9 for pensioners who were found in the Prince William Minute and Order Books.

[65] NARA, *Grayson's Additional Continental Regiment, compiled service records*, M 881 (http://www.footnote.com)

[66] Sanchez-Saavedra, 79.

[67] Ibid., 102.

Chapter 5's treatment of the 1778–1784 court minutes uncovered three men in Colonel Lee's Legion. *George Newman* and *John Bristoe* were both men who died while in Lee's Legion while *David Blackwell*, a former Prince William Militia officer, had the opportunity to join the Legion as commissary and quartermaster.

- **Identified Prince William officers in the 1st Continental Light Dragoons.**

Congress raised four regiments of cavalry during the Revolution, three from Virginia. These units came to be known as light dragoons for their ability to fight on horseback, using a saber as their primary weapon. Light dragoons were among Washington's most versatile troops and were used in a variety of roles. They served as scouts, flank troops, messengers, sentinels on horseback, and military police. The first Regiment of Continental Dragoons was commanded by Colonel Theodorick Bland. There were three captains from Prince William in the 1st Continental Dragoons: *Henry Lee* was perhaps the most well-known, and was later rewarded with his own command. *Cuthbert Harrison* was another captain, of the 4th troop of this regiment, commissioned in February 1777.

Most of the dragoons' enlistments were up by the end of 1778 and by March 1779, only eight men were fit for duty. However, the regiment was recruited up to full strength in the fall of 1779 and sent south to Savannah, Georgia. Early in 1780, the dragoons were detached and sent to Charleston with orders to remove military stores from the threat of British capture. The regiment managed to get themselves and the stores to safety before the British took the city and capture the Continental army stationed there.[68]

Andrew Nixon was one of the captains who was commissioned in 1780 and served in this capacity until his retirement in November 1782. It appeared that he returned to Virginia with Lieutenant Colonel White, who had assumed the command of the regiment in 1780. White was successful in raising a further 200 men but was only able to equip sixty for active service. This was due to the British invasion of Virginia in 1781.

The reconstructed regiment fought at Spencer's Ordinary, Green Spring, and Yorktown. After the victory at Yorktown, the regiment was ordered to reinforce General Greene at Charleston. At that point, Major John Swan took over the reins of the regiment. The dragoons were assigned to the Cherokee expeditions under Generals Pickens and Wayne.[69]

In the October 1841 Prince William Court session, it was satisfactorily proven to the court that *Andrew Nixon*, a late Captain Virginia Continental line, died intestate in 1790 in Prince William. His nearest collateral heir at law was Daniel A. Nixon, who lived in Pennsylvania.[70]

John Massey was another officer of the 1st Continental Dragoons, mentioned in the Prince William Court Minutes in December 1834.[71] He was a cornet and paymaster for the regiment in 1781. He transferred over to Baylor's Consolidated Regiment of Dragoons in November 1783.[72]

Massey's heirs, the children of Henry Massey decd., were entitled to military land scrip for his service as a cornet. The Court thought it would be better to sell the scrip and have their guardian, Robert Massey, use the proceeds for their benefit.[73]

- **Identified Prince William veterans in the 4th Continental Light Dragoons.**

The 4th Continental Light Dragoons came into being when Congress authorized Washington to appoint officers of the 2nd, 3rd, and 4th regiments of light dragoons. Steven Moylan was commissioned the colonel of the 4th regiment in January, 1777. *Strother Settle* or *Suttle*, as his name was sometimes spelled, was a private in this regiment. His service can be found in Chapter 5's treatment of military records from 1778–1784.

---

[68] Sanchez-Saavedra, 100–103.
[69] Ibid., 104.
[70] See Chapter 9, Sanchez-Saavedra, 103, and Heitman, 414.
[71] See Chapter 9.
[72] See Chapter 9 and Heitman, 384.
[73] See Chapter 9: LVA, *PWCOB*, December 1, 1834 Court session.

- **Identified Prince William officers in the 1st Continental Artillery.**

Virginia raised two artillery regiments during the Revolution. One was utilized for Continental Service while the other was designated for local defense purposes. The artillery rarely fought as a single organization. Instead one or more field guns and personnel accompanied an infantry regiment.

Because of the specialized nature of the artillery, enlisted men were often given designations as bombardiers, gunners, or matrosses. Bombardiers and gunners were men who were skilled in engineering and mathematics with the ability to estimate the range necessary for cannon to hit their target. These men were also the ones with the responsibility of loading, sighting, and firing the cannon. Matrosses were usually privates who "manhandled" the guns.

After the loss of Fort Washington in November 1776, it became obvious that more cannon were needed in defense of New York. Together with Henry Knox, General Washington drew up a plan to enlarge the artillery branch. The two began with the creation of an artillery regiment in Virginia.

In November 1776, Congress resolved that such a regiment be raised in Virginia, with the men being armed with muskets and bayonets rather than fusees. They issued commissions to Charles Harrison, Edward Carrington, and Christian Holmer.

While Congress could commission the field and staff officers and captain, the state was given the responsibility to appoint the subaltern officers of this Artillery unit. As the year 1777 opened, Washington was desperate for artillery men. The Massachusetts artillery's enlistment had ended and those men had gone home. Harrison was requested to recruit as many men as he could as soon as possible. The new artillery unit was designated the 1st Regiment of Continental Artillery in the summer of 1777. Only Harrison's regiment was raised exclusively in Virginia.[74]

One of the captains, *Nathaniel Burwell,* a Prince William resident, was in this regiment. He had begun his career as an ensign in the 1st Virginia and was promoted to a captaincy in this Artillery Regiment in November, 1776. In May 1779, he was promoted to major and became an aide-de-camp to General Robert Howe. In 1782, he was back in Prince William and submitted a public service claim for three beeves in March of that year.[75]

3. In December 1776, the Virginia General Assembly authorized Virginia State Infantry, Artillery, and State Troops

In December 1776, the Virginia legislature created groups of regular troops to be used for local defense. Three state infantry regiments were authorized to serve within the boundaries of the state. Within a year, however, these three regiments were attached to the Virginia Continental Line, in order to replace the loss of the 9th Virginia to the British.

When the Virginia Continental line was reorganized in September 1778, the three State line regiments were able to come back to Virginia. However, there were constant recruitment problems in filling out the three regimental lines mainly due to the priority given to raising men for the Continental units.

- **Identified Prince William men in the Virginia State Line.**

In December 1776, the Virginia General Assembly authorized three battalions of eight companies each—the *1st Virginia State Regiment*, the 2nd Virginia State Regiment, and the 3rd Virginia State Regiment—which were **not** to serve outside the state's boundaries. Then, in October 1777, at Germantown, Virginia Continental troops suffered their worse defeat since the capture of a Rawling's Rifle regiment in December 1776. The entire 9th Virginia Continental Regiment was either captured or killed at Germantown. Congress then ordered their replacement by the 1st and 2nd Virginia State Line who were sent to join the main army in Pennsylvania in late 1777. The two State Regiments served with the Continentals until late 1779.

---

[74] Sanchez-Saavedra, 97–98.
[75] See Chapter 5 and Heitman, 136.

In 1780, the **1st Virginia State Regiment** returned to Virginia, in time to take part in the Yorktown campaign. In February 1782, the regiment had shrunk to 195 men who had enlisted for the war so they were merged with another Virginia unit—Dabney's Legion.

Prince William contributed both men and officers to the 1st Virginia State Regiment. Chapter 5's treatment of the revolutionary war Court records from 1778–1784, revealed two Prince William residents who served in this regiment. *Alexander Jones* was a private in Captain Thomas Winder Ewell's Company; and *Edward Whitfield* was another soldier who saw action with this State line Regiment.

Chapter 9's pensioners provided several officers and men for this State Regiment. *Captain Thomas Winder Ewell* was the commanding officer of the 4th company. In February 1834, it was proved to the satisfaction of the Prince William Court that Captain Thomas Ewell served in the 1st Virginia State Regiment until the close of the war. He died in Dumfries in Prince William. His heirs were certified at the same Court session.[76]

Thomas Hutchison was a sergeant in Captain Ewell's Company while *William McIntosh, Elijah Green, Alexander Maddox, Patrick McCune,* and *John Carr* all served in his company. Their service can be found in Chapter 9.

Lucy Fortune, widow of *Garner Fortune,* was a resident of Prince William in 1835, when she was granted a half pay pension under the July 4, 1835 Congressional Act for widows of soldiers with Revolutionary War service. Her husband Garner Fortune had served in Captain Thomas Armistead's company of Grenadiers in the 1st Virginia State Regiment.[77]

The **2nd Virginia State Regiment** also had two Prince William residents among its field and staff and officers. *Lieutenant-Colonel Thomas Blackburn,* mentioned in the public service claims, in the Prince William Minutes from 1778–1784 in Chapter 5, served in this state line unit from December 1776 to June 1777. So did *William Brent,* a lieutenant-colonel in the regiment from June 1777–January 1779.[78]

- ♦ **Identified Prince William men in George Roger Clark's Illinois Regiment of Virginia State Troops**

The largest unit raised by either Congress or the state was *George Roger Clark's Illinois Regiment.* Originally this regiment had been composed of frontiersmen. In four years of recruiting, from 1778–1783, Colonel Clark and his successors' recruitment policies were very successful. They were able to enlarge this force into an army almost as large as the main Continental Army under Washington prior to Yorktown. Clark's Illinois Regiment was then reinforced by Joseph Crockett's Western Battalion.[79]

Clark's Illinois Regiment was by far the most complex unit raised in the state during the war. It began, in January 1778 as a special militia regiment raised for the defense of the Western department. Governor Henry instructed Lieutenant Colonel Clark, in January 1778, to raise seven companies of fifty men each and attack the British fort Kaskaskia on the Mississippi. The Governor gave further orders to establish a fort on the Falls of the Ohio.[80]

Colonel Clark and his forces operated almost exclusively in the old Northwest against the British and the Indians. In February 1779, they captured Fort Vincennes. The regiment also participated in an expedition against the Shawnee, which took place from 1780–1782.[81]

---

[76] See Chapter 9 and Sanchez-Saavedra, 111.

[68] See Chapter 9 and NARA, *Garner Fortune's Pension File* W 24233 M 804 (http://www.footnote.com), 1–9, Images 19405789 to 1940582. Garner Fortune was soldier who served for three years Captain Thomas Armistead's 1st Virginia State Regiment. Garner had enlisted in Caroline County in January 1777 and was discharged in January or February 1780. A fuller description of his service can be found in Chapter 9, note 36.

[78] Sanchez-Saavedra, 112.

[79] Ibid., 108–110.

[80] Ibid., 128.

[81] Ibid.

Lynaugh or *Leonard Helm* of Prince William was a captain of the 3rd Company in Clark's Illinois Regiment in June 1778.[82] In March 1782, he was back in Prince William, having submitted a public service claim for seven beeves. His service in the regiment is found in note 68, in Chapter 5.

Two Prince William pensioners were part of Clark's Illinois Regiment: *William Wright* and *Jesse Evans*. *William Wright decd.*, was in "the N.W. Army in the war of the Revolution," according to the Court minutes. His heirs appeared August 3, 1835 in the Prince William Court to prove his service and be certified.[83]

Jesse Evans was *Captain Jesse Evans,* who died around 1814 intestate and served in "the Virginia Military service in the war of the Revolution." His surviving heirs came into Court on August 5, 1835 to prove his death and to have their heirship certified.[84] Jesse Evans had served in Clark's Regiment as a captain from July 1778–December 1782.[85]

The Virginia State Navy

Virginia's civilian leaders recognized the lack of defense along the coast and took measures to provide for their security. At least seventy-seven commissioned vessels made up the state navy, along with nearly 100 privateers.

◆ **Identified Prince William men in the Virginia State Navy.**

Chapter 9's treatment of Prince William pensioners revealed two men who were active in Virginia's Navy. *Henry Tyler* was a midshipman in the State Navy. His heirs were certified in September 1834. *Charles DeKay* was a sailing master in the Virginia Navy. His death, occurring in August 1839, was certified by the Court in a February 7, 1842 entry.

CONCLUSIONS

As can be seen by the men mentioned here, Prince William contributed officers and men to all branches of the Continental, State and Naval service. However, it must be remembered that this is only a partial listing, combining entries from the county court minutes and other derivative sources.

The County Court minutes which follow also underline the importance of the county militia as the primary unit for the local defense of the county, especially near the rivers where British ships could commit depredations.

---

[82] Ibid., 129.

[83] See Chapter 9 and NARA, *William Wright's compiled service records,* M 881 MR 1086, *Clark's Illinois Regiment* (http://www.footnote.com), 1–2, Images 2329499 to 23229501. William Wright served as a soldier in Clark's Illinois Regiment of Virginia State Troops. He appeared on an undated payroll for soldiers who received their pay up to the end of December 1781.

[84] See Chapter 9 and Marcus Gaius Brumbaugh, *Revolutionary War Records: Virginia* , 1936 Reprint (Baltimore: Genealogical Publishing Company, 1995), 531. Jesse Evans was a captain in the Virginia State Troops in Colonel George Rogers Clark's Illinois Regiment. A payroll of the officers of the regiment showed Colonel Clark as commander, Lieutenant Colonel John Montgomery, **Captain Jesse Evans,** Lieutenant Anthony Crockett, Ensign William Campbell, and Colonel Christian.

[85] Sanchez-Saavedra, 129.

THE REVOLUTIONARY WAR PERIOD

CHAPTER 5

MILITARY RECORDS FROM PRINCE WILLIAM COUNTY VIRGINIA ORDER BOOK 1778–1784

May 1778 Court, pg. 4.

Charles Lee, Gent., was recommended to his Excellency the Governor as a Captain of Militia in this County for the Company lately commanded by Captain Samuel Peachey, who took the oath prescribed by law.

July 1778 Court, pg. 8.

John Linton,[1] Gent., took the oath prescribed by Law as a Captain of Militia of this County.

Robert Warren took the oath prescribed by Law as a 1st Lieutenant in Captain Linton's Company.

Samuel Love[2] was recommended to his Excellency the Governor as a 2nd Lieutenant in Captain Linton's Company.

William Linton,[3] Gent., took the oath prescribed by Law as an Ensign in Captain Linton's Company.

Peter Conway[4] took the oath prescribed by Law as an Ensign in Captain John Whitledge's Company.

July 1778 Court, pg. 9.

William Brown took the oath prescribed by Law as 1st Lieutenant in Captain Bernard Hooe's Company.

Lewis Reno Jr took the oath prescribed by Law as 2nd Lieutenant in Captain John Hedges's Company.

On Hearing the Petition of Ruth Holifield, Widow of **Daniel Holifield**[5], **late a Soldier in the 3rd Virginia Regiment in Continental Service**, she was allowed the sum of ten Pounds for the support of herself and one child which was ordered to be certified to the Treasurer.

---

[1] John Linton had previously served in Colonel William Grayson's Additional Continental Regiment of Infantry. He was listed as a sergeant in March 1777, a sergeant-major, in October 1777, an ensign in November of that year and a 2nd Lieutenant in April 1778. He had been promoted after his resignation in March 1778. In April 1779, Linton was a cornet in the 3rd Continental Dragoons. He was promoted to Lieutenant in May 1780. He transferred to Baylor's Consolidated Regiment of Dragoons in November 1782 and served until the close of the war. He died in 1824. See Heitman, 352.

[2] Samuel Love was another 3rd Virginia veteran. He served as a sergeant in Captain Philip Richard Francis Lee's company from July 1777 until his discharge in January 1778. Colonel Grayson received Sergeant Love's certificate for the balance of his full pay in January 1785 for £18 15s 15d. See NARA, *Samuel Love's compiled service records*, 3rd Virginia Regiment, M 881 MR 954.

[3] William Linton had served in Grayson's Additional Continental Regiment as a cadet, commissioned on May 28, 177. He was promoted to ensign in November 1777 and resigned in March 1778. See Heitman, 352.

[4] This may be the Peter Conway who was a private in Captain William Blackwell's Culpeper Minute Battalion in 1775. See John K. Gott and T. Triplett Russell, *Fauquier County in the Revolution* (Warrenton: Warrenton Printing & Publishing Company, 1977), 454.

[5] NARA, *Daniel Holifield's compiled service records*, 3rd Virginia Regiment, M 881 MR 954. Daniel Holifield was a private in Captain Charles West's company in February, 1777. That month's payroll for this company awarded him service for only one-half a month, so he either enlisted in this company around February 14th or died then. There were no further records for this soldier in the service records for the 3rd Virginia.

July 1778 Court, pg. 9.
On Hearing the Petition of **Nancy Davis, Wife of Thomas Davis,**[6] **a soldier ... in the Continental Army,** she was allowed the sum of twenty Pounds for the support of herself and four children, which was ordered to be certified to the Treasurer.
On the Petition of **Ann Cornwell, widow of John Cornwell**[7] decd., late a regular Soldier in the Continental Army, ordered that she be allowed the sum of twelve Pounds for the support of herself and two small children ... [The Court ordered this] to be certified to the Treasurer.

October 1778 Court, pg. 19.
On the motion of **John Crook**, ordered that the Churchwardens of Dettingen Parish bind Susanna Mahew, a baseborn child to him according to law.
John Crook[8] was allowed the sum of five Pounds, he being an aged man & having lost his Son in the Service of his Country, which was ordered to be certified to the Treasurer.
Sarah Grant was allowed the sum of five Pounds for her Present Support, her husband being a Soldier in the Continental Service. The Court ordered this to be certified to the Treasurer.

November 1778 Court, pg. 21.
Samuel King,[9] having two sons in the Continental Service is allowed the sum of five Pounds towards his support, which was ordered to be certified to the Treasurer and was exempted for the future from Public County & parish levies.
Mary Sidebottom[10] was allowed the sum of three Pounds for her support, her sons being on the Continental Service, which was ordered to be certified to the Treasurer.
Reginald Graham Gent., took the oath prescribed by Law as a Lieutenant of the Militia of this County.

---

[6] There were several soldiers named Thomas Davis in the Virginia Continental Line. See NARA, *Thomas Davis's compiled service records* for 1st and 10th Virginia, 6th and 10th Virginia, and 7th Virginia on http://www.footnote.com. It is not known whether any of these men were the soldier from Prince William.

[7] Gott and Russell, 30. There was a John Cornwell in the Prince William County Militia during the French and Indian War. He was a trooper in Richard Taylor's company of horse. This would not appear to be the John Cornwell mentioned above as he would probably be too old to serve in the Continental forces in 1778.

[8] John Crook's son was probably Zachariah Crook, who enlisted in Captain John Peyton's 3rd Virginia Company. He was found on payrolls from October 8, 1776 to January 1, 1777 for two months and twenty-three days. He was also found on company payrolls for January through March 1, 1777 for fifteen day's service with the remark: "Dead." See NARA, *Zachariah Crook's compiled service records*, M 881 (http://www.footnote.com) page 3, Image 21954605. (Accessed June 23, 2008).

[9] NARA, *John King (2) Compiled Service Records*, M 881 MR 954, *3rd Virginia Regiment*. John King was a private in Captain John Ashby and Captain Val Peyton's company from September 1777 until at least December 1778. He enlisted in September 1777 for three years or the war. See also Virginia Genealogical Society, *Virginia State Revolutionary War Pensions* (1982; reprint, Greenville: Southern Historical Press, 1992), File 233, 66–67. In this file is a military pass issued in Salisbury North Carolina in March 1780 by Brigadier General Smallwood for John King, wounded in the action of Colonel Buford along with a request by his father **Samuel King** to issuing commissaries to furnish rations. John King has lost both arms at Colonel Buford's defeat at the Waxhaws.

[10] Mary Sidebottom's two sons were probably John and Joseph Sidebottom. John Sidebottom, spelled "Sidebotham" in the 3rd Virginia compiled service records, was a private and corporal in Captain Charles West's company of that regiment. He was found on company pay rolls from February 1777 until November 1777 and on muster rolls from Jun 1777 until his discharge in February 1778.See NARA, *John Sidebottom's compiled service records*, M 881 MR 956. His pension, file W 8775 may be found in NARA, *John Sydbotham's Pension File W 8775*, M 804 MR 2333.

Joseph Sidebotham was a private in Captain Charles West and Reuben Briscoe's 3rd Virginia company. He served the same term: payrolls showed service from February to November 1777 while muster rolls indicated service from June 1777 until his discharge in February 1778. See NARA, *Joseph Sidebotham's compiled service records*, M 881 MR 956. He also filed for a pension, File W 8727, found in NARA, *Joseph Sidebottom's Pension*, M 804 MR 2183.

February 1779 Court, pg. 29.
William Linton[11] was appointed 2nd Lieutenant in Captain Brent's Company and **John Ross**, ensign in the same company. **William Reeve** was appointed ensign in Captain Linton's Company in the place of Wm. Linton.

Upon the petition of **Bertrand Ewell**, he was allowed the sum of forty Pounds towards the support of two children, orphans of **John Gunyon**,[12] who died a soldier in the service and the same was ordered to be certified to the Treasurer.

On the **Petition of Thomas Hines**[13], a soldier in the Continental Army, he was allowed the sum of ten Pounds towards the support of his wife and child and the same was ordered to be certified to the Treasurer.

March 1779 Court, pg. 30.
Isaac Wickliff was appointed Captain of the Company lately commanded by **John Whitledge of the Militia of this County**.

June 1779 Court, pg. 41.
William Carr Gent., produced to the Court an account against the State of Virginia for sundries furnished wives, widows etc and aged parents of Soldiers in the Continental Army, amounting to £85 9s 2d, which being examined by the Court was allowed and ordered to be certified to the Treasurer.

William Carr Gent., presented to the Court an account against the State of Virginia for sundries furnished for wives, etc of soldiers in the Continental Army, amounting to £714 which, being examined and allowed, was ordered to be certified to the Treasurer.

June 1779 Court, pg. 42.
At a Court called and held at the Courthouse of Prince William County, 22nd June 1779 for the Examination of **Joseph Sidebotham**[14] for having and passing forged money. He was brought to the bar of the Court. The court heard several evidences and fully considered all the circumstances.

---

[11] Heitman, 352. William Linton began his career in the Continental service as a cadet, commissioned in late May 1777 in Colonel William Grayson's Additional Continental Regiment. He was promoted to ensign on November 1, 1777 and resigned in March, 1778.

[12] John Gunyon was a soldier in the 3rd Virginia. See Louis A. Burgess, *Virginia Soldiers of 1776* (1927; reprint, Baltimore: Clearfield Publishing Company, 2004), I: 112. His name was *not* found in the compiled service records of the 3rd Virginia. See NARA, *Compiled Service Records* M 881 MR 953, *3rd Virginia Regiment (1776–1778)*.

[13] NARA, *Thomas Hines's compiled service records*, M 881 MR 962, *3rd and 4th Virginia*. Thomas Hines, also spelled "Hinds," was a private in Captain John Peyton's company from July 1778 until December 1778. When John Peyton retired in September, 1778, his first lieutenant, Valentine Peyton, took over the company. Private Hines was part of Captain Val Peyton's company from October to December 1778. He apparently reenlisted in December as he was listed as being "on furlough" in December.

[14] This was the first of several brushes with the law and Court system that Joseph Sidebotham or "Sidebottom," was to have in Prince William. He was another veteran of the 3rd Virginia Regiment, serving as a private in Captain Charles West's company. He had enlisted for two years. Company payrolls and muster rolls showed his service from February 1777 until February 1778. In August 1777, Private Sidebotham was "with Colonel." See NARA, *Joseph Sidebotham's compiled service records*, M 881 MR 956.

See also Heitman, 1777 for identity of Colonel Crawford. He began as a Lieutenant Colonel in the 5th Virginia, commissioned on February 13, 1776. He was promoted to be the Colonel of the 7th Virginia in August of that year. While he resigned in March 1777, he was subsequently involved along the Virginia frontier. It is likely that Private Sidebotham served with him in that capacity in August. In September 1777, he had returned to his company, now under the Captaincy of Reuben Briscoe of the 3rd Virginia. A Mr. Peyton received his certificate fro the balance of his full pay in December 1783 for £16 6s 4d. See also NARA, *Joseph Sidebottom's Pension File W* 8727, M 804 MR 2183 for his pension, filed in Henry County Kentucky in August 1818.

It was the opinion of the Court that Sidebotham was not guilty and was acquitted of this charge.

July 1779 Court, pg. 45.
Robert Warren was recommended to the Governor as a fit person to be Captain of a Company of Militia lately commanded by Captain John Linton,[15] who has resigned. Warren took the oath prescribed by law.

July 1779 Court, pg. 45.
Samuel Love[16] was recommended as a 1st Lieutenant, William Reeve, as a 2nd Lieutenant, and Isaac Smith as an Ensign. William Reeve took the oath of a Lieutenant of the Militia of this County.
Ordered that the Churchwardens of Dettingen Parish bind **Tommy Calvert, orphan of Reuben Calvert**[17] to George Newman Brown, accorded to Law to learn the trade of a carpenter or joiner.

August 1779 Court pg. 46.
Peter Evans,[18] Gent., was recommended to the Governor as a 1st Lieutenant. **Steven Howison**, as a 2nd Lieutenant and **James Peake** as an Ensign in the Company commanded by Captain Charles Lee. James Peake took the oath prescribed by law.

August 1779 Court, pg. 54.
Charles Lenox,[19] **a wounded soldier**, appeared before the Court and showed his wound. **The Court was satisfied that he was "unable to labour and becomes properly a pensioner to be provided for, for Life"** as a wounded soldier of the Continental Army by the State of Virginia.

---

[15] Heitman, 352. John Linton had already served in the army before being appointed to the Prince William Militia. He had formerly served as a Sergeant, Ensign, and 2nd Lieutenant in Grayson's Additional Continental Regiment, from which he resigned in March 1778. He then served as a cornet in the 3rd Continental Dragoons, commissioned in April 1779 and was promoted to Lieutenant in May 1780. He transferred into Baylor's Consolidated Regiment of Dragoons in November 1782 and served there until the close of the war. He died in 1824.

[16] NARA, *Samuel Love's compiled service records*, M 881 MR 954, *3rd Virginia Regiment*. Samuel Love was Sergeant Samuel Love in Captain Philip Richard Francis Lee's company of the 3rd Virginia. Company muster rolls and pay rolls placed him in this company from July 1777 until January 1778. His time had expired in January and he was, accordingly, discharged. Colonel Grayson received Sergeant Love's certificate for the balance of his full pay in January 1785 for £15s 15d.
As the war was winding down, in March 1782, Samuel Love presented a public service claim to the Prince William Court for one beef weighing 625 pounds. He was allowed 4d per pound.

[17] NARA, *Reuben Calvert's compiled service records*, 3rd Virginia Regiment, M 881 MR 952. Reuben Calvert served as a sergeant in Captain John Peyton's company. He appeared on company payrolls beginning in January 1777. He was reported "dead" on January 15, 1777. See also Lloyd Dewitt Bockstruck, *Revolutionary War Bounty Land Grants Awarded by State Governments* (Baltimore: Genealogical Publishing Company, 1996), 83. Reuben Calvert was awarded 100 acres as a private in the Virginia Continental Line in June 1820.

[18] Heitman, 219. Peter Evans was a 1st Lieutenant in the Virginia Militia in 1779. It is not known when the Prince William County Militia was attached to the Continental Line. A search for his name and place did not show any results on footnote.com.

[19] NARA, *Charles Lenox's compiled service records*, 3rd Virginia Regiment, *M* 881 MR 954. Charles Lenox was yet another 3rd Virginia veteran who served in Captain John Peyton's company. He enlisted in February 1776 and appeared on payrolls beginning in October 1776. Muster rolls from September through January 1778 indicated that he was "wounded," and "absent, wounded." It is likely that he was disabled at Brandywine in September 1777. In July 1783, Henry Lee received Charles Lenox's certificate for the balance of his full pay as a soldier in the infantry. That pay amounted to £15 12s.

By order of this Court, **Captain Carr** has **advanced for Charles Lenox's present relief £30,** to be refunded Carr by the Treasurer and to be deducted out of his (Lenox) allowance. The Court ordered this to be certified to the Governor of Virginia.

August 1779 Court, pg. 56.
Commonwealth v. John Dunbar
 John Dunbar was brought before the Court, charged with coming into Virginia from some one of the other United States. He did not apply to one of the nearest Justices after he entered the state. He did not take or subscribe an oath or affirmation renouncing all allegiance to the King of Great Britain or promise that he would do anything prejudicial to the independence of the United States.
 It appeared to the Court that the charge is a just one and Dunbar now was refusing to take or subscribe to the oath or affirmation.
 The Court ordered that John Dunbar be committed to the Jail of the county and remain there without bond or *mainprise*[20] until he either took or subscribed to the oath or affirmation and gave bond or security for £1000 and immediately depart from Virginia.

September 1779 Court, pg. 59.
 (Note: pgs. 57–58 are missing as is the first portion of this payment to a widow with young children. The widow and the soldier's name were not found on pg. 59.)
 "…**in the Continental Army** and **left her a widow with five young Children.** Ordered the same be certified to the Treasurer."
 An affidavit of Allegiance to the United States of America of **John Dunbar** was returned to the Court and admitted to record.
 William Anderson, Wm. Brewer, and George Thomas were **bound over by a warrant** from William Carr Gent. It appeared, upon proof, that **they advised** a certain **Cada Ramey, a soldier, to desert and forced him to play at all fours and unlawfully took from him $200.00.**
 On hearing the evidence, the Court ordered that the three men be bound over to their good behavior in the sum of £500 each and their securities for £250 and that they stand committed and each pay their costs.

September 1779 Court, pg. 60.
 George Thomas, Benjamin Thomas and Spencer Anderson[21] came into Court and severally acknowledged themselves indebted to the Governor… George Thomas, for £500, Benjamin Thomas and Spencer Anderson, for £250 each. The recognizance was conditioned for the good behavior of George Thomas for a year and a day. If violated then Benjamin Thomas and Spencer Anderson could have their bonds levied on their own goods and chattels, lands and tenements…
 Stephen Howison took the oath prescribed by law as a **Militia officer of this County.**

October 1779 Court, pg. 77.
Commonwealth v. **Joseph Sidebotham**[22] On a Presentment

---

[20] *Mainprise* is the delivery of a person to someone called a *mainpernor* who acted as security for the appearance of the person under arrest. In this Commonwealth cause, John Dunbar was remanded to jail without a security bond and without the right to find someone who could guarantee his future appearance into Court. See Henry Campbell Black, *Black's Law Dictionary* (St Paul: West Publishing Company, 1990), 953.

[21] NARA, *Spencer Anderson's compiled service records*, 3rd Virginia Regiment, M 881 MS 951. Spencer Anderson served as a private in Captain Philip Richard Francis Lee's 3rd Virginia company from April 1777 until he "enlisted in the Light Horse Dec. 23/77." He had enlisted in Captain Lee's company on February 15, 1776.

[22] See note 14.

It appears to the Court that Joseph Sidebottom was legally summoned and failed to appear. It is considered that he make his fine by the payment of five pounds and the costs of this prosecution.

April 1780 Court, pg. 85.
Charles Simms[23] produced to the court a Certificate relative to lands with sundry other papers, which being read and examined by the Court, the came is ordered to be certified.

George Bearmore, a soldier, swears he served a campaign with **Major Douglas**[24] mentioned in the papers and that he had reason to believe Douglas served the time for which the Regiment he belonged to was raised.

On the motion of Cuthbert Bullett and proof being made, it was ordered it to be certified that there is still due to him as devisee of the late **Colonel Thomas Bullett**[25] **730 acres of land** for the services of Thomas Bullett as a **Captain** in the **first Virginia Regiment** during the last French war.

An Inventory and Appraisement of the Estate of Andrew **Leitch**[26] deceased was returned to the Court by John Murray ... and on his motion, was admitted to record.

April 1780 Court, pg. 86.
Ordered it be certified that **George Bearmore**[27] came into court and made oath that in the Late French War, he enlisted as a soldier in the State of New Jersey for six months which time he duly served and at this time and for 10 years past, he is and has been an inhabitant of Virginia.

It was ordered that it be certified (appearing upon proof) that **Leonard Murphy**[28] was entitled to the lands due for service as a **soldier belonging to this State in the Continental**

---

[23] Heitman, 497. Charles Simms had served as a major in the 12th Virginia, commissioned in November 1776. He was promoted to be a Lieutenant-Colonel of the 6th Virginia in September 1777. In September 1778, after the Battle of Brandywine, he transferred into the 2nd Virginia. He resigned his commission in December 1779 and died in 1819.

[24] Heitman, 202. Major Douglas was taken prisoner at Briar Creek on March 3, 1779. This battle was one of the American's attempts to retake Georgia. It was fought by North Carolina militia and Georgia Continentals. It was a costly operation. The Americans lost between 150 and 200 killed or drowned and more than 170 men captured. See Mark M. Boatner, III, *Encyclopedia of the Americah Revolution* (Mechanicsburg: Stackpole Books, 1994), 113–114.

[25] "Thomas Bullitt." *Wikipedia, The Free Encyclopedia* (http://en.wikipedia.org/wike/Thomas_Bullit) Bullitt was born in Prince William County and became active in the militia there. By 1754, he was a captain in the Prince William County Militia. He led part of his company with Colonel Washington's expedition in 1754 which ended with the defeat at Great Meadows. In 1755, he marched against Fort Duquesne and was defeated again at the Battle of Monongahela in July.

In 1758, Captain Bullitt led a militia company and was a part of a large advance party of British regulars and Virginia militia commanded by Major James Grant. His party was ambushed by the French and Indians in September 1758. Grant was captured but Bullitt took to the woods and rallied the militia. He led a successful counter attack on the enemy. He remained in the militia service and, by the end of the French and Indian War, he was the adjutant general of the Virginia militia.

[26] Andrew Leitch was an early Captain in the 3rd Virginia who was promoted to be the major of the 1st Virginia. He died a lingering death, from lockjaw, in early October 1776 from wounds suffered at Harlem Heights in September. See NARA, *Andrew Leitch's compiled service records*, M 881 MR 951 *Officers of the 3rd Virginia*. See also Dr. David Griffith's letter to Richard Henderson, announcing Leitch's death of lockjaw. Virginia Historical Society, *David Griffith to Richard Henderson*, October 3, 1776, Mss 2 G8755b, *Letters &c of David Griffith*, VHS, Richmond, Virginia.

[27] George Bearmore had already appeared at the April 1780 Court and sworn that he had seen service with Major Douglas, captured at Briar Creek in March 1779. See note 22. Now he was testifying regarding his service in the French and Indian War when he served six months in the New Jersey militia.

[28] This is *Leander* Murphy, who served in the 11th Virginia in Captain Charles Gallahue's company, Colonel Daniel Morgan's Regiment, from May 1777 until May 1778. Then the 11th and 15th Virginia were temporarily consolidated and Murphy served in Captain George Rice's Company. He had enlisted in November 1776 for 3 years or the war. He served for three months in the artillery, according to company muster rolls.

Army. He duly **served out his time of enlistment for three years** and never claimed his right to land before.

It was ordered to be certified (appearing upon proof) that **George White**[29] was entitled to lands due for service **as a soldier belonging to this State in the Continental Army**. He duly **served out his time of enlistment for three years** and never claimed his right to land before this time.

May 1780 Court, pg. 92.

Jane Bradley, wife to Richard Bradley,[30] **a soldier in the Continental Army** was allowed a barrel of corn towards supporting herself and a child. The corn was valued at thirty pounds. The Court ordered this to be certified to the auditors.

Ann Brent, widow of Willoughby Brent[31] deceased, late a soldier in the Continental Army, was allowed a barrel of corn, valued at thirty pounds. The Court ordered that this be certified to the auditors.

The Court ordered that **orphans of soldiers whose widows were unable to maintain them, be bound out by the Churchwardens of the several parishes where they reside.**

Peter Evans Gent., is **appointed Captain** of a company of militia formerly commanded by **Captain Charles Lee and was sworn accordingly.**

June 1780 Court, pg. 95.

On the motion of **John Hedges** Gent., **proof was made that there is due to him 2000 acres of land** under the proclamation of the King **for the services of Francis Eppes, during the last French war.**

---

[28] After September 1778, the reorganization placed Murphy in the 7th Virginia in Captain Philip Slaughter's Company. In May 1779, Lieutenant James Wright took over the company and Murphy served with him in the 7th Virginia until his discharge on November 1, 1779. In February 1782, he received his own certificate for the balance of his full pay, for £54 and again in September 1783. At that time he received another £51 18s 6d. See NARA, *Leander Murphey's compiled service records,* M 881 (http://www.footnote.com) 2-64, images 23156202 to 22843642. He filed his pension in Spencer County, Kentucky in November 1832. See NARA, *Leander Murphey's Pension File* S 11126, M 804 MR 1794.

[29] George White was another soldier who served in the 11th, 15th and 7th Virginia as a private in Captain Charles Gallahue's company, Captain George Rice's Company and Lieutenant James Wright's company. . He had enlisted in November 1776 for three years or the war. He, too, served a stint in the Artillery and was discharged in November 1779. See NARA, *George White's compiled service records,* M 881 (http://www.footnote.com) 2-65, Images 28198290 to 23187417. He made a pension application, at age seventy-two in Pickaway County, Ohio. The application was rejected, evidently because he could not be found on the rolls and could not produce a discharge or witnesses to his service. See NARA, *George White's Pension File* R 11413, M 804 (http://footnote.com), 3-7 ff., images 27928789 to 27928794.

[30] The only Richard Bradley found as a soldier in the Virginia Continental Line was a private in the 2nd Virginia. He appeared in that rank on payrolls for Captain John Peyton Harrison's company from May to December 1777. The December roll remarked that he "des. 18th Dec." On an undated account due the dead, deserted and prisoners of the 2nd Virginia to the last of May 1778, Richard Bradley's name appeared as a member of Captain J. Peyton Harrison's Company. The remarks on this Account stated that he "deserted 28 Dec'r 1777."

However, the payroll for December 1777 has "Next Muster roll on file Aug. 1779." This muster roll was not found in Bradley's file. It appears that he either returned to the Army or reenlisted, in order for this remark on the December payroll to have been made. There are no rolls extant for the 2nd Virginia for 1780–1783. See NARA, *Richard Bradley's compiled service records,* M 881 MR 939 (http://www.footnote.com) 1-9, images 22717090 to 22417131 (Accessed June 25, 2009).

[31] NARA, *Willoughby Brent's compiled service records,* 3rd Virginia Regiment, M 881 MR 952. Willoughby Brent was a sergeant in Captain John Peyton's company from October 1776 until his death on February 1, 1777. His name appeared on Peyton's payrolls from October 1776 to January 1777. He was given credit for two months and twenty three days service. The company payroll from January 1, 1777 to March 1, 1777 only gave him credit for a month's service and had the remark: "Dead." This remark and length of service strongly suggests a death date of February 1, 1777.

Francis Eppes[32] **was a Lieutenant in the Second Virginia Regiment** in that war and **assigned his right** to this land to Hedges. Neither Frances Eppes nor John Hedges has received any satisfaction of land. The Court ordered this to be certified.

Thomas Lawson produced and **account** to the Court against the Commonwealth for £151 19s **for sundries furnished to soldiers' wives and children.** The court ordered this to be certified to the auditors.

July 1780 Court, pg. 99.
Commonwealth v. **John Sidebottom**— On Information
It appeared to the Court upon oath that John Sidebottom threatened the lives of **Lewis Reno**[33] and **Vester Moss.**[34] The Court ordered that he be bound to his good behavior for twelve months and a day, himself in the sum of ten thousand pounds and his two securities in the sum of five thousand pounds each and that Sidebottom pay costs.

John Sidebottom, Charles Sidebottom and **John Randolph**[35] came into Court and severally acknowledged themselves indebted to the Governor, John for ten thousand pounds and Charles Sidebottom and **John Randolph**[36] for five thousand pounds each, to be made and levied on their and each of their goods and chattels, lands and tenements for the use of the Commonwealth.

The condition of this bond was that John Sidebottom shall be of good behavior towards all the good people of the Commonwealth for 12 months and a day.

If this occurs, the above recognizance was to be void; otherwise it was to remain in full force and virtue.

July 1780 Court, pg. 100.
It appeared, upon proof, that at the request of the Deputy Attorney for Prince William County, that John James attended four days at the county court of Shenandoah from Fauquier, 75 miles and returning, to give evidence against **Joseph Sidebottom "a Notorious horse thief "** who had broken out of jail before his trial.

The Court ordered this to be certified.

---

[32] Lloyd Dewitt Bockstruck, *Bounty and Donation Land Grants in British Colonial America* (Baltimore: Genealogical Publishing Company, 2007), 117. Francis Eppes was a lieutenant in William Byrd's 2nd Virginia regiment. He married Elizabeth Hill. His only child, Elizabeth Hill Eppes married Thomas Woodlief. It was Woodlief who assigned the warrant for 2000 acres, issued in 1779 in Prince William.

[33] This was Lewis Reno **Jr** who had been appointed as a 2nd Lieutenant in Captain John Hedges Militia company in 1778. John Sidebottom, as has been already noted, served as a corporal in the 3rd Virginia company of Captain Charles West and Reuben Briscoe. He had enlisted for two years and had appeared on company payrolls and muster rolls from February 1777 until his discharge in January 1778. Corporal Sidebottom had seen action at Brandywine and Germantown. Lieutenant Reno's company of the Prince William Militia did not appear to have ever been attached to the Continental Army. His militia company did not appear in any of the militia that saw service with the Virginia Continental Line. See NARA, *Compiled Service Records* M 881 M 1087, 1088, 1089, 1090.

[34] NARA, *Vester Moss's compiled service records,* M 881 MR 955, 3rd *Virginia Regiment.* Vester Moss was a private in Captain Philip Richard Lee's company from February 1777 until January 1778. He had enlisted for two years. He spent his **entire** enlistment "sick in Virginia."

[35] NARA, *John Randolph's compiled service records,* 3rd Virginia Regiment, M 881 MR 955. John Randolph served as a soldier in Captain John Peyton's 3rd Virginia company. He appeared on company pay rolls, beginning in October 1776 and on muster rolls, in June 1777. He served with Captain Peyton until December 23, 1777 when he reenlisted in the Light Horse.

[36] See note 35.

September 1780 Court, pg. 104.
Catherine Davis,[37] John Sidebottom, Anne Randolph,[38] Margaret Moore,[39] Marianne Mc Mahan[40] and **Charles Lenox**[41] were found guilty of an assault on Lewis Renoe and riotously meeting at his house.

The Court ordered that they be bound over to the next Grand Jury, each of them in the sum of 2000 pounds and their securities in the sum of 1000 pounds each and that they be of good behavior in the meantime and pay costs.

Catharine Davis, John Graham and Wm. Farrow came into Court and severally acknowledged themselves indebted to the Governor ... Catharine Davis for £2000 and John Graham and Wm. Farrow for £1000 each to be made and levied upon their goods and chattels, lands and Tenements...

Upon condition that Catharine Davis makes her personal appearance at the next Grand Jury to answer a complaint alleged against her by Lewis Reno and not depart without the leave of the Court. She was also to be of good behavior in the mean time. If Catharine Davis does this, this appearance bond was to be void; otherwise the bond was to remain in full force and virtue.

September 1780 Court, pgs. 104-105.
The Court ordered that the Attorney prosecute **John Sidebottom** on his former Recognizance.

Charles Lenox and Scarlet Madden came into Court and severally acknowledged themselves indebted to the Governor... for £2000. Scarlett Madden acknowledged himself indebted for £1000 ... to be made of goods and chattels, lands and Tenements...

Upon condition that Charles Lenox shall make his personal appearance at the next Grand Jury to answer a complaint against him by Lewis Reno and not to depart without the leave of the court. He was to be of good behavior in the mean time.

As long as Charles Lenox obeyed the conditions in this appearance bond, the bond was to be void. Otherwise, it was to remain in full force and virtue.

September 1780 Court, pgs. 104-105.
John Sidebottom, Alexander Hume and **Stephen Howison**[42] came into Court and severally acknowledged themselves indebted to the Governor...John Sidebottom, for 2000 pounds and Alexander Hume and Stephen Howison for 1000 pounds each.

---

[37] Ibid., *John Davis's compiled service records,* M 881 MR 953. John Davis was a soldier in Captain John Peyton's company, who appeared on company payrolls from October 1776 until March 1777. The March payroll gave his service for two months. The April payrolls stated that this soldier was "not to be accounted for." This was a euphemism for a soldier having died in service. Since John Peyton had other soldiers from Prince William in his company, it is more likely that Catharine's husband was this John Davis.

Since it was a regular occurrence for veterans (and their wives or widows) of the same regiment to interact socially, it is likely that Catharine Davis's husband was in the 3rd Virginia. The only other Davis that would fit as her husband was a John Davis in the 3rd Virginia company of Captain John Ashby. He appeared on those company payrolls beginning in February 1777 and continued to be found on company rolls until August 1777. Muster rolls for June through July 1777 showed him "sick in Virginia." He had enlisted until March 18, 1778.

[38] It is very likely that Ann Randolph's husband was John Randolph, formerly of Captain John Peyton's company of the 3rd Virginia. See note 34.

[39] Margaret Moore's husband has not yet been identified.

[40] There *was* a Thomas McMahon who served briefly as a corporal in Captain David Arell's 3rd Virginia company. He appeared on Captain Arell's company payroll for November 1777 and was given credit for a month's service. It is not know whether this soldier was Marianne's husband. It is given here to show that there was at least one soldier of that surname serving in the 3rd Virginia. See NARA, *Thomas McMahon's compiled service records,* M 881 MR 955.

[41] See note 19.

[42] Stephen Howison was a lieutenant in the Militia in August 1779.

These sums were to be levied on their goods and chattels, lands and tenements... upon the condition that John Sidebottom make his personal appearance at the next Grand Jury to answer a complaint against him and not to depart without the leave of the court and be of good behavior in the meantime.

If John Sidebottom followed these conditions, this appearance bond was to be void. Otherwise, it was to remain in full force and virtue.

Mary McMahan, Thomas Harris and Wm. Scott took out a bond to the governor, Mary McMahan for 2000 pounds and Thomas Harris and Wm. Scott, for 1000 pounds each. These sums were to be levied on their goods and chattels, lands and tenements...

Upon the conditions that Mary McMahan made her personal appearance before the next Grand Jury to answer a complaint against her and not to depart without the leave of the court and to be of good behavior in the meantime.

If Mary McMahan followed these conditions, this appearance bond was to be void. Otherwise, it would remain in full force and virtue.

September 1780 Court, pg. 106.

On the motion of **Elizabeth McGinnis, wife of Peter McGinnis,**[43] **a soldier in the Continental Army**, it was ordered that she be allowed 120 pounds for three barrels of corn and 80 pounds for 150 pounds of pork **for the support of herself and two small children.**

The court ordered this to be certified to the auditors.

September 1780 Court, pg. 107.

Thomas Lawson Gent presented to the Court **an account for sundries furnished the soldiers' wives and children**, amounting to £380 1s, which being proved and examined by the Court, it was ordered to be certified to the auditors.

October 1780 Court, pg. 109.

At a Court called and held at the Court house for Prince William County on September 1, 1780, for the **examination of John Sidebottom**, who stands committed for a felony.

John Sidebottom was committed to the jail of the county by precept under the hand of John Hooe Gent, **being charged with feloniously stealing a saddle,** valued at 200 pounds, the property of William Hall or otherwise concerned in this theft.

The evidence for the Commonwealth was not able to be heard since witnesses were sick so the Court ordered that Sidebottom be bound with good security to appear at the Courthouse on the following Monday in October. Meanwhile, he was to take out a bond for £2000 and his securities were to take out bonds for £1000 each.

John Sidebottom, Humphrey Calvert and Richard Taylor came into court and took out bonds, Sidebottom for £2000 and Calvert and Taylor each for £1000, to be levied against their goods and chattels and lands and tenements...

The conditions of the bonds were that Sidebottom make his personal appearance at the next Court on the first Monday in October to answer what shall be then there alleged against him and not depart without leave of the Court. If he does this, this appearance bond would be void. Otherwise it was to remain in full force and virtue.

Vester Moss and William Hall also took out appearance bonds to the Governor for L500 each on their goods and chattels and lands and tenements.

---

[43] Peter McGinnis served as a private in Captain Thomas Wills's company (and others) in the 11th Virginia and the 11th and 15th Virginia, from February 1778 through May 1779. He had originally enlisted in June, 1777 for three years. He reenlisted in December, 1778 for the war and went home on furlough until April 1779. See NARA, *Peter McGinnis's compiled service records,* 11th Virginia Regiment, M881 (http://www.footnote.com) , 1–42, Images 22856264 to 22856447. (Accessed June 25, 2008).

Their conditions were to appear to give evidence against John Sidebottom, who was committed for a felony and not to depart the Court without its leave. If they appeared, then this bond would be void. Otherwise it would remain in full force and virtue.

November 1780 Court, pg. 115.

Commonwealth v. Catharine Davis, John Sidebottom, Ann Randolph, Margaret Moore, Mary Ann McMahan and Charles Lenox—Upon an Indictment for Riot, etc.

The defendants Catharine Davis, John Sidebottom and Mary Ann McMahon came into court and severally pleaded not guilty and prayed time until the next term for the trial which was granted them, upon entering into recognizances with securities for their personal appearance at that term and that they would not depart thence without the leave of this Court and be of good behavior in the mean time.

Anne Randolph, Margaret Moore and Charles Lenox were called and failed to appear. The Court ordered that an attachment issue to force their appearance and that the Attorney prosecute their recognizance unless they appeared at the next term.

The Court further ordered that Catharine Davis, John Sidebottom and Margaret McMcMahon give a bond for 2000 pounds each and that the securities for 1000 pounds each.

Alexander Keith and John Waters came into court and gave their bond for 1000 pounds each to be made and levied on their goods and chattels and lands and tenements... on the condition that Catharine Davis make her personal appearance at the next term to answer the complain against her...

Roger McMahan[44] and **James Hays**[45] came into Court and gave their bonds for 1000 pounds each to be made and levied on their goods and chattels and lands and tenements... on the condition that Mary McMahon make her personal appearance at the next term to answer the complain against her.

John Sidebottom, **George Purcell**[46] and William Marshall came into court and took out bonds... John Sidebottom, for 2000 pounds and his two securities for 1000 pounds each on the condition that John Sidebottom makes his personal appearance at the next term to answer the complaint against him...

Lewis Reno came into Court and **took out a bond** for 5000 pounds... on the condition that he appear at the next term to testify and give evidence against Catharine Davis, John Sidebottom, Marianne McMahan, Ann Randolph, Margaret Moore and Charles Lenox, indicted for a riot...

November 1780 Court, pg. 116.

Commonwealth v. John Sidebottom – on an indictment for receiving and purchasing stolen goods.

---

[44] Roger McMahan was a former private in Captain Charles Gallahue's company, 11th and 15th Virginia Regiment commanded by Colonel Daniel Morgan. He appeared on rolls of Captain Gallahue's company in May 1777. See W. T. R. Saffell, *Records of the Revolutionary War* (1894; reprint, Bowie: Heritage Press, 1999), 257.

[45] James Hays' name was found on an undated list of men who enlisted or was reenlisted by officers belonging to the **11th Virginia**, under the command of Colonel Abraham Buford. Sergeant Hatcher was responsible for his enlistment. See *Virginia Troops*, (http://www.footnote.com), 1-2, images 23348399 to 23348402 (Accessed June 26, 2008).

[46] George Purcell served as an ensign in Captain George McCarmick's Company of the 13th Virginia from December 1776 to April 1778. Company muster rolls for October listed him as "wounded." In April 1778, he was "on command to Fort Pitt." See NARA, *George Purcell's compiled service records*, 13th Virginia, M 881 (http://www.footnote.com) 1-19, Images 23975777 to 23975812.

He was living in Fauquier when he made his pension declaration in March 1822. See Joan W. Peters, *Military Records, Certificates of Service, Discharge, Heirs, & Pension Declarations and Schedules from the Fauquier County, Virginia Court Minute Books, 1784–1840* (Westminster: Willow Bend Books, 1999), 71.

John Sidebottom came into court and pleaded not guilty and prayed time until the next term which is granted him upon his entering into a recognizance with security for his personal appearance at the next term...

John Sidebottom, George Purcell and Wm. Marshall came into Court and took out bonds, John Sidebottom for 2000 pounds and George Purcell and Wm. Marshall for 1000 pounds each.

The bonds were conditioned so that John Sidebottom was to appear at the next term of the court...

Commonwealth v. Sibi Weeks, alias Reno & Margaret Weeks, alias Reno – on an Indictment for an **Assault made on Catharine Davis**

Margaret Weeks, alias Renoe, came into court and acknowledged herself guilty and submitted to the judgment of the Court. It is thereupon considered by this court that she be fined five pounds... and she stand committed until she pays the fine and costs.

Sibi Weeks, alias Reno, was summoned but failed to appear. The Court ordered that an attachment be issued and the attorney prosecutes her recognizance unless she appears at the next court.

Vester Moss, Thomas Massey and William Hall came into Court and severally acknowledged a bond for 5000 pounds each, to be made and levied on their and each of their goods and chattels, land and tenements... on condition that they make their personal appearance at the next term **to give evidence against John Sidebottom who is indicted for receiving and purchasing a stolen saddle** and not depart without leave of the Court....

Roger McMahan came into Court and took out a bond for five thousand pounds to be made of his goods and chattels, lands and tenements... on condition that he make his personal appearance at the next term to give evidence against **Catharine Davis, John Sidebottom, Anne Randolph, Margaret Moore and Charles Lenox who were indicted for riot** and not to depart without leave of the Court. This recognizance was to be void else to remain in full force and virtue.

[Margaret Weaks alias Reno & John Cannon came into Court and severally acknowledged themselves indebted to the Governor of Virginia in the sum of one thousand pounds to be made of their goods & chattels, lands & tenements ... Upon Condition that if the said Margaret shall be of good behaviour towards all the good subjects of this state for twelve months. Then this Recognizance to be void, else to remain in full force & virtue.][47]

[page 117 and all of page 118 is missing from this Court Order Book]

April 1781 Court, pg. 123.
William Farrow is appointed Captain of the company lately commanded by James Triplett who resigned.

April 1781 Court, pg. 124.
Ordered that the Churchwardens of Dettingen Parish bind out **William Gunyon, orphan of John Gunyon**[48] deceased to John Murray according to law.

July 1781 Court, pg. 127
The Gentlemen of the Court proceeded to inquire into the several classes for the purpose of furnishing clothes etc for the soldiers agreeable to law.[49]

---

[47] The bracketed portion of the November 1780 Court session in the Prince William Order Book was extracted from Marty Hiatt, "Prince William County Court Order Books 1778–1785," *Northern Virginia Genealogy* 7 (2002): 1040–1041.

[48] John Gunyon served in the 3rd Virginia. See note 12.

Class No. 21. Bernard Hooe, Gent., produced receipts for clothes and beef for this class and was discharged. He was allowed six days at L10 per day.

Class No. 27. **Thomas Blackburn**[50] produced a receipt for clothing, receipt for beef wanted and to be produced at the next Court.

Class No. 16. John Fitzhugh, Gent., receipts for clothes and beef for this class and was discharged. He was allowed four days at ten pounds per day.

Class No. 2. **David Blackwell**,[51] Gent., produced a receipt for clothes for this class, the receipt for beef to be sent to the next court. He was allowed 8 days at ten pounds per day.

Class No. 10. William Skinker, Gent., a receipt for clothes for this class, the receipt for beef was to be sent to the next Court. He was allowed 6 days at ten pounds per day.

Class No. 17. Stephen Lee produced receipts for clothing and beef for this class and was discharged. He was allowed 3 days at ten pounds per day.

Class No. 18 & 19. Alexander Brown, Gent., produced a receipt for clothing for these classes and was to produce a receipt at the next court for three beeves.

Class No. 11. **Matthew Whiting**[52] produced a receipt for clothes for this class; his receipt for beef was to be produced at the next court.

July 1781 Court, pg. 128

Class No. 30. Richard Graham, Gent., produced a receipt for clothes for this class. The beef was ready for marched troops. He was allowed 2 days at 10 pounds per day. The Money was to be assigned and payable to Evan Williams.

Class No. 35. William Carr, Gent., produced a receipt for clothes for this class and also for a beef weighing 301 pounds and was discharged. He was to have a certificate for the overplus of ten pounds of beef.

---

[49] The Court's furnishing of clothing to the soldiers, "according to law," may refer to the provisions in the act to raise two legions for the defense of the state in March 1781. This act provided, among other things, that all persons who agreed to serve in the legions, except the commissioned officers, would be clothed at the expense of the state. The clothes were to be used only while the legions were on duty or in service. All camp utensils, arms, and military "apparatus for the non-commissioned offices and soldiers," were to be furnished at the expense of the state as well. See "An Act to Raise two legions for the defense of the State, March 1781," *Hening's Statutes at Large* (http://www.vagenweb.org/hening/vol10-19.htm) (Accessed June 25, 2008).

Also passed in March 1781 was an act to "remedy the inconveniencies" arising from the invasion of Virginia by Cornwallis's forces and the march of the Continental forces upon Yorktown. Further time was given to recruit the state's quota of troops for the continental forces and to supply the army with clothes, provisions, and wagons. The time factor proved to be critical as many of the counties had completely suspended the collection of clothing and supplies. Then there was the stipulation relating to the provision of "live beef" to the Continental troops. It was decided that the Governor should be the one to call for the "live beef" to be furnished the army whenever "publick necessities demanded it." See "An Act to remedy the inconveniencies ... for recruiting ... troops... and for supplying the army with clothes, provisions, and wagons, March, 1781," *Hening's Statutes at Large* (http://www.vagenweb.org/hening/wol10-19htm) (Accessed June 25, 2008).

[50] Thomas Blackburn had served in the State line as the lieutenant colonel of the 2nd Virginia State Regiment from December 1776 to June 1777. See Sanchez-Saavedra, 112.

[51] Gott and Russell, 451. David Blackwell (1753–1841) served in Captain John Chilton's company of the Culpeper Minute Battalion in 1775. David Blackwell filed a pension W 9358 in 1833 in which he stated that he had enlisted in 1776 or 1777 in a militia company that marched to the Potomac River to put a stop to the British depredations there. In September, 1780, he spent time in Captain John Brett's company, destined for North Carolina. Before he departed, he was given the opportunity to be commissioned a Lieutenant in Colonel Henry Lee's Regiment. He eventually received pay as a Commissary and Quartermaster. He was granted a pension under the act of June 1832. See NARA, *David Blackwell's Pension File* W 9358, M 804 (http://www.footnote.com), 1-20, Images 11704899 to 11704920 (Accessed June 25, 2008).

[52] Heitman, 589. Matthew Whiting was commissioned a 2nd Lieutenant in the 3rd Virginia on March 19, 1776. He resigned a year later.

Class No. 32, 33 & 34. Thomas Lawson, Gent., produced receipts for beeves and clothing and was discharged. He was allowed 9 days at ten pounds per day, to be paid to Wm. Murphy.

July 1781 Court, pg. 128.
Class No. 31. Robert Lawson, Gent., produced to the Court a receipt for a beef for this class. He also delivered a suit of clothes as required by law.

Class No. 15. James Ewell, Gent., presented to the court a receipt for clothes for this class except a hat, which with the receipt for beef, was to be delivered at the next Court. The beef received weighed 240 Net. He was allowed 6 days at ten pounds per day.

Class No. 18. Moses Moss presented to the court receipts for clothes and beef for this class, beef weighing 375 pounds. The court ordered that he have a receipt for 75 pounds overplus and be allowed 6 days at ten pounds per day.

Class No. 39. **Isaac Wickliffe** [53] presented to the Court receipts for clothes and beef for this class and was discharged. He was allowed 6 days at ten pounds per day.

Class No. 38. John Pope, Gent., Having failed to produce the hat and overalls to the receiver, and having advertised at sundry times to let the furnishing to the lowest bidder, no person agreed to undertake to furnish the hat and overalls. It was the opinion of the court that Pope should furnish these himself and give his account to the Constable to collect according to law.

Class No. 37. Simon Luttrell produced receipts for clothes and beef for this class and was discharged.

Class No. 26. Robert Moseby produced receipts for clothes and for 450 pounds of beef for this class and was discharged. The Court ordered that he have a certificate for the overplus of 150 pounds of beef.

Class No. 36. Robert Hedges produced receipts for clothes and beef for this class and was discharged. He was allowed 6 days at ten pounds per day.

Class No. 12. William Alexander, Gent., produced a receipt for clothes for this class to the Court with one pair of stockings wanting. He also produced a receipt for one beef weighing 280 pounds.

Class No. 14. Hugh Brent, Gent., produced receipts for 235 lbs of beef and clothing for this class and was discharged. He was allowed 7 days at ten pounds per day.

August 1781 Court, pgs. 130–131.
Class No. 29. Henry Lee, Gent., produced to the Court receipts for Beef and clothing for this class and was discharged. He was allowed six days at ten pounds per day.

Class No. 13 having furnished clothing and beef by Thomas Chapman, William Brent, Esquire, the head of this class was discharged and allowed 6 days at ten pounds per day.

Ordered that **Valentine Peyton**[54], **Robert Warren**[55], William Powell Jr and James White, or any three of them, being first sworn, do inventory and appraise the estate of Henry Peyton Gent...

---

[53] Isaac Wickliffe had served as a Captain in the Prince William Militia in March 1779, replacing John Whitledge.

[54] Valentine Peyton was the former 1st Lieutenant in Captain John Peyton's 3rd Virginia Company. He succeeded to the captaincy of this company when John Peyton retired after the September 1778 reorganization of the Continental Line. This Valentine Peyton was *not* the Valentine Peyton who was killed at Charleston in May 1780. That Valentine Peyton had been a lieutenant in Captain John Ashby's company and been promoted to Captain when John Ashby was forced to resign due to wounds in October 1777. See Joan W. Peters, *The Third Virginia*, II: iii–vi.

[55] Robert Warren had been appointed as a 1st Lieutenant in Captain Linton's Prince William County Militia company in July 1778 and Captain of the Prince William Militia in July 1779. See pages 63 and 65.

All delinquent districts for the clothing & provisions, Ordered they be proceeded against as the law directs and all those who have failed to pay their dividend as required by law be distressed for the same.

September 1781 Court, pg. 132.
Class # 22 returned receipt for clothes and beef acknowledged to be received by the County and to be allowed 6 days @ £1 per day.

March 1782 Court, pg. 137. (Public Service Claims)
Francis Floyd presented a certificate for 1 beef weighing 356 lbs @ 4d.
William Sandford ... 1 beef weighing 325 lbs @ 4d.
Norman Matthews ... for 1 beef weighing 300 lbs @ 4d.
Charles Neile, assignee of Cuthbert Bullitt ... 1 beef weighing 400 lbs @ 4d.
Benjamin Tennell[56] ... 2 beeves weighing 675 lbs @ 4d.
George King ... for 3 beeves weighing 1075 lbs @ 4d.
William Landrum ... 2 beeves weighing 325 lbs @ 4d.
George Newman Brown ... 1 beef weighing 400 lbs @ 4d.
John Ferguson ... 1 beef weighing 200 lbs @ 4d.

March 1782 Court, pg. 137. (Public Service Claims)
David Lee ... 2 beeves weighing 400 lbs @ 4d.
Benjamin Dixon for 2 beeves weighing 550 lbs @ 4d.
David Lee ... for wagon & 2 horses hauling cornt of Continental Army 8 days @ 6/ pr day.
Peter Ringoe ... for 18 days driving Cattle.
Samuel Cawood ... for 2 wagons & 2 horses hauling corn for Continental Army 11 days @ 6/ per day.
Thomas Sandford is appointed 1st Lieutenant; Benjamin Tennell, 2nd Lieutenant; and William Linton Jr., Ensign of Capt. Wm. Brown's company.

March 1782 Court, pg. 138. (Public Service Claims)
Henry Lee[57] presented certificates for beeves weighing 2795 and allowed 4d pr lb; 1091 lbs of fine flour at 2d pr lb; 4800 lbs of Marsh Hay @ 2/6 pr C^t W^t [?]; 846 lbs of Midling @ 2/10 pr C^t.

March 1782 Court, pg. 144.
Alexander Lithgow, Gent., is **appointed Captain of** company of Militia of the County in the place of **Reginald Graham**, Gent., deceased.

March 1782 Court, pg. 145. (Public Service Claims)
William Grayson[58] presented to the Court a certificate for 100 lbs Beef impressed for which the Court allowed 4d pr lb.

---

[56] NARA, *Benjamin Tennell's compiled service records,* 3rd Virginia Regiment, M 881 MR 856. Benjamin Tennell served as a sergeant in Captain Philip Richard Lee's company from June 1777 until his discharge in January 1778. A Francis Graves received Tennel's certificate for the balance of his full pay in March 1785 for £17 5s.

[57] Henry Lee had a distinguished career in the Continental service. His last military command was as the commanding officer of Lee's Partizan Legion. See Sanchez-Saavedra, 22, 79, 95–96, 102, 103, and 181 for more details about his career.

[58] Heitman, 359. William Grayson began his career as the assistant secretary to General Washington, appointed to that post in June 1776. He was promoted in August, 1776 to be a Lieutenant-Colonel and Aide-de-Camp to the commander-in-chief. In January 1777, he became the commanding officer of Grayson's Additional Continental

Ordered that Benjamin Scandland be summoned to appear at the next Court to **answer a complaint against him by Col. Grayson for impressing more beeves from his Estate than required by law.**

Enoch Reno presented to the Court a certificate for a beef weighing 235 lbs.

Francis Reno ... beef weighing 325 lbs.

Thomas Bird ... 4 beeves weighing 1200 lbs.; for 2 beeves weighing 625 lbs; allowed 4 d pr lb.

March 1782 Court, pg. 146. (Public Service Claims)

Thomas Bird presented to the Court a Certificate for one hundred & thirty bushels of rye for which he is allowed 3/ per bushel.

Thomas Fitzhugh presented to the Court a certificate for two beeves weighing 600 lbs for which he is allowed 4d per lb.

Thomas Fitzhugh presented a certificate for 2 head of cattle weighing 550 lbs and allowed 4d per lb.

James Gwatkin presented two certificates for 2 beeves weighing 800 lbs and allowed 4d per lb. He also presented a certificate for Pasturage for 9 head of cattle, per head 130 days & allowed 4d per day.

James Byrn presented a certificate for a beef weighing 200 lbs & allowed 4d per lb.

William Skinker presented a certificate for a beef weighing 400 lbs & allowed 4d per lb.

Wm. Leach ... 1 beef weighing 203 lbs & allowed 4d per lb.

William Creel ... 1 beef weighing 75 lbs & allowed 4d per lb.

Revd. Isaac Campbell ... 1 beef weighing 375 lbs & allowed 4d per lb.

Obed Harriss ... 1 beef weighing 350 lbs & allowed 4d per lb.

General Nelson[59]... 4 beeves weighing 975 lbs & allowed 4d per lb.

Henry Hampton ... 1 beef weighing 350 lbs. & allowed 4d per lb.

John Carter ... 2 beeves weighing 650 lbs & allowed 4d per lb.

John Armstead ... 13 beeves weighing 4320 lbs. & allowed 4d per lb.

James Wiatt ... 1 beef weighing 275 lbs. & allowed 4d per lb.

Francis Feagan ... 2 beeves weighing 525 lbs. & allowed 4d per lb.

Solomon Jones[60]... 2 beeves weighing 675 lbs & allowed 4d per lb.

Jerry Foster ... 1 beef weighing 325 lbs & allowed 4d per lb.

Samuel Love[61]... 1 beef weighing 625 lbs & allowed 4d per lb.

Conquest Wiatt ... 1 beef weighing 225 lbs & allowed 4d per lb.

Matthew Whiting[62]... 4 beeves weighing 1170 lbs & allowed 4d per lb.

Alexander Campbell ... 1 beef weighing 200 lbs & allowed 4d per lb.

Anthony Seale[63] ... 1 beef weighing 215 lbs & allowed 4d per lb.

Regiment. He retired in April 1779 and became a commissioner to the Board of War in December of that year. He resigned that post in September 1781. He died in March, 1790.

[59] See note 66.

[60] Lloyd DeWitt Bockstruck, *Virginia Colonial* Soldiers (Baltimore: Genealogical Publishing Company, 1988), 57. This may have been the Solomon Jones who served as a soldier in Captain Thomas Waggener's Company, in January 1756, in the French and Indian War. He appeared on Captain Waggener's payroll for that month. Afterwards, Bockstruck, *Virginia Colonial Soldiers.*

[61] See note 2. In addition to his 3rd Virginia service, Samuel Love had also served in the Prince William County Militia, as a 2nd Lieutenant in Captain John Linton's company in July 1778.

[62] See note 52.

[63] Bockstruck, *Virginia Colonial Soldiers,* 30. Anthony Seale had been a Prince William County Militia officer, appointed in May 1753.

March 1782 Court, pg. 146. (Public Service Claims)
James Wiatt... 2 beeves weighing 400 lbs & allowed 4 d per lb.
William Lynn ... 1 beef weighing 275 lbs & allowed 4d per lb.
James Able ... 1 beef weighing 375 lbs & allowed 4d per lb.
William Lynn presented a certificate for himself & horse 6 days, driving Cattle; allowed 5s per day.
James Wiatt, a Certificate for 2 bushels Indian corn @ 2/ 100 bundles, fother [fodder]@ 5/ and 7lbs beef @ 4d & seven pound flour @ 2d.
Jacob Garoon Pierce presented to the court a certificate for a gun and is allowed 25/.
David Jameson, a certificate for 6 bushels wheat, allowed 4/.
William Lynn a certificate for his expenses from Winchester on public service & is allowed seven shillings.
John Fitzhugh Jr presented a receipt for 2 beeves weighing 575 lbs; allowed 4d per lb.
John Fitzhugh ... 7 beeves weighing 2350 lbs; allowed 4d per lb.

March 1782 Court, pg. 147. (Public Service Claims)
Thomas Holmes ... 2 beeves weighing 475 lbs; allowed 4d per lb.
William Brown ... 1 beef weighing 220 lbs; allowed 4d per lb.
John Seale ... 1 beef weighing 475 lbs; allowed 4d per lb.
Mrs. Margaret Peyton .. 1 beef weighing 330 lbs; allowed 4d per lb.
William Skinker ... 2 horses and is allowed £75 for one & £50 for the other.
Anthony Seale Jr ... 1 beef weighing 350 lbs; allowed 4d per lb.
Francis Floyd had a horse impressed by Nemenus Bullitt who acted under the direction of **Francis Triplett**[64] to impress horses for **General Morgan's**[65] Core [Corps] by order of **General Nelson**[66] and the Court to find the horse was taken for the use of this State, ^ the certificate being lost, [the court] appraises it to thirty pounds ^ Ordered the same to be certified.

March 1782 Court, pg. 149. (Public Service Claims)
James Triplett presented to the Court a certificate for 3 beeves weighing 1000 lbs & allowed 4d per lb.
John Pope[67] ... 1 beef weighing 190 lbs: allowed 4d per lb.

---

[64] Francis Triplett (1728–1794) was an Adjutant for the Fauquier Militia in 1777. He was a captain in the Fauquier County Militia in March 1778 and a Major of Fauquier's militia in December 1780 at Cowpens. He was appointed a Colonel in June 1781 in Colonel Daniel Morgan's Virginia State Regiment. He served until 1783. See Gott and Russell, 476.

[65] Heitman, 401. General Morgan was, of course, Brigadier General Daniel Morgan who began his Revolutionary War service as a Captain of a Virginia Rifle company in July 1775. He was taken prisoner at Quebec in late December 1775. He became the Colonel of the 11th Virginia in November 1776. In June 1777, he received permission from Washington to recruit his own independent rifle command. In the September 1778 reorganization of the Continental Line, his regiment was redesignated as the 7th Virginia. He was promoted to Brigadier General in October 12780. He and his men were recognized by Congress for their defeat of Colonel Banastre Tarleton at Cowpens. He died in July, 1802.

[66] Heitman, 411. General Nelson was Thomas Nelson Jr., a signer of the Declaration of Independence. He began his revolutionary war career as a captain in the 1st Virginia, commissioned in February 1776. He resigned in August 1777 to become the commander of the Virginia State forces and served in that capacity from 1778–1782. By an Act of Congress in August 1778, it was 'resolved that the thanks of Congress be given to the Honorable General Nelson and the officers and gentlemen for their brave, generous, and patriotic efforts in the cause of their country.' He served as a Governor of Virginia in 1782 and was a participant in the siege at Yorktown. General Nelson died on January 4, 1789.

[67] Bockstruck, *Virginia Colonial Soldiers*, 85. John Pope was a corporal in Captain Mercer's Company on a size roll in August 1756. He enlisted in December 1754 from Prince William County when he was eighteen years old. He had been born in Virginia, was five feet seven, with a fair complexion and hair, and a fresh look. He was a carpenter.

March 1782 Court, pg. 149. (Public Service Claims)
Capt. Lynaugh Helm[68]... 7 beeves weighing 3057 lbs; allowed 4d per lb.
Bernard Hooe[69]... 1 beef weighing 450 lbs; allowed 4d per lb.
Seth McMillian ... 2 beeves weighing 585 lbs; allowed 4d per lb.
William Alexander ... 10 beeves weighing 3350 lbs; allowed 4d per lb.
William Ashmore ... 1 beef weighing 250 lbs; allowed 4d per lb.
George Bussell ... 1 beef weighing 250 lbs; allowed 4d per lb.
Richard Melton ... 1 beef weighing 200 lbs; allowed 4d per lb.
Matthew Harrison ... 1 beef weighing 450 lbs; allowed 4d per lb.
Ignatius Mitchell ... 1 beef weighing 300 lbs; allowed 4d per lb.
John Murray[70]... 3 bushels alum salt @ 3/ per bushel
John McMillian[71]... 81 lb bacon delivered at Dumfries at 9d per lb.
John McMillian ... 100 bushels of wheat delivered at Mr. Lawson's Mill at 4/3 per bushel.
Revd. James Scott ... 1 beef weighing 250 lbs; allowed 4d per lb.
Mrs. Ann Downman ... 2 beeves weighing 500 lbs; allowed 4d per lb.
John Highwarden ... 1 beef weighing 250 lbs; allowed 4d per lb.
Frances Botts ... 1 beef weighing 250 lbs; allowed 4d per lb.
Frances Botts ... 134 lbs bacon @ 9d per lb.
Landon Carter ... 6 beeves weighing 1100 lbs; allowed 4d per lb.
William Alexander ... a bay horse 14 hands 3 inches high, 4 years old @ £40.
Alexander Lithgow[72]... 447 lbs of bread at 10/ per Ct. [count?]
Capt. William Tebbs[73]... 1 beef weighing 250 lbs at 4d per lb.
Robert Luttrell[74]... 38 days in collecting & driving cattle at 1/4 per day.
Robert Garrett ... 37 days in collecting & driving cattle at 1/4 per day.
James Grinstead ... 1 beef weighing 312 lbs at 4d per lb.
John Willcocks[75] ... for himself, cart & 2 horses, 13 days at 6/ per day.

In August 1757, Corporal Pope, who had enlisted in Prince William in November 1754, was found on a size roll for Colonel George Washington's company. See Bockstruck, *Virginia Colonial Soldiers,* 103.

[68] Gott and Russell, 460. Lynaugh (or Leonard) Helm was a captain in Clark's Illinois Regiment in 1778. He was captured at Vincennes. He soon after the war. In 1782, he would have been about forty years old. See also Gott and Russell, 251. In 1796, his son Achillis Helm deed 750 acres of his Illinois grant to Colonel Simon Triplett of Loudoun in consideration of the trouble and expense that Colonel Triplett went to in getting a law passed by the Virginia Assembly to recognized his father's claim to 3334 acres as a captain in the Illinois Regiment.

See also Gott and Russell, 76. Lynaugh Helm's daughter Celia (Helm) Foote, the widow of Henry Foot married William Blackwell of Fauquier sometime around 1780. He was the son of Colonel William and Elizabeth (Crump) Blackwell.

[69] This may be the Bernard Hooe who was a Captain in the Prince William County Militia in July 1778. See page 63.

[70] Bockstruck, *Virginia Colonial Soldiers,* 162. John Murray was another veteran of the French and Indian War in the Prince William County Militia, a trooper with sixty-six days service according to the Militia claims for Prince William. Indeed, he made a claim for payment as a blacksmith in September 1768 which was rejected. He had, he stated, been sent out with drafted militia from Prince William and had been employed as a blacksmith for ninety days. He requested payment for that service rather than that of a common soldier which rate had already been paid him.

[71] Ibid. John McMillion had served 66 days as a trooper in the Prince William County Militia according to that county's militia claims before the Virginia colonial legislature. His claim for service was allowed.

[72] Alexander Lithgow had been appointed a captain in the Prince William Militia in February 1782 to replace Reginald Graham who had died. See entry for March 1782 Court on page 77.

[73] William Tebbs was not found in Heitman, 535, so it is likely that he is a Prince William County Militia captain.

[74] Robert Luttrell may be the Robert Luttrell who served as a private in Captain John Ball's Fauquier County Militia Company in 1781. See Gott and Russell, 466.

March 1782 Court, pg. 149. (Public Service Claims)
  Evan Williams for Mrs. Rawlings... for 1 axe 7/6 State.
  Moses Moss ... 1 beef weighing 275 lbs; allowed 4d per lb.
  John Lynn ... 1 beef weighing 225 lbs; allowed 4d per lb.

March 1782 Court, pg. 150. (Public Service Claims)
  Strother Suttle[76] ... 1 beef weighing 375 lbs; allowed 4d per lb.
  Nicholas Ware ... 1 beef weighing 300 lbs; allowed 4d per lb.
  James Matson ... 1 beef weighing 310 lbs; allowed 4d per lb.
  George Green Sr ... 3 beeves weighing 875 lbs; allowed 4d per lb.
  David Renoe ... 1 beef weighing 175 lbs; allowed 4d per lb.
  George Bussell ... 1 beef weighing 250 lbs; allowed 4d per lb.
  James Roach ... 2 beeves weighing 1025 lbs; allowed 4d per lb.
  James Anderson ... 1 beef weighing 250 lbs; allowed 4d per lb.
  Joseph Petty ... 1 beef weighing 235 lbs; allowed 4d per lb.
  John Sidebottom... for forage 4/.
  Jacob Minitree ... 1 bushel corn 2/ & fother [fodder] for 4 horses 2/ for 1 night.
  Jacob Minitree ... 2 ½ bushels of oats at 2/; 100 bundles fodder 5/. 9 lbs beef at 4d & 9 lbs flour @ 2d.
  Jonathan Latham ... a gun left at Lancaster 70/.
  John Hedges[77]... 19775 lbs of Timothy Hay @ 4/ per Ct; for pasturage of 9 horses 2 nights & a day @ 4d for 24 hours each; for pasturage of 75 oxen & horses two days and a night. At 4d for twenty-four hours. Also for Pasturage of 19 horses & 340 oxen for 1 night at 4d; 3 horses and 22 oxen for 24 hours @ 4d; pasturage of 222 cattle & 1 horses 2 ½ hours; Pasturage for 5 horses for 2 nights and a day @ 4d per 24 hours; Pasturage for 6 horses 24 hours @ 4d.
  James Brown ... 3 beeves weighing 1375 lbs @ 4d per lb.
  Nathaniel Burwell[78]... 3 beeves weighing 786 lbs @ 4d per lb.
  James Brown ... 230 lbs of hay @ 4/ per Ct; 200 lbs of hay @ 4/ per Ct; pasturage for 9 horses & 103 head of Cattle @ 4d per 24 hours; for a shoat @ 6/; for 200 lbs Hay @ 4/ pr Ct; for 8 lbs of bacon @ 9d & 10 lbs Indian Bread @ 1d; for supper for 6 men 6/; for 515 lbs hay @ 4/ per Ct & for shoeing horses 1/3; for an account settled February 1781 for £295 is £3 13s 9d; for 235 lbs salt beef at 6d.
  William Melton ... 4595 lbs Timothy hay @ 4/ per Ct.
  Daniel Moore ... for hauling 34 Beeves, Corn delivered Gerrard Conn 2 days at 10/ per day & for hauling 35 bees [?] Corn delivered Gerrard Conn 2 days @ 10/ per day.
  Mrs. Burwell ... 3 beeves weighing 787 lbs @ 4 d per lb; for 2 horses 6 days @ 2/6 Each per day.

---

[75] Bockstruck, *Virginia Colonial Soldiers*, 92. John Willcocks had served as soldier in the French and Indian War in Captain George Mercer's company where his name appeared in the September and October 1756 payrolls.

[76] Gott and Russell, 474. Strother Settle (or Suttle, as it was sometimes spelled) was a private in Colonel Steven Moylan's 4th Regiment of Light Dragoons. Joan W. Peters, *Military Records, Patriotic Service & Public Service Claims from the Fauquier County Minute Books, 1759–1784* (Westminster: Willow Bend Books, 1999), 116. In September 1782, Strother Settle swore an oath that he and seven others had been inhabitants of Virginia when they had enlisted in the 4th Regiment of Light Dragoons.

[77] John Hedges was a captain in the Prince William County Militia. See July 1778 Court entry on page 9 of this book.

[78] Heitman, 136. Nathaniel Burwell served as an Ensign in the 1st Virginia Continental Regiment. He was commissioned in September 1775. In November 1776, Burwell was promoted out of the regiment to a captaincy in the 1st Continental Artillery. In May 1779, he was promoted to Major and became an aide-de-camp to General Robert Howe. He retired in January 1783 and died in 1801.

March 1782 Court, pg. 150. (Public Service Claims)
Daniel Moore ... 7 bar: Corn 2 days at 10/ per day, delivered Gerrard Conn; for hauling 7 bar; Corn 2 days at 10/ ; delivered Gerrard Conn; for 1 beef weighing 175 lbs @ 4d per lb.
George Purcell,[79] assignee of Samuel Jackson presented a certificate for a black horse £50.
Alexander Henderson ... Certificates for 4 steers weighing 1475 lbs & 4 beeves weighing 1350 lbs @ 4d per lb.

March 1782 Court, pg. 151. (Public Service Claims)
William Powell ... 1 beef weighing 335 lb; allowed 4d per lb.
Leonard Leachman ... 1 beef weighing 475 lbs; allowed 4d per lb.
James Foster ... 1 beef weighing 275 lbs; allowed 4d per lb.
John Hooe, Gent., ... 1 beef weighing 350 lbs; allowed 4d per lb.
John Brett[80]... 1 beef weighing 350 lbs; allowed 4d per lb.
William French... 1 beef weighing 350 lbs; allowed 4d per lb.
James French... for cash expended driving beeves 6/
Wm. Sidebottom... beef weighing 200 lbs; allowed 4 d per lb.
Asa Reeves... for waggon & team, 4 days @ 10/ per day.
Francis Jackson Jr... 1 beef weighing 350 lbs; allowed 4d per lb.
Francis Jackson (son of Frank)... 1 beef weighing 150 lbs; allowed 4d per lb.

Alexander Tarte presented Certificates for 1 cord of wood @ 10/; pasturage for 90 horses & 34 Cattle [for] 24 hours @ 4d each; for 150 lbs Hay @ 4/ & 150 lbs fodder @ 5/; Pasturage [for] 34 cattle [for] 18 hours @ 4d pr 24 hours; Pasturage for 5 cattle 1 night @ 2d; Pasturage for 24 waggon horses 1 night at 2d each; D° [ditto] for 6 horses 1 night @ 4d per 24 hours; D° for 7 horses 1 night at 4d per 24 hours; D° for 2 horses 2 nights & a day at 4d per 24 hours and 17 horses [for] 24 hours; D° for 3 horses [for] 3 days and nights at 4d pr 24 hours; D° for 18 horses 24 hours , each at 4d; d° for 70 horses [for] 18 hours, each a 4d pr 24 hours;
Alexander Tarte presented Certificates for 2 horses 4 days and 4 nights at 4d pr 24 hours; d° for 2 horses 24 hours, each at 4d; d° for 5 horses 24 hours, each at 4d; d° for 3 horses 12 hours each; d° for 10 horses at 12 hours each at 4 d pr 24 hours; d° for 85 Cattle and 12 horses 6 hours each at 4d pr 24 hours; for pasturage at different times 580 days and nights for horses and Cattle at 4d ; for storage 2 horses 56 days L6; for lodging and pasturage for the Marquis troop £4.
William Rookard ... 1 beef weighing 225 lbs; allowed 4d pr lb.
John Randolph[81] ... ½ bushel of corn 1/ & 30 lbs fodder at 5/.
John Grinstead ... a waggon & team 4 days, for the Marquis at 10/.
Peter Cockerill ... 1 beef weighing 175 lbs; allowed 4d pr lb.
Margaret Peyton ... 11 diets to Wagener and Drovers @ 1/ & 4 ½ lbs flour @ 2d.
John Steel ... 1 beef weighing 331 lbs; allowed 4d pr lb.
William Munday... for pasturage 11/ 8d.
Peter Cockerill ... for repairing arms for the State of Virginia 62/.
John Grinstead ... for black horse ab^t 14 hands high, 8 years old, £15.
Margerum & Moore, assignees of George Hill... beef £4 11s.
William Munday ... 2 beeves weighing 575 lbs; allowed 4d pr lb.

---

[79] George Purcell was an ensign in Captain George McCarmick's 13th Virginia Regiment from December 1776 until April 1778. NARA, *George Purcell's compiled service records,* M 881 (http://www.footnote.com), 1-18, Images 23975777 to 23975812. See also Joan W. Peters, *Military Records ... from Fauquier County, Virginia Court Minute Books, 1784–1840* (Westminster: Heritage Books, 2007), 71. George Purcell made a pension declaration in March 1822 in Fauquier County, Virginia

[80] Heitman, 119. John Brett was a captain in the Virginia Militia, 1777–1778.

[81] See note 35.

March 1782 Court, pg. 151. (Public Service Claims)
    Ann Downman ... 2 beeves weighing 400 lbs; allowed 4d pr lb.
    Thomas Blackburn ... 300 lbs hay @ 4/ & 500 lbs hay @ 4/; 1 beef weighing 510 lbs at 4d pr lb; 2 beeves weighing 600 lbs @ 4d; 2 beeves weighing 500 lbs @ 4d pr lb.

March 1782 Court, pg. 152 (Public Service Claims)
    William Gains ... 1 beef weighing 310 lbs; allowed 4d pr lb.
    Berkley & Company... 2 beeves weighing 1200 lbs; allowed 4d pr lb.
    William Edward Wiatt ... a black horse ab^t 14 ½ hands high, 5 yrs old, £35.
    John Tyler,[82] Gent., ... for 13 lbs bacon at 9d; 1 Bushel oats 2/ & 50 lbs Hay at 4/ pr C^t; 2 meals at 1/; 1 bushel oats 2/; for fire wood & lodging for 30 men 1 night at 6d each, 15/; for 1 cord of wood 10/; for half cord of wood 5/ (for 8 ½ cords wood at 10/;
    John Tyler, Gent ... **house room for 53 Officers and privates** at 3d; Stablege for 32 horses for 2 days & nights at 3d pr 24 hours; 2 ½ bushel oats at 2/; fodder for 8 horses 1 Night, 4/; & **Stabledge for 19 horses of Col^o Gists Regiment**[83] @ 4/9, L6 7s 6d; for diets for **6 Men belonging to Morgans Infantry**[84]; for 25 diets at 1/; forage & Pasturage for 25 horses for 1 Night @ 6d each, L1 7s 6d; for 200 bundles of fodder at 5/ pr C^t; pasturage for five horses at 4d; **State Militia** 12/8; for 94 horses 1 night at 2d each, 15/8; for 11 1/2 Bushels corn at 2/; 1 gallon oats 3d & pasturage for 9 horses 1 night at 2d, 4/9; for 1 bushel & 3 pecks of oats at 2/, 3/6; 70 lbs fodder at 5/, 3/6; 10 lbs beef at 4d, ¾ & 10 lbs of flour at 2d, 1/8... 12/0.
    Hugh McKillup... a blanket furnished the **11th Virginia Regiment, Capt. Gallahues Comp^y**[85] 20/; for a Dutch oven 60 lbs & a pot 55 lbs @ 4d pr lb; for **Loudoun Militia** for 4 bushel oats at 2/; 100 Bundles fodder @ 5/; 7lbs beef at 4d; 7 lbs flour at 2/.
    John Williss, Esqr., ... 3 beeves weighing 1000 lbs at 4d pr lb.
    Snowden Horton... 2 beeves weighing 675 lbs at 4d pr lb.
    William Grant ... 2 beeves weighing 675 lbs at 4d pr lb.
    William Whitledge Jr ... 1 beef weighing 275 lbs at 4d pr lb
    Anthony Seale ... 100 lbs hay at 4/; State **Loudoun Militia**; for pasturage 21 horses 1 night for **Wayne's Troops**[86] at 2d; for 2500 lbs hay at 4/.
    James Brown ... 1 ton of hay at 4/ pr C^t; for hay 1 nigh for 39 horses at 6d pr night & 2 barrells corn at 10/.
    Anthony Seale ... 70 lbs hay at 4/ per C^t.
    Lawrence Suthard ... for forage 1 night for 4 horses at 6d each.
    Lewis Reno ... for 74 bushel oats at 6d; died [?] 1/.
    Cornelius Kincheloe ... 1 beef weighing 225 lbs at 4d pr lb.
    Thomas Stone ... 1 beef weighing 212 lbs at 4d pr lb.
    Henry Marjorum[87] ... 1 beef weighing 350 lbs at 4d pr lb.

---

[82] Heitman, 553. John Tyler had been a 1st lieutenant in the 3rd Virginia Continental Regiment, commissioned in February 1776. He resigned in August.

[83] Sanchez-Saavedra, 75–76. Colonel Gist's Regiment was one of the Additional Continental Regiments, raised at large as a supplementary force, early in the war. After the surrender of the American forces at Charleston, his regiment was the only one still active. Grayson's Additional Regiment had been decimated by smallpox and its survivors had been absorbed by Colonel Gist's regiment.

[84] Heitman, 401. Daniel Morgan was made a Brigadier-General of the Continental Army in October 1780.

[85] Sanchez-Saavedra, 64–66. This public service claim must have been used by the 11th Virginia early in the war since Captain Charles Gallahue was a captain of this Prince William County company between November 1776 and February 1777. The 11th Virginia was then under the command of Colonel Daniel Morgan. The regiment ceased to exist after February 12, 1781 when the Virginia Continental Line was reduced to eight regiments.

[86] Wayne's Troops referred to General Anthony Wayne's Pennsylvania Line troops who joined Lafayette in Virginia at Yorktown. See Boatner, 1175–1177.

March 1782 Court, pg. 152 (Public Service Claims)
   Humphry Calvert ... 2 days driving 2/8
   William Scott ... for an axe for Fairfax Militia 6/.
   Alexander Doyle ...for 12 gallons rum at 12/ pr Gallon.
   Charles Cornwell [88]... 1 beef weighing 275 lbs at 4d pr lb.

March 1782 Court, pg. 153 (Public Service Claims)
   Ezekiel Cornwell ... 1 beef weighing 225 lbhs at 4d pr lb.
   Thomas Sincock ... 1 beef weighing 225 lbs at 4d pr lb.
   Colin Campbell ... 4 barrels for State [of] Virginia at 5/.
   Mark Tharp... for 1 beef weighing 310 lbs at 4d pr lb.
   William Lyndsey... 2 beeves weighing 775 lbs at 4d pr lb.
   Peter Evans[89]... 1 beef weighing 350 lbs at 4d pr lb.
   James Shelton ... 1 beef weighing 200 lbs at 4d pr lb.
   George Graham ... 2 beeves weighing 500 lbs at 4d pr lb.
   Landon Carter ... 6 beeves weighing 1560 lbs at 4d pr lb.
   Richard Graham ... for 3 beeves weighing 1070 lbs at 4d pr lb.
   Wormley Carter ... for a bay horse 6 years old near 14 ½ hands high, £40
   Richard Graham ... for a sorrel horse 4 yrs old, 14 ½ hands high, £40.
   Alexander Keith[90] ... for 3 breakfasts at 1/; 3 horses fed 1/6; for 7 meals 7/ & lodging 3/6 for Balt dragon.
   Christian Bower, Assignee of Richard Stonell... for hire of a horse 6 days @ 6/6...
   Thomas Attwell ... 2 beeves weighing 775 lbs @ 4d pr lb.
   John Chancellor ... 2 beeves weighing 525 lbs @ 4d pr lb.
   Matthew Harrison ... 1 beef weighing 500 lbs @ 4d pr lb.
   Stephen Lee ... 1 beef weighing 256 lbs @ 4d pr lb.
   Burr Harrison... 2 beeves weighing 700 lbs @ 4d pr lb; hauling corn 6 days at 10/; 2 tons Timothy Hay @ 4/ pr C^t
   Samuel Jackson Sr ... two beeves weighing 600 lbs @ 4d pr lb & for an overplus in Class beef 50 lbs @ 4d...
   Robert Mosely furnished a beef for Class 26, overplus 150 lbs at 4d pr lb.
   John Calvert Sr ... 1 beef weighing 250 lbs @ 4d pr lbs.
   Jesse Ewell ... 1 beef weighing 524 lbs @ 4d pr lb.

March 1782 Court, pg. 154. (Public Service Claims)
   William Carr... for a bay horse ab^t 15 hands high, 8 yrs of age, £72; 1 beef weighing 450 lbs @ 4d pr lb.
   Isaac Farrow... 1 beef weighing 375 lbs @ 4d pr lb; for 2060 lbs Timothy Hay @ 4/ pr C^t.

---

[87] Henry Marjorum had served as a conductor in the Artillery, in Colonel Wadsworth's Regiment, Rochambeau's Brigade, involved with the transportation of the artillery from Yorktown to Boston. See John Bell's Pension Declaration, filed in November 1819 in Fauquier County in Joan W. Peters, *Neglected and Forgotten: Fauquier County, Virginia, French and Indian War, Revolutionary War, and War of 1812 Veterans 1759–1825* (Westminster: Willow Bend Books, 2004), 41. Afterwards, Peters, *Lost and Forgotten.*

[88] Bockstruck, *Virginia Colonial Soldiers,* 167. Charles Cornwell appeared on a list of deserters from the Prince William County Militia who never returned when ordered out in June 1759 to a frontier post on the South Branch of the Potomac.

[89] Peter Evans had been appointed a 1st Lieutenant in Captain Charles Lee's Militia company in August 1779. See note 17. In May 1780, he replaced Lee as the Captain of this Militia Company.

[90] Heitman, 328. Alexander Keith served as a cadet in the 3rd Virginia, commissioned in August 1776. He transferred to the 10th Virginia and was promoted to a 1st Lieutenant in March 1777. In September, 1778, he transferred into the 6th Virginia. He resigned his commission in October 1778. Alexander Keith died in 1824.

March 1782 Court, pg. 154. (Public Service Claims)
  Howson Hooe Sr… for 3 beeves weighing 1050 lbs @ 4d pr lb; for 2 beeves weighing 750 lbs @ 4d pr lb.
  Robert Luttrell… 1 beef weighing 312 lbs @ 4d pr lb.
  Rev[d] Mr. Scott… 2 beeves weighing 750 lbs @ 4d pr lb.
  Dan[l] Carroll Brent… 4 beeves weighing 1325 lbs @ 4d pr lb.
  John Stisle … 50 lbs mutton @ 4d pr lb.
  William Farrow… a black horse ab[t] 14 hands high, 4 yrs old £78.
  Bernard Hooe… 1 beef weighing 375 lbs and also an overplus of his Class beef of 62 lbs @ 4d pr lb.
  John Orear… 1 beef weighing 250 lbs; 1 beef , 350 lbs @ 4d pr lb.
  Charles Love… 96 lbs Hay @ 4/; 2 ½ bushels corn @ 2/; 6 lb flour @ 2d; beef @ 4/.
  Anthony Lucas… 1 beef weighing 200 lbs @ 4d pr lb.
  Thomas Bland… for a cart & 2 horses 1 day; Drawing provision 6/.
  Zephaniah Ratcliffe… 1 beef weighing 350 lbs @ 4d pr lb.
  William Montgomerie… 2 beeves weighing 575 lbs @ 4d pr lb.
  Moses Jeffries… 1 beef weighing 200 lbs @ 4d pr lb.
  Obed Calvert… 1 beef weighing 100 lbs @ 4d pr lb.
  Vester Moss… for 10 days collecting & driving Cattle 5/.
  William Hazlerigg… 1 beef weighing 300 lbs @ 4d pr lb.
  Benjamin Cooper … 1 beef weighing 200 lbs @ 4d pr lb.
  William Hampton… 1 beef weighing 225 lbs @ 4d pr lb.
  Robert Carter Esq[r] 2 beeves weighing 600 lbs @ 4d.
  Ben: Wigginton… 2 beeves weighing 675 lbs @ 4 d.
  Sarah Williams… 1 beef weighing 225 lbs @ 4d pr lb.
  John Derrington… 1 beef weighing 375 lbs @ 4d pr lb.
  Carty Wells… 1 beef weighing 250 lbs @ 4d pr lb; 1 beef weighing 250 lbs @ 4d pr lb.
  Rutt Johnston… 1 beef weighing 325 lbs @ 4d pr l; for 200 lbs Hay @ 4/.
  John Farrow… 1 beef weighing 375 lbs @ 4d pr lb.
  Rutt Johnston… 45 lbs of hay @ 4/
  Robert Hutchinson… 1 beef weighing 225 lbs @ 4d pr lb.
  Thomas Bland… 1 beef weighing 400 lbs @ 4d pr lb.
  William Ross … 1 beef weighing 250 lbs @ 4d pr lb.
  Sarah Calvert … 1 beef weighing 300 lbs @ 4d pr lb.

March 1782 Court, pg. 155. (Public Service Claims)
  Benjamin Wood… 1 beef weighing 250 lbs @ 4d pr lb.
  Obed Calvert Sr … 1 beef weighing 120 lbs @ 4d pr lb.
  Jesse Calvert … 1 beef weighing 110 lbs @ 4d pr lb.
  Obed Calvert Sr … for pasturage for 238 h[d] Cattle 3 hours @ 4d pr 24 hours.; 1 ½ bushel corn 3/; 20 bundles fodder/; breakfast for 4 men 4/.
  Mich[l] Lynn … 1 beef weighing 225 lbs @ 4d pr lb.
  Elizabeth Holmes … 1 beef weighing 400 lbs @ 4d pr lb.
  William Mitchell … for a wagon & 4 horses hauling corn 6 days @ 10/; for 1 beef weighing 265 lbs @ 4d pr lb.
  Spilsby Stone … 1 beef weighing 225 lbs @ 4d pr lb.
  Thomas Davis … 1 beef weighing 250 lbs @ 4d pr lb.
  Spilsby Stone … 1 beef weighing 275 lbs @ rd pr lb.
  Jos: Stone … 1 beef weighing 225 lbs @ 4d pr lb.
  Francis Cornwell … 1 beef weighing 215 lbs @ 4d pr lb.

March 1782 Court, pg. 155. (Public Service Claims)
  Stephen Howison[91] ... 1 beef weighing 225 lbs. @ 4d pr lb.
  Richard Gray... 1 beef weighing 300 lbs @ 4d pr lb.
  Elizabeth Holmes ... for 2 beeves weighing 455 lbs @ 4d pr lb.
  Cuthbert Bullitt ... 6 beeves weighing 1900 lbs; for 3 beeves [weighing] 1100 lbs @ 4d pr lb; for 184 lbs hay @ 4/; 3 ½ bushels corn @ 10/; 13 lb beef at 4 d; & 13 lb flour @ 2d.
  Thomas Norman ... 1 days carting with 2 horses 6/...
  Thomas Lawson ... for Wagonage acct settled Rob.[?]
  Richard Young, a Deputy Quarter Master Genl..£19 10s for 5 pr horse shoes at 2/6 pr p^r for 192 lbs hay @ 4/; 1 bushel corn 2/; for a wagon, 5 horses for 5 days & driver 2 10/; for wagon & 5 horses 38 days @ 10/; for wagon, 4 horse & driver 7 days @ 10/; for a wagon, 4 horses & Driver 73 days @ 10/; for a large black dray mare 5 years old & upwards of 15 hands high, £50; for a black horse ab^t 5 or 6 years... upwards of 14 hands high, £35.
  Samuel Love Sr ... a milk and cider horse 10 or 11 years old next spring, upwards of 14 hands high, £15; for 10 bushels Indian Meal @ 2/; & 6 flour barrels @ 2/.
  Thomas Lawson ... 10 beeves weighing 4068 lbs @ 4d pr lb; for wagonage 4 days with 4 horses @ 10/; pasturage for 60 men & 20 horses 1 Night @ 2d each; 6 bundles rye @ 3/; pasturage for 264 head cattle and two horses 1 night @ 2 d each; for 500 lbs fodder @ 5/; for 900 lbs hay @ 4/; for 40 bundles fodder @ 5/; 1 bundle corn 2/; for 4 beeves weighing 1075 lbs @ rd; for [illegible number] lbs marsh hay @ 2/6; pasturage for 102 horses 1 Night @ 6d each; for 8 horse shoes @ 1/3; for 1 barrel flour, 275 lbs @ 2d pr lb.

March 1782 Court, pg. 156 (Public Service Claims)
  William Davis Jr ... 1 beef weighing 250 lbs; allowed 4d pr lb.
  Rhodham Blancett ... 1 beef weighing 200 lbs; allowed 4d pr lb.
  John Smith... 1 beef weighing 300 lbs; allowed 4d pr lb.
  Robert Lawson ... for 17 trips over the Occoquan with 64 horses and a cart & 2 horses @ 3d pr horse & cart; 6 days [for] a wagon & team @ 10/; 3 frying pans 2 [illegible word] 32 ½ lb @ 1/; 6 bushels Charcoal @ 6d; 32 horse shoes @ 2/6 pr pair; pasturage for 320 oxen & 17 horses 1 Night @ 2 d each; 1 beef weighing 400 lbs @ 4d pr lb.
  Thomas Chapman presented a certificate dated 2nd Feby 1781 from **John Herndon, D^y Muster Master** under **Col^o Finnie, Q^r Master,**[92] for £347 10s which in Specie is £4 6s for 250 lbs Marsh hay @ 2/6; 3 cords wood @ 10/; 6 Quarts & 6 gills of whiskey @ 6/ pr Gallon; half a cord of wood 5/; Pasturage for 22 oxen & 3 horses 1 night @ 2d each; pasturage for 223 head cattle & 7 horses 1 night @ 2d each; 1 beef weighing 234 lbs @ 4d pr lb; 2 bushels of Country salt @ 18/ pr bushel.
  William Carr, assignee of Stephen Sanger presented a certificate from John Herndon, D^y Q^r Master for £224 January 1779 is £28 Specie.
  Wm. Carr, assignee of ... Stephen Sanger presented a certificate from John Herndon, D^y Q^r Master dated 28th of January 1781 for £354 and Affidavit being made by the assignee that a certificate in consequence of which the same was issued... dated in January 1780 which such with depreciation is L8 8s.
  Wm. Carr presented a certificate for 1 q^r [quire] of paper for **Prince Wm Militia** @ 3/.
  William Carter ... for 11 ½ lbs bacon for **Prince Wm Militia**.
  John Holliday ... for 9 lbs bacon for **Prince W^n Militia**.
  John Earls ... for 11 ½ lbs bacon for **Prince W^n Militia** @ 9d; & ½ bushel Meal 1/.

---

[91] See Note 42.
[92] Heitman, 227. Colonel Finnie was William Finnie, Colonel and Deputy Quartermaster General of the Southern Department from March 1776. He served until the close of the war.

March 1782 Court, pg. 156 (Public Service Claims)
Nat^l Wickliffe ... 2 beeves weighing 763 lbs @ 4d & 37 lbs bacon @ 9d; 1 bushel of Indian meal.
William Davis Sr ... 1 beef weighing 200 lbs @ 4d.
William Davis Jr ... for 1 beef weighing 200 lbs; allowed 4d pr lb.
Robt Carter Esqr... 2 beeves weighing 650 lbs @ 4d.
Ben: Wigginton... 2 beeves weighing 675 lbs @ 4d.
John Friar ... 2 beeves weighing 525 lbs @ 4d.
Robert Carter ... 3 beeves weighing 975 lbs @ 4d.
William Wiatt ... 1 beef weighing 300 lbs @ 4d.
William Carter Jr ... 1 beef weighing 300 lbs @ 4d.
Thomas Ramey ... 2 beeves weighing 700 lbs @ 4d.

May 1782 Court, pg. 163. (Public Service Claims)
Philip Dawes is allowed **for keeping British prisoners 45/; ordered the same be certified.**
John McMillian for receiving & storing 325 bushels specific grain £5 & Pasturing & 375 h^d Cattle, £20; for 3 horses valued at £95 specie which the Court think[s] reasonable (to wit) 1 chestnut sorrel 9 yrs old 15 ½ hands high; 1 black horse 14 ½ hands high, 8 yrs old; 1 bay horse 15 yrs old, 14 hands high.
Alexander Keith ... furnishing stable & hay for 6 horses 1 night... allowed 6/.
Mann Page, Esqr. ... for 2 horses impressed £180 specie & for a beef weighing 160 lbs & allowed 4d pr lb.
William Carr, Gent., ... allowed per account for sundries £14 13s, to wit, for a blanket 15/ 2 bushels salt 28/ and for rent of a lumber house 11 months, £11.
William Martin is discharged from paying taxes &c in [the] future.

May 1782 Court pg. 164.
David Lee presented a certificate for a wagon & 2 horses, 8 days @ 6/ pr day.
James Gwatkin ... for 8000 lb hay @ 4/ pr C^t.
James White ... 1 beef weighing 200 lbs @ 4d.
William Skinker ... for 2 beeves weighing 700 lbs @ 4d.
James Brown... 1 beef weighing 200 lbs @ 4d.
Seth Peyton ... 1 beef weighing 225 lbs @ 4d.
Valentine Peyton ... 1 beef weighing 125 lbs @ 4d.
James Stark ... 1 beef weighing 300 lbs @ 4d.
John Chancellor ... 1 beef weighing 225 lbs @ 4d.
Asa Reeves ... 1 beef weighing 225 lbs @ 4d.
John Brown ... 1 beef weighing 225 lbs @ 4d.
Robert Brown ... 1 beef weighing 250 lbs @ 4d.
William Herndon ... 3 beeves weighing 600 lbs @ 4d.

September 1782 Court, pg. 176.
Administration of the Estate of **Valentine Peyton**[93] deceased is granted to Timothy Peyton, who took the oath of an Administrator and executed a bond with security according to law.

---

[93] Peters, *The Third Virginia Regiment*, II: 82. Captain Valentine Peyton was killed at the Siege of Charleston, June 1780. He began his career as a 1st lieutenant in Captain John Ashby's company and was promoted to the captaincy of this company after the resignation of Captain Ashby in October 1777. Another 3rd Virginia veteran, James Alverson, recalled the American's march to Charleston. He confirmed Captain Peyton's death in a pension declaration filed in October 1826 in Chester District, South Carolina. See also NARA, *James Alverson's Pension File* W 8236, M 804 MR 48.

Ordered that John Brett, Thomas Sandford, Wm. Powell & Wm. Sandford, or any three… inventory and appraise the Estate of Valentine Peyton, according to law.

Samuel Jackson (son of Sam) is appointed **guardian to Thomas & Richard Calvert, orphans of Rheuben Calvert**[94] **decd**, who executed a bond with Security according to law.

September 1782 Court, pg. 177.
Ordered that John Thorn & Samuel Byrne do **divide the estate of Rhubin Calvert decd between the orphans and the widow and set apart the widow's dower** & report to the Court.

September 1782 Court, pg. 177.
Ordered that **Alexander Lithgow**[95], Thomas Chapman & Evan Williams set apart the dower of Mrs. Mary Graham in the personal estate of Reginald Graham decd in this county

September 1782 Court, pg. 188.
Valentine Peyton[96] **Plaintiff v. Vester Moss**[97], **Defendant** in Trespass, Assault & Battery. Suit abated **Plaintiff dead.**

November 1782 Court, pg. 195.
Isaac Wickliffe[98] Deputy Sheriff is allowed 55 shillings for his extraordinary trouble in summoning the Justices to elect Commissioners of the Land Tax, agreeable to law.
Isaac Wickliffe & Richard Neale severally took the oaths prescribed by law as Deputy Sheriffs of this County.

December 1782 Court, pg. 197. (Public Service Claims)
William Skinker presented a certificate No. 1 for forage for use of Guards and prisoners & is allowed £7; No. 2, for pasturage of 410 horses @ 2d I £3 8s 4d; No.3, for 500 rails @ 10/ destroyed £2 10s; No. 4, for 500 Battons [?] Eye Straw, £1; No. 5, for 300 Corn blades 15/; No. 6 for a Gun, £4 5s; No. 7 for two guns, £4 10s.

Richard Graham presented Certificates: No. 1 for one barrel beef & Quire paper, is allowed L5 10/; No. 2, for 4 barrels, £1; No 3 for 74 lbs beef @ 4d, £1 4s; No. 4 for ropes, 7/6; No. 5 for 3 pots, 2 Dutch ovens, ironware AND Helve [???] and 2 quires paper, £5 3s; No. 6 as assignee of Moses Lunsford for 205 lbs pork @ 6d, £5 2/6.

Thomas Love… for 5 bushels corn, 10/; forage of 5 horses 2/6.
Burr Harrison… 2 trace ropes, 5/.
William Leach… 1 bushel corn & 6 bushels oats @ 2/-- 16/.
Robert Brent… pasturage of 118 horses @ 2d, 19/8.
George Graham, **Admr of Reginald Graham** … 1 beef weighing 350 lbs @ 4d pr lb, £5 16s 6d.
Thomas Chapman… for a flat 6 days carrying French troops over Occoquan @ 6/.
William Carr Gent… for tar & Junk—£1 5/.

December 1782 Court, pg. 199.

---

[94] NARA, *Reuben Calvert's compiled service records*, M 881 MR 952, *3rd Virginia Regiment*. Rueben Calvert was a sergeant in Captain John Peyton's company who died on January 1, 1777.

[95] Alexander Lithgow was a captain in the Prince William Militia in February 1782. He replaced Reginald Graham who had died. See note 71. See also entry for February 1782 Court on page 22 of this book.

[96] This is the Valentine Peyton who died at the siege of Charleston in May 1780. See Peters, *History of the 3rd Virginia*, II: 82.

[97] Vester Moss had enlisted in the 3rd Virginia but spent his entire enlistment "sick in Virginia. See note 34.

[98] See note 53.

On the motion of Philip Dawe, assignee of **Philip Connor**[99], it is ordered to be certified to the Register of the Land Office that... Connor was **a Sergeant in the third Virginia Regiment of this state for three years**. [He] served the time of his inlistment duly and was entitled to the lands for the service by the resolves of Congress and Acts of Assembly of this state.

March 1783 Court, pg. 203.
Alexander Lithgow took the oath of a Justice of the Peace for this County and also a Justice of Oyer & Terminer.
On the motion of Philip Dawe, assignee of **Philip Connor**, it is ordered to be certified to the Register of the Land Office that... Connor was **a Sergeant in the third Virginia Regiment of this state for three years**. [He] served the time of his inlistment duly and was entitled to the lands for the service by the resolves of Congress and Acts of Assembly of this state.

May 1783 Court ? (Court and page number missing. This page appears before pg. 209 and the top half of the page is missing.)
...Moses Davis presented to the Court a certificate for a gun impressed for the Militia marching to headquarters and valued to L3 10s which is allowed and ordered to be certified.
Benjamin Jones presented to the Court a certificate for a gun impressed as is allowed for the law three pounds fifteen shillings and the same is ordered to be certified.

May 1783 Court, pg. 209.
John King,[100] **formerly a soldier in the American Army, having lost both his arms,** appearing in Court, ordered the same be certified.
Alexander Jones,[101] **formerly a soldier in the American army, being wounded in the knee,** ordered the same be certified...
On the motion of **Evan Williams, Burser of the Militia of Prince William County**, judgment is granted him against the Estate of Henry Peyton, Gent, [illegible word] for one thousand four hundred & sixty six pounds, fifteen shilling, which is agreeable to the scale of depreciation in November one thousand seven hundred and eighty, nineteen pounds sixteen shillings and five pence Specie for fines imposed by the Court Martial in the said County at different periods & put into the said Peyton's hands to collect as per his Receipt.

May 1783 Court, pg. 210.
Charles Lenox,[102] **formerly a soldier in the Continental Army, being wounded in the knee**, ordered the same to be certified.
May 1783 Court, pg. 211.

---

[99] Peters, *The Third Virginia Regiment*, II: 408. Phillip Connor had originally enlisted for two years as a private in Captain Charles West and Reuben Briscoes' 3rd Virginia company. He was wounded in September 1777 at the Battle of Brandywine. He reenlisted in the 3rd Virginia in December 1777 for three years. In August 1778, he was promoted to Sergeant in Captain Briscoe's company. After the reorganization of the Continental Line, Sergeant Connors was transferred into Captain Robert Powell's 3rd Virginia Company.

[100] See note 9.

[101] NARA, *Alexander Jones's Pension File* S 34939, M 804 (http://www.footnote.com) 1-4, images 24152431 to 24152434. Alexander Jones was living in Prince George's County, Maryland when he made his pension declaration in March 1818. He stated that he had enlisted in 1779 in Captain Thomas Ewell's company which was attached to the 1st Virginia State Regiment. He saw action at Guilford Courthouse and served principally in the southern campaign, under General Greene. He was severely wounded, enough so that it was necessary for him to apply for assistance from his country under the Pension Act of March 1818. See also NARA, *Alexander Jones' compiled service records*, 1st Virginia State Regiment, M 881 (http://www.footnote.com), 1-5, Images 21852073 to 21852079.

[102] See note 19.

On the **motion of the County Lieutenant in behalf of the Commonwealth against Robert Warren, Collector of the Class No. 7** for money due from [this] Class under the Act of Assembly entitled and Act for Recruiting the States Quota of Troops to Serve in the Army of the United States.

It appeared to the Court that the Deft had legal Notice and failing to appear, it is ordered that the Commonwealth have their execution against the Defendant for the sum of one pound fourteen shillings and three pence one farthing, being the balance due from the class, as^d [assessed] with the costs of this motion and damages at the rate of five per centum.

On the **motion of the County Lieutenant in behalf of the Commonwealth against Burr Peyton, Collector of the Class No. 11** for money due from [this] Class under the Act of Assembly entitled and Act for Recruiting the States Quota of Troops to Serve in the Army of the United States.

It appeared to the Court that the Deft had legal Notice and failing to appear, it is ordered that the Commonwealth have their execution against the Defendant for the sum of ten shillings and seven pence, being the balance due from the class, as^d [assessed] with the costs of this motion and damages at the rate of five per centum.

On the **motion of the County Lieutenant in behalf of the Commonwealth against John Newman, Collector of the Class No. 12** for money due from [this] Class under the Act of Assembly entitled and Act for Recruiting the States Quota of Troops to Serve in the Army of the United States.

It appeared to the Court that the Deft had legal Notice and failing to appear, it is ordered that the Commonwealth have their execution against the Defendant for the sum of five pounds four shillings and a half penny, being the balance due from the class, as^d [assessed] with the costs of this motion and damages at the rate of five per centum.

On the **motion of the County Lieutenant in behalf of the Commonwealth against Valentine Peyton, Collector of the Class No. 13** for money due from [this] Class under the Act of Assembly entitled and Act for Recruiting the States Quota of Troops to Serve in the Army of the United States.

It appeared to the Court that the Deft had legal Notice and failing to appear, it is ordered that the Commonwealth have their execution against the Defendant for the sum of four pounds nineteen shillings and seven pence, being the balance due from the class, as^d [assessed] with the costs of this motion and damages at the rate of five per centum.

May 1783 Court, pg. 212.

On the **motion of the County Lieutenant in behalf of the Commonwealth against Thomas Sandford, Collector of the Class No. 18** for money due from [this] Class under the Act of Assembly entitled and Act for Recruiting the States Quota of Troops to Serve in the Army of the United States.

It appeared to the Court that the Deft had legal Notice and failing to appear, it is ordered that the Commonwealth have their execution against the Defendant for the sum of one pound nine shillings and three pence, being the balance due from the class, as^d [assessed] with the costs of this motion and damages at the rate of five per centum.

On the **motion of the County Lieutenant in behalf of the Commonwealth against John Redman, Collector of the Class No. 14** for money due from [this] Class under the Act of Assembly entitled and Act for Recruiting the States Quota of Troops to Serve in the Army of the United States.

It appeared to the Court that the Deft had legal Notice and failing to appear, it is ordered that the Commonwealth have their execution against the Defendant for the sum of two pounds eleven shillings and eight pence half penny, being the balance due from the class, as^d [assessed] with the costs of this motion and damages at the rate of five per centum.

On the motion of the County Lieutenant in behalf of the Commonwealth against William Gaines, Collector of the Class No. 19 for money due from [this] Class under the Act of Assembly entitled and Act for Recruiting the States Quota of Troops to Serve in the Army of the United States.

It appeared to the Court that the Deft had legal Notice and failing to appear, it is ordered that the Commonwealth have their execution against the Defendant for the sum of one pound six shillings and seven pence being the balance due from the class, as^d [assessed] with the costs of this motion and damages at the rate of five per centum.

On the motion of the County Lieutenant in behalf of the Commonwealth against William Linton, Collector of the Class No. 20 for money due from [this] Class under the Act of Assembly entitled and Act for Recruiting the States Quota of Troops to Serve in the Army of the United States.

It appeared to the Court that the Deft had legal Notice and failing to appear, it is ordered that the Commonwealth have their execution against the Defendant for the sum of one pound three shillings and three pence, being the balance due from the class, as^d [assessed] with the costs of this motion and damages at the rate of five per centum.

On the motion of the County Lieutenant in behalf of the Commonwealth against John Cannon, Collector of the Class No. 21 for money due from [this] Class under the Act of Assembly entitled and Act for Recruiting the States Quota of Troops to Serve in the Army of the United States.

It appeared to the Court that the Deft had legal Notice and failing to appear, it is ordered that the Commonwealth have their execution against the Defendant for the sum of seven pounds six shillings and five pence, being the balance due from the class, as^d [assessed] with the costs of this motion and damages at the rate of five per centum.

May 1783 Court, pgs. 212-213

On the motion of the County Lieutenant in behalf of the Commonwealth against Thomas Newman, Collector of the Class No. 22 for money due from [this] Class under the Act of Assembly entitled and Act for Recruiting the States Quota of Troops to Serve in the Army of the United States.

It appeared to the Court that the Deft had legal Notice and failing to appear, it is ordered that the Commonwealth have their execution against the Defendant for the sum of two pounds six shillings and one penny half penny, being the balance due from the class, as^d [assessed] with the costs of this motion and damages at the rate of five per centum.

On the motion of the County Lieutenant in behalf of the Commonwealth against Samuel Byam, Collector of the Class No. 25 for money due from [this] Class under the Act of Assembly entitled and Act for Recruiting the States Quota of Troops to Serve in the Army of the United States.

It appeared to the Court that the Deft had legal Notice and failing to appear, it is ordered that the Commonwealth have their execution against the Defendant for the sum two pounds seven shillings and six pence half penny, being the balance due from the class, as^d [assessed] with the costs of this motion and damages at the rate of five per centum.

On the motion of the County Lieutenant in behalf of the Commonwealth against James Dalton, Collector of the Class No. 34 for money due from [this] Class under the Act of Assembly entitled and Act for Recruiting the States Quota of Troops to Serve in the Army of the United States.

It appeared to the Court that the Deft had legal Notice and failing to appear, it is ordered that the Commonwealth have their execution against the Defendant for the sum of six shillings and two pence three farthings, being the balance due from the class, as^d [assessed] with the costs of this motion and damages at the rate of five per centum.

May 1783 Court, pg. 213.
On the motion of the County Lieutenant in behalf of the Commonwealth against Colin Campbell, Collector of the Class No. 39 for money due from [this] Class under the Act of Assembly entitled and Act for Recruiting the States Quota of Troops to Serve in the Army of the United States.

It appeared to the Court that the Deft had legal Notice and failing to appear, it is ordered that the Commonwealth have their execution against the Defendant for the sum of one pound two shillings and ten pence, being the balance due from the class, as^d [assessed] with the costs of this motion and damages at the rate of five per centum.

On the motion of the County Lieutenant in behalf of the Commonwealth against Solomon Ewell, Collector of the Class No. 40 for money due from [this] Class under the Act of Assembly entitled and Act for Recruiting the States Quota of Troops to Serve in the Army of the United States.

It appeared to the Court that the Deft had legal Notice and failing to appear, it is ordered that the Commonwealth have their execution against the Defendant for the sum of seven pounds six shillings and four pence half penny, being the balance due from the class, as^d [assessed] with the costs of this motion and damages at the rate of five per centum.

On the motion of the County Lieutenant in behalf of the Commonwealth against Jacob Marshall, Collector of the Class No. 42 for money due from [this] Class under the Act of Assembly entitled and Act for Recruiting the States Quota of Troops to Serve in the Army of the United States.

It appeared to the Court that the Deft had legal Notice and failing to appear, it is ordered that the Commonwealth have their execution against the Defendant for the sum of three pounds two shillings and eight pence, being the balance due from the class, as^d [assessed] with the costs of this motion and damages at the rate of five per centum.

May 1783 Court, pg. 214.
Valentine Peyton Gent took the oaths prescribed by Law as a Justice of the peace for the County and also as Justice of Oyer & Terminer.

June 1783 Court, pg. 218.
On the motion of the County Lieutenant in behalf of the Commonwealth against John Lynn, Collector of the Class No. 23 for money due from [this] Class under the Act of Assembly entitled and Act for Recruiting the States Quota of Troops to Serve in the Army of the United States.

It appeared to the Court that the Deft had legal Notice and failing to appear, it is ordered that the Commonwealth have their execution against the Defendant for the sum of seven pounds five shillings and eleven pence lea [?] farthing, being the balance due from the class, as^d [assessed] with the costs of this motion and damages at the rate of five per centum.

Robert Overall is recommended to the Governor as a **Captain in the room of Wm. Brent who has resigned.**

June 1783 Court, pg. 226.
    Commonwealth v. John Sidebottom & als.   On an indictment
        The prosecution is discontinued.
    Commonwealth v. John Sidebottom-- The prosecution is discontinued.
    Commonwealth v. **John Randolph**[103]-- On indictment. Prosecution is discontinued.

---

[103] See note 35.

Commonwealth v. Sibi Renoe, alias Weekes -- On indictment. Prosecution is discontinued.

August 1783 Court, pg. 241
It being proved to the Court that Valentine Peyton is heir at law **to George Peyton deceased, formerly an Ensign in the third Virginia Regiment,** came into Court and claimed his right to the lands promised by Act of Assembly to the officers and soldiers in the Virginia line.
It appearing to the Court that **George Peyton died in the year 1777[104] and at the time of his death, was in the Continental Service.** Ordered that the same be certified.
It being proved to the court that Valentine Peyton is heir at law to **Robert Peyton[105] deceased, formerly a Lieutenant in the third Virginia Regiment,** came into Court and claimed his right to the lands promised by an Act of Assembly to the officers and soldier of the Virginia Line.
It appearing to the Court that **Robert Peyton was killed at the Battle of Brandywine** and at that time [was] in the Continental Service. Ordered that the same be certified.

October 1783 Court, pg. 256.
On the motion of Nathaniel Wickliff, ordered that it be certified (the Court being fully satisfied of the truth thereof) that Nathaniel [Wickliff is] the heir at law to **Robert Wickliff decd,** late a resident of Westmoreland County, Pennsylvania.
Ordered that it be certified that **Elizabeth Whitfield, is the widow of John Whitfield and mother of Edward Whitfield,[106] who died in the service of the United States.**

December 1783 Court, pg. 282.
William Payne produced a certificate granted to **Colonel George Mason** for two thousand six hundred and fifty five pounds paper money, dated August 12, 1780. Ordered the same be certified.

March 1784 Court, pg. 288.
Ordered to be certified that W. Davis is entitled to the Bounty in Lands which would have been due to **John Davis, his brother,** to [illegible word] that William is heir at law to the said **John, having enlisted in the Virginia Continental line for three years and died in the service[107]** which facts, having been made, appear to the Court by Evidence.
March 1784 Court, pg. 289.

---

[104] NARA, *George Peyton's compiled service records*, M 881 MR 951, *Officers of 3rd Virginia*. George Peyton was an ensign in Captain Gustavus Brown Wallace's 3rd Virginia company. He appeared on the payrolls from October to December 1776 and from December 7, 1776 to January 1, 1777. The latter payroll remarked that his name was "cancelled on the roll." He was marked "deceased" in a list of officers who had receive their certificate for the balance of their full pay, agreeable to an Act of Assembly in November 1781. Elisha Price received the George Peyton deceased certificate in March 1784 for £10.

[105] NARA, *Robert Peyton's compiled service records*, M 881 MR 955, *3rd Virginia Regiment*. Robert Peyton was an ensign and 2nd lieutenant in Captain John Peyton's company from October 1776 to August 1777. He transferred into Captain Phill Lee's company of the 3rd Virginia in August 1777 and was killed at Brandywine on September 11, 1777. Mr Price received his certificate for the balance of his full pay in November 1783 for £37 16s.

[106] Ibid., *Edward Whitfield/Whitefield compiled service records*, 1st Virginia State Regiment, M 881 (http://www.footnote.com) 2–15, Images 21913323 to 21913404.

[107] This may be the John Davis who was a soldier in Captain John Peyton's company of the 3rd Virginia from October 1776 until March 1777. The payroll from January 1, 1777 to March 1, 1777 gave him credit for service for two months. Thus, he may have died on March 1, 1777 as the April payroll states that he was "not to be accounted for." This was the usual terminology for soldiers who had died in the service. See NARA, *John Davis's compiled service records*, 3rd Virginia Regiment, M 881 MR 953.

James Ewell[108] Gent took the oaths of a **Lieutenant Colonel in the Militia of the County.**

Ordered that it be certified that **Joseph Blanchett** is entitled to the Bounty in lands that should have been due to **William Blanchett, his brother**, to whom the said Joseph [is] heir at law. **William [Blanchett] enlisted in the Virginia Continental line for three years & died in the service**, which facts having been made, appear to the Court by evidence.

March 1784 Court, pg. 290.

Ordered that it be certified that **Hugh Davis**[109] **enlisted & served three years in the Continental line for this Commonwealth as a Sergeant and had his discharge, which is lost, proved by the testimony of George Pearl the Officer who enlisted him.**

May 1784 Court, pg. 301.

Mr. Landon Carter, having produced to the Court a certificate for fifteen hundred & sixty pounds of beef furnished the Commissioners, ordered the same be certified.

Ordered that it be certified that **John Posey Newman is heir at law to George Newman who enlisted in Lieutenant Colonel Lee's Legion in the Continental service during the war and died in the service.**

November 1784 Court, pg. 402.

It appeared to the Court, upon oath [and] ordered [to] be certified that **Thomas Bristow is heir at law to John Bristoe**[110] **who died a soldier in the continental service under Colonel Henry Lee, late of the horse.**

---

[108] Heitman, 220. James Ewell was a major in the Virginia Militia 1776–1778.

[109] NARA, *Hugh Davis's compiled service records,* 13th Virginia Regiment, M 881 MR 1078 (http://www.footnote.com), 1–21, images 23091308 to 23091366. Hugh Davis served as a sergeant in Captain George McCarmick's 13th Virginia company from January 1777 to October 1778. In October 1778, he was in Colonel Campbell's 13th Virginia company until February 1779. On February 16, 1779, he was demoted to the ranks and served until May 1779 as a private in Colonel Campbell's Company. He was at Fort Pitt from October 1778 until March 1779. Colonel Grayson received his certificate for the balance of his full pay as a soldier in the infantry in July 1784, for £74 8s 6d.

[110] Ibid., *John Bristoe's compiled service records,* Continental Troops: Lee's Legion, M 881 MR 94 (http://www.footnote.com), 1–5, images 13049518–13049528. John Bristo's name appeared on receipt rolls for October 1778, having received his pay and subsistence from Captain Forsythe, the Paymaster for Lee's Legion in full for July 1778. He had enlisted in May 1778 for three years. His name was omitted from the rolls in November 1779. He may have died then.

Part III

The War of 1812 Period
1804–1806, 1812–1814

Chapter 6

Historical Introduction

The Two Prince William Virginia State Militia Regiments in the War of 1812

Chapter 7

Military Records from the Prince William County Court Order Book 1804–1806, 1812–1814

THE WAR OF 1812 PERIOD

CHAPTER 6

HISTORICAL INTRODUCTION

The War of 1812 actually encompassed a struggle with the French and the British over impressments of American sailors,[1] a naval war with the British on the Great Lakes[2] and the high seas,[3] the British Navy's blockade of the American east coast,[4] two unsuccessful invasions of Canada,[5] and engagements on land with the British in Canada and along the Canadian border,[6] for forts throughout the old Northwest, and along the borders of New York[7] and New England.[8] The British invasion of the Chesapeake brought about the burning of the nation's capital in August 1814 and the bombardment of Fort McHenry in Baltimore in September.

In addition there were expeditions against Native American tribes in the old Northwest[9] and throughout the southern frontier.[10] Unfortunately, those expeditions are outside the scope of this present study.

However, the British invasion of the Chesapeake *is* relevant since it involved militia from Virginia and Maryland. Before examining this invasion and its impact upon the militia system in Virginia, it is necessary to look at the United States military establishment prior to the War.

The American Military Establishment 1798–1814

1. In 1798, during John Adam's presidency Congress created a Provisional Army.

Congress created legislation for a 10,000-man provisional army to be raised in the event of war. The President was given the power to accept volunteer companies into national service. Then, Congress went a step further. They authorized the President to raise a New Army immediately, to be composed of twelve infantry regiments and six troops of dragoons. They also proposed what they called an "Eventual Army," to be raised only in an emergency.

Thus, there were now five different armies: the "old" Army, on the frontier; the Provisional Army, the volunteer units, the "New Army," and the Eventual Army.[11] Only the New Army was organized for the impending war. The so-called "old" Army remained in the west. The War department, for all intents and purposes, ignored the Provisional, volunteer and Eventual forces. They prevailed upon Washington to

---

[1] Carl Benn, *The War of 1812* (Oxford: Osprey Publishing Company, 2002), 11–12.
[2] Commodore Perry's naval battle of Lake Erie and his subsequent attack on Fort George is discussed in Donald R. Hickey, *The War of 1812: A Forgotten Conflict* (Chicago: University of Illinois Press, 1995), 132–135 and 136–140.
[3] The *Constitution* and *HMS Guerriere's* sea battle in August 1812 is discussed in Walter R. Borneman, *1812: The War That Forged a Nation* (New York: Harper Collins, 2004), 84–88. For a map of naval operations on the high seas, see Benn, 54.
[4] Benn, 58.
[5] A.J. Langguth, *Union 1812: The Americans Who Fought the Second War of Independence* (New York: Simon & Shuster, 2006), 173–180, 262–270. See also Benn, 28–31.
[6] Benn, 31.
[7] Ibid., 37–42.
[8] In September 1814, the British occupied Maine along the Penobscot River up to Bangor, giving them effective control over 100 miles of the Maine coast. See Hickey, 94–95.
[9] William Henry Harrison's expedition against Tecumseh and the Shawnee, and the victory at Tippecanoe in 1811 is described in Borneman, 28–37. See also Langguth, 257–270.
[10] The Creek nation rose up against American encroachment on their lands in Georgia, Alabama, and Louisiana. Andrew Jackson's expedition against the Creeks is related in Borneman, 143–152. See also Langguth, 271–290.
[11] Arthur R. Millett & Maslowski, Peter, *For the Common Defense: A Military History of the United States of America* (New York: The Free Press, 1994), 101.

command the New Army although he would not take the field until both the new and old army had been combined. Alexander Hamilton was to be his chief subordinate.

The military policy which evolved during the last decade of the eighteenth century "basically remained intact for a century." The country would keep a small professional army, augmented by militia and federal volunteers during a war. The nascent system of arsenals, shipyards, drydocks, and coastal fortifications would be increased and a small Navy would be created to protect American shipping and allow for plundering of enemy commerce during a war.

While impressments of American sailors and trade issues between the British and Americans heated up during Jefferson's administration, he viewed the army from a local perspective. He believed that the militia should be the first line of defense and could buy time to raise a regular force.

2. The Federal Militia Act of 1802.

Congress used this act to completely revamp and reorganize the army. In an economy move, disguised as a partisan effort to erase Federalist control from the army, legislation reduced the officer corps by eliminating eighty-eight positions. However, the Act did establish the United States Military Academy, thus creating a Corps of Engineers distinct from the Artillery.[12]

3. Virginia's Militia Acts

The Virginia legislature passed a series of militia acts between 1803 and 1808 which gave greater clarity to the duties and responsibilities of the militia and its officers and men. The 1803 act organized the militia into brigades and divisions and set out precise instructions for the appointment of slave patrols. The 1806 act, by and large, regulated the use and distribution of arms among the various companies. The Act also prohibited officers from resigning their commissions for five years. The 1807 law regulated the distribution of public arms throughout the state. The 1808 Act authorized regimental commanders to appoint their own musicians, authorized the governor to let contracts for rifles and capped voluntary enlistment terms to not less than three but more than five years.

In order to understand the importance of the slave patrols dealt with in Chapter 7 and the appendix, along with the makeup of the two Prince William Militia Regiments, a brief synopsis of these acts is presented here.

- ♦ **Virginia Militia Act of 1803**

Virginia's Militia Act came about in the words of its preamble when it became obvious that it was "expedient to carry into effect the laws of the Congress of the United States, providing for the national defence, by establishing a uniform militia throughout the United States."

The Assembly passed legislation in 1803 to revamp the Virginia Militia. Among the more important parts of this act were the following:
- The legislators divided the state into divisions and brigades. Prince William, Fauquier, Stafford, and King George were to form one brigade in the second division of State troops. Loudoun and Fairfax were to put together another brigade, Culpeper, Madison, Orange, Spotsylvania, and Caroline formed a third brigade, while Louisa, Goochland, Fluvanna, Albemarle, and Amherst were to create the final brigade in the 2nd division.[13]
- The Governor was given the authority to consolidate and divide the regiments in the counties, as he thought necessary. Field Officers of the State Regiment were appointed. The Adjutant General was to have overall oversight of the State Militia. Each division was to be commanded by a major general; brigades were to have a brigadier general. These officers were to be appointed by joint ballot of both houses of the legislature.

---

[12] Ibid., 103–104.
[13] Samuel Shepherd, *Statutes at Large of Virginia from October 1792 to December 1806*, (1835; reprint, New York: AMS Press, 1970), III: 3.

- The Governor, with the advice of council, is authorized and required to appoint and commission one lieutenant colonel commandant and two majors for artillery and cavalry annexed to each division. Returns were to be made by the commanding officers of the regiments, battalions, and companies.
- The Company officers were to be recommended by the County Courts in each division. Divisions, brigades, and regiments were to be numbered and registered in the Office of the State Adjutant General.
- Commanding officers of regimental companies had the responsibility for numbering their companies from one to ten for the purpose of a "regular rotine" of duty when called into service. Officers were also to return a roster of each division and its number in rotation to their commanding officers within fifteen days. The battalion officer was then to transmit this to the clerk of the court of enquiry.
- These regulations were to be observed by every commanding officer of a company, battalion, and regiment on enrolling soldiers in their units.[14]
- The governor, with the advice of council, could cause the companies of artillery, cavalry, grenadiers, light infantry, and riflemen to be allotted by entire companies into divisions from one to ten. Every able-bodied white male citizen, from eighteen to forty-five was required to serve in the state militia.

There were exemptions— members of the council of state, judges of superior and inferior courts, clerks of both houses of the general assembly, the state attorney general, the state treasurer and his clerks, the auditor of public accounts, the register of the land offices and his clerks, inspectors of tobacco, professors and students at the college of William and Mary, professors and students at all other public seminaries, ministers of the gospel who have taken an oath of fidelity to the Commonwealth, keepers of the jails and public hospitals, millers, and ferrymen. All of these occupations were exempt from military service in the State Militia.[15]

- The Governor could commission officers on the advice of his council or by recommendations from the County Courts. Commissions were to be granted for at least one captain, one lieutenant, and one ensign, for each battalion. These officers were then to proceed, by voluntary enlistment within their battalion, to enrolla sufficient number of men to complete their companies. Companies were to be distinguished by denominations of grenadiers, light infantry or riflemen at the discretion of the commanding officer of the regiment.
- The governor could also issue commissions for officers of one or more troops of cavalry to each regiment and, with the advice of council at their own discretion, appoint and commission the necessary officers for one or more companies of artillery in each brigade. These officers were then to enlist, by voluntary enlistment a company or companies of cavalry or artillery
- If officers fail to complete their quota of men within six months of receiving their commissions, then their commissions were to be discontinued, unless they could present a good reason for their failure. No person enlisting in any of the volunteer companies was to serve for more than five years. Muster regulations were given for militia gathering and regimental gatherings.[16]
- Each captain or commanding officer of a company was to appoint to his company, four sergeants, four corporals, a drummer and fifer. These appointments were to be approved by the battalion commander.[17]
- The lieutenant colonel commandant was to purchase a set of colours for each regiment and for each battalion. He was also to procure a drum, fife or bugle horn for each company. These

---

[14] Ibid., III: 4–6.
[15] Ibid., III: 6.
[16] Ibid.. III: 6–7.
[17] Ibid., III: 8.

accoutrements were to be marked with the number of the regiment and battalion and the name of the county. The money for the colors, drums, fifes and bugles was to come from court martial fines.[18]

- In the event of an invasion or insurrection or a probable prospect of one, the governor with the advice of his council, was empowered to call up the militia.
- When the Virginia State militia was in actual service of the United States, they were to be governed by the articles of war which govern the regular troops of the U.S.[19]
- Battalion commanding officers were, from time to time, to appoint an officer or non-commissioned officer and as many men of the militia as he thinks appropriate to patrol and visit all negro quarters and other places "suspected of entertaining unlawful assemblies of slaves, servants, or others strolling from one plantation to another without a pass …"
- Patrols were to take place once a month or more often if required. The patrollers had the authority to take those thus captured before a justice of the peace. If the justice saw cause to admonish the captured Negroes, then he was required to order them to receive at least twenty lashes on their backs.
- After every patrol, the officer in charge was to return a report in writing upon oath to the county court. These reports were to be made once in every three months or more often if necessary. If the county court decided that the patrollers had performed their duty, then the court could levy on the county seventy-five cents for every twelve hours of patrol.[20]
- The Lieutenant colonels in the regiments were required to appoint a regimental staff, consisting of one adjutant, one quartermaster, on paymaster, one surgeon, and one surgeon's mate.[21]
- The governor was authorized to distribute two thirds of all the arms and accoutrements provide that on delivery, each musket and cartridge box was stamped with the name of the county and number of the regiment to which they were allotted.
- It was up to the commanding officer of the regiment to receive the arms and accoutrements and give a receipt of their delivery to the governor. Company commanders were to inspect the public arms in the possession of the non-commissioned officers and privates of their companies.[22]
- The governor was authorized to provide all of the arms for the artillery, grenadiers, light infantry, riflemen, and cavalry troopers.[23]

♦ **Virginia Militia Act of 1806**

In 1806 the General Assembly passed another militia act that regulated the distribution and arms of the militia and detailed the duties of commanding officers. Among the salient features of this act were the following:

- The Militia was to be armed by companies. These arms were to be distributed by the major or commandant of the battalion at a battalion muster. If there was a light or flank company attached to a battalion, they were to be armed first.
- Company commanders were to carry out fines for non-attendance at musters or for refusing to receive company arms. Officers commanding battalions were to attend musters at least once a year to review companies and inspect their arms at that time.
- Officers were prohibited from resigning their commissions for five years.[24]

---

[18] Ibid., III: 15.
[19] Ibid., III: 16.
[20] Ibid., III: 17.
[21] Ibid., III: 18.
[22] Ibid., III: 19–20.
[23] Ibid., III: 20.
[24] Ibid., III: 208–209.

- **An Act concerning the distribution of Public Arms**

Another act associated with the militia was passed in January 1807 dealing with the distribution of public arms. The governor was given the authority to distribute public arms in the capitol, barracks and armory. He was authorized to forward them to the colonel commandant of each regiment so that there would not be more than 3000 muskets, 150 rifles, 150 pistols, and 150 swords left undistributed at any one time.

Arms would be delivered to any freeholders of family members on militia rolls. Light companies in the militia were to be armed by entire companies with arms manufactured for their use. Likewise, rifle companies were to be armed with rifles.

Other provisions in this act provided for examination of the arms by captains of militia companies, duties of officers to prevent their loss. There was even a fine assessed for any freeholder or housekeeper, who was not a Quaker, Dunker, or Mennonite, who refused to receive public arms when tendered.[25]

- **Militia Act of 1808**

This act dealt with the appointment of musicians, fines assessed for not attending musters, Court martial regulations and fines, issuance of government contracts for arms, and voluntary enlistment terms for the militia.

Evidently, there were problems in filling the regimental quotas for musicians so the legislature decided that commanding officers of battalions or companies could employ a drummer and fifer to attend musters. Captains of light companies, likewise, were authorized to enlist musicians for service in their companies although the musician would not be entitled to compensation unless he saw actual service. Cavalry troop captain could also employ a trumpeter to attend on any regular parade. He was to be paid from muster fines.

The governor was authorized to contract for making 300 rifles annually. He was to order payment for the rifles from the treasury when there was evidence that the contract had been satisfactorily completed. However, the cost of rifles was capped at $15.00.

Enlistments in volunteer companies in the militia were to be for at least three years but no more than five. The governor was further prohibited from commissioning officers unless authorized by law. Anyone who had been employed by a lieutenant colonel commandant as an express, to carry out orders from the governor or a major general or brigadier general, was to be paid from militia fines of the regiment.[26]

4. Congressional legislation in 1812 increased the Army to 35,000 men.

Despite clamors for war with Great Britain during the first decade of the nineteenth century, the government made few preparations for war. So the November 1811 declaration of war and legislation for an army and navy in January 1812 came almost simultaneously.

In early 1812, Congress decided to act. They increased the army to 35,000 men and provided for some 50,000 volunteers and 100,000 militia. When the war actually began, however, the regular army amounted to only 12,000 men and the volunteers and militia forces remained unorganized. The Navy had sixteen ships.

5. In addition to a lack of preparations, four challenges became apparent in the overall operations of the war.
- **James Madison, as President and commander-in-chief.**

James Madison faced a political crisis in his re-election bid in the 1812 election. His perceived weakness in governing the country and his lack of understanding of the events on the international scene led to some bad decisions when he decided to trust the French under Napoleon Bonaparte.

---

[25] Ibid., III: 305–307.
[26] Ibid., III: 365–369.

Basically, Madison wanted to run the government cheaply and did not want to run up a large national debt that a war would entail. He did not like the idea of a standing army either. His appointments to fill the officer corps were aging revolutionary war veterans who were selected for their past accomplishments rather than for their existing leadership abilities. Many of these men had returned to civilian life and now, approaching or exceeding sixty years of age, were called back into service of their country.[27]

The president began to realize that he needed to take a stronger stand against the British in order to keep his party leadership intact. Thus he either had to negotiate a settlement with Britain over impressments and trade issues or go to war. When negotiations with the British ended in failure, he had little choice but to ask Congress to declare war in November 1811. Madison thought this might effectively unite his supporters and his critics while increasing pressure on the British over trade and sailor's rights. If the British failed to do this, then Madison would go ahead and provide the resources for a war with Great Britain.[28]

Unfortunately, these resources called for some type of federal taxation policy to support it and Madison and his administration failed to come up with a policy to adequately fund the army and navy.

- ♦ **Factionalism and partisanship permeated all aspects of the war.**

In the field, generals rarely cooperated with one another and paid little attention to each other's concerns or their officer's apprehensions. To add to this confusion, there was no mechanism in place to plan or coordinate any kind of intra-service cooperation. Then, too, Madison's own cabinet was deeply divided regarding the wisdom of the war and Congress reflected that view. The Federalists in Congress opposed the war almost to the man.

- ♦ **Disagreement about the fundamental aims of the war hampered the administration.**

Madison's strategic aims were built around a successful invasion of Canada, hoping that its conquest would force the British to the bargaining table. Unfortunately, local concerns did not agree with this strategy.

Residents along the coastal areas were more worried about naval raids and a possible British invasion, especially along the Atlantic coast and the Canadian border of New York. The settlers living in the old Northwest were apprehensive about the military situation on Lake Ontario and Lake Erie and about the Indian situation— primarily Tecumseh and his confederacy while the south worried over keeping their trade access along the Mississippi open to New Orleans and the situation with the Creek Indians.[29]

The divergence of a national strategy for the war and the partisan politics that went along with it made for a difficult time for Madison and his cabinet as they struggled to wage a war for the right of the American navy not to be boarded by the British or the French as well as the right to trade independently with European nations during the Napoleonic wars.

- ♦ **Despite Madison's efforts to concentrate on Canada, the war became a regional one, fought in three theatres: the Northern theatre, along the Great Lakes and New York; the Gulf and New Orleans, and the Chesapeake Bay Region.**

While the other theatres were famous for generals and commanders, it is the Chesapeake Bay area that is the focus of this particular work. The British invasion force consisted of both naval and land forces. The American response was made primarily by militia units from Maryland and Virginia.

- • **Infantry tactics in the War of 1812**

The land war was essentially an infantry struggle, fought by men organized into regimental or battalion size formations, numbering between 500–800 men. The infantry on both sides used a

---

[27] Millet and Maslowski, 101.
[28] Benn, 19.
[29] Millett and Maslowski, 107.

smoothbore, muzzle-loaded, single-shot flintlock musket. American soldier utilized paper cartridges containing a ball and powder and sometimes, buckshot. Soldiers could load and fire his musket two or three times a minute. The musket's range alternated between an accurate shot at sixty yards to a deadly one at 175 feet.

In order to gain maximum accuracy from musket fire, troops were placed in tightly packed lines. They fired massed volleys into the enemy at close range. The intent was to thin out the enemy lines so that a bayonet charge could be made.

- **Light Infantry acted as auxiliary troops for ambushes, skirmishes, and scouting.**

However, these tactics could not be used in all situations, so adaptations had to be made. The army would use light infantry for skirmishes and for ambushes. Light infantry deployed in long chains of men and were utilized to preserve the main body of troops by providing cover for their approach towards the enemy. In a retreat, the light infantry would be used to hold off pursuing troops long enough to allow the main force to escape. The light infantry used both muskets and rifles. Rifles had a larger range of accuracy, often still a dangerous weapon at 350 feet. There were drawbacks to using them however, since they took longer to load and were often fouled by gunpowder.[30]

The British invasion of the Chesapeake 1813–1814

1. <u>In February 1813, the British navy and army commanders launched destructive raids against the Chesapeake region, close to Washington, D.C.</u>

Admiral Sir George Cockburn had the command of the British Navy in the Chesapeake. He spent the spring of 1813 plundering along the Chesapeake, guided through the area by runaway slaves. His immediate goal was three-fold: 1) to destroy American warships, 2) to burn American government supplies, and 3) to ruin the coasting trade. He wanted to demonstrate the futility of resisting British naval power.

In April 1813, Cockburn sailed into the Upper Chesapeake and attacked and burned Frenchtown, Maryland, destroying all the ships that were docked there. In May, he looted and burned Havre de Grace, Georgetown and Fredericktown. He destroyed sixty-eight cannons at Principio.

In mid-June 1813, the British planned to attack Norfolk where the frigate *Constellation* was docked. General Robert B. Taylor, in charge of the local defenses there, he called out 700 militia and fortified the island commanding the entrances to Norfolk. The British ran into heavy armed resistance and were forced to withdraw.

Undeterred, the enemy went on to attack Hampton, Virginia with 2000 men. The militia was again turned out, this time with 450 men. They did not fare as well and Hampton was occupied where atrocities on the civilian population were committed by French prisoners of war who had enlisted with the British.[31] It is likely that two of Colonel Renno's companies, those of Captain Alexander Howison and those of Captain Joseph Gilbert were called up as part of the American response to the British attacks on Norfolk and Hampton.[32]

2. <u>In 1814, the British Navy extended its blockade from southern and mid-Atlantic States to the coast of New England.</u>

While Madison denounced the blockade as illegal, it did not encourage neutral European nations to trade with the United States. As a result, American exports plummeted to one-tenth of their value in 1811 and imports shrunk to a quarter of their prewar total.

---

[30] Benn, 24–25.
[31] Hickey, 153–154.
[32] See pages 110–111 for muster roll dates of these two 36th Regiment captains.

3. The British intensified their efforts as they order raids along the eastern coast line in order to disrupt shipping and destroy naval vessels

Then Vice Admiral Sir Alexander Cochrane ordered a number of punitive hit-and-run raids along the eastern coast line. Some of the ports like Baltimore had coastal fortifications. Others did not.

Among several dozen naval operations along the eastern coast, six boats from the blockading force sailed up the Connecticut River and burned seven privateers, twelve large merchantmen, and ten coastal vessels. A month long naval bombardment of Stonington, Connecticut took place in May 1814. The British thought the town was harboring men who planned to sail "booby-trapped vessels" into Royal Navy ships and blow them up.[33] Even Nantucket, off the coast of Massachusetts felt the Royal Navy's wrath. It was cut off and so ravaged those living there were forced into neutrality.[34]

4. In late summer 1814, The British, under Admiral Cockburn expanded their raids into an invasion force in the Chesapeake Bay region with army and naval forces.

After the raid on Havre de Grace, just north of Annapolis, Cockburn was alleged to have stated that on his next visit ashore, "he planned to bow to Dolly Madison in her drawing room and then set fire to her home."[35]

Dolly was not particularly impressed by the threat when it was relayed to her and wrote that she was "not trembling at the prospect but *did* resent Cockburn making his threat personal." Since the British did not have land troops or artillery in position around the capital, Secretary of State Armstrong dismissed the threat as unlikely. He had overruled concerns of the District of Columbia's Militia commander, Major General John Van Ness, in June when Van Ness pointed out the dangers of the British navy to the Patuxent River. Armstrong thought that Baltimore was much more likely to engage British interest, rather than the Patuxent and the capital.

- **The American Response: Creation of a new military command to include militia from the District of Columbia, Maryland, and northern Virginia.**

That was June. Now it was July and the British fleet's arrival in the Chesapeake was imminent. While Madison's cabinet refused to take the fleet seriously, the President did. He asked Maryland's Federalist Governor, Levin Winder, to add 1500 militia to Fort McHenry and to send two regiments from the regular army to Norfolk.

Then the President created a new military command to include the District of Columbia, Maryland, and northern Virginia. He even put the Governor's nephew Brigadier-General William Winder in charge of these forces to ensure the Governor's support.[36]

The role of the militia once again took center stage. Brigadier-General Winder wanted 4000 men called up for three months. However, Secretary of War Armstrong did not want to pay them if they were not actually fighting. He thought instead, that the militia could be called up "on the spur of the moment" and then sent into combat. So he told General Winder to request men only in "case of actual or menaced invasion of the District."[37]

When the British sailed again into the Patuxent, Winder called up three companies of militia but then sent them home.

- **Events leading to the Battle of Bladensburg.**

Winder settled on Bladensburg, four miles northeast of Washington, as the muster ground for the Maryland militia. In late July, he sent arms and supplies there and inspected regular army detachments

---

[33] Benn, 57.
[34] Borneman, 217.
[35] Langguth, 295.
[36] Langguth, 295–296.
[37] Ibid., 297.

from the 36th and 38th regiments. At the beginning of August, he set up his headquarters in the town. One thousand regular army troops and 4000 militia had been promised. They had yet to appear.

Sixteen days later, the British fleet *did* appear, carrying an infantry brigade under Major General Robert Ross, with the fleet. Ross had orders not to conduct "any extended operation at a distance from the coast." Instead, his forces were to act as a diversionary measure along the coast to draw American forces away from a planned British counter-strike in Lake Champlain.

Nothing in Ross's orders encouraged the destruction of civilian property or the burning of non-military public buildings. Admiral Cockburn, however, had different ideas and was acting on orders from Admiral Cochrane.[38]

- **August 15, 1814: The British fleet with infantry troops on board pass into the Chesapeake**

On August 15, 1814, Ross's brigade of some 3400 men passed through the Virginia Capes on British transports to meet up with the Royal Navy. Seven hundred marines were also assigned to Ross's troops, bringing his forces to more than 4000 men.

The next day, more than twenty ships entered the Chesapeake and separated, with half sailing towards Baltimore and the other half heading towards the Potomac.[39] Ross successfully rendezvoused with Cochrane and Cockburn and, three days later, the British entered the mouth of the Patuxent. Their aim was to trap the gunboats of Commodore Joshua Barney, who had been "buzzing about the bay like pesky horseflies." Fortunately, Barney was successful in eluding British capture and moved still further up the river.[40]

Meanwhile, the Navy Department sprang into action. They ordered General Winder to summon Maryland's 3rd Militia Division and directed General Van Ness to set up camp in Alexandria with two militia brigades from the District of Columbia. Rather than take orders from General Winder, Van Ness resigned.[41]

The American forces were in a state of confusion. General Winder was slow to organize his forces and sent no orders out to destroy bridges to slow down the British or harass British forces upon their expected landing.[42] Since the militia were crucial to the defense of the capital, it is difficult to understand General Winder's inaction. Then politics raised its head once more and pleas from the General to Secretary of War Armstrong went unanswered. It seems that Armstrong was annoyed that his own advice had not been taken; so he disregarded Winder's pleas for assistance.[43]

General Winder's forces expected to defend the capital were made up of just 900 regular army enlistees and 400 cavalry. His artillery consisted of twenty-six cannons, all small six-pounders.[44] Although he had been promised 6000 militia, his uncle, Governor Levin Winder, moved slowly and only 250 men answered the call-up.[45]

- **August 19, 1814: The British land at Benedict, Maryland**

The British affected a successful landing at Benedict, Maryland on August 19th. They met no resistance as they marched through the small towns along the Patuxent. As Ross and Cockburn moved north, they were followed British launches and barges. Alarmed that Barney's small flotilla of gunboats would be captured by the Royal Navy, Barney received orders to burn his gunboats.

---

[38] Ibid., 297–298. See also Millett and Maslowski, 115 and Borneman, 219–220.
[39] Langguth, 298.
[40] Borneman, 222.
[41] Langguth, 298.
[42] Millett and Maslowski, 114.
[43] Borneman, 224.
[44] Langguth, 298.
[45] Borneman, 224.

The British faced their first resistance outside the village of Marlborough. After a heated exchange, the Americans gave way and the British moved on to a fork in the road. One branch went to Alexandria, the other to Washington.

- **August 24, 1814: The Americans finally chose to do the expected—blow up bridges on the Potomac while the British countered with the unexpected—a march towards Bladensburg and Washington, D.C.**

In the early morning hours of August 24th, the Americans *finally* decided it was time to slow down the British march. So they blew up two bridges over the east branch of the Potomac.[46] At the same time, the British did the unexpected. In a successful effort to deceive the Americans, the British marched down the road towards Alexandria just long enough for the scouts observing them to turn their horses towards that town. Then the British marched back the way they had come and proceeded on the road to Washington.

Although the British General, Robert Ross, was reluctant to attack the capital Admiral Cockburn finally persuaded him that the American militia would never stand up to the British army.[47]

General Winder was still trying to organize the militia and concentrated these forces near the navy yard, fearing an attack from the south.

> Incredibly, however, as a small British army marched quite leisurely through the Maryland countryside towards the nation's capital, no attempt was made to impede its progress by felling trees, sniping at its flanks, or attacking it supply wagons. Perhaps, most significantly, the bridge across the East Branch at Bladensburg was left intact. The upstart American rebels, who had taught the British a thing or two about guerilla tactics a generation before, seemed to have momentarily forgotten them.[48]

While the British were moving towards Bladensburg without meeting any resistance, General Winder was conferring with the President and members of his cabinet in the capital. It became obvious to everyone there that Bladensburg was the British short term objective and Washington, the long term one. The President ordered most of the government records moved out of the city. As rumors spread of danger to the city, a number of linen bags had been filled with government documents and sent aboard carts and wagons to Leesburg.

In order to raise morale among the American troops deployed at Bladensburg, Madison and his cabinet decided to pay a visit to the troops there. In this entourage were General Winder, Secretary of War Armstrong, and Secretary of State James Monroe. Dolly Madison stayed behind to do what she could to protect the White House and the President's records.

In his haste to get to the presumed battlefield before the rest of the cabinet and the President, Secretary of State James Monroe went on ahead. Once Monroe arrived, he redirected the deployment of some of the militia. This prompted a twenty-first century historian to make this comment: "Certainly the secretary of state had no direct command authority to do so, and his movements of two units of Baltimore militia so that they no longer supported the front ranks showed that he had no military acumen, either."[49]

On August 22, 1814, the President arrived at Bladensburg. He was not worried since the British lacked both cavalry and artillery. Both he and General Winder thought that their forces would send the British back to their fleet.[50]

August 24, 1814: Defeat at Bladensburg opens up the Capital to the British

The American forces— perhaps numbering 7000 in all, and comprised of regulars, militia and nearly 500 sailors under Barney's command— were arrayed in three lines facing the east branch of the Potomac.

---

[46] Ibid., 226.
[47] Langguth, 298–299. See also Borneman, 225–226.
[48] Borneman, 226.
[49] Ibid.
[50] Langguth, 300–301.

The third line was too far away to support the first two and, thanks to Monroe's redeployment, the second line could not support the first. A recipe for a disaster in the making.

The president and his cabinet arrived just before the battle began and were on the verge of crossing the bridge straight into the British forces. Fortunately they were warned off in time. The battle commenced an hour after noon, just as the last militia took their places. The British were not impressed.

Two British brigades crossed the river and outflanked the first American line, causing it to fall back. Just as the British were attacking the second line, General Winder ordered it to fall back. That withdrawal turned into a rout. Caught in this retreat were the President and his cabinet, who prudently left the lines and moved to the rear.

The third line was made up of Barney's seamen who held firm. However, the British were successful in routing the militia protecting his flank and stormed his position. Now out of ammunition, Barney ordered a retreat. Although he was wounded and made a British prisoner, most of his men managed to escape. In a little over three hours, the British were in complete control of the battlefield.[51]

By the time the battle was over, most of the residents of Washington had left the city. Dolly Madison remained, overseeing the removal of cabinet records. House clerks lamented later that "everything belonging to the office ... might have been removed in time if carriages could have been procured."[52]

In the event a departure from the District became necessary, the President and his advisors made arrangements to meet together in Frederick, Maryland. However, these plans were changed when Madison and his Attorney General Richard Rush, and joined by Secretary James Monroe, left for Virginia, instead.[53]

August 24, 1814: The British burn the capital

The British moved into the capital at eight in the evening. While Ross looked in vain for someone to discuss a surrender, another group of officers headed by Admiral Cockburn entered the White House. There, they found a meal that had been left uneaten and quickly consumed it. After looting the White House, they set fire to the building. Nothing survived but 'unroofed, marked walls, cracked, defaced, blackened with the smoke of fire.'[54]

The British burned the Capitol building, the treasury and the building housing the war and state departments. Only the patent office was saved, thanks to the quick thinking of Dr. William Thornton. The navy yard and two new ships under construction also went under the torch. The newspaper office of the *National Intelligencer* was destroyed. Fires burned all night. Violent storms the next day blew down several more buildings. Then, the British left the city the following day, leaving their wounded behind.[55]

Aftermath

The President and his cabinet returned to the devastated city on August 27th. It was a somber sight that greeted them. Residents blamed the President and Secretary of War Armstrong for the destruction. Local militia refused to take any further orders from the Secretary of War. After meeting with Madison, Armstrong resigned and retired to Baltimore. He blamed everything on Madison.

Madison, in the meantime, did not come out of this unscathed. Graffiti appeared on the walls of the Capitol that read: "George Washington founded this city after a seven years' war with England—James Madison lost it after a two years' war."[56]

General Winder was court-martialed. The court of inquiry, presided over by Winfield Scott, found extenuating circumstances provided by the lack of support from his secretary of war and the Madison administration and the troublesome issue of command and control of an independent militia. In their

---

[51] Hickey, 197–198.
[52] Ibid., 199.
[53] Ibid.
[54] Ibid., 199
[55] Ibid., 200–201.
[56] Ibid., 202.

findings, they stated that General Winder was "entitled to no little commendation, notwithstanding the result..."[57]

The destruction of the capital was denounced on both sides of the Atlantic. Opposition newspapers in London joined in the criticism as did some members of Parliament. Most Englishmen, however, rejoiced at the embarrassment of the Americans and considered the destruction of Washington as a just desert for American depredations, looting and burning of towns in Canada.

September 11–14, 1814: The British land at North Point to attack Baltimore and Fort McHenry

British decided to cap this success with an attack on Baltimore, both from land and from sea. Baltimore was the home of much of the privateering fleet that had formerly plagued the British navy. On September 11, the navy sailed to the mouth of the Patapsco, and prepared to land troops to attack Baltimore and then head on for Fort McHenry.

September 12, 1814: The Battle of North Point

The army disembarked at North Point at three in the morning of September 12th. About half way to the city, the British forces met up with a force of 3200 militia under the command of General John Strickler. On the way, an advanced party was ambushed by American forces. Although the British forced the Americans to retreat, their commander, General Ross was killed by a sharpshooter.[58] Although North Point was officially deemed a British victory, it was a costly one. The Americans lost 215 men, the British 340 along with their General.

September 13, 1814: The British attack Baltimore and Fort McHenry

The British pressed on, now under the command of Colonel Arthur Brooke. They came within sight of Baltimore but realized that the defenders were well entrenched behind defensive works. Brooke decided not to attack due to the fact that they were unsuccessful in procuring the naval support needed and they were not able to lure the Americans from their fortifications.

Admiral Cochrane was already busy shelling Fort McHenry. Fort McHenry was defended by a 1000 man garrison under the command of Major George Armistead. The British fired more than 1600 rounds at the fort over the next twenty-five hours. The Americans were unable to respond because their guns were not as powerful. The British were hampered in their efforts to get close enough to the fort to cause maximum damage, largely because the citizens of Baltimore had sunk twenty-four merchant ships to block their way. At the same time, a squadron of American gunboats was threatening the Royal Navy's rear. Cochrane decided to pull back and sent word to the army that a withdrawal was in order. The army departed for the ships the next day.

Fortunately, the overall damage to the fort was minimal. Four Americans were killed and twenty-four were wounded while the resultant anthem by Francis Scott Key became an instant hit throughout the city. Fort McHenry had held out. Baltimore had been saved.[59]

THE TWO PRINCE WILLIAM VIRGINIA STATE MILITIA REGIMENTS IN THE WAR OF 1812

There were two Virginia State Militia Regiments with Prince William men who fought in the War of 1812. The first unit was Lieutenant Colonel Enoch Renno's 36th State Regiment of Militia. Colonel Renno or "Renoe" and "Rennoe" as his name was sometimes spelled, was found in a paymaster's account for the

---

[57] Borneman, 242.
[58] Hickey, 202–203. See also Benn, 60–61.
[59] Benn, 61 and Hickey, 203.

Regiment, found in a Prince William Deed book between 1805–1807,[60] and as a resident of Prince William in 1810[61] and 1820 [62]

The 36th Regiment, Virginia Militia

A complete roster of Colonel Renno's 36th Regiment may be found in Ancestry.com's military records collection. This roster revealed a field staff consisting of Colonel Renno and two Majors, Samuel Ashby[63] and Thomas Chapman.[64] Officers included captains, lieutenants, ensigns, cornets, and surgeons. The roster also revealed the musicians, non-commissioned officers, and rank and file. Only the officers and musicians are shown here.

There were eleven captains of companies in the 36th Regiment: William Dulin,[65] **Joseph R. Gilbert,**[66] **James Hayes,**[67] **John Linton,**[68] **Joseph R. Lynn,**[69] **John Merchant,**[70] William Obannon,[71] **Joseph Smith,**[72] Barton S. Stone,[73] and Richard Weedon.[74]

This regiment had thirteen lieutenants: **William Brundige**[75], James Crane, Travers Davis, **William Dawe,**[76] **William French,**[77] John Gibson,[78] Alfred C. Hayes,[79] Peter Holmes,[80] William McInteer,[81] William Kemper, **William Nelson,**[82] George Waller, and William Thompson.

---

[60] *Prince William County Deed Book 1805–1807*, 337–338. MR 8

[61] Elizabeth Petty Bentley, *Index to the 1810 Census of Virginia* (Baltimore: Genealogical Publishing Company, 1980), 270.

[62] Jeanne Robey Felldin, *Index to the 1820 Census of Virginia* (Baltimore: Genealogical Publishing Company, 1981), 356.

[63] Ancestry.com, *War of 1812 Service Records: Samuel Ashby, Major, 36th Reg't (Renno's) Virginia Militia* (http://search.ancestry.com/cgi-bin/sse.dll?indiv=1&rank=1gsfn=Samuel&gsln=Ashby...) Afterwards, *War of 1812 Service Records* (http://search.ancestry.com) (Accessed July 25, 2008).

[64] Ibid., *Thomas Chapman, Major 36th Reg't (Renno's) Virginia Militia* (http://search.ancestry.com).

[65] This *may* be the same William Dulin *Jr* who was sworn in as an ensign in the 85th Virginia Regiment in Fauquier in July 1805. See Peters, *Military Records, Certificates of Service, Discharges, Heirs, & Pension Declarations and Schedules from the Fauquier County Court Minute Books 1784–1840*, (1999; reprint, Westminster: Heritage Books, 2007), 34. Afterwards, Peters, *Military Records, 1784–1840*.

A William Dulin sold 481 acres of land in Fauquier to Edward Dulin, as recorded in the 1808 Fauquier County Tax Records. Library of Virginia, *1809 Thomas Robinson's Land Tax Records, District 2*, under "D", (LVA, MR 95, Richmond, Virginia.) This may have been the future Captain in the 36th Regiment in 1812. However, a William Dulin *was* recorded as living in Fauquier in the 1810 Virginia Census, along with five others of the same surname. There were no Dulins living in Prince William in 1810. See Bentley, 97.

[66] Joseph R. Gilbert was recommended as a Captain of the 1st Battalion of the 36th Regiment in September 3, 1804. See Chapter 7 on the War of 1812 from the Prince William County Court Minutes.

[67] James Hayes had been promoted from a lieutenancy to Captain in the Infantry belonging to the 36th Regiment, as early as September 1804, according to the Court Minutes in Chapter 7.

[68] In May, 1813, John Linton received money from the county levy for 24 ½ hours of patrolling the slave quarters in the county, according to the court minutes in Chapter 7. He was recorded as a resident of Prince William in the 1810 Virginia Census. See Bentley, 199–200. He evidently survived the war because he was still living in Prince in 1820. See Felldin, 263.

[69] In June 1813, Joseph R. Lynne, as the assignee of Charles Reno and others, received money from the county levy for patrolling. His hours were recorded in the Court Minutes for that date, as found in Chapter 7.

[70] In May 1813, former Lieutenant John Merchant was promoted and received a commission as a captain in the 36th Regiment, replacing Philip Dawe who "vacated his commission," when he accepted the Clerkship of the Prince William County Court. See Chapter 7.

[71] In June 1804, a William Obannon was appointed as an ensign in the 1st Battalion, 44th Regiment in Fauquier County. See Peters, *Military Records 1784–1840*, 32. William Obannon was a resident of Fauquier County according to the 1810 Virginia Census. While there here were no Obannon families living in Prince William at that time, there was an Elias *Obanian* in the county then. See Bentley, 243.

[72] Joseph Smith was commissioned as a captain of the 36th Regiment in September 1813, according to the Prince William County Court Minutes reported in Chapter 7.

[73] While there were three Stone families in Prince William in 1810 (John S., Josiah, and Manoah) Barton Stone was found in Stafford in this census. See Bentley, 311.

[74] No Weadon or Weeden families were recorded in Prince William in 1810. Only one Richard Weadon was listed, in Loudoun County, in the 1810 Census. See Bentley, 343, 344.

[75] In the May 1813 Court Minutes recounted in Chapter 7, William Brundige was promoted to lieutenant in the 36th Regiment, Virginia Militia.

There were ten ensigns commissioned in the 36th Regiment of Virginia Militia. They were **Samuel Adams**,[83] Abner R. Alcock, Barnaby Cannon, **William S. Colquhoun**, [84] **William French**,[85] Rawleigh Hickerson, **Philip Langfitt**,[86] George Lansdown, John Marr, and John Tippett.

The surgeons included **John Bronaugh,** who began his service as a private and ended it as a surgeon in the 36th Regiment. He lived in Prince William resident.[87] John Spence, also a Prince William resident in 1810, served as a surgeon for the regiment.[88] **Thomas Thornton** began as a surgeon's mate and was promoted to surgeon. He, too, lived in Prince William in 1810.[89] Thomas F. Tebbs, who began his military career in the 36th Regiment as a corporal, eventually served as a surgeon's mate in the regiment.[90]

The cornet of the regiment was Burr Harrison.[91] Musicians included Drum Major **Allen Duffy**, [92] Drummers Thomas Barton, Cary Cox, Alexander Hill, and Abraham Wikcoff; Fife Major **William Purnell**,[93] and Fifer Samuel Elliott.

Muster rolls of some of the companies in the 36th Regiment suggest deployment in the defense of Washington as several captains of the regiment filed muster rolls with the Auditor's Office in Richmond. Captain **Joseph R. Gilbert's** Company muster rolls dated from July 20–July 26, 1813 and August 24–August 30, 1814. Captain Gilbert's company may have been part of the American response to the British attack on Norfolk and Hampton in June and July 1813.[94] It is also likely they were called up when the British were attacking Bladensburg.[95] **John Linton** was a captain of a cavalry troop whose muster rolls

---

[76] William Dawe was a resident of Prince William in 1810. See Bentley, 87.

[77] In September 1813, in the Court Minutes found in Chapter 7, William French was promoted from ensign to lieutenant in the 36th Regiment, Virginia Militia.

[78] John Gibson was living in Prince William in 1810. See Bentley, 124.

[79] Alfred C. Hayes was mentioned twice in the Court Minutes found in Chapter 7. In May 1813, he was promoted to Ensign in the Light Infantry attached to the 1st Battalion, 36th Regiment; in September he was promoted to lieutenant in the same unit.

[80] A Peter Holmes was living in Fauquier in 1810. See Bentley, 159. In the February 1814 Fauquier County Court, a certificate of Peter Holmes's oath as a lieutenant in the militia was returned and ordered recorded. See Peters, *Military Records 1784–1840*, 43.

[81] William McInteer's name was not found in the Index to the 1810 Virginia Census. However, there was a William *McIntire* living in Stafford at that time. See Bentley, 219.

[82] William Nelson was living in Prince William in 1810. See Bentley, 239.

[83] In the May 1813 Prince William Court Minutes, reported in Chapter 7, Samuel Adams was appointed ensign in the 36th Regiment, to replace William Brundige who had been promoted to a vacant lieutenancy.

[84] William S. Colquhoun began as a sergeant in the 36th Regiment. See Ancestry.com, *War of 1812 Service Records,* M 602, MR 44 (http://search.ancestry.com). In the May 1813 Court Minute Books in Chapter 7, Colquhoun had been assigned various patrol accounts for Samuel Anderson and others. In September he had been commissioned as an ensign in the Light Infantry attached to the 1st Battalion of the 36th Regiment of the Virginia State Militia.

[85] See note 61.

[86] Ancestry.com, *War of 1812 Service Records,* M 602 MR 121 shows Philip Langfitt as an ensign in this regiment. In September 1813, the Prince William Court minutes, as recounted in Chapter 7, recorded Philip Langfitt's appointment as ensign in the 36th Regiment.

[87] Ancestry.com, *War of 1812 Service Records,* M 602 MR 25 (http://search.ancestry.com) He was living in Prince William in 1810. See Bentley, 40.

[88] Ibid., M 602 MR 196; Bentley, 305.

[89] Ibid., M 602 MR 208; Bentley, 324.

[90] Ibid., M 602 MR 205.

[91] Ibid., M 602 MR 93.

[92] Ibid., M 602 MR 61. Allan Duffy's name appeared in a Paymaster's Account for 1805–1807, for November 1805, recorded in Chapter 7, from the *Prince William Deed Book 1805–1807*.

[93] Ibid., M 602 MR 169. William Purnell was another member of the 36th Regiment whose name appeared in the paymaster accounts of the 36th Regiment as reported in Chapter 7. He received cash from Paymaster Thomas Page in October 1806.

[94] See page 100 for details on British attacks on Norfolk and Hampton.

[95] Auditor's Rolls, Richmond, *Virginia Militia in the War of 1812* (1851; reprint, Baltimore: Genealogical Publishing Company, 2001), I: 357–358.

dated from August 21–August 27, 1814 and August 30–September 7, 1814. His company may have seen action at Bladensburg on August 24, 1814.[96]

Captain **Alexander Howison's** Company muster rolls dated from July 21–July 26, 1813, July 31–August 7, 1814, and August 24–August 30, 1814.[97] This company, too, may have been involved as a response to the British attack on Norfolk and Hampton in the summer of 1813[98] and the British campaign against Washington in August 1814.

Captain **Richard Weadon's** Company was called into service at Dumfries on orders from Colonel Rennoe and served from August 24–August 30, 1814.[99] Captain **Joseph Smith's** Company, in Prince William County, was also called up on the same regimental orders by Colonel Renno on August 24, 1814 and served from that date to August 30, 1814.[100] It is likely that these companies were called into service of the United States during the British campaigns against the capital.

The 89th Regiment, Virginia Militia, 1804–1806

The command structure of the **89th Regiment** in the 1804-1806 time frame was considerably different than that of the regiment that fought during the war. In 1805, the 89th Regiment's Officer and Field staff consisted of Colonel Thomas Lee Sr as the commanding officer. When he died in that year,[101] Major **William Tyler**[102] was promoted to the colonelcy of this regiment. This took effect in November 1806.[103] **Washington John Washington**, another Prince William resident was then promoted from captain to major in the 2nd battalion of the 89th Regiment in place of William Tyler who had just been promoted.[104]

In September 1805, the Prince William County Court justices recommended these captains be appointed to the 89th Regiment: **John Kincheloe**,[105] William Kincheloe, Robert **Little**[106], and **Elias Obannion**.[107]

The Court also filled vacancies in the regiment during the same court date for lieutenants. **Gerard Alexander**, who was later to command the 89th during August and September 1814,[108] was appointed a lieutenant in the light infantry. **Lynaugh Fitzhugh**[109] was appointed a lieutenant in the 1st battalion of the 89th Regiment during the same court session. Other appointments for lieutenants in the 89th were Daniel Kincheloe, **Richard Brett**,[110] and **Daniel Rose**.[111]

The September 1805 Court also recommended ensigns to the governor for the 89th Regiment. John Chesley was recommended as an ensign of the Light Infantry attached to the 89th while John Brawner, **William Lewis**[112], **Elisha Jenkins**,[113] William B. Saunders, Henry Brewer and James Rose Jr[114] also received the nod from the Prince William Court as worthy of accepting a commission into the regiment.

---

[96] Ibid., I: 548.
[97] Ibid., I: 452–453. Alexander Howison was another resident of Prince William in 1810. See Bentley, 163.
[98] See page 100 for details on British attacks on Norfolk and Hampton.
[99] Ibid., I: 820.
[100] Ibid., I: 728.
[101] Thomas Lee was the son of Richard Henry Lee of Westmoreland and his first wife Ann (Aylett). See Wikipedia, "Richard Henry Lee," (http://en.wikipedia.org/wiki/Richard_Henry_Lee).
[102] William Tyler was living in Prince William in 1810. See Bentley, 332.
[103] See Chapter 7, November 4, 1805 County Court session for this appointment.
[104] Ibid. Washington John Washington was living in Prince William in 1810. See Bentley, 341.
[105] John Kincheloe resigned his commission as captain of the 89th Regiment in 1813. See September 6, 1813 Court entry in Chapter 7.
[106] Robert Little *may* be the same man as Robert *H.* Little who was a resident in Prince William in 1810. See Bentley, 200.
[107] Elias Obanian was living in Prince William in 1810. See Bentley, 243.
[108] Auditor's Rolls, Richmond, Virginia *Militia in the War of 1812*, II: 791.
[109] Bentley, 111. In 1810, Lenaugh H. Fitzhugh was living in Prince William.
[110] Richard Brett was another Prince William resident, found in the 1810 Virginia Census. See Bentley, 38.
[111] Ibid., 279. Daniel Rose also lived in Prince William in 1810.
[112] Bentley, 198. William Lewis was living in Prince William in 1810.
[113] Ibid., 173. Elisha Jenkins was another Prince William resident in 1810 who had seen service in the 89th Regiment in the 1804–1806 time period.

The 89th Regiment, Virginia Militia 1812–1814

By the time the War of 1812 was declared, the 89th Regiment had undergone several changes. The service records for this regiment gave Philip Klepstine, as the commanding colonel.[115] However, the auditor's office in Richmond recognized **Gerrard Alexander** as the colonel of the Regiment.[116]

While Captains John Brawner and **Robert Brown**[117] are listed in the service records as officers in the 89th during the War of 1812,[118] the Auditor's office recognized Captains **John Merchant** and Benjamin Tyler as officers during the war of 1812.[119] Both filed muster rolls in 1814. Captain Merchant's muster roll dated from August 24–September 7, 1814. Captain Benjamin Tyler's muster roll dated from August 30– September 7, 1814. Men found on both of these rolls may be found in Appendix 3 along with the service records of officers, non-commissioned officers and rank and file which were part of the service records of the war.[120]

The 89th Regiment muster rolls and service records both suggest a role in the defense of Washington, D.C, although it is not known for certain exactly where the regiment was deployed. Their service records are dated from July to September 1814, which would intimate a possible role in the unsuccessful defense of the capital since the British burned Washington on August 24, 1814. John Merchant's musters dated from the burning of the capital until September 7, 1814. Captain Tyler's company was not called up until six days later, on August 30, 1814. This company also served until September 7, 1814.

However, neither Merchant's or Tyler's company were involved with the successful defense of Baltimore and Fort McHenry since the British attack took place six days after their tours of service were over, between September 11–14, 1814.

Conclusions

The early nineteenth century Virginia Militia Acts revealed that Prince William, Fauquier, Stafford, and King George provided one brigade for the second division of the State Militia. Preliminary census work appears to support this as both the 36th Regiment and the 89th Regiment seem to have been recruited from Prince William and other nearby counties. While the census is not a particularly good determinate for identifying men in the regiment with men of the same name in a different county, the residence of men in the regiment can be verified by examining county tax and land records. Unfortunately, the recruitment pattern and research needed to confirm this is outside the scope and survey nature of this book.

In addition, there may have been other men from Prince William who served in other regiments during the war. It is impossible to know who they are unless or until more research has been done on Prince William in the War of 1812.

A complete roster of the officers and men of the 36th Virginia State Regiment and the 89th Regiment may be found in Appendix 3.

---

[114] Bentley, 279. A James Rose was living in Prince William in 1810. It is not known whether this was the same man as James Rose Jr, who had previously served in the 89th Regiment in 1806.

[115] Ancestry.com, *War of 1812 Service Records,* 89th Regiment (http://search.ancestry.com).

[116] There are two muster rolls from the Auditor's Rolls, Richmond, of Captains in the 89th Regiment commanded by Lieutenant-Colonel Gerrard Alexander. One is a muster roll of Captain John Merchant's Company, dating from August 24–September 7, 1814 and the other is Captain Benjamin Tyler's Company, dating from August 30–September 7, 1814. See Auditor's Rolls, Richmond, I: 583–584, and 791.

[117] Bentley, 41–44. Robert Brown was living in Prince William in 1810.

[118] Ancestry.com., *War of 1812 Service Records,* 89th Regiment (http://search.ancestry.com).

[119] Auditor's Rolls, Richmond, *Virginia Militia in the War of 1812,* I: 583, 791.

[120] Ancestry.com, *War of 1812 Service Records,* 89th Regiment (http://search.ancestry.com)

CHAPTER 7

THE WAR OF 1812 PERIOD

MILITARY RECORDS FROM PRINCE WILLIAM COUNTY VIRGINIA ORDER BOOK 1804–1806, 1812–1814

Prince William County Order Books 1804–1806

September 3, 1804 Court, pg. 6
At the request of the commanding officer of the 36th Regt, it is ordered that the following persons be recommended to the Executive as Militia officers in the 1st Battln of the 36th Regt:
John M. Muschett as Major in the room of **Enoch Reno,**[1] promoted.
James Hayes, Captain, in the Infantry, in the room of **Jno. W. Muschett promoted.**
Joseph R. Gilbert,[2] **Captain** [in place of] **George Williams, resigned.**
Charles McCaughan, Lieutenant in the Infantry, in place of **James Hayes, promoted.**
Isham E. Hedges, Lieutenant, in place of **Joseph Gilbert promoted.**
Allan Bland, Lieutenant, in place of **John Carr, resigned.**
Thomas A. Smith, Ensign, in place of **Charles McCaughan, promoted.**
James DeNeale Jr, Ensign, in place of **Isham E. Hedges, promoted.**
Levi Scott, Ensign, in place of **Allen Bland promoted.**

September 3, 1804 Court, pg 7.
At the request of **Major Townshend Dade of the 2nd Battalion, 36th Regiment, by Captain Allen Sowden,** it is ordered that the following persons be recommended to the Executive as **Militia Offices in the 2nd Battalion of the 36th Regiment:**
Francis Jackson, Captain in place of **William Grayson, Esquire, resigned.**
John Davis, Lieutenant in place of **Francis Jackson promoted.**
William T. Reardon, Lieutenant, in place of **George Jackson resigned.**
Philip Davis, Lieutenant, in place of **Enoch Jameson, resigned.**
Samuel Cole, Ensign, in place of **John Davis promoted.**
Peter Jett, Ensign in place of **William T. Reardon, promoted.**
Joseph Lynn,[3] **Ensign** in place of **Philip Harrison resigned.**
Warren Cooksey, Ensign, in place of **Braddock Richmond resigned.**

October 1, 1804 Court, pg. 22.
The rule against **Charles Purcell, to shew cause why he should not be removed from his office of constable for improper conduct,** is continued until the next Court.

---

[1] NARA, *Index to the Compiled Service Records for Volunteer Soldiers Who Served During the War of 1812*, M 602, MR 173 (http://searchancestry.com/cgi-bin/sse.dll?indiv=1& rank=1&gsfn=Enoch&gsln=Renno&=&fe =36th+Regit+(Renno)+Virginia + Militia ...) (Accessed June 30, 2008). Afterwards, Ancestry.com, *War of 1812 Service Records* (http://www.ancestry.com). Enoch Renno was the commanding officer of this regiment of Virginia Militia, with the rank of Lieutenant Colonel.

[2] Ibid., 36th Regiment, M 602, MR 80 (http://search.ancestry.com). Joseph R. Gilbert, was a Captain, in the 36th Regiment (Renno's) Virginia Militia, according to the index of compiled service records as found on ancestry.com.

[3] Ibid., 36th Regiment. Joseph R. Lynn was a Captain in the Lieutenant Colonel Enoch Renno's 36th Virginia Regiment of Militia.

Francis Jackson produced a commission from the Governor **appointing him a Captain in the 36th Regiment of Virginia Militia**. He took the oath to support the Constitution of the United States, the oath of fidelity to the Commonwealth of Virginia, and the oath of a captain in the 36th Regiment.

April 2, 1805 Court, pg 129.

On the motion of Moses Moss, it is ordered that Mary Lewis and **David Blackwell**,[4] as Executor of Zachariah Lewis decd, be summoned to the next Court to give Moss counter security for their administration on Lewis's estate, or to deliver the estate to Moss.

The Administration of Estate of **Thomas Love**[5] is granted to **Philip Love**,[6] he having taken the oath of an administrator and entered into and acknowledged a bond with security according to law.

On the motion of Philip Love, it is ordered that William Love, Margaret Love, **Samuel Love**,[7] **John Love**,[8] and Lucinda Love be summoned to the next Court to shew cause whey the **lands which descended to them by the death of Thomas Love** should not be sold according to law and the money distributed among the heirs of Thomas Love deceased. It appears to the Court that these lands will not exceed $100.00 to each of the representatives.

May 6, 1804 Court, pgs 138–139.

On the motion of Philip Love, it is ordered that Craven Horton and William Brook do sell upon such reasonable credit as they think fit the tract of land lately the property of Thomas Love,

---

[4] David Blackwell's military experience began as a member of Captain John Chilton's company in the Culpeper Minute Battalion back in 1775. He also spent time on the Potomac in a militia company and in 1780, became an officer in Colonel Henry Lee's Regiment. See chapter 3, note 51, page 21.

[5] The family and heirs of Thomas Love decd of Prince William County mentioned here could have been of an age to have served in the Revolutionary War. There *was* a Thomas Love who served as a corporal in the 13th Virginia in Captain George McCarmick's Company, stationed at Fort Pitt who was entitled to bounty lands due to his enlistment for the war. See NARA, *Thomas Love's compiled service records,* M 881 (http:// www.footnote.com) 2–7, images 23055508 to 23055521. While at Fort Pitt, he volunteered to go on a naval expedition to New Orleans in December 1777 on the ship *Rattletrap,* commanded by Navy Captain James Willing.

There was also a Thomas Love who served in the 1st Virginia State Regiment. See Hamilton J. Eckenrode, *Virginia Soldiers of the American Revolution* (1913; reprint, Richmond: Virginia State Library and Archives, 1989), 189. Unfortunately, there did not appear to be a compiled service record for Thomas Love in the 1st Virginia State Regiment as found on footnote.com. See http://www.footnote.com, Virginia, First State Regiment, Individual, L, page 4. John Love is there. Thomas Love is not. If the land the Court referenced in April 1804 was bounty land, there is no mention of that in Bockstruck, *Revolutionary War Bounty Land Grants Awarded by State Governments* (Baltimore: Genealogical Publishing Company, 1996), 322. Afterwards, Bockstruck, *Revolutionary War Bounty Land Grants.*

This being said, it is more likely that Samuel, Philip, William, Thomas, Margaret, and Lucinda were all the *children* of Thomas Love of Prince William. If Thomas Love had brothers named Philip, William, John, and Samuel, he may well have named his sons after them. All fought in the Revolution. Only one of the Loves did not survive the war. William Love, a private in the 7th Virginia, in Captain Benjamin Biggs's company, died at Fort Pitt in July 1782. See NARA, *William Love's compiled service records,* M 881 (http://www.footnote.com), 1–18, images 23055621 to 2304848 (Accessed June 29, 2008).

[6] See note 2. A Philip Love served in the Revolutionary war, as a Brigade Major of the Virginia Militia in 1777. See Heitman, 358.

[7] See note 2. Samuel Love of Prince William served as a sergeant in Captain Philip Richard Francis Lee's 3rd Virginia company from 1776 to 1778 and as a lieutenant in the Prince William County Militia from July 1778 to July 1779. See Chapter 3, notes 2, 16, and 60.

[8] See note 2. See also Hamilton J. Eckenrode, *Virginia Soldiers of the American Revolution* (Richmond: Virginia State Library, 1989), II: 189. John Love also served in the Revolution as a private in the 1st Virginia State Regiment. See also NARA, *John Love's compiled service records,* M 881 (http://www.footnote.com), 1– 57, images 21872030 to 21872239 (Accessed June 29, 2008).

and do make an equal distribution of the proceeds of the sale amongst the representatives: William Love, John Love, Samuel Love, Lucinda Love, and Philip Love.

On the motion of Philip Love, administrator of Thomas Love decd., it is ordered that Jesse Barron be summoned to the next Court to settle his accounts as guardian of Thomas Love.

June 3, 1805 Court, pg 149.
Daniel Rose and Colin Campbell are appointed constables in this County within the District of the 2nd Battalion of the 89th Regiment. Rose and Campbell, having taken the oaths prescribed by law and entered into and acknowledged a bond with securities, according to law, it is ordered that the bond be recorded.

Benjamin Reeves and Hugh Attwell are appointed constables in this County within the District of the 1st Battalion of the 89th Regiment. Reeves and Attwell, having taken the oath prescribed by Law and entered into bonds with securities, according to law, it is ordered that the bond be recorded.

June 6, 1805 Court, pg 170.
Ordered that the Magistrates of this County be summoned to the first day of August Court next to recommend proper persons to the Executive as Officers to fill up vacancies in the 36h and 89th Regiments of Virginia Militia.

June 6, 1805 Court, pg 174.
For reasons appearing to the Court, **Charles Lee** is excused from paying taxes, levies, and poor rates in the future for negroes Beck, Yellow Moll, and Pickett.

August 8, 1805 Court, pg 217.
Ordered that the Magistrates of this County be summoned to the first day of the next Court to recommend proper persons to the Executive as officers to fill up the vacancies in the 36th and 89th Regiments of Virginia Militia and that the commanding officers of the two Regiments in this County be summoned to the next Court also to make their nominations of persons to fill up the vacancies in the regiments.

September 2, 1805 Court, pg 240.
Ordered that the following persons be recommended to the Executive as proper persons to be commissioned as **Militia officers in the 36th Regiment**:
George W. Lindsay, Captain, in place of Allen Sowden removed out of the county.
James Deneal, Lieutenant in place of John Ware, decd.
Elijah Cockrell, Ensign, in place of Peter Jett, removed.
Warren Cooksey, Lieutenant in place of Philip Dawes, removed.
Samuel Cole, Lieutenant in place of William Reardon, removed.
Robert Howison, Ensign in place of [illegible name], removed
Philip D. Dawe, Ensign in place of John Carter, resigned.
Obed Cooksey, Ensign, in place of Warren Cooksey, promoted.
James Gallagher, Ensign, in place of James Deneale, Jr., promoted
John Plant, ensign, in place of Levi Scott who refuses to accept his commission.

September 2, 1805 Court, page 240–241.
Ordered that the following persons be recommended to the Executive as proper persons to be commissioned as **Militia officers in the 89th Regiment**:
Jno Kincheloe, Captain in place of Francis Montgomerie resigned.
William Kincheloe, Captain in place of George Florence, resigned.

Garrard Alexander, Lieutenant of Light Infantry and Jno Chesley, Ensign of Light Infantry.
Daniel Kincheloe, Lieutenant in place of John Kincheloe promoted.
Thomas Brawner, Lieutenant in place of William Kincheloe promoted.
John Brawner,[9] Ensign in place of William Hixon, resigned.
William Lewis, Ensign in place of Daniel Kincheloe, promoted.
Elisha Jenkins, Ensign, in place of Strother Reno resigned.
Robert Little, Captain, in place of Jno Hutchinson, resigned.
Richard Brett, Lieutenant, in place of George Whiting resigned.
William B. Saunders, Ensign in place of Wm. Rogers who refused to act.
Daniel Rose, Lieutenant in place of Philip Chapman who refuses to act.
Henry Brewer, Ensign in place of Daniel Rose promoted.
Elias Obannion, Lieutenant in place of John Glassell, who refuses to act.
James Rose Jr, Ensign in place of William Love, removed.

On the recommendation of Colonel E. Renoe, it is ordered that **John H. Peyton, be recommended to the Executive as Captain of a Troop of Cavalry to be annexed to the 36th Regiment and Wm. A. G. Dade, [become the] Lieutenant and John Carr, [serve] as Cornet in this troop of Cavalry.**

September 3, 1805 Court, pg 248.
From County Levy, for patrolling:
To **Jeremiah Brammell** for 65 hours; **Richard Glover**, for 44 hours; **John Pilcher**[10] for for 65 hours; **James Allen**,[11] for 64 hours; **George Roach**, for 58 hours; **Philip Love**, for 69 ½ hours; **George Colliss**, for 46 ½ hours; **James Sparks**, for 46 ½ hours; **Jesse Petty**, for 40 ½ hours; **Thomas Elliott**, for 75 hours; **John Harris**, for 75 hours; **David Davis**,[12] for 40 hours; **Philip D. Dawe**, for 17 hours; **Joseph Butler**, for 32 hours; and **John Nash**, for 33 hours.

October 7, 1805 Court, pg 259.
William Payne,[13] for reasons appearing to the Court, is excused from paying levies and poor rates in the future.
Ordered that the Magistrates of this County be summoned to the next Court to recommend Officers to fill up vacancies in the **36th and 89th Regiments of Virginia Militia.**

October 8, 1805 Court, pg 261.
From the County Levy: for patrolling:
To **Stephen Howison Jr.**,[14] for 99 hours; **Isaac Milstead**,[15] for 99 hours; **Stephen Shaw**, for 61 hours; and **Jesse Dowell**,[16] for 40 hours.

---

[9] Ancestry.com, *War of 1812 Service Records*, 36th Regiment M 602, MR 24 (http://www.ancestry.com) (Accessed June 30, 2008). John Brawner had been promoted to a captaincy in Lieutenant Colonel Enoch Renno's 36th Regiment of Virginia Militia by the time of the war.

[10] Ibid. M 602 MR 166. John Pilcher, a patroller in September 1805, became a private in Lieutenant Colonel Enoch Renno's 36th Regiment, Virginia Militia.

[11] Ibid., M 602 MR 3.James Allen also served as a private in Renno's 36th Regiment, Virginia Militia during the War of 1812.

[12] Ibid, M 602 MR 53. David Davis was another War of 1812 veteran who served as a private in Renno's 36th Regiment, Virginia Militia during the War of 1812.

[13] This may be the William Payne who was a Captain in the 1st Virginia State Regiment in 1777–1778. See Heitman, 431.While Captain Payne's company was raised in Fauquier County, his successor, Charles Ewell, recruited this company from Prince William County. See Sanchez-Saavedra, 111.

October 8, 1805 Court, pg. 264.
    From the County Levy: for patrolling:
        To **Jno Rolls**,[17] for 89 hours; **Joseph Barker**, for 78 hours; **Clane Martin**, for 53 hours per order of Mr Cole; **Mr. James**, for 75 hours per order of Mr. Cole; **William Norman**, for 75 hours; **John Burros**, for 68 hours; and **Hedgman Murphy**, for 57 ½ hours.

Colonel James Ewell, one of the Commissioners for letting the building of bridges over Cedar Run and Broad Run, having this day informed the Court there is no probability of making an agreement for building the bridge in ant short time.

The Court is unwilling under the distress occasioned by a failure in crops [for] the present year to add thereto by a levy for payment of the debts due by the County.

It is ordered that out of the money in his hands for building the bridges, the Collector of the County levy (laid on October 7, 1801) pay to the several creditors the amount of their respective claims, amounting to a total of $598.36 to be replaced at the laying of the County levy next after the Bridge over Broad Run shall be contracted for.

November 4, 1806, pg 268
    From the County Levy, for patrolling
        To **John Graham**, for 75 hours; **George Robinson**, for 75 hours; **James Woods**, for 75 hours; **John Alexander**, for 41 hours; **Nathaniel Triplett**, for 22 hours; and **Warren Davis**, for 10 hours.

Ordered that the following persons be recommended to the Executive as proper persons **to be commissioned and to fill vacancies in the 36th Regiment of Virginia Militia:**
    Allen Bland, Captain, in place of Francis Johnston, removed.
    Edward Dickinson, Lieutenant, in place of Lewis Dickenson, resigned.
    Richard Allen, Lieutenant, in place of Allen Bland, promoted.
    Richard Weedon,[18] **Ensign, in place of Edward Dickinson, promoted.**

Ordered that the following persons be recommended to the Executive as proper persons to be **commissioned as Officers and to fill up vacancies in the 89th Regiment of Virginia Militia:**
    William Tyler, Colonel in place of Thomas Lee Sr., deceased.
    Washington John Washington, Major, in 2nd Battalion, in place of Wm. Tyler promoted.
    Elias O'Bannon, Captain in place of Washington John Washington, promoted.
    Lynaugh Fitzhugh, Lieutenant in the 1st Battalion, in place of Jesse Ewell, resigned.

NOTE: Prince William County Court Minute and Order Books for 1806–1812 are missing.

---

[14] Ancestry.com, *War of 1812 Service Records*, 36th Regiment, M 602 MR104 (http://www.ancestry.com) (Accessed July 1, 2008). Stephen Howison, without the Jr., became a private in Renno's 36th Regiment, Virginia Militia during the War of 1812.

[15] Ibid. M 602 MR 145. Isaac Milstead was yet another member of Renno's 36th Regiment, Virginia Militia— a private in his regiment during the War of 1812.

[16] Ibid., M 602 MR 60. Jesse Dowell too was a private in the same regiment during the War of 1812.

[17] Ibid., M 602 MR 178. John Rolls also served as a private in Renno's 36th Regiment, Virginia Militia during the War of 1812.

[18] Ibid., M 602 MR 40. Richard Weedon had been promoted to Captain in Lieutenant Colonel Enoch Renno's 36th Regiment, Virginia Militia sometime between 1806 and the War of 1812.

Military Records from Prince William Order Books 1812–1814

October 6, 1812 Court, pg 9.
An address from a Committee appointed by a Meeting of the Citizens of Richmond and Manchester, together with the proceedings of this meeting on the subject of Voluntary contributions for support to the families of drafted men and Volunteers for the Country's Service [was] directed to the County Court of Prince William. It was presented and read. The members here present, considering the application improper, being barely a quorum. They consider the application improper yet will not determine thereon but from respect to the Meeting in Richmond and their Motives.

It is ordered that the Justices be summoned to the 2d day of the next Court to take the same into consideration.

November 3, 1812 Court, pgs. 14–15.
The Magistrates of this County, having been convened by an order of the Court of the 6th day of October last, to take into consideration a letter addressed to the Court by the Central Committee of the Society denominated "The Society for promoting the Success of the War against Great Britain," having, according to the order and notification proceeded to discharge that duty. And being of opinion that the said letter was in fact addressed to them in their individual And they are of opinion that the Court of the 6th day of October ought not to have made the communication the subject of their official notice and being of opinion that the letter was in fact addressed to them in their individual, and not in their Judicial or ministerial capacity, they refuse to act further upon it as a Court.

April 6, 1813 Court, pg 86.
Ordered that the Magistrates of this County be summoned to the first day of the next Court to recommend proper persons as Officers to supply vacancies in the 36th and 89th Regiments of Virginia Militia.

May 3, 1813 Court, pg 94.
Ordered that the following gentlemen be recommended to the Executive as proper persons to be commissioned as officers in the **36th Regiment**, Virginia Militia:

John Merchant,[19] **Captain** in place of Philip D. Dawe who has vacated his commission by accepting the Clerkship of Prince William Court.

William Brundige,[20] **Lieutenant** in place of John Merchant, promoted.

Samuel Adams,[21] **ensign**, in place of Wm. Brundige promoted.

James G. Evans, Lieutenant in place of **Walter G. Hayes**[22] who [is] **in the United States service.**

William Fairfax, ensign in place of John McIntosh decd.

James Gwatkin, Ensign in place of Wm. B. Summons removed.

---

[19] Ibid., M 602, MR 143. John Merchant was a Captain in the 36th Regiment of Virginia Militia under the command of Lieutenant Colonel Enoch Renno. (http://www.ancestry.com) (Accessed June 30, 2008).

[20] Ibid., M 602, MR 28. William Brundige was a lieutenant and adjutant of Lieutenant Colonel Enoch Renno's 36th Regiment of Virginia Militia.

[21] Ibid., M 602 MR 1. Samuel Adams was an ensign in Renno's 36th Regiment, Virginia militia.

[22] Francis Heitman, *Historical Register and Dictionary of the U.S. Army 1789–1903*, (1903; reprint, Baltimore: Genealogical Publishing Company, 1994), I: 515. Afterwards, Heitman, *Historical Register and Dictionary, 1789–1903*. Walter G. Hayes was a 1st Lieutenant in the 20th Infantry, commissioned on March 19, 1812. He was promoted to captain on March 2, 1814 and was honorably discharged on June 15, 1815.

  Alfred C. Hayes,[23] Ensign in Light Infantry attached to 1st Battalion, 36th Regiment, in place of James G. Evans promoted.
  Richard Davis, Lieutenant in place of George Weedon removed.
  George Lansdown,[24] ensign in place of Richard Davis promoted.

May 4, 1813 Court, pg. 99.
  From the County Levy for patrolling:[25]
   To **Maryann Cave, assignee of Samuel M. Hodges** for patrolling, 72 hours; **as assignee of Wm. Moore**, for 72 hours; as **assignee of George Melton,** for 72 hours; as **assignee of Larkin Cave,** for 72 hours; **as assignee of Thomas Clarke,** 87 hours; as **assignee of William Laid,** 87 hours; as **assignee of William Hutchison**, 87 hours; as **assignee of Moses Pilcher,** 73 hours.
   To **Henry Brawner**, for 64 hours.
   To **George Hutchison**, 75 hours.
   To **Daniel King, assignee of John Webster,** 128 hours; **as assignee of James Smith,** 128 hours.
   To **Samuel Cornwell, assignee of Harrison Cornwell**, 128 hours.
   To **Samuel Cornwell,** for patrolling, 128 hours.
   To **William S. Colquhoun, assignee of Samuel Anderson,** 120 hours; **as assignee of George Keys**, 120 hours; as **assignee of Robert Keys**, 120 hours; as **assignee of George Smallwood,** 120 hours; as **assignee of Thomas Keys, 120 hours.**
   To **Benoni E. Harrison,** 30 hours
   To **John Cocke,** 4 ½ hours.
   To **Thomas Lawson**, 30 hours.
   To **John Linton,** 24 ½ hours.
   To **Patton S. Philbrick**, 13 ½ hours.
   To **Benoni E. Harrison, assignee of George Carney,** 64 ½ hours; as **assignee of Richard Gaines**, 36 ¾ hours; as **assignee of Benson Jewell**, 64 ¼ hours; as **assignee of Moses Duffy,** 110 hours; as **assignee of Tannly Guy**, 110 hours; as **assignee of Wm. Calvert,** 104 hours; as **assignee of Samuel Mitchell,** 86 hours.

May 4, 1813 Court, pg. 100.
  From County Levy: Patroller accounts
   Benoni E. Harrison, assignee of Wm. Smith, 100 hours; as **assignee of Wm. Cornwell,** 136 hours; as **assignee of James Smith**, 118 hours; as **assignee of Daniel King**, 117 hours; as **assignee of Mathias Cole,** 101 hours; as **assignee of William Tansil**, 101 hours; as **assignee of Jesse Dowell**, 101 hours, as **assignee of George Tansil**, 101 hours; as **assignee of Wm. Boswell**, 98 hours, as **assignee of Jesse Patterson**, 98 hours; as **assignee of John Bland**, 88 hours; as **assignee of Samuel Boswell**, 96 hours; as **assignee of George Dewal**, 88 hours; as **assignee of Samuel Anderson,** 121 hours; as **assignee of George Smallwood,** 121 hours; as **assignee of James Thomas**, 111 hours; as **assignee of Thomas Keys**, 114 hours; as **assignee of Alexander Brawner**, 97 hours; **as assignee of John Webster**, 140

---

  [23] Ancestry.com, *War of 1812 Service Records,* 36th Regiment, M 602, MR 95. Alfred C Hays had been promoted to a lieutenant during the War of 1812. See NARA, *Index to Compiled Service Records of Volunteer Soldiers who served during the War of 1812,* M 602 MR 95 (http://search. ancestry.com.)
  [24] Ibid., 36th Regiment, M 602, MR 121. George Lansdown, or "Lansdowne" was an ensign in Lieutenant Colonel Enoch Renno's 36th Regiment of Virginia Militia.
  [25] There are so many men who were patrollers in May and June 1813 who ended up in Lieutenant Colonel Enoch Renno's 36th Regiment, Virginia Militia that I have placed them in a separate Appendix. See Appendix 3 for their names and ranks.

hours; as **assignee of William Cornwell**, 140 hours; as **assignee of Samuel Cornwell**, 140 hours; as **assignee of James Smith**, 133 hours.
    Philip Carter, for patrolling, 101 hours.

June 9, 1813 Court, pg. 113.
    From County Levy: Patroller accounts[26]
        To **William Fairfax**, for patrolling 126 hours
        To **Peyton Read**, 104 hours.
        To **Francis Wood**, 120 hours.
        To **Thompson Bird**, 108 hours.
        To **Martin Mills**, 114 hours.
        To **Joseph R. Lynne, assignee of Charles Reno**, 67 hours; as **assignee of Benson Lynn**, 51 ½ hours; as **assignee of James Norman**, 57 hours; as **assignee of Bernard Botts**, 54 ½ hours.
        To **Edward Norman**, 64 hours.
        To **James Arnold**, 130 hours.
        To **Seth Brawner**, 129 hours.
        To **John Davis**, 54 hours.
        To **Jesse Davis**, 62 hours.
        To **James Arnold**, 107 hours.
        To **Moses Arnold**, 107 hours.
        To **Thomas McCuin**, 98 hours.
        To **William Cornwell**, 98 hours.

August 3, 1813 Court, pg. 128.
    Ordered that the Magistrates of this County be summoned to the first day of the next Court to recommend proper persons to be commissioned as officers to supply vacancies in the 36th Regiment, Virginia Militia.

September 6, 1813 Court, pg. 147
Ordered that the following Gentlemen be nominated to the Executive as proper persons to be commissioned as officers to supply vacancies in the **36th Regt**, Virginia Militia:
    Joseph Smith,[27] **Captain in place of Posey D. Grant decd.**
    William Renno[28] **Ensign in place of William French promoted.**
    Alfred C. Hayes,[29] **Lieutenant in Light Infantry attached to 1st Battalion, in place of Colin Campbell decd.**
    William S. Colquhoun,[30] **Ensign in the Light Infantry attached to the 1st Battalion, in place of Alfred C. Hayes promoted.**

---

[26] Every one of these patrollers, listed in June 1813, ended up in Enoch Renno's 36th Regiment, Virginia Militia and saw action in the War of 1812. See Appendix 3.

[27] Ancestry.com, *War of 1812 Service Records*, 36th Regiment, M 602 MR 193 (http://www.ancestry.com) (Accessed July 1, 2008).

[28] Ibid., 36th Regiment, M 602 MR 173. There was a William Rennoe in the 36th Regiment, who served as a private, during the war. There was no record for a William Renno, as an ensign.

[29] Ibid., 36th Regiment, M 602 MR 95.

[30] Ibid., 36th Regiment, M 602, MR 44. William S. Colquhoun began as a sergeant in the 36th Regiment and was promoted to ensign.

Philip Langfitt,[31] Ensign in place of James Gwatkin who refused to accept his commission.

Ordered that James G. Evans[32] be summoned to the next Court to declare whether or not he intends to qualify to the commission in the Militia delivered to him.

Ordered that the following Gentlemen be nominated to the Executive as proper persons to be commissioned as officers to supply vacancies in the **89th Regt, Virginia Militia**:[33]

Noah English, Captain in place of Lynaugh Fitzhugh resigned.
Henry Payne,[34] **Lieutenant in place of Noah English promoted**
William P. Dunnington, Ensign[35] **in place of H. Payne promoted.**
Benjamin Marshall to be Lieutenant in place of Stephen Joy Compton decd.
Benjamin Pridmore to be ensign in place of Benjamin Marshall promoted.
John Lee Captain in place of John Kincheloe resigned.
Thomas Brewer Lieutenant in place of John Lee promoted.
John Lee Jr Ensign in place of Thomas Brewer promoted.

October 4, 1813 Court, pg. 155.

Ordered that **James G. Evans**[36] be recommended to the Executive as a Lieutenant in the 36th Regiment, Virginia Militia in place of Walter G. Hayes in the United States Service. It appears that James Evans was recommended at May Court last, and had lost his commission before he qualified thereto.

John Lee appeared in Court and **took the oath to support the Constitution of the United States, the oath for giving assurance of Fidelity to this State, the oath of Captain in the Militia of this County, and the oath to suppress dueling.**

October 4, 1813 Court, pg. 156.

Thomas Brewer appeared in Court and **took the oath to support the Constitution of the United States, the oath for giving assurance of Fidelity to this State, the oath for Lieutenant in the Militia of this County, and the oath to suppress dueling.**

---

[31] Ibid., 36th Regiment, M 602, MR 121.
[32] James G. Evans was not found in Ancestry.com, *War of 1812 Service Records*, as members of the 36th Regiment or 89th Regiment, M 602.
[33] None of these officers appeared in Ancestry.com, *War of 1812 Service Records*, as members of the 36th or 89th Regiment, M 602.
[34] Henry Payne *may* be the H. R. Payne, who was a lieutenant on a muster roll of Captain Benjamin Tyler's Company of the 89th Regiment, then under the command of Gerard Alexander, from August 30 to September 7, 1814. See Auditor's Rolls, *Virginia Militia in the War of 1812*, II: 791
[35] Ibid. William P. Dunnington appeared as an ensign on Captain Benjamin Tyler's muster roll for the same period.
[36] See note 32.

An Account of the Paymaster for the 36th Regiment, Thomas T. Page, appeared in the *Prince William County, Virginia Deed Book 1805–1807*, 336–337. The account was listed as follows:

An Account of the Paymaster for the 36th Regiment, Thomas T. Page 1805–1807.

Thomas T. Page, Paymaster, 36th Regiment

Sept. 22, 1805	To amt of fines rec'd from the Sheriff	$56.19
October 17, 1806	Ditto	$25.00
	Ditto	$53.85
		$126.54
	Balance due	$12.24

An Account of the Paymaster for the 36th Regiment, Thomas T. Page 1805–1807.[37]

1805	Contra	
August 1805	Cash paid Colin Camnibeels [Campbell] Admrs	$2.00
October 7, 1805	Cash pd Allan Duffy	$8.00
ditto	Cash pd Randolph & Renoe	$2.00
ditto	Cash pd Negro Boy	$2.00
ditto	Cash pd Thomas Turner	$2.00
ditto	Cash pd Travers McJoy	$2.00
Nov 19, 1805	Cash pd A. Duffy	$2.00
Mar 3, 1806	Cash pd Colonel Renno	$2.00
Mar 3, 1806	Cash pd ditto	$2.00
Mar 4, 1806	Cash pd Richard Cole	$8.00
Oct 17, 1806	Cash pd ditto	$2.00
ditto	Cash pd Negro Moses	$3.00
ditto	Cash pd William Purnell	$2.00
ditto	Cash pd A. Duffy	$2.00
ditto	Cash pd Ro. Keys	$2.00
ditto	Cash pd R. Rawlins	$3.00
ditto	Cash pd T. Turner	$4.00
ditto	Cash pd Jo. Gilbert	$10.00
ditto	Cash pd [blank] Keys	$2.00
ditto	Cash pd Capt. Orear	$ .75
1807	Cash pd Jo. Gilbert	$9.50
May 16, 1807	Cash pd Randall Rollings	$8.00
ditto	Cash pd Thomas Turner	$2.00
Nov. 15, 1806	Cash pd Randall Rollings	$12.00
Ditto	Cash pd Jno. Weston	$4.00
Ditto	Cash pd Posey D. Grant	$15.00
Mar 7, 1806	Cash pd Moses Tarlton	$8.00
May 16, 1807	Cash pd Posey Grant	$3.00
	Cash pd Negro Cash	$2.00
	Cash pd Moses Tarlton	$12.00
	Cash pd William Purnell	$ 2.00
		$138.25

---

[37] LVA, MR 8, *Prince William County Deed Book 1805–1807*, 337–338, (LVA, Richmond, Virginia)

By virtue of an order of the worshipful Court of Prince William, we have examined the within acct and vouchers of T. Page Paymaster to the 35th Regt of this County and do find that there appears to be a balance due Thomas T. Page of $12.21. Given under our hands 7 December 1807.

(Signed) Ch^s Ewell, James Wigginton

At a court held for Prince William County December 7, 1807.

This Acct of the Paymaster of the 36th Regiment with the Regiment was presented to the Court and ordered to be recorded.

Teste   J. Williams, CC Cur.

Part IV

Prince William Pensioners
1833–1850, 1853–1856

Chapter 8

Historical Introduction

Neglect Sets In:
I. Federal Pension Legislation
II. Federal Bounty Land Legislation 1776–1858
A Brief Overview

The State's Response:
I. Virginia Pension Legislation
II. Virginia's Bounty Land Legislation

Chapter 9

The Pensioners
Military Records from the Prince William Virginia
County Court Order Books
1833–1850, 1853–1856

The General Service Pension

4 (Stat.) 529 [& 530].
TWENTY-SECOND CONGRESS. Sess. 1. 1832.

Chap. CXXVI. *An Act supplementary to the "Act for the relief of certain surviving officers and soldiers of the revolution."*

Be it enacted by the Senate and House of Representatives, of the United States of America, in Congress assembled, That each of the surviving officers, non-commissioned officers, musicians, soldiers and Indian spies, who shall have served in the continental line, or state troops, volunteers or militia, at one or more terms, a period of two years, during the war of the revolution, and who are not entitled to any benefit under the act for the relief of certain surviving officers and soldiers of the revolution, passed the fifteenth day of May, eighteen hundred and twenty-eight, be authorized to receive, out of any money in the treasury not otherwise appropriated, the amount of his full day in the said line, according to his rank, but not exceeding, in any case, the pay of a captain of said line.

Such pay [is] to commence from the fourth day of March, one thousand eight hundred and thirty-one, and shall continue during his natural life;

and that any officer, non-commissioned officer, musician, or private, as aforesaid, who shall have served in the continental line, state troops, volunteers or militia, a term or terms in the whole less than the above period but not less than six months, shall be authorized to receive out of any unappropriated money in the treasury, during his natural life, each according to his term of service, an amount bearing such proportion to the annuity granted to the same rank for the service of two ears, as his term of service did to the term aforesaid; to commence from the fourth day of March, one thousand eight hundred and thirty-one.

Sec. 2, *And be it further enacted,* That no person, receiving any annuity or pension under any law of the United States providing for revolutionary officers and soldiers, shall be entitled to the benefits of this act, unless he shall first relinquish his further claim to such pension; and in all payments under this act, the amount which may have been received under any other act as aforesaid, since the date at which the payments under this act shall commence, shall first be deducted from such payment.

Sec. 3, *And be it further enacted,* That the pay allowed by this act shall, under the direction of the Secretary of the Treasury, be paid to the officer, non-commissioned officer, musician or private, entitled thereto, or his or their authorized attorney, at such places and times as the Secretary of the Treasury may direct, and that no foreign officer shall be entitled to said pay, nor shall any officer, non-commissioned officer, musician or private, receive the same until he furnish the said Secretary satisfactory evidence that he is entitled to the same in conformity to the provisions of this act; and the pay hereby allowed shall not be in any way transferable or liable to attachment, levy, or seizure, by any legal process whatever, but shall inure wholly to the person benefit of the officer, non-commissioned officer, musician, or soldier, entitled to the same.

Sec. 4, *And be it further enacted,* That so much of the said pay as accrued before the approval of this act, shall be paid to the person entitled to the same as soon as may be, in the manner and under the provisions above mentioned; and the pay shall accrue thereafter shall be paid semi-annually, in the manner above directed; and, in case of the death of any person embraced by the provisions of this act, or of this act to which it is supplementary, during the period intervening between the semi-annual payments directed to be made by said acts, the proportionate amount of pay which shall accrue between the last preceding semi-annual payment, and the death of such person, shall be paid to his widow, or, if he leave no widow, to his children.

Sec. 5, *And be it further enacted,* That the officers, non-commissioned officers, mariners, or marines, who served for a like term in the naval service during the revolutionary war, shall be entitled to the benefits of this act, in the same manner as is provided for the officers and soldiers of the army of the revolution.

Approved, June 7, 1832.

Source: Christine Rose, *Military Pension Laws, 1776–1858* (San Jose: Rose Family Association, 2001), 23–24.

PRINCE WILLIAM PENSIONERS
1833–1850, 1853–1856

CHAPTER 8

HISTORICAL INTRODUCTION

Most of the veterans whose records appear in Chapter 9 fought in the American Revolution as part of four commands: on the Continental Establishment, in a Virginia State Regiment, in an independent command, or as part of the county militia. Most were young. Many were poor, with dependent wives and families in need of the county's beneficence for support while their soldier was off fighting. Others came from families who were yeoman farmers—small landowners working small farms.

These men had different reasons for going to war. Some fought to be free of taxes and government regulation of their lives. Taxes touched all phases of their life. The state government could, and did, tax any legal documents. Deeds, wills, marriage licenses were among taxable documents; even ordinaries and taverns needed licenses to operate. Playing cards were to be printed on special embossed paper. Newspapers, too, were to be printed on expensive government-issued paper. Advertisers had to pay a tax to print a forthcoming sale of a piece of property, a reward for a runaway servant, or an announcement of a new patent medicine. The taxes angered the wealthy and fostered a simmering resentment among farmers, tradesmen, and merchants in towns along Virginia's rivers and along the burgeoning frontier settlements.

To many of the soldiers, this war was a life-changing event. Soldiers from Prince William fought in New York, New Jersey, and Pennsylvania. They survived Valley Forge. Others fought in the south only to be captured at Charleston. Still others made it to Yorktown and were participants in the final victory over Lord Cornwallis.

They arrived home as heroes. Over time, their status changed. As a result of their wartime experiences, many were not nearly as willing to return to eke out an existence on a small farm hold. So some veterans and their families headed west into Kentucky, Tennessee, and the Old Northwest. Others, who could not afford to move, stayed and as their reward, were left to take their chances at survival. Very few soldiers thrived after the war.

Wounded veterans supplemented their subsistence, living on a disability pension or on the bounty of neighbors. A fortunate few received a small state pension for their disability. As Virginia worked to stabilize its economy and to rework its infrastructure in a peacetime setting, these veterans, those in need and those on disability, began to drop from the scene and from the memories of both the state and federal government.

It is against this backdrop that pension legislation was enacted. It was a slow process for veterans who were in need, unable to support their families with meaningful work. The war had been over for more than thirty years before the United States Congress enacted any meaningful legislation for these veterans. This legislation was restricted to veterans who had service in the Virginia Continental Line. Veterans, who served in any other service, including the militia, were not eligible. So many veterans from the Virginia Continental service applied for assistance in 1818 that Congress put further restrictions on these men in 1820 that removed many of them from pension lists because, even as poor as they were, they were deemed to have too much property to qualify. In 1823, Congress finally enacted another pension act that restored many of these men to the pension lists.

It took another ten years before the Congress enacted a more inclusive general service pension for veterans who served in the Army of the Revolution. In 1832, the Congress opened up pension benefits to veterans of the Continental Line, volunteers, state units, rangers, Indian spies, and militia who fought for at least six months in the war.

While the federal government did give disability pensions to wounded veterans, they all but ignored those in need and those who had served in other units outside the Continental Line. This was neglect on a massive scale for these men who had fought for the country's freedom.[1]

NEGLECT SETS IN: FEDERAL PENSION AND BOUNTY LAND LEGISLATION HISTORY
A BRIEF OVERVIEW

I. FEDERAL PENSION LEGISLATION

Federal pension legislation for veterans may be divided into four different areas: 1) Disability Pensions, 2) Need-based Pensions, 3) the General Service Pension, and 4) Half-pay pensions to officers, soldiers, widows and orphans.

Disability Pensions 1776–1814.

This legislation dealt with relief for wounded or disabled revolutionary war veterans and War of 1812 veterans. During the Revolutionary War, Congress passed several acts for the relief of wounded and disabled veteran. Three of the more important acts appear here.

- **Continental Congress Pension Acts, 1776–1785.**

  - **The National Pension Act, August 1776.**

This act applied to wounded or disabled veterans whose wounds were so severe that they rendered him incapable of earning a livelihood. Every commissioned or non-commissioned officer and private soldier or seaman in the United States Army or Navy who lost a limb or was disabled in the war was eligible. However, there was a catch— he had to be able to perform guard duty and then join an "invalid corps." Once these conditions were met, the veteran would then receive half his monthly pay for his life or for as long as the disability continued.[2]

  - **Extension of invalid provisions for soldiers, September 1778**

The provisions of this act extended the eligibility of disabled or wounded veterans to those in service from April 1775 with the same provisos regarding garrison duty and joining an invalid corps.

If an eligible veteran refused to perform garrison duty or join an invalid corps, he was to be struck of the pension list, unless he had a family for which he needed to provide. State governors were given the authority to make exceptions to this law and could grant exemptions from further service. The soldier could then produce his certificate and obtain a pension.

If a soldier received his disability when he was a prisoner or if he was unable to produce the required certificate due to the death of his officer, physicians, or surgeon, he could still apply to the Governor for a disability pension. Once he showed satisfactory proof that he was disabled or maimed in the service of his country or as a prisoner, along with a certificate from the Governor, he would receive his pension.[3]

---

[1] Joan W. Peters, *Neglected and Forgotten: Fauquier County, Virginia, French & Indian War, Revolutionary War, & War of 1812 Veterans ... from the Military Records Series of the Fauquier County, Virginia Clerks Loose Papers, 1759–1825* (Westminster: Willow Bend Books, 2004), i. Afterwards, Peters, *Neglected and Forgotten*.
[2] Christine Rose, *Military Pension Laws, 1776–1858* (San Jose: Rose Family Association, 2001), 1.
[3] Peters, *Neglected and Forgotten,* ii.

- **Disability Pensions for men still in Continental Service, April 1782.**

In 1782, Congress resolved that sick and wounded soldiers who were unfit for duty either in the field or garrison and who applied for a discharge rather than serve in the invalid corps could be discharged. They were then entitled to a pension of $5.00 per month. Congress recommended that the state where the veteran resided administer these pensions on a yearly basis from a United States Pension Agency, set up there.[4]

- **Congressional resolutions relating to officers and supernumeraries, November 1778–November 1780.**

Included in these wartime acts were eight Congressional resolutions relating to pensions for commissioned officers and supernumeraries. Basically, these acts stipulated half pay for commissioned officers for seven years.

In May 1778, all military officers who had been commissioned by the Continental Congress, and who continued in the Continental service, were eligible for half pay for seven years.[5]

In November 1778, as a result of the reorganization of the Continental Line, many officers became supernumeraries. In acknowledging their "faithful services," officers so designated were to be entitled ton a year's pay. Two years later, in October 1780, half pay for seven years was allotted to supernumerary officers.

In August 1780, Congress extended half pay benefits to commissioned officers who served until the close of the war and to widows, until they died or remarried, and orphans of soldiers who died in service. In November of the same year, Congress extended these benefits to majors and brigadiers who served until the end of the war.[6]

- **The Commutation Act, March 1783.**

In March 1783, Congress passed this act for officers who had remained in service until the close of the war. They were entitled to five year's full pay, or to securities at six per cent per year, instead of the earlier half pay for life. The act was also extended to state militia that did not belong to the State Lines. Officers could not individually accept or refuse these payments; they could only do so collectively at the option of the respective state lines. The state lines had six months to after the passage of the legislation to act.[7]

One other piece of important pension legislation was passed after the war had ended. In **June, 1785,** Congress passed the **Disabled Veteran's Pension Act.** Congress recommended to the states that they make provisions for officers, soldiers or seaman, who had been disabled in the service of the United States. Congress set forth these eight conditions to be followed by the states:

- The state was to assign someone to make a list of all officers, soldiers or seamen who lived in the state, who served in the army or navy of the United States or in the militia in the service of the U.S. who have been disabled.
- Their disability must have been severe enough to incapacitate them from military duty or from obtaining their livelihood by labor.
- The list was to include the name of the invalid, his pay, age, and disability, along with the regiment, corps, or ship to which he belonged.

---

[4] Rose., 2. See also Peters, *Neglected and Forgotten,* ii.
[5] Ibid., 1.
[6] Rose, 2–3.
[7] Ibid., 4.

- A copy of this list was to be sent to the office of the Secretary of war within a year after the state passes a law for this purpose. After that, the pensioner's list was to be transmitted annually to the officer of the Secretary of War.
- To be eligible for this pension, officers, soldiers and seaman, must produce a certificate from the commanding officer or surgeon of the regiment, ship, corps or company in which he served. He can also procure a certificate from a physician or surgeon of a military hospital or "other good and sufficient testimony, setting forth his disability," and that it was incurred while he was in the U.S. service.
- All commissioned officers, disabled in service of the United States who were "wholly incapable of military duty" or of working for a living, were to be allowed a yearly pension equal to half of their pay.
- All commissioned officers who were not disabled to such a degree were allowed a yearly pension according to the severity of their disability.
- All non-commissioned officers and privates, disabled in the service of the U.S. who were incapable of military duty in a garrison or working for a living, were allowed a sum not more than $5.00 per month. Those veterans, who were not immobilized to that extent, were allowed a sum depending on the degree of their disability.[8]

♦ **Military Pension Laws enacted by the U.S. Congress from the U.S. Statutes at Large: Selected Acts.**

The U.S. Congress, from its inception, continued to be concerned about its officers, its wounded and disabled pensioners, and widows and orphans of deceased army and naval officers. In 1789, Congress continued the provision of funding for state pensions, which had been executed under the previous Continental Congresses, for a year, These were pensions that had been allotted to "invalids who were wounded and disabled" during the Revolution.

Revolutionary War Disability Pensions.

Between 1789 and 1806, Congress passed a numerous disability pensions to care for wounded and disabled revolutionary war veterans. While some of the laws expanded coverage to militia and volunteers, the bulk of the legislation served to tighten the existing law to prevent pension fraud and abuse.[9] In May 1792, pension relief was expanded to include wounded or disabled revolutionary war officers and soldier belonging to the militia called into service. These veterans were to be "taken care of and provided for at the public expense."[10]

In March 1796, Congress provided for disability pensions for commissioned officers, non-comms, privates, and musicians who had been wounded or disabled in service while in the militia or while a volunteer.[11]

- **The Consolidated Pension Act, April 10, 1806.**

In April 1806, the ninth Congress consolidated the previous disability and invalid pension acts to include any commissioned or non-commissioned officer, musician, soldier, marine or seaman, or member of a state militia regiment. This pension act served as the basis for all subsequent acts. To be eligible, the veteran could

1) have received his disability while the service of the United Sates or in the line duty.

---

[8] Ibid., 4.
[9] Ibid., 5-12.
[10] Ibid., 7.
[11] Ibid., 9.

2) have received his wound or disability in the revolution.
3) have not deserted.
4) have either resigned his commission or taken a disability discharge.
5) have received his disability when a prisoner of war

Finally, as a result of the wounds he received, he must have become so disabled that he could not perform manual labor.

On substantiating his claim, the veteran would be placed on the pension list of the United States for either the continuance of his disability or for his life. He would then be entitled to a pension.

Congress also spelled out how the veteran was to prove his claim. First, he needed an affidavit concerning his disability. The affidavit could be issued by his commanding officer or two other credible witnesses. Secondly, he had to prove, by at least one credible witness, that he had continued in service unless he had been discharged. If the veteran was an officer, he had to prove he resigned because of his disability. If a prisoner, he had to proved that he had been disabled while a captive of the enemy. Finally, he had to state, under oath, that he was not on a pension list of any state.[12]

The Prince William Court Minutes for 1804–1806 do not show any revolutionary war pension applicants for disability relief.

War of 1812 Disability Pensions.

Congress approved disability pensions for War of 1812 veterans in January, 1812. The legislators granted pensions for wounded veterans who had been officers, non-comms, musicians, or privates, while in the line of duty. Compensation was limited for officers, to half their monthly pay at the time they were wounded; for non-comms, musicians, and privates, compensation was not to exceed $5.00 per month.[13]

In April 1816, Congress extended pensions to include officers and soldiers of the militia, while in the service of the U.S.[14]

The Revolutionary War need-based pensions, 1818–1823.

There were three pensions acts associated with federal government relief for revolutionary war veterans in need of assistance from their country. The first was passed in March 1818 which were to go only to veterans in the Continental Line. The second act, passed in May 1820, placed severe restrictions on the financial status of previous pension holders under the 1818 act. The net result was that many veterans lost the only financial assistance they had which provided support for themselves and their families. This pushed them over the brink and into poverty. Then, in March 1823, Congress lifted restrictions in the 1820 act and as a result, pensioners stricken from the rolls were returned to pension lists.

- **Relief for revolutionary war veterans in reduced circumstances, March 18, 1818.**

This pension act applied to revolutionary war land and naval service veterans who were in such reduced circumstances that they needed the assistance of their country. To be eligible, veterans must have served for at least nine months in a Continental regiment. Militia service did not count.

Veterans were to make an application for a pension before a Judge of a District or County Court of records. They were to supply the court with the details of their revolutionary war service—enlistment dates, names of company officers, regimental commanders, battles,

---

[12] Ibid., 12.
[13] Ibid., 15.
[14] Ibid., 17.

tours of duties, names of officers who discharged them, and other facts that would clearly establish their service in the Continental Army.

If the Judge was satisfied that the applicant had indeed served in the revolution, he would hen certify the application and send it along to the War Department. Witnesses were required to give depositions regarding the financial status of the applicant and swear, under oath, that the veteran was in such reduced circumstances that he needed help from the federal government.[15]

While Prince William's Court Minutes from are missing from 1815–1832, one of the pensioners in the 1833 Court Minutes was **John Bell**, who had applied in Fauquier County for a pension in November 1819. He was fifty-eight years old.

His pension declaration revealed that he had enlisted for a year in January 1782, with the rank and pay as a captain, under Captain Henry Margarum. Margarum was a conductor of the Artillery. Captain Bell and his company belonged to Rochambeau's Brigade. Bell's artillery regiment was commanded by Colonels Wadsworth and Carter, who were responsible for supervising the transportation of the artillery from York, Virginia to Boston. In early 1783, Captain Bell received a written discharge from Major Alcott, while stationed at Sheffield, Massachusetts.[16]

Charles Atwell attested to Captain Bell's service. Atwell had also served as a Captain of Artillery and stated that John Bell enlisted for a year as a soldier under Captain Margarum.

Nathaniel Grigsby, Baylis Grigsby, and Peter Adams testified as to his need. He was "aged and infirm, [with] a family of children. [He is] a man of truth and respectability ..."[17]

Spencer Anderson was another veteran who made an application for a pension from Prince William in September 1818.[18] He was sixty-eight at the time of his declaration. He had, he stated, enlisted in Prince William in a company commanded by Captain Philip Richard Francis Lee of the 3rd Virginia Regiment.

He served in this company for two years until the expiration of his enlistment. He was discharged from the service in Pennsylvania. He was action at York Island, White Plains, Brandywine, and Germantown. Elijah Wood gave his affidavit in September 1818 that he, too, was a soldier in Captain Lee's Company in 1776. Wood stated that Spencer Anderson was a soldier in the 3rd Virginia. He had enlisted in Captain Lee's Company. Wood believed that he served his time faithfully in that regiment.[19]

In May 1819, Spencer Anderson made another pension declaration before William A. G. Dade of the General Court. He had enlisted in January 1776 in Dumfries under Captain Philip Richard Francis Lee of the 3rd Virginia Regiment, commanded by Colonels Thomas Marshall and William Heth.

He had received an honorable discharge from Colonel Heth at the expiration of his term. Unfortunately, he had lost his discharge while on a militia tour in 1778. He had been wounded over the eye at Princeton and had fought at Brandywine and Germantown. His original declaration had been made in the spring of 1819. His pension certificate number was 12459.

---

[15] Ibid., 18. See also Peters, *Neglected and Forgotten*, iv-v.

[16] See chapter 9, June 1833 Court. See Peters, *Neglected and Forgotten*, 41 for his November 1819 pension application. John Bell received a pension S 12986 while a resident of Prince William. See Virgil White, *Genealogical Abstracts of Revolutionary War Pension Files* (Waynesboro: The National Historical Publishing Company, 1990), I: 222.

[17] Peters, *Neglected and Forgotten*, v, 41–42.

[18] NARA, *Spencer Anderson's Pension File* S 37672, M 804 MR 58. See also Peters, *The Third Virginia*, II: 127–128.

[19] Peters, *Neglected and Forgotten*, 44–45. See also Peters, *The Third Virginia*, II: 127–128.

He presented a schedule of his property to the court. Valued at $7.00, his property contained a set of coarse carpenter tools, a black walnut table and a garden hose.[20]

Another veteran who had enlisted in Prince William during the Revolutionary war was **John Powell**. He made his pension declaration in 1818 while living in Fauquier. He was sixty-two years old. He had enlisted in Prince William for more than three years under Captain Thomas Ewell of Prince William. Captain Ewell's company was attached to the 1st Virginia State Regiment, commanded by Colonel Gibson. Afterwards, Powell transferred to Colonel Buford's regiment after its defeat and marched south. He was "taken sick" and left at Hillsboro.

Upon his recovery, he joined General Daniel Morgan on the field after Cowpens. He then returned to Virginia and was attached to the 1st Virginia regiment commanded by Colonel Dabney. Powell saw action at Yorktown. He continued in service until the declaration of peace when he received his discharge.

He made the requisite oaths of citizenship in March 1818 and that he had not disposed of his property or had any placed in trust. His schedule, dated July 1820, was annexed to this pension application. He had no real estate. His personal estate consisted of one hog, a broad axe, two narrow aces, a handsaw, a draw knife, two froes, a chisel, and two hoes, all of which were worth $ 52.42. He has less than $20.00 in debts due him.

His occupation was that of a rough carpenter, but he had "little bodily strength to pursue it." He had a wife, age fifty-seven and "sickly," a daughter, Francis, age thirteen, also "sickly," a son Robert, age eleven; and a grand daughter, Kitty, age three.[21]

These veterans were just three examples of the pensioners who applied in Prince William under the Pension Act of 1818. It is indeed unfortunate that the court minutes for this period are no longer around. It is likely that there were many more veterans living in Prince William during that time who came into court to make a pension application.[22]

- **Pension Act of 1820, May 1820.**

Pensioners, who had received benefits according to the 1818 act and had received payments to March 1820, would now have to submit to a court of record in the county, city, or borough in which he resided, a schedule subscribed by him, of his whole estate and income in order to continue on the pension rolls.

Applicants must subscribe and take a written oath of affirmation that he was 1) a resident citizen of the United States on March 18, 1818; 2) he had not disposed of any part of his property by sale or gift or any other way in order to remain eligible for his pension; 3) he had no property in trust, nor has he placed property, securities, contracts, or debts in a trust held by some one else for him; 4) he had only the income contained in a schedule annexed to his application..

Then the Clerk of the Court, if satisfied regarding the claim, was to certify the schedule, give an appraisal of the property, and sent certified copies of the papers to the Secretary of War. The original papers were to stay with the Court.

On receipt of the copy of the application, schedule, appraisal of the property, and oath of affirmation, the Secretary of War could strike from the pension list the names of any applicant, who, in his opinion, was not in indigent enough circumstances as to be unable to support himself without further financial assistance from the federal government.

---

[20] Ibid.

[21] Peters, *Neglected and Forgotten*, 38–39.

[22] If Fauquier Court Minutes are any indication of the applicants, then Prince William probably had many veterans who applied for this need-based pension. Nearly two dozen veterans in Fauquier availed themselves of this opportunity to apply for the 1818 benefits. See Peters, *Fauquier County Military Records 1784–1840*, 55–59.

Veterans, who had been placed on the pension lists because of a disability from a known wound in the revolution and had relinquished the disability pension in order to qualify for the 1818 pension, were restored to the disability pension lists, if they had been taken off.[23]

Two Prince William veterans, John Bell and Spencer Anderson, who had received benefits from the 1818 pension act, were back in Court in Fauquier to present schedules to the Court and have their property appraised.

John Bell's 1820 pension declaration was filed in Fauquier on the day after Christmas in 1820. He was fifty-nine years old. He had enlisted in Prince William for one year as a captain under Henry Margaram, a conductor of the Artillery. He served for fourteen months and was on the Continental Establishment the entire time. He received a written discharge from Major Alcott, in Sheffield, Massachusetts. He has since lost that discharge.

He stated, under oath, that he was a resident citizen of the United States on March 18, 1818 and that he had not disposed or sold his property. Nor did he have property in trust. The only property he had was his wearing apparel. He was a cooper by trade although "crippled and very infirm, a waggon having run over [him] and disabled [him]."

He did not have a wife living, although he had four children: James, age twelve; Landy, age fourteen, Moses, age sixteen, and Mary Ann, age eighteen. His sons had been bound out to learn trades while his daughter lived with Landy Calvert. He did not receive any assistance from his children and obtained "subsistence by working at [his] trade when [he] was able."[24]

In September 1838, John Bell, a former private, and resident of Fauquier for two years appointed James E. Heath as his attorney to collect his pension due from March 4, 1838 to September 4, 1838. John Bell had lived in Prince William prior to his two year residence in Fauquier. Heath traveled to Richmond, and on September 25, 1838, collected $20.00 for Bell.[25]

The Fauquier County Minute Book for 1820–1821 noted Spencer Anderson's pension declaration and schedule of property offered to the court. The court was of the opinion that his property was worth $7.00 and ordered that to be certified.[26]

In September 1834, Spencer Anderson, a former private, eighty-four years of age, and a resident of Fauquier County for more than nine years gave a power of attorney to John G. Hull of Richmond. Mr. Hull was empowered to collect Anderson's pension due from March 4, 1834 to September 4, 1834. He did so, collecting $48.00 for Anderson.[27]

- **Pension Act of 1823, March 1, 1823.**

This act returned some of the revolutionary war pensioners to the pension lists. Basically, this legislation restored pensioners to the rolls if they had already satisfied the Secretary of War regarding their circumstances under the 1818 act. The applicants still had to swear, under oath, that they had not disposed or transferred any property in order to keep their pension. Applicants who were not able to attend Court because of bodily infirmity,[28]

The General Service Pension Act, June 7, 1832.

Nearly forty years after the end of the revolutionary war, Congress finally decided to award pensions for general service in the revolution.

---

[23] Rose, 19–20.
[24] Peters, *Neglected and Forgotten*, 61.
[25] Alycon Trubey Pierce, *Selected Final Pension Payment Vouchers, Virginia, 1818–1864* (Athens: Iberian Publishing Company, 1996), I: 38.
[26] Peters, *Fauquier County Military Records, 1784–1840*, 68.
[27] Pierce, I: 11.
[28] Peters, 20–21.

Upon application and proof, pensions would be paid to revolutionary war officers, soldiers, musicians, and Indian spies who had served for at least six months in the continental line, in state troops, as volunteers, or in the militia.

Those veterans who had served one or more terms for two years received a pension equal to their full pay according to his rank for his lifetime. Those who served less than two years but more than six months received a proportionate amount of their pay for their lifetime.

Pension applicants had to relinquish their claims to any other pension to be eligible to this one. Officers, non-comms, mariners, and marines who served a like term in the naval service during the revolution were also entitled to these benefits.[29]

By the time this act was passed, many of the Revolutionary War veterans were in their sixth or seventh decade.

Five veterans availed themselves of this pension act according to the Prince William County Court Minutes for 1833–1835. One was a familiar name, John Bell, who had already applied for an earlier need-based pension in Fauquier. His Prince William application, filed in June 1833, was presented to the court, sworn to and ordered certified. Thankfully, John Bell's other pension applications were found in other documents in Fauquier that detailed his service and his economic situation in the 1818–1820 period.[30]

Thomas Arrington,[31] **John Lowe,**[32] **Daniel Orear,**[33] and **Joseph Bobo**[34] were the other veterans who applied for pension benefits as Prince William soldiers in the Revolutionary War.

Revolutionary War and War of 1812 Relief for officers, widows and orphans, 1778–1858

Revolutionary War and War of 1812 relief for officers, widows and orphans provided a number of acts, primarily for the relief of widows and orphans of deceased veterans. Upon the expiration of the act in question, Congress simply extended the act for another period of years.

- **Revolutionary War Legislation, 1778–1780**

Congress passed five important acts for the relief of officers and their widows and orphans during the Revolutionary War. In May 1778, the first half-pay pensions for commissioned officers of the Continental Line were passed. These officers were to receive half pay every year for seven years. General officers were entitled to the half pay of a colonel. An addition condition in the act stated that all officers must have taken an oath of allegiance to the United States in order to be eligible for their pension benefits.[35]

In **August 1780,** the Continental Congress passed legislation for half pay pensions for widows and orphans of commissioned officers who died while in the *Continental* service. They were to receive the half pay due their deceased husband or father for seven years.

In October the legislators extended half pay benefits to supernumerary officers. In the same month, another act extended half pay benefits to officers who served until the end of the war. This act differed from the previous ones in one important aspect—these officers were entitled to half pay for *life*.

---

[29] Ibid., 23–24.
[30] See Chapter 9, June 3, 1833 Court.
[31] Ibid., May 2, 1836 entry. This was a supplemental declaration for his service in the Revolution.
[32] Ibid., February 5, 1839. He was seventy-nine when he made his declaration. He died on June 15, 1843. See September 4, 1843 court entry.
[33] Ibid., April 6, 1846 court entry.
[34] Ibid.
[35] Rose, 1.

In November, half pay was extended to brigadiers and major generals who continued in the service of the United States until the close of the war. They, too, were to receive these benefits for life.[36]

- **Indian Wars (1790s) Legislation to provide relief to widows and orphans.**

In **March 1798**, Congress extended pension benefits to widows and orphans of commissioned officers in service of the United States and of the militia who have died of wounds received since March 1789. However, there was a catch—these widows and orphans must apply for a pension within two years of the passage of this act.[37]

This act was passed to provide some pension relief for families of the Indian wars fought in the last decade of the eighteenth century. It provided relief for families of men who served in both regular and militia troops.

- **War of 1812 Legislation to provide relief to widows and orphans.**

Fifteen years were to pass before Congress turned its attention once again to providing pension relief for widows and orphans. In **August 1813**, the thirteenth Congress passed legislation to provide for half pay pensions for widows and orphans of commissioned officers who served as a volunteer or in the militia while in the service of the United States. If an officer left a widow, or if no widow, a child or children under the age of sixteen, then the survivor(s) are entitled to receive half the monthly pay of the deceased for five years. If the widow remarried, the pension went to the child. The pension ceased on the death of the child or children.[38]

In March 1814, half pay pensions were extended to widows and orphans of seamen or marines belonging to the United States Navy. In **April 1816,** pensions were awarded to widows and orphans of commissioned officers in the regular army, private soldiers of the militia, including rangers, sea-fencibles, and volunteer or non-comms, musicians, and privates.

These men must have enlisted for a term of one year or eighteen months and died of wounds. Their deaths, whether after their discharge or mustering out, or return to their home, must have been caused by wounds received during the "late war." [the War of 1812].

If a widow survived them, or if no widow, a child or children, under sixteen, then the survivor(s) were entitled to half the deceased officer's monthly pay for five years. If the widow died or married again, before the five years was up, the half pay was to go to the surviving child or children.

There was an important proviso to this act as it referred to half pay pension relief for widows and orphans. The Secretary of War had the responsibility for putting together the standard of proof in pension applications under this act.[39]

In **March 1819**, Congress extended pensions to widows and orphans of officers, seamen, or marines who died of wounds since June 1812. This act was extended for another five years in January and May, 1824.[40]

- **Pension Relief for surviving officers and soldiers of the Revolutionary Army, May 1828.**

In May 1828, Congress passed legislation to benefit the surviving officers and soldiers of the Revolutionary Army. Officers in the Continental Line, who had been entitled to half pay by legislation in October 1780, were now entitled to his *full* pay, according to his rank, for his

---

[36] Ibid., 2–3.
[37] Ibid., 9.
[38] Ibid., 15.
[39] Ibid., 16–17.
[40] Ibid., 19, 21, 22.

natural life. This act was to commence on March 3, 1826. However, the officer's full pay was limited to that of a captain in the Continental line. [41]

- **Pension Relief for widows and orphans of Revolutionary War veterans who died between March 1831 and June 1832. Passed March 1836.**

The first part of this act dealt with officers, non-comms, musicians, or privates in the militia, including rangers, sea fencibles, and volunteers who died in the service or of wounds while in service, since April 1818. If a widow survived of if no widow, any surviving children under sixteen were entitled to receive half the deceased veteran's monthly pay for five years.

The second part of the act provided for special provisions for widows and orphans of revolutionary war veterans who have died since March 1831 and June 1832. Any pension payment owed to the deceased veteran may now be collected by the widow and her surviving children.[42]

The Prince William County Court minutes show one widow who applied under the provisions of this act. In **July 1839**, **Lucy Fortune** applied for coverage for benefits under the provisions of this act. She made her declaration in open court and the Court ordered it and the certificates annexed with it, be certified to the War department.[43]

- **Pension Relief for widows and orphans, 1838–1848.**

In **July 1838**, Congress passed legislation to provide half pay to widows of deceased revolutionary war veterans who had married before January 1, 1794.[44] Fifteen more years were to pass before Congress, in **February 1853**, extended this same benefit to widows who had married after 1800.[45]

Widows in Prince William Court Minutes who applied under this act.

The Prince William Court minutes show three widows who applied for benefits under this act. In **August 1838, Lydia Mills,** the widow of George Mills, a soldier in the Prince William Militia during the Revolution, stated, under oath, that she and George were married prior to January 1, 1794.[46]

In **October 1838, Dekandra Mattingly** also made a declaration to receive pension benefits. She was the widow of John Mattingly, a private in the 3rd Virginia. She, too, had been married to her husband prior to January 1, 1794.[47]

The final widow who applied under this act according to the Prince William County Court Minutes was **Sarah Florence.** She made her declaration in December 1838.[48]

In **March 1843**, Congress extended the widow's half pay pension benefits for an additional year under three previous pension acts: 1832, 1838, and 1842. It also extended the five year half pay pension under the 1836 act for one more year. Then in **June 1844**, they extended half-pay for widows another four years.[49]

---

[41] Ibid., 22–23.
[42] Ibid., 25.
[43] See Chapter 7, Prince William Court Minutes, July 1, 1839 entry.
[44] Rose., 27.
[45] Ibid., 30.
[46] See Chapter 7, Prince William Court Minutes, August 6, 1838, July 4, 1853, August 2, 1853 entries.
[47] Ibid., October 12, 1838, and July 6, 1840
[48] Ibid., December 3, 1838 entry.
[49] Rose., 27.

In **March 1845, March 1847,** and again, in **August 1848,** half pay pensions for widows of naval veterans were extended in increments of five years.[1]

Then in **February 1848**, Congress acted to restrict half pay pensions to widows of revolutionary war veterans. If the widow remarried, her pension was discontinued.

In **July, 1848**, three further restrictions were enacted. Widows of all officers, non-comms, musicians, soldiers, mariners or marines, and Indian spies, who served in the State troops, volunteers, militia, or in the naval service in the revolutionary war were entitled to a pension during their widow hood.

This pension would be equal to the yearly amount their deceased husbands were entitled to under the existing pension law. These pension benefits were to begin in March 1848.

No widow now receiving a pension was entitled to receive a further pension under the provision of this act. Further, no widow married after January 1800 was entitled to receive a pension under this act.[2]

- **The Pension Act of 1853.**

In **February 1853**, Congress approved yet another act to continue half pay to certain widows and orphans. All widows and orphans granted and allowed half pay for five years under the 1848 and 1849 acts were granted a further five years of coverage.

There was one important proviso. If the widow remarried within the five years of coverage, then the benefits were to go to the surviving children under the age of sixteen. Once those children reached their seventeenth birthday, the pension coverage ceased.

The half pay pension was limited to the pay of a lieutenant colonel. This act extended coverage to widows and minor heirs of officers, non-comms, musicians, and privates in the regular service, volunteer service, and militia service in the War of 1812 and the various Indian conflicts since 1790.

Widows of all officers, non-comms, musicians, and privates in the Revolutionary War army, married before January 1800, were also entitled to a pension.[3]

The **Prince William Court Minutes** for **1853–1856** showed **one widow, Lettice Gill,** who applied for a half pay pension under this act. Her declaration was filed with the Court in **October 1854**. She was the widow of John Gill, a private and sergeant in Captain Brent's Company, Colonel Churchill's Regiment in the Virginia Line for eleven months. He had died in 1842 or 1843. She was not married to her husband as Lettice Lee, prior to January 1, 1800.[4]

- **Pension Act of 1855.**

In February 1855, Congress provided pension benefits to widows of officers, non-comms, marines or mariners who served in the Naval service during the revolutionary war who were married after January 1, 1800.[5]

CONCLUSIONS

As can be seen by the foregoing synopsis of federal pension legislation, there were significant gaps in pension coverage for revolutionary war veterans. While disability pensions were enacted early-on for revolutionary war veterans, virtually nothing was done to assist those

---

[1] Ibid., 27, 29–30.
[2] Ibid., 28–29.
[3] Ibid., 30.
[4] See Chapter 7, October 2, 1845 Court Minutes.
[5] Ibid., 30.

veterans who returned home and had trouble making ends meet in a peacetime economy still reeling from the effects of war.

It was not until March 1818 that those veteran's needs were addressed. However, only veterans who had served in the Continental Line were eligible for these benefits. The first General Service pension did not occur until 1832. These benefits were open to veterans in the Continental service, volunteers, and State and militia units.

While half pay pension benefits to widows and orphans of revolutionary war and War of 1812 veterans was sporadic, the very least that can be said is that these women and children were covered in legislation during the nineteenth century.

While this legislation appeared as part of the Congressional resolves and federal law, these laws did not reflect the difficulties in procuring pensions for those who were entitled. To understand those challenges, a closer examination of the actual pension applications would be needed. Here are the names of some of the **3rd Virginia veterans** who applied for federal pensions.

They either lived in Prince William at the time of their enlistment or resided there when they made their declaration: John Athey, Robert Alvey, Spencer Anderson, Moses Daulton, John Davis, William Davis, Benjamin Hamrick, James Holliday, Cornelius Hurley, Thomas Hutchinson, Francis Kendall, William King, John Lary, Charles Lenox, Samuel Love, John Mathews, Vester Moss, John Sidebottom, Joseph Sidebottom, Samuel Stribling, Evan Thomas, John Thomason, William Thurman, and David Wickliffe.[55]

Officers of the 3rd Virginia from Prince William included: William Brent, Philip Richard Francis Lee, Andrew Leitch, William Nelson, Valentine Peyton, and John Tyler.[56]

Some received pensions in a short time. Others waited for years[57] and some, though entitled, *never* received the benefits promised them.[58]

II. FEDERAL BOUNTY LAND LEGISLATION

The Federal government was much more forthcoming with land for its revolutionary war and war of 1812 veterans. The United States Military District was set up in the Northwest Territory and veterans of both wars were given military warrants to be surveyed and located there. Widow's rights to military bounty land was also recognized, albeit belatedly. It was not until 1850 the widows were recognized as being entitled to military land owed their deceased husbands for service.

Revolutionary War Bounty Land Legislation.

The Continental Congress, in a resolution dated September 16, 1776, made grants to officers and soldiers who would continue in Continental service until the close of the war, or were discharged by Congress. Grants would also be given to representatives of officers and soldiers who had died in the war.

The United States was to provide the land. The state was to provide the funding to purchase the land. Grants were made in proportion to rank. A colonel received 500 acres; a lieutenant colonel, 450 acres; a major, 400 acres; a captain, 300 acres, a lieutenant, 200 acres, an ensign, 150 acres; and a non-comm and soldier, 100 acres.

---

[55] Peters, *The Third Virginia Regiment,*, II: 125-128, 189–190, 192, 194–195, 234–235, 241–242, 245, 268–269, 274–275, 284–285, 290–291, 294–295, 302–205, 326–327, 372–383, 392–293, 405–409, 412–414, 437–438.
[56] Ibid., 23–24, 47–63, 79–80, 83, 100.
[57] Ibid., *II*: 48–63.
[58] Ibid., II: 302–305.

In August 1780, the Continental Congress resolved that the 1776 act be extended to include major generals, who would receive 1100 acres; and brigadiers, who would be granted 850 acres.[59]

Revolutionary War Warrants in the United States Military District: Ohio.

In June 1796, Congress set apart a tract of land in the Northwest Territory, now in an area encompassing the state of Ohio. This land was set aside for officers and soldiers serving in the Revolutionary War.

It was known as the U.S. Military District of Ohio and contained some 4,000 square miles, or 2,560,000 acres. It included, in full or in part, the counties of Tuscarawas, Guernsey, Muskingum, Monroe, Coshocton, Holmes, Knox, Licking, Franklin, Delaware, and Lake. Some 14,220 United State bound land warrants from 100 to 1100 acres were issued for location in the U.S. Military District of Ohio.[60]

Revolutionary War Warrants in The United States Military District: Ohio, Indiana, and Illinois.

This military district was exclusively set up for Revolutionary war veterans until the passage of the scrip act of May 1830. After that date, any revolutionary war warrant issued either by the federal government or the Commonwealth of Virginia could be exchanged for scrip and the warrant could be located in Ohio, Indiana, or Illinois. Other U.S. military warrants could also be located in these three states until July 1832 when Congress provided that all the vacant land there would now be open to private sale.[61]

War of 1812 Bounty Land Warrants: Michigan, Illinois, and Louisiana Territory

Congress's act of December 1811 provided bounty land for non-comm and soldiers in the War of 1812. Upon their discharge, these veterans were entitled to 160 acres and an additional cash bounty. The land so designated was to be surveyed and laid off at public expense.

The May 1812 Act set apart some 6,000,000 acres of land in Michigan, Illinois, and Louisiana territories to satisfy the War of 1812 land bounties. Some 28,085 160 acre warrants and 1101 320 acre warrants were surrendered for location in these states by War of 1812 veterans.[62]

Other U.S. military bounty land warrants for U.S. public lands

In February 1847, September 1850, March 1852, and March 1855, the Congress passed legislation to provide for issuing and locating military bounty land warrants on any public lands subject to appropriation. The acreage in these warrants depended on the rank of the veteran and varied from forty to 160 acres. In February 1847, 7,585 warrants of 40 acres were issued along with 80,689 warrants for 160 acres.

The September 1850 act saw 103,978 warrants for forty acres, 57,715 warrants for eighty acres, and 27,450 warrants for 160 acres. In the March 1852 act, 9,070 forty acre warrants were issued. In addition, 1,699 eighty acre warrants, and 1,222 warrants for 160 acres were given out. Finally, the March 1855 act granted 542 warrants for forty acre parcels, 359 warrants for sixty

---

[59] Gauis Marcus Brumbaugh, *Revolutionary War Records: Virginia* (1936; reprint, Baltimore: Genealogical Publishing Company, 1995), v.
[60] Ibid., v-vi.
[61] Ibid., vi.
[62] Ibid..

acres, 52,000 warrants for 80 acres, 100,000 warrants for 120 acres, and 115,785 warrants for 160 acres.[63]

Military Land Warrants issued to heirs of Revolutionary War veterans in the Prince William Court Minutes.

The bulk of entries in the Court Minutes from 1830 through the 1856 minutes dealt with the certification of heirs at law to veterans of the revolutionary war. Unfortunately, it can not be stated with any certainty whether bounty land entitlement was that which was part of the federal legislation or that which was part of the State military bounty land legislation.

THE STATE'S RESPONSE: VIRGINIA'S
PENSION AND MILITARY LAND WARRANTS

I. VIRGINIA PENSION LEGISLATION

Background

In the spring of 1775 Virginia was embroiled in an altercation with their royal governor, John Murray, Lord Dunmore. The altercation quickly became much more than that when the governor removed gunpowder from the magazine at Williamsburg in April, 1775. The governor had ordered the removal hoping to put an end to any armed resistance to British policies in Virginia.

This, of course, brought about an immediate chorus of disapproval from the colonists. The disapproval quickly moved from voiced concern to military action. Independent militia companies, authorized by the 2nd Virginia Convention, including those of Prince William, under the command of William Grayson,[64] prepared to march on the capital. The Prince William company, along with companies from Fredericksburg and Fairfax, turned back only when George Washington persuaded them to do so.[65]

By the end of May, things had quieted down a bit. Dunmore realized he was not in a position to fight without British help, who were in New England reeling from Concord and Lexington, while the Virginia patriot leadership realized that their militia forces were in no condition to fight the British.

Then in June, Dunmore made the decision to leave Williamsburg with his family for the safety of the British Navy. He had not been successful in arousing the loyalists to come to his aid, especially after he promised Virginia's slaves their freedom if they enlisted in his cause.[66]

- ♦ **Pensions for wounded and disabled veterans, July 1775**

In July, the Virginia Assembly appointed a committee of safety, who were charged with putting together the defense of the colony. The assembly passed legislation that authorized two regiments of regular troops and fifteen battalions of minute men to defend the colony against invasion and insurrection.[67]

As part of this legislation, "for the greater encouragement and farther promotion of the service," pensions were promised to men who enlisted as a result of the legislation. Pensions

---

[63] Ibid., vii. See also Kenneth Hawkins, *Research in the Land Entry Files of the General Land Office, Record Group 49* (Washington: National Archives and Records Administration, 2001), 11.
[64] Sanchez-Saavedra, 9.
[65] Ibid., 8–9, 11.
[66] *JCC*, 3, image 403 (http://www.loc.gov/ammem/amlawlwjclink.html).
[67] M. Lee Minis, *The First Virginia Regiment of Foot, 1775–1783* (Westminster: Willow Bend Books, 1998), 3.

were to be given to veterans "so maimed or disabled as to be rendered incapable of maintaining [themselves]. Upon their discharge, they were to "be supported at the expense of the publick." [68]

Pensions for a Prince William disabled veteran in the Court Minutes: Charles Lenox.
The Prince William Court Minutes showed at least one wounded veteran who took advantage of this legislation. In August 1779, **Charles Lenox**, a wounded soldier, appeared in Court and exhibited his wound. The Court was satisfied that he was "unable to labour and [became] properly a pensioner to be provided for, for life, as a wounded soldier of the Continental Army by the State of Virginia. The Court ordered that the £30 advanced by Captain Carr for his relief be refunded to the Captain and be deducted from Lenox's pension allowance. The Court ordered all of this to be certified to the Governor." He appeared in Court again in May 1783 when the Court certified that he was a former soldier in the Continental Army and had been wounded in the knee.[69]

♦ **Relief and support of distressed wives and families of soldiers enlisted in service of Commonwealth extended to families of volunteer soldiers, May 1778.**
This provision was part of an act to raise volunteers to join the Grand Army under General Washington. The act was passed in response to Continental requests for further troops for the main army. Four additional volunteer battalions were authorized by the General Assembly. In August 1778, however, Congress advised the commonwealth that these troops would not be needed and the partially formed units were then disbanded.[70]

While no repeal of this legislation was found, there did not appear to be any other legislation in Henings that touched on the support for wives, parents, and families of soldiers until October 1779.

The Prince William Court minutes from 1778–1784 show that wives, widows, parents, and families were indeed given support from the county beginning in July 1778. Their pages are filled with illustrations of this relief and support.

Families allowed support in Prince William Court Minutes
In **July 1778, Ruth Holifield, the widow of Daniel Holifield**, a 3rd Virginia soldier who had died in the service, petitioned the county for relief. She was allowed £10 for support for herself and her child. The Court ordered this certified and sent to the Treasurer.[71]

Nancy Davis, the wife of Thomas Davis, a soldier in the Continental Army, was allowed £20 for her support and support for her four children.[72] **Ann Cornwell, the widow of John Cornwell**, was granted £12 to support herself and her two small children.[73] The justices granted John Crook £5. He was an "aged man" and had lost his son "in the service of his country."

Sarah Grant was allowed the same amount for her support. Her husband was a soldier in the Continental service.[74]

Samuel King was allowed £5 towards his support. He, too, had two sons in the Continental Army. The Court further ruled that he was to be exempted from future public, county, or parish

---

[68] Hening, "Ordinances of the Convention," *Statutes At Large,* July 1775 (http://vagenweb.org/hening/vol09-01.htm) 9: 14.
[69] See Chapter 5, August 1779 and May 1783 Court entry.
[70] Sanchez-Saavedra, 89.
[71] See Chapter 5, July 1778 Court entry.
[72] Ibid.
[73] Ibid.
[74] Ibid., October 1778 Court entries

levies. **Mary Sidebottom** was allowed £3 for her support because her sons were in the Continental Army.[75]

In **February 1779**, Bertrand Ewell petitioned the justices on behalf of the **two children of John Gunyon**, who died as a soldier in the Service. He was allowed £40 for their support. **Thomas Hines,** another 3rd Virginia soldier, petitioned the County for support of his wife and child. He was allowed £10 for their support.[76]

♦ **Relief provided for widows of officers and soldiers of the army or navy raised by any act of the General Assembly, October 1778.**

Buried within an act to establish a board of auditors for public accounts were provisions laying out the responsibility of public auditors. Among those responsibilities detailed by this act, was one that gave the auditors the authority to allow annual pensions to officers and soldiers of the army or navy raised by any act of the General Assembly and disabled in the service and to widows of those officers or soldiers killed by the enemy.[77]

♦ **Support for wives, parents, and families were repealed in favor of legislation in favor of those in indigent circumstances, October 1779.**

In **October 1779**, the General Assembly repealed the previous acts empowering the county courts to provide for the support of wives, parents, and families of soldier of the state in service to the commonwealth or to the U.S.

Instead, the legislature authorized county courts to grant allowances to wives, parents, and families of soldiers then in service, on proof that they were so poor they could not "maintain themselves." The allowance was not to "exceed one barrel of corn and fifty pounds of nett pork for each person, annually."[78]

Families allowed support in Prince William Court Minutes

In **May 1780**, the Court saw to it that **Jane Bradley,** wife of Richard Bradley, a soldier in the Continental Army, received a barrel of corn valued at £30, for the support of herself and her child. The Court ordered this to be certified to the auditors. **Ann Brent, widow of Willoughby Brent,** a 3rd Virginia soldier who died in the Continental Army, was also given a barrel of corn, with the same value.[79]

In **September 1780, Elizabeth McGinnis,** wife of Peter McGinnis, a soldier in the Continental Army, was allowed £120 for three barrels of corn and £80 for 150 pounds of pork for the support of herself and her two small children. The Court ordered this to be certified to the auditors.[80]

♦ **Pension Act of 1782, October 1782.**

In October 1782, the General Assembly passed legislation for the examination of wounded and disabled pensioners by the County Courts. In April and May 1783, Courts were to enquire into "the condition and state of bodily ability of all pensioners and persons receiving an annual

---

[75] Ibid., November 1778 Court entries.
[76] Ibid., February 1779 Court entries.
[77] Hening, "An act for establishing a board of auditors for public accounts," October 1778, 10: 537.
[78] Hening, "Act to repeal ... acts of assembly which empower county courts to [provide] for support of wives, parents, and families of soldiers ..." *Henings Statutes at Large,* October 1779 (http://vagenweb.org/hening/vol10-10.htm), 10: 212.
[79] See Chapter Chapter 5, May 1780 Court entries.
[80] See Chapter 5, September 1780 Court entry.

allowance" from Virginia in consequence of their wounds. The Court was then to report the results of these enquiries to the state legislature.[81]

Wounded and disabled veterans in the Prince William Court Minutes: Charles Lenox and John King.

In **May 1783**, three wounded veterans appeared in Court to present evidence of their wounds. **Charles Lenox,** formerly a soldier in the Continental Army, appeared, having been "wounded in the knee.[82] **John King,** formerly a soldier in the American Army, **having lost both his arms,** appeared in Court. The Court ordered this to be certified.[83] **Alexander Jones**, formerly a soldier in the American Army, appeared in Court and, "being **wounded in the knee**," the Court ordered that to be certified.[84]

♦ **Legislation to provide for allowances to wives, parents, and families of poor soldiers, May 1782.**

This legislation was part of tax legislation passed in May 1782. It was passed because the provisions in the October 1779 act had "become inconvenient." To remedy this, the General Assembly prescribed a multi-step process for collection. The allowances were now to be paid by any specific tax commissioner in the county, upon application from wives, parents, or families of poor soldiers.

The applicants must have produced a copy of the order for the allowance witnessed by the clerk of the county. The clerk was directed to grant this order without charging a fee for it. Then the commissioner would pay the allowance from his accounts.

The governor had the authority to examine the charges for expenses incurred in executing the orders for the allowance.[85]

♦ **Various pension acts extend and amend pension relief to invalid veterans 1784–1786.**

The General Assembly passed various pension acts to continue and amend invalid pensions. In **October 1784**, the legislature continued the Pension Act of 1784 for three more years. The governor was authorized to place all wounded or disabled regular soldiers and militia officers and soldiers who applied on a pension list.

The Courts were to transmit their opinion of the wounds of soldiers to the governor instead of the legislature. The governor was then authorized to continue or discontinue the allowances.[86]

In **October 1785**, the legislature amended and reformed the previous pension acts. This was due to Congressional legislation that recommended the state make provisions for their officers, soldiers, and seaman who were disabled in the service of the United States. The legislature decided that the previous State acts were "very defective." So they reformed the legislation to bring the state into compliance with the Congressional directives.

---

[81] Hening, "An Act concerning Pensioners," *Henings Statutes at Large*, October 1782 (http://vagenweb.org/hening/vol11-07.htm), 11: 146–147.

[82] Chapter 5, May 1783 Court entry.

[83] See Chapter 5, May 1783 Court entry. For John King's story of his service and how he lost both arms, see Peters, *History of the Third Virginia*, II: 274, and Virginia Genealogical Society, *Virginia Revolutionary War State Pensions* (1980; reprint, Greenville: Southern Historical Press, 1992), 66.

[84] See Chapter 5, May 1783 Court entry.

[85] Henings, "Act for … paying allowances to wives, parents, and families of soldiers …" *Henings Statutes at Large,* May 1782 (http://vagenweb.org/hening/vol11-01.htm), 11: 11.

[86] Ibid., "An Act for further continuing the act entitled An Act concerning Pensioners," October 1784   11: 446–447.

The auditors of public accounts were authorized to keep a book, updated every January, of a complete list of all wounded or disabled officers, soldiers, and seamen, who served in the army or navy of the U.S., or in the militia in service to the US. Their names, pay, age, regiment, corps or ship, along with their disability were to appear on the list.

To be eligible, applicants must be so disabled that he was incapable of military duty or of obtaining a livelihood by labor. He was required to produce a certificate from a commanding officer or surgeon setting forth his disability.

All commissioned officers in the army, navy, or militia, disabled in the service of the U.S., or of the commonwealth who fell into the above description, were to be allowed a yearly pension equal to half their pay. Those who were not that disabled were allowed a pension corresponding to the degree of their disability.

Non-commissioned officers and privates who were so disabled they could not perform military duty or work for a living were to be allowed a sum up to $5.00 per month and no more. Non-comms and privates who were not disabled to that degree were allowed a pension according to the degree of their disability.

The Governor, with the advice of council, was authorized to examine all claimants for pensions. If he found that applicant to be an invalid and disabled while in service, he was to present him with a pension certificate specifying the regiment, corps or vessel to which he belonged and whether he was in the service or the U.S. or of the commonwealth when he was disabled. The certificate was also to state the degree of disability and the pensioner's pay.

A duplicate of the certificate was to be transmitted to the auditors of public accounts who would then place the invalid on the pension list. Then, a six step process was initiated to carry out for the payment of the pension on the county level.

First, the auditors transmitted the general list of pensioners to the clerks of the court. Secondly, every pensioner, in each May or June of the year, was to apply in person to the court in the county in which he resided. Third, he had to show the certificate and swear, on oath, that he was the person named in the certificate. If an orphan, then his or her guardian was required to do this.

Fourth, the Court was to compare the certificate to the auditor's list of pensioners, and if correct, order it recorded. Fifth, the Court was then to direct the sheriff to pay the pension. The claimant was to be given a copy of that order. Sixth, the sheriff, once the payment had been made, was to take a receipt of the order and was then entitled to credit in the settlement of his account with the auditors.

In order to protect against pension fraud, certificates were to be countersigned by the governor. The governor was also authorized to grant certificates for admission onto the pension list for widows and orphans of all officers, soldiers, and seamen, who died in the service of the U.S., or of this commonwealth in the army, navy, or militia. The widows and/or orphans must have certificates issued by their local county court. However, there was a proviso: "No allowances shall be made except indigency of circumstances shall render the same necessary." To that end, all invalid's widows and orphans on the pension list may have their allowances adapted to the degree of disability. They may also be removed from the list when their allowances "become no longer requisite."

All pensioners were to undergo a reexamination of their disability whenever the governor directed. On a reexamination, the governor was authorized to either raise or lower the allowance according to the situation. If the governor thought the allowance no longer applied, he had the authority to remove the pensioner from the pension list.

Auditors were then to make up accounts of all payments made to invalids for their pensions to the end of the year which ought to be charged to the United States. They were to charge those amounts against the quotas of the years the pensions had already been made. No sum greater than half the pay of any soldier was to be charged to the account of the United States.[87]

In **October 1786**, the General Assembly passed another act dealing with pensioners. In this act, the auditor of public accounts was authorized to send a general list of pensioners in January to the clerks of the county courts in the commonwealth.

Pensioners had February or April to apply in person in his local court, exhibit his certificate, and swear, by oath, that he was the claimant to whom the certificate was granted. If an orphan, then his or her guardian was to follow the same steps. If the claimant was unable to attend, he or she could make the same oath before a magistrate.

Then the court was to compare the certificate with the auditor's list, and if correct, order it to be recorded. The court would then direct the sheriff to pay the pension. A copy of this order was to be given to the pensioner. When the sheriff paid the pension amount, he was to take the receipt of the order and then be entitled for credit in the settlement of his accounts with the auditor.[88]

II. VIRGINIA'S BOUNTY LAND LEGISLATION

Background

Land Grants and Bounty Warrants were first offered to men to encourage enlistments. As a soldier completed his agreed upon service, usually three years or for the war, he was issued a warrant for at least 100 acres of land, depending on his rank.

Bounty Warrants were issued all through the course of the war and then as late as 1850. During this seventy year period, applications often named children and grandchildren of the veteran and give information about their residence. While an number of veterans lived to be quite elderly and may have been living somewhere in the Northwest territory, they usually remembered who enlisted them, where and when they enlisted, and what their regiment was.

By 1850, Virginia veterans were applying from all over the east coast, the south, Kentucky and Tennessee, and the Old Northwest Territory.[89]

♦ **State Bounty land legislation, in October 1776 referred to federal land bounties.**

In October 1776, the Continental Congress thought it was necessary to augment Continental forces to eighty regiments from the different states. These battalions were to be enlisted for the war. Fifteen of the eighty were to come from the commonwealth.

In order to encourage enlistment, among the provision in this package was one relating to a land bounty. Congress, by resolution, had provided land at the close of the war or whenever discharged, to officers and soldiers in the Continental service, or their representatives, if killed by the enemy.

Every non-commissioned officer or soldier was to receive 100 acres; every ensign, 150 acres; every lieutenant, 200 acres; every captain, 300 acres, every major, 400 acres; every lieutenant colonel, 450 acres; and every colonel, 500 acres.[90]

---

[87] Ibid., "An Act to amend the act concerning pensioners," October 1785, 12: 102–106.

[88] Ibid., "An act to amend the act entitled An act to amend the act concerning pensioners," October 1786, 12: 276–277.

[89] William Lindsay Hopkins, *Virginia Revolutionary War Land Grant Claims, 1783–1850 (Rejected)* (Richmond: William L. Hopkins, 1988), i.

[90] Hening, "An act for raising six additional battalions of infantry on the continental establishment," October, 1776, 9: 179.

- **Bounty land legislation, October 1776.**

Later that month, the General Assembly passed an act to amend the act for raising six additional regiments of infantry on the continental establishment. The assembly had already passed the original act to raise six additional regiments of infantry for continental service, together with the nine others, formerly raised by the commonwealth which were directed to be enlisted for service during the war.

Then the Continental Congress, since the above act was passed, resolved that all non-commissioned officers and soldiers who do not enlist for the war but for three years instead, would be entitled to the same bounty and pay as those who enlisted for the war. However, they would *not* be entitled to the 100 acres of land. That land was to be granted to only those who enlisted without a time limitation.[91]

- **Bounty land legislation, October 1778.**

In October 1778, the General Assembly passed legislation for the speedy recruitment of the Virginia regiments on the continental establishment. Among the provisions in the act was one for bounty land for each person who enlisted for three years. They would be entitled to a bounty of $400.00 along with the continental bounty of lands.[92]

The Journal of the House of Delegates for October 1778 also referred to bounty land for officers and soldiers with three years service and recommended setting off a tract of land for officers and soldiers of the Virginia line that lay between the Green and the Ohio.

> Mr. Lyne from the committee to whom the memorial of the general and field officers was referred, reported that the committee had, according to order, had the same under their consideration, and had agreed upon a report...
>
> *Resolved*, That it is the opinion of this committee, that a certain tract of country to be bounded by the Green river and the south east course from the head thereof to the Cumberland mountains, with the said mountains to the Carolina line, with the Carolina line to the Cherokee or Tennessee river, with the said river to the Ohio river, and with the Ohio river to the said Green river, ought to be reserved for supplying the officers and soldiers in the Virginia line with the respective proportions of land which have been or may be assigned to them by the general assembly, saving and reserving the land granted to Richard Henderson and company, and their legal rights to such person as have heretofore actually located land and settled thereon within the bounds aforesaid.
>
> *Resolved*, That it is in the opinion of this committee that the said officers and soldiers, or any of them, may be at liberty to locate their proportions of land on any other vacant and ungranted lands within this commonwealth.
>
> *Resolved*, That it is the opinion of this committee, that the allowance of two hundred acres of land over and above the continental bounty, be given to all the soldiers in the Virginia line, who have heretofore enlisted or shall hereafter enlist for the terms of three years or during the war.[93]

The Senate agreed to this resolution for reserving certain lands on the waters of the Ohio and the Green for the use of officers and soldiers, by amendment and sent it to the House. The House considered and passed it.[94]

---

[91] Hening, "An Act to amend the act for raising six additional battalions of infantry on the continental establishment," October 1776, 9: 214.

[92] Ibid., "An act for speedily recruiting the Virginia regiments on continental establishment," October 1778, 9: 588-589.

[93] Ibid., "from the Journal of the House of Delegates, October 1778, six pages from the end—the volume not being paged." May 1779, 10:55-57.

[94] Ibid., from the "Journal of the House of Delegates, October 1768, 3rd and 4th pages from the end," May 1779.

* **Bounty land legislation, May 1779.**

In **May 1779**, the Virginia legislature tackled the challenges associated with declining enlistments in Continental army, navy, state regiments, and militia. Additional bounties were given to soldiers who reenlisted in the service.

In addition, every soldier, sailor, and marine who continued in service, was, at the end of the war, entitled to a grant of 100 acres of any unappropriated land within the commonwealth. Every officer was entitled to a grant equal in quantity to land allowed officers of the same rank in the Virginia regiments on continental establishment. No purchase money would be required.[95]

In the same act, the General Assembly provided bounty land for the men in Colonel George Rogers Clarke's men who enlisted in Colonel George Rogers Clarke's Illinois Regiment, Virginia State Forces.

Men who enlisted to serve for the war in Clarke's Illinois Regiment were also entitled, to bounty money, and at the end of the war, to a bounty of 200 acres of unappropriated lands in Virginia. Those who enlisted for two year received 100 acres of unappropriated land in the commonwealth.[96]

Anyone could acquire title to as much waste land as they desire to purchase, conditioned on paying £40 for every 100 acres and on obtaining a certificate from the public auditors. Once title has been obtained and that certificate has been placed in the land office, the register would then grant a printed warrant under his and seal, specifying the quantity of land and the rights upon which it is due. A surveyor was authorized to lay off and survey the land. Warrants were good and valid until executed by the actual survey or exchanged. [97]

* **Bounty land legislation, October 1779.**

In October 1779, the General Assembly passed an act which provided bounty land to chaplains, surgeons, and surgeon's mates of regiment raised by the state and for those raised for the continental establishment.

The officers had to serve for three years or the war to be eligible. They were entitled to the same quantity of land allowed by law to commissioned officer receiving the same pay and rations.[98]

* **Bounty land legislation, November 1781.**

In November 1781, the General Assembly passed bounty land legislation that extended bounty land given to officers and soldiers of the Virginia line in continental service and regulations for surveying it to state officers, state infantry, and officers and soldiers of the state cavalry. Officers and seamen of the state navy were also entitled to the same grants.[99]

* **Bounty land legislation, May 1782.**

In May 1782, buried in an act for providing funds for the redemption of certificates granted officers and soldiers raised by the state, were provisions for bounty land for three years service for officers and soldiers. While these veterans could not have been cashiered or superceded, they did have an absolute and unconditional title to their land.

---

[95] Ibid., "An act concerning officers, soldiers, sailors, and marines," May 1779. 10: 23–24.
[96] Ibid., 10: 26–27.
[97] Ibid., "An act for establishing a Land office ..." May 1779, 10: 50–65. This act is much too complex to abstract here. See Hening for the recitation of the complete act.
[98] Ibid., "An act for giving a bounty of lands to chaplains, surgeons, and surgeon's mates ..." October 1779, 10: 141.
[99] Ibid., "An act to adjust and regulate the pay and accounts of officers and soldiers of the Virginia line on continental establishment ..." November 1781, 10: 467.

For every year beyond a term of six years, an officer or soldier was entitled to a one sixth part, dependent on his rank, in addition to the quantity he had already received. Officers and soldiers were to procure their land from the register of the land office.[100]

Veteran's representatives claiming bounty land in the Prince William Minutes 1778–1784

In **August 1783**, Valentine Peyton, the heir at law of **George Peyton decd.**, a late ensign in the 3rd Virginia, appeared in Court and claimed his right to the lands promised by an Act of Assembly to the officers and soldiers of the Virginia line. George Peyton died in 1777 while in Continental service.

As the heir at law of **Robert Peyton**, another deceased officer of the 3rd Virginia, Valentine Peyton claimed *his* right to lands promised by the General Assembly. Robert Peyton was killed at the Battle of Brandywine in September 1777 while he was in the . The Court ordered both of these actions certified.[101]

In **March 1784**, The Court ordered it certified that **William Davis** was entitled to the bounty in land due his brother **John Davis** who had enlisted in the Virginia Continental Line for three years and died in the service.[102]

In the same month, the Court ordered it certified that **Joseph Blanchett** was the heir at law and entitled to the bounty lands due his brother **William Blanchett** who enlisted in the Virginia Continental Line for three years and died in the service.[103]

CONCLUSIONS

This overview of Pension and Bounty land legislation for both the Federal and state legislation illustrates the complexity of these laws. For the most part, state and federal pensions were limited to disability ones. The state did not enact any pension legislation for general service.

Bounty land legislation by both state and federal statutes did set up differing tracts of land for veterans who had to have served a minimum of three years. The federal bounty lands were located in the Northwest Territory. The commonwealth's bounty lands were located among the unappropriated lands in Virginia and in the district between the Green and Ohio rivers.

---

[100] Ibid., "An act or providing funds for the redemption of certificates granted officers and soldiers raised by the state," May 1782, 11: 83–84.
[101] See Chapter 5, August 1783 Court entry.
[102] Ibid., March 1784 Court entry.
[103] Ibid.

The Pension Act of 1848

9 (Stat.) 265 [&266].
THIRTIETH CONGRESS. Sess. I. 1848.

Chap. CXX. *An Act for the Relief of certain surviving Widows of Officers and Soldiers of the Revolutionary Army.*

Be it enacted ... That the widows of all officers, non-commissioned officers, musicians, soldiers, mariners, or marines, and Indian spies, who shall have served in the Continental line, State troops, volunteers, militia, or in the naval service, in the revolutionary war with Great Britain, shall be entitled to a pension during such widowhood, of equal amount per annum that their husbands would be entitled to, if living, under existing pension laws; to commence on the fourth day of March eighteen hundred and forty-eight, and to be paid in the same manner that other pensions are paid to widows.

But no widow now receiving a pension shall be entitled to receive a further pension under the provisions of this act. No widow married after the first day of January, one thousand eighteen hundred, shall be entitled to receive a pension under this act.

Sec. 2. *And be it further enacted*, That any pledge, mortgage, sale, assignment, or transfer of any right, claim, or interest, in any way granted by this act, shall be utterly void and of no effect, nor shall the annuities or pension granted by this act be liable to attachment, levy, or seizure by any process of law or equity, but shall enure wholly to the personal benefit of the pensioner or annuitant entitled to the same.

The same rules of evidence, regulations, and prescriptions shall apply and govern the Commissioner of pensions and pension agents under this act as now prevail under existing pension laws which relate to widows of revolutionary officers and soldiers

Sec. 3. *And be it further enacted*, That this act shall take effect immediately.

Approved July 29, 1848.

The Pension Act of 1853

10 (Stat.) 154
THIRTY-SECOND CONGRESS. Sess. II. 1853.

Chap. XLI. *An Act to continue Half-Pay to certain Widows and Orphans.*

[Provides that all widows and orphans that were granted and allowed five years half-pay by the provisions of acts of July 21, 1848, February 22, 1849, are granted a continuance of said half-pay, "under like limitations and restrictions, for a further period of five years to commence at the expiration of the half-pay provided for by the aforesaid acts ..."]

Provided however, That in case of the death or marriage of such widow before the expiration of said term of five years, the half-pay for the remainder of the term shall go to the child or children of the deceased officer or soldier, whilst under the age of sixteen years.

In like manner, the child or children of such deceased when there is no widow, shall be paid no longer than while there is a child or children under the age aforesaid.

Provided further, That the act approved the twenty-second of February, eighteen hundred and forty-nine, "granting five years half-pay to certain widows and orphans of officers, non-commissioned officers, musicians, and privates, both regular and volunteers," be so extended and construed as to embrace the widows and min or heirs of the officers, non-commissioned officers, musicians, and privates of the regulars, militia, and volunteers of the war of eighteen hundred and twelve, and of the various Indian war since seventeen hundred and ninety."

Sec. 2. *An be it further enacted*, That the widows of all officers, non-commissioned officers, musicians, and privates of the Revolutionary army, who were married subsequent to January, anno Domini eighteen hundred, shall be entitled to a pension in the same manner as those who were married before that date.

Approved February 3, 1853.

Source: Christine Rose, *Military Pension Laws 1776–1858, 28–29. 30.*

Chapter 9

THE PENSIONERS

MILITARY RECORDS FROM PRINCE WILLIAM COUNTY VIRGINIA ORDER BOOKS 1833–1850, 1853–1856

Prince William County Virginia Court Order Book 1833-1835

June 3, 1833 Court, pg. 5.
A **Declaration of John Bell**[1], in order to obtain the benefit of the provision made by the act of Congress passed June 7th 1832 was presented to the court, sworn to and ordered to be certified.
Ordered to be certified that it was proven to the entire satisfaction of the Court by the testimony and examination of Hugh Davis on oath, that William Davis was sole heir at law of **John Davis**,[2] **who died in the service of the United States during the Revolutionary War,**, and also that John Davis died intestate and further it was proven by Hugh Davis that the land due John Davis has never been drawn.

July 1, 1833 Court, pg. 28.
The Court ... certifies, by the oath of witnesses examined in open Court, that **Thomas White**[3], formerly a resident of Prince William County, **entered the service as a Sergeant in the first Virginia Regiment, State line in the Revolutionary War in the month of November... 1776** and acted as a Sergeant until he was promoted to a Lieutenancy in that Regiment. That Thomas White served as sergeant and lieutenant from the time of his entering the service until 1780 when he was still in the service.
That he, after the close of the war, returned to Prince William, near Greenwich where he remained for a short period and then he removed to the southern part of the State of Virginia.

July 1, 1833 Court, pg. 30.
Satisfactory evidence having been adduced to the Court that Nathl Tyler, **heir of John Tyler**[4] **decd** and brother of John Tyler, Charles Tyler, William Tyler and George G. Tyler decd and also brother

---

[1] Peters, *Neglected and Forgotten*, 41. John Bell filed a pension declaration in November 1819 in Fauquier County. He was fifty-eight at the time and applied under the March 1818 Pension Act. He had enlisted in January 1782, under Captain Henry Margaram, a Conductor of the Artillery, for a year as a Captain.
Captain Margarum was under the command of Colonel Wadsworth and Carter, who were responsible for supervising the transportation of the artillery from York, Virginia to Boston. Captain Bell and his company belonged to Rochambeau's Brigade. He served for two months longer than his enlistment so that sometime in early 1783 he received a written discharge from Major Aliott, at Sheffield, Massachusetts.
In December 1820, he made another declaration in Fauquier, now fifty-nine years. He was a cooper by trade but unable to work because he was crippled when a wagon ran over and disabled him. At the time he did not have a wife living, although he had four children: James, age twelve; Landy, age fourteen; Moses, age sixteen; and Mary Ann, age eighteen. His sons had been bound out to trades. His daughter lived with Landy Calvert. See Peters, *Lost and Forgotten*, 61.

[2] This *may* be the John Davis who died in March 1777, as a private in Captain John Peyton's company of the 3rd Virginia Regiment. See Peters, *The Third Virginia Regiment of Foot, 1776–1778*, II: 192.

[3] Heitman, 587. Thomas White was a corporal and sergeant in the 1st Virginia State Regiment in March 1777. He was promoted to 2nd Lieutenant in December 1778 and to 1st Lieutenant in August 1779. He served until January 1783. He died in 1839.

[4] Heitman, 553. This was Ensign John Tyler, of the 3rd Virginia who died in January 1777. His heirs were eligible for bounty land because Ensign Tyler died while in service.

of Sally Linton, formerly Sally Tyler, departed this life previous to the year 1796. On the motion of Henry B. Tyler, it is ordered that the same be spread on the records of this court.

July 1, 1833 Court, pgs 32-33.

The Court ... order[s] and authorizes Henry Taliaferro as Gd^n of his infant daughter Helen Taliaferro, by his wife Mary Ann Taliaferro, formerly Mary Ann Tyler, to sell or transfer all right, title and interest of his war in and to a **military land bounty warrant which issued to Nathl Tyler decd from the land office of V^a on the 1st day of July 1784 for 2666 2/3 acres of No. 3301 for the revolutionary service of John Tyler decd, a Lieutenant of the Continental Line for three years.**

December 2, 1833 Court, pg. 77.

Satisfactory evidence is this day adduced before the Court now sitting that **William[5] and Douglas Conner[6] (brothers)** enlisted under **Captn Andrew Leach[7] in the Continental Army for 3 years in the early part of the year 1776, and marched to the north and joined the 3^d Virginia Regiment. Douglas died in the army, intestate without issue.**

William Conner returned in 1779, after the expiration of his term of enlistment, **and married and left** as issue **an only son Douglas Conner Jr., the present** applicant now before the Court, and who the Court is perfectly satisfied is sole heir and only heir at law of his father Wm. Conner and of his uncle Douglas Conner who died in the service...

The court have no hesitation in saying they are convinced that ... Douglas Jr. is only and sole heir at law of his father and Uncle and is entitled to the Bounty in land due each of them and also that William Conner died intestate.

Satisfactory evidence is this day adduced before the Court now sitting that **Wm. Dowell[8] enlisted under Capt. George McCormick[9] in the Continental Army in 1776 for 3 years**
That he served out his term with fidelity and bravery and returned to Prince William and is since dead, leaving no legitimate (if any) issue. **He died intestate.**

Jeremiah Dowell, his only brother and heir and sole heir at law (late of our county) **is dead, leaving three sons, Wm. D, James** and **Jesse Dowell**, all of our county, who are their heir and ... **entitled to the Bounty in land owed William Dowell for his services in the Continental army.**

Satisfactory proof is this day adduced on oath in open court that **Wm. Garner, George Garner, Hezekiah Garner, Theodosia Garner (now the wife of Silas Beach)** and **Elizabeth Garner (now the wife of John Dyson Mills)** are the **only surviving children** of **Wm Garner decd, a soldier of the Revolution[10]**—and **are** the only and **sole heirs at law** of ... Wm. Garner and also that ... **William Garner died intestate.**

---

[5] Peters, *The Third Virginia Regiment*, II: 178. William Conner enlisted in February 1776 as a private for two years in Captain John Peyton's company. He was discharged in January, 1778.

[6] Ibid., II: 177. Douglas Conner was a corporal in Captain John Peyton's company from January 1, 1777 until his death on January 15th 1778.

[7] Andrew Leitch was an early captain in the 3rd Virginia. He was promoted out of the regiment and died in early October 1776 from lockjaw, as a result of wounds suffered at Harlem Heights in September 1776. John Peyton, his lieutenant was promoted to the captaincy of his company.

[8] William Dowell served as a private and corporal in Captain George McCarmick's 13th Virginia company from January 1777 until September 1778. He was promoted to corporal in October 1777. In October 1778, he was in Colonel Campbell's 9th Virginia and remained there through December 1779. He spent that time at Fort Pitt. He was promoted to sergeant in August 1779. See NARA, *William Dowell's compiled service records*, M 881 MR (http://www.footnote.com), 2–24, Images 23092605 to 23092658 (Accessed July 2, 2008).

[9] Heitman, 366. George *McCormick* was commissioned as a captain in the 13th Virginia in December 1776. He retired from the Army in September 1778. He died in January 1820.

[10] A William Garner assigned a bounty land warrant no. 12147–100, issued on April 13, 1791, to James Reynolds, for Garner's service as a private in Colonel Henry Lee's Legion. This William Garner may be the same veteran of that name whose heirs came into the Prince William court to be certified as such in the above entry. See Virgil D. White,

Satisfactory proof is this day adduced on oath in open Court that **Thompson Hutchison** is the only child of **Thos Hutchison** decd a **Sergeant in Captn Thomas Ewell's Company,**[11] **1st V^a Reg^t, State line, George Gibson, Colonel** and is the only and sole Heir at Law of his father and that Thos Hutchison died intestate.

Satisfactory proof is this day adduced on Oath in open court, that **Elizabeth Hamil**, widow of John Hamil decd, **is the only surviving child of Wm. McIntosh**[12] **decd, a soldier in the Revolution in Captain Thomas Ewell's Company of the 1st V^a Regt, State line, George Gibson Col; and is the only and sole heir at law of her father Wm. McIntosh decd. William [McIntosh] died intestate.**

December 2, 1833 Court, pg. 78.

On due application made to the Court and upon satisfactory evidence appearing to them, it is ordered to be certified that **Peggy Abel, formerly Peggy Green and Sally Rolls, formerly Sally Green** of Prince Wm County V^a and **Elijah Green** of the District of Columbia are the only **surviving heirs** of **Elijah Green decd,**[13] **late of Prince William and a United States pensioner at the time of his death.**

December 2, 1833 Court, pg. 80.

Satisfactory evidence is this day adduced in open court that **Capt. Thos Ewell**[14] **of the 1st V^a Regiment, State line, Col. Geo. Gibson's reg^t. He continued in the service until the close of the War and that he died in the Town of Dumfries V^a ... in 1784 or 1785.**

February 3, 1834 Court, pg. 96.

On the motion of Jesse E. Weems, it is ordered to be certified that it was proved to the satisfaction of this court, that **Thos Ewell decd was a Captain in the first Virginia State Regiment, commanded by Col. Geo. Gibson during the Revolutionary war, and that he served until the close of the war.**

He died in the Town of Dumfries in [Prince William] County... in ... 1784, having previously duly constituted & appointed his Father Bertrand Ewell & his mother & Brothers & Sisters his only heirs & devisees.

It is further certified that shortly after his death, his... heirs & devisees conveyed by Deed all their interest in his estate to **Sarah Ewell** and that she is since dead. She previously duly constituted & appointed her **niece Sarah E. Hays as her heir at law**. Sarah E. Hayes now resides in Botetourt County Virginia. **Sarah E. Hayes is the only person entitled to the benefit of the Military claim of Thomas Ewell for his Revolutionary services.**

Genealogical *Abstracts of Revolutionary War Pensions* (Waynesboro: National Historical Publishing Company, 1990) III: 1314.

[11] Heitman, 220. Thomas Ewell was a Captain in the 1st Virginia State Regiment from January 3, 1777 until January 1781. The only Thomas Hutchison/Hutchenson/Hutchinson/*Hutcherson* I could find in the 1st Virginia State Regiment was a corporal who served in Captain William Payne Jr's company and Captain Charles Ewell's company from March 1777 to November 1779. See *Thomas Hutcherson's compiled service records* M881 MR 913 (http://www.footnote.com), 1-33. Images 21843173 to 2184323 (Accessed July 2, 2008).

[12] NARA, *William McIntosh's compiled service records,* M 881 MR 915 (http://www.footnote.com), 1-62. Images 21837701 to 21838401. William McIntosh enlisted in March 1777 as a private for three years in Captain Thomas W. Ewell's company, 1st Virginia State Regiment. He remained in this regiment under Captain Ewell until November 1779.

[13] NARA, *Elijah Green's Pension File* S 37961, M 804 (http://www.footnote.com), 3-55. Images 22615740 to 22616523 (Accessed July 2, 2008). Elijah Green enlisted in 1776 in Captain Thomas Ewell's company, 1st Virginia State Regiment, Colonel Gibson's Regiment of Virginia troops and served in this regiment until 1780 when he was discharged in Alexandria. See Appendix 2 for an abstract of this pension, issued in 1818 and suspended until 1832.

[14] Sanchez-Saavedra, 111. Thomas Winder Ewell was a captain of the 4th company of the 1st Virginia State Regiment, under the command of Colonel George Gibson. He was commissioned in January 1777. He served until January 1781. See also Heitman, 220.

It is also certified that Charles Ewell, the Executor of Sarah Ewell, is dead and that administration has not since been granted on the Estate of Sarah Ewell.

September 1, 1834 Court, pg. 173.

On the motion of Alice P. Tyler and Mary Ann Beard & upon satisfactory evidence being exhibited before the Court, it is ordered to be certified that they… are the sole heirs at law of **Henry Tyler who is reputed to have been a Midshipman in the Virginia State Navy in the war of the Revolution** and also that Henry Tyler died testate. His last will & testament is of record in the Clerks office of this county.

On the motion of Alexander H. Waters, and it appearing to the Court upon Satisfactory proof that … Alex^r H. Waters is the sole heir at law of **Lieut. John Galloway,**[15]**who was an Officer in the Virginia Continental Line in the war of the Revolution,** the same is accordingly ordered to be certified and that John Galloway died intestate.

September 1, 1834 Court, pg. 174.

On the motion of John S. Ross, and it appearing to the court on satisfactory evidence, it is ordered to be certified that … John S. Ross is the sole heir of **John & Wm. Ross, reputed to have been Virginia Continental soldiers in the war of the Revolution.** It is further certified that John and William Ross both died intestate.

October 6, 1834 Court, pg. 179.

Satisfactory evidence was this day adduced in open court, that Nathl Carter, John Carter & Francis Carter are the legal rep^s & only heirs at law in fee to **Nathaniel Carter**, late of Prince William County, Virginia.

October 7, 1834 Court, pg. 182.

It is satisfactorily proven and the Court does order it to be certified that **Elijah Green**[16] **died without leaving a widow** and that Peggy Abel (formerly Peggy Green) and Sally Rolls (formerly Sally Green) and Elijah Green are the only surviving children of Elijah Green deceased.

December 1, 1834 Court, pg. 197.

Wm. D. Massey & John H. Massey, orphans of Henry Massey decd, with the approbation of this court, made choice of Robert Massey for their guardian… and with Peter Trialor his security, entered into and acknowledged a bond in the penalty of $1200., conditioned according to law.

It was represented to the Court that the infants are entitled to some military land scrip, in lieu of warrants received from the United States & the State of Virginia in consideration of the services of **John Massey,**[17] **as a cornet in the revolution**.

It appears to the Court that it would be to the interest of the… infants, that the scrip should be sold, rather than located. The Court does therefore authorize and advise… Robert Massey to receive, sell & assign the scrip of his… wards and put the money at interest for [their] benefit.

January 5, 1835 Court, pg. 205.

It is satisfactorily proved and the Court foes order it to be certified that the surviving **children of Elijah Green decd, as named in the order of Oct. 7th 1834, are all of age.**

---

[15] Heitman, 241. John Galloway was a lieutenant "in a Virginia Regiment" in 1780. Unfortunately, Heitman did not identify the regiment.

[16] See note 12.

[17] Heitman, 384. John Massey was a cornet and paymaster for the 1st Continental Dragoons in 1781. He transferred to Baylor's Consolidated Regiment of Dragoons in November 1783 and served until the close of the war.

On the motion of Jesse E. Weems, it is ordered to be certified that it was proven to the satisfaction of the court on the 3ᵈ day of July 1834 that **Thomas Winder Ewell decd** (and not Thomas Ewell decd as mentioned in the order) was **a Capt. in the first Virginia State Regiment, commanded by Col. Geo. Gibson during the Revolutionary War..**

That he served until the close of the … war and that he **died in the town of Dumfries in the County of Prince William in the year 1784,** having previously duly constituted & appointed his father Bertrand Ewell & his mother and brothers & sisters his only heirs and devisees.

It is further certified that shortly after his death his… heirs & devisees conveyed by deed all their interest in the Estate of Thomas Winder Ewell to Sarah Ewell & that she is since dead, having previously duly constituted & appointed her Niece Sarah E. Hayes her heir at law, and that … Sarah E. Hayes, now residing in Bottetourt County Virgᵃ is the only person entitled to the benefit of the Military claim of … Thomas Winder Ewell for his Revolutionary Services. It is also certified that Charles Ewell. the Exor of Sarah Ewell is dead and that Administration has not since been granted on the estate of Sarah Ewell.

April 7, 1835 Court, pg. 229.

Satisfactory evidence is this day adduced in open Court, to prove that Catharine Williams is the only and sole heir at law of **Edward Williams**[18] **decd a soldier of the Revolutionary War in Capt. Thomas Triplet's**[19] **company** … [Edward] Williams died without issue… intestate.

Satisfactory evidence is this day adduced in open Court, to prove that James Mitchell is the only surviving brother of **William Mitchell**[20] **decd, a soldier of the Revolutionary army in Captain Thomas Triplet's Company…** James is the only & sole heir at law of William Mitchell decd… William [Mitchell] died without issue… intestate.

Satisfactory evidence is this day adduced in open Court, to prove that Jesse Davis is the only and sole heir at law of **Presley Davis**[21] **decd, a soldier of the Revolutionary war in Captain Thomas Triplet's company**… Presley Davis died without issue & intestate.

June 1, 1835 Court, pg. 241.

Ordered that it be certified that satisfactory proof is this day adduced before the Court to prove that Fanny Gossom is the only and sole heir at law of **Alexʳ Maddox**[22] **a soldier in the Revolutionary War in Captⁿ Thomas Ewell's Company,** Virginia state line.. [Alexander] Maddox died without issue and intestate.

---

[18] NARA, *Edward Williams's compiled service records,* M 881 MR 75, *Grayson's Additional Continental Regiment* (http://www.footnote.com), 1–11. Images 11304444 to 11304523 (Accessed July 2, 2008). Edward Williams enlisted February 18, 1777 for three years as a sergeant in Captain Thomas Triplett's Company, Grayson's Additional Continental Regiment. Muster rolls and payrolls show him with service from February 18, 1777 until his death on December 1, 1777.

[19] Heitman, 548. Thomas Triplett was a Captain in Grayson's Additional Continental Regiment, commissioned on January 13, 1777. He resigned on April 29, 1778. He died in February 1833.

[20] NARA, *William Mitchell's compiled service records,* M 881 MR 75, *Grayson's Additional Continental Regiment* (http://www.footnote.com), 1–50, Images 14064393 to 11167013. William Mitchell was a drummer in Captain Thomas Triplett's , and Ensign William Triplett's , Colonel Grayson's regiment from March 1777 until March 1779. In April 1779, Grayson's regiment was absorbed by Colonel Nathaniel Gist's unit. Mitchell continued as a drummer in Captain Joseph Smith's , Colonel Nathaniel Gist's regiment until October 1779.

[21] Presley Davis was not found in Captain Thomas Triplett's in Grayson's Additional Continental Regiment as recorded on footnote.com. He was not found on any roster in Gist's Additional Continental Regiment either. Grayson's Regiment was absorbed by Colonel Nathaniel Gist's Additional Continentals in April 1779. See Sanchez-Saavedra, 74.

[22] NARA, *Alexander Maddox's compiled service records,* M 881 MR 914 (http://www.footnote.com), 1–31, Images 21872579 to 2187264. Alexander Maddox served as a private in the 1ˢᵗ VSR under four different captains: Captain Ewell's company, Captain Thomas Meriwether, Captain John Shield, and Captain William Campbell from March 1777 to June 1779.

August 3, 1835 Court. Pg. 276.
Satisfactory evidence is this day adduced in open Court, to prove that **Jesse Davis** is the only & sole **heir at law of Presley Davis**[23] **decd, a soldier of the revolutionary War in Captain Andrew Leach's company, Continental line... Presley Davis died without issue and intestate.**

August 3, 1835 Court, pg. 277.
On the motion of William Wright and it appearing to the Court on satisfactory proof exhibited that **Fanny Settle and Jane Lee (if living), Thomas Wright, John Wright, William Wright, Mary Wright, Lucy W. Wright** are great nephews and nieces of **William Wright**[24] **decd of the N.W. Army in the war of the Revolution**... **Francis Loveless** and **Molly Reno** are nieces of William Wright ... they, the... great nephews & nieces and [Francis] Loveless and [Molly] Reno are the sole heirs at law of ... **Wm. [Wright] who died intestate**.

It also appearing to the court that **Fanny Settle and Jane Lee (if living), Thomas Wright, John Wright, William Wright, Mary Wright** and **Lucy W. Wright** are the **children of John Wright decd** and nephews & nieces of **Richard Wright decd** & their sole surviving heirs at law... **John & Richard [Wright] were reputed soldiers in the war of the Revolutionary, and ... they died intestate.**

August 5, 1835 Court, pg. 284.
On the motion of William D. Dowell and it appearing to the satisfaction of the Court that Gracy Jackson and Cloe M. Dowell are the sole surviving heirs at law of the late **Captain Jesse Evans**[25]... **who died in or about 1814 intestate**, the same is ordered to be certified.

It appears from evidence before the Court that **Captain Jesse Evans was the same person who served in the Virginia Military service in the war of the Revolution** in the capacity of a Captain ... which is also ordered to be certified.

On the motion of Rhodam Carter and the court being satisfied on exhibited proof that **Lucy Carter** and **Hannah Hughlett are the sole heirs at law (being his daughters) of William Hughlett,**[26] late of this County... William Hughlett was **reported to be a soldier in the Virginia Continental Line** in the war of the Revolution... **He died intestate** [which] is ordered to be certified.

---

[23] Ibid., *Presley Davis's compiled service records,* M 881 MR 953, *3rd Virginia Regiment.* Presley Davis served as a sergeant in Captain John Peyton's 3rd Virginia company. Company payrolls show service from October 8, 1776 until his death on February 1, 1777. John Peyton took over Andrew Leitch's 3rd Virginia company.

[24] Ibid., *William Wright's compiled service records,* M 881 MR 1086, *Clarke's Illinois Regiment* (http://www.footnote.com), 1–2, Images 23229499 to 23229501. William Wright served as a soldier in Clarke's Illinois Regiment of Virginia State Troops. He appeared on an undated payroll for soldiers receiving their pay up to the last of December 1781.

[25] Marcus Gaius Brumbaugh, *Revolutionary War Records: Virginia* (1936; reprint Baltimore: Genealogical Publishing Company, 1995), 531. Jesse Evans was a captain in the Virginia State Troops in Colonel George Rogers Clarke's Illinois Regiment. A payroll of the officers of the regiment showed Colonel Clarke as commander, Lieutenant Colonel John Montgomery, Captain Jesse Evans, Lieutenant Anthony Crockett, Ensign William Campbell, and Colonel Christian.

[26] NARA, *William Hughlett's compiled service records,* M 881, *Virginia Troops* (http://footnote.com), 1–2. William Hughlett served as a sergeant in the infantry. His name as a soldier appeared in a book of a list of soldiers of the Virginia Line on Continental Establishment who received Certificates for the balance of their full pay, agreeable to an Act of Assembly, passed in November 1781. J. Marshall received his certificate on October 20, 1783 for £54. William Hughlett's name was also spelled as *Hulett*. He appeared as a private in Benjamin Harrison's company of Fauquier Militia in 1777. See Gott and Russell, 461. See also *William Hulett's compiled service records* M 881 MR 1089 (http://www.footnote.com), 1–2, Images 23541998 to 235452001. He was a wagoner in Captain Benjamin Harrison's Fauquier County Militia company.

September 7, 1835 Court, pg. 287.
On the motion of Thomas Nelson... it appears to the Court on satisfactory proof [being] exhibited that Catharine Ewell, Alexander Ewell, Cordelia Ewell, Anny Slade (formerly Anny Ewell), Ellen Ewell & Elizabeth Ewell, children of Bertrand Ewell decd; Cordelia Ring (formerly Cordelia Ewell) & Olivia Martindale (formerly Olivia Ewell), children of James Ewell decd; Rebecca Ewell, Benjamin Ewell, Elizabeth Ewell, Virginia Ewell, Richard Ewell, Thomas Ewell & William Ewell, children of Thomas Ewell decd; Fanny Weems (formerly Fanny Ewell), Sarah B. Davis (formerly Sarah B. Ewell) Alfred Ewell, Jesse Ewell and Emma Ewell are the only and sole **heirs at law of Col. Jesse Ewell decd.**[27]

Prince William County Virginia Order Book 1836-1839.

May 2, 1836, pg. 22.
Thomas Arrington,[28] a resident of this County who was **a Revolutionary soldier**, personally appeared in open Court and presented his **supplemental declaration** in order to obtain the benefit of the provision of the Act of Congress of June 1832 providing for the payment of pensions for service in the war of the Revolution. [He was] duly sworn, according to law, [and] testified to the truth of the statements contained in the annexed declaration, whereupon the same was ordered to be certified.

December 5, 1836, pg. 78.
Satisfactory evidence has been adduced [?] to the court, that the "late **Thomas W. Ewell**[29] **of P. Wm Cty, who was an officer in the Revolutionary War," died leaving nine brothers & sisters Viz; Charles, Solomon, Ann, Charlotte, Susannah, Hannah, Mary Ann, Elizabeth** and **Sally;** that **Susannah** married a Mr. Chapman, by whom she had three children, viz: **Carr, Jane & Charles T;**

Mary Ann married a Mr. Thos. Thornton, by whom she had three children viz: Sarah, Ann & Thomas; that **Sarah Thornton** the **daughter of Thomas & Mary Ann**, married Carr Chapman, the son of her aunt Susannah above named by who she **had one child named Susan**. [Susan] married a Mr. Francis Lowry (and now both are living in Fredericksburg).

That **Mary Ann Thornton**, who survived her husband, and by his will became entitled to his estate, **died leaving all her property to her daughter Sarah Chapman during her life; & after her death, to her grand daughter Susan**, appointing her daughter Sarah (now Sarah Southard) her Executrix...

Sarah Southard is [thus] entitled to one ninth of Capt. Thomas W. Ewell's Est. under the will of her mother for life, and that after her death, it falls to Francis Lowry in right of his wife Susan ...

---

[27] Hamilton J. Eckenrode, *Virginia Soldiers of the American Revolution*, (1912; reprint, Richmond: Virginia State Library and Archives, 1989), I: 157. Jesse Ewell was a Colonel in the Prince William County Militia. The source for this was the *Council Journals, 1777–1778*, and *1788*.

[28] NARA, *Thomas Arrington's Pension File* R 269, M 804 (http://www.footnote.com). Thomas Arrington's rejected pension was interfiled on footnote with pensions for Samuel Arrington and Richard Arrington. Thomas Arrington stated that he was called out with a company of Fairfax Militia in the fall of 1776 and served with Captain Dennis Ramsay of Alexandria for three months. In early 1777, he was drafted again from the Fairfax Militia to begin service in June 1777 under Captain Thomas West. This draft, for the war, was to fill up the 10th Virginia Continental Regiment. He procured a substitute since he wanted to return home at the application of his mother. He was drafted again from the Fairfax Militia company of Captain William Thompson of Colchester and was stationed in and around Alexandria. See his pension file, pages 26–28, Images 10939542, 10939560, and 10939587 in Samuel and Richard Arrington's pension papers.

Thomas Arrington's name was not found in the 10th Virginia Continental Regiment on footnote.com.

[29] See note 10.

that Francis Lowry is entitled to 1/3 of another ninth part which she, his ... wife Susan, inherits from her father the late Carr Chapman.

August 6, 1838 Court, pg. 246.

It appears by satisfactory testimony to the court, that **Lydia Mills**, a resident of [Prince William County] is the **widow of George Mills,**[30] **a Revolutionary Pensioner of the United States** and it further appears that **Lydia was marred to George Mills prior to the first day of January 1794** which is ordered to be certified.

October 12, 1838 Ct, pg. 267.

On this 6th day of August 1838, personally appeared before [a]... justice of the Peace, **Mrs Dekeandra Mattingly,** a resident of [Prince William County]... aged 77 years. [She was] duly sworn... [and] on her oath, make[s] the following **declaration** in order to obtain the benefit of the provision made by the act of Congress passed July 7th 1838 entitled an act granting half pay and pensions to certain widows; that she is the widow of **John Mattingly,**[31] **who was a soldier in the Revolution, on pension at his death.**

He served in the Virginia line under Capt. P. T. T. Lee.[32] She further declares that she was married to... John Mattingly on the 6th day of March, in... 1781 or about that time. Her husband... John Mattingly, died on the [day left blank] February 1824. That she was not married to him prior to his leaving the service, but the marriage took place previous to the 1st of January 1794...

Samuel H. Janney certified that he attended the house of Dekeandra Mattingly and took her declaration, finding that her infirmities prevented her from attending the Courthouse. He further certified that the bible with the family record was found in the house and has been forwarded to Washington.

J. Williams Clerk of the County Court, certified that Samuel H. Janney was a Justice of the Peace for Prince William and that his signatures on the above records is genuine.

Dekeandra Mattingly's declaration with certificates were received and admitted to record in Prince William on October 12, 1838.

December 3, 1838 Court, pg. 285.

The declaration of **Sarah Florance,**[33] "made under the provision of an act of Congress passed July 7th 1838 entitled an act granting half pay and pensions to certain widows", was made August 17, 1838 and annexed, with the certificate of Charles Meng, a magistrate for Prince William

---

[30] NARA, *George Mills's Pension File* W 7449, M 804 (http://www.footnote.com), 1–6, images 25115561 to 25115573. George Mills entered the service as a militia man in September 1777, for six months, in a company commanded by Captain Valentine Peyton, Colonel Jesse Ewell's Regiment. Major James Ewell and Captains Hugh Brent, John Brett, and John Judges were part of Colonel Ewell's Prince William County Militia company.

[31] Ibid., *John Mattingly's compiled service records,* 11th, 15th, and 7th Virginia, M 881 (http://www.footnote.com), 1–64, images 23999376 to 22836939. John Mattingly served as a private in Captain Charles Gallahue's 11th Virginia company from May 1777 to May 1778. In June 1778, he was a private in Captain George Rice's company of the 11th Virginia and served until November 1778 in that capacity. In December 1778, the 11th was redesignated the 7th Virginia and Private Mattingly found himself in Captain Slaughter and Lieutenant James Wright's company until his discharge in November 1779.

See also White, II: 2228. John Mattingly originally applied for a pension in Prince William County in March 1819, at the age of fifty-eight. He had enlisted in Prince William. He married Kykeander Boswell on March 6, 1781. He died February 23, 1824.

[32] The only Captain P. Lee in Heitman, 345–346 was Captain Philip Richard Francis Lee of the 3rd Virginia. John Mattingly was not found in the compiled service records for this regiment.

[33] NARA, *Garner Florence or Florance's Pension* File W 7291, M804 (http://www.footnote.com), 1–22, Images 19661553 to 19662774. Sarah Florance was the widow of Garner Florance, who enlisted and served eighteen months as a private in Colonel Buford's Virginia Regiment. In April 1784, he married Sarah Hutchinson in Prince William. The marriage bond was found in the file. Her husband died October 22, 1822.

County, Virginia. [The declaration] was produced in open court, upon an examination of the declaration and certificate, it is ordered to be certified to the War Department that the declaration, certificates and proceeding were approved by the Court.

February 5, 1839 Court, pg. 298.

The declaration of **John Lowe**[34] in order to obtain the benefit of the act of Congress passed June 7, 1832, was presented to the Court and ordered to be certified.

The Court declares their opinion, after the investigation of the matter & after putting the interrogatories prescribed by the War Department, that [John Lowe] **was a revolutionary soldier** and served as he states.

The Court further certifies that it appears to them that Jesse E. Weems, who has signed the preceding certificate, is a clergyman, resident in this County and that Washington H. Norvell is a credible person and that their statement is entitled to credit.

March 4, 1839 Court, pg. 300.

It has been satisfactorily proven to the Court [and] ordered to be certified that **Thos Bowne,**[35]... **a Captain in the Virginia Continental service in the revolutionary war, died intestate**, about ... **1808**, leaving only one child, viz: **Elizabeth Bowne**, who had, previously to the death of her father, **intermarried with George Jansen** of New York City.

It is also certified that George Jansen died in ... 1800 and his... wife **Elizabeth Jansen died intestate in... 1824, leaving the following children and only heirs at law: Thos Bowne Jansen; Benj^a G. Jansen, Helen M. Jansen and Mary S. Jansen, now the wife of Thos. Powers.**

It is further certified that **Thomas Bowne Jansen died intestate, unmarried & without issue in August 1838** and that his surviving brother and sisters—**Benj. G** and **Helen M. Jansen** and **Mary S. Powers are the only heirs at law of Captain Thomas Bowne.**

July 1, 1839 Court, pg. 341.

The declaration of **Lucy Fortune**[36] made under the provisions of the third section of an act of Congress passed July 4, 1836 entitled "An act granting half pay to widows and orphans when their husbands or fathers have died of wounds received in the Military Service of the United States, in certain cases & for other purposes, was made September 21, 1838, together with certificates of James D. Tennille, Jesse E. Weems & Thos. B. Hamilton, magistrates in Prince William County.

[The declaration] as produced in open court & upon examination of the declaration and certificates, it is ordered to be certified to the War department that the declaration, certificates and proceedings are approved by this Court.

---

[34] Ibid., *John Lowe's Pension File* S 8859, M 804 (http://www.footnote.com), 1–35, images 27316720 to 27316754. John Lowe served as a private in Captain Thomas's company of the 3rd Maryland Line for two years. He had been born in St Mary's County, Maryland in February, 1760. He had enlisted in Captain Thomas's company in February 1776. He received a discharge at Germantown in February 1779. He returned home to St Mary's County, only to move to Prince William in 1786.

[35] Heitman, 113. Thomas Bowne began his career as a 2nd lieutenant in the 10th Virginia, commissioned in April 1777. He was promoted to 1st lieutenant and regimental adjutant in October. In September 1778, Lieutenant Bowne transferred to the 1st Virginia. He was promoted to Captain in 1780 and taken prisoner at Charlestown in May of that year. He transferred to the 6th Virginia in February 1781 and served until the close of the war.

[36] NARA, *Garner Fortune's Pension File* W 24233, M 804 (http://www.footnote.com), 1–9, images 19405789 to 19405852. Lucy Fortune was the widow of Garner Fortune, a soldier for three years in Captain Thomas Armistead's 1st Virginia State Regiment. He had enlisted in Caroline County in January 1777. He was discharged in January or February 1780 and returned home. That fall, he was drafted from the Caroline Militia and participated in the siege of Yorktown and capture of Cornwallis. He returned to the service for a short while after Yorktown, as a guard for the British prisoners. Lucy was Lucy Hartgrove, the daughter of Humphrey Hargrove, according to the family record in the pension papers. She was born in August 1758. Her husband, Garner, was the son of Richard Fortune and was born in March 1758. The couple were married in November 1780.

Prince William County Court Minute Book 1839-1843

July 6, 1840 Court, pg. 107.
Ordered that be certified that satisfactory evidence was exhibited to the Court, that **John Mattingly**[37] **was a pensioner of the United States** at the rate of ninety six dollars per annum, [and] was a resident of ... Prince William... [He] **died in Prince William on February 23, 1824 and** ... **left a widow** whose name is **Dykeander Mattingly**.

January 1, 1841 Court, pg. 141.
Ordered that it be certified that satisfactory evidence has been exhibited to the Court that **Patrick McEwin**[38] was a **pensioner of the U.S.** at the rate of $8. per month, [and] was a resident of Prince William County. He **died in Prince William on February 11, 1840** [and] **left two children** whose names are **Mary** and **William McEwin**.

March 1, 1841 Court, pg. 151.
Ordered that it be certified that satisfactory evidence has been exhibited to the Court that **Patrick McEwin** was a **pensioner of the U.S.** at the rate of $8. per month [and] was a resident of Prince William... [He] **died February 11, 1841** [and] **did not leave a widow**... he left **two children** only whose names are **Mary** and **William McEwin**.

August 1, 1841 Court, pg. pgs. 207-208.
The last will & testament of **John Dickinson Sr** decd was presented to the Court and being proved by the oaths of John Thompson, Richard Amiss and George H. Cockrell, is ordered to be recorded.

On the motion of John Dickinson, Jr & Pricey Dickinson, widow of John Dickinson Sr, the Court certifies that it has been fully proved to their satisfaction, in open Court, that **John Dickinson the elder**[39] **was a soldier in the Revolutionary war, that he died intestate in Prince William some time after ...1787**; that he left an only child named John Dickinson, lately called **John Dickinson Sr, who also [died] on July 15, 1841,** leaving a last will and testament which, has been admitted to probate in this Court; that the last named John Dickinson decd **left a widow** named **Pricey Dickinson** and four children... **John Dickinson Jr, Catharine Money, wife of John Money; Nancy Dickinson** and **Pricy Ann Dickinson;** [These] four children of John Dickinson [the son of John Dickinson the elder] are the **only heirs at law of their grandfather, John Dickinson the elder.**

---

[37] See note 31.
[38] NARA, *Patrick McCune's compiled service records,* M 881, *1ˢᵗ Virginia State Regiment* (http://www.footnote.com), 1–19, selected images 21830844 to 21831063. Patrick McCune (also spelling McEwing), was a private in Captain Thomas Ewell's . He enlisted in March 1777 for three years. See also NARA, *Patrick McEwing's Pension File,* R16267, M 804 (http://www.footnote.com), 1–17, images 27557025 to 27265027. He did eventually receive a pension, which was issued in June 1831 for his service as a private in Captain Ewell's , Colonel Gibson's Regiment, for three years from January 1777 until December 1779. His original pension declaration was filed in November 1818, when he was seventy years old. He stated that he had enlisted in Prince William under Captain Thomas Ewell in 1776 in a State Regiment commanded by Colonel George Gibson. He continued in service unti 1780 when he was discharged in New Jersey. He saw action at Stony Point and Monmouth.
[39] John Dickinson, or *Dickerson,* as his name is sometimes spelled was probably the private in Captain Charles Gallahue's 11ᵗʰ Virginia company, recruited from Prince William See Sanchez-Saavedra, 65 and NARA, *John Dickinson/Dickerson's compiled service records,* M 881, *11th Virginia* (http://www.footnote.com).

October 4, 1841 Court, pg. 226.
It being satisfactorily proven to the Court, it is ordered to be certified that **Andrew Nixon**[40]**... a Captain of the Virginia Continental line in the revolution, died intestate in... 1790** and without issue... [His] nearest collateral relation and only heir at law is Daniel A. Nixon of the Town of Manayunk, Pennsylvania.

It being satisfactorily proven to the Court, it is ordered to be certified that **William Hickman, who was the owner of sundry military surveys in the Virginia Military districts in Ohio and Kentucky, died intestate in Jefferson County Virginia on or about ... 1827**, leaving the following children and grand children who are his only lawful heirs: Rebecca Hickman, Julia Hickman, S. J. C. Hickman, Mary Taylor, Lucretia Hickman, Ellen D. Davenport, William Talbott and Lavinia Brand.

February 7, 1842 Court, pg. 255.
It being proven to the satisfaction of the Court, it is ordered to be certified that **Charles Dekay, who was a sailing master in the Virginia Navy in the Revolutionary war, died... August 1, 1829.**

Prince William County Order Book 1843-1846

September 4, 1843 Court, pg. 29.
On satisfactory evidence, it is ordered to be certified that **Thomas Ransdell,**[41] **who was a Captain in the Virginia Continental Line in the Revolution, died intestate in... 1796,** leaving only two children: **John** and **Maria Ransdell**; ... both of [these] children died intestate & without issue; that the brothers & sisters of Thomas Ransdell were then his only legal heirs [which] were: **Mary Ball, Ursula Ransdell, Horace C. Ransdell, John M. Ransdell** and **Agnes Ransdell, the only children of Chilton Ransdell.**

John Ransdell [was?] the only issue of **Stephen Ransdell**; **Nat N. Gray, Sarah & Caroline C Gray, Maria F. Davis, Hannah S. Nichols & Elizabeth Guthrie, Margaret E. Maddox, James Maddux** and **Nat W. Maddux [the] only heirs of Elizabeth Gray, a sister of Thomas Ransdell.**

John W. Moore, Charles C. Moore, Thomas R. Moore, Hannah J. Moore, Samuel R. Moore and **Lucy Lofland, [the] heirs of Hannah Moore,** another **sister of Thomas Ransdell.**

Thomas J. Ransdell, Benj. T. Ransdell, John C. Ransdell and **Wm. H. Ransdell & Mary Dawkins, Lucy Powell, Letitia Waters, Sarah E. Scott, Eveline H. Martin & Jane Chilton, Letitia Adams, Joseph Martin, Felicia Martin, Nancy Martin** and **Maria Martin** [were] the **only heirs of John Ransdell, another brother of Thomas Ransdell.**

---

[40] Heitman, 414 lists only one Andrew Nixon. He was an ensign in a Delaware Regiment from June 76 to January 1777. He was promoted to be a lieutenant and adjutant of the 1st Continental Dragoons in February 1777. He became a Captain in 1780 and retired in November 1782. See also W. T. R. Saffell, *Records of the Revolutionary War*, (1894; reprint, Bowie: Heritage Books, 1999), 428. Among the officers entitled to half–pay was one Captain Andrew Nixon of the Virginia Line.

[41] Ibid., 458. Thomas Ransdall began his career as a 3rd lieutenant in the 11th Virginia, commissioned in July 1776. He was promoted to 2nd lieutenant in February 1777 and 1st lieutenant in July, 1777. The 11th Virginia was designated the 7th Virginia in the September 1778 reorganization of the Virginia line. Ransdall transferred to the 3rd Virginia in February 1781 and was promoted to a captaincy in October 1781. He retired in January 1783.

September 4, 1843 Court, pg. 30.
On satisfactory evidence, it is ordered to be certified that **Benjamin Stubblefield**[42] who was heir of **George Stubblefield**, died in 1795 leaving the following persons his nearest of kin & only heirs at law; **Eliza Owens, George B. [?] Herndon, Edward Herndon, Richard W. Herndon, Frazier D. Herndon, Catharine B. Woodruff, Thomas Herndon, Martha T. Berry, Mary Shortridge, Carter Stubblefield** and **Robert A. Stubblefield**.

Upon satisfactory evidence exhibited to the Court, it is ordered to be certified that **Nancy Sidebottom** and **Sarah Anderson** are the only legal **heirs at law** of **Elias Wingate**[43] decd, late of Prince William County.

Upon satisfactory evidence exhibited to the Court, it is ordered to be certified that **Anna Arrington, George Johnston** and **Davis Johnston** are the only legal **heirs at law** of **Francis Johnston**[44] who died, late of Prince William County.

Upon satisfactory evidence exhibited to the Court, it is ordered to be certified that **John Lowe**[45] was **a pensioner of the United States,** at the rate of $80. per year; ... that... Lowe was a resident of.. Prince William County ... & **died ... June 15, 1843**. He left no widow or children living.

April 6, 1846 Court, pg. 302.
The **declaration of Daniel O'Rear**[46] **for a pension** under the act of June 7, 1832, was received in Open Court & ordered to be certified to the War office in Washington...

The **declaration of Joseph Bobo,**[47] **for a pension** under the act of June 7, 1832, was received in Open Court, & ordered to be certified to the War Office in Washington...

---

[42] Brumbaugh, 497. Benjamin Stubblefield, as the heir of George Stubblefield, received a Continental Line Warrant number 1171 in the Virginia Military District of Ohio for George's service as an ensign for the war. See also Bockstruck, 511. George Stubblefield Jr, an ensign in the Virginia Line, received a bounty land grant for 2666 2/3 acres o land in June 1783.

[43] Saffell, 247–248. Elias Wingate was a corporal on the rolls of Captain John Danbridge's company, Colonel Charles Harrison's Regiment of Artillery in June 1778 at Valley Forge and in July 1779 at Smith's Clove. See also Sanchez-Saavedra, 106. Colonel Charles Harrison's Artillery was the 1st Continental Artillery.

[44] Ibid., 282. This may have been the Francis Johnston, in Colonel John Gibson's Detachment in the Western Department. He was killed in March 1781. See also Sanchez-Saavedra, 130. Five companies of Colonel Gibson's Detachment were at Fort Pitt from January 1780 until December 6, 1781.

[45] NARA, *John Lowe's Pension File* S 8859, M 804 (http://www.footnote.com), 1–35, images 27316720 to 27316754. John Lowe was a private in Captain Thomas's company in the 3rd Maryland Continental Regiment. He served for two years. He was inscribed on the Rolls at Richmond at $80.00 per year beginning on March 4, 1831. His certificate of pension, number 32051, was issued on June 13, 1843.

He first applied for a pension in Prince William in February 1839, ag age seventy-eight. He had enlisted in the 3rd Maryland sometime in May 1777 and served for three years as a corporal. He had been born in St. Mary's County, Maryland, where he enlisted. He removed with his father to Prince William County, Virginia in 1785.He had died June 15,1843, without leaving a widow or children, Wileman Thomas qualified as his administrator and traveled to Richmond to collect the arrears due on his pension. Thomas collected nearly $1000.00 in arrears from March 1831 until his death in September 1843. See Pierce, II: 351.

[46] Ibid., *Daniel Orear's Pension File* S 7376, M 804 (http://www.footnote.com), 1–63, images 25322056 to 25321680. File contained 104 pages. He received a pension as a private in Captain Hedges's company, Colonel Ewell's Virginia Militia for sixteen months. He was inscribed on the Rolls at Richmond at $53.33 per year, beginning on March 4, 1831. His certificate of pension, number 32660, was issued on September 3, 1840. He received an increase from his original pension of $26.66. He also served in Captain Leonard Helm's company, Colonel Clarke's Illinois Regiment in 1778 with his two brothers, Jesse and John O'Rear.

[47] Ibid., *Joseph Bobo's Pension File* R 981, M 804 (http://www.footnote.com), 2–11, images 11270317 to 11270370. Joseph Bobo made his pension declaration in Prince William in April 1846, when he was eighty-six years old. His first tour was one of six months, raised to go south in September 1780. He was drafted into the company Captain John Britt [Brett] of Prince William and marched to North Carolina. Solomon Ewell was an orderly sergeant of this company. William Farmer was the lieutenant. He was discharged at Hillsborough. His application was rejected.

Prince William County Minute Book 1846-1850

February 5, 1849 Court, pg. 269.
On the motion of Pricilla Robertson, satisfactory evidence appearing, having been exhibited to the Court, the Court certifies that **George Robertson,**[48] **a pensioner of the United States at the rate of six dollars per month,** was a resident of Prince William County when he **died November 30, 1841**; **he left a widow, Priscilla Robertson.**

April 6, 1850 Court, pg. 445.
On the motion of Wileman Thomas, it is ordered to be certified that satisfactory evidence has been exhibited to the Court that **John Carr**[49] **was a pensioner of the United States** at the rate of eight dollars per month; he was a resident of Prince William when he **died September 9, 1837** he **left** no widow but **three children: Nancy Godfrey, Jane Godfrey** and **Elizabeth Jones.**

Prince William County Court Minute Books 1853-1856

July 4, 1853 Court, pg. 25.
Satisfactory evidence was this day exhibited before the Court that **George Mills,**[50] **late of this county, was a pensioner of the United States** at the rate of twenty dollars per annum; he was a resident of Prince William county when he died in [year left blank]; he **left a widow, Lydia Mills** who was a resident of Prince William and died ... some years after her husband, leaving these children: **John D. Mills, age 67; Caty Russell, age 64; Ann Woodyard, age 58.**

August 2, 1853 Court, pg. 33.
Satisfactory evidence was this day exhibited before this Court that **George Mills,** late of this county, **was a pensioner of the U.S.** at the rate of twenty dollars per annum; he was a resident of Prince William when he **died in 1838**; he **left a widow, Lydia Mills**, who was a resident of Prince William when **she died March 20, 1844**; she left **three children: John D. Mills, age 67; Caty Russell, age 64;** and **Ann Woodyard, age 58.**

September 5, 1853, pg. 45.
Ordered that it be certified that satisfactory evidence was this day produced before the Court showing that **Amos T. Fisher,**[51] **late a private in Captain Corse's Company of Virginia Volunteers** who is inscribed in the pension rolls, Richmond Virginia Agency is still living.

---

[48] NARA, *Index to Compiled Service Records of Volunteer Soldiers ... in War of 1812*, M 602 MR 177 (http://www.ancestry.com). George Robertson served as a private in Colonel Enoch Renno's 36th Virginia Militia. See also NARA, *Index to War of 1812 Pension Application Files*, M 313 MR 80, Robe-Rol (http://ancestry.com), image 198. "Old War, Invalid, and Widow Rejected: File 17464. The claimant was Priscilla Robertson, widow of George Robertson. He was in Captain Jackson's, 36th Virginia Militia.

[49] NARA, *John Carr's Pension File* S 39274, M 804 (http://www.footnote.com), 1–25, images 15196068 to 15196195. John Carr was granted a pension for his service as a private in Captain Ewell's, Colonel Gibson's Regiment for three years from 1776–1779. He was inscribed on the Virginia Rolls at $8.00 per month beginning in June 1831. His certificate of pension, number 20344, was issued on July 21, 1831. His pension application was originally rejected because his first application was under the Act of March 1818 which was only for Continental Service. His pension was restored in March 1831.

[50] See note 30.

[51] Amos T. Fisher was a private in Captain *Montgomery* Corse's, in the 1st Regiment of Virginia Volunteers, commanded by Colonel John F. Hamtramck, called into service for the Mexican War. See Auditor's Office, *Virginia Militia in the War of 1812*, (1852; reprint, Baltimore: Genealogical Publishing Company, 2001), II: 67.

February 6, 1854, pg. 83.
Satisfactory evidence has this day been made before this Court that **Catharine A. Thomas married Thomas Buyene [?]; Malinda Thomas married Leroy W. Lynn; John W. Thomas** is now 21 years old; **Newton F. Thomas** is 21 years old; **Joseph B. Thomas died a minor; Catharine Buyene, Malinda Thomas, John W. Thomas, Newton F. Thomas** and **Joseph B. Thomas are the heirs** of **J. Bullitt, Colonel in the Continental Line.**

October 2, 1854 Court, pg. 154.
In order to obtain the benefit of the 2nd Section of the Act of 3rd February 1853, also of the joint Resolutions Act of Congress passed 1838, 1843 and 1844, explaining the acts that no pension shall be withheld from any widow when her husband has died since the passage of either of these acts provided and that no pension shall be granted to these widows for the same time her husband [next word illegible] our [?]...

On this 2nd day of October 1854, personally appeared before the County Court... **Lettice Gill**, age 53, a resident of Prince William County, who first being duly sworn, makes the following declarations in order to obtain the benefits of the joint resolutions passed by Congress... 1838, 1843 and 1844 and the act of Congress passed February 3, 1853.

She is the widow of **John Gill,**[52] **who served during the Revolutionary war with the State line of Virginia as orderly Sergeant.**

She further declares that **she was married to John Gill** on [day left blank] **July 1824**; her **husband died November 29, 1843**; she was not married to him prior to January 2, 1800 and that she has remained a widow since her husband's death.

(Signed) Lettice (x) Gill

Satisfactory evidence was this day produced before this Court by the oath of Thomas Lee that Lettie Gill is the widow of **John Gill, who served as an Orderly Sergeant in the Virginia State Line during the Revolutionary War.**

December 5, 1854 Court, pg. 181.
Euphan M. Washington, widow of the late **Col. John M Washington**[53] yesterday made the following declaration in open Court, the entry of which, was for want of time, adjourned by the Court to this day...

On this 4th December 1854, personally appeared before the Prince William County Court... Mrs Euphan M. Washington, resident of Prince William County, age 52 years.

---

[52] NARA, *John Gill's Pension File* W 7520, M804 (http://www.footnote.com), 1–49, images 21868350 to 21868835. John Gill received a revolutionary war pension as a private and sergeant in Captain Brent's company, Colonel Churchill's Regiment in the Virginia Line for eleven months in 1776. He was inscribed on the Virginia Rolls at $43.33 per month, beginning in March 1831. His certificate of pension was issued in July 1832 and delivered to him. He died in November 1842 or 1843. He had married Letitia Gill in 1824.

His service included three months in 1776 as a private (he substituted for his father) in Captain Robert Overall's, Colonel Churchill's Regiment. In 1781, he spent four months as a sergeant in Captain William Brent's company, Colonel Richard Brent's Regiment and another four months as a private in Captain Robert Warren's company, Colonel Churchill's Regiment.

Letitia (Lee) Gill was allowed a pension on her application executed in June 1854, when she was fifty-three years old. She needed to fill out a loyalty oath in May 1867 to continue on the U. S. Pension Rolls. She died in August 1879.

[53] Heitman, *Historical Register and Dictionary of US Army, 1789–1903*, I: 1007. This is John Macrae Washington, who was a cadet at the Military Academy in October, 1814. By July, 1817, he was a 3rd lieutenant in a Corps of Artillery, then a 2nd lieutenant in March 1818. He served as a captain and assistant Quartermaster General for his regiment from July 1838 to April 1839. He was promoted to major in July 1847 because he had been a brevet Captain in May 1830. He was promoted for ten years faithful service in one grade. In February 1847 he was promoted to Lieutenant Colonel for gallantry and meritorious conduct at the Battle of Buena Vista in the Mexican War. He drowned on the steam ship San Francisco on Christmas Eve, 1853.

She was duly sworn and made the following declaration in order to obtain the benefit of the 2nd section of the Act of Congress, passed March 27, 1854 entitled an "Act for the relief of the United States troops who were sufferers by the recent disaster to the Steam ship *San Francisco*.

She was the widow of **John M. Washington, who was an officer of the rank of Brevet Lt. Colonel in the Army of the United States**, and was on board the Steamship *San Francisco* on December 24, 1853; he remained on board this ship until the disaster by which the ship was lost; in consequence of this disaster, her husband perished on December 24 1853.

She further declares she was married to John M. Washington on April 3, 1828 and that she is still his widow.

(Signed) Euphan M. Washington

March 5, 1855 Court, pg. 199.
Ordered that it be certified that satisfactory evidence was this day exhibited before this Court that **John Gill was a pensioner of the United States** at the rate of $433 1/3 per annum; he was a resident of Prince William County when **he died November 29, 1842**.

March 6, 1855 Court, pg. 202.
On the motion of Isaiah Fisher, it is certified that he is the acting committee of **Amos T. Fisher, a pensioner** inscribed on the pension list roll of the Virginia agency… It is further certified that Amos T. Fisher is still living.

November 5, 1855 Court, pg. 269.
On the motion of William T. Washington, the Court orders it certified on the record that it has been this day proved by competent witnesses to the satisfaction of the court that **John M. Washington, late Brevet Col. of Artillery in the United States Army**, died on or about December 24, 1853, have been lost in the steamship *San Francisco*; he left at the time of his death, a widow Euphan M. Washington and two sons, William T. Washington and H. W. M. Washington, his sole heirs at law; both of his sons are of lawful age.

APPENDICES

INTRODUCTION

There are three appendices in this section. Appendix 1 covers the French and Indian War time period. It contains information about officers and soldiers, identified as either enlisting or living in Prince William, many of whom were not mentioned in the County Court Minutes during this time period.

Appendix 2 includes extracts from Elijah Green's Revolutionary War Pension file, containing an 1818 pension application. This pension is important because Prince William's Court Minute Books are missing from 1815–1831. The Pension Law of 1818, for the first time, gave Continental Line Revolutionary War veterans in need, a chance for assistance from the federal government they helped form.

Appendix 3 provides information about Prince William's two Virginia Militia Regiments in the War of 1812. Colonel Enoch Rennoe headed up the 36th Virginia Militia Regiment while Colonels Philip Klipstine and Gerard Alexander commanded the 89th Virginia Militia Regiment.

APPENDIX 1

A Partial Listing of Identified Prince William soldiers and officers in the French and Indian War from other Source Records

1. Sources for this list of men, identified from Prince William, who served in the French and Indian War

This listing of men from Prince William, who served in the French and Indian War, primarily on frontier duty, has been extracted from these four sources:

- Bockstruck, Lloyd deWitt. *Bounty and Donation Land Grants in British Colonial America* Baltimore, Genealogical Publishing Company, 2007.
- —— *Virginia's Colonial Soldiers,* Baltimore: Genealogical Publishing Company, 1998.
- Clark, Murtie June. *Colonial Soldiers of the South 1732–1774,* Baltimore: Genealogical Publishing Company, 1999.
- *Virginia Military Records from the Virginia Magazine of History and Biography, the William and Mary College Quarterly, and Tyler's Quarterly.* 1925, Reprint, Baltimore: Genealogical Publishing Company, 2007.

It is by no means an exhaustive list and should be viewed as a beginning for identifying Prince William militia in the French and Indian War.

2. Military Biographies of Men identified as serving from Prince William in the French and Indian War

- **Joseph Ale (aka Ails, Ailes, Ales, Ayle, Ayles)**

Joseph **Ails** appeared as a private in Captain Robert McKenzie's Company on July 13, 1756. He had enlisted in Prince William when he was thirty-four years old. He was 5 feet 6 inches tall; his description was that of a "ruddy, well made" man, with a "free, open countenance." His occupation was that of a bricklayer. He was English.[1] He appeared as Joseph **Ayle** on a July 1756 payroll for Captain McKenzie.[2]

His name appeared again as Joseph **Ale** on a return for August [year not given] of Necessaries belonging to Captain Robert McKenzie's 10th Company of the Virginia Regiment.[3]

An undated Size Roll for Captain McKenzie's company listed him as Joseph **Ale**, who was recruited by Lieutenant Bullett. Joseph Ale was thirty-four years old, 5 feet 6 inches tall, English and a bricklayer. He had a "ruddy complexion, dark hair, [and was] well made."[4]

A size roll for Captain McKenzie's Company, dated 1757–1758, listed Joseph Ale as having enlisted in Prince William. He was thirty four years old at the time of his enlistment and was 5 feet 6 inches tall. In this listing Joseph Ale's occupation was that of a mason.[5]

He did not appear on any other rolls after this time with service in the French and Indian War. He did not receive bounty land for his service.

---

[1] Lloyd deWitt Bockstruck, *Virginia's Colonial Soldiers*, 76.
[2] Ibid., 84.
[3] Ibid., 102.
[4] Ibid., 122.
[5] Clark, 486.

◆ **John Askins (1)**

John Askins first appeared in Captain Thomas Waggener's company as John **Ashings** on a payroll for two days in December 1756 and January and February 1755.[6] His next appearance was not until January 1756 payroll for subsistence in Captain Thomas Waggener's Company when he was listed as Private John **Asking**.[7] He made his next appearance on a June 1, 1756 payroll for Captain Thomas Waggener Company as John **Askins**.[8] His name also appeared with the same spelling on Captain Waggener's July 7, 1756 payroll.[9] On July 9, 1756, Captain Thomas Waggener's payroll for a bonus for service at the Battle of Monongahela, he appeared as John **Arskins**. The men were paid £5 currency, the premium granted by the colonial assembly for participating in this battle.[10]

Then, in August, 1756, John Askins was listed on Captain George Mercer's Size Roll. This roll revealed that he had enlisted in October 1754 in Prince William. He was 26 years old in August 1756; 5 feet 10 inches tall, and a planter; he was "brown, sturdy, well set [with] dark hair." He was a Virginian.[11]

Captain Mercer's monthly return for September 1756 mentions that John Askins joined his company on August 7th.[12] Private Askins continued to appear on Captain Mercer's payrolls for both September and October 1756.[13] After October 1756 his name disappeared from the Virginia Regiment rolls.

◆ **John Askins (2)**

This John Askins showed up on a size roll of Colonel George Washington's, for August 28, 1757. This man had also enlisted from Prince William but in **December** 1754 when he was twenty-two years of age and 5 feet 7 inches tall. He was a carpenter and native of Virginia. He had a "dark complexion, [with] sandy hair."[14]

It is doubtful that the John Askins who served with Captains Waggener and Mercer was the same John Askins whose name was on Colonel Washington's 1757 roll. Their descriptions, ages, and occupations are different. In addition, it strains all credibility to think that the John Askins in Colonel Washington's company in August 1757 could have gained three inches in height and gone from having been brown, sturdy well set up with dark hair to being dark complected with sandy hair. Thus it appeared that there were two men of this name serving with the Virginia Regiment during the French and Indian war, *both from Prince William County.*

One of the purposes of a size roll was to identify soldiers who deserted. While this may have been helpful to the eighteenth century military establishment, it has proved to be far more advantageous to present-day historians seeking to distinguish between two soldiers with the same name.

To confuse matters even further, *another* John Askins, who, in October 1779, was living in Augusta County, had his service certified by that Court for service as a soldier in the 1st Virginia Regiment under **Colonel William Byrd**. Alexander McClenachan came into court and swore, on oath, to John's service. At the same time, Francis Long, as the assignee of the soldier, received a bounty land warrant for Askins's service in the French and Indian War.[15]

---

[6] Bockstruck, *Virginia Colonial Soldiers*, 51.
[7] Ibid., 319.
[8] Bockstruck, *Virginia Colonial Soldiers*, 61.
[9] Clark, 378; Bockstruck, *Virginia Colonial Soldiers*, 63.
[10] Clark, 379.
[11] Ibid., *Virginia Colonial Soldiers*, 88; *Virginia Military Records*, 393; Clark, 404.
[12] Clark, 417.
[13] Clark, 420, 423.
[14] Bockstruck, *Virginia Colonial Soldiers*, 104.
[15] Ibid., 243.

- **Philemon** or **Phillip Askins**

Phill Askins had a similar history to John Askins. He first appeared on a Captain Thomas Waggener's company payroll in January 1756 as Philip: **Askings**.[16] A payroll for subsistence for Captain Waggener's Company, in January 1756, showed him as Phill: **Asking**.[17] When his name showed up again on Captain Waggener's payroll, in July 1756, he was Philip **Askins**.[18]

In August, 1756, **Philemon** Askins's name appeared on a size roll taken for Captain George Mercer's Company. Philemon had enlisted in September 1755 in Prince William. He was twenty-two years old at the time he enlisted. His height was 5 feet 8 inches. He was a planter and native of Virginia. He had a "brown complexion, [was] well set [and had] dark hair."[19]

On all the remaining returns of rolls for Captain George Mercer's Company, Philemon Askins's given name is abbreviated to Phill or Phil. In one instance, he is Phillip Askins. On a monthly return for Captain Mercer's Company taken on September 1, 1756, **Phil** Askins name appeared.[20] This return stated that Phil Askins had joined the company on August 7th.[21] His name appeared on company payrolls for both September and October 1756, in September as Philip Askins, private; and in October, as Phillip Askins.[22]

The next appearance of Phillip Askins is in August 1757 when his name appeared on a size roll for Colonel George Washington. This roll reported that he had enlisted in January 1755 in Prince William when he was twenty-two years old. He was 5 feet 9 inches. His occupation was that of a carpenter. He was a native of Virginia. He had a "brown complexion and hair, [and was a] stout, robust fellow,"[23] according to the description in this size roll.

The description of the Philemon Askins who appeared in Captain George Mercer's size roll in August 1756 was similar enough to the Phillip Askins of Col Washington's size roll in August 1757 to identify the two individuals as the same person.

- **Francis Austin (aka Austing, Ostin)**

Francis Austin first appeared on Captain Thomas Waggener's Company payroll for two days in December 1754 and for the months of January and February 1755.[24] His next appearance was not until Captain Waggoner's payroll for January 1756 when he was a sergeant.[25] Captain Waggoner also turned in a payroll for subsistence for his company in the same month. Francis Austin appeared on this roll as a sergeant.[26]

The next surviving roll for this company was a payroll dated June 1, 1756. On this roll, Francis Austin was a private in Captain Waggener's Company.[27] He appeared with the same rank on a payroll dated July 7, 1756 for Captain Waggener's unit. As a private, he was given a bonus of £5 by the colonial assembly for participating at the Battle of Monongahela on July 9, 1756.[28] He appeared on Captain Waggener's payrolls for July and August 1756 as well.[29]

He appeared as Francis **Ostin** in a size roll for Captain Waggener's Company, dated September 19, 1756. He was a sergeant and 49 years old. He was 5 feet 9 ½ inches tall and a native of England. A

---

[16] Ibid., 57.
[17] Clark, 349.
[18] Bockstruck, *Virginia Colonial Soldiers*, 63.
[19] Ibid., 88; Clark, 404
[20] Bockstruck, *Virginia Colonial Soldiers*, 90.
[21] Clark, 417.
[22] Ibid., 420, 423.
[23] Bockstruck, *Virginia Colonial Soldiers*, 105.
[24] Ibid., 51.
[25] Ibid., 57; Clark, 310.
[26] Clark, 348.
[27] Ibid., 372.
[28] Ibid., 378–379.
[29] Bockstruck, *Virginia Colonial Soldiers*, 89.

shoemaker by trade, he had been enlisted by Lieutenant Thomas Bullet. He was "well made, [with] short black hair, full faced [and his] right leg [was] larger than his left."[30]

Rolls for this company are missing for the fall and early winter of 1756. However, with a few exceptions, the rolls for this company for 1757 are fairly complete. Francis Austin appeared on the payrolls for Captain Waggener's company from January to May 1757.[31] In August 1757, Francis Austin was a sergeant on the size roll filed by Captain Waggener at Fort Holland on the South Branch of the Potomac. Sergeant Austin had enlisted, when he was forty-nine years, in Prince William. He was 5 feet 9 ½ inches tall. A native of England, he was a shoemaker by occupation. His complexion was "dark."[32]

In September, his name was the first entry on the Necessary Roll for Captain Waggener's Company at Fort Hopewell, dated September 14, 1757.[33] Unfortunately, the October 1757 rolls for Captain Waggener's Company are no longer extant. However, the November and December 1757 necessary rolls are. Francis Austin appeared on the November roll[34] as well as the necessary roll, dated December 4, 1757, on the South Branch of the Potomac.[35]

He appeared on the January 21, 1758 payroll for Captain Waggener as a private.[36] His final appearance on one of Captain Waggener's rolls came in March, 1758, when his name was spelled Francis **Austing** on a necessary roll at Fort Hopewell.[37] Items issued to soldiers in this roll included a flintlock, bayonet, cartridge boxes, cartridges, belt and frogs, coats, waistcoats, breeches, a hat, a cockade, shirts, shoes, stockings, socks, shoe, knee and garter buckles, haversacks, knapsacks, blankets, combs, canteens, swords, and sashes.[38]

In September, 1779, in Frederick County, Virginia, a warrant for 200 acres was issued to Charles M. Thruston, as the assignee of Bryan Bruin, who was the assignee of Francis Austin, a sergeant in the 1st Virginia Regiment.[39]

- ♦ **William Bear (aka Bare)**

William Bear appeared on Captain Robert Spotswood's Size Roll in July 1756. He was 41 years of age, 5 feet 11 inches tall, born in Virginia and a planter. He enlisted November 1, 1754 in Prince William. He had a dark complexion and short brown hair.[40] In Captain Spotswood's October 1757 Size Roll at Fort Young, William *Bare* was 45 years old, 5 feet 11 inches, born in Virginia and a planter. No date is given for his enlistment, which took place in Virginia.[41] More details were given in his description. Still with a dark complexion and short brown hair, now he was "lame in one leg."[42]

---

[30] Ibid., 90.
[31] Ibid., 93.
[32] Ibid., 107.
[33] Clark, 467.
[34] Bockstruck, *Virginia Colonial Soldiers,*, 124.
[35] Clark, 482.
[36] Ibid., 489.
[37] Bockstruck, *Virginia Colonial Soldiers*, 125.
[38] Clark, 494.
[39] Bockstruck, *Virginia Colonial Soldiers*, 271. See also Lloyd deWitt Bockstruck, *Bounty and Donation Land Grants*, 12.
[40] Bockstruck, *Virginia Colonial Soldiers*, 79.
[41] Ibid., 474.
[42] Bockstruck, *Virginia Colonial Soldiers*, 224.

♦ **Doctor Bowles (aka Bowls)**
Doctor Bowles appeared on a size roll for Captain Thomas Waggener's Company at Fort Holland on the South Branch of the Potomac in August, 1757. He was 24 years old, 5 feet 4 inches tall, born in England and was a planter. He had a brown complexion and had enlisted in Prince William.[43]
He appeared on several necessary rolls for Captain Waggener's Company, the first ones in September 1757, while on the South Branch of the Potomac.[44] He appeared on another of these rolls in November[45] and December 1757.[46] In January, 1758 he appeared on a payroll for Captain Waggener's Company, while stationed at Fort George.[47] He made his final appearance on yet another necessary roll for March 1, 1758 in Captain Thomas Waggener's Company at Fort Hopewell on the South Branch of the Potomac.[48]

♦ **Francis Braunaugh (aka Bronaugh)**
Francis Braunough of Prince William was allowed 16s 8d for an express, according to a schedule attached to the October 1765 Militia Act. That act allowed the appointment of Commissioners to examine and state the various accounts of Militia who were ordered into actual service during the French and Indian War. Braunough's name was found in the Prince William Militia Accounts.[49]

♦ **William Bronaugh**
William Bronaugh appeared on a roll of officers and soldiers who saw service before the Battle of the Meadows in July 1754. He was an ensign and had been commissioned in the Prince William Militia in March 1754.[50] By January 6, 1756, Bronaugh had been promoted to the Captain of a Virginia Regiment.[51] As an officer in the French and Indian War, William Bronaugh received bounty land for some 3000 acres which he assigned. [52]

♦ **Benjamin Bullitt (aka Bullett)**
In May, 1753, Benjamin Bullet took the oath and subscribed the test in the Prince William County Court as a militia officer.[53] He served as an ensign in a Virginia Regiment and was killed in April 1757. His right to 2000 acres of bounty land for service in the French and Indian War was devised to his heir Thomas Bullet.[54]
In October 1779, Abraham Hite and Burr Harrison gave satisfactory proof that Benjamin Bullet decd., was an ensign in one of the Virginia regiments and was killed in April 1757. The right to bounty land was devised to Cuthbert Bullet, the devisee of Benjamin and Thomas Bullet.[55]

♦ **Thomas Bullitt (aka Bullett)**
Thomas Bullitt began his career as a cadet in the French and Indian War. His name appeared on a Roll of Officers in that capacity who saw service before the Battle of the Meadows in July 1754.[56] His name also appeared on a roll of a party of recruits, as a cadet, who joined at Will's Creek after the Battle of the

---

[43] Ibid., 108. See also Clark, 464.
[44] Bockstruck, *Virginia Colonial Soldiers,*, 109, 113.
[45] Ibid., 117.
[46] Clark, 483.
[47] Bockstruck, *Virginia Colonial Soldiers,* 124.
[48] Ibid., 125.
[49] Ibid., 214.
[50] Clark, 589. Bockstruck, *Virginia Colonial Soldiers,* 30–31.
[51] Bockstruck, *Virginia Colonial Soldiers,* 15.
[52] Ibid., 46.
[53] Ibid., 30–31.
[54] Ibid., 52–53.
[55] Ibid, 270.
[56] Clark, 589.

Meadows.[57] By September 1756, he was a lieutenant in Captain Thomas Waggener's Company, and recruited soldiers Francis Austin and John Haley for Waggener's Company.[58] His name appeared as a lieutenant on a August 1757 roll of a Company belonging to the late Captain Peter Hogg.[59] In January 1764, he was Captain Bullett in a petition to the legislature for reimbursement of £ 30 18s which he had advanced Richard Smith. Smith acted as an interpreter to a party of Indians under the care of Captain Bullett at Fort Chiswell.[60]

A size roll for Major Andrew Lewis, dated 1757–1758, was signed by Lewis, Thomas Bullitt, and two other officers.[61]

Captain Bullett petitioned the legislature in January 1764 for reimbursement of £ 30 18s he advanced to Richard Smith as an interpreter to a party of Indians under his care at Fort Chiswell. The legislature allowed this claim with the proviso that it be deducted out of the sum of £71 due to Smith. Bullett had an order for that deduction from Smith's executor.[62]

Captain Bullitt received bounty land for his service, which he located in Botetourt County. He devised the bounty land to Cuthbert Bullet, who patented the land in Greenbrier County in November 1779.[63]

- **Thomas Burris (aka Burras, Burroughs)**

Thomas "Burras" first appeared on a May 29, 1754 Payroll for the Virginia Regiment from his enlistment until the May 1754 date.[64] He was a private soldier in Captain George Mercer's Company. He appeared as Thomas *Burris*, with the rank of private on Captain George Mercer's Pay Bill of the Virginia Regiment, made by Colonel Washington to Officers and Soldiers in 1754.[65]

In early July 1754, his name, still spelled "Burris," was found on a return of Captain George Mercer's Company, dated on July 9th, at Will's Creek.[66] Thomas Burris's name was also part of the Roll of Officers and soldiers who were engaged in the service before the Battle of the Meadows. He was a soldier in Captain Mercer's Company.[67] Towards the end of July, on the 29th of the month, he was found on another payroll for Captain George Mercer's Company, this time at Alexandria.[68]

In early September 1754, Captain Mercer, in a return of his company, showed Thomas Burris as fit for duty.[69] Later the same month Private Burris was paid £2 8d for his service, according to a pay bill submitted by Captain George Mercer.[70] He received his bounty money for his enlistment in 1754.[71]

In May 1757, Thomas *Burras* was paid £ 10 for the loss of an arm in service of his country.[72]

- **Benjamin Cage**

In March, 1760, Benjamin Cage petitioned the colonial legislature for his pay when he was sent out in the militia to the frontier. He served a total of 108 days but his name was omitted by mistake from the

---

[57] Bockstruck, *Virginia Colonial Soldiers*, 128.
[58] Ibid., 90.
[59] Ibid., 102.
[60] Ibid., 81.
[61] Clark, 484.
[62] Bockstruck, *Virginia Colonial Soldiers*, 181.
[63] Bockstruck, *Bounty and Donation Land Grants*, 53.
[64] Bockstruck, *Virginia Colonial Soldiers,*, 133.
[65] Clark, 310.
[66] Bockstruck, *Virginia Colonial Soldiers,*, 130.
[67] Clark, 597.
[68] Bockstruck, *Virginia Colonial Soldiers*, 132.
[69] Ibid., 46.
[70] Ibid., 48.
[71] Ibid., 50.
[72] Ibid., 165.

company roll. In March 1761, the legislature allowed him £5 8s for his service in the Prince William Militia.[73]

♦ John Cole

John Cole was a corporal on a size roll for Captain Thomas Waggener's Company, filed in August, 1757 at Fort Holland on the South Branch of the Potomac. He had enlisted in Prince William. He was 21 years old, 5 feet 3 inches tall, with a ruddy complexion. He have been born in Scotland and was a planter.[74]

An abstract of an earlier size roll, in August 1754, for this company did not give his place of enlistment although it did state this recruiting officer, Lieutenant John Wright. This size roll also gave more details about Corporal Cole. In September 1754, he was 21 years old and 5 feet 2 inches tall. He had a ruddy complexion, brown curling hair and was had a pock pitted full face.[75] His name appeared on payrolls for Captain Thomas Waggener's Company from July to August, 1756 as a private[76] and from January through May, 1757 when his rank was not given.[77] He was probably a corporal during those months as he served in that capacity according to the September 1756 size roll alluded to earlier.

He appeared on necessary rolls for Captain Waggener's Company in July, November,[78] and December, 1757.[79] In April 1762, he presented a petition to the colonial legislature as a "sergeant in the Virginia Regiment," for the payment for a horse pressed into service by Captain Bullet. Captain Bullet appraised his horse at £15. It was captured by the enemy. He also requested payment for his services as a tailor to several soldiers in the regiment.[80]

♦ Cornelius Colman (aka Coleman)

Cornelius Colman was a soldier in Captain Henry Woodward's Company. His name appeared on a size roll for the company in September 1757. He had been born in Ireland and was 25 years of age at the time of his enlistment. He was 5 feet 6 inches tall, with a brown complexion, brown eyes, and thick set. He had enlisted from Prince William.[81] His name also appeared on an "exact necessary roll," filed by Captain Henry Woodward at Fort Lytleton, in August 1757.[82]

♦ Joseph Evans (aka Evins)

This *may* be the Joseph *Evins* whose name appeared on an August 1756 payroll as a private in Captain Henry Woodward's Company.[83] In September 1758, Joseph Evans, of Prince William, petitioned the legislature for relief for a disability suffered as a soldier with the Prince William Militia. He had marched the previous April to garrison Fort Loudoun at Winchester. He had been wounded in the leg and "made a cripple."[84]

In the last week of September 1758, Joseph Evans petitioned the legislature for relief. He had, in April 1758, marched out with the Prince Militia to garrison Fort Loudoun at Winchester. He was wounded in the leg and made a cripple.[85]

---

[73] Ibid., 172, 173.
[74] Clark, 463. See also Bockstruck, *Virginia Colonial Soldiers*, 107.
[75] Bockstruck, *Virginia Colonial Soldiers,*, 90.
[76] Clark, 415.
[77] Bockstruck, *Virginia Colonial Soldiers*, 93.
[78] Ibid., 109, 124.
[79] Clark, 482.
[80] Bockstruck, *Virginia Colonial Soldiers*, 175.
[81] Ibid., 110. See also *Virginia Military Records*, 394.
[82] Bockstruck, *Virginia Colonial Soldiers*, 103.
[83] Clark, 416.
[84] Bockstruck, *Virginia Colonial Soldiers*, 167.
[85] Ibid., 167

In November 1740, a James Evans took out a three lives lease from William Low, in Prince William. The lease was made to James, his wife Mary and his son *Joseph* Evans.[86] The son may be the Joseph Evans of the Prince William Militia who was crippled on the way to Fort Loudoun. He would be about the right age to have been a member of the militia.

- **Duncan Ferguson (aka Farguson)**

Duncan Ferguson was first found as a soldier in Captain Peter Hogg's Company in 1754, who had received bounty money for his enlistment.[87] His next appearance was as a drummer in Major Andrew Lewis's Company. He was among the party of recruits who arrived at Will's Creek after the Battle of the Meadow. His enlistment date was given as March 29th.[88]

A 1757–1758 size roll for this company revealed that Dunkin *Farguson*, a drummer, was 20 years old. He was 5 feet 9 inches tall and had been born in Scotland. He enlisted from Prince William.[89] He had a fair complexion sandy colored hair and a spare frame with good limbs.[90]

- **Henry Francis**

Henry Francis's name first appeared on a necessary roll for Captain Robert Spotswood's Company in August 1757.[91] His next appearance on a roll for Captain Spotswood was a size roll, dated October 4, 1757 at Fort Young. This roll disclosed that he was a corporal and had enlisted from Prince William. He was 24 years old, 5 feet 6 inches tall, with a dark complexion and black hair. He was "well-set." He had been born in Virginia and was a planter.[92]

In May 1780, Henry Frances appeared in the Montgomery County Court and declared that he had served as a sergeant in the 1st Virginia Regiment under different commanders in the French and Indian War. He served a total of six and a half years and was discharged by Colonel Adam Stephen. In August, 1780, it was determined that he was entitled to 200 acres of bounty land for his service.[93]

In May, 1780, he also told the Court that he was the oldest brother and heir at law to John Francis decd., a soldier in the 1st Virginia Regiment under Colonel Washington. His brother served for about three years and was killed by the Indians. He was also heir at law to William Francis decd., a soldier for three years in the 1st Battalion of the Royal American Regiment. William Francis died in the service.[94]

He received a warrant for fifty acres as the brother and heir at law of John Francis and another fifty acres as the eldest brother and heir at law of William Francis in May 1780 while living in Montgomery County.[95] He also received a fifty acre warrant in his own right as a sergeant in the 1st Virginia Regiment.[96]

- **John Frogg**

John Frogg saw service in the French and Indian War as a major and colonel in the Prince William Militia. As a major, he submitted a claim for twenty-three days service to the colonial legislature which was allowed.[97] In March 1780, the Augusta County Court was satisfied that John Frogg had served as a "colonel or major ... for a considerable time."[98]

---

[86] *Prince William County Deed Book* E, 141–142.
[87] Bockstruck, *Virginia Colonial Soldiers*, 50.
[88] Ibid., 129.
[89] Clark, 482. See also *Virginia Military Records*, 364.
[90] Bockstruck, *VCS*, 118.
[91] Ibid., 103.
[92] Clark, 474 and Bockstruck, *Virginia Colonial Soldiers*, 113.
[93] Ibid., *Virginia Colonial Soldiers*, 259.
[94] Ibid., *260.*
[95] Ibid., 306–307.
[96] Ibid.
[97] Ibid., 162.
[98] Ibid., 245.

He was an early settler of Prince William, having purchased fifty acres in June 1740 from William and Francis Thornton.[99] In April, 1741, he bought another 235 acre tract on a branch of the Occoquan River from Richard Blackburn.[100] In June, 1741, he purchased another 200 acres in the Elk Run Valley, on Horsepen Branch.[101] This land is now in Fauquier, in the southern end of the county.

♦ **John Hally (aka Haly, Hawley)**

John *Hawley* made his first appearance on a payroll for Captain Thomas Waggener's Company in June, 1756.[102] He also appeared on a July, 1756 payroll as John Hawley.[103] Payroll receipts for Captain Waggener's Company, dated July and August 1756 showed him as Private John Hawley.[104]

John *Haly* appeared on a size roll of Captain Thomas Waggener's Company in September, 1756. He was 24 years old, 5 feet 3 ½ inches tall, born in Virginia and a planter. He was recruited by Thomas Bullet. He had a full face, black straight hair and "remarkable thick legs."[105]

In May 1757, a payroll for Captain Waggener's showed Private John *Hally* as part of his company.[106]

Another size roll for Captain Waggener's Company, taken at Fort Holland on the South Branch of the Potomac in August 1757, confirmed John *Hally*'s enlistment in Prince William. His age at the time of his enlistment was 24, his height was the same as the September 1756 size roll. There were no remarks about his legs on this size roll.[107]

When he appeared on Captain Waggener's payroll dated January to May 1757 his name was spelled as John *Hally*.[108] In yet another variation of his surname, he appeared as John *Hawley* on four different necessary roll for Captain Waggener's Company in September 1757, December 1757 and March 1758.[109]

♦ **William Istobe**

In March 1759, William Istobe petitioned the colonial legislature. He had been a soldier in Captain Ashby's Company of Rangers. He was taken prisoner at Patterson's Creek in April 1756 and was taken to Quebec where he remained for nineteen months. He was then transported to England where he was exchanged.

He had a certificate signed by Captain John Ashby that he had enlisted on September 8, 1755 and served until April 1, 1756. He was due two month's pay at the time he was captured by the French and Indians. He had lived in Prince William and was gone from home nearly twenty-two months as a prisoner, at Fort Duquesne, at Montreal, and at Quebec. The colonial legislature allowed his claim for pay of £21.[110]

♦ **Moses Johnston (aka Johnson)**

Moses Johnston served in Captain David Bell's Company and is found on size rolls and payrolls for that company in 1756. He appeared on payrolls in May and June 1756 as Moses Johnston and Moses *Johnson*.[111] A size roll for July 1756 for this company showed him as Moses *Johnston*. He had enlisted in

---

[99] *Prince William County Deed Book* D, 394–398.
[100] *Prince William County Deed Book* E, 249–241.
[101] Ibid., 284–289.
[102] Bockstruck, *Virginia Colonial Soldiers,*, 61.
[103] Ibid., 62.
[104] Ibid., 415.
[105] Ibid., 90.
[106] Ibid., 435.
[107] Ibid., 107.
[108] Ibid., 93.
[109] Ibid., 109, 112, 117, 125.
[110] Ibid., 169–170.
[111] Ibid., 61, 62.

Prince William in March 1756 at age 33. He was 5 feet 8 inches tall, born in Virginia, and a planter. His description stated that he was "black as a mulatto with black hair."[112]

◆ **Solomon Jones**

Solomon Jones first appeared on a payroll for Captain Thomas Waggener, for two days in December, 1754, and for the months of January and February 1755. [113] He then appeared on a payroll for Captain Thomas Waggener, eligible for a bonus for being in the Battle of Monongahela on June 9, 1755. He was a private according to this roll.[114]

Solomon Jones was carried on a January 1756 payroll of Captain Waggener's Company.[115] His next appearance on a company payroll was in June 1756,[116] when he appeared as a private in Captain Thomas Waggener's Company. He showed up again in July of the same year on Captain Waggener's payroll which was filed as part of a return of stores and provision, while the company was stationed at Fort Cumberland.[117]

His name was *not* found on the size roll of Captain Waggener's Company at Fort Holland on the South Branch of the Potomac in August 1757, nor was he found on necessary rolls for Waggener's company filed in September and December 1757.[118] He may not have been in service when these rolls were taken in 1757.

While Solomon Jones did not appear on a size roll for Captain Thomas Waggener that revealed his county of enlistment, he *may* have lived in Prince William. There *was* a Solomon Jones of Prince William who was referenced in a Fauquier County Minute Book in 1771.[119] Without further research in Prince William Deeds and early tax records, it is not possible to identify the Solomon Jones who served in Captain Thomas Waggener's Company with the Solomon Jones of Prince William who appeared in Fauquier in 1771.

◆ **Thomas Lattin**

Thomas Lattin appeared on Captain George Mercer's size roll for August 2, 1756. He had enlisted in Prince William on November 1, 1755 when he was 24 years old. He was 5 feet 2 inches tall, born in Ireland and was a malster by trade. He had a brown complexion, and was a "sturdy, low man, very brisk, [and] talks much on the brogue." [120]

◆ **Leonard Leachman**

In November, 1759, Leonard Leachman presented a petition to the colonial legislature for payment for service in the Prince William militia. In 1758, he was drafted into the Prince William militia. He served for 108 days but his name was omitted by mistake from the payrolls.

On March 10, 1761, the legislature took up his petition for payment for 108 days of service in the Prince William militia. A week later, they authorized £4 17s as payment for his service in the county militia.[121]

---

[112] Ibid., 64.
[113] Ibid., 51.
[114] Clark, 379.
[115] Bockstruck, *VCS*, 56–57.
[116] Ibid., 61.
[117] Clark 372, 378.
[118] Bockstruck, *Virginia Colonial Soldiers*, 108, 108, 117.
[119] See John P. Alcock, *Fauquier Families 1759–1799* (Athens: Iberian Publishing Company, 1994), 198. Alcock refers to Solomon Jones as "Solomon Jones of PW," according to a Fauquier County Minute Book 4, 319.
[120] Bockstruck, *Virginia Colonial Soldiers,*, 87. See also *Virginia Military Records*, 393.
[121] Ibid., 171, 172. 173.

- ### Henry Lee

Henry Lee was the Colonel of the Prince William Militia. His militia account was among those considered by a legislature-appointed committee in June 1754. His account dealt with pay for county militia and their provisions.[122]

He also corresponded with Colonel George Washington on matters relating to his post as County Lieutenant. In October 1755, Colonel Washington wrote Colonel Lee from Fredericksburg.

> As I understand Lord Fairfax has had great reason to order one hundred of the Militia of your County [Prince William] to march, to assist in the protection of our Frontiers; I must desire, that you will see that they come on Horse-back, as they will thereby be enable to make Dispatch and to carry Provisions with them, which must be done, as the scarcity of Bread between this and Fort Cumberland, renders it absolutely necessary. I must earnestly recommend dispatch to you, as you must be truly sensible, that the present situation of Affairs, will not admit of the least delay.
>
> I shall be at Winchester tomorrow, and shall expect to see your Detachment there the next Day or the day after, at the farthest.[123]

In a May 1756 incident at Winchester, when Colonel Lee was present, members of the Prince William militia became so abusive towards the soldiers of the Virginia Regiment that one militia man was seized and ordered to cool his heels in the guardhouse. The Prince William, incensed at this treatment of one of their own, stormed the guard house and released the prisoner. To compound this, another of the officers swore that all the officers of the Virginia Regiment were "scoundrels."

This insult to the Regiment did not sit well and the militia officer was reprimanded and informed of the possible consequences to his and his militia's action under military law. Shaken by the reprimand, the officer went to Washington and apologized. The Colonel decided not to court martial the officer since the Virginia Regiment had made him sufficiently aware of the culpability of his actions.[124]

Still, Washington thought it prudent to deploy the Prince William Militia elsewhere, so he sent them off to build stockades and storehouses on the Little Cacapon and Paterson Creeks.[125]

In July 1757, Colonel Washington wrote to Colonel Lee, with orders for him to proceed to Fredericksburg where he was to remain until the arrival of the drafts for the Regiment. Washington ordered him to take the drafted men's "names, size, complexion, age, country, and former employment," along with the names of the officers who delivered them. Lee was to specify the number of men received from each officer and give him a receipt for them.

Washington did not want any men accepted into the Regiment who were subject to fits, had ulcers or old sores on their legs or any other disease that would render them incapable of service. He put a cap on the height of the men as well—no one less than 5 feet 4 inches was to be accepted *unless* they were active and well-built.

Lee was then to order the men "up here in parties" and transit an exact muster roll of the command to him. "You are to give the Officers of these commands," he went on, "orders to be particularly careful, and to use every precaution to prevent desertion."

Colonel Lee was to obtain provisions for the draftees "upon the best terms" available and he was to see the men were properly supplied. Once this requisitioning had been completed, Lee was to continue to Fredericksburg. If any of the draftees should desert, Lee was to write the appropriate commanding officer

---

[122] *Virginia Military Records*, 44.
[123] Robert Hedges, Colonel George Washington to Colonel Henry Lee, dated Fredericksburg, October 8, 1755," *The Encyclopedia of Dumfries, Virginia 1740–1759* (http://www.ecsd.com/~rhhedgz1/1740--49.HTML
[124] Sandra Mayo, "Fairfax and Prince William Counties in the French and Indian War," *Northern Virginia Heritage*, February 1987 (Vol. IX No. 1) (http://www.historic princewilliam.org).
[125] Ibid.

of the county from which the man or men came and request aid in apprehending and sending the deserters to the Regiment.[126]

In October 1765, Commissioners were appointed to examine various Militia Accounts associated with the French and Indian War service. Colonel Lee's name, with others, appeared in a schedule attached to the October 1765 Militia Act providing for the appointment of Commissioners to examine and state the Militia Accounts of militia men ordered into actual service during the French and War. Colonel Lee was allowed £479 6s 4d to pay Captains William Tebbs and Thomas McClenaham for their service as well as that of the Prince William Militia to August 30, 1758.[127]

Henry Lee lived at "Leesylvania," near Dumfries. He served a short stint in the colonial legislature from 1756–1758.[128] He stood for election, as a representative from Prince William, for the House of Burgesses in May. While it was considered "bad form" to ask for a vote outright, candidates were permitted to have their friends encourage others to vote for them.

Food and drink were permitted at the Courthouse for all voters. Individuals called out their votes publicly. It was not unusual for as many as three or four candidates to stand for election. Two Burgesses would be then be selected to represent the county. Lee initially won the election in 1756.

However, Henry Peyton successfully appealed the election with the result that Lee was expelled by the House of Burgesses in March 1756, for bribing voters. Henry Peyton then took Lee's place in the colonial legislature. However, Lee was successful in accruing enough votes to win in 1758, and returned with his old rival, Henry Peyton to serve until 1761. He ultimately served as a member of the colonial assembly from Prince William from 1761 through 1774.[129]

♦ Archibald Lockard (aka Lockhart, Lockett)

Archibald Lockard, or Lockhart as his name was sometimes spelled, was a soldier in Captain George Mercer's Company. He appeared on a size roll for this company in August 1756. He had enlisted October 19, 1755 in Prince William, when he was 23 years old. He was 5 feet 6 inches tall and a planter. Lockard was born in Scotland. He had a dark complexion, smooth face, and short curled hair. He "speaks upon the brogue."[130]

His name next appeared, still spelled Archibald Lockard, on a payroll for Captain Mercer's Company in September 1756.[131] He was Archibald *Lockhart* on the August 28, 1757 size roll for Colonel George Washington's Company. He had enlisted in October 1757 at age 25 in Prince William County. His height in this size roll was given as 5 feet 4 ½ inches and his occupation was that of a carpenter. He was born in Scotland. He had a brown complexion and brown hair.[132]

Archibald Lockhart, or *Lockett* proved his right to bounty land in Kentucky County in February 1788 for service as a soldier in the 1st Virginia Regiment in the French and Indian War. He assigned his warrant for 50 acres.[133]

♦ Michael Lynn

Michael Lynn petitioned the legislature in November 1761. He stated that in 1756 he was one of the militiamen detached from Prince William. He was wounded in an engagement with the Indians on the

---

[126] Hedges, "Colonel George Washington to Colonel Henry Lee, dated July 1, 1757," *The Encyclopedia of Dumfries* (http://www.ecsd.com).
[127] Bockstruck, *Virginia Colonial Soldiers*, 214.
[128] Wikipedia, "Henry Lee II," Wikipedia, the free encyclopedia (http://en.wikipedia.org/wiki/Henry_Lee_II). Henry Lee's full biography may be found here.
[129] Historic Prince William, "Burgesses of Prince William County," (http://www.historicprincewilliam.org/burges.html),2.
[130] Bockstruck, *Virginia Colonial Soldiers*, 86. See also *Virginia Military Records,* 391.
[131] Bockstruck, *Virginia Colonial Soldiers,*, 92.
[132] Ibid., 105.
[133] Bockstruck, *Bounty Land and Donation Grants,* 233.

South Branch and is now unable to do any work. There was considerable expense associated with his recovery.

In November 1761, he was allowed £15 for wounds received in the engagement with the Indians on the South Branch of the Potomac.[134]

♦ **Thomas Muccaboy (aka Macaboy)**

Thomas Maccaboy proved his service in the French and Indian War in the Fauquier County Court, in March 1780. He served in the 47th British Regiment of Foot and produced a certificate signed by Colonel William Russell that he had been discharged as unfit for duty.[135]

♦ **Thomas McClanahan (aka McClanachan)**

Captain Thomas McClanahan petitioned the colonial legislature in September 1758 for payment of one of his horses lost on an express to Henry Lee. The captain was the commanding officer of a detachment of Prince William militia ordered out to Fort George on the south branch of the Potomac. One of his horses was lost by an express rider to Henry Lee, the commanding officer of the Prince William militia. He requested compensation.[136]

In Hening's *Statutes,* Captain McClanahan's name appeared on a schedule attached to the October 1765 Militia account for Prince William. "Thomas McClanaham, for his pay and that of guards conducting drafted soldiers to Winchester, £2 4s."[137]

In February, 1780 in Culpeper County, six[138] bounty land warrants for 50 acres each were issued to Captain Thomas McClanachan assignee of five soldiers in the 1st and 2nd Virginia Regiments for their service in the French and Indian War.

♦ **Lochlan McLean (aka McLain)**

Lochlan McLean was a soldier in Colonel George Washington's Company. He appeared on a roll for Colonel Washington's Company in August 1756. He had enlisted in January 1755 in Prince William when he was 24 years old. He was 5 feet 8 inches tall, born in Scotland, and a planter. He had a brown complexion and dark hair.[139]

His last appearance on a roll of Colonel Washington's was in August 1757. On this roll, his name was Lauchlin McLain. He enlisted in January 1755 at age 25. His height was 5 feet 8 inches. He was born in Scotland, and a planter. He had a brown complexion and brown hair.[140]

♦ **Gabriel Nevil**

Gabriel Nevil's name appeared on Captain George Mercer's size roll, dated August 2, 1756. He had enlisted December 15, 1754 in Prince William when he was 24 years old. He was 5 feet 11 inches, born in Virginia. His occupation was that of a tailor. His description was as follows: a "grinning look and snuffles, [with] a scar in [his] left eye."[141]

He also made two appearances on Captain Mercer's payrolls, for September and November, 1756.[142]

---

[134] Bockstruck, *Virginia Colonial Soldiers,*, 163, 174.
[135] Peters, *Fauquier County Military Records 1759–1784,* 61.
[136] Bockstruck, *Virginia Colonial Soldiers,* 167.
[137] Ibid., 214.
[138] Ibid., 293.
[139] Ibid., 85. See also *Virginia Military Records,* 390.
[140] Bockstruck, *Virginia Colonial Soldiers,* 104.
[141] Ibid., 87. See also *Virginia Military Records,* 393.
[142] Bockstruck, *Virginia Colonial Soldiers,* 92.

♦ **Henry Nevil**

Henry Nevil was another soldier in Captain George Mercer's Company who appeared on Mercer's size roll dated August 2, 1756. He had enlisted November 1, 1755 in Prince William when he was just 20 years old. He was 5 feet 7 inches, born in Virginia, and a planter. He had a brown complexion and dark skin and "snuffles."[143] He, too, appeared on Captain Mercer's payrolls for September and October, 1756.[144]

A Henry *Nevils* proved his right to bounty land for service in the French and Indian War in September 1779 in Rockbridge County. He stated that he was a soldier in the Virginia Regiment commanded by Colonel George Washington. He received fifty acres and assigned it.[145]

♦ **Clement Norman**

Clement Norman was a trooper in the Prince William Militia whose claim for 66 days of service was allowed by the colonial legislature.[146] On March 10, 1760, he petitioned the legislature for reimbursement of £5 paid to Dr Parker for attending his son who was shot and died in the service. The legislature allowed the £ 5 reimbursement to Norman two days later, on March 12, 1760.[147]

He appeared on a 1751 "List of Taxpayers in Elk Run and vicinity,", then located in Prince William. When Fauquier County was formed from Prince William in 1759, the Elk Run Valley became part of Fauquier. In 1796, Clement Norman received 1320 pounds of tobacco as payment for his services as a trooper in the Prince William Militia during the French and Indian War.[148]

♦ **Henry Peyton**

Henry Peyton was the Lieutenant-Colonel of the Prince William Militia, and in that capacity, acted as the second-in-command to Colonel Henry Lee. In the election of 1756 to the House of Burgesses, for the right to represent Prince William, he successfully challenged Colonel Lee's election to that body. The end result was that Lee's election was thrown out because he allegedly bribed voters to vote for him. Peyton took his place in the legislature.

However, it is unlikely that he ever attended the legislature in 1756 since he was active on the frontier, building forts along the Cacapon and Patterson Creeks. In May 1756 Prince William Militia had been chastised severely for their insubordination after an altercation broke out between the militia and the Virginia Regiment. This resulted in the Prince William Militia being sent to build stockades and storage facilities on frontier. Washington had originally intended for Captain Baylis to lead this contingent out to the Little Cacapon and Patterson Creeks.

However, Lieutenant Colonel Peyton insisted on going as well. Washington issued orders for Peyton to strengthen the garrisons at Cocke's and Ashby's Forts and to erect another fort in order to secure the pass at the mouth of the Little Cacapon.

Then, Colonel received the embarrassing news that a sergeant and fourteen of his privates had deserted a loss of one sixth of his enlisted strength. Washington countered these desertions at once, with an order that if any militia ordered to the small forts on the South Branch deserted, they would immediately be drafted into the Virginia Regiment.[149]

In mid-May, 1756, Washington issued orders to the militia contingents on the frontier as a result of a Council of War. Colonel Peyton, a captain, four subalterns, four sergeants and ninety men from the Prince

---

[143] Ibid., 86.
[144] Ibid., 92.
[145] Bockstruck, *Bounty Land and Donation Grants,*, 294.
[146] Bockstruck, *Virginia Colonial Soldiers,*, 162.
[147] Ibid., 171–172.
[148] V. Layne Moffett, "Clement Norman" (http://files.usgwarchives.org/wv/harrison/bios/norman.txt) (Accessed September 17, 2008).
[149] Mayo, "Fairfax and Prince William Counties in the French and Indian War" (http://historicprincewilliam.org).

William Militia were ordered posted at the mouth of the Little Cacapon.[150] He wrote Peyton ordering him "to proceed with the whole of your Militia, to the mouth of Little Capecapon."[151]

During the same month, Washington wrote again to Peyton, ordering him to consult with Governor Innes on the most expedient way to pursue the Indians in his vicinity. Washington found it "requisite [for Peyton] to continue [his] command on these waters [the Little Cacapon and Patterson Creeks], to range and scout about, and to secure the grain and cattle of the inhabitants from the enemy; [rather] than to build that Fort on Cacapon [Creek]. ... If you learn any further intelligence about the strength and motions of the Enemy, which you may think worth regarding, I desire you would lose no time in communicating it to me."[152]

In late June 1757, Washington wrote Colonel Peyton from Fort Loudoun. In this letter he told Peyton that he had discharged John Wood, who employed Doctor Bowles in his place as well as John Highwarden "who, thro' age and consequent infirmity, is altogether unfit to undergo the fatigues of a soldier." He went on to chastise Peyton for the small number of drafts received from Prince William. Colonel Washington recommended that Peyton "use the most speedy and effectual means of sending [his] quota; for we stand greatly in need of them."[153]

It is not known whether Colonel Peyton was successful in filling his quota for the militia in June 1757. He did return to Virginia to serve out his term in the House of Burgesses, though. He went on to become one of the incorporators of Dumfries, and served terms as a justice and Sheriff of the county.[154]

In March 1761, Henry Peyton, Thomas Slaughter and William Green petitioned the colonial legislature for their trouble and expenses in settling the accounts for pay and provisions for the militia and the damages done in Prince William, Stafford, Orange, and Culpeper. The legislature allowed the three officers £15 each for their trouble.[155]

♦ John Pope

John Pope was a corporal in Captain George Mercer's Company. He appeared on two size rolls of this company. The first roll was dated August 2, 1756. He had enlisted in Prince William on December 22, 1754 at age eighteen He was 5 feet 7 inches tall, and had been born in Virginia. He was a carpenter. His description showed him to be "fair, [with] a fresh look, [and] fair hair."[156]

The second size roll for Captain Mercer's Company was dated August 28, 1757. In this roll he enlisted in Prince William, but on a slightly earlier date— November 1754. His age was still eighteen while his height was given as 5 feet 8 inches. Still listed as a corporal, he was a planter, born in Virginia, according to this roll. He had a "dark complexion, [and] light brown hair."[157]

♦ Prince William Militia

Problems with discipline and desertion in May 1756 in the Prince William Militia have already been discussed.[158] Suffice it to say that Washington issued orders to supply Captain John Baylis with tools to construct a small fort at the mouth of the Cacapon in mid May. Two months later, Baylis, now a Major in the Prince William Militia, and his men were ordered to bring in the harvest left on neighboring abandoned plantations.

---

[150] Hedges, "Orders for the Militia, [May 15, 1756,]" *The Encyclopedia of Dumfries* (http://www.ecsd.com/~rhhedgz1/1740-59.HTML) (Accessed September 18, 2008).
[151] Ibid., "Colonel George Washington to Colonel Henry Peyton, dated Winchester, May 16, 1756."
[152] Ibid., "Colonel George Washington to Colonel Henry Peyton, dated Winchester May 17, 1756."
[153] Ibid., "Colonel George Washington to Colonel Henry Peyton, dated Fort Loudoun, June 30, 1757."
[154] Ibid. [dated 17 November 1779 entry].
[155] Bockstruck, *VCS*, 174.
[156] Ibid., 85.
[157] Ibid., 103.
[158] See entries under Colonel Henry Lee and Lieutenant-Colonel Henry Peyton.

Then in July 1756, John's brother, Captain William Baylis, led a contingent of Prince William Militia in a confrontation with the Indians at Fort Pearsall.[159] This fort had been built in 1756 in what is now Romney, West Virginia, to protect local settlers from Indian raids along the South Branch of the Potomac. It had been erected originally as a log house with a stockade by Job and John Pearsall on their plantation.[160]

In March 1767, Job Pearsall of Hampshire County presented a petition to the legislature. In 1756 he had a large fort erected on his land by order of Colonel Washington. The timber was cut down in great quantities and used by the inhabitants and garrison until the end of General Forbes's campaign in 1758. When the wars began with the Indians in 1763, the fort was repaired and Pearsall "pitched on" for a garrison until 1764. He piloted officers and parties many times across the creek and had to return at night for security reasons. In April, 1767, and again in May, the legislature referred the petition to its next session. Six months later, in November 1767, the petition had still not been resolved.[161]

After harvesting the crops on the abandoned plantations, the Prince William Militia was to be discharged. Captain Baylis was advised by Washington not to impress horses for his men. "There have," Washington said, "been many complaints made to me of the militia officers impressing horses to dome down here and ride about upon their own business."[162]

In a June 1757 letter to Governor Dinwiddie, Washington wrote of the "odd behavior" of the militia from Fairfax, Prince William, and Culpeper counties. Not only were the men without arms, they also had no ammunition or provisions.

In June 1758, Washington found the militia to be negligent in the care of their ammunition. They wasted in hunting and firing on targets for wagers. He instructed Captain Thomas McClanahan of Prince William to "maintain a careful accounting of the ammunition used, and for what purpose." While an additional supply of ammunition was issued to the Prince William militia stationed at South Branch, the commanding officer was directed to take "proper care that a more frugal use be made, or the expense ... will be deducted from their pay."[163]

In May 1758, the County Lieutenant for Prince William was ordered to send 100 militia under the command of two captains to garrison Fort Loudoun at Winchester and to continue their duty there until December 20, 1758.

On the June 19, 1757, they were ordered out to the frontier along the South Branch. At that order, Charles Ward, Henry Kelly, William Kelly, Peter Lawrence, John Priest, Rawleigh Hopper, Anthony Orchard, Edward Lawrence, and Benjamin Neal deserted.

Isaac Suttle, John Thomas, James Davis, Joshua Shumake, Thomas Carter, Humphrey Grub, Samuel Luttrel, John Robertson, Moses Hopper, Joseph Taylor, and Charles Cornwell deserted and never returned. In September 1758, the legislature decided to pay the first nine men for the time they continued in the service. However the latter thirteen who did not return to their posts were not to be paid.[164]

In June 1758, Colonel Washington wrote Francis Fauquier from Fort Loudoun. He talked about the Prince William Militia in this letter.

> This day the Prince William Militia are to march for the South Branch, to relieve two companies of my Regiment, agreeably6 to orders. I shou'd think myself difficient in my duty were I to pass over in silence the transactions of and state of this company from their first coming out, about the 20th...
>
> One hundred Militia then, were order'd from Prince William County (but at what time I can't exactly say ...) instead of that number, they sent 73 and everyone of them unprovided with either arms or ammunition, as the Law directs. By which means they were useless but burthensome to the Country, as they receiv'd true Allowance of Provisions and had their pay running on.

---

[159] Mayo, "Fairfax and Prince William Counties in the French and Indian War" (http://historicprincewillilam.org).
[160] Wikipedia, "Fort Pearsall," Wikipedia, the free encyclopedia (http://en.wikipedia.org/wiki/Fort_Pearsall).
[161] Bockstruck, *VCS*, 192–194.
[162] Mayo, "Fairfax and Prince William Counties in the French and Indian War" (http://historicprincewilliam.org).
[163] Ibid.
[164] Bockstruck, *Virginia Colonial Soldiers*, 167.

This matter was represented to Colo. Henry Lee, Lieut't of that County, by Sir Jno. St. Clair, then commanding officer here. The consequence of this representation was that about the first of this Inst't, near 100 arms were sent up by his order, out of which number scarce 5 were serviceable. Not more than 30 cou'd possibly be made to Fire.

This was also represent'd to Colo. Lee, who after professing a concern for it said, they expect'd arms from England, (I think) every day, and took no further Acct of the matter that I have yet heard of. I immediately set Smiths to repairing their arms, and have at last, with the assistance of 36 old muskets which I caus'd to be deliver'd out of the store here, got this company, which shou'd consist of 100 men (tho' there is but 68) at last completed.

Till this time, they have been a dead expence to the Publick, and no service to the Inhabitants. This Sir, are serious facts, and really merits [reprehension[for, if the Country, as is in the present case for instance, if the troops had march'd agreeable to my first Orders, the companies on the South Branch wou'd have been drawn off and the inhabitants left either destitute of relief, or have come off with them, which they determin'd to do.

This I understand actually happen'd in Augusta County, when Maj'r Lewis came from thence, by the negligence, I suppose of the County Lieutenants.[165]

♦ Prince William Militia Claims

The House of Burgesses allowed these militia claims for service for soldiers and officers in the Prince William Militia:

To **John Frogg, Major**, for 23 days service;

To **Captain William Baylis**, for 80 days service;

To these officers for 93 days service:
Lieutenant of Horse, **Richard Taylor** and Lieutenant of Horse **William Splane**.

To Cornet **William Farrow**, and Corporal **Samuel Porter**, Corporal **Jacob Spillman**, Corporal **William Whalley**, and Corporal **Lewis Reno**, all for 93 days service.

To these men for 66 days service: Sergeant **Henry Floyd**, Corporal **William Buchanan**, Corporal **Thomas Hoard**, and Corporal **George Kenner**.

To **Foushee Tebbs** for 13 days service

To Captain **John Baylis** and Lieutenant of Foot **James Seaton** for 26 days

To Lieutenant of Foot **Richard Hampton** for 22 days.

These troopers were allowed their claims for 93 days service: **Joseph Nevill, Richard Matthews, Benjamin Wilson, Stephen Morris, Thomas Marshall, Richard Marshall, John Luttrell, Thomas Doyle, Joshua Welch, Nathaniel Freeman, Stanley Singleton, Samuel Balson, John Murray, William Fielder,** and **Andrew Cannaird.**

These troopers were allowed their claim for 66 days service: **John McMillon, Henry Kemper, John Fishback, Clement Norman, Joseph Martin, Richard Byrns, Peter Pierce, Michael Lynn, John Cornwell, John Dowell, William Key, Robert Nevill, Thomas Gardiner, Charles Smith, Isaac Gibson, Benjamin Edwards, John Coreham, Griffith Matthews, John Bland Jr., William Peak,** and **William Berry.**

To **Gilbert Crupper**, and **Samuel Grigsby**, troopers for 9 days service

To **William Barr**, a trooper with 8 days service.

To **Nathaniel Overall**, a trooper with 13 days service.

These foot soldiers claims were allowed for 93 days service:
Nicholas Hill, John Bolling, Edward Oneal, Joseph Neal, John Carter, Thomas Shirley, Lewis Oden, John Green, Martin Suttle, David Parsons, George Rose, John Low, James Crockett, William Suttle, and **William Bowling.**

These foot soldiers claims were allowed for 66 days service:
Isaac Settle, William Jennings, Valentine Barton, William Crouch, Moses Coppage, and **John Rice.**

---

[165] Hedges, "Letter from Colonel Washington to Francis Fauquier, dated Fort Loudoun, June 19, 1758," *The Encyclopedia of Dumfries Virginia* (http://www.ecsd.org).

George Calvert Jr's claim for an express was also allowed.[166]

* **Prince William Militia Petitions**

In May 1757, **David Parsons, John Morgan, John Munk, John Darnal, Josiah Fishback, Leonard Davis, Thomas Conway Jr., William Turner, John Twentyman, James Corder,** and **Joshua Welsh** petitioned the legislature. They had been drafted from the Prince William Militia for 79 days service on the frontier. The men returned home without the consent of their commissioned officers in order to provide themselves with clothes and other necessaries. The legislature thought the petition was reasonable and payment was to be made for service.[167]

In September 1758, **John Markham** petitioned the colonial legislature for his pay as a corporal in the Prince William Militia. He was sent out in 1755 with a detachment of county militia and served 66 days as a corporal. His name was inadvertently left off the list certified by the late Assembly. His claim was allowed and he received £4 2s 6d for his service as a corporal in the county militia.[168]

In the same month, **John Murray's** petition for payment for service as a blacksmith was rejected. It seems that in 1757 he was sent out with drafted militia from PWC and employed as a blacksmith in the service for 90 days. He requested payment at the rate of 50 lbs of tobacco per diem rather than that of a common soldier which he has already received.[169]

In November 1762, **William Purcell** petitioned the legislature for going as an express rider to the South Branch of the Potomac to a captain of the Prince William militia on the orders of the commanding officer of the county's militia and returning immediately. The legislature allowed £ 2 5s 8d for his claim, as the assignee of Giles Burdett, for the express.[170]

On April 28, 1757, **Francis Triplett** petition the legislature. He was a volunteer in the Prince William Militia sent out in June 1756 to the frontier. In a skirmish with the enemy, he was wounded in the right arm and went to considerable expense in the care of his limb. The next day, the legislature allowed him £55 for his expenses in caring for his arm.[171]

* **Daniel Robinson**

Daniel Robinson was a private soldier in Lieutenant Colonel Adam Stephen's Company. His name appeared on a size roll for that company dated July 13, 1756. Robinson had enlisted on October 22, 1755, in Prince William, at age nineteen. He was 5 feet 3 inches tall, born in Virginia, and a planter. He had "black hair, a brown complexion, [and was] well made."[172]

* **John Scott**

John Scott was a private and a corporal in Captain Harry Woodward's Company. His name appeared on a size roll for this company dated July 13, 1756. Scott had enlisted in December 1745 in Prince William when he was twenty-eight years old. He was 5 feet 3 ½ inches tall, and a sailor. He had been born in Scotland. He had a brown complexion, and was "thick and well set." [173]

His name appeared on payrolls for Captain Woodward's Company, in July and August 1756. The August payroll showed his rank as a corporal.[174] He also appeared on an "exact necessary roll," of Captain Woodward's when the company was stationed at Fort Lyleton, in August 1757.[175] His last

---

[166] Bockstruck, *Virginia Colonial Soldiers,* 162.
[167] Ibid., 164.
[168] Ibid., 168, 214.
[169] Ibid., 167.
[170] Ibid., 176–177.
[171] Ibid., 163.
[172] Ibid., 80. See also *Virginia Military Records,* 377 which gives the identical information minus the description.
[173] Bockstruck, *Virginia Colonial Soldiers,* 81.
[174] Ibid., 83, 89. See also Clark, 416.
[175] Ibid., 103.

appearance on a roll in this company took place in September 1757 when he showed up on another size roll. On this roll, he was a corporal, a "Scotchman," thirty-nine years old, and 5 feet 4 inches tall. He had enlisted in Prince William. He was a planter. He had a dark complexion and "quiet [of] speech."[176]

+ **George Seaton**

George Seaton appeared on only one roll, a size roll for Captain George Mercer, dated August 2, 1756. He had enlisted in Prince William on November 8, 1755 when he was seventeen. He was 5 feet 6 inches tall and a sawyer. He had been born in Virginia. He had a "brown complexion, brown skin, thin visage, [and] looks brisk, [with] small legs."[177]

+ **William Smith**

William Smith served as a corporal who had enlisted from Prince William in Major Andrew Lewis's Company, according to a size roll dated 1757–1758. He was twenty-seven years old when he enlisted in Prince William and 5 feet 8 inches tall. He was a shoemaker.[178] An undated size roll for Major Lewis's Company gave more details about him. He was a corporal, born in Virginia, 5 feet 8 ½ inches tall, and a shoemaker. He had "large well made limbs, [and] fair hair."[179] He was a corporal on an August 1757 size roll for the company and found on a return of Major Lewis's Company wanting necessaries in September 1757.[180]

In March 1780, William Smith, now living in Fauquier, appeared in the County Court there and produced a certificate from General Stephen that he served five or six campaigns in the 1st Virginia Regiment in the last war [the French and Indian War]. Smith swore, on oath, that his certificate was authentic and that he had never before claimed or proved his right to land for this service. The Court ordered this to be certified.[181]

During the same Court session, William Smith was certified as the heir at law to Robert Smith, who also served as a soldier in the 1st Virginia Regiment in the last war. A certificate from General Stephen attested to this and was proved to be authentic by the oath of William Smith. He swore, on his oath, that Robert had died in the war without ever having claimed or proved his right to land for this service. The Court ordered this certified as well.[182]

+ **Edward Thompson (aka Tompson)**

Edward Thompson served as a private in Captain Thomas Waggener's Company. He appeared on necessary rolls for Waggener's Company July, 14, 1757, September 14, 1757, November 1757, and December 4, 1757.[183]

It was the size roll for August 1757 for Captain Waggener's Company stationed at Fort Holland on the South Branch that revealed Edward Thompson as a soldier who enlisted from Prince William. He was twenty-three at the time of his enlistment and 5 feet 4 inches tall. He had been born in England and was a sailor. He was of a fair complexion.[184]

His name was also found on a payroll, as Edward *Tompson,* for Captain Waggener's Company at Fort George from November 12, 1757 to January 21, 1758.[185] His last appearance on a roll for Captain

---

[176] Ibid., 109.
[177] Ibid., 86.
[178] Clark, 484.
[179] Ibid., *Virginia Colonial Soldiers,* 118.
[180] Ibid., 106. No details regarding other information for soldiers was found in this abstract. See also *VCS,* 112.
[181] Peters, *Fauquier County Military Records, 1759–1784,* 29.
[182] Ibid.
[183] Bockstruck, *Virginia Colonial Soldiers,* 109, 124, and Clark, 467, 482.
[184] Bockstruck, *Virginia Colonial Soldiers,* 108.
[185] Ibid., 124.

Waggener's Company came in a necessary roll dated March 1, 1758 at Fort Hopewell. In this roll his name was spelled *Tompson*.[186]

♦ Joshua Wells

Joshua Well was found on one undated size roll of Captain Joshua Lewis's 7th Company of the Virginia Regiment. He had enlisted in Prince William, by Lieutenant Wright. He was thirty-two at the time of his enlistment and a planter. He had been born in England. He had a brown complexion and black hair.[187]

♦ Ezekiel Young

Ezekiel Young's name appeared on a size roll for Captain Thomas Waggener's Company, stationed at Fort Holland on the South Branch, August 1757. He had enlisted in Prince William when he was twenty years old. He was 5 feet 2 1/2 inches tall, born in England, and a farmer. He had a brown complexion.[188] Young appeared on Captain Waggener's necessary rolls on the South Branch, of which two were filed in September 1757, one in November 1757, and one in December 1757.[189] He also showed up on a payroll for this company from November 12, 1757 to January 21, 1758.[190] His final appearance on a roll for Captain Waggener was on a necessary roll filed at Fort Hopewell on the South Branch on March 1, 1758.[191]

---

[186] Ibid., 125.
[187] Ibid., 96.
[188] Ibid., 108. See also Clark, 484 whose information shows his height to be 5 feet 5 rather than 5 feet 2 ½.
[189] Bockstruck, *Virginia Colonial Soldiers*, 109, 113, 117, and 124.
[190] Ibid., 124.
[191] Ibid.

APPENDIX 2

Elijah Green's Pension File S 37961

Historical Background
Prince William County's Minute and Order Books from 1814–1832 are no longer extant. This means that those revolutionary war veterans from Prince William who applied for need-based assistance under the Pension Act of March 1818 are as of yet unknown.

While these missing minute and order books have made it difficult to discover Prince William County veterans, one such pension has come to light while researching the Court entries involving Elijah Green for December 2, 1833, October 1834, and January 1835.

In the December 1833 entry, the Court certified that "Peggy Abel, formerly Peggy Green and Sally Rolls, formerly Sally Green of Prince William, and Elijah Green of the District of Columbia were the only surviving heirs of Elijah Green decd, late of Prince William and a pensioner at the time of his death."

In October 1834, The Court certified that Elijah Green died "without leaving a widow" and once again named Peggy Abel, Sally Rolls, and Elijah Green as his surviving children. In the final entry, in January 1835, the Court certified that Elijah Green's children were all of age.

Armed with this information I went on footnote.com and downloaded Elijah Green's pension file. The abstract that follows underscores the importance of researching beyond the Court Minutes for further information about a pensioner and soldier. In this instance, an elusive 1818 pension declaration was uncovered in a large pension file that also contained other information that helped draw a clearer picture of this Revolutionary War veteran.

Abstract of Elijah Green's Pension File S 37961
His original pension declaration in November 1818 was made before Judge William A. G. Dade, a Judge of the General Court whose jurisdiction extended to Prince William. Mr. Green was sixty-six at the time of his declaration. His declaration was made to receive benefits under the Act of Congress entitled "An act to provide for certain persons engaged in the Land and Naval service of the United States in the Revolutionary war," passed in March 1818.

He stated that he had enlisted in Prince William in 1776 in Captain Thomas Ewell's company of Virginia Troops in Colonel Gibson's Regiment. He served in the same company and regiment until 1780 when he was discharged in Virginia. He fought at Stony Point, Monmouth, and many other battles. He was in reduced circumstances and needed the assistance of his country.

Charles Ewell's affidavit accompanied Green's pension declaration. Charles Ewell was another captain in the 1st Virginia State Regiment under the command of Colonel George Gibson from 1776 until the end of the war.

Captain Ewell confirmed that Elijah Green was a soldier in this regiment and had enlisted under Captain Thomas Ewell, who was now dead. Green enlisted for three years and served faithfully during that time.

Both he and Judge Dade testified that Green was in reduced circumstances and the Judge was satisfied that Green had, indeed, served in the Revolutionary War as he stated in his declaration "against the common enemy for the term of three years … on the Continental establishment."

The pension declaration and affidavits were sent to the Secretary of War with the seal and sworn statement of the Clerk of Court, Philip Dawe, that William A. G. Dade was still a Judge of the General Court and full faith and credit ought to be given to his statements.

Elijah Green's pension was initially granted for his service as a private for eight months in the Virginia Line. The pension certificate, number 4859, was issued in December 1818 and sent to Judge Dade. Then it was rescinded when it was found that he had served in the State Line, not the Continental Line. The need-based pension act of March 1818 only applied to those Continental Line veterans who were in reduced circumstances.

Thirteen years later, in June 1831, John W. Williams, a Justice of the Peace for Prince William County, wrote to William S. Colquhoun. Attached to the letter was an affidavit from Patrick McEwing that Elijah Green had enlisted in 1777 and served for three years in Captain Thomas Winder Ewell's company in the 1st Virginia State Regiment under the command of Colonel George Gibson. McEwing stated that Green had faithfully served out his term of enlistment.

Williams told Colquhoun that, if Colquhoun would prepare Green's papers in proper form, then the Justice of the Peace would sign a certificate embracing the evidence of McEwing. He went on to say "I am not acquainted with the mode of preparing old soldiers papers or I would prepare Mr Greens for him with a great deal of cheerfulness. I know of no one," he told Colquhoun, "more willing than yourself to aid old soldiers in obtaining their rights." He hoped, that between the two of them, "Mr Green will be able to accomplish his wishes."

Two months later, in August 1831, Elijah Green appeared once again in the Prince William County Court to make a further declaration, this time under the Pension Act of March 1818 and the Act of May 1820. By this time, he was eighty-one years old.

He enlisted for three years in January 1777 in Virginia in Captain Thomas Ewell's company, Colonel George Gibson's Regiment in the line of the state of Virginia on Continental Establishment. He continued in this company and regiment until the expiration of his term when he was discharged from the service in Alexandria.

He relinquished any claim whatever to a pension except the present one. His name had been placed on the pension list; He had lost his certificate of pension and had never exhibited a schedule of his property because "from his extreme age, infirmity, and ignorance of business he did not know how to proceed, and till now, could not find a friend."

In pursuance of the May 1820 Act, he swore that he was a resident citizen of the U. S. in March 1818 and that he had not, since that time, by gift, sale, or in any manner disposed of his property or an part of it with the intent to diminish it to the point he would be within the provisions of the March 1818 Pension Act. He had not, nor had any person, place in trust any property or securities, contracts, or debt due him no did he have any income other than what was contained in the annexed schedule subscribed by him in the Prince William Court on August 2, 1831.

Real Property: None. Mixed Property: None. Personal Property: a pair of old irons wedges, an old bed and rug and counterpane. A drawing knife, iron pot, butter pot, old table and chest, an old sugar box and bell, 2 claw hammers which are old, and one pair of old flesh forks.
Witness: George W. Macrae   (Signed) Elijah (x) Green

Since March 18, 1818 the following changes had been made to his property: No changes that he could "call to mind, if any, very immaterial."

(Signed) Elijah (x) Green

Philip D. Dawe, the Clerk of the Prince William County Court, certified that it appeared to his satisfaction that Elijah Green did serve in the Revolutionary War as he stated "against the common enemy for the term of nine months, under one engagement, on the Continental Establishment."

The Clerk further certified that the oath and annexed schedule were true copies from the Court records and that the total amount of value of the property in the schedule was worth $4.00. The declaration, schedule, and the certified statement of the Clerk and seal were placed on record on August 16, 1831.

In March 1832 he wrote the pension agency in Washington, saying that Mr. Green had been informed by him that his name had been enrolled on the pension list about September 1, 1831.

However, Green had never received a Certificate informing him that he was properly enrolled. "Mr. Green is an old man in great need and if [he] is properly enrolled," then Williams wanted the certificate to prove that.

In June 1832, John W. Williams, now acting clerk of the County Court, certified that he had, in August 1831, sent a copy of Elijah Green's oath, schedule, and certificate to the Secretary of War. Green was answered by letter which stated that, while he did not have a certificate under seal with the letter, nevertheless he had been enrolled on the pension list.

On June 6, 1832 Elijah Green appeared before again before John W. Williams, to make an affidavit regarding his service. He stated that he was the same person who formerly belonged to Captain Thomas Ewell's company in the regiment commanded by Colonel George Gibson in the service of the United States. His name had been placed on the Pension Roll of Virginia, as he was informed in August 1831 but he had never received a formal certificate. He now wished to obtain one.

Attached to this sworn statement was an affidavit by Moses Copin who certified that he was well acquainted with Elijah Green and knew him to be the same person described in his affidavit. John W. Williams, as the Clerk *pro tempore* of the County Court, certified that Moses Copin was a man of "honesty and truth."

A new certificate of pension was issued on June 27, 1832 and sent to the Honorable C. J. Mercer of the House of Representatives. His certificate number 4859 showed that he was continued on the Roll of Virginia on August 31, 1831. Notification of this was sent to the pensioner at Brentsville. The pension was to commence on August 23, 1831.

However, there was a catch. An undated note in the pension file said

> The Pensioner has made a mistake in claiming his pension from the 4th day of <u>March 1821.</u> His pension commences from the 23d day of Augt 1831. He will therefore be paid here from the 23 Augt 1831 to the 4th day of Sep. 1832.
>
> He will have to make out new papers dated and executed in or after the 4th Sep. 1832 and with the additional proof of identity, the form of which is on the other side. This is now required as more than one years pension will be due next pay day. (4 Sept).
>
> The clerk's certificate under seal must be ensealed on the claim verifying the Magistrates Signature.

Once again Elijah Green appeared before a Justice of the Peace, James Foster on August 22, 1832, to make another sworn declaration. He swore that "he[was] the identical Elijah Green named in the Certificate now in his possession." The original certificate was lost. The following was a true copy of that certificate, a duplicate issued by the War Department:

> I certify that, in conformity with the Laws of the United States of the 18th March 1818 and May 1, 1820, Elijah Green, late a private in the Army of the Revolution, Virginia line, is inscribed on the Pension list Roll of the Virginia Agency at the rate of eight dollars per month, to commence on the second day of November One thousand eight hundred and eighteen.
>
> This Certificate is issued in lieu of one dated December 11th 1818, supposed to be lost or destroyed, which if it should hereafter be presented at the Bank, the agent will please transmit to this department.
>
> Given at the War Office of the United States, this twenty-seventh day of June one thousand eight hundred and thirty two.

The certificate was signed by the Secretary of War, Lewis Cass, examined and counter signed by Pension Agent J. L. Edwards.

Elijah Green was entitled to a pension of $8.00 per month for services rendered the United States during the Revolutionary War. He served in Captain Thomas Ewell's Company and General Muhlenberg's Regiment. He now resided in Prince William County and has resided there for sixty-five or seventy years. Previous to that, he resided in Baltimore where he was born. Elijah Green signed this endorsement with his mark.

In December 1833, the Prince William County Court certified the heirs at law of Elijah Green as Peggy Abel, Sally Rolls, and Elijah Green. In October 1834, the court further certified that Elijah Green died without leaving a widow and again stated the heirs at law were Peggy Abel, Sally Rolls, and Elijah Green. In January 1835, the Court certified that the heirs were all of legal age. These entries appeared in the Prince William County Court Minute Book.

In February 1835, Jacob and Sally Rolls, Elijah Green, and James and Peggy Able appointed Thomas G. Moncure their attorney to collect the arrears in pension due from September 4, 1832 to January 15, 1833 the day of the pensioner's death. Thomas Moncure went to Richmond on February 18, 1835 and collected $34.83.[1]

On March 1, 1836, the heirs of Elijah Green decd, a soldier of the Revolution and a pensioner of the United States at the time of his death, petitioned Congress for relief. Their father had been placed on the Pension Roll of the Virginia Agency in 1818, they stated, and under the law of that year at the rate of $8.00 per month. The records at the Pension Agency would show this fact. He drew his pension under this certificate and at the same semi-annual period. In due form, he applied again at Richmond where his application was rejected and returned unissued ... Being thus deprived of his only productive means of support and being old and unable to labor, he was place in the hands of his children where he remained from 1819 until 1828 or perhaps longer.

When his family was no longer able to support him, being poor themselves and having families of small children to support, Elijah was taken to the Poor Lands in Prince William where he remained, until, through the interposition of Captain Williams, he was restored to the Pension list and remained so until his death in 18–.

The heirs, being informed now that "the rejection of Elijah's pension in 1819 was contrary to the spirit, meaning, and true intent and construction of the law of 1818 under which his first certificate was issued, would respectfully suggest" to Congress that "if such is the fact, there can be no doubt that all arrears of Pension accruing from the period for which ... Elijah applied in 1819 up to the date of his restoration to the Pension list, in [blank] constitutes a debt due to him under the law, at the time of his death. If due to him, necessarily now due to us ... his true and only heirs ..."

The heirs respectfully asked Congress to grant them the arrears of Pension as well on account of the Justice of the claim as the circumstances of their scanty substance, being applied to Elijah's support during the time of his rejection, from 1819 to the date of his restoration.

On April 9, 1836, J. L. Edwards of the Pension Agency wrote the Honorable H. J. Janes, of the House of Representatives in response to his inquiry into the matter of the arrears of pension the heirs thought were owed their father Elijah Green for his services during the Revolutionary War.

Edwards explained that Elijah Green had been pensioned under the act of March 18, 1818 at $8.00 per month, beginning on November 2, 1818. He was dropped from the rolls in 1819 because when certain lists received after his claim was admitted, were searched, it was discovered that the regiment of Colonel George Gibson, to which he was attached, was composed of State troops and did not belong to the Continental line.

The Act of 1818 provided for only those who belonged to the continental establishment. He had been paid to March 4, 1819 before the pension was stopped. Then, in August 1831, he was restored to the rolls. The Secretary of War decided that Gibson's regiment was a continental one. He based his decision on an act of the Legislature of Virginia which directed Colonel Gibson's regiment to "supply the place" of the 9th Virginia, which had been captured at Germantown. The pension, under this decision, was to begin on August 23, 1831.

---

[1] This power of attorney was not found in the pension file. See instead Pierce, I: 227.

After Mr. Janes received this letter from the Pension Agency, H. R. 645 was passed on May 17, 1836 by the 25th Congress, 1st Session. This was a Bill for the relief of Peggy Abel, Sally Rolls, and Elijah Green.

> *Be it enacted by the Senate and House of Representatives of the United States of America in Congress assembled*, That the Secretary of War be, and he is hereby, directed to pay to Peggy Abel, Sally Rolls, and Elijah Green, in the State of Virginia, children and heirs at law of Elijah Green, late of said State, deceased, the sum of nine hundred and sixty dollars, it being the amount of ten years' pension in arrear to the said Elijah Green, senior, in consequence of his name having been stricken from the pension roll by a decision of the Department of War, and afterwards restored by a reversal of said decision.

A report, Number 684, accompanied HR 645. It was issued on May 17, 1836 by Mr Janes, from the Committee on Revolutionary War Pensions.

Summarizing its contents, the report showed that Elijah Green had been pensioned, in November, 1818 under the act of March 18, 1818 at $8.00 per month for revolutionary services as a private soldier in Colonel George Gibson's regiment of the Virginia Line. His pension was paid him up to March 4, 1819 when his name was stricken from the rolls. This was done because the War Department had decided that Gibson's regiment did not belong to the Continental Line but were state troops and not within the provisions of the 1818 Act.

Elijah Green was a poor man and unable to take care of himself so his children provided for and supported him from the time his pension ceased until 1828 or 1829. At that time, when his family could no longer do this, Elijah was taken to the Poor House.

In January 1830, the Secretary of War reversed his decision and determined that Colonel Gibson's regiment did indeed belong to the Continental Line. On August 31, 1831, the Secretary of War restored Elijah Green to the rolls and paid him from that time until his death.

> The committee are of opinion, that as the said Elijah Green was wrongfully, and without and default on his part, stricken from the roll, and the payment of his pension withheld, and he supported by the petitioners, that they are justly entitled to so much of the arrearage of pension as should have been paid during the time they actually supported the said pensioner out of their own means, viz. from March 4, 1819 to March 4, 1829, being ten years and to that effect report a bill.

Included in the report was a note from Lewis Cass, Secretary of War.

> SIR: Agreeably to your request, I have to inform you, that the regiment commanded by Col. George Gibson, of the Virginia line, was, on the 12th January 1830, decided by the late Secretary of War to be a continental regiment from October 1777; it appearing to his satisfaction that by an act of the Virginia Assembly, that it was put in the place of the 9th Virginia continental regiment, which was nearly destroyed at the battle of Germantown.

In August 1836, William S. Colquhoun certified the identity of the three heirs in three separate certificates of identity so that they could receive the benefits of the claim approved by Congress in May of that year.

Elijah Green, he stated, was the identical and true heir of Elijah Green decd and entitled to receive the amount of the claim granted by Congress in May 1836. In a separate certificate, William S. Colquhoun certified the identity of Sally Green, who intermarried with Jacob Rolls, the bearer of the certificate in right of his wife. He was also entitled to receive the amount of the claim granted by Congressional Act. Finally, Colquhoun certified the identity of Peggy Abel, who intermarried with James Able about nineteen years ago. James Able, the bearer of this certificate was entitled, in right of his wife, to the claim granted by Congress in May 1836.[2]

Conclusions

This pension file illustrated several points about the necessity of thorough research in regard to entries in the County Court Minute and Order Books. The pension file underscored the importance of the relationship of the Pension Act to the actual pension declaration. In this instance, at the time of the 1818 Pension Act, State troops were not eligible for this pension, no matter how needy or in what economic straits the veteran found himself.

In Elijah Green's case, it took an act of the Virginia Legislature in 1830 to overturn the pension denial. The legislature determined that the 1st Virginia State Regiment was a continental one since it replaced the 9th Virginia, decimated and capture at Germantown in October 1777. Had that legislation not been passed, Elijah Green would have not had his pension restored no matter how worthy his circumstances were.

Once there was legal authority for the 1st Virginia State Regiment being a continental one, it cleared the way for the Secretary of War to make his ruling and for Congress to pass the necessary legislation awarding the arrears in Elijah's pension to his heirs.

This pension file also showed the importance of the discovery of little known information in the file concerning the pensioner himself. For example, his duplicate pension certificate revealed his birthplace as Baltimore, Maryland where he lived as a boy before moving to Prince William County where, in 1831, he had lived for sixty-five to seventy years.

This file also demonstrated the importance of looking at other records associated with the pensioner. Since the Minute Book entry did not specify Elijah Green's service it was not within the scope of this inquiry to verify it. He already was a pensioner according the Court Order Book entries. However, Elijah Green's service records are on footnote.com, all sixty-three of them, in Captain Thomas Ewell's company of the 1st Virginia State Regiment.

The last point to be made about this pension file demonstrated the determination and unflagging persistence of the Prince William County Justices in pursuing this pension claim doggedly and without a let-up until Elijah was restored to the Rolls. Judge Dade, John W. Williams, and William S. Colquhoun certainly played their part in seeing that this old soldier was restored to the Rolls. At least he received some of his pension before he died.

His heirs carried the claim one step further when they successfully petitioned Congress for the arrears in their father's pension from 1819 to 1831. Of course, the family was immeasurably helped by the Virginia legislature's decision to make the 1st Virginia State Regiment a continental unit. This made the Secretary of War's 1830 reversal of Elijah's pension denial in 1819 and Congress's subsequent awarding of the arrears of pension in 1836, to date from 1819 to 1831 an easy decision for everyone.

---

[2] NARA, *Elijah Green's Pension File* S 37961, M 804 (http://www.footnote.com), 3–54, images 22615740 to 22616421 (Accessed July 2, 2008 and July 14, 2008).

APPENDIX 3

Patrollers from 1804–1806 Minute Book in Colonel Enoch Renno's 36th Regiment, War of 1812

36th and 89th Regiments, Virginia Militia, War of 1812

Major Townsend Dade's Court Martial, November 1807

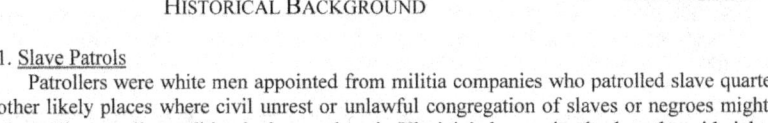

HISTORICAL BACKGROUND

1. Slave Patrols

Patrollers were white men appointed from militia companies who patrolled slave quarters or other likely places where civil unrest or unlawful congregation of slaves or negroes might take place. The patroller tradition had roots deep in Virginia's law, going back to the mid eighteenth century. It was then, in February 1727, that the colonial legislature created the first law establishing formal slave patrols.

Slaves in Virginia usually congregated together in large numbers at holidays, like Christmas, Easter and Whitsuntide, when they did not have to work. The 1727 slave patrol law directed the county lieutenant or any other commanding officer in the militia to appoint any of their members, where the officer thought fit, to patrol and disperse "all unusual concourse of negros or other slaves"… in order to prevent any kinds of "dangerous combinations" which might be made among them.

The white patrols that were sent out had full power to take up any slaves who were thus assembled and deliver them to the county's constable for punishment.[1]

After a succession of insurrections scares between 1729–1738, the legislature broadened the powers conferred on militia commanders. Now, they could order white men to be armed when they went to church and they appointed patrollers to visit all negro quarters suspected of entertaining unlawful assemblies of slaves, servants, and other disorderly persons.

Patrollers could also take up slaves who "strolled" about between plantations without passed. These unfortunate bondsmen were to be taken to a Justice of the Peace who, depending on the circumstance, could order a whipping of up to twenty lashes, well-laid on, on their bare backs.[2]

By the beginning of the nineteenth century, the slave patrol laws had not materially changed from those of the eighteenth century. Legislation was passed in December 1803, as part of the Act regulating the Militia of the Commonwealth that was very nearly identical to those slave patrol laws passed in the second and third decade of the eighteen century.

The legislature directed commanding officers of every militia battalion to appoint an officer or non-commissioned officer, and as many men in the militia, as the officer thought necessary, to "patrol and visit all negro quarters and other places suspected of entertaining unlawful assemblies of slaves, servants, or other disorderly persons … unlawfully assembled …" The patrols were also given the power to take up and deliver to a Justice of the Peace any one going from one plantation to another without a pass, whether a slave, servant, "stroller," or other disorderly person. The Justice of the Peace could then, if he thought there was cause, order the

---

[1] William Waller Hening, *Hening's Statutes at Large*, February 1727 (http://vagenweb.org/hening/vol104-09.htm), 202–203 (Accessed July 14, 2008).

[2] Sally E. Hadden, *Slave Patrols: Law and Violence in Virginia and the Carolinas* (Cambridge: Harvard University Press, 2001), 30–31.

detained slaves, strollers, servants, or the disorderly, to be whipped— up to twenty lashes well-laid upon their bare backs.

After every such patrol, the officers were required to return a report in writing to the county court. The Court was then authorized to levy seventy-five cents for every twelve hours to pay the patrollers.[3]

The renewal of conflict with the British during the War of 1812 ignited fears of slave insurrections again and addition slave patrols were posted, especially during the holidays. Virginia's white population was reluctant to use their militia against the British primarily because they were afraid of a slave insurrection one the militia had left the area. The lack of slave patrols would make their bondsmen more apt to move about or congregate unlawfully.[4]

During this war, many slave owners were also worried about the possibilities that their slaves could be captured by, or escape to, the British, especially along Virginia's coastal areas or rivers. So they increased patrols in these areas during the war. Prince William's Minute and Order Books for the 1813–1814 period reflect this increase.

2. Patrollers who appeared in 1805 and 1813 Court Minutes who were in Lieutenant Colonel Renno's 36th Virginia Regiment during the War of 1812

The following men who served as patrollers in September and October 1805 were all members of Colonel Renno's 36th Regiment which saw action in the War of 1812: James Allen, Joseph Barker, David Davis, Jesse Dowell, and John Pilcher

There were even more patrollers, mentioned in May and June 1813, who appeared in Colonel Renno's 36th Regiment during the War of 1812: Samuel Anderson, James Arnold, Moses Arnold, Thompson Bird, John Bland, Bernard Botts, William Boswell, Seth Brawner, William Calvert, George Carney, Mathias Cole, William S. Colquhoun, Harrison Cornwell, Samuel Cornwell, William Cornwell, John Davis, Jesse Dowell, Moses Duffey, George Hutchison, William Hutchison, Benson Jewell, George Keys, Daniel King, Thomas Lawson, Joseph R. Lynne, Martin Mills, Thomas McCuin, William Moore, Edward Norman, James Norman, Moses Pilcher, Peyton Read, Charles Reno, George Smallwood, James Smith, William Smith, George Tansil, William Tansil, and John Webster.[5]

Muster Rolls and Rosters of 36th Regiment, Virginia Militia

There are both service records and muster rolls still in existence for the 36th Regiment of Virginia Militia. The service records may be found on Ancestry.com, *War of 1812 Service Records*, 36th Regiment, which were extracted from micro publication 602, *Index to Compiled Service Records of Volunteer Soldiers ... [in] the War of 1812*, part of the National Archives *Records of Volunteer Soldiers Who Served in the War of 1812*.[6]

The extant muster rolls for this regiment were filed in Richmond in the Auditor's Office. Those rolls comprise the publication *Virginia Militia in the War of 1812*, reprinted in 2001 by the Genealogical Publishing Company.

---

[3] Samuel Shepherd, *Laws of Virginia*, December 1803 (http://book.google.com), 17 (Accessed July 14, 2008).
[4] Hadden, 162–164.
[5] Ancestry.com, *War of 1812 Service Records*, M 602 (http://www.ancestry.com) (Accessed July 1, 2008).
[6] National Archives Trust Fund Board, *Military Service Records: A Select Catalog of National Archives Microfilm Publications* (Washington: National Archives and Service Administration, 1985), 31–34.

1. Field and Staff Muster Rolls of 36th Regiment, Virginia Militia
The auditor of accounts in Richmond had a muster roll of the Field and Staff Officers of this regiment during 1813 and 1814.[7] They were:

Enoch Rennoe	Lieutenant Colonel	for 7 days service
Thomas Chapman	Major	for 22 days
Thomas Thornton	Surgeon	for 15 days
John Spence	Surgeon	for 6 days
Thomas Thornton	Surgeon's Mate	for 6 days
John Bronaugh	Surgeon's Mate	for 7 days
Peyton Norvell	Surgeon's Mate	for 7 days
David Davis	Surgeon's Mate	for 7 days
James Hays	Adjutant	for 21 days
Thomas Tebbs	QM Sergeant	for 2 days
Robert Doughnahan	QM Sergeant	for 21 days
William Barron	QM Sergeant	for 6 days
David Boyle	Paymaster	for 21 days
Henry Fairfax	Quartermaster	for 15 days
George Smith	Quartermaster	for 6 days
William Purnell	FM	for 15 days
Peyton Norvell	FM	for 8 days
Allen Duffey	DM	for 15 days
Thomas Montgomery	Sergeant Major	for 6 days

2. Muster rolls for the 36th Regiment
There are five company muster rolls filed in Richmond for this regiment.
- **Captain Joseph R. Gilbert's Muster Roll, from the 36th Regiment, Virginia Militia commanded by Lieutenant-Colonel Enoch Rennoe, for service from July 20–July 26, 1813, and August 24–August 30, 1814.**[8]

Joseph R. Gilbert	Captain	for 12 days service	
William Dawe	Lieutenant	for 6 days	
William Brundige	Lieutenant	for 6 days	
William French	Ensign	for 6 days	
Samuel Adams	Ensign	for 6 days	
William Colquhoun	Sergeant	for 6 days	
Henry M. Smoote	Sergeant	for 6 days	
William C. Williams	Sergeant	for 6 days	
Jon'a C. Gibson	Sergeant	for 6 days	
Judah Lord	Sergeant	for 6 days	
Thomas F. Tebbs	Sergeant	for 4 days	Transferred to staff Aug. 25, 1814
Geo. F. Huber	Sergeant	for 6 days	
Lemuel M. Hedges	Corporal	for 6 days	
Bayly Taylor	Corporal	for 6 days	
Francis Purnell	Corporal	for 6 days	
David Moore	Corporal	for 6 days	
Wansford Evans	Corporal	for 6 days	
James D. Bohannon	Corporal	for 6 days	

---
[7] Auditors Rolls, Richmond, *Virginia Militia in the War of 1812*, , II: 16.
[8] Ibid., II: 357–358.

♦ **Captain Joseph R. Gilbert's Muster Roll, from the 36th Regiment, Virginia Militia commanded by Lieutenant-Colonel Enoch Rennoe, for service from July 20–July 26, 1813, and August 24–August 30, 1814.**
(Cont.)

John S. Harrison	Corporal	for 6 days service
Robert Alexander	Private	for 12 days
Richard Allen	Private	for 6 days
Willis Athey	Private	for 6 days
Hugh Adie	Private	for 6 days
Levi Athey	Private	for 6 days
Zachariah Allen	Private	for 6 days
Spencer Bird	Private	for 6 days
James Bradley	Private	for 6 days
Henry Brawner	Private	for 6 days
Jesse Bobo	Private	for 6 days
Samuel Boswell	Private	for 6 days
Silvanus Crosby	Private	for 6 days
William Cannon	Private	for 6 days
Larkin Carr	Private	for 6 days
William Carter	Private	for 6 days
James Curry	Private	for 6 days
James Chick	Private	for 6 days
William Carney	Private	for 6 days
Daniel Cole	Private	for 6 days
Thomas Cocke	Private	for 6 days
Alexander Crosby	Private	for 11 days
Charles Cook	Private	for 6 days
John Carney	Private	for 6 days
Charles Calhoun	Private	for 6 days
Charles G. Cannon	Private	for 6 days
James Crismond Jr.	Private	for 6 days
Jessee Davis	Private	for 6 days
Hugh C. Davis	Private	for 6 days
Richard Dunnington	Private	for 6 days
David Davis	Private	for 6 days
Charles Edrington	Private	for 6 days
William Evans	Private	for 6 days
Robert Forgie	Private	for 12 days
Matthew Guy	Private	for 6 days
Hezekiah Gray	Private	for 11 days
Townly Gray	Private	for 6 days
John P. Harrison	Private	for 6 days
Walter Harrison	Private	for 6 days
Zacheus Holliday	Private	for 6 days
Cuthbert V. Harrison	Private	for 6 days
Philip Harrison	Private	for 6 days
Thomas W. Hewett	Private	for 6 days
James Jordan	Private	for 6 days
Thomas Johnston	Private	for 6 days
Robert Keys	Private	for 6 days

♦ **Captain Joseph R. Gilbert's Muster Roll, from the 36th Regiment, Virginia Militia commanded by Lieutenant-Colonel Enoch Rennoe, for service from July 20–July 26, 1813, and August 24–August 30, 1814**
(Cont.)

John Keys	Private	for 6 days service
Archibald Lawson	Private	for 12 days
John Landsdown	Private	for 6 days
Joseph B. Linebough	Private	for 6 days
Thomas Lawson	Private	for 6 days
William Moore	Private	for 6 days
Isaac Murphy	Private	for 6 days
Geo. Maddox	Private	for 6 days
James Merchant	Private	for 6 days
Thomas Montgomery	Private	for 6 days
William Phillips	Private	for 6 days
William Patterson	Private	for 6 days
Arthur S. Robertson	Private	for 6 days
Alexander P. Ralls	Private	for 6 days
Peyton Reid	Private	for 6 days
William Rennoe	Private	for 6 days
John Stroke Jr.	Private	for 6 days
Wilford D. Sidebotham	Private	for 6 days
James Smith	Private	for 6 days
Lemuel Stone	Private	for 6 days
James Sincox	Private	for 6 days
William Smithers	Private	for 6 days
George Scott	Private	for 6 days
Henry Tasker	Private	for 6 days
Thomas F. Tibbs	Private	for 6 days
Charles Thomas	Private	for 6 days
Thomas Tomlin	Private	for 6 days
John H. W. Wardie	Private	for 6 days
James Watson	Private	for 6 days
Elistett Umberfield	Private	for 6 days
Nicholas Young	Private	for 6 days

♦ **Captain Alexander Howison's Muster Roll, 36th Regiment, under the command of Lieutenant-Colonel Enoch Renno, for service from July 21–July 26, 1813 and from July 31–August 7, 1814, and August 24–August 30, 1814.**[9]

Alexander Howison	Captain	for 20 days service
William Brundige	Lieutenant	for 6 days
Travers Davis	Lieutenant	for 6 days
Benjamin Cannon	Ensign	for 6 days
Philip Langfitt	Ensign	for 6 days
Daniel Grant	Sergeant	for 8 days
Joseph B. Lunebough	Sergeant	for 8 days
Charles Rennoe	Sergeant	for 4 days
James D. Boughanan	Sergeant	for 8 days

---

[9] Ibid., II: 452–453.

♦ **Captain Alexander Howison's Muster Roll, 36ᵗʰ Regiment, under the command of Lieutenant-Colonel Enoch Renno, for service from July 21–July 26, 1813 and from July 31–August 7, 1814, and August 24–August 30, 1814.**
(Cont.)

Name	Rank	Service	Notes
John Webster	Sergeant	for 6 days service	
William Allen	Sergeant	for 6 days	
John Bland	Sergeant	for 6 days	
Thos. Burroughs	Sergeant	for 6 days	
John Lynn	Sergeant	for 6 days	
James Arnold	Sergeant	for 6 days	
Vincent Calvert	Sergeant	for 6 days	
William Phillips	Corporal	for 8 days	
John Bridwell	Corporal	for 8 days	
John S. Harrison	Corporal	for 8 days	
James Jourdan	Corporal	for 8 days	
Geo. Boswell	Corporal	for 6 days	
William Dowell	Corporal	for 6 days	
Allison Johnston	Corporal	for 6 days	
Thomas Molair	Corporal	for 6 days	
Thomas Able	Private	for 14 days	
James Able	Private	for 14 days	
Richard Allen	Private	for 14 days	
Thomas Addams	Private	for 14 days	
John Arnold	Private	for 14 days	
Larkin Arrington	Private	for 6 days	Joined the Cavalry
Moses Arnold	Private	for 6 days	
Leroy Athy	Private	for 6 days	
George Appleby	Private	for 12 days	
Washburn Arrington	Private	for 6 days	
Sandford Anderson	Private	for 6 days	
James Allen	Private	for 6 days	
Horatio Athey	Private	for 6 days'	
John Athey	Private	for 6 days	
Rowland Bates	Private	for 8 days	
Henry Brawner	Private	for 8 days	Sub. For W. F. Moore
Fantly Ball	Private	for 14 days	Sub. For Aug. Ball
Doctor John Bronaugh	Private	for 8 days	
William S. Parker	Private	for 6 days	
John Brammel	Private	for 6 days	
Thomas Burroughs	Private	for 6 days	
Seth Brawner	Private	for 6 days	
Joseph Brawner	Private	for 6 days	
William Carter	Private	for 8 days	
Geo. Cornwell	Private	for 11 days	
William Cornwell	Private	for 20 days	
James Carter	Private	for 8 days	
William Calvert	Private	for 8 days	
Peter Cockrell	Private	for 14 days	
Alexander Chick	Private	for 8 days	

- **Captain Alexander Howison's Muster Roll, 36th Regiment, under the command of Lieutenant-Colonel Enoch Renno, for service from July 21–July 26, 1813 and from July 31–August 7, 1814, and August 24–August 30, 1814.**
(Cont)

Nimrod Carr	Private	for 14 days	Substituted himself previous to this call.
David Carter	Private	for 8 days	Sub. For James. Smith
John Cornwell	Private	for 6 days	
Peyton Calvert	Private	for 6 days	
Bland Currie	Private	for 6 days	
Harrison Cornwell	Private	for 6 days	
Richard Calvert	Private	for 6 days	
Geo. Crosby	Private	for 6 days	
Willis Chicks	Private	for 6 days	
Jessee Dowell	Private	for 6 days	
John Disney	Private	for 8 days	
Jessee Davis	Private	for 8 days	
Walter Dodson	Private	for 14 days	
Presley Davis	Private	for 8 days	Sub. For Seth Brown
Walter Davis	Private	for 8 days	
William Davis	Private	for 8 days	
John P. Duvall	Private	for 6 days	
William H. Duvall	Private	for 6 days	
Geo. Duvall	Private	for 6 days	
John B. Davis	Private	for 6 days	
Nathaniel Ellicot	Private	for 6 days	
John English	Private	for 6 days	
Alfred Ewell	Private	for 6 days	Joined the cavalry
James Epps	Private	for 6 days	
Wm. Foxworthy	Private	for 8 days	
Edmond Fair	Private	for 8 days	
Harrison Fox	Private	for 6 days	
Michael Floudy	Private	for 6 days	Or Floridy. [surname]
John Goslin	Private	for 8 days	Sub for Wm. Selickman
Townley Guy	Private	for 8 days	
Charles Guy	Private	for 8 days	
Cuthbert Harrison	Private	for 8 days	
Corbin Hall	Private	for 8 days	
John Hancock	Private	for 14 days	
Thomas Homes	Private	for 8 days	
John Harrison	Private	for 6 days	
William Harris	Private	for 6 days	
James Hopwood	Private	for 6 days	
Stephen Harrison	Private	for 6 days	
Rhodam Henry	Private	for 6 days	
Richard Johnston	Private	for 6 days	
Fielding Jewill	Private	for 8 days	
Jacob Janny	Private	for 8 days	
James Keys	Private	for 8 days	
Michael Koon	Private	for 8 days	

♦ **Captain Alexander Howison's Muster Roll, 36th Regiment, under the command of Lieutenant-Colonel Enoch Renno, for service from July 21–July 26, 1813 and from July 31–August 7, 1814, and August 24–August 30, 1814.**
(Cont)

Geo. Kees	Private	for 8 days service	
Thomas Keys	Private	for 6 days	
William King	Private	for 6 days	
Richard Lee	Private	for 8 days	
Michael Lennox	Private	for 8 days	Sub. For Stephen Howison
William Martin	Private	for 8 days	
Ignatious Milsted	Private	for 8 days	
Geo. Maddox	Private	for 8 days	Sub. for D. Davis
Walter Maddox	Private	for 6 days	
Elias McCuin	Private	for 6 days	
Thomas McQueen	Private	for 6 days	
Thomas Nelson	Private	for 14 days	
Geo. Norman	Private	for 8 days	
Thomas Pearson	Private	for 6 days	
Wm. Patterson Jr.	Private	for 14 days	
Richard Pell	Private	for 6 days	
Jessee Pilcher	Private	for 6 days	
Wm. Patterson Sr.	Private	for 6 days	
William Pierson	Private	for 6 days	
Hugh Petty	Private	for 14 days	
William Purnell	Private	for 8 days	
John Patterson	Private	for 8 days	
John Pinson	Private	for 8 days	
Alexander Pattison	Private	for 8 days	
Travis Payne	Private	for 8 days	
Cumberland Pinson	Private	for 8 days	Sub. For Wm. Pinson
Madden Rennoe	Private	for 14 days	
Arthur S. Robinson	Private	for 8 days	
William Robey	Private	for 8 days	
Jacob Rolls	Private	for 6 days	
Geo. Renoe	Private	for 6 days	
James Rison	Private	for 6 days	
John Smith	Private	for 6 days	
Townley Smith	Private	for 14 days	
William Smith	Private	for 8 days	
James Smith	Private	for 14 days	
Larkin Strawther	Private	for 8 days	
James Scott	Private	for 6 days	
Raleigh Spinks	Private	for 6 days	
Charles Shaw	Private	for 6 days	
Jesse Sincoks	Private	for 6 days	
Peter Trone	Private	for 6 days	
Henry Tasker	Private	for 6 days	Joined the cavalry.
Thomas Tebbs	Private	for 8 days	Appointed surgeon's mate, transferred to the staff.
Joseph Tyler	Private	for 8 days	

♦ **Captain Alexander Howison's Muster Roll, 36th Regiment, under the command of Lieutenant-Colonel Enoch Renno, for service from July 21–July 26, 1813 and from July 31–August 7, 1814, and August 24–August 30, 1814.**
(Cont)

David Willett	Private	for 8 days	Sub. for John Willett
Geo. Woodward	Private	for 8 days	
Philip Wurchoof	Private	for 8 days	
Randolph Welch	Private	for 8 days	
Thomas West	Private	for 6 days	
Henry West	Private	for 6 days	
Zachariah Winne	Private	for 6 days	
Geo. Britain	Private	for 8 days	Sub. for John Britain
Uriah Bell	Private	for 8 days	
Thomas Burroughs	Private	for 8 days	Sub. for D. Larkin
Elijah Campbell	Private	for 8 days	
Jonathan Campbell	Private	for 8 days	Sub. for Moses Cockrell
Josiah Copen	Private	for 8 days	Sub. for John F. Jackson
John Franklin	Private	for 8 days	
Elijah Fryer	Private	for 8 days	
William Graham	Private	for 8 days	
William Gardiner	Private	for 8 days	Sub. for D. Cannon.
James Hope	Private	for 8 days	
John Hill	Private	for 8 days	
William Hope	Private	for 8 days	Sub. for Joshua Huff
Thomas Huff	Private	for 8 days	
James Keach	Private	for 8 days	
John King	Private	for 8 days	
Henry Langfitt	Private	for 8 days	
James Mason	Private	for 8 days	
Thomas Mason	Private	for 8 days	
Charles Ogden	Private	for 8 days	
Richard Payne	Private	for 8 days	
Martin Robertson	Private	for 8 days	
William Riley	Private	for 8 days	
David Ramie	Private	for 8 days	
James Roach	Private	for 8 days	
William Larkin	Private	for 8 days	

♦ **Captain John Linton's Troop of Cavalry, from the 36th Regiment, Virginia Militia, commanded by Lieutenant Colonel Enoch Rennoe, for service from August 21– August 27, 1814 and August 30– September 7, 1814.**[10]

John Linton	Captain	for 12 days service
John Gibson	Lieutenant	for 12 days
James E. Heath	Lieutenant	for 12 days
Burr Harrison	Cornet	for 12 days
Wm. C. Williams	Sergeant	for 12 days
Lemuel Stone	Sergeant	for 12 days
Geo. Norman	Sergeant	for 12 days

---

[10] Ibid., II: 548.

♦ **Captain John Linton's Troop of Cavalry, from the 36th Regiment, Virginia Militia, commanded by Lieutenant Colonel Enoch Rennoe, for service from August 21– August 27, 1814 and August 30– September 7, 1814**

Jonathan C. Gibson	Sergeant	for 8 days service
Hugh Adie	Corporal	for 8 days
Thomas Dowell	Corporal	for 18 days
Larkin Arrington	Private	for 12 days
Geo. Bell	Private	for 7 days
Thomas Charlton	Private	for 12 days
David Carter	Private	for 12 days
John Carney	Private	for 12 days
Alexander Chick	Private	for 12 days
Richard Davis Jr	Private	for 12 days
Alfred Ewell	Private	for 12 days
Henley Groves	Private	for 12 days
Matthew Guy	Private	for 7 days
Harrison Graham	Private	for 7 days
James Harrison	Private	for 12 days
James Hawley	Private	for 12 days
Colin Hays	Private	for 12 days
Thos. W. Hewit	Private	for 9 days
Lemuel Hedge	Private	for 11 days
Philip Harrison	Private	for 7 days
Robert Hamilton	Private	for 7 days
Allison Johnston	Private	for 5 days
Elias King	Private	for 5 days
James McAboy	Private	for 12 days
Thos. J. Newman	Private	for 5 days
William Patterson	Private	for 5 days
John C. Stone	Private	for 12 days
John Stoke	Private	for 12 days
William H. Tebbs	Private	for 12 days
Peter Trone	Private	for 12 days
Thomas Turner	Private	for 12 days
Warden Walter	Private	for 7 days

♦ **Captain Joseph Smith's Muster Roll, 36th Regiment, Virginia Militia in the County of Prince William, called into actual service under the regimental orders of August 24, 1814, from August 24–August 30, 1813.**[11]

Joseph Smith	Captain	for 7 days service
William French	Lieutenant	for 7 days
George Lansdowne	Ensign	for 7 days
John Webster	Sergeant	for 7 days
Edward Austin	Sergeant	for 7 days
John Athy	Private	for 7 days
Willis Bridwell	Private	for 7 days
Chapman Copen	Private	for 7 days
James Cooper	Private	for 7 days

---

[11] Ibid., II: 728. The date is as state above in the Auditor's Rolls.

♦ **Captain Joseph Smith's Muster Roll, 36th Regiment, Virginia Militia in the County of Prince William, "called into actual service under the regimental orders of 24 August 1814, from the 24th to the 30th August 1813."**

Harrison Cornwell	Private	for 7 days service
Alexander Chick	Private	for 7 days
Peter Cockrell	Private	for 7 days
Elijah Dawson	Private	for 7 days
Harrison Fox	Private	for 7 days
Edward Fair	Private	for 7 days
Samuel Florence	Private	for 7 days
Michael Floriday	Private	for 7 days
Daniel Grant	Private	for 7 days
George Godfrey	Private	for 7 days
Cathbert V. Harrison	Private	for 7 days
Thomas Homes	Private	for 7 days
Benson Jewel	Private	for 7 days
Sandy Keys	Private	for 7 days
William F. Moore	Private	for 7 days
Isaac Murphy	Private	for 7 days
William Norman	Private	for 7 days
Edward Norman	Private	for 7 days
Watson Person	Private	for 7 days
John Person	Private	for 7 days
Whittenton Person	Private	for 7 days
George Person	Private	for 7 days
Cumberlain Person	Private	for 7 days
George Rennoe Sr.	Private	for 7 days
George Rennoe Jr.	Private	for 7 days
Madden Rennoe	Private	for 7 days
Matthew H. Smoote	Private	for 7 days
Willis Turner	Private	for 7 days
Henry Webster	Private	for 7 days

♦ **Captain Richard Weadon's Muster Roll of Company called into the Service of the United States, at Dumfries, under an order of August 24th by Colonel Enoch Rennoe, Lieutenant Colonel commandant of the 36th Regiment, from August 24–August 30, 1814.**[12]

Richard Weadon	Captain	for 7 days service
Barnaby Cannon	Ensign	for 7 days
Hugh Adie	Sergeant	for 7 days
Ignatius Mitchel	Sergeant	for 7 days
Larkin Carr	Corporal	for 7 days
Moses Duffee	Corporal	for 7 days
William Bell	Private	for 7 days
James Carter	Private	for 7 days
William Cannon	Private	for 7 days
William Calvert	Private	for 7 days
Jesse Carpenter	Private	for 7 days

---

[12] Ibid., I: 820.

- Captain Richard Weadon's Muster Roll of Company called into the Service of the United States, at Dumfries, under an order of August 24th by Colonel Enoch Rennoe, Lieutenant Colonel, Commandant of the 36th Regiment, from August 24–August 30, 1814. (Cont.)

John Dickerson	Private	for 7 days service
Edward Evans	Private	for 7 days
Matthew Guy	Private	for 7 days
Townley Guy	Private	for 7 days
Corben Hales	Private	for 7 days
Richard Lee	Private	for 7 days
James McDaniel	Private	for 7 days
Edward Mitchell	Private	for 7 days
Samuel Mitchell	Private	for 7 days
William Moore	Private	for 7 days
Ignatius Milstead	Private	for 7 days
George Mattox	Private	for 7 days
William Smith	Private	for 7 days

- A Roster of 36th Regiment, Virginia Militia: Officers, non-commissioned officers and rank and file from Ancestry.com *War of 1812 Service Records*, extracted from NARA, *Index to Compiled Service Records of Volunteer Soldiers ... in the War of 1812*, M 602. 234 rolls.[13]

Field and Staff Officers
    Lieutenant Colonel Enoch Renno
    Major Samuel Ashby
    Major Thomas Chapman

Captains
    William Dulin
    Joseph R. Gilbert
    James Hayes, Adjutant, Promoted to Captain
    John Linton
    Joseph R. Lynn
    John Merchant
    William Obannion/Obannon
    Barton S. Stone
    Joseph Smith
    Richard Weadon

Lieutenants
    William Brundige, Adjutant
    Daniel Boyle, Paymaster
    James Crane
    Travers Davis
    William Dawe
    William French
    John Gibson
    Alfred C. Hayes
    Peter Holmes
    William McInteer

Lieutenants (Cont)
    William Kemper
    William Nelson, 1st Lieutenant
    William McInteer
    John H. Prosser
    William Thompson, promoted to PM
    George Waller

Ensigns
    Samuel Adams
    Abner R. Alcock
    Barnaby Cannon
    Burn (?) Cannon
    William S. Colquhoun
    William French, promoted
    Rawleigh Hickerson
    Philip Langfitt
    Daniel Larkin
    George Lansdowne
    John Marr
    Reuben Rogers
    John Ross
    Francis Smith

---

[13] Ancestry.com, *War of 1812 Service Records*, 36th Regiment, Virginia Militia (http://search.ancestry.com).

♦ **A Roster of 36th Regiment, Virginia Militia: Officers, non-commissioned officers and rank and file from** Ancestry.com *War of 1812 Service Records,* extracted from NARA, *Index to Compiled Service Records of Volunteer Soldiers ... in the War of 1812*, M 602. 234 rolls. (Cont.)

Ensigns (Cont.)
  John Tippett
Cornet
  Burr Harrison
Quartermaster
  George Smith
Surgeon Mates
  David Davis
  Thomas F. Tebbs
Surgeons
  Dr. John Bronaugh, Private, promoted to Surgeon
  John Spence
  Thomas Thornton
Musicians
  Thomas Barton, Drummer
  Cary Cox
  Allen Duffy, Musician, promoted to Drum Major
  Samuel Elliott, Fifer
  Allen Hill, Drummer
  Henry Marvel
  Gustavus Muschett
  William Purnell, promoted to Fife Major
  Abraham Wyckoff, Drummer
Sergeants
  William Allen
  Edward Austin
  William Barron, Orderly Sgt, to QM Sgt
  John Bland
  James Bohannon, reduced to prvt.
  Robert Bohannon, QM Sgt
  Alsop Boswell
  Anderson Boughton
  Thomas Burroughs
  Vincent Calvert, reduced to prvt.
  William Carney
  John P. Claxton, QM Sgt
  Daniel Cole
  William S. Colquhoun promoted to Ensign.
  Charles Duncan, 1st Sgt
  Dillard Duncan
  Jonathan Gibson
  George Jameson
  John Kerr
  John L. Kincaid
  Thomas Lawson, promoted from prvt.
  Hancock Lee, promoted from prvt.

Sergeants (Cont.)
  Judah Lord
  John Lynn
  James McLennan
  Robert Miller
  Ignatius Mitchell, reduced to prvt.
  William Monroe
  Thomas Montgomerie, Sgt. Major
  George Norman, promoted from prvt
  Peyton Norville, Sgt Major,
    Promoted to Forage Master
  Joseph Parmer
  Valentine Potes (?)
  Charles Rennoe
  Henry W. Richardson
  Andrew Sale
  Lemuel Stone, prvt, promoted to Sgt.
  Henry Smoote
  Ephraim Templeman
  Gustavus M. Ware, 1st Sgt.
  Elias Utterback
  William Walker
  William C. Williams, Sgt. to 1st Sgt.
  Henry Webster, prvt.,
    Promoted to Sgt.
Bowman for the Regiment
  Daniel Boyd
Rank and File: Corporals
  Benjamin Adie
  Hugh Adie
  Thomas Brannan
  Willis Bridwell
  Lewis Brown
  Daniel Bruin
  Vincent Calvert, reduced to prvt.
  William H. Duvall
  Wansford Evans
  George Jeffries
  James Jourdan, reduced to prvt.
  Edmund McCormick
  James Merchant
  Thomas Molair, reduced to prvt.
  David Moore
  Alexander OBannon
  William Phillips, reduced to prvt.
  Silem (?) Phillips

♦ **A Roster of 36th Regiment, Virginia Militia: Officers, non-commissioned officers and rank and file** from Ancestry.com *War of 1812 Service Records,* extracted from NARA, *Index to Compiled Service Records of Volunteer Soldiers ... in the War of 1812*, M 602. 234 rolls. (Cont.)

Rank and File: Corporals (Cont.)
  Samuel Anderson
  Samuel Boswell
  Francis Purnell, reduced to prvt.
  Joseph Rakestraw
  James P. Roe
  Francis Simpson
  Bailey Taylor
  Thomas F. Tebbs, promoted to Surgeon's Mate

Rank and File: Privates
  Thomas Able
  James Able
  Levi Athey
  Willis Athey
  John Atwood
  Elisha Baker
  Augustine Ball
  Fauntley Ball
  John Ball
  Lamath Barbee
  William S. Barker
  Charles Barton
  Rowland Bates
  Moses Batley
  John Beach
  Daniel Bell
  Francis Bell
  George Bell
  Thomas Bell
  Uriah Bell
  William Bell
  Richard Berry
  Zachariah Berryman
  Spencer Bird
  Thomas Biscoe
  William Blackwell
  Jesse Bobo
  James D. Bohannon, reduced to prvt from Sgt.
  John Bowen
  Abijah Bowling
  James Bowling
  George Bowling
  Daniel Boyd
  William Boyd
  George Bozel [Bussell?]

Rank and File: Privates (Cont.)
  Samuel Bozel [Bussell?]
  William Bozel [Bussell?]
  James Bradley
  John Brammell Jr.
  John Brammell Sr.
  Henry Brawner Sr.
  Ignatius Brawner
  Joseph Brawner
  Seth Brawner
  William Brawner
  William Briant
  Isaac Bridwell
  Lewis Bridwell
  Richard Bridwell
  William Bridwell
  Willis Bridwell, promoted
  George Brittain
  John Brittain
  John S. Brown
  Wesley Brown
  William Brown
  Samuel Browne
  William Browne
  Frederick Burdett
  William Burdett
  Thomas Burrough
  William Butler
  Thompson Byrd
  William Byrd
  Charles Calhoun
  Elias Calvert
  Geyton Calvert
  Richard Calvert
  William Calvert
  Vincent Calvert
  Elijah Calvert
  Jonathan Calvert
  Charles Cannon
  D. Cannon
  John B. Cannon
  William Cannon
  Benjamin Carney
  George Carney
  John Carney

♦ **A Roster of 36th Regiment, Virginia Militia: Officers, non-commissioned officers and rank and file from** Ancestry.com *War of 1812 Service Records,* extracted from NARA, *Index to Compiled Service Records of Volunteer Soldiers ... in the War of 1812*, M 602. 234 rolls. (Cont.)

Rank and File: Privates (Cont.)
  Silas Carney
  William Carney
  Jesse Carpenter
  John Carr
  Larkin Carr, promoted.
  Nimrod Carr
  William Carr
  David Carter
  James Carter
  John Carter
  Nathaniel Carter
  Philip Carter
  Sanford Carter Jr.
  William Carter
  Zachariah Carter
  George Carver
  Samuel Cave
  Thomas Charlton
  Alexander Chick
  Charles Chick
  James Chick
  Willis Chick
  Richard Clark
  Alpheus Clarke
  John Clarke
  Rodney Clowe
  William Clowe
  Jeremiah Cockrell
  Moses Cockrell
  Peter Cockrell
  Benjamin Cole
  Harrison Cole
  Charles Colquhoun
  Charles Cook
  James Cooksey
  James Cooper
  Chapman Copen
  Joshua Copen
  Mason Corben
  Elijah Cornwell
  George Cornwell
  Harrison Cornwell
  John Cornwell
  Samuel Cornwell
  William Cornwell

Rank and File: Privates (Cont.)
  William Cox
  Zachariah Cox
  Zachariah Crim
  Alexander Crosby
  George Crosby
  Silvanus Crosby
  Elijah Croson
  Coleman Crutcher
  William Culverhouse
  John Cummins
  Bland Curry
  James Curry
  Asa Davis
  Charles W. Davis
  David Davis
     Promoted to Surgeon's Mate
  Hugh R. Davis
  Jesse Davis
  John B. Davis
  Presley Davis
  Richard Davis
  Walter Davis
  Joseph Daws
  Elijah Dawson
  Henry Dawson
  John Dickerson
  Edmund Dishman
  John Disney
  Travis Dodd
  Walter Dodson
  Richard Dorsey
  Jesse Dowell
  Thomas Dowell
  Moses Duffey
  Jarvis Dunaway
  Joseph Dunaway
  Leroy Duncan
  Richard Dunnington
  George Duvall
  John Duvall
  John P. Duvall
  William Duvall, promoted.
  James Ebbs
  Thomas Edmonds
  Thornton Edmonds

♦ **A Roster of 36th Regiment, Virginia Militia: Officers, non-commissioned officers and rank and file from** Ancestry.com *War of 1812 Service Records,* extracted from NARA, *Index to Compiled Service Records of Volunteer Soldiers ... in the War of 1812*, M 602. 234 rolls. (Cont.)

Rank and File: Privates (Cont.)
    Champ Corum
    Leonard Courtney
    James Cox
    George Embrey
    Joseph Embrey
    Reuben Embrey
    Hadius English
    John English
    John English Jr.
    John K. Ensey
    Rhodham Ensey
    Edward Evans
    Alfred Ewell
    William W. Fant
    Higby Fayre
    Daniel Feagan
    Henry Feltner
    William Ferguson
    John Fewell
    Dennis Griffith
    Travis Groves
    Alexander Hall, Drummer, Prvt.
    James Halley
    Robert Hamilton
    Eliphalet Humphreys
    John F. Jackson
    Fontine Jacobs
    George Jameson
    Townsend Jameson
    Asa Jeffries
    Pleasant Jeffries
    Burkett Jett
    Peter Jett
    Benson Jewell
    Fielding Jewell
    Allison Johnson/Johnston
    William Johnson/Johnston
    Richard Johnston
    Thomas Johnston
    Daniel Jones
    Fielding Jones
    Gustavus Jones
    John Jones
    Noah Jones
    Starling Jones

Rank and File: Privates (Cont.)
    Charles Edrington
    William Edwards
    Philip L. Elkins
    John Kenny
    George Keys
    James Keys
    Archibald Kincaid/Kincade
    Thomas Kincaid/Kincade
    Daniel Kincheloe
    Robert Kincheloe
    Elias King
    Elias King Jr.
    Daniel King
    George King
    William King
    Solomon Kinsey
    Hugh Kirkpatrick
    John Kirkpatrick
    Thomas Kirkpatrick
    Michael Koon
    Henry Langfitt
    John Lansdowne
    William Lansford
    Daniel Latham
    James Latham
    John Latham
    Thornton Latham
    Thomas Lawson,
        Promoted to Sgt.
    George Leach
    Thornton K. Leach
    George Ledman (?)
    Hancock Lee
        Promoted to Sgt.
    Henry Lee
    Joseph Lee
    Richard Lee
    Michael Lenox
    William Leonard
    George W. Leslie
    John Limbrick
    Joseph B. Linebough
    John Lloyd
    Joseph A. Lloyd
    Judah Lord, promoted to Sgt.

♦ **A Roster of 36th Regiment, Virginia Militia: Officers, non-commissioned officers and rank and file from** Ancestry.com *War of 1812 Service Records,* extracted from NARA, *Index to Compiled Service Records of Volunteer Soldiers ... in the War of 1812,* M 602. 234 rolls. (Cont.)

Rank and File: Privates (Cont.)
    Thomas Jones
    James Jourdan, Corporal reduced to prvt.
    James Keach
    James Kelley
    Spencer Kemper
    Charles Kendall
    John Kennedy
    Robert Lyon
    James MacAboy
    William Mack
    George Maddox
    Walter Maddox
    Solomon W. Mallory
    Allan Manuel
    John Manuel
    William C. Martin
    James Mason
    Nelson Mason
    Thomas Mason
    William McBee
    William McClanahan
    Benjamin McCoy
    Alexander McCuin/McEwen
    Elias McCuin/McEwen
    Thomas McCuin/McEwen
    William McCuin/McEwen
    James McDaniel
    Theodosius McDonald
    Timothy McGuin
    Daniel McLean
    Thomas McMorris
    Peter C. McPherson
    Robert Metcalf
    Timothy Milburn
    John I. Miller
    John D. Mills
    Ignatius Milstead
    Isaac Milstead
    Samuel Milstead
    Edward Mitchell
    Samuel Mitchell
    Thomas Molair, Corporal, reduced to prvt.
    Robert Monday
    John Montgomery
    Thomas Moore

Rank and File: Privates (Cont.)
    Nicholas Young
    Richard Luckett
    Benjamin Lunceford
    Simon Luttrell
    Lewis Lyder (?)
    John Lynn
    Moses Lynn
    Heaven (?) Oliver
    Josiah Owens
    William Pair
    Joseph Palmer
    Thomas Parmer (Palmer?)
    William Parr
    Aaron Patterson
    Alexander Patterson/Pattison
    John Patterson Jr.
    William Patterson Jr.
    William Patterson Sr.
    Larkin Patton
    Benjamin Payne
    Daniel Payne
    John Payne
    Lewis Payne
    Richard Payne
    Sanford Payne
    Travis Payne
    William Payne
    Craven Peake
    Lloyd Peake
    Asa Pearson
    Cumberland Pearson
    George Pearson
    John Pearson
    Thomas Pearson
    Watson Pearson
    Whittington Pearson
    William Pearson
    Richard Pell
    John Penquite
    Eli Petty
    Hough Petty
    John S. Phillips
    William Phillips
        Corporal, reduced to prvt.
    Jesse Pilcher

♦ **A Roster of 36th Regiment, Virginia Militia: Officers, non-commissioned officers and rank and file from** Ancestry.com *War of 1812 Service Records,* extracted from NARA, *Index to Compiled Service Records of Volunteer Soldiers ... in the War of 1812,* M 602. 234 rolls. (Cont.)

Rank and File: Privates (Cont.)
    William Moore
    Thomas Morton
    Keland Moss
    Isaac Murphy
    Frederick Muschett
    Thomas Nelson
    Edward Norman
    George Norman, promoted to Sgt.
    James Norman
    Thornton Ocain
    Charles Ogden
    George Quisenberry
    John Quisenberry
    John Ragans
    Alexander P. Ralls
    Charles Ralls
    Abraham Ramey
    David Ramey
    Augustus Randall
    William Ransdell
    Lewis Rector
    Andrew Reed
    John Reed
    Richard Reed
    Thomas Reed
    James Reeves
    Peyton Reid
    William Reid
    George Reno
    Maddin Reno
    William Richardson
    Edward Riley
    William Riley
    William Rimus (?)
    James Rison
    William Rison
    James Roach
    Robert Roach
    Arthur J. Robertson
    Arthur S. Robertson
    George Robertson
    Thomas Robertson
    Martin Robinson
    William Roby
    George Rockinbaugh

Rank and File: Privates (Cont.)
    John Pilcher
    Moses Pilcher
    John Plant
    Humphrey Pope
    John Porter
    Ashford Posey
    William Primm
    Hugh Purcell
    Barnaby Purnell
    Francis Purnell
        Corporal, reduced to prvt.
    Charles Shaw
    James Shilkett
    Wilford Sidebotham
    Frederick Sifle/Stifle
    Isaac Silvey
    Presley Simms
    Rhodham Simpson
    Alexander Sinclair
    Jesse Sinclair
    Marmaduke Sisson
    Phineas Skinner
    George Smallwood
    Harris Smith
    James Smith
    John Smith
    Mourning Smith
    Townly Smith
    William Smith
    William Smithers
    George Smoote/Smoot
    Matthew H. Smoote/Smoot
    William Snelling
    William Snipe
    Alexander Sorrel
    Richard Speak
    Frederick Stifle/Sifle
    John C. Stone
    Lemuel Stone
        Promoted to Sgt.
    Fauntley Roy Stone.
    Vincent Stonnell
    John Storke Jr.
    Larkin Strother
    Henry Suttle Sr.

♦ **A Roster of 36th Regiment, Virginia Militia: Officers, non-commissioned officers and rank and file from** Ancestry.com *War of 1812 Service Records,* extracted from NARA, *Index to Compiled Service Records of Volunteer Soldiers ... in the War of 1812,* M 602. 234 rolls. (Cont.)

Rank and File: Privates (Cont.)
    Henry Rogers
    Russell Rollow (?)
    Jacob Rolls
    John Rolls
    Isaac Rose
    Jeremiah Rust
    Jacob Rye
    William Rymes
    Wesley Sanders
    John L. Saunders
    Presley Saunders
    George Scott
    James Scott
    William Selecman
    Robert Shackleford
    Sampson Turley
    Henry Turner
    John Turner
    Levi Turner
    Lewis Turner
    Thomas Turner
    Willis Turner
    Joseph Tyler
    James Vowles
    James Waddell
    Thomas Wade
    Caleb Walker
    William Walker
    Thomas Walters
    John Warder
    Walter Warder
    James Watson
    Thomas Watts
    John Way
    Henry Weaver
    Henry Webster, promoted to Sgt.
    William Webster
    William Weeks
    Joseph Welch
    Randolph Welch
    Thomas West
    Isaac Wharton
    Lawson Wheatley
    George White

Rank and File: Privates (Cont.)
    Thornton Swarts
    George Tansil
    William Tansil
    Henry Tasker
    Pendleton Taylor
    Joseph Teagle
    William H. Tebbs
    James Tharpe
    Charles Thomas
    John Thompson
    Vincent Thompson
    John Timberlake
    Thomas Tomlin
    Bayliss Tracey
    Peter Trone
    George White Sr.
    John White
    Thomas Wilkins
    David Willet
    John Willet
    Thomas Williams
    William Williams
    George Willingham
    John Wilson
    Philip Winchoof [Winekoop]
    Thomas Windsor
    William Windsor
    George Wine
    William Winn
    Zacharias Winn
    Elijah Wood
    Hezekiah Wood
    George Woodward
    Joseph Woodward
    Jabaz Woodyard
    John B. Wright
    Thomas B. Wright
    Vincent Wyatt
    David Yates

One salient fact emerges from a perusal of these muster rolls and rosters: the men often served in more than one company and under more than one company commander. Sometime they may have served in both Prince William regiments at different times. Note, too, that despite my best efforts to avoid this, duplicate entries may have snuck into these rosters.

Muster Rolls and Rosters of 89th Virginia Regiment (1813 and 1814)

There are two extant muster rolls from the 89th Virginia Regiment. Both companies served in the August–September 1814 campaign. These muster rolls were filed with the Auditor's Office in Richmond and first published in 1852. They may be found in volume II of *Virginia Militia in the War of 1812*.

- **Captain John Merchant's Company Muster Roll, from the 89th Regiment, Virginia Militia, commanded by Lieutenant Colonel Gerrard Alexander, in the service of the U.S. from August 24 to September 7, 1814.**[14]

John Merchant	Captain	14 days service
William French	Lieutenant	8 days
Barnaby Cannon	Ensign	8 days
Thomas Burrough	Sergeant	8 days
Cuthbert Harrison	2nd Sergeant	8 days
Daniel Cole	3rd Sergeant	14 days
William Martin	Corporal	8 days
James Merchant	2nd Corporal	8 days
Otley Crosby	3rd Corporal	8 days
Matthias Cole	Corporal	6 days
Lewis Athey	Private	8 days
James Abel	Private	8 days
Samuel Anderson	Private	6 days
John Arnold	Private	8 days
James Arnold	Private	8 days
Thomas Abel	Private	8 days
Richard Allen	Private	[blank]
Zephaniah Brawner	Private	8 days
Fantley Ball	Private	8 days
Benjamin Carney	Private	[blank]
Vincent Calvert	Private	8 days
Thomas Cock	Private	[blank]
Alexander Crosby	Private	6 days
William Cornwell	Private	8 days
Harrison Cornwell	Private	8 days
Jesse Dowell	Private	14 days
Walter Davis	Private	14 days
John B. Davis	Private	8 days
Walter Dodson	Private	8 days
Jessee Davis	Private	6 days
Thomas Davis	Private	6 days
Edward Fair	Private	8 days
Cuthbert Harrison	Private	8 days

---

[14] Auditor's Rolls, Richmond, *Virginia Militia in the War of 1812*, II: 582–583.

♦ **Captain John Merchant's Company Muster Roll, from the 89th Regiment, Virginia Militia, commanded by Lieutenant Colonel Gerrard Alexander, in the service of the U.S. from August 24 to September 7, 1814.** (Cont.)

Zacheus Harrison	Private	14 days
Stephen Harrison	Private	8 days
James Jordan	Private	8 days
William King	Private	8 days
George Keys	Private	14 days
James Keys	Private	14 days
Archibald Lawson	Private	8 days
William Moore	Private	8 days
Ignatius Milstead	Private	8 days
Thomas Nelson	Private	14 days
William Murphy	Private	6 days
William Martin	Private	6 days
William Mauck	Private	[blank]
Alexander Patterson	Private	14 days
John Payne	Private	14 days
William Phillips	Private	8 days
George Pierson	Private	8 days
Hugh Petty	Private	8 days
Ashford Posey	Private	6 days
Ace Pierson	Private	6 days
John Patterson	Private	6 days
Travis Payne	Private	6 days
John Roles	Private	6 days
Arthur S. Robertson	Private	14 days
Maddin Rennoe	Private	8 days
George Rennoe	Private	8 days
William Ryme	Private	6 days
John Smith	Private	14 days
James Smith	Private	8 days
Smallwood Truman	Private	6 days
Henry Tasker	Private	8 days
Eliphalet Umberfield	Private	8 days

♦ **Captain Benjamin Tyler's Company Muster Roll, from the 89th Regiment, Virginia Militia, commanded by Lieutenant Colonel Gerrard Alexander, in the service of the U.S. from August 30 to September 7, 1814.**[15]

Benjamin Tyler	Captain	9 days service
H. R. Payn	Lieutenant	9 days
William P. Dunnington	Ensign	9 days
Silas Foster	Sergeant	9 days
Francis T. Fitzhugh	Sergeant	9 days
Joseph Tyler	Sergeant	9 days
James Cowls	Sergeant	9 days
Alexander Anderson	Corporal	9 days
Joshua Hoff	Corporal	9 days

---

[15] Ibid., II: 791–792.

♦ **Captain Benjamin Tyler's Company Muster Roll, from the 89th Regiment, Virginia Militia, commanded by Lieutenant Colonel Gerrard Alexander, in the service of the U.S. from August 30 to September 7, 1814.**
(Cont.)

Robert Therman	Corporal	9 days
Reuben Francis	Corporal	9 days
William Briant	Private	9 days
Joseph Butler	Private	9 days
William Brawner	Private	9 days
John Brown Jr.	Private	9 days
Thomas Bradfield	Private	9 days
Elijah Camerl [Campbell?]	Private	9 days
Jonathan Camerl [Campbell?]	Private	9 days
William Davis	Private	9 days
Robert Dunnington	Private	9 days
Solomon Ewell Jr.	Private	9 days
David Franklin	Private	9 days
Elijah Fryer	Private	9 days
Presley Fryer	Private	9 days
George Garner	Private	9 days
William Garner	Private	9 days
William Graham	Private	9 days
Thomas Hoff	Private	9 days
James Hixon	Private	9 days
John Hall	Private	9 days
John Jackson Jr.	Private	9 days
Bailey Jackson	Private	9 days
Pleasant Jeffreys	Private	9 days
John King Jr.	Private	9 days
John King Sr.	Private	9 days
John Kinchelow	Private	9 days
Benjamin King	Private	9 days
John Kirkpatrick	Private	9 days
Thomas Kirkpatrick	Private	9 days
William Learkin [Larkin]	Private	9 days
Daniel Learkin [Larkin]	Private	9 days
Henry Langfelt	Private	9 days
John Milstead Jr.	Private	9 days
Thomas Mason	Private	9 days
Martin Moredock	Private	9 days
Burket Newman	Private	9 days
Albert Newman	Private	9 days
Richard Payne	Private	9 days
Joseph Parmer	Private	9 days
David Ramie	Private	9 days
William Rollins	Private	9 days
Strother Reno	Private	9 days
James Suttle	Private	9 days
Westward Smithers	Private	9 days
Edmond Thermon [Thurman]	Private	9 days

♦ **Captain Benjamin Tyler's Company Muster Roll, from the 89th Regiment, Virginia Militia, commanded by Lieutenant Colonel Gerrard Alexander, in the service of the U.S. from August 30 to September 7, 1814.**
(Cont.)

Thomas Waring	Private	9 days
Philip Winekoop	Private	9 days
Randolph Welsh	Private	9 days
Jesse Woodyard	Private	9 days
John Woodyard	Private	9 days
George Woodyard	Private	9 days

♦ **Roster of the 89th Regiment, (July–September 1814) Virginia Militia: Officers, non-commissioned officers and rank and file** from Ancestry.com, *War of 1812 Service Records*, extracted from NARA, *Index to Compiled Service Records of Volunteer Soldiers ... in the War of 1812*, M 602. 234 rolls.

It should be remembered that the roster here, include **only** the men found on Ancestry.com's compilation of 1812 service records.

Field and Staff Officers
    Colonel Philip Klepstine
Captains
    John Brawner
    Robert Brown
Lieutenants
    Daniel Foster, 2nd Lieutenant
    Augustine Gaines
    Howson Hooe
Ensign
    Moses Davis
Cornet
    Reuben Burton
Surgeon
    John Severo
Musician
    Thomas McClanahan, Trumpeter, Musician
Non-Commissioned Officers: Sergeants
    John B. Bailey, 1st Sgt.
    Henry Brooks
    Charles Chloe
    Edward Fitzhugh, 1st Sgt., Sgt.
    John P. Harrison, 1st Sgt.
    Josiah B. Harrison
    John Moore
    John P. Montgomery, QM Sgt.
    Abraham Penquite
    Jarvis Shaw
Rank and File: Corporals
    Giles Carter
    Thompson Green
    Cornelius Hoff

Rank and File: Corporals (Cont.)
    Robert Kincheloe
    John Latham
    Charles McClanahan
    William Thurman
Rank and File: Privates
    Elisha Adams
    Henry Allen
    John Barron
    Thomas Barron
    Joshua Beckley
    Bailey Bell
    Greenberry Belt
    William E. L. Belt
    Alexander Blackwell
    John Blackwell
    William Blake
    Francis Bowen
    George Bradfield
    Richard Brady
    Richard A. Brett
    John N. Brooks
    Pursus R. A. Brown
    John L. Bryan
    Joshua Buckley
    James Burdett
    Edward E. Carter
    Reuben Chick
    Elijah Chloe
    William Creel
    Francis Crouch

♦ **Roster of the 89th Regiment, (July–September 1814) Virginia Militia: Officers, non-commissioned officers and rank and file** from Ancestry.com, *War of 1812 Service Records*, extracted from NARA, *Index to Compiled Service Records of Volunteer Soldiers ... in the War of 1812,* M 602. 234 rolls.
(Cont.)

Rank and File: Privates (Cont.)
    Bernard Crowson
    Simpson Crowson
    Samuel S. Davis
    Bradford Dawson
    Amos Dye
    Benjamin Ellis
    John Ellis Jr.
    Joseph Ellis
    Charles Ewell
    James Fewell
    Sinah Fitzhugh
    Richard Flemming
    James Florence
    Redman Foster
    George Garner
    John I. Gill
    Thomas Graham
    Uriah Graham
    Horton Green
    James Green
    John L. Green
    John Hall
    Zachariah Halsey
    Thomas B. Hamilton
    Nathan Helsop
    John Hoff
    John Hooe
    Gavin Horton
    Hawkins Howard
    Forsythe Jackson
    Dennis M. Johnson
    James Keach
    Moses Kembler (?)
    Charles W. King
    John King
    William W. King
    Jeremiah Lee
    William Maddox
    John Manuel
    Robert Mason
    Thomas McAboy
    Alexander McEwen

Rank and File: Privates (Cont.)
    James W. Morehead
    Charles D. Nalley/Nally
    Daniel Norman
    Leonard Oliver
    Travis Petty
    William Petty
    John Powell
    Samuel Purcell
    William Read/Reed
    Charles Renno
    Eli Renno
    William Riley
    William Roach
    Henry Rollins
    John Rollins
    John Ross
    William S. Saunders
    George Shirley
    Wilford Sidebotham
    William Simpson
    Thomas A. Smith
    Henry Smoot
    Francis Taylor
    Thomas Thurman
    Levi Turner
    Gustavus B. Tyler
    John M. Tyler
    Richard B. Tyler
    Stark Washington
    Isaac Weeks
    Benjamin Welsh
    Jacob Wilson
    Thomas Windsor
    John Woodyard
    Thomas Wright

The two regiments belonged to the 5th Brigade, 2nd Division of Virginia Militia forces. The regimental command for the 36th Regiment consisted of Lt. Colonel Enoch Renno, in August 1804, Major Enoch O'Rear and Major Thomas Chapman, in May 1809. One of the Captains of the 36th Regiment, Virginia Militia was Captain **Joseph R. Gilbert**. His company saw service from July 20–26, 1813 and January 10–April 20, 1814. The company was split between to Colonel Richard Parker's command and Colonel Daniel Coleman's 6th Virginia Militia.

Captain **James Hayes's Light Infantry** was called into service in August and September 1814. Captain **Alexander Howison's Company** had two tours of duty: one in July and August 1813, the other in the last week of August 1814. Captain **George W. Jackson's Company** was stationed at Ellicott Mills, Maryland between the last of August and November 24, 1814. Captain **John Linton's Cavalry** was called up in the last of August, until the first week in September 1814. Captain **Joseph R. Lynn's Company** was called out by General Hungerford and stationed at Fredericksburg and Mattox Bridge for a month between August 2 and September 2, 1814. Captain **Joseph Smith's Company** and Captain **Richard Weedon's Company** were called up during the last week of August 1814.

The 89th Regiment of Virginia Militia was led, first by Major **W. L. Washington**, in December 1805 and then by Lieutenant Colonel **Gerard Alexander**, in March 1812. There were five Captains in the 89th Regiment. Captain **Robert Brown's Cavalry** were called up in the last of August through the first week of September 1814.

Captain **John Brawner's Company** was on duty from the last day in July until September 2, 1814. They marched to Mattox Bridge in early August 1814 where they remained until ordered to King George on August 15, 1814. At that time, Major **Enoch Orear** of the 36th Regiment took charge of the company and marched them to Round Hill Church where they reported to Colonel Austin Smith. In early September this company was consolidated with General Madison's Brigade.

Captain **John Merchant's Company** of the 89th Regiment of Virginia Militia was called out in late August and served until September 7, 1814. Captain **Benjamin Tyler's Company** served from August 30–September 7, 1814.

Most of the Prince William militia either remained in Virginia or took part in the Baltimore campaign. Regimental orders in July 1813 and General Orders in August 1814 directed Major **Thomas Chapman**, of the 36th Regiment, to take charge of a detachment of Prince William militia at Dumfries. Other Prince William companies were called out by General Hungerford in the summer of 1814 to assist in the defense of the Northern Neck.[16]

One final note. While these rosters and muster rolls are by no means a complete list of Prince William men who served in the War of 1812, it is outside the survey nature of this book to identify all of those officers and men in this war. More research is indicated which would include, at a minimum, federal pension and bounty land applications and an 1810–1850 census research, along with a closer examination of the Prince William record base.

A good case in point follows.

♦ The Court Martial of Major Townsend Dade, 2nd Battalion, 36th Regiment, Virginia Militia, November, 1807.[17]

In the Clerks Loose Papers of the Fauquier County Court is an interesting court martial of a field officer in the 36th Virginia Militia commanded by Colonel Enoch Rennoe.

---

[16] Stuart Lee Butler, *A Guide to Virginia Militia Units in the War of 1812* (Athens: Iberian Publishing Company, 1988), 180–181.

[17] Peters, *Neglected and Forgotten*, 20–22, 1807-001 Court-martial of Major Townsend Dade, 2nd Battalion, 36th Regiment.

John Wills, John Williams, Enoch Aram, Luke Cannon, Levi Scott, Joseph Smith, Walter Ashmore and John McRae were summoned to the Fauquier Courthouse on the third Monday in November to attend a court martial convened by Brigadier General Thomson Mason as witnesses for the Commonwealth.

The summons specified a dispute between the Commonwealth and Major Townsend Dade. It was signed by Major General James Williams, 2nd Division of the Virginia Militia. Other names of officers appeared on the summons as well: Collin Campbell, George Carney, Richard Cole, Beverley W. Booner, Seth Botts, John Hays, George Wedon, and Joseph Brady.

The court martial began Monday morning, November 16, 1807 at the Fauquier Courthouse. Major Townsend had been arrested and faced four counts against him. First, for disobeying orders; second, for ungentlemanly conduct; third, for being intoxicated while on duty; and fourth, for opening letters addressed to the commandant of the 36th Regiment.

Officers in the regiment were present: General Thompson Mason was the president of the proceedings. Colonels William Tyler, Thornton Buckner, Thomas Broadus, and Hugh Douglas attended. So did Majors Owen Sullivan and Thomas Spindle. Also in attendance were four captains, Thomas Brooke, John Obannon, Stanton Slaughter, and Thomas White. Hugh R. Campbell was the Judge Advocate and Benjamin V. Lakin, the Provost Martial.

Unfortunately not enough officers had appeared which necessitated an adjournment until the next day. On Tuesday, Major Thomas Gibson and Major Gillison appeared and the Court Martial was officially in session.

Major Dade's attorney required the separate charges exhibited along with the time they were allegedly committed. The court obliged. The Commonwealth Attorney brought forth three charges: He disobeyed orders while he was in Dumfries on September 5, 1807 when he rode into the Prince William Courthouse while on duty, making a return of draft. This was contrary to the orders he received. He was charged with ungentlemanly conduct because he raised his sword against his superior officer. Furthermore, he was intoxicated during the September 5, 1807 incident.

On hearing the testimony from the Commonwealth and from Major Dade, the court was of the opinion that of the charges leveled against Major Dade, some were frivolous and others were not sufficiently supported. Therefore Major Dade was reinstated.

The Court then ordered that George Renoe who had summoned the sixteen witnesses receive $9.00 for his service. The Court also granted Richard Weedon, $6.00 for retrieving the Articles of War; Philip Daw, $12.000, for summoning witnesses; Richard Roy, $6.00 for furnishing a room (probably for the witnesses); Hugh Campbell, the Judge Advocate, $40.00; and Benjamin Lakin, the Provost Martial, $9.00.

Having concluded all the business brought before them, the Court was dissolved.

There was one other document of interest in the Military Series of the Clerk Loose Papers 1759-1825. In May 1815, Captain William Obannon of the 36th Regiment gave a copy of a receipt for camp equipment to Samuel F. Adams, the Quartermaster of the Regiment. Among the items on the receipt were six common tents, two wall tens, four pick axes, three felling axes, four shovels, four spades, nine iron pots, twenty mess pans, seven camp kettles, five ovens, one scale, a six pound weight and eight oven leads. The receipt was signed by Samuel F. Adams and witnessed by 1st Lieutenant Peter Holmes and Charles Duncan. Captain Obannon certified that the copy was a true one and that he had the original.[18]

These two examples demonstrate the importance of examining records in nearby counties for officers in the 36th and 89 Virginia Militia during the war of 1812 time period.

---

[18] Peters, *Neglected and Forgotten*, 29. 1815-001 Receipt for Camp Equipage.

Index

Abel, Able

Peggy (Green) — 189
  As daughter of Elijah Green decd, certified as heir at law, Dec 1833, Oct 1834 — 153–154
  Certified as heir at law to Elijah Green, decd, a soldier in Captain Thomas Ewell's 1 VSR, December 1833, February 1835 — 192
  Appointed Thomas G. Moncure as attorney to collect arrears in pension for Elijah Green decd from September 1832 until his death January 15, 1833 — 192
  As wife of James Able, identified and certified as heir at law to Elijah Green, August 1836 — 194

James, PSC — 79
James, Prvt 36th Rgt, Virginia Militia, War of 1812 Roster — 208
James, Prvt. Captain John Merchant's Company Muster Roll, 89th Rgt Virginia Militia, War of 1812 — 214

Thomas, Prvt Captain Alexander Howison's Company Muster Roll, 36th Rgt Virginia Militia, War of 1812 — 200
Thomas, Prvt 36th Rgt., Virginia Militia, War of 1812 Roster — 208

Adams, Addams

Elisha, Prvt 89th Rgt, Virginia Militia, War of 1812 Roster — 217

George, Ensign, 36th Rgt, Virginia Militia, War of 1812 Roster — 206

John, Patrol Accounts — 37, 39

Letitia, certified as heir of John Ransdell decd, and heir at law to Captain Thomas Ransdell decd, of Virginia Continental Line, September 1843 — 161

Peter — 132

Samuel, Ensign, 36th Rgt, Virginia Militia, 1813 — 110, 118
Samuel, Ensign, Captain Joseph R. Gilbert's Company Muster Roll, 36th Rgt, Virginia Militia, War of 1812 — 197

Samuel F, as QM, 36th Rgt, Virginia Militia in Camp Equipage Papers, May 1815 Fauquier County Clerks Loose Papers — 220

Thomas, Prvt Captain Alexander Howison's Company Muster Roll, 36th Rgt, Virginia Militia, War of 1812 — 200

Adie

Benjamin, Corporal, 36th Rgt, Virginia Militia, War of 1812 Roster — 207

Hugh, Prvt, Captain Joseph R. Gilbert's Company Muster Roll, 36th Rgt, Virginia Militia, War of 1812 — 198
Hugh, Corporal, Captain John Linton's Muster Roll of Cavalry Troops, 36th Rgt, Virginia Militia, War of 1812 — 204
Hugh, Sgt, Captain Richard Weedon's Company Muster Roll, 36th Rgt, Virginia Militia, War of 1812 — 205

Aix-la-Chapelle, Treaty of — 14

Index

Albany, New York	10, 14
Treaty of	11

Alcock
Abner R. Ensign, 36th Rgt, Virginia Militia, 1813	110
Abner R. Ensign, 36th Rgt, Virginia Militia, War of 1812 Roster	206

Alcott,
— Major	132, 134

Ails, Ailes, Ale, Ales, Ayle, Ayles
Joseph, Prvt, Captain Robert McKenzie's Company, Virginia Rgt, Fr and Indian War	169

Alexander
Garrard, Lt, Light Infantry, 89th Virginia Rgt, 1805	111, 115
Gerard, Lt, 89th Rgt, Virginia Militia, 1804–1806	111
Gerard, Lt Colonel, 89th Rgt, Virginia Militia, 1812	219
Gerrard, Lt Colonel, 89th Rgt, Virginia Militia, 1814	111–112
John, Patrol Acct, 1806	117
Robert, Prvt, Captain Joseph R. Gilbert's Company Muster Roll, 36th Rgt, Virginia Militia, War of 1812	198
William	43, 76
William, 2 PSCs	80

Allan
Henry, Prvt, 89th Rgt, Virginia Militia, War of 1812 Roster	217
James, Patrol Acct, 1805	116
James, as Prvt, 36th Rgt, Virginia Militia, War of 1812	116, note 11
James, Patrol Acct, 1805, and Prvt, 36th Rgt, Virginia Militia, War of 1812	196
James, Prvt, Alexander Howison's Company Muster Roll, 36th Rgt, Virginia Militia, War of 1812	200
John, Captain	40
Richard, Lieutenant, 36th Rgt, Virginia Militia, 1806	117
Richard, Prvt, Captain Joseph R. Gilbert's Company Muster Roll, 36th Rgt, Virginia Militia, War of 1812	198
Richard, Prvt, Captain Alexander Howison's Company Muster Roll, 36th Rgt, Virginia Militia, War of 1812	200
Richard, Prvt, Captain John Merchant's Company Muster Roll, 89th Rgt, Virginia Militia, War of 1812	214
William, Sgt, Captain Alexander Howison's Company Muster Roll, 36th Rgt, Virginia Militia, War of 1812	200
William, Sgt, 36th Rgt, Virginia Militia, War of 1812 Roster	207
Zachariah, Prvt, Captain Joseph R. Gilbert's Company Muster Roll, 36th Rgt, Virginia Militia, War of 1812	198

Index

Allerton
    Isaac, Major   5

Alvey
    John, Prvt, Captain Philip Richard Francis Lee's Company, 3rd Virginia Rgt,   56
        Revolutionary War

    Robert, Prvt, Captain John Mercer's Company, 3rd Virginia Rgt,   56, 139
        Revolutionary War

Anderson
    Alexander, Corporal, Captain Benjamin Tyler's Company Muster Roll, 89th Rgt,   215
        Virginia Militia, War of 1812

    James, PSC   81

    Samuel, Patrol Acct, 1813, assigned to William S. Colquhoun   119
    Samuel, Patrol Acct, 1813, assigned to Benoni Harrison   120
    Samuel, Patrol Acct, 1813 and soldier in 36th Rgt, Virginia Militia, War of 1812   196
    Samuel, Corporal, 36th Rgt, Virginia Militia, War of 1812 Roster   208

    Samuel, Prvt, Captain John Merchant's Company Muster Roll, 89th Rgt,   214
        Virginia Militia, War of 1812

    Sanford, Prvt, Captain Alexander Howison's Company Muster Roll, 36th Rgt,   196
        Virginia Militia, War of 1812

    Sarah, certified as heir at law to Elias Wingate, decd, a soldier in the Virginia   162
        State Artillery, Revolutionary War, September 1843

    Spencer, Prvt, Captain Philip Richard Francis Lee's Company, 3rd Virginia Rgt,   56, 139
        Revolutionary War
    Spencer, as Prvt, Captain Philip Richard Francis Lee's Company, 3rd Virginia Rgt,   56, note 45
        Revolutionary War
    Spencer, security on recognizance for George Thomas   67
    Spencer, Security on recognizance for George Thomas   67
    Spencer, Revolutionary War Pension Application, September 1818   132
    Spencer, Revolutionary War Pension Declaration and Schedule, 1820–1821   134, 139

    William, Commonwealth cause against, for advising a soldier to desert and fleecing him   67
    in an illegal card game, September 1779 Court

Appleby
    George, Prvt, Captain Alexander Howison's Company Muster Roll, 36th Rgt,   200
        Virginia Militia, War of 1812

Aram
    Enoch, in Major Townsend Dade's Court martial Proceedings, November, 1807   219
        From Fauquier County Clerk's Loose Papers

Armistead, Armstead
    George, Major in charge of defense of Fort McHenry   108

Index

Armistead, Armstead (Cont.)
John, PSC, Revolutionary War 78

Thomas, Captain of Grenadiers, 1st Virginia State Regiment, Revolutionary War 61

Armstrong
— Secretary of War under President James Madison 104, 107

Arnold
James, Patrol Acct and as Privt, 36th Rgt, Virginia Militia, War of 1812 196
James, Prvt, Captain Alexander Howison's Company Muster Roll, 36th Rgt, Virginia Militia, War of 1812 200
James, Prvt, Captain John Merchant's Company Muster Roll, 89th Rgt, Virginia Militia, War of 1812 214
James, 2 Patrol Accts, 1813 220

John, Prvt, Captain Alexander Howison's Company Muster Roll, 36th Rgt, Virginia Militia, War of 1812 200
John, Prvt, Captain John Merchant's Company Muster Roll, 89th Rgt, Virginia Militia, War of 1812 214

Moses, Patrol Acct, 1813 120
Moses, Prvt, Captain Alexander Howison's Company Muster Roll, 36th Rgt, Virginia Militia, War of 1812 200

Arrington
Anna, certified as heir at law to Francis Johnston, decd, a Revolutionary War Soldier, September 1843 162

Larkin, Prvt, Captain Alexander Howison's Company Muster Roll, 36th Rgt, Virginia Militia, War of 1812 200
Larkin, Prvt, Captain John Linton's Muster Roll of Cavalry Troops, 36th Rgt, Virginia Militia, War of 1812 204

Thomas, Revolutionary War Pension Application noted in Court Minutes, May 1836 ..... 135, 157
Thomas, Revolutionary War Pension Application, May 1836 ..... 157, note 28

Washburn, Prvt, Captain Alexander Howison's Company Muster Roll, 36th Rgt, Virginia Militia, War of 1812 200

Ashby
John, Captain, Ranger Company, Virginia Rgt, French and Indian War 177

Ashmore
Walter, in Major Townsend Dade's Court martial Proceedings, November 1807 219

William, PSC 80

Askins, Ashings, Asking, Askings, Arskins
John (1), Prvt, Captain George Mercer's Company, Virginia Rgt, French and Indian War 33
John (1), Prvt, Captain George Mercer's Company, Virginia Rgt, French and Indian War ..... 33, note 129
John (1), Prvt, Captain Thomas Waggener's Company, Virginia Rgt, French and Indian War 170

Index

Askins, Ashings, Asking, Askings, Arskins (Cont.)
  John (1), Prvt, Captain George Mercer's Company, Virginia Rgt, French and Indian War   170
  John (2), Prvt, Colonel George Washington's Virginia Rgt, French and Indian War   170
  John (3?), Prvt, Colonel William Byrd's Virginia Rgt, French and Indian War   170

  Philemon Prvt, Captain George Mercer's Company, Virginia Rgt,   33, 171
    French and Indian War
  Philemon Prvt Thomas Waggener's Company, Virginia Rgt,   171
    French and Indian War

  Philip, Prvt, Colonel George Washington's Virginia Rgt,   33, 171
    French and Indian War

  William, Patrol Acct   39

Athey, Athy
  Horatio, Prvt, Captain Alexander Howison's Company Muster Roll, 36th Rgt,   200
    War of 1812

  John, Corporal, Captain Philip R. F. Lee's Company, 3rd Virginia Rgt,   139
    Revolutionary War

  John, Prvt, Captain Alexander Howison's Company Muster Roll, 36th Rgt,   200
    Virginia Militia, War of 1812
  John, Prvt, Captain Joseph Smith's Company Muster Roll, 36th Rgt,   204
    Virginia Militia, War of 1812

  Leroy, Prvt, Captain Alexander Howison's Company Muster Roll, 36th Rgt,   200
    Virginia Militia, War of 1812

  Levi, Prvt, Captain Joseph R. Gilbert's Company Muster Roll, 36th Rgt,   198
    Virginia Militia, War of 1812
  Levi, Prvt, 36th Rgt, Virginia Militia, War of 1812 Roster   208

  Lewis, Prvt, Captain John Merchant's Company Muster Roll, 89th Rgt,   214
    Virginia Militia, War of 1812

  Willis, Prvt, Captain Joseph R. Gilbert's Company Muster Roll, 36th Rgt,   198
    Virginia Militia, War of 1812

Atwell, Attwell
  Charles, Captain Revolutionary War Artillery, Affidavit in John Bell's Pension Papers   132
    November 1819 in Fauquier County

  Hugh, Constable, in 1st Battn, 89th Rgt District, June 1805 Court   115

  Thomas, PSC   84

Atwood
  John, Prvt, 36th Rgt, Virginia Militia, War of 1812 Roster   208

Austin, Austing, Ostin
  Edward, Sgt, Captain Joseph Smith's Company Muster Roll, 36th Rgt,   204
    Virginia Militia, War of 1812

Index

Austin, Austing, Ostin (Cont.)
    Edward, Sgt, 36th Rgt, Virginia Militia, War of 1812 Roster   207
    Francis, Prvt, Colonel George Washington's Virginia Rgt, French and Indian War   33
    Francis, Prvt, Colonel George Washington's Virginia Rgt, French and Indian War   33, note 130
    Francis, Sgt, Captain Thomas Waggener's Company, Virginia Rgt, French and Indian War   171–172

Bacon
    Nathaniel   4–5

Bacon's Rebellion   3–5

Bailey
    John B., 1st Sgt, 89th Rgt, Virginia Militia, War of 1812 Roster   217

Bailis, Baylis
    — , Captain, Prince William Militia, French and Indian War   50, 182
    John, Oath as Prince William Militia Officer 1755, French and Indian War   36
    John, Captain of Cavalry Troop, 1755, Prince William Militia, French and Indian War   37, 39
    John, Captain, Prince William Militia, 1756   37
    John, Captain, Prince William Militia, Militia claim for service, French and Indian War   37, note 8
    John, Captain, Prince William Militia Accounts on frontier, 1756, French and Indian War   38
    John, Captain, Militia Account for service, French and Indian War   185
    John, Captain, Prince William Militia, French and Indian War   183
    John, Major of Foot, Prince William Militia, French and Indian War   38, 183
    John, Major, Prince William Militia, excused from attending Council of War   39

    Samuel, Oath as Prince William Militia Officer 1756, French and Indian War   38

    William, Oath as Prince William Militia Officer 1754, French and Indian War   36
    William, Officer, Prince William Militia, 1756, militia claim for service   36, note 2
    William, Captain, Prince William Militia   38, note 11
    William, Captain, Prince William Militia Account, 1757, French and Indian War   39
    William, Captain, Prince William Militia, French and Indian War   183–185

Baker
    Elisha, Prvt, 36th Rgt, Virginia Militia, War of 1812 Roster   208

Ball
    Augustine, Prvt, 36th Rgt, Virginia Militia, War of 1812 Roster   208

    Fantley (aka Fauntley), Prvt, Captain Alexander Howison's Company Muster Roll Virginia Militia, War of 1812   200
    Fantley (aka Fauntley), Prvt, 36th Rgt, Virginia Militia, War of 1812 Roster   208
    Fantley (aka Fauntley), Prvt, Captain John Merchant's Company Muster Roll, Virginia Militia, War of 1812   214

    Mary, d/o Chilton Ransdell and heir at law to Captain Thomas Ransdell, decd. of Continental Line, September 1843 Court   161

Balson
    Samuel, Trooper, Prince William Militia, Militia Claim for service, French and Indian War   185

Baltimore Campaign, War of 1812   219

Index

Barbee
Lamath, Prvt, 36th Rgt, Virginia Militia, War of 1812 Roster — 208

Barker
Joseph, Patrol Acct, 1805 — 117
Joseph, Patrol Acct, 1805 and Prvt, 36th Rgt, Virginia Militia, War of 1812 — 196

William S., 36th Rgt, Virginia Militia, War of 1812 Roster — 208

Barney
Joshua, Commodore, gunboats in Chesapeake, War of 1812 — 105, 108
Joshua, burns small flotilla of gunboats to avoid capture by British, War of 1812 — 105
Joshua, POW of British — 108

Barr
William, Ensign, Prince William Militia 1755, French and Indian War — 37
William, Ensign, Prince William Militia, militia claim for service, French and Indian War — 37, note 6
William, Lt, Prince William Militia 1762, French and Indian War — 41

William, Trooper, Prince William Militia, Militia Claim for service — 185

Barron
John, Prvt, 89th Rgt, Virginia Militia, War of 1812 Roster — 217

Jesse, summoned to Court to settle guardianship acct for Thomas Love, May 1804 Court — 115

Thomas, Prvt, 89th Rgt, Virginia Militia, War of 1812 Roster — 217

William, Orderly Sgt, QM Sgt, 36th Rgt, Virginia Militia, War of 1812 Roster — 196, 207

Barton
Charles, Prvt, 36th Rgt, Virginia Militia, War of 1812 Roster — 208

Thomas, Drummer, 36th Virginia Militia, War of 1812 Roster — 110, 207

Valentine, Soldier, Prince William Militia, Militia Claim for service, French and Indian War — 185

Bates
Rowland, Prvt, Captain Alexander Howison's Company Muster Roll, 36th Rgt, Virginia Militia, War of 1812 — 200
Rowland, Prvt, 36th Rgt, Virginia Militia, War of 1812 Roster — 208

Batley
Moses, Prvt, 36th Rgt, Virginia Militia, War of 1812 Roster — 208

Battle of Bladensburg, Events leading to — 104–106

Beach
John, Prvt, 36th Rgt, Virginia Militia, War of 1812 Roster — 208

Theodosia (Garner), w/o Silas Beach, d/o William Garner, a Revolutionary War Soldier Certified as heir at law to William Garner, December 1833 Court — 162

Index

Bear, Bare
    William, Prvt, Captain Robert Spotswood's Company, Virginia Rgt, French and Indian War   33
    William, Prvt, Captain Robert Spotswood's Company, Virginia Rgt, French and Indian War   33, note 131
    William, Patrol Acct, French and Indian War   37
    William, Prvt, Captain Robert Spotswood's Company, Virginia Rgt, French and Indian War   171

Beard
    Mary Ann, certified as heir at law to Henry Tyler, decd, reputed Midshipman, Virginia State Navy, Revolutionary War   154

Bearmore
    George, Oath that he served with Major Douglas   68
    George, New Jersey Solider, French and Indian War   68
    George, as New Jersey Soldier, French and Indian War   68, note 27

Beckley
    Joshua, Prvt, 89th Rgt, Virginia Militia, War of 1812 Roster   217

Bedford, Duke of   12

Bell
    Bailey, Prvt, 89th Rgt, Virginia Militia, War of 1812 Roster   217

    Daniel, Prvt, 36th Rgt, Virginia Militia, War of 182 Roster   208

    David, Captain, Virginia Rgt, French and Indian War   177–178

    Francis, Prvt, 36th Rgt, Virginia Militia, War of 1812 Roster   208

    George, Prvt, Captain John Linton's MR of Cavalry, 36th Rgt, Virginia Militia War of 1812   204
    George, Prvt, 36th Rgt, Virginia Militia, War of 1812 Roster   208

    James, s/o John Bell, in John Bell's 1820 Pension Papers   134

    John, Oath as Prince William Militia Officer 1753, French and Indian War   35
    John, Major of Horse, Prince William Militia 1756, French and Indian War   38
    John, as delegate to House of Burgesses   38, note 16

    John, Revolutionary War Pension Application, 1819 in Fauquier   132
    John, Revolutionary War Pension Application and Schedule, 1820, in Fauquier   134
    John, Revolutionary War Pension Application, 1833 in Prince William   151
    John, Revolutionary War Pension Application, 1833, in Prince William   151, note 1

    Landy, s/o John Bell, in Bell's Pension Papers, 1820   134

    Mary Ann, d/o John Bell, in Bell's Pension Papers, 1820   134

    Moses, s/o John Bell, in Bell's Pension Papers, 1820   134

    Thomas, Prvt, 36th Rgt, Virginia Militia, War of 1812 Roster   208

    Uriah, Prvt, Captain Alexander Howison's Company Muster Roll, 36th Rgt, Virginia Militia, War of 1812   203

Index

Bell (Cont.)
    Uriah, Prvt, 36th Rgt, Virginia Militia, War of 1812 Roster   208

    William, Prvt, Captain Richard Weedon's Company Muster Roll, 36th Rgt,   205
    William, Prvt, 36th Rgt, Virginia Militia, War of 1812 Roster   208

Belt
    Greenberry, Prvt, 89th Rgt, Virginia Militia, War of 1812 Roster   217

    William E. L, Prvt, 89th Rgt, Virginia Militia, War of 1812 Roster   217

Benedict, Maryland,   British landing at, August 1814   105

Bennett
    William, Captain, Prince William Militia 1762, French and Indian War   40

Berkley, Governor   4–5

Berkley & Company, PSC   83

Berry
    Martha T, certified as heir at law to George Stubblefield, Ensign, Virginia Continental   162
        Line, Revolutionary War

    Richard, Prvt, 36th Rgt, Virginia Militia, War of 1812 Roster   208

    William, Trooper Prince William Militia, Claim for service, French and Indian War   185

Berryman
    Zachariah, Prvt, 36th Rgt, Virginia Militia, War of 1812 Roster   208

Bethel
    Valentine, Patrol Acct   39

Beverly
    William, Colonel   12

Bird, Byrd
    Spencer, Prvt, Captain Joseph R. Gilbert's Company Muster Roll, 36th Rgt,   198
        Virginia Militia, War of 1812
    Spencer, Prvt, 36th Rgt, Virginia Militia, War of 1812 Roster   208

    Thomas, 2 PSCs, Revolutionary War   78

    Thompson, Patrol Acct 1813   120
    Thompson, Patrol Acct 1813 and Prvt, 36th Rgt, Virginia Militia, War of 1812   196
    Thompson, Prvt, 36th Rgt, Virginia Militia, War of 1812 Roster   208

Biscoe
    Thomas, Prvt, 36th Rgt, Virginia Militia, War of 1812 Roster   208

Blackburn
    Edward, Oath as Prince William Militia Officer 1757, French and Indian War   38–39

Index

Blackburn (Cont.)
    Richard, Oath as Prince William Militia Officer 1753, French and Indian War   36
    Richard, sold land in Prince William, April 1741   176

    Thomas, Captain, Prince William Militia 1762, French and Indian War   41
    Thomas, Captain, Prince William Militia, 1763, French and Indian War   42

    Thomas, Receipt for clothing, etc for Class 27, 1781, Revolutionary War   75
    Thomas, as Lt Colonel, 2 VSR, Revolutionary War   61, 75, note 50
    Thomas, PSC   83

Blackwell
    Alexander, Prvt, 89th Rgt, Virginia Militia War of 1812 Roster   217

    David, as Commissary and QM, Lee's Legion   59
    David, as member of Captain John Chilton's Culpeper Minute Men   75, note 51
    David, Receipt for clothing, etc for Class 2, 1781, Revolutionary War   75
    David, summoned to Court as Exor of Zachariah Lewis, 1805   114
    David, as service in Revolutionary War detailed   114, note 4

    John, Prvt, 89th Rgt, Virginia Militia, War of 1812 Roster   217

    William, Oath as Lt Colonel of Foot, Prince William Militia 1756, French and Indian War   38

    William, Prvt, 36th Rgt, Virginia Militia, War of 1812 Roster   208

Bladensburg, Battle of, August 1814   106–107

Blake
    William, Prvt, 89th Rgt, Virginia Militia, War of 1812 Roster   217

Blancett
    Rhodham, PSC, Revolutionary War   86

Blanchett
    Joseph, certified as entitled to bounty land of brother William Blanchett   94
    Joseph, certified as heir at law to brother William Blanchett, decd, soldier in Virginia Continental line; claims bounty land, March 1784   149

    William, decd, soldier in Continental Army; brother Joseph entitled to bounty Lands for Revolutionary War service   94
    William, decd, soldier in Continental Army, enlisted for 3 years, died in service   149

Bland
    Allan, Ensign, Lt, 36th Rgt, Virginia Militia, 1804   113
    Allan, Lt, Captain, 36th Rgt, Virginia Militia, 1806   117

    John Jr, Trooper, Prince William Militia, Claim for service, French and Indian War   185

    John, Patrol Acct 1813, assigned to Benoni Harrison   120
    John, Sgt, Captain Alexander Howison's Company Muster Roll, 36th Rgt, Virginia Militia, War of 1812   200
    John, Sgt, 36th Rgt, Virginia Militia, War of 1812 Roster   207

Index

Bland (Cont.)
    Theodorick, Colonel, 1st Continental Dragoons, Revolutionary War   58–59

    Thomas, 2 PSCs, Revolutionary War   85

Bobo
    Jesse, Prvt, Captain Joseph R. Gilbert's Company Muster Roll, 36th Rgt, Virginia Militia, War of 1812   198
    Jesse, Prvt, 36th Rgt, Virginia Militia, War of 1812 Roster   208

    Joseph, Revolutionary War Pension Application, 1846   135
    Joseph, Revolutionary War Pension Application, 1846   135, note 34
    Joseph, Revolutionary War Pension Application, 1846   162
    Joseph, service in Captain John Brett's Company, Prince William Militia, Revolutionary War   162, note 47

Bohannon
    James, Sgt, Prvt, 36th Rgt, Virginia Militia, War of 1812 Roster   207
    James D., Sgt, Prvt, 36th Rgt, Virginia Militia, War of 1812 Roster   208

    Robert, QM Sgt, 36th Rgt, Virginia Militia, War of 1812 Roster   207

Bolling
    John, Soldier, Prince William Militia, militia claim for service, French and Indian War   185

Boswell
    Alsop, Sgt, 36th Rgt, Virginia Militia, War of 1812 Roster   207

    George, Corporal, Captain Alexander Howison's Company Muster Roll, Virginia Militia, War of 1812   200

    Samuel, Corporal, 36th Rgt, Virginia Militia, War of 1812 Roster   208

    William, Patrol Acct 1813, assigned to Benoni Harrison   120
    William, Patroller and Prvt, 36th Rgt, Virginia Militia, War of 1812   196

Botts
    Bernard, Patrol Acct 1813, assigned to Joseph R. Lynn   120
    Bernard, Patroller and Prvt, 36th Rgt, Virginia Militia, War of 1812   196

    Francis, 2 PSCs, Revolutionary War   80

Boughanan (See Bohannon)
    James D., Sgt, Captain Alexander Howison's Company Militia, 36th Rgt, Virginia Militia, War of 1812   199

Boughton
    Anderson, Sgt, 35th Rgt, Virginia Militia, War of 1812 Roster   207

Bounty Land
    Continental, Revolutionary War Legislation   139–140
    Federal Legislation   139–141
        War of 1812   140
        Public Lands, 1847–1855   140

Index

Bounty Land, Federal Legislation (Cont.)	
U.S. Military District of Ohio	140
U.S. Military District of Ohio, Indiana, and Illinois	140
Virginia Legislation	146–149

Bowen
Francis, Prvt, 89th Rgt, Virginia Militia, War of 1812 Roster	217
John, Prvt, 36th Rgt, Virginia Militia, War of 1812 Roster	208

Bower
Christian, assignee of PSC of Richard Stonnell	84

Bowles
Doctor, Prvt, Captain Thomas Waggener's Company, French and Indian War	33, 173
Doctor, French and Indian War service detailed	33, note 132
Doctor, as substitute for John Wood, French and Indian War	183

Bowling,
Abijah, Prvt, 36th Regt, Virginia Militia, War of 1812 Roster	208
George, Prvt, 36th Regt, Virginia Militia, War of 1812 Roster	208
James, Prvt, 36th Regt, Virginia Militia, War of 1812 Roster	208
William, Prvt, Prince William Militia, Militia claim for service, French and Indian War	185

Bowne
Thomas, Lieutenant, 10th Virginia Rgt, Revolutionary War	57
Thomas, Revolutionary War service	57
Thomas, decd, Captain Virginia Continental Line, Revolutionary War death certified ca 1801, March 1893 Court	159
Thomas, decd, Captain Virginia Continental Line, Revolutionary War	159, note 35

Boyd
Daniel, Bowman for the Rgt, Prvt, 36th Rgt, Virginia Militia, War of 1812 Roster	207, 208
William, Prvt, 36th Rgt, Virginia Militia, War of 1812 Roster	208

Boyle
Daniel, Paymaster, 36th Rgt, Virginia Militia, War of 1812 Roster	206

Bozel (Buzzell, Bussell? See Bussell)
George, Prvt, 36th Rgt, Virginia Militia, War of 1812 Roster	208
Samuel, Prvt, 36th Rgt, Virginia Militia, War of 1812 Roster	208
William, Prvt, 36th Rgt, Virginia Militia, War of 1812 Roster	208

Braddock's Defeat, French and Indian War	33
Braddock, Edward, British Major General, French and Indian War	27–29, 31–33, 49
Braddock Expedition, French and Indian War	29–32

Index

Bradfield
George, Prvt, 89th Rgt, Virginia Militia, War of 1812 Roster — 217

Bradfield (Cont.)
Thomas, Prvt, Captain Benjamin Tyler's Company Muster Roll, 89th Rgt, Virginia Militia, War of 1812 — 216

Bradley
James, Prvt, 36th Rgt, Virginia Militia, War of 1812 Roster — 208

Jane, w/o Richard Bradley, a revolutionary war soldier, allowed support for herself and her child, May 1780 Court, Revolutionary War — 69, 143

Richard, husband of Jane Bradley; Prvt, Captain John Peyton Harrison's Company, 2nd Virginia Rgt, Revolutionary War — 55

Richard, husband of Jane Bradley; Prvt, Captain John Peyton Harrison's Company, 2nd Virginia Continental Rgt, Revolutionary War — 69, note 30

Brady
Richard, Prvt, 89th Rgt, Virginia Militia, War of 1812 Roster — 217

Brammel, Brammell
Jeremiah, Patrol Acct, 1805 — 116

John Jr, Prvt, 36th Rgt, Virginia Militia, War of 1812 Roster — 208

John Sr, Prvt, 36th Rgt, Virginia Militia, War of 1812 Roster — 208

Brand
Lavinia, certified as heir at law to William Hickman, decd, who held various military surveys in Virginia Military Districts in Ohio and Kentucky, October 1841 Court — 161

Brannan
Thomas, Corporal, 36th Rgt, Virginia Militia, War of 1812 Roster — 207

Brawner
Alexander, Patrol Acct, 1813, assigned to Benoni Harrison — 120

Henry, Patrol Acct, 1813 — 119

Henry, Prvt, Captain Joseph R. Gilbert's Company Muster Roll, 36th Rgt, Virginia Militia, War of 1812 — 198

Henry, Prvt, Captain Alexander Howison's Company Muster Roll, 36th Rgt, Virginia Militia, War of 1812 as substitute for W. F. Moore — 200

Henry Sr, Prvt, 36th Rgt, Virginia Militia, War of 1812 Roster — 208

Ignatius, Prvt, 36th Rgt, Virginia Militia, War of 1812 Roster — 208

John, Ensign, 89th Rgt, Virginia Militia, 1804–1806 — 111
John, Captain, 89th Rgt, Virginia Militia, 1814 — 112
John, Captain, 89th Rgt, Virginia Militia, 1814 — 112, note 118
John, Captain, 89th Rgt, Virginia Militia, War of 1812 Roster — 217

Index

Brawner (Cont.)
    John, Captain, 89th Rgt, Virginia Militia, ordered to King George County,   219
        August 1814, War of 1812
    John, Captain, 89th Rgt, on orders, marched to Mattox Bridge, Virginia, August 1814,   219
        War of 1812

    Joseph, Prvt, Captain Alexander Howison's Company Muster Roll, 36th Rgt,   200
        Virginia Militia, War of 1812
    Joseph, Prvt, 36th Rgt, Virginia Militia, War of 1812 Roster   208

    Seth, Prvt, Captain Alexander Howison's Company Muster Roll, 36th Rgt,   200
        Virginia Militia, War of 1812
    Seth, Prvt, 36th Rgt, Virginia Militia, War of 1812 Roster   208

    Thomas, Lt, 89th Rgt, Virginia Militia, 1805   116

    William, Prvt, Captain John Merchant's Company Muster Roll, 89th Rgt,   214
        Virginia Militia, War of 1812

    William, Prvt, 36th Rgt, Virginia Militia, War of 1812 Roster   208

    Zephaniah, Prvt, Captain John Merchant's Company Muster Roll, 89th Rgt,   214
        Virginia Militia, War of 1812

Brent
    —, Captain, Prince William Militia, 1779, Revolutionary War   65

    Ann, wid/o Willoughby Brent, decd, 3rd Virginia Rgt, allowed support, May 1780   69, 143
        Revolutionary War

    Daniel Carroll, PSC, Revolutionary War   85

    George, Proprietor of Brenton, 1686   6

    Hugh, receipts for clothing and beef for class 14, July 1781 Court, Revolutionary War   76

    Robert, PSC, Revolutionary War   88

    William, Lt Colonel, 2 VSR, from June 1777–January 1779, Revolutionary War   61
    William, furnished clothing and beef for class 13, August 1781 Court   76
        Revolutionary War
    William, Captain, Prince William Militia, resigned June 1783 Court,   92
        Revolutionary War

    William, cadet, 3rd Virginia Rgt, Revolutionary War   139

    Willoughby, decd husband of Ann Brent, Sgt, 3rd Virginia, Revolutionary War   56
    Willoughby, decd husband of Ann Brent, Sgt, 3rd Virginia, Revolutionary War   69
    Willoughby, decd husband of Ann Brent   69, note 31

Brent Town   6

Brenton Grant   6–7

Index

Brett
John, 2 PSCs, Revolutionary War	82
John, as Captain, Virginia Militia, Revolutionary War	82, note 80
John, Court appointed as appraiser of Valentine Peyton decd estate	88
Richard, Lt, 89th Rgt, Virginia Militia, 1804–1806	111
Richard, as resident of Prince William in 1810	111, note 110
Richard, Lt, 89th Rgt, Virginia Militia, 1805	116
Richard A, Prvt, 89th Rgt, Virginia Militia, War of 1812 Roster	217

Brewer
Henry, Ensign, 89th Rgt, Virginia Militia, 1804–1806	111
Thomas, Ensign, Lt, 89th Rgt, Virginia Militia, 1813	121
William, arrested on warrant from William Carr for advising Cada Ramey a soldier, to desert and fleecing him in an illegal card game, September 1779 Court	67
William, Prvt, 36th Rgt, Virginia Militia, War of 1812 Roster	208

Briant, Bryant
William, Prvt, 36th Rgt, Virginia Militia, War of 1812 Roster	208
William, Prvt, Captain Benjamin Tyler's Company Muster Roll, 89th Rgt, Virginia Militia, War of 1812	216

Bridges
Benjamin, security for guardian bond for Benjamin Rush's guardianship of Robert Peyton, December 1762 Court	42

Bridges, Potomac, Blown up by Americans to slow down British advance on Capitol, War of 1812   106

Bridwell
Isaac, Prvt, 36th Rgt, Virginia Militia, War of 1812 Roster	208
John, Corporal, Captain Alexander Howison's Company Muster Roll, 36th Rgt, Virginia Militia, War of 1812	200
Lewis, Prvt, 36th Rgt, Virginia Militia, War of 1812 Roster	208
Richard, Prvt, 36th Rgt, Virginia Militia, War of 1812 Roster	208
William, Prvt, Captain Joseph Smith's Company Muster Roll, 36th Rgt, Virginia Militia, War of 1812	204
William, Prvt, 36th Rgt, Virginia Militia, War of 1812 Roster	208
Willis, Prvt, Corporal, 36th Rgt, Virginia Militia, War of 1812 Roster	207–208

Bristoe, Bristow
John, Soldier, Lee's Legion who died in service, Revolutionary War	59
John, decd, former soldier in Lee's Legion, who enlisted for 3 years, died in Revolutionary War; Thomas Bristow certified as heir at law, November 1784 Court	94

Index

Bristoe, Bristow (Cont.)
    John, decd, former soldier, Lee's Legion, Revolutionary War   94, note 110

    Robert, Proprietor of Brenton, 1686   6

    Thomas, certified as heir at law to John Bristoe, soldier in Lee's Legion who died in Revolutionary War   94

Britain, Britton
    George, Prvt, Captain Alexander Howison's Company Muster Roll, 36th Rgt, Virginia Militia, War of 1812   203
    George, Prvt, 36th Rgt, Virginia Militia, War of 1812 Roster   208

    John, 36th Rgt, Virginia Militia, War of 1812 Roster   208

British Attack on Baltimore, War of 1812   108
British Regiments,
    44th, for French and Indian War   27–28, 30
    48th, for French and Indian War   27–28, 30

Broadus
    Thomas, mentioned in Major Townsend Dade's Court martial Proceedings, Nov 1807 From Fauquier County Clerks Loose Papers   219

Bronaugh, Branough
    Francis, Express rider, French and Indian War, Militia Claim for service,, October 1765   173

    John, Dr, Prvt, Captain Alexander Howison's Company Muster Roll, 36th Rgt, Virginia Militia, War of 1812   200
    John, Prvt, Surgeon, 36th Rgt, Virginia Militia, 1812   110
    John, Prvt, Surgeon, 36th Rgt, Virginia Militia, 1812   110
    John, as resident of Prince William in 1810   110, note 87
    John, Surgeon's Mate, 36th Rgt, Virginia Militia, War of 1812   196
    John, promoted to Surgeon, 36th Rgt, Virginia Militia, War of 1812 Roster   207

    William, Oath as Prince William Militia Officer 1754, French and Indian War   36
    William, Ensign, Captain, Prince William Militia, Military Biography, French and Indian War   173
    William, Ensign, Captain, Prince William Militia, Bounty Land, French and Indian War Service   173

Brook
    William, Court order to sell land of Thomas Love, decd, May 1804 Court   114–115

Brooke
    Arthur, British Colonel, War of 1812   108

    Thomas, Captain, mentioned in Major Townsend Dade's Court martial proceedings, November 1807, from Fauquier County Clerks Loose Papers   219

Brooks
    Henry, Sgt, 89th Rgt, Virginia Militia, War of 1812 Roster   217

    John N. Prvt, 89th Rgt, Virginia Militia, War of 1812 Roster   217

Index

Brown
 Alexander, Receipts for clothing, etc. for Classes 18 and 19, July 1781 Court,   75
  Revolutionary War

 George Newman, OP Indenture for Tommy Calvert, orphan of Reuben Calvert, decd, 66
  former soldier, 3rd Virginia, who died in Revolutionary War
 George Newman, PSC, Revolutionary War   77

 James, 2 PSCs, Revolutionary War   81
 James, PSC, Revolutionary War   83, 87

 John, PSC, Revolutionary War   87
 John Jr. Prvt, Captain Benjamin Tyler's Company Muster Roll, 89th Rgt,   216
  Virginia Militia, War of 1812
 John S, Prvt, 36th Rgt, Virginia Militia, War of 1812 Roster   208

 Lewis, Corporal, 36th Rgt, Virginia Militia, War of 1812 Roster   207

 Pursus R. A, Prvt, 89th Rgt, Virginia Militia, War of 1812 Roster   217

 Robert, PSC, Revolutionary War   87

 Robert, Captain, 89th Rgt, Virginia Militia, 1814   112, note 118
 Robert, as resident of Prince William in 1810   112, notes 117
 Robert, Captain, 89th Rgt, Virginia Militia, War of 1812 Roster   217
 Robert, Captain, Cavalry Troop, 89th Rgt, Virginia Militia, War of 1812   219

 Wesley, Prvt, 36th Rgt, Virginia Militia, War of 1812 Roster   208

 William, 1st Lt, Captain Bernard Hooe's Company, Prince William Militia, July 1778 Court, 77
  Revolutionary War
 William, PSC, Revolutionary War   79

 William, Prvt, 36th Rgt, Virginia Militia, War of 1812 Roster   208

Browne
 Samuel, Prvt, 36th Rgt, Virginia Militia, War of 1812 Roster   208

 William, Prvt, 36th Rgt, Virginia Militia, War of 1812 Roster   208

Bruin
 Daniel, Corporal, 36th Rgt, Virginia Militia, War of 1812 Roster   207

Brundige
 William, Ensign, Lt, 36th Rgt, Virginia Militia, 1812   109
 William, Ensign, Lt, 36th Rgt, Virginia Militia, 1812   109, note 75
 William, Ensign, Lt, 36th Rgt, Virginia Militia, 1813   118
 William, Lt, 36th Rgt, Virginia Militia, 1813   118, note 20
 William, Lt, Captain Joseph R. Gilbert's Company Muster Roll, 36th Rgt,   197
  Virginia Militia, War of 1812
 William, Lt, Captain Alexander Howison's Company Muster Roll, 36th Rgt,   206
  Virginia Militia, War of 1812
 William, Adjutant, 36th Rgt, Virginia Militia, War of 1812 Roster   206

Index

Bryan
    John L, Prvt, 89th Rgt, Virginia Militia, War of 1812 Roster   217

Buchanan
    William, Oath as Prince William Militia officer, 1756, French and Indian War   38
    William, as corporal in 1756 for militia claim for service, French and Indian War   39, note 17

Buckley
    Joshua, Prvt, 89th Rgt, Virginia Militia, War of 1812 Roster   217

Buckner
    Thornton, mentioned in Major Townsend Dade's Court martial proceedings, November 1807, from Fauquier County Clerks Loose Papers   219

Buford
    — Colonel, mentioned in John Powell's Revolutionary War Pension papers, filed in Fauquier, 1818, Revolutionary War   133

Bullett, Bullitt, Bullet, Bullit
    Benjamin, Oath as Prince William Militia Officer, 1753, French and Indian War   35
    Benjamin, Ensign, Prince William Militia, killed April 1757   173
    Benjamin, rights to bounty land for French and Indian war service devised to his heir, Thomas Bullett   173

    —, Lt, Captain Robert McKenzie's Company, Virginia Rgt, French and Indian War   169

    Cuthbert, devisee of bounty lands due Colonel Thomas Bullett, decd, Captain in 1st Virginia Rgt, French and Indian War, April 1780 Court   68, 174
    Cuthbert, PSC, Revolutionary War   86

    J. Colonel, Virginia Continental Line, Heirs at law certified, February 1854 Court   164

    Nemenus, mentioned in Francis Floyd's PSC, Revolutionary War   79

    Thomas, Captain, 1st Virginia Rgt, French and Indian War   42, 68
    Thomas, Captain, 1st Virginia Rgt, French and Indian War   68, note 25
    Thomas, cadet, Lt, Captain, French and Indian War
    Thomas, Lt, Captain Thomas Waggener's Company, Virginia Rgt, French and Indian War   173
    Thomas, Captain, Petition to Legislature, January 1764   173
    Thomas, Lt, Captain Peter Hogg's Company, Virginia Rgt, French and Indian War   174
    Thomas, received bounty land for service, located in Botetourt, which he devised to his heir Cuthbert Bullitt   174
    Thomas, Captain, Virginia Rgt, French and Indian War   175

Burd
    James, Colonel, French and Indian War   23

Burdett, Burditt
    Frederick, Privt, 36th Rgt, Virginia Militia, War of 1812 Roster   208

    James, Prvt, 89th Rgt, Virginia Militia, War of 1812 Roster   217

    William, Prvt, 36th Rgt, Virginia Militia, War of 1812 Roster   208

Index

Burroughs, Burrough, Burras, Burris, Burros
    John, Patrol Acct, 1805   117

    Thomas, Soldier, Captain George Mercer's Company, Virginia Rgt, French and Indian War   174
    Thomas, received £10 for loss of an arm from Colonial Assembly, May 1757,   174
        French and Indian War

    Thomas, Prvt, Captain Alexander Howison's Company Muster Roll, 36th Rgt,   200
        Virginia Militia, War of 1812
    Thomas, Prvt, Captain Alexander Howison's Company Muster Roll, 36th Rgt   203
        Virginia Militia, War of 1812, as substitute for D. Larkin
    Thomas, Sgt, 36th Rgt, Virginia Militia, War of 1812 Roster   207

    Thomas, Sgt, Captain John Merchant's Company Muster Roll, 89th Rgt,   214
        Virginia Militia, War of 1812

Burton
    Reuben, Cornet, 89th Rgt, Virginia Militia, War of 1812 Roster   217
Burwell
    Mrs, PSC, Revolutionary War   81

    Nathaniel, PSC, Revolutionary War   81
    Nathaniel, as Ensign, Captain 1st Continental Artillery, Revolutionary War   60, note 75; 81, note 78
Bussell
    George, PSC, Revolutionary War   80

Butler
    Joseph, Patrol Acct, 1805   116
    Joseph, Prvt, Captain Benjamin Tyler's Company Muster Roll, 89th Rgt,   216
        Virginia Militia, War of 1812

    William, Prvt, 36th Rgt, Virginia Militia, War of 1812 Roster   208

Buyene
    Catharine A. (Thomas), w/o Thomas Buyenne and heir at large to J. Bullitt,   164
        Colonel, Virginia Continental Line, February 1854 Court

    Thomas, husband of Catharine A. (Thomas) Buyene, who was certified as heir   164
        at large to J. Bullitt, Colonel, Virginia Continental line in February 1854 Court

Byam
    Samuel, Judgment against as collector of class 25, for money due, May 1783 Court   91

Byrne
    Samuel, ordered by Prince William Court to divide the estate Reuben Calvert decd,   88
        among widow and children, September 1782

Byrns
    Richard, trooper Prince William Militia, Militia claim for service, French and Indian War   185

Cage
    Benjamin, soldier, Prince William Militia, petitioned legislature for pay, March 1760,   174–175
        French and Indian War

Index

Calhoun
    Charles, Prvt, Captain Joseph R. Gilbert's Company Muster Roll, 36th Rgt,   198
        Virginia Militia, War of 1812
    Charles, Prvt, 36th Rgt, Virginia Militia, War of 1812 Roster   208

Calvert
    Elias, Prvt, 36th Rgt, Virginia Militia, War of 1812 Roster   208

    George the Younger, Patrol Accts, 1755, 1756   37, 39
    George the Younger, Oath to service in French and Indian War, 1756   38
    George the Younger, with claim for express, French and Indian War   38, note 12
    George the Younger, appointed as Constable, 1761   40
    George, Soldier, Prince William Militia, Militia Claim as express rider,   186
        French and Indian War

    Geyton, Prvt, 36th Rgt, Virginia Militia, War of 1812 Roster   208

    Humphrey, one of securities for John Sidebottom's appearance before grand jury, 1780   72
    Humphrey, PSC, Revolutionary War   78

    Jesse, PSC, Revolutionary War   85

    John, Patrol Acct   39

    John Sr, PSC, Revolutionary War   84

    Jonathan, Prvt, 36th Rgt, Virginia Militia, War of 1812 Roster   208

    Landy, in John Bell's Pension Papers, 1820; daughter Mary Ann Bell living with   134
        Landy Campbell

    Obed, Patrol Acct   39
    Obed, PSC, Revolutionary War   85

    Obed Sr, 2 PSCs, Revolutionary War   85

    Peyton, Prvt, Captain Alexander Howison's Company Muster Roll, 36th Rgt,   201
        Virginia Militia, War of 1812

    Reuben, Appointed constable   42
    Reuben, Sgt, Captain John Peyton's Company, 3rd Virginia Regiment,   42, note 22
        Revolutionary War
    Reuben, decd, died in Revolutionary War; son Tommy indentured, July 1779   56
    Reuben decd, Sgt, Captain John Peyton's Company, died in service   56, note 46
    Reuben decd, Son Tommy indentured to George Newman Brown as a carpenter, July 1779   66
    Reuben decd, 3rd Virginia service records   66, note 17
    Reuben decd, Division of estate, September 1782   88

    Richard, s/o Reuben Calvert, Court appointed Samuel Jackson his guardian, 1782   88
    Richard, Privt, Captain Alexander Howison's Company Muster Roll, 36th Rgt,   201
        Virginia Militia, War of 1812
    Richard, Prvt, 36th Rgt, Virginia Militia, War of 1812 Roster   208

    Sarah, PSC, Revolutionary War   85

Index

Calvert (Cont.)
    Thomas, s/o Reuben Calvert decd, Court appointed Samuel Jackson as his guardian, 1782   88
    Thomas, (aka Tommy), s/o Reuben Calvert decd, OP Indenture to George   66
        Newman Brown, as carpenter, July 1779

    Vincent, Sgt, Alexander Howison's Company Muster Roll, 36th Rgt,   200
        Virginia Militia, War of 1812
    Vincent, Corporal, Prvt, 36th Rgt, Virginia Militia, War of 1812 Roster   207–208
    Vincent, Prvt, Captain John Merchant's Company Muster Roll, 89th Rgt,   214
        Virginia Militia, War of 1812

    William, Constable, replaced by Reuben Calvert, April 1763   42

    William, Patrol Acct, 1813, assigned to Benoni Harrison   119
    William, Patroller, 1813 and soldier, 36th Rgt, Virginia Militia, War of 1812   196
    William, Prvt, 36th Rgt, Virginia Militia, War of 1812 Roster   208

Campbell
    Alexander, PSC, Revolutionary War   78

    Colin, PSC, Revolutionary War   84
    Colin, Judgment against as collector for class 39, May 1783 Court Revolutionary War   92

    Colin, appointed Constable, district of 2nd Battn, 89th Rgt, Virginia Militia, 1805   115
    Colin, decd, as part of his admr's acct in 1805 Paymaster Acct, 36th Rgt   122

    Colin, decd., former Lieutenant in Light Infantry, 1st Battn, 36th Rgt, Virginia Militia   120
        replaced by Alfred C. Hayes, September 1813

    Elijah, Prvt, Alexander Howison's Company Muster Roll, 36th Rgt,   203
        Virginia Militia, War of 1812
    Elijah, Prvt, Captain Benjamin Tyler's Company Muster Roll, 89th Rgt,   216
        Virginia Militia, War of 1812

    Hugh R., in Major Townsend Dade's Court martial proceedings, November 1807   219–220
        in Fauquier County Clerks Loose Papers

    Isaac, Reverend, PSC, Revolutionary War   78

    Jonathan, Prvt, Captain Alexander Howison's Company Muster Roll, 36th Rgt,   203
        Virginia Militia, War of 1812, as substitute for Moses Cockrell
    Jonathan, Prvt, Captain Benjamin Tyler's Company Muster Roll, 89th Rgt,   216
        Virginia Militia, War of 1812

Cannaird
    Andrew, Trooper, Prince William Militia, Militia claim for service, French and Indian War   185

Cannon
    Barnaby, Ensign, 36th Rgt, Virginia Militia, War of 1812   110
    Barnaby, Ensign, Captain Richard Weedon's Company, Muster Roll 36th Rgt,   205
        Virginia Militia, War of 1812
    Barnaby, Ensign, 36th Rgt, Virginia Militia, War of 1812 Roster   206
    Barnaby, Ensign Captain John Merchant's Company Muster Roll, 89th Rgt,   214
        Virginia Militia, War of 1812

Index

Cannon (Cont.)
    Benjamin, Ensign, Captain Alexander Howison's Company Muster Roll, 36th Rgt,   199
        Virginia Militia, War of 1812

    Burn (?), Ensign, 36th Rgt, Virginia Militia, War of 1812 Roster   206

    Charles G, Prvt, Captain Joseph R. Gilbert's Company Muster Roll, 36th Rgt,   198
        Virginia Militia, War of 1812

    Charles, Prvt, 36th Rgt, Virginia Militia, War of 1812 Roster   208

    D, Prvt, 36th Rgt, Virginia Militia, War of 1812 Roster   208

    John, Judgment against as collector for class 21, May 1783 Court, Revolutionary War   91

    John B, Prvt, 36th Rgt, Virginia Militia, War of 1812 Roster   208

    Luke, in Major Townsend Dade's Court martial proceedings, November 1807   220
        in Fauquier County Clerks Loose Papers

    William, Prvt, Captain Joseph R. Gilbert's Company Muster Roll, 36th Rgt,   198
        Virginia Militia, War of 1812
    William, Prvt, Captain Richard Weedon's Company Muster Roll, 36th Rgt,   205
        Virginia Militia, War of 1812
    William, Prvt, 36th Rgt, Virginia Militia, War of 1812 Roster   208

Carney
    Benjamin, Prvt, 36th Rgt, Virginia Militia, War of 1812 Roster   208
    Benjamin, Prvt, Captain John Merchant's Company Muster Roll, 89th Rgt,   214
        Virginia Militia, War of 1812

    George, Patrol Acct, 1813, assigned to Benoni Harrison   196
    George, Patroller, 1813 and Prvt, 36th Rgt, Virginia Militia, War of 1812   196
    George, Prvt, 36th Rgt, Virginia Militia, War of 1812 Roster   208

    John, Prvt, Captain Joseph R. Gilbert's Company Muster Roll, 36th Rgt,   198
        Virginia Militia, War of 1812
    John, Prvt, Captain John Linton's Company Muster Roll of Cavalry, 36th Rgt,   204
        Virginia Militia, War of 1812
    John, Prvt, 36th Rgt, Virginia Militia, War of 1812 Roster   208

    Silas, Prvt, 36th Rgt, Virginia Militia, War of 1812 Roster   209

    William, Sgt, Prvt 36th Rgt, Virginia Militia, War of 1812 Roster   207
    William, Prvt, 36th Rgt, Virginia Militia, War of 1812 Roster   209

Carpenter
    Jesse, Prvt, Captain Richard Weedon's Company Muster Roll, 36th Rgt,   205
        Virginia Militia, War of 1812
    Jesse, Prvt, 36th Rgt, Virginia Militia, War of 1812 Roster   209

Carr
    —, Captain, advanced pension relief to Charles Lenox, a solider wound in the   67, 142
        Revolutionary war, August 1779 Court

Index

Carr (Cont.)
    John, Prvt, Captain Thomas Ewell's 1st VSR   61
    John, decd, certified by Court as US Pensioner when he died in September 1837,   163
        leaving no widow or children surviving him; death certified, April 1850 Court
    John, decd, Pension and Revolutionary War service detailed   163, note 49

    John, Lieutenant, 36th Rgt, Virginia Militia, Resignation of, 1804   113
    John, Cornet, in cavalry unit attached to 36th Rgt, Virginia Militia, 1805   116
    John, Prvt, 36th Rgt, Virginia Militia, War of 1812 Roster   209

    Larkin, Prvt, Joseph R, Gilbert's Company Muster Roll, 36th Rgt,   198
        Virginia Militia, War of 1812
    Larkin, Corporal, Captain Richard Weedon's Company Muster Roll, 36th Rgt,   205
        Virginia Militia, War of 1812
    Larkin, Prvt, Corporal, 36th Rgt, Virginia Militia, War of 1812 Roster   209

    Nimrod, Prvt, 36th Rgt, Virginia Militia, War of 1812 Roster   209

    William, Oath as Prince William Militia Officer, August 1755, French and Indian War   37

    William, 2 Accts presented to Court re relief to wives, widows and families of soldiers in   65
        Revolutionary War, June 1779 Court
    William, bound over by warrant, William Anderson, William Brewer, and George Thomas   67
        for advising Cada Ramey, a soldier to desert and took his money in an unlawful
        card game, September 1779
    William, receipt for clothes and beef as collector for class 35, July 1781, Revolutionary War   75
    William, 3PSCs, Revolutionary War   84, 87–88
    William, PSC for Prince William Militia, Revolutionary War   86
    William, PSC, as assignee of Stephen Sanger, Revolutionary War   86

    William, Prvt, 36th Rgt, Virginia Militia, War of 1812 Roster   209

Carrington
    Edward, Lt Colonel, 1st Continental Artillery, Revolutionary War   60

Cartagena, American capture of   11

Carter
    David, Prvt, Captain Alexander Howison's Company Muster Roll, 36th Rgt,   201
        Virginia Rgt, War of 1812, substituted himself previous to this call
    David, Prvt, Captain John Linton's Company Muster Roll, Cavalry, 36th Rgt,   204
        Virginia Rgt, War of 1812
    David, Prvt, 36th Rgt, Virginia Militia, War of 1812 Roster   209

    Edward E, Prvt, 89th Rgt, Virginia Militia, War of 1812 Roster   217

    Francis, certified as heir at law to Nathaniel Carter, decd, October 1834   154

    Giles, Corporal, 89th Rgt, Virginia Militia, War of 1812 Roster   217

    James, Prvt, Captain Alexander Howison's Company Muster Roll, 36th Rgt,   200
        Virginia Militia, War of 1812
    James, Prvt, Captain Richard Weedon's Company Muster Roll, 36th Rgt,   205
        Virginia Militia, War of 1812

Index

Carter (Cont.)
James, Prvt, 36th Rgt, Virginia Militia, War of 1812 Roster	209
John, soldier, Prince William Militia, Militia claim for service, French and Indian War	185
John, PSC, Revolutionary War	78
John, Ensign, 36th Rgt, Virginia Militia, Resignation of, 1805	115
John, Prvt, 36th Rgt, Virginia Militia, War of 1812 Roster	209
John, certified as heir at law to Nathaniel Carter decd, October 1834	154
Landon, 2 PSCs, Revolutionary War	80, 84
Lucy, d/o William Hughlett decd, soldier in Continental Line certified as his heir at law, August 1835 Court	156–157
Nathaniel, certified as heir at law to Nathaniel Carter, decd	154
Nathaniel, Prvt, 36th Rgt, Virginia Militia, War of 1812 Roster	209
Nathaniel, decd, heirs at law certified, October 1834 Court	154
Philip, Patrol Acct, 1813	120
Philip, Prvt, 36th Rgt, Virginia Militia, War of 1812 Roster	209
Rhodam, on his motion, Court certified heirs at law of William Hughlett, decd, a soldier in Virginia Continental Line, August 1835 Court	156–157
Robert, Agent Fairfax Proprietary, 1702	9
Robert, 3 PSCs, Revolutionary War	85, 87
Sanford Jr, Prvt, 36th Rgt, Virginia Militia, War of 1812 Roster	209
Thomas, soldier, Prince William Militia, deserted in June 1757 and never returned to duty, French and Indian War	184
William, PSC, for Prince William Militia, Revolutionary War	86
William, Jr, PSC, Revolutionary War	87
William, Prvt, Captain Joseph R. Gilbert's Company Muster Roll, 36th Rgt, Virginia Militia, War of 1812	198
William, Prvt, Captain Alexander Howison's Company Muster Roll, 36th Rgt, Virginia Militia, War of 1812	200
Wormley, PSC, Revolutionary War	84
Zachariah, Prvt, 36th Rgt, Virginia Militia, War of 1812 Roster	209

Carver
George, Prvt, 36th Rgt, Virginia Militia, War of 1812 Roster	209

Cavalry Units, Revolutionary War, created for defensive purposes by 2nd Virginia Convention, Revolutionary War	51

Index

Cave
Larkin, Patrol Acct 1813, assigned to Mary Ann Cave   119

Mary Ann, Patrol Acct, 1813, as assignee of Larkin Cave   119
Mary Ann, Patrol Acct, 1813, as assignee of George Melton   119
Mary Ann, Patrol Acct, 1813, as assignee of Moses Pilcher   119
Mary Ann, Patrol Acct, 1813, as assignee of Samuel Hodges   119
Mary Ann, Patrol Acct, 1813, as assignee of Thomas Clarke   119
Mary Ann, Patrol Acct, 1813, as assignee of William Hutchison   119
Mary Ann, Patrol Acct, 1813, as assignee of William Laid   119
Mary Ann, Patrol Acct, 1813, as assignee of William Moore   119

Samuel, Prvt, 36th Rgt, Virginia Militia, War of 1812 Roster   209

Cawood
Samuel, PSC, Revolutionary War   77

Chancellor
John, 2PSCs, Revolutionary War   84, 87

Chapman
Carr, husband of Sarah (Thornton,) d/o Thomas and Mary Ann (Ewell) Thornton, and heir   157
    of Thomas W. Ewell, Revolutionary War officer, December 1836 Court

Carr, s/o Susannah Chapman, heir of Thomas W. Ewell, Revolutionary War officer,   157
    December 1836 Court
Carr, s/o Susannah Chapman and husband of Sarah (Thornton), d/o Thomas and Mary Ann   157
    (Ewell) Thornton, and heir to Captain Thomas W. Ewell, Revolutionary War officer,
    December 1836 Court

Charles T, s/o Susannah Chapman, and heir to Thomas W. Ewell, Revolutionary War   157
    officer, December 1836 Court

Jane, d/o Susannah Chapman, and heir to Thomas W. Ewell, Revolutionary War officer,   157
    December 1836 Court
Nathaniel, Proprietor of Ohio Company, 1747   12

Philip, Appointed lieutenant, 89th Rgt, Virginia Militia, 1805, refused to act   116

Sarah, d/o Thomas and Mary Ann (Ewell) Thornton, and w/o Carr Chapman, and heir to   157
    Captain Thomas W. Ewell, revolutionary war officer, December 1836 Court

Susan, d/o Carr and Sarah (Thornton) Chapman and grdn/o Mary Ann (Ewell) Thornton   157
    and heir to Captain Thomas W. Ewell, Revolutionary war officer, December 1836
    Court; she married Francis Lowry of Fredericksburg

Susannah (Ewell), sister to Captain Thomas W. Ewell, revolutionary war officer,   157
    December 1836 Court

Thomas, Beef and clothing furnished for Class 13, August 1781 Court, Revolutionary War   76
Thomas, 2 PSCs, Revolutionary War   86, 88

Index

Chapman (Cont.)
Thomas, ordered by Court to set apart dower of Mary Graham, wid/o Reginald Graham, decd. — 88

Thomas, Major, 36th Rgt, Virginia Militia, War of 1812 — 196
Thomas, Major, 36th Rgt, Virginia Militia, War of 1812 Roster — 206
Thomas, Major, 36th Rgt, commanding officer, May 1809, Virginia Militia, War of 1812 — 219
Thomas, Major, 36th Rgt, directed to take charge of detachment of Prince William Militia at Dumfries, 1813 — 219 and 184

Charlton
Thomas, Prvt, Captain John Linton's Company Roll, Cavalry, 36th Rgt, Virginia Militia, War of 1812 — 204
Thomas, Prvt, 36th Rgt, Virginia Militia, War of 1812 Roster — 209

Chesapeake Bay, British move into, August 1814, during War of 1812 — 105

Chesley
John, Ensign, Light Infantry, 89th Rgt, Virginia Militia, 1804–1806 — 111
John, Ensign, Light Infantry, 89th Rgt, Virginia Militia, 1805 — 115

Chick, Chicks
Alexander, Prvt, Captain John Linton's Company Muster Roll, Cavalry, 36th Rgt, Virginia Militia, War of 1812 — 204
Alexander, Prvt, Captain Alexander Howison's Company Muster Roll, 36th Rgt, Virginia Militia, War of 1812 — 200
Alexander, Prvt, Captain Joseph Smith's Company Muster Roll, 36th Rgt, Virginia Militia, War of 1812 — 205
Alexander, Prvt, 36th Rgt, Virginia Militia, War of 1812 Roster — 209

Charles, Prvt, 36th Rgt, Virginia Militia, War of 1812 Roster — 209

James, Prvt, Captain Joseph R. Gilbert's Company Muster Roll, 36th Rgt, Virginia Militia, War of 1812 — 198
James, Prvt, 36th Rgt, Virginia Militia, War of 1812 Roster — 209

Reuben, Prvt, 89th Rgt, Virginia Militia, War of 1812 Roster — 217

Willis, Prvt, Captain Alexander Howsion's Company Muster Roll, 36th Rgt, Virginia Militia, War of 1812 — 201
Willis, Prvt, 36th Rgt, Virginia Militia, War of 1812 Roster — 209

Chickacoan, Indian District of — 3

Chilton
Jane (Ransdell), heir of John Ransdell, and heir at law to Captain Thomas Ransdell, decd, of Virginia Continental Line, September 1843 Court — 161

Chloe (see also Clowe)
Charles, Sgt, 89th Rgt, Virginia Militia, War of 1812 Roster — 217

Elijah, Prvt, 89th Rgt, Virginia Militia, War of 1812 Roster — 217

Index

Clark (See also Clarke)
  George Rogers, Lt Colonel, Illinois Rgt of Virginia State Troops, Revolutionary War — 61–62

  Richard, Prvt, 36th Rgt, Virginia Militia, War of 1812 Roster — 209

Clarke (See also Clark)
  Alpheus, Privt, 36th Rgt, Virginia Militia, War of 1812 Roster — 209

  John, Prvt, 36th Rgt, Virginia Militia, War of 1812 Roster — 209

  Thomas, Patrol Acct, 1813, assigned to Mary Ann Cave — 119

Clark's Illinois Rgt, Formation of — 61
Clark's Illinois Rgt, Formation of — 61, note 79
Clark's Illinois Rgt, Prince William men in — 62

Claxton
  John P, QM Sgt, 36th Rgt, Virginia Militia, War of 1812 Roster — 207

Clowe (see also Chloe)
  Rodney, Prvt, 36th Rgt, Virginia Militia, War of 1812 Roster — 209

  William, Prvt, 36th Rgt, Virginia Militia, War of 1812 Roster — 209

Cochrane, Sir Alexander, British Vice Admiral, War of 1812 — 104–105, 108

Cock, Cocke
  John, Patrol Acct, 1813 — 119

  Thomas, Prvt, Captain Joseph R. Gilbert's Company Muster Roll, 36th Rgt, Virginia Militia, War of 1812 — 198

  Thomas, Prvt, Captain John Merchant's Company Muster Roll, 89 Rgt, Virginia Militia, War of 1812 — 214

Cockburn, Sir George, British Admiral, War of 1812 — 104–105, 107

Cockrell, Cockerill
  Jeremiah, Prvt, 36th Rgt, Virginia Militia, War of 1812 Roster — 209

  Moses, 36th Rgt, Virginia Militia, War of 1812 Roster — 209

  Peter, 2 PSCs, Revolutionary War — 82

  Peter, Prvt, Captain Alexander Howison's Company Muster Roll, 36th Rgt, Virginia Militia, War of 1812 — 200

Cockrell, Cockerill (Cont.)
  Peter, Prvt, Captain Joseph Smith's Company Muster Roll, 36th Rgt, Virginia Militia, War of 1812 — 205

Codd, St Ledger, —, British Colonel, to furnish supplies for garrison at Neabsco, 1679 — 5

Index

Cole
    Benjamin, Prvt, 36th Rgt, Virginia Militia, War of 1812 Roster   209

    Daniel, Prvt, Captain Joseph R. Gilbert's Company Muster Roll, 36th Rgt, Virginia Militia, War of 1812   198

    Daniel, 3rd Sgt, Captain John Merchant's Company Muster Roll, 89th Rgt, Virginia Militia, War of 1812   214

    Daniel, Sgt, 36th Rgt, Virginia Militia, War of 1812 Roster   207

    Harrison, Prvt, 36th Rgt, Virginia Militia, War of 1812 Roster   209

    John, Prvt, Corporal, Captain Thomas Waggener's Company, Virginia Rgt, French and Indian War   33, 175

    John, Prvt, Corporal, Captain Thomas Waggener's Company, Virginia Rgt,   33, note 133

    John, Petition to legislature for reimbursement of impressed horse captured by the enemy, French and Indian War   175

    Mathias, Patrol Acct, 1813, assigned to Benoni Harrison   120

    Mathias, Patroller, 1813 and Prvt, 36th Rgt, Virginia Militia, War of 1812   196

    Richard, in Paymaster Acct, 36th Rgt, 1806   122

Collis
    George, Patrol Acct, 1805   116

Coleman, Colman
    Cornelius, soldier, Captain Henry Woodward's Company, Virginia Regiment, French and Indian War   175

    Cornelius, solider, Captain Henry Woodward's Company, Virginia Regiment,   175

    Daniel, Colonel, 6th Rgt, Virginia Militia, War of 1812   219

Colonial Regiments, French and Indian War, 50th and 51st to be raised in colonies   27

Colquhoun
    Charles, Prvt, 36th Rgt, Virginia Militia War of 1812 Roster   209

    William, Sgt, Captain Joseph R. Gilbert's Company Muster Roll, 36th Rgt, Virginia Militia, War of 1812   197

    William S, Patrol Acct, 1813, as assignee of George Keys   119

    William S, Patrol Acct, 1813, as assignee of George Smallwood   119

    William S, Patrol Acct, 1813, as assignee of Robert Keys   119

    William S, Patrol Acct, 1813, as assignee of Samuel Anderson   119

    William S, Patrol Acct, 1813, as assignee of Thomas Keys   119

    William S, Patroller 1813, and soldier, 36th Rgt, Virginia Militia, War of 1812   196

    William S, Ensign, 36th Rgt, Virginia Militia, 1812   110

    William S, Ensign, Light Infantry, 1st Battn, 36th Rgt, Virginia Militia, 1813   120

    William S, Ensign, Light Infantry, 1st Battn, 36th Rgt, Virginia Militia, 1813   120

    William S, Sgt., Ensign, 36th Rgt, Virginia Militia, War of 1812 Roster   206–207

    William S, correspondence with John Williams, JP, in Elijah Green's Pension Papers   190

    William S, certified identities of her at law of Elijah Green decd, a revolutionary war Soldier, August 1836 Court   193

Index

Colville
    Thomas, Colonel, representative from Maryland to Treaty of Lancaster with Iroquois, 1744   12

Committee of Safety, appointed by Virginia Convention   53

Compton
    Stephen Joy decd, former lieutenant, 89th Rgt, Virginia Militia, 1813   121

Congressional Legislation, 1812, to increase Army   101

Conner
    Douglas decd, Corporal Captain Andrew Leach [Leitch], 3rd Virginia Rgt, who died in   152
        Revolutionary War, intestate and w/o issue, December 1833 Court
    Douglas, decd, Revolutionary war service proved, December 1833 Court   152
    Douglas decd, Revolutionary War service detailed   152, note 6

    Douglas Jr, s/o William Conner, certified as heir at law to Douglas Conner decd,   152
        former Corporal, 3rd Virginia Rgt, Revolutionary War
    Douglas Jr, entitled to bounty land due for revolutionary war service of Douglas Conner,   152
        Corporal in Andrew Leitch's Company, Revolutionary War
    Douglas Jr, entitled to bounty land due for revolutionary war service of his father, William   152
        Conner, December 1833 Court

    Philip, 3rd Virginia Rgt, Revolutionary War   56
    Philip, Sgt, 3rd Virginia Rgt, Revolutionary War service certified by Court, December 1782   89
    Philip, Revolutionary War service in 3rd Virginia detailed   89, note 99
    Philip, Sgt, 3rd Virginia Rgt, entitled to bounty land for his service, December 1782   89

    William, 3rd Virginia Rgt, Revolutionary War   56
    William decd, 3rd Virginia soldier who returned home at expiration of his enlistment   152
        in 1779, married and left son Douglas Conner Jr as his only heir, December 1833 Court
    William decd, Revolutionary war service proved, December 1833 Court   152
    William, Revolutionary War service detailed   152, note 5
    William decd, service in revolutionary war and death, intestate, certified by Court,   152
        December 1833

Continental Artillery,
    1st Regiment, Formation of, Revolutionary War   60
    1st Regiment, Prince William men in, Revolutionary War   60

Continental Dragoons
    1st Regiment, Cherokee Expedition   59–60
    1st Regiment, Formation of   59–60

Continental Forces, Transition in Virginia to   55

Continental Regiments   53–56
    Virginia,
        1st Virginia Continental Rgt, Creation of   53
        1st Virginia Continental Rgt,, Prince William men in   55
        2nd Virginia Continental Rgt, Creation of   53
        2nd Virginia Continental Rgt, Prince William men in   55

Index

Continental Regiments (Continental)
  Virginia
    3rd Virginia Continental Rgt, Prince William men in   55
    3rd Virginia Continental Rgt, Campaigns   56

Conway
  Peter, oath as Ensign, Captain John Whitledge's Company, Prince William Militia,   63
      July 1778 Court, Revolutionary War
  Peter, further service detailed   63, note 4

  Thomas Jr. soldier, Prince William Militia, Militia claim for service, May 1757   186
      French and Indian War

Cook
  Charles, Prvt, Captain Joseph R. Gilbert's Company Muster Roll, 36th Rgt,   198
      Virginia Militia, War of 1812
  Charles, Prvt, 36th Rgt, Virginia Militia, War of 1812 Roster   209

Cooksey
  James, Prvt, 36th Rgt, Virginia Militia, War of 1812 Roster   209

  Obed, Ensign, 36th Rgt, Virginia Militia, 1805   115

  Warren, Ensign, 2nd Battan, 36th Rgt, Virginia Militia, 1804   113
  Warren, Lieutenant, 36th Rgt, Virginia Militia, 1805   115

Cooper
  Benjamin, PSC, Revolutionary War   85

  James, Prvt, Captain Joseph Smith's Company Muster Roll, 36th Rgt,   204
      Virginia Militia, War of 1812
  James, Prvt, 36th Rgt, Virginia Militia, War of 1812 Roster   209

Copin, Copen
  Chapman, Prvt, Captain Joseph Smith's Company Muster Roll, 36th Rgt,   204
      Virginia Militia, War of 1812
  Chapman, Privt, 36th Rgt, Virginia Militia, War of 1812 Roster   209

  Joshua, Prvt, 36th Rgt, Virginia Militia, War of 1812 Roster   209

  Josiah, Prvt, Captain Alexander Howison's Company Muster Roll, 36th Rgt,   203
      Virginia Militia, War of 1812

  Moses, affidavit of service attached to Elijah Green's June 1832 statement of   191
      service in revolutionary war, affirming his identity

Coppage
  Moses, soldier, Prince William Militia, claim for service, French and Indian War   185
Corben, Corbin
  Gavin, County Lt, Prince William Militia, July 1755 Court, French and Indian War   35

  Mason, Prvt, 36th Rgt, Virginia Militia, War of 1812 Roster   209

Index

Corder
    James, Prince William Militia, Petition to colonial legislature for service,   186
        French and Indian War

Coreham (see also Corum)
    John, trooper, Prince William Militia, Militia claim for service, French and Indian War   185

Cornwell
    Ann, wid/o John Cornwell, decd, regular soldier in Continental Army, provided relief   64
        for herself and two small children. July 1778 Court
    Ann, wid/o John Cornwell decd, regular soldier in Continental Army, provided relief   142

    Charles, soldier Prince William Militia, deserted June 1757 and never returned,   184
        French and Indian War
    Charles, PSC, Revolutionary War   84

    Elijah, Prvt, 36th Rgt, Virginia Militia, War of 1812 Roster   209

    Ezekiel, PSC, Revolutionary War   84

    Francis, PSC, Revolutionary War   85

    George, Prvt, Captain Alexander Howison's Company Muster Roll, 36th Rgt,   200
        Virginia Militia, War of 1812
    George, Prvt, 36th Rgt, Virginia Militia, War of 1812 Roster   209

    Harrison, Patrol Acct, 1813, assigned to Samuel Cornwell   119
    Harrison, Patroller, 1813 and Prvt, 36th Rgt, Virginia Militia, War of 1812   196
    Harrison, Prvt, Alexander Howison's Company Muster Roll, 36th Rgt,   201
        Virginia Militia, War of 1812
    Harrison, Prvt, Joseph Smith's Company Muster Roll, 36th Rgt,   205
        Virginia Militia, War of 182
    Harrison, Prvt, 36th Rgt, Virginia Militia, War of 1812 Roster   209

    John, trooper, Prince William Militia, Militia claim for service, French and Indian War   185

    John decd , regular soldier in Continental Army, husband of Ann Cornwell   64
    John decd, Revolutionary War service detailed   64, note 7

    John, Prvt, Captain Alexander Howison's Company Muster Roll, 36th Rgt,   201
        Virginia Militia, War of 1812
    John, Prvt, 36th Rgt, Virginia Militia, War of 1812 Roster   209

    Samuel, Patrol Acct, 1813, as assignee of Harrison Cornwell   119
    Samuel, Patrol Acct, 1813   119
    Samuel, Patrol Acct, 1813, assigned to Benoni Harrison   120
    Samuel, Patroller, 1813 and soldier, 36th Rgt, Virginia Militia, War of 1812   196
    Samuel, Prvt, 36th Rgt, Virginia Militia, War of 1812 Roster   209

    William, Patrol Acct, 1813   120
    William, 2 Patrol Accts, 1813, assigned to Benoni Harrison   120
    William, Prvt, 36th Rgt, Virginia Militia, War of 1812 Roster   209

Index

Corse
    Montgomery, Captain 1st Rgt, Virginia Volunteers, Mexican War, September 1853   163
    Montgomery, as Captain, 1st Rgt, Virginia Volunteers, Mexican War   163, see note 52

Corum (see also Coreham)
    Champ, Prvt, 36th Rgt, Virginia Militia, War of 1812 Roster   210

County Levy (Prince William)
    Patrollers in   37, 39, 40
    Patrollers in   37, note 7

Courtney
    Leonard, Prvt, 36th Rgt, Virginia Militia, War of 1812 Roster   210

Cowles, Cowls
    James, Sgt, Captain Benjamin Tyler's Company Muster Roll, 89th Rgt,   214
        Virginia Militia, War of 1812

Cowpens, Battle at, Revolutionary War   133

Cox
    Cary, Drummer, 36th Rgt, Virginia Militia, 1812   110
    Cary, Musician, 36th Rgt, Virginia Militia, War of 1812 Roster   207

    James, Prvt, 36th Rgt, Virginia Militia, War of 1812 Roster   210

    William, Prvt, 36th Rgt, Virginia Militia, War of 1812 Roster   209

    Zachariah, Prvt, 36th Rgt, Virginia Militia, War of 1812 Roster   209

Crane
    James, Lt, 36th Rgt, Virginia Militia, 1812   109
    James, Lt, 36th Rgt, Virginia Militia, War of 1812 Roster   206

Crawford
    —, Colonel, Virginia Rgt, Revolutionary War   65, see note 14

Creel
    William, PSC, Revolutionary War   78

    William, Prvt, 89th Rgt, Virginia Militia, War of 1812 Roster   217

Cresap
    Daniel, Proprietor of Ohio Company, 1747   12

    Michael, Proprietor of Ohio Company, 1747   12

Crimm, Crim
    Zachariah, Prvt, 36th Rgt, Virginia Militia, War of 1812 Roster   209

Crismond
    John Jr, Prvt, Captain Joseph R. Gilbert's Company Muster Roll, 36th Rgt,   198
        Virginia Militia, War of 1812

Index

Crockett
James, soldier, Prince William Militia, Militia claim for service, French and Indian War   185

Joseph, Colonel, Western Battalion, Revolutionary War   61

Crook
John, relief provided for, as he lost his son in the service of his country, October 1778   64
John, probable identification of his son who died in service, October 1778   64, note 8

Zachariah, 3rd Virginia soldier who died in Revolutionary War; may have been s/o John Crook   56

Crosby
Alexander, Alexander, Prvt, Captain Joseph R. Gilbert's Company Muster, Roll, 36th Rgt, Virginia Militia, War of 1812   198
Alexander, Prvt, 36th Rgt, Virginia Militia, War of 1812 Roster   209
Alexander, Prvt, Captain John Merchant's Company Muster Roll, 89th Rgt, Virginia Militia, War of 1812   214

George, Prvt, Captain Alexander Howison's Company Muster Roll, 36th Rgt, Virginia Militia, War of 1812   201
George, Prvt, 36th Rgt, Virginia Militia, War of 1812 Roster   209

Otley, 3rd Corporal, Captain John Merchant's Company Muster Roll, 89th Rgt, Virginia Militia, War of 1812   214

Silvanus, Prvt, 36th Rgt, Virginia Militia, War of 1812 Roster   209

Croson, Crowson
Bernard, Prvt, 89th Rgt, Virginia Militia, War of 1812 Roster   218

Elijah, Prvt, 36th Rgt, Virginia Militia, War of 1812 Roster   209

Simpson, Prvt, 89th Rgt, Virginia Militia, War of 1812 Roster   218

Crouch
Francis, Prvt, 89th Rgt, Virginia Militia, War of 1812 Roster   217

Crump
Benjamin, Surveyor of Road, May 1757 Court   40

John, Oath as Prince William Militia Officer, July 1753, French and Indian War   35

Crupper
Gilbert, Trooper, Prince William Militia, Militia Claim for service, French and Indian War   185

Crutcher
Coleman, Prvt, 36th Rgt, Virginia Militia, War of 1812 Roster   209

Culpeper,
Lord Thomas, Proprietor of Northern Neck, grants Brenton Grant to Nicholas Hayward, George Brent, Richard Foote, and Robert Bristow, January 1686   6

Index

Culverhouse
    William, Prvt, 36th Rgt, Virginia Militia, War of 1812 Roster   209

Cumberland, Duke of (Prince William Augustus), Proposal to send Major General Edward   27
    Braddock to Virginia for French and Indian War

Cummins, Cummings
    John, Prvt, 36th Rgt, Virginia Militia, War of 1812 Roster   209

Curry, Currie
    Bland, Prvt, Captain Alexander Howison's Company Muster Roll, 36th Rgt,   201
        Virginia Militia, War of 1812
    Bland, Prvt, 36th Rgt, Virginia Militia, War of 1812 Roster   209

    James, Prvt, Captain Joseph R. Gilbert's Company Muster Roll, 36th Rgt,   198
        Virginia Militia, War of 1812
    James, Prvt, 36th Rgt, Virginia Militia, War of 1812 Roster   209

Dabney
    Charles, Colonel, Virginia Forces, Revolutionary War   133

Dade
    Townsend, Major, 2nd Battn, 36th Rgt, Virginia Militia, 1804   113
    Townsend, Major, 36th Rgt, Virginia Militia, Court Martial Proceedings, November 1807   219–220
        From Fauquier County Clerks Loose Papers

    William A. G, Lt, Cavalry, 36th Rgt, Virginia Militia, 1805   116
    William A. G, Judge General Court, in Spencer Anderson's 1819 Pension Papers   132
    William A. G, Judge, General Court, in Elijah Green's Pension Papers   189

Dalton
    James, Judgment against, as collector for Class 34, May 1783, Revolutionary War   91–92

Darnall, Darnal
    John, Soldier, Prince William Militia, Petition to colonial legislature for pay for service,   186
        French and Indian War

D'Arnouville, Jean Baptiste de Machault, French politician for whom the French fort,   17
    Fort Machault was named, in French and Indian War

Daulton, Dalton
    Moses, of 3rd Virginia Continental Rgt, Revolutionary War   56, 139
    Moses, of 3rd Virginia Continental Rgt, Revolutionary War   56, note 47
    Moses, 3rd Virginia Continental Rgt, Revolutionary War   136

Davenport
    Ellen D, certified as heir at law to William Hickman, decd, who held sundry military   161
        Surveys in Virginia Military Districts of Ohio and Kentucky, October 1841 Court

Davis
    Asa, Prvt, 36th Rgt, Virginia Militia, War of 1812 Roster   209

    Catharine, Commonwealth Cause against, for assault on Lewis Reno, September 1780   71
    Catharine, Commonwealth Cause against, for assault on Lewis Reno, September 1780   71, note 37

Index

Davis (Cont.)

Catharine, found guilty of assault on Lewis Reno, September 1780	71
Catharine, Commonwealth cause against for riot, November 1780 Court	74
David, Patrol Acct, 1805	116
David, Patroller, 1805 and Prvt, 36th Rgt, Virginia Militia War of 1812	116, note 12; 196
David, Surgeon's Mate, 36th Rgt, Virginia Militia, War of 1812	196
David, Prvt, Captain Joseph R. Gilbert's Company Muster Roll, 36th Rgt, Virginia Militia, War of 1812	198
David, Prvt, Surgeon's Mate, 36th Rgt, Virginia Militia, War of 1812 Roster	207, 209
Hugh, Sgt, Captain George McCormick's Company, 13th Virginia Continental Rgt, Revolutionary War	58
Hugh, Sgt, Captain George McCormick's Company, 13th Virginia Continental Rgt, Service for 3 years proved although his discharge was lost, proved by George Pearl, his recruiting officer, March 1784 Court	94
Hugh, as Sgt, Captain George McCormick's Company, 13th Virginia Continental Rgt, Revolutionary War, March 1784	94, note 109
Hugh, Sworn evidence that William Davis was sole heir at law of John Davis, who died in Revolutionary War, intestate, June 1833 Court	151
Hugh, Testimony that John Davis's revolutionary war bounty lands had not been drawn, June 1833 Court	151
Hugh C. Prvt, Captain Joseph R. Gilbert's Company Muster Roll, 36th Rgt, Virginia Militia, War of 1812	198
Hugh R, Prvt, 36th Rgt, Virginia Militia, War of 1812 Roster	209
Isaac, Patrol Acct	33
James, Soldier, Prince William Militia, deserted June 1757 and never returned to duty, French and Indian War	184
Jesse, Patrol Acct, 1813	120
Jesse, Prvt, Captain Joseph R. Gilbert's Company Muster Roll, 36th Rgt, Virginia Militia, War of 1812	198
Jesse, Prvt, 36th Rgt, Virginia Militia, War of 1812 Roster	209
Jesse, Prvt, Captain John Merchant's Company Muster Roll, 89th Rgt, Virginia Militia, War of 1812	214
Jesse, certified as heir at law to Presley Davis, Prvt, Captain Thomas Triplet's Company, Grayson's Additional Continental Infantry, April 1835, Revolutionary War	155
Jesse, certified as heir at law to Presley Davis, Prvt, Captain Andrew Leach's Company, 3rd Virginia Continental Regiment, August 1835, Revolutionary War	156
John, of 3rd Virginia Continental Rgt, Revolutionary War	56, 139
John decd, Revolutionary War soldier who enlisted for 3 years and died in service; Brother William Davis entitled to his bounty land, March 1784	93, 139
John decd, possible identification as 3rd Virginia soldier	93, note 107
John decd, died in service of the US in Revolutionary War, intestate; brother William sole heir at law, June 1833 Court	151
John decd, died in service of US, may have been prvt, 3rd Virginia, who died in March 1777	151, note 2

Index

Davis (Cont.)

John, Lt, 2nd Battn, 36th Rgt, Virginia Militia, 1804	113
John, Patrol Acct, 1813	120
John B, Prvt, Captain Alexander Howison's Company Muster Roll, 36th Rgt, Virginia Militia, War of 1812	201
Leonard, Soldier Prince William Militia, Petition to colonial legislature for pay for service, May 1757, French and Indian War	186
Maria F (Gray), d/o Elizabeth Gray, and heir at law to Captain Thomas Ransdell, decd, of Virginia Continental Line, September 1843 Court	161
Moses, PSC, Revolutionary War	89
Moses, Ensign, 89th Rgt, Virginia Militia, War of 1812 Roster	217
Nancy, w/o Thomas Davis, revolutionary war soldier, relief provided for, July 1778	142
Philip, Lt, 2nd Battn, 36th Rgt, Virginia Militia, 1804	113
Presley decd, Heir at law (Jesse Davis) certified, April 1835	155
Presley decd, Service corrected in footnote	155, note 21
Presley decd, Prvt, Captain Andrew Leach's Company, 3rd Virginia Continental Rgt, Died intestate w/o issue, death certified, August 1835 Court	156
Presley decd, Prvt, Captain Andrew Leach's Company, 3rd Virginia Continental Rgt,	156, note 23
Presley, Prvt, Captain Alexander Howison's Company Muster Roll, 36th Rgt, Virginia Militia, War of 1812	201
Presley, Prvt, 36th Rgt, Virginia Militia, War of 1812 Roster	209
Richard, Ensign, Lt, 36th Rgt, Virginia Militia, 1813	119
Richard, Prvt, 36th Rgt, Virginia Militia, War of 1812 Roster	209
Richard Jr, Prvt, Captain John Linton's Company Muster Roll, Cavalry, 36th Rgt, Virginia Militia, War of 1812	204
Samuel S, Prvt, 89th Rgt, Virginia Militia, War of 1812 Roster	218
Sarah B (Ewell), certified as heir at law to Colonel Jesse Ewell, decd, September 1835	157
Thomas, soldier in Virginia Continental Army, husband of Nancy Davis; wife allowed support for herself and 4 children, July 1778 Court	64
Thomas, as soldier in Virginia Continental Army	64, note 6
Thomas, PSC, Revolutionary War	85
Thomas, Prvt, Captain John Merchant's Company Muster Roll, 89th Rgt, Virginia Militia, War of 1812	214

Index

Davis (Cont.)
    Travers, Lt, 36th Rgt, Virginia Militia, 1812 — 109
    Travers, Lt, Captain Alexander Howison's Company Muster Roll, 36th Rgt, Virginia Militia, War of 1812 — 199
    Travers, Lt, 36th Rgt, Virginia Militia, War of 1812 Roster — 206

    Walter, Prvt, 36th Rgt, Virginia Militia, War of 1812 Roster — 209
    Walter, Prvt, Captain John Merchant's Company Muster Roll, 89th Rgt, Virginia Militia, War of 1812 — 214

    Warren, Patrol Acct, 1806 — 117

    William, Ensign Prince William Militia, July 1762, French and Indian War — 41

    William, of 3rd Virginia Continental Rgt, from Prince William — 56, 139
    William, of 3rd Virginia Continental Rgt — 56, note 47

    William Jr, 3 PSC, Revolutionary War — 86–87

    William, Prvt, Captain Benjamin Tyler's Company Muster Roll, 89th Rgt, Virginia Militia, War of 1812 — 216

    William, certified as entitled to bounty lands due to brother John Davis, March 1784 — 93
    William, claimed bounty land due brother John Davis for revolutionary war service in March 1784 — 149
    William, certified as heir at law to John Davis, a revolutionary war soldier who died in the Revolutionary War, June 1833 Court — 151

Dawe, Dawes, Daw
    Joseph, Prvt, 36th Rgt, Virginia Militia, War of 1812 Roster — 209

    Philip, PSC for keeping British prisoners, Revolutionary War — 87

    Philip, former Lt, 36th Rgt, Virginia Militia, 1805 — 115
    Philip, in Major Townsend Dade's Court Martial proceedings, November 1807 From Fauquier County Clerks Loose Papers — 219

    Philip D, Patrol Acct, 1805 — 116
    Philip D, Ensign, 36th Rgt, Virginia Militia, 1805 — 115
    Philip D, Captain, 36th Rgt, Virginia Militia, 1813, Resignation of to become Clerk of Prince William County Court — 118
    Philip D, Clerk of Prince William County Court, certified Elijah Green's revolutionary War service in pension, August 1831 — 190

    William, Lt, 36th Rgt, Virginia Militia, 1812 — 109
    William, as resident of Prince William in 1810 — 110, note 76
    William, Lt, Captain Joseph R. Gilbert's Company Muster Roll, 36th Rgt, Virginia Militia, War of 1812 — 197
    William, Lt, 36th Rgt, War of 1812 Roster — 206

Dawson
    Bradford, Prvt, 89th Rgt, Virginia Militia, War of 1812 Roster — 209

Index

Dawson (Cont.)
    Elijah, Prvt, Captain Joseph Smith's Company Roster, 36th Rgt,   205
        Virginia Militia, War of 1812
    Elijah, Prvt, 36th Rgt, Virginia Militia, War of 1812 Roster   209

    Henry, Prvt, 36th Rgt, Virginia Militia, War of 1812 Roster   209

De Bienville, Celeron, French and Indian War commander   15

De Contrecouer, — French commandant at Fort Duquesne, French and Indian War   21–22

De Saint Pierre, Jacques Legardeur, Captain of French forces, French and Indian War   18

De Villiers,
    —, Captain of French forces, French and Indian War   25–26
    Louis Coulon, Captain of French forces, French and Indian War   22

DeKay
    Charles, Sailing Master, Virginia State Navy, Revolutionary War   62, 161
    Charles, Sailing Master, VSN, death in August 1829 certified, February 1842 Court   161

DeNeal, Deneale
    James, Ensign, Lt, 36th Rgt, Virginia Militia, 1804   113
    James Jr, Ensign, Lt, 36th Rgt, Virginia Militia, 1805   115

Dewal, (see also Duvall)
    George, Patrol Acct 1813, assigned to Benoni Harrison   120

Dickerson (see also Dickinson)
    John, Prvt, Captain Richard Weedon's Company Muster Roll, 36th Rgt,   206
        Virginia Militia, War of 1812
    John, Prvt, 36th Rgt, Virginia Militia, War of 1812 Roster   209

Dickinson (see also Dickerson)
    Edward, Ensign, Lt, 36th Rgt, Virginia Militia, 1806   117

    John [the Elder] in Captain Gallahue's Company, 11th Virginia Continental Rgt,   57
        Revolutionary War
    John the Elder, decd, service in Revolutionary War proved, death after 1787 in   160
        Prince William certified
    John the Elder decd, as prvt, Captain Gallahue's Company, 11th Virginia Continental Rgt,   160, note 39
        Revolutionary War

    John Sr, decd, s/o John Dickinson the Elder, John Sr died in July 1841, probate of will   160
        in August 1841

    John Jr, s/o John Sr and Pricey Dickinson and heir at law to John Dickinson the Elder, a   160
        Revolutionary War soldier, August 1841 Court

    Lewis, Lt, 36th Rgt, 1806, resignation of   117

    Nancy, d/o John Sr and Pricey Dickinson and heir at law to John Dickinson the Elder, a   160
        Revolutionary War soldier, August 1841 Court

Index

Dickinson (see also Dickerson) (Cont.)
    Pricey, wid/o John Dickinson Sr and heir at law to John Dickinson the Elder, a Revolutionary 161
        War soldier, August 1841 Court

    Pricey, d/o John Sr and Pricey Dickinson and heir at law to John Dickinson the Elder, a   161
        Revolutionary War soldier, August 1841 Court

Dinwiddie
    Robert, Governor of Virginia   12, 17–19, 21, 28, 33–34, 47–49

Dishman
    Edmund, Prvt, 36th Rgt, Virginia Militia, War of 1812 Roster   209

Disney
    John, Prvt, Captain Alexander Howison's Company Muster Roll, 36th Rgt,   201
        Virginia Militia, War of 1812

Dixon
    Benjamin, PSC, Revolutionary War   77

Dodd
    Travis, Prvt, 36th Rgt, Virginia Militia, War of 1812 Roster   209

Dodson
    Walter, Prvt , Captain Alexander Howison's Company Muster Roll, 36th Rgt,   201
        Virginia Militia, War of 1812
    Walter, Prvt, 36th Rgt, Virginia Militia, War of 1812 Roster   209
    Walter, Prvt, Captain John Merchant's Company Muster Roll, 89th Rgt,   214
        Virginia Militia, War of 1812

Dorsey
    Richard, Prvt, 36th Rgt, Virginia Militia, War of 1812 Roster   209

Doughnahan, Donahan
    Robert, QM Sgt, 36th Rgt, Virginia Militia, War of 1812 Roster   196

Douglas
    —, Major, probably Continental Forces, taken prisoner at Briar Creek, in Georgia, 1779   68
    —, Major, Continental Forces   68, note 24

    Hugh, in Major Townsend Dade's Court martial proceedings, November 1807   220
        From Fauquier County Clerks Loose Papers

Dowell
    Cloe, certified as heir at law to Captain Jesse Evans decd, August 1835 Court   156

    James, s/o Jeremiah, entitled to bounty land due William Dowell for Continental   152
        Army service, December 1833 Court

    Jeremiah decd, brother and sole heir at law to William Dowell, a revolutionary war   152
        Soldier; Jeremiah's death certified, December 1833

    Jesse, Patrol Acct, 1805   116
    Jesse, Patroller and Prvt, 36th Rgt, Virginia Militia, War of 1812   116, note 16; 196

Index

Dowell (Cont.)
Jesse, Patrol Acct, 1813, assigned to Benoni Harrison	120
Jesse, Prvt, 36th Rgt, Virginia Militia, War of 1812 Roster	200
Jesse, Prvt, Captain Alexander Howison's Company Muster Roll, 36th Rgt, Virginia Militia, War of 1812	201
Jesse, Prvt, Captain John Merchant's Company Muster Roll, 89th Rgt, Virginia Militia, War of 1812	214
Jesse, s/of Jeremiah, entitled to bounty land due William Dowell for Continental Army service, December 1833 Court	152
John, Trooper, Prince William Militia, Militia claim for service, French and Indian War	185
Thomas, Patrol Acct, French and Indian War	39
Thomas, Corporal, Captain John Linton's Company Muster Roll, Cavalry, 36th Rgt, Virginia Militia, War of 1812	204
Thomas, Prvt, 36th Rgt, Virginia Militia, War of 1812 Roster	209
William, as soldier in Captain George McCormicks' Company, 13th Virginia Continental Rgt, Revolutionary War	58
William, as soldier in Captain George McCormick's Company, 13th Virginia Continental Rgt, Revolutionary War	58, note 62
William, service as soldier under Captain George McCormick, 13th Virginia Continental Rgt, in 1776 for 3 years proved, December 1833 Court	152
William, as soldier in Captain George McCormick's Company, 13th Virginia	152, note 8
William, on his motion, Court certified heirs at law of Captain Jesse Ewell decd, as Grace Jackson and Cloe Dowell, August 1835 Court	156
William, Corporal, Captain Alexander Howison's Company Muster Roll, 36th Rgt, Virginia Militia, War of 1812	200
William D, s/o Jeremiah, entitled to bounty land due William Dowell for Continental Army service, December 1833 Court	152

Downman
Ann, Mrs 2 PSCs Revolutionary War	80, 82

Doyle
Alexander, PSC, Revolutionary War	84
David, Paymaster, 36th Rgt, Virginia Militia, War of 1812	196
Thomas, Trooper, Prince William Militia, Militia claim for service, French and Indian War	185

Drouillion, Pierre-Jacques, Ensign, French forces, French and Indian War — 21

Duffey, Duffy
A, in Paymaster Acct, 36th Rgt, Virginia Militia, 1806	122
Allen, Drum Major, 36th Rgt, Virginia Militia, 1812	110
Allen, in Paymaster Acct, 36th Rgt, Virginia Militia, 1805	110, note 92; 122
Allen, Drum Major, 36th Rgt, Virginia Militia, War of 1812	196
Allen, Musician, Drum Major, 36th Rgt, Virginia Militia, War of 1812 Roster	207

Index

Duffey, Duffy (Cont.)
   Moses, Patrol Acct, 1813 assigned to Benoni Harrison — 119
   Moses, Patrol Acct, 1813 and Prvt, 36th Rgt, Virginia Militia, War of 1812 — 196
   Moses, Corporal, Captain Richard Weedon's Company Muster Roll, 36th Rgt, Virginia Militia, War of 1812 — 205
   Moses, Prvt, 36th Rgt, Virginia Militia, War of 1812 Roster — 209

Dulin
   William, Captain, 36th Rgt, Virginia Militia, 1812 — 108
   William, Captain, 36th Rgt, Virginia Militia, War of 1812 Roster — 206

Dumas, —, French Captain, French and Indian War — 31

Dunaway
   Jarvis, Prvt, 36th Rgt, Virginia Militia, War of 1812 Roster — 209
   Joseph, Prvt, 36th Rgt, Virginia Militia, War of 1812 Roster — 209

Dunbar
   John, Committed to jail for refusing to take oath of allegiance, August 1779 — 67
   John, Affidavit of Allegiance returned to Court and ordered recorded, September 1779 — 67
   Thomas, British Colonel, French and Indian War — 32

Duncan
   Charles, appointed Surveyor of Road from the Fort on Thumb Runt to meet the lower Road at Carter's Run, March 1757 Court — 40
   Charles, 1st Sgt, 36th Rgt, Virginia Militia, War of 1812 Roster — 207
   Dillard, Sgt, 36th Rgt, Virginia Militia, War of 1812 Roster — 209
   Leroy, Prvt, 36th Rgt, Virginia Militia, War of 1812 Roster — 208

Dunmore, Lord, Colonial Governor of Virginia — 50, note 18; 52

Dunnington
   Richard, Prvt, Captain Joseph R. Gilbert's Company Muster Roll, 36th Rgt, Virginia Militia, War of 1812 — 198
   Richard, Prvt, 36th Rgt, Virginia Militia, War of 1812 Roster — 209
   Robert, Prvt, Captain Benjamin Tyler's Company Muster Roll, 89th Rgt, Virginia Militia, War of 1812 — 216
   William P, Ensign, 89th Rgt, Virginia Militia, 1813 — 121
   William P, Ensign, Captain Benjamin Tyler's Company Muster Roll, 89th Rgt, Virginia Militia, War of 1812 — 215

Duquesne, — French Governor-General of New France, French and Indian War — 22

Duvall (see also Duwal)
   George, Prvt, Captain Alexander Howison's Company Muster Roll, 36th Rgt, Virginia Militia, War of 1812 — 201
   George P, Prvt, 36th Rgt, Virginia Militia, War of 1812 Roster — 209

Index

Duvall (See also Duwal)
John P, Prvt, Captain Alexander Howison's Company Muster Roll, 36th Rgt, Virginia Militia, War of 1812 — 201

John P, Prvt, 36th Rgt, Virginia Militia, War of 1812 Roster — 209

William H, Prvt, Captain Alexander Howison's Company Muster Roll, 36th Rgt, Virginia Militia, War of 1812 — 201

William H, Prvt, Corporal, 36th Rgt, Virginia Militia, War of 1812 Roster — 207, 209

Dye
Amos, Prvt, 89th Rgt, Virginia Militia, War of 1812 Roster — 218

Earls
John, PSC for Prince William Militia, Revolutionary War — 86

Ebbs (See also Epps)
James, Prvt, 36th Rgt, Virginia Militia, War of 1812 Roster — 209

Edmonds
Thomas, Prvt, 36th Rgt, Virginia Militia, War of 1812 Roster — 209

Edrington
Charles, Prvt, Captain Joseph R. Gilbert's Company Muster Roll, 36th Rgt, Virginia Militia, War of 1812 — 198

Charles, Prvt, 36th Rgt, Virginia Militia, War of 1812 Roster — 210

Edwards
Benjamin, Trooper, Prince William Militia, Militia claim for service, French and Indian War — 185

J. L, of US Pension Agency, letter to H. J. Janes of House of Representatives, giving background for pension agency's treatment of Elijah Green's Pension Declarations, April 1836 — 192–193

John, soldier, 3rd Virginia Continental Rgt, Revolutionary War — 56
John, as soldier, 3rd Virginia — 56, note 47

William, Prvt, 36th Rgt, Virginia Militia, War of 1812 Roster — 210

Elkins
Philip L, Prvt, 36th Rgt, Virginia Militia, War of 1812 Roster — 210

Elk Run Church — 6

Ellicot Mills, Maryland — 219

Ellicott, Ellicot
Nathaniel, Prvt, Captain Alexander Howison's Company Muster Roll, 36th Rgt, Virginia Militia, War of 1812 — 201

Jesse, Patrol Acct, 1805 — 116

Samuel, Fifer, 36th Rgt, Virginia Militia, 1812 — 110
Samuel, Fifer, 36th Rgt, Virginia Militia, War of 1812 Roster — 207

Index

Ellis
    Benjamin, Prvt, 89th Rgt, Virginia Militia, War of 1812 Roster   218

    John Jr, Prvt, 89th Rgt, Virginia Militia, War of 1812 Roster   218

    Joseph, Prvt, 89th Rgt, Virginia Militia, War of 1812 Roster   218

Ellzey, Ellzy
    William, Captain, Prince William Militia, resignation of, July 1762   41

Embrey
    George, Prvt, 36th Rgt, Virginia Militia, War of 1812 Roster   210

    Joseph, Prvt, 36th Rgt, Virginia Militia, War of 1812 Roster   210

    Reuben, Prvt, 36th Rgt, Virginia Militia, War of 1812 Roster   210

English
    Hadius, Prvt, 36th Rgt, Virginia Militia, War of 1812 Roster   210

    John, Prvt, 36th Rgt, Virginia Militia, War of 1812 Roster   210
    John Jr, Prvt, 36th Rgt, Virginia Militia, War of 1812 Roster   210

    Noah, Captain, 89th Rgt, Virginia Militia, 1813   121
    Noah, Captain, 89th Rgt, Virginia Militia, 1813   121

Ensey
    John K, Prvt, 36th Rgt, Virginia Militia, War of 1812 Roster   210

    Rhodham, Prvt, 36th Rgt, Virginia Militia, War of 1812 Roster   210

Eppes, Epps
    Francis, Lt, 2nd Virginia Rgt, French and Indian War, June 1780   70
    Francis, as Lt, Captain William Byrd's Company, 2nd Virginia Rgt, French and Indian War   70, note 32
    Francis, Officer, French and Indian War, bounty land to John Hedges, June 1780   69–70
Epps (See also Ebbs)
    James, Prvt, Captain Alexander Howison's Company Muster Roll, 36th Rgt,   201
        Virginia Militia, War of 1812

Eustace
    William, Oath as Prince William Militia Officer, 1753, French and Indian War   35

Evans
    Edward, Prvt, Captain Richard Weedon's Company, 36th Rgt, Virginia Militia   206
        War of 1812
    Edward, Prvt, 36th Rgt, Virginia Militia, War of 1812 Roster   210

    Jesse, Captain, Clark's Illinois Rgt, Revolutionary War   62
    Jesse, as Captain, Clark's Illinois Rgt, Revolutionary War   62, notes 84, 85

    James G, Lt, 36th Rgt, Virginia Militia, 1813   118, 121
    James G, summoned to Court on whether he intends to qualify for commission   121

    Joseph, prvt, Captain Henry Woodward's Company, Virginia Rgt, French and Indian War   175

Index

Evans (Cont.)
    Joseph, 2 petitions to colonial legislature for relief for wound in leg, September 1758`   175
    Joseph, Three lives lease from William Low to Joseph, wife Mary and son Joseph,   176
        Lease in Prince William, November 1740

    Peter, 1st Lt, Captain Charles Lee's Company, Prince William Militia, August 1779 Court   66
        Revolutionary War
    Peter, as 1st Lt, Virginia Militia, 1779, Revolutionary War   66, note 18
    Peter, Captain, Prince William Militia, Revolutionary War   69
    Peter, PSC, Revolutionary War   84

    Walter G, former Lt, 36th Rgt, Virginia Militia, 1813, now in U. S. Army   121

    Wansford, Prvt, Corporal, Captain Joseph R. Gilbert's Company Muster Roll, 36th Rgt   197–198
        Virginia Militia, War of 1812
    Wansford, Corporal 36th Rgt, Virginia Militia, War of 1812 Roster   207

Ewell
    Alfred, Prvt, Captain Alexander Howison's Company Muster Roll, 36th Rgt,   201
        Virginia Militia, War of 1812
    Alfred, Prvt, Captain John Linton's Company Muster Roll, Cavalry, 36th Rgt,   204
        Virginia Militia, War of 1812
    Alfred, Prvt, 36th Rgt, Virginia Militia, War of 1812 Roster   210
    Alfred, certified as heir at law to Colonel Jesse Ewell, decd, September 1835 Court   157

    Ann, sister to Captain Thomas W. Ewell, decd, a Revolutionary War Officer,   157
        December 1835 Court

    Benjamin, s/o Thomas Ewell, decd, certified as heir at law to Colonel Jesse Ewell, decd,   157
        December 1835 Court

    Bertrand, Oath as Prince William Militia Officer, June 1756 Court   38
    Bertrand, removed from office as Surveyor of Prince William, April 1767 Court   42
    Bertrand, On his petition, relief paid for support of orphans of John Gunyon, a decd   65, 143
        soldier in Revolutionary War, February 1779 Court

    Catharine, d/o Bertrand Ewell, certified as heir at law to Colonel Jesse Ewell, decd,   157
        September 1835 Court

    Charles, examined Paymaster's Acct, 36th Rgt, Virginia Militia, 1805–1807   123

    Charles, Prvt, 89th Rgt, Virginia Militia, War of 1812 Roster   218

    Charles, brother to Captain Thomas W. Ewell, decd, a Revolutionary War officer,   157
        December 1836 Court
    Charles, Captain, 1st Virginia State Regiment, affidavit of service for Elijah Green's   189
        Pension Application, 1818

    Charles, decd, Exor of Sarah Ewell, decd; no new admr for Sarah appointed,   154–155
        January 1835 Court

    Charlotte, sister to Captain Thomas W. Ewell, decd, a Revolutionary War Officer,   157
        December 1836

Index

Ewell (Cont.)

Cordelia, d/o Bertrand Ewell, certified as heir at law to Colonel Jesse Ewell decd, September 1835 Court	157
Elizabeth, sister to Captain Thomas W. Ewell decd, a Revolutionary War Officer December 1836 Court	157
Elizabeth, d/o Bertrand Ewell, certified as heir at law to Colonel Jesse Ewell decd, September 1835 Court	157
Elizabeth, d/o Thomas Ewell decd, certified as heir at law to Colonel Jesse Ewell decd, September 1835 Court	157
Ellen, d/o Bertrand Ewell, certified as heir at law to Colonel Jesse Ewell decd, September 1835 Court	157
Emma, certified as heir at law to Colonel Jesse Ewell decd, September 1835 Court	157
Hannah, sister to Captain Thomas W. Ewell decd, a Revolutionary War Officer, December 1836 Court	157
James, Receipt as Collector for Class 15, July 1781, Revolutionary War	76
James, Oath as Lieutenant Colonel, Prince William Militia, March 1784 Revolutionary War	94
James, as Lt Colonel, Prince William Militia, March 1784, Revolutionary War	94, note 108
James, Colonel, in charge of contract for letting the building of bridges on Cedar Run and Broad Run, October 1805 Court	117
James, Prvt, 89th Rgt, Virginia Militia, War of 1812 Roster	218
Jesse, PSC, Revolutionary War	84
Jesse, Captain, Revolutionary War, death in 1814 intestate certified, August 1835 Court	156
Jesse, as Captain, Clark's Illinois Rgt, Revolutionary War	156, note 25
Jesse, Lt, 1st Battn, 89th Rgt, Virginia Militia, 1806, resignation of	117
Jesse, certified as heir at law to Colonel Jesse Ewell, Prince William Militia, Revolutionary War, September 1835 Court	157
Jesse, as Colonel, Prince William Militia, Revolutionary War	157, note 27
Rebecca, d/o Thomas Ewell decd, certified as heir at law to Jesse Ewell, Colonel, Prince William Militia, Revolutionary War, September 1835 Court	157
Sally, sister to Captain Thomas W. Ewell decd, Revolutionary War officer, December, 1836 Court	157
Sarah decd, no new admr appointed for her estate, December 1833 Court	154
Sarah decd, heirs of Thomas W. Ewell previously conveyed their interests to, February 1834, January 1835 Court	153, 155
Solomon Jr, Prvt, Captain Benjamin Tyler's Company Muster Roll, 89th Rgt, Virginia Militia, War of 1812	216

Index

Ewell (Cont.)
    Solomon, brother to Captain Thomas W. Ewell decd, Revolutionary War officer,   157
        December 1836 Court

    Thomas W, Captain 1 VSR, Revolutionary War   61
    Thomas, Captain 1 VSR, Revolutionary War   133
    Thomas W. decd, Captain 1 VSR, service in Revolutionary War proved,   153, 155
        February 1834, January 1835 Courts
    Thomas W. decd, Revolutionary War officer, February 1834 Court   153
    Thomas W. decd, as Captain 1 VSR, Revolutionary War   153, note 11; 157, note 29
    Thomas W. decd, Revolutionary War officer, heirs at law, February 1834 Court   153
    Thomas W. decd, Revolutionary War officer, death in 1784 certified, January 1835 Court   155
    Thomas W. decd, Captain 1 VSR, Revolutionary War   156
    Thomas W, decd, Captain 1 VSR, heirs of, December 1836 Court   157
    Thomas W. decd, Captain 1 VSR, Revolutionary War   189

    Thomas, s/o Thomas Ewell decd, certified as heir at law to Jesse Ewell decd,   157
        Colonel, Prince William Militia, Revolutionary War, September 1835 Court

    Virginia, d/o Thomas Ewell decd, certified as heir at law to Jesse Ewell decd,   157
        Colonel, Prince William Militia, Revolutionary War, September 1835 Court

    William, s/o Thomas Ewell decd, certified as heir at law to Jesse Ewell decd,   157
        Colonel, Prince William Militia, Revolutionary War, September 1835 Court

Fair (See also Fayre)
    Edmond, Prvt, Captain Alexander Howison's Company Muster Roll, 36th Rgt,   201
        Virginia Militia, War of 1812

    Edward, Prvt, Captain Joseph Smith's Company Muster Roll, 36th Rgt,   205
        Virginia Militia, War of 1812
    Edward, Prvt, Captain John Merchant's Company Muster Roll, 89th Rgt,   214
        Virginia Militia, War of 1812

Fairfax Militia, axe provided for by William Scott's PSC, Revolutionary War   84

Fairfax
    George, Proprietor of Ohio Company, 1747   12

    Henry, QM, 36th Rgt, Virginia Militia, War of 1812   196

    William, Patrol Acct, 1813   120
    William, Ensign, 36th Rgt, Virginia Militia, 1813   118

Fairfax Proprietary   9, 13

Fant
    William W, Prvt, 36th Rgt, Virginia Militia, War of 1812 Roster   210

Farrow
    Isaac, PSC, Revolutionary War   84

    John, Patrol Acct, French and Indian War   39

Index

Farrow (Cont.)
    William, Cornet, Prince William Militia, Militia claim for service, French and Indian War   185

    William, security for Catharine Davis's appearance before Grand Jury, September 1780   71
    William, Captain, Prince William Militia, April 1781, Revolutionary War   74

Fauquier, Francis, Correspondence with Colonel George Washington, June 1758,   184–185
    Re: Prince William Militia, French and Indian War

Fayre (See also Fair)
    Higby, Prvt, 36th Rgt, Virginia Militia, War of 1812 Roster   210

Feagan
    Daniel, Prvt, 36th Rgt, Virginia Militia, War of 1812 Roster   210

    Francis, PSC, Revolutionary War   78

Federal Militia Act, 1802   98

Feltner
    Henry, Prvt, 36th Rgt, Virginia Militia, War of 1812 Roster   210

Ferguson, Farguson
    Duncan, Prvt, Captain Peter Hogg's Company, Virginia Rgt, French and Indian War   176
    Duncan, Drummer, Major Andrew Lewis's Company, Virginia Rgt, French and Indian War   176

    John, PSC, Revolutionary War   77

    William, Prvt, 36th Rgt, Virginia Militia, War of 1812 Roster   210

Fewell
    John, Prvt, 36th Rgt, Virginia Militia, War of 1812 Roster   210

Fielder
    William, Trooper, Prince William Militia, Militia claim for service, French and Indian War   185

Finnie
    William, Colonel and QM, in Thomas Chapman's PSC, Revolutionary War   86
    William, as Colonel and deputy QM General of Southern Department   86, note 92

Fishback
    John, Trooper, Prince William Militia, Militia claim for service, French and Indian War   185

    Josiah, Soldier, Prince William Militia, petition to colonial legislature for pay for service,   186
    May 1757

Fisher
    Amos T, Prvt, Captain Corse's Company, Mexican War, certified as U. S. Pensioner, still   163, 165
    living, September 1853 Court
    Amos T, as Prvt, Captain Corse's Company, Mexican War   163, note 51

    Isaiah, as Committee for Amos T. Fisher, moves for certification of Amos as US Pensioner   165
    on rolls at Richmond, and still alive, March 1855 Court

Index

Fitzgerald
    John, Captain, 3rd Virginia Continental Rgt, Revolutionary War   53, 55
    John, as Captain, 3rd Virginia Continental Rgt, Revolutionary War   53, note 25

Fitzhugh
    Edward, 1st Sgt, Sgt, 89th Rgt, Virginia Militia, War of 1812 Roster   217

    Francis T, Sgt, Captain Benjamin Tyler's Company Muster Roll, 89th Rgt, Virginia Militia, War of 1812   215

    John, receipts as collector for Class 16, July 1781 Court, Revolutionary War   75
    John, PSC, Revolutionary War   79

    John Jr, PSC, Revolutionary War   79

    Lynaugh, Lt, 1st Battn, 89th Rgt, Virginia Militia, 1804–1806   111
    Lynaugh, as resident of Prince William, 1810   111, note 109
    Lynaugh, Captain, 89th Rgt, Virginia Militia, 1813, resignation of   121

    Sinah, Prvt, 89th Rgt, Virginia Militia, War of 1812 Roster   218

    Thomas, PSC, Revolutionary War   78

Fleming, Flemming
    Richard, Prvt, 89th Rgt, Virginia Militia, War of 1812 Roster   218

Florance, Florence
    Sarah, Revolutionary War Pension Declaration in December 1838   137
    Sarah, Revolutionary War Pension Declaration, December 1838 Court   158

    George, Captain, 89th Rgt, Virginia Militia, 1805, resignation of   115
    George, husband of Sarah Florence, Revolutionary War Pension File   158, note 33

    James, Prvt, 89th Rgt, Virginia Militia, War of 1812 Roster   218

    Samuel, Prvt, Captain Joseph Smith's Company Muster Roll, 36th Rgt, Virginia Militia, War of 1812   205

Floriday, Floudy
    Michael, Prvt, Captain Alexander Howison's Company Muster Roll, 36th Rgt, Virginia Militia, War of 1812   201
    Michael, Prvt, Captain Joseph Smith's Company Muster Roll, 36th Rgt, Virginia Militia, War of 1812   205

Floyd
    Francis, 2 PSCs, Revolutionary War   77, 79

    Henry, Sgt, Prince William Militia, Militia claim for service, French and Indian War   185

Folsom
    Israel, Patrol Acct, French and Indian War   39

Foote
    Richard, one of original patentees of the Brenton Grant from Thomas Lord Culpeper, 1686   6

Index

Forgie
    Robert, Prvt, Captain Joseph R. Gilbert's Company Muster Roll, 36th Rgt,   198
        Virginia Militia, War of 1812

Fort McHenry   104, 108

Fort Washington, Loss of, November 1776   60

Forts, in French and Indian War
    Fort Cumberland   29, 33
    Fort Duquesne   16, 21–22, 24, 26, 30, 32–33
    Fort Le Boeuf   14, 16, 18
    Fort Necessity   23–27
    Fort Niagara   27
    Fort Presque Isle   16
    Fort Prince George   20
    Fort Saint Frederic   27

Fortune
    Garner, as Prvt, Captain Thomas Armistead's Company of Grenadiers, 1st VSR,   61, 159, note 36
        Revolutionary War
    Lucy, Pension Declaration, July 1839 Court   61, 159–160

Foster
    Daniel, 2nd Lt, 89th Rgt, Virginia Militia, War of 1812 Roster   217

    George, Patrol Acct, French and Indian War   37

    James, PSC, Revolutionary War   82

    James, Justice of Peace, Prince William County, took Elijah Green's affidavit of   191–192
        identity and service, August 1832 Court

Foster (Cont.)
    Jerry, PSC, Revolutionary War   78

    Redmon, Prvt, 89th Rgt, Virginia Militia, War of 1812 Roster   218

    Robert, Ensign, Captain Daniel Kincheloe's Company, Commission and Oath,   41
        May 1762 Court, French and Indian War

    Silas, Sgt, Captain Benjamin Tyler's Company Muster Roll, 89th Rgt,   215
        Virginia Militia, War of 1812

Fox
    Harrison, Prvt, Captain Alexander Howison's Company Muster Roll, 36th Rgt,   205
        Virginia Militia, War of 1812

Foxworthy
    William, , Prvt, Captain Alexander Howison's Company Muster Roll, 36th Rgt,   205
        Virginia Militia, War of 1812

Francis
    Henry, Prvt, Captain Robert Spotswood's Company, Virginia Rgt, French and Indian War   176
    Henry, French and Indian War service proved, Montgomery County, Virginia, May 1780   176

Index

Francis (Cont.)
Henry, received 50 acres bounty land for French and Indian War service	176
Henry, discharged by Colonel Adam Stephen, French and Indian War	176
Henry, proved service as Prvt, Sgt, 1st Virginia Rgt, French War, while living in Montgomery County, Virginia, May 1780	176
Henry, entitled to 200 acres bounty land for service in French and Indian War	176
Henry, oldest brother and heir at law to John Francis decd, soldier, 1st Virginia Rgt, French and Indian War	176
Henry, as heir at law to John Francis decd, received 50 acres Bounty Land for John's Service in French and Indian War	176
Henry, as heir at law to William Francis decd, received 50 acres Bounty land for William's service in French and Indian War	176
John, Prvt, Colonel George Washington's 1st Virginia Rgt, served ca 3 years and was killed by Indians in French and Indian War	176
Reuben, Corporal, Captain Benjamin Tyler's Company Muster Roll, 89th Rgt, Virginia Militia, War of 1812	216
William, Soldier for 3 years in 1st Battn, Royal American Rgt, died in service, French and Indian War	176

Franklin
David, Prvt, Captain Benjamin Tyler's Company Muster Roll, 89th Rgt, Virginia Militia, War of 1812	216
John, , Prvt, Captain Alexander Howison's Company Muster Roll, 36th Rgt, Virginia Militia, War of 1812	203

Fredericktown, British raids on, War of 1812	104
Fredericksburg, Virginia, Captain Joseph Lynn's Company, 36th Rgt, Virginia Militia stationed there during War of 1812	219

Freeman
Nathaniel, Trooper, Prince William Militia, militia claim for service	185

French
James, PSC, Revolutionary War	82
William, PSC, Revolutionary War	82
William, Ensign, 36th Rgt, 1812	109–110
William, Lt, 36th Rgt, 1813	120
William, Lt, Captain Joseph Smith's Company Muster Roll, 36th Rgt, Virginia Militia, War of 1812	204
William, Lt, Captain John Merchant's Company Muster Roll, 89th Rgt, Virginia Militia, War of 1812	214
William, Ensign, Lt, 36th Rgt, Virginia Militia, War of 1812 Roster	206

French and Indian War, Lessons learned from	47–48
French Huguenots	6–7

Index

French Troops, carried over Occoquan, Revolutionary War	88

Friar
John, PSC, Revolutionary War	87

Frogg
John, Oath as Prince William Militia Officer, April 1756 Court, French and Indian War	38
John, Major, Colonel, Prince William Militia, French and Indian War	39
John, Major, Colonel, Prince William Militia, militia claim, as Major, French and Indian War	39, note 18
John, Major, Colonel, Prince William Militia, brief biography of	176–177
John, Major, Prince William Militia, Militia claim allowed, French and Indian War	176, 185
John, Major, Colonel, Militia service proved, Augusta County, March 1780	176
John, as early settler of Prince William; land purchases, 1740 and 1741	176

Fry
Joshua, Colonel, Virginia Rgt, French and Indian War	19–20
Joshua, Colonel, Virginia Rgt, death of, French and Indian War	24

Fryer
Elijah, , Prvt, Captain Alexander Howison's Company Muster Roll, 36th Rgt, Virginia Militia, War of 1812	203
Elijah, Prvt, Captain Benjamin Tyler's Company Muster Roll, 89th Rgt, Virginia Militia, War of 1812	216

Gage
Thomas, British Lt Colonel, French and Indian War	30–31

Gaines
Augustine, Lt, 89th Rgt, Virginia Militia, War of 1812 Roster	217
Richard, Patrol Acct, 1813, assigned to Benoni Harrison	119

Gaines (Cont.)
William, PSC, Revolutionary War	83
William, Judgment against as collector for class 19, Revolutionary War	91

Gallagher
James, Ensign, 36th Rgt, Virginia Militia, 1805	115

Gallahue
Charles, Captain, 11th Virginia, death of	57
Charles, as Captain, 11th Virginia Continental Rgt, Revolutionary War	57, note 55

Galloway
John, Lt , Virginia Continental Line, death intestate, certified September 1834 Court	154
John, Lt, Virginia Continental Line	154

Gardiner
Thomas, Trooper, Prince William Militia, Militia claim for service, French and Indian War	185
William, Prvt, Captain Alexander Howison's Company Muster Roll, 36th Rgt, Virginia Militia, War of 1812	203

Index

Garner
George, Prvt, 89th Rgt, Virginia Militia, War of 1812 Roster	218
George, Prvt, Captain Benjamin Tyler's Company Muster Roll, 89th Rgt, Virginia Militia, War of 1812	216
George, s/o William Garner, Revolutionary War soldier, certified as heir at law, December 1833 Court	152
Hezekiah, s/o William Garner, Revolutionary War soldier, certified as heir at law December 1833 Court	152
William decd, Revolutionary War soldier, death intestate certified, leaving heirs at law, December 1833 Court	152–153
William decd, as Prvt, Lee's Legion, Revolutionary War	153, note 10
William, s/o William Garner, Revolutionary War soldier, certified as heir at law December 1833 Court	152

Garrett
Robert, PSC, Revolutionary War	80

General Assembly, Acts for Recruiting State Quota of Troops, Revolutionary War — 80–92

Georgetown, British raids on, during War of 1812 — 104

Gibson,
George, Colonel, 1 VSR, in John Powell's 1818 Pension Application	133
George, Colonel, 1 VSR	153, 155, 159, 189
Isaac, Trooper, Prince William Militia, militia claim for service, French and Indian War	185
John, Lt, 36th Rgt, 1812	109
John, Lt, 36th Rgt, 1812	109, note 78
John, Lt, 36th Rgt, Virginia Militia, War of 1812 Roster	206
John, Lt, Captain John Linton's Company Muster Roll, Cavalry, 36th Rgt, Virginia Militia, War of 1812	203
Jonathan C, Sgt, Captain Joseph R. Gilbert's Company Muster Roll, 36th Rgt, Virginia Militia, War of 1812	197
Jonathan C, Sgt, Captain John Linton's Company Muster Roll, Cavalry, 36th Rgt, Virginia Militia, War of 1812	204
Jonathan, Sgt, 36th Rgt, Virginia Militia, War of 1812 Roster	207
Thomas, Major, in Major Townsend Dade's Court martial proceedings, November 1807 From the Fauquier County Clerks Loose Papers	219

Gilbert
Joseph, Lt, Captain, 36th Rgt, Virginia Militia, 1804	113
Joseph, Captain, in Paymaster's Acct, 36th Rgt, 1806 and 1807	122
Joseph R, Captain, 36th Rgt, Virginia Militia, 1812	109
Joseph R, Captain, 36th Rgt, Virginia Militia, Muster Rolls	110
Joseph R, Captain, 36th Rgt, Virginia Militia, War of 1812	197, 219
Joseph R, Captain, 36th Rgt, Virginia Militia, Muster Rolls, 1813 and 1814	197–199

Index

Giles
    Jacob, Proprietor of Ohio Company, 1747   12

Gill
    John, decd, Orderly Sgt, VSR, died November 1843, October 1854 Court   164
    John, decd, Pension as Prvt and Sgt, Captain Brent's Company, Revolutionary War   164, note 52
    John decd, death in November 1842 as U. S. Pensioner certified, October 1854 Court   165

    John I, Prvt, 89th Rgt, Virginia Militia, War of 1812 Roster   218

    Lettice, wid/o John Gill, Orderly Sgt, VSR, Pension Declaration, October 1854 Court   164

Gillison
    John, Major, in Major Townsend Dade's Court martial proceedings, November 1807   219
        From the Fauquier County Clerks Loose Papers

Gist
    Christopher, Surveyor for Ohio Company   15
    Christopher, American officer, French and Indian War   18, 20, 24–25, 30
    Nathaniel, Colonel, Gist's Additional Continental Rgt, Revolutionary War,   58, 83

    Gist's Additional Continental Rgt, Capture at Charleston, S.C.   58

Glascock
    Peter, Lt, Prince William Militia, February 1762 Court, French and Indian War   41

Glassell
    John, appointed Lt, 89th Rgt, Virginia Militia, 1805, refused to act   116

Glover
    Richard, Patrol Acct, 1805   116

Godfrey
    George, Prvt, Captain Joseph Smith's Company Muster Roll, 36th Rgt,   205
        Virginia Militia, War of 1812

    Jane (Carr), d/o John Carr, U. S. Pensioner at time of his death in September 1837,   163
        April 1850 Court

Gooch, Colonel, American Regiment, Cartagena Expedition, 1748   11

Goslin
    John, Prvt, Captain Alexander Howison's Company Muster Roll, 36th Rgt,   201
        Virginia Militia, War of 1812

Gossom
    Fanny, certified as heir at law to Alexander Mattox, a soldier in Captain Thomas   156
        W. Ewell's Company, 1 VSR, Revolutionary War, June 1835 Court

Graham
    George, PSC, Revolutionary War   84
    George, as admr of Reginald Graham, decd, PSC, Revolutionary War   88

Index

Graham (Cont.)
    Harrison, Prvt, Captain John Linton's Company Muster Roll, Cavalry, 36th Rgt,   204
        Virginia Militia, War of 1812

    John, security for Catharine Davis's appearance before Grand Jury, September 1780 Court   71

    John, Patrol Acct, 1806   117

    Reginald, Oath as Lt, Prince William Militia, November 1778, Revolutionary War   64
    Reginald decd, Captain, Prince William Militia, replaced by Alexander Lithgow,   77
        March 1782, Revolutionary War

    Richard, receipts as collector for Class 30, July 1781, Revolutionary War   75
    Richard, 2 PSCs, Revolutionary War   84, 88

    Thomas, Prvt, 89th Rgt, Virginia Militia, War of 1812 Roster   218

    Uriah, Prvt, 89th Rgt, Virginia Militia, War of 1812 Roster   218

    William, Prvt, Captain Alexander Howison's Company Muster Roll, 36th Rgt,   203
        Virginia Militia, War of 1812
    William, Prvt, Captain Benjamin Tyler's Company Muster Roll, 89th Rgt,   216
        Virginia Militia, War of 1812

Grant
    Daniel, Sgt, Captain Alexander Howison's Company Muster Roll, 36th Rgt,   199
        Virginia Militia, War of 1812

    Daniel, Prvt, Captain Joseph R. Gilbert's Company Muster Roll, 36th Rgt,   205
        Virginia Militia, War of 1812
    Posey, Captain, in Paymaster's Acct, 36th Rgt, Virginia Militia 1807   122
    Posey D, decd, Captain, 36th Rgt, Virginia Militia, replaced by Joseph Smith,   120
        September 1813 Court

    Sarah, husband of soldier in Continental Army, granted relief, July 1778   64, 142

    William, Oath as Prince William Militia officer, June 1756 Court, French and Indian War   38
    William, excuse accepted for not attending Council of War, September 1756 Court,   39
        French and Indian War
    William, appointed to settle tithes of road where Captain John Allen and Benjamin   40
        Crump are surveyors, May 1757
    William, PSC, Revolutionary War   83

Gray
    Caroline, d/o Elizabeth Gray and heir at law to Captain Thomas Ransdell, decd,   161
        Virginia Continental Line, September 1843 Court

    Elizabeth decd, sister to Captain Thomas Ransdell decd, Virginia Continental Line   161
        September 1843 Court

    Hezekiah, Prvt, Captain Joseph R. Gilbert's Company Muster Roll, 36th Rgt,   198
        Virginia Militia, War of 1812

Index

Gray (Cont.)

Nathaniel N, s/o Elizabeth Gray, and heir at law to Captain Thomas Ransdell, decd, Virginia Continental Line, September 1843 Court	161
Sarah, d/o Elizabeth Gray, and heir at law to Captain Thomas Ransdell, decd, Virginia Continental Line, September 1843 Court	161
Townly, Prvt, Captain Joseph R. Gilbert's Company Muster Roll, 36th Rgt, Virginia Militia, War of 1812	198

Grayson

William, Captain, Prince William Independent Militia Company, 1774	51
William, Colonel, Prince William Minute Battalion, 1775, Revolutionary War	54
William, Colonel, Prince William Minute Battalion, resignation of	54
William, Colonel, PSC, Revolutionary War	77
William, Colonel, Revolutionary War service detailed	77, note 58
William, Colonel, Plaintiff in suit against Benjamin Scanland, May 1782	78
William, Military biography of	54
William, Captain 2nd Battn, 36th Rgt, 1804, resignation of, September 1804 Court	113
Grayson's Additional Continental Rgt	58
Great Meadows, Battle of, French and Indian War	20

Green

Elijah, Pension File S 37961, 1818–1836	189–194
Elijah, Prvt, Captain Thomas W. Ewell's Company, 1 VSR	61
Elijah, Revolutionary War Pension Declaration, November 1818	189
Elijah, Revolutionary War Pension Declaration, August 1831	190
Elijah, Certificate of Pension issued June 1832 and sent to C. J. Mercer, of House of Representatives; pension to begin in August 1831	191
Elijah, Note from Pension Agency stating new papers needed with additional proof of identity, August 1831	191
Elijah decd, Act of Virginia Legislature determined 1 VSR part of Continental Army, thus allowing Green his pension under Act of 1818	194
Elijah, decd, Court certified Elijah Green as U. S. Pensioner at his death, December 1833 Court	153
Elijah, decd, Court certified as U.S. Pensioner at his death	153
Elijah, decd, Court certified heirs certified, December 1833 Court	153
Elijah, decd, Court certified no surviving widow, October 1834 Court	154
Elijah decd, Heirs in October 1834 Court Orders, all of age, January 1835 Court	155
Elijah decd, Heir's petition Congress for relief, March 1836 and HR 635 passed, May 1836	193
Elijah, s/o Elijah Green decd, affidavit of identity before James Foster, Justice of Peace, in order to collect pension benefits, August 1832 Court	191
Elijah, s/o Elijah Green decd, appointed Thomas G. Moncure as attorney to collect arrears In pension from September 4, 1832 to January 15, 1833 when his father died	192
Elijah, s/o Elijah Green decd, a U.S. Pensioner at his death, certified as heir at law, October 1834 Court	154

Index

Green (Cont.)
    Elijah, s/o Elijah Green decd, certified as heir at law to Elijah Green, decd, a soldier in   192
        Captain Thomas Ewell's Company, 1 VSR, Revolutionary War, December 1833,
        February 1835
    Elijah and others, Heirs petition Congress for relief: HR 645 passed May 17, 1836   193
    Elijah, s/o Elijah Green decd, certified as heir at law by William Colquhoun,   193
        August 1836 Court

    George Sr, PSC, Revolutionary War   81

    Horton, Prvt, 89th Rgt, Virginia Militia, War of 1812 Roster   218

    James, Prvt, 89th Rgt, Virginia Militia, War of 1812 Roster   218

    John, soldier, Prince William Militia, militia claim for service, French and Indian War   185

    John L, Prvt, 89th Rgt, Virginia Militia, War of 1812 Roster   218

    Peggy, d/o Elijah Green decd, certified as heir at law, December 1833 Court   153

    Thompson, Corporal 89th Rgt, Virginia Militia, War of 1812 Roster   217

    William, Petition, March 1761 to legislature, for expenses in settling militia accts   183
        for pay and provisions for Prince William militia and for damages done in
        Prince William, French and Indian War

Griffith
    Dennis, Prvt, 36th Rgt, Virginia Militia, War of 1812 Roster   210

Grigsby
    Baylis, Affidavit of need for John Bell's 1818 pension, filed in Fauquier County   132

    Nathaniel, Affidavit of need for John Bell's 1818 pension, filed in Fauquier County   132

    Samuel, Trooper, Prince William County, militia claim for service   185

Grinstead
    James, PSC, Revolutionary War   80

    John, 2 PSCs, Revolutionary War   82

Groves
    Henley, Prvt, Captain John Linton's Company Muster Roll, Cavalry, 36th Rgt,   204
        Virginia Militia, War of 1812

    Travis, Prvt, 36th Rgt, Virginia Militia, War of 1812 Roster   210

Grubb, Grub
    Humphrey, soldier, Prince William Militia,, deserted June 1757 and never returned to duty,   184
        French and Indian War

Gunyon
    John, decd, Soldier, Revolutionary War soldier, who died in war   56, 65
    John, decd, orphans of, relief for, February 1779 Court   65

Index

Gunyon (Cont.)
    John, Revolutionary War service detailed   65, note 12
    John, decd, Revolutionary war Soldier who died in service, 2 children granted relief   143

    William, orphan of John Gunyon decd, revolutionary war soldier; CW Indenture to John Murray   74

Guthrie
    Elizabeth (Gray), d/o Elizabeth Gray and heir at law to Captain Thomas Ransdell, decd, Virginia Continental Line, September 1843 Court   161

Guy
    Charles, , Prvt, Captain Alexander Howison's Company Muster Roll, 36th Rgt, Virginia Militia, War of 1812   201

    Matthew, Prvt, Captain Joseph R. Gilbert's Company Muster Roll, 36th Rgt, Virginia Militia, War of 1812   198

    Matthew, Prvt, Captain John Linton's Company Muster Roll, Cavalry, 36th Rgt, Virginia Militia, War of 1812   204

    Matthew, Prvt, Captain Richard Weedon's Company Muster Roll, 36th Rgt, Virginia Militia, War of 1812   206

    Tanley, Patrol Acct, 1813, assigned to Benoni Harrison   119
    Tanley, Prvt, Captain Alexander Howison's Company Muster Roll, 36th Rgt, Virginia Militia, War of 1812   201
    Tanley, Captain Richard Weedon's Company Muster Roll, 36th Rgt, Virginia Militia, War of 1812   206

Gwatkin
    James, 2 PSCs Revolutionary War   78, 87

    James, Ensign, 36th Rgt, Virginia Militia, 1813   118

Hales (see also Hall)
    Corben, Prvt, Captain Richard Weedon's Company Muster Roll, 36th Rgt, Virginia Militia, War of 1812   206

Halket
    Peter, killed at Braddock's Defeat, French and Indian War   31

Hall (see also Hales)
    Alexander, Prvt, Drummer, 36th Rgt, Virginia Militia, War of 1812 Roster   210

    Corben, Prvt, Captain Alexander Howison's Company Muster Roll, 36th Rgt, Virginia Militia, War of 1812   201

    John, Prvt, Captain Benjamin Tyler's Company Muster Roll, 89th Rgt, Virginia Militia, War of 1812   216

    William, appearance bond as Commonwealth witness against John Sidebottom, October and November 1780 Court   72–74

Index

Halley, Haly, Hawley
    John, soldier, Captain Thomas Waggener's Company, Virginia Rgt, French and Indian War   177

    James, Prvt, Captain John Linton's Company Muster Roll, Cavalry, 36th Rgt, Virginia Militia, War of 1812   204

Halsey
    Zachariah, Prvt, 89th Rgt, Virginia Militia, War of 1812 Roster   218

Hamil, Hamill
    Elizabeth, wid/o John Hamil decd, certified as sole heir at law to her father, William McIntosh, decd, Revolutionary War soldier   153

    John decd, husband of Elizabeth Hamil, heir at law to William McIntosh   153

Hamilton
    Robert, Prvt, Captain John Linton's Company Muster Roll, Cavalry, 36th Rgt, Virginia Militia, War of 1812   204

    Robert, Prvt, 36th Rgt, Virginia Militia, War of 1812 Roster   210

    Thomas B, 89th Rgt, Virginia Militia, War of 1812 Roster   218

Hampton, Virginia, British Raid on, War of 1812   104

Hampton
    Henry, 2 Patrol Accts, French and Indian War   37, 39
    Henry, PSC, Revolutionary War   78

    Richard, Oath as Prince William Militia officer, July 1753, French and Indian War   35
    Richard, Lt, Prince William Militia claims, April 1756 French and Indian War   35, note 1

    William, PSC, Revolutionary War   85

Hamrick
    Benjamin, Prince William veteran in 1818 Pension, for service in 3rd Virginia Continental Rgt, Revolutionary War   139
    Benjamin, 3rd Virginia Continental Line, Revolutionary War   56

Hanbury
    John, London Merchant, Proprietor of Ohio Company, 1748   12

Hancock
    John, Lt, Captain Thomas Blackburn's Company, April 1763 Court, French and Indian War   42

    John, Prvt, Captain Alexander Howison's Company Muster Roll, 36th Rgt, Virginia Militia, War of 1812   201

Harper
    George, Patrol Acct, French and Indian War   39

Index

Harris, Harriss
John, Patrol Acct, 1805	116
Obed, PSC, Revolutionary War	78
Thomas, security for appearance of Mary McMahan before grand jury, July 1780 Court	72
William, , Prvt, Captain Alexander Howison's Company Muster Roll, 36th Rgt, Virginia Militia, War of 1812	201

Harrison
Benoni, Patrol Acct, 1813	119
Benoni, Patrol Acct, 1813, as assignee of Alexander Brawner	119
Benoni, Patrol Acct, 1813, as assignee of Benson Jewell	119
Benoni, 3 Patrol Acct, 1813, as assignee of Alexander Brawner	119
Benoni, Patrol Acct, 1813, as assignee of Daniel King	119
Benoni, Patrol Acct, 1813, as assignee of Alexander Brawner	119
Benoni, Patrol Acct, 1813, as assignee of George Carney	119
Benoni, Patrol Acct, 1813, as assignee of George Dewall	119
Benoni, Patrol Acct, 1813, as assignee of Alexander Brawner	119
Benoni, Patrol Acct, 1813, as assignee of George Smallwood	119
Benoni, Patrol Acct, 1813, as assignee of George Tansill	119
Benoni, Patrol Acct, 1813, as assignee of James Smith	119
Benoni, Patrol Acct, 1813, as assignee of James Thomas	119
Benoni, Patrol Acct, 1813, as assignee of Jesse Dowell	119
Benoni, Patrol Acct, 1813, as assignee of Jesse Patterson	119
Benoni, Patrol Acct, 1813, as assignee of John Bland	119
Benoni, Patrol Acct, 1813, as assignee of Matthias Cole	119
Benoni, Patrol Acct, 1813, as assignee of Moses Duffy	119
Benoni, Patrol Acct, 1813, as assignee of Richard Gaines	119
Benoni, Patrol Acct, 1813, as assignee of Samuel Anderson	119
Benoni, Patrol Acct, 1813, as assignee of Samuel Boswell	119
Benoni, Patrol Acct, 1813, as assignee of Samuel Mitchell	119
Benoni, Patrol Acct, 1813, as assignee of Tanley Guy	119
Benoni, Patrol Acct, 1813, as assignee of Tomas Keys	119
Benoni, Patrol Acct, 1813, as assignee of William Boswell	119
Benoni, Patrol Acct, 1813, as assignee of William Calvert	119
Benoni, Patrol Acct, 1813, as assignee of William Cornwell	119
Benoni, 2 Patrol Accts, 1813, as assignee of William Smith	119
Benoni, Patrol Acct, 1813, as assignee of William Tansill	119
Benoni, Patrol Acct, 1813, as assignee of Benson Jewell	119
Benoni, Patrol Acct, 1813, as assignee of Benson James Smith	119
Benoni, Patrol Acct, 1813, as assignee of James Smith	120
Benoni, Patrol Acct, 1813, as assignee of John Webster	120
Benoni, Patrol Acct, 1813, as assignee of Samuel Cornwell	120
Burr, proved Benjamin Bullitt's service as ensign, Virginia Rgt and death in April 1757	173
Burr, 2 PSCs, Revolutionary War	84, 88
Burr, Cornet, 36th Rgt, Virginia Militia, War of 1812	110
Burr, Cornet, Captain John Linton's Company Muster Roll, Cavalry, 36th Rgt, Virginia Militia, War of 1812	203
Burr, Cornet, 36th Rgt, Virginia Militia, War of 1812 Roster	207

Index

Harrison (Cont.)

Charles, Colonel, 1st Continental Artillery, Revolutionary War	60
Cuthbert, Oath as Prince William Militia Officer, September 1753 Court, French and Indian War	36
Cuthbert, Captain, Prince William Minute Battalion, Revolutionary War	53
Cuthbert, Captain, 1st Continental Dragoons, Revolutionary War	53, 59
Cuthbert, Prvt, Captain Alexander Howison's Company Muster Roll, 36th Rgt, Virginia Militia, War of 1812	201
Cuthbert, Prvt, QM Sgt, Captain John Merchant's Company Muster Roll, 89th Rgt, Virginia Militia, War of 1812	214
Cuthbert V, Prvt, Captain Joseph R. Gilbert's Company Muster Roll, 36th Rgt, Virginia Militia, War of 1812	198
Cuthbert V, Prvt, Captain Joseph Smith's Company Muster Roll, 36th Rgt, Virginia Militia, War of 1812	205
James, Prvt, Captain John Linton's Company Muster Roll, Cavalry, 36th Rgt, Virginia Militia, War of 1812	204
John, Prvt, Captain Alexander Howison's Company Muster Roll, 36th Rgt, Virginia Militia, War of 1812	201
John P, 1st Sgt, 89th Rgt, Virginia Militia, War of 1812 Roster	217
John Peyton, Captain, 2nd Virginia Continental Rgt, Revolutionary War	55, 69, note 30
John S, Corporal, Captain Joseph R. Gilbert's Company Muster Roll, 36th Rgt, Virginia Militia, War of 1812	198
John S, Corporal, Captain Alexander Howison's Company Muster Roll, 36th Rgt, Virginia Militia, War of 1812	200
Josiah B, Sgt, 89th Rgt, Virginia Militia, War of 1812 Roster	217
Matthew, 2 PSCs, Revolutionary War	80, 84
Philip, Ensign, 2nd Battn, 36th Rgt, Virginia Militia, 1804, resignation of	113
Philip, Prvt, Captain Joseph R. Gilbert's Company Muster Roll, 36th Rgt, Virginia Militia, War of 1812	198
Philip, Prvt, Captain John Linton's Company Muster Roll, Cavalry, 36th Rgt, Virginia Militia, War of 1812	204
Stephen, Prvt, Captain Alexander Howison's Company Muster Roll, 36th Rgt, Virginia Militia, War of 1812	201
Stephen, Prvt, Captain John Merchant's Company Muster Roll, 89th Rgt, Virginia Militia, War of 1812	215
Thomas, Oath as Prince William Militia officer, August 1753 Court, French and Indian War	36

Index

Harrison (Cont.)
    Walter, Prvt, Captain Joseph R. Gilbert's Company Muster Roll, 36th Rgt,   198
        Virginia Militia, War of 1812

    Zacheus, Prvt, Captain John Merchant's Company Muster Roll, 89th Rgt,   215
        Virginia Militia, War of 1812

Havre de Grace, Maryland, British raids on, War of 1812   104

Hayes, Hay
    Alfred C, Ensign, Light Infantry, 1st Battn, 36th Rgt, Virginia Militia, 1813   119–120
    Alfred C, Lt, 36th Rgt, Virginia Militia, 1812   109, 110, note 79
    Alfred C, 36th Rgt, Virginia Militia, War of 1812 Roster   206

    Colin, Prvt, Captain John Linton's Company Muster Roll, Cavalry, 36th Rgt,   204
        Virginia Militia, War of 1812

    James, Prvt, 11th Virginia Continental Rgt, Revolutionary War   57, 73, note 45
    James, security for Mary McMahan's appearance at Court on charge of riot,   73
        November 1784 Court

    James, Captain, 36th Rgt, Virginia Militia, 1812   109
    James, Lt, Captain, 36th Rgt, Virginia Militia, 1804   113
    James, Adjutant, Captain, 36th Rgt, Virginia Militia, War of 1812 Roster   206
    James, Captain, Light Infantry, 36th Rgt, Virginia Militia, War of 1812   219

    John, Adjutant, 36th Rgt, Virginia Militia, War of 1812   196
    Sarah E, niece to Sarah Ewell of Botetourt, certified as heir at law to Sarah Ewell,   153
        February 1834 Court
    Sarah E, only heir entitled to bounty land claims of Thomas W. Ewell for service as   153, 155
        Revolutionary War officer, February 1834 Court, January 1835

    Walter G, former Lt, 36th Rgt, Virginia Militia, now in U. S. Service, May 1813 Court   118
    Walter G, as 1st Lt, 20th U. S. Infantry, War of 1812   118, note 22

Hayward
    Nicholas, Patentee of Brenton Grant from Thomas, Lord Culpeper, 1686   6

Hazlerigg, Hazelrigg
    William, PSC, Revolutionary War   85

Heath
    James, Attorney for John Bell, to collect arrears in pension, September 1838   134

    James E, Lt, Captain John Linton's Company Muster Roll, Cavalry, 36th Rgt,   203
        Virginia Militia, War of 1812

Hedges, Hedge
    Isham E, Ensign, Lt, 36th Rgt, Virginia Militia, 1804   113

    John, Captain Prince William Militia, July 1778, Revolutionary War   63
    John, entitled to bounty land of Francis Eppes for his service in French and Indian War,   69–70
        June 1780 Court
    John, 2 PSCs, Revolutionary War   81

Index

Hedges, Hedge (Cont.)
    Lemuel, Corporal, Captain Joseph R. Gilbert's Company Muster Roll, 36th Rgt,   197
        Virginia Militia, War of 1812
    Lemuel, Prvt, Captain John Linton's Company Muster Roll, Cavalry, 36th Rgt,   204
        Virginia Militia, War of 1812

    Robert, receipt for clothes and beef as collector for Class 36, July 1781 Court,   76
        Revolutionary War

Helm
    Leonard [Lynaugh], Commission and oath as Captain of Foot, October 1755 Court,   37
        French and Indian War
    --- [Lynaugh?] Captain, to allot tithes from road on Fauquier line to bridge on Slaty Run,   43
        June 1767 Court
    Leonard [Lynaugh], Captain, Clark's Illinois Rgt, Revolutionary War, 1778–1782   62, 88, note 68
    Leonard [Lynaugh], 2 PSCs, Revolutionary War   80

Helsop
    Nathan, Prvt, 89th Rgt, Virginia Militia, War of 1812 Roster   218

Henderson
    Alexander, PSC, Revolutionary War   82
Hendricks
    James, Offered command of Prince William Minute Battalion, but refused, 1776   54

Henry
    Patrick, Governor of Virginia   51

    Rhodam, Prvt, Captain Alexander Howison's Company Muster Roll, 36th Rgt,   201
        Virginia Militia, War of 1812
Herndon
    Benjamin decd, heir at law to George Stubblefield, Ensign, Virginia Continental Line   162

    Frazier D, certified as heir at law to George Stubblefield, decd, Ensign, Virginia   162
        Continental Line, Revolutionary War, September 1843 Court

    George, certified as heir at law to George Stubblefield, decd, Ensign, Virginia   162
        Continental Line, Revolutionary War, September 1843 Court

    John, as Deputy Muster Master under Colonel William Finnie, in Thomas Chapman's   86
        PSC, March 1782
    John, as Deputy Muster Master under Colonel William Finnie, Revolutionary War   86, note 92

    Richard W, certified as heir at law to George Stubblefield, decd, Ensign, Virginia   162
        Continental Line, Revolutionary War, September 1843 Court

    Thomas, certified as heir at law to George Stubblefield, decd, Ensign, Virginia   162
        Continental Line, Revolutionary War, September 1843 Court

    William, PSC, Revolutionary War   87

Index

Hewett, Hewitt
    Thomas W, Prvt, Captain Joseph R. Gilbert's Company Muster Roll, 36th Rgt,   198
        Virginia Militia, War of 1812
    Thomas W, Prvt, Captain John Linton's Company Muster Roll, Cavalry, 36th Rgt,   204
        Virginia Militia, War of 1812

Hickerson
    Rawleigh, Ensign, 36th Rgt, Virginia Militia, 1812   110
    Rawleigh, Ensign, 36th Rgt, Virginia Militia, War of 1812 Roster   206

Hickman
    Julia, certified as heir at law to William Hickman, decd, who held various military   161
        surveys in Virginia Military Districts in Ohio and Kentucky, October 1841 Court

    Lucretia, certified as heir at law to William Hickman, decd, who held various military   161
        surveys in Virginia Military Districts in Ohio and Kentucky, October 1841 Court

    Julia, certified as heir at law to William Hickman, decd, who held various military   161
        surveys in Virginia Military Districts in Ohio and Kentucky, October 1841 Court

    Rebecca, certified as heir at law to William Hickman, decd, who held various military   161
        surveys in Virginia Military Districts in Ohio and Kentucky, October 1841 Court

    S. J. C, certified as heir at law to William Hickman, decd, who held various military   161
        surveys in Virginia Military Districts in Ohio and Kentucky, October 1841 Court

    William decd, owner of various military surveys in Virginia Military Districts in Ohio   161
        and Kentucky; died intestate in Jefferson County, Virginia ca. 1827, leaving heirs,
        October 1841 Court

Higgins
    Charity, Grand Jury Presentment for living in adultery with Nathaniel Overall,   41
        May 1762 Court

Highwarden
    John, Soldier, Virginia Rgt, discharged by Colonel Washington due to age and infirmity,   183
        June 1757, French and Indian War
    John, PSC, Revolutionary War   80

Hill
    Alexander, Drummer, 36th Rgt, Virginia Militia, 1812   183

    Allen, Drummer, 36th Rgt, Virginia Militia, War of 1812 Roster   207

    George, PSC, Revolutionary War, assigned to Margerum & Moore   82

    John, Prvt, Captain Alexander Howison's Company Muster Roll, 36th Rgt,   203
        Virginia Militia, War of 1812

    Nicholas, soldier, Prince William Militia, militia claim for service, French and Indian War   185

    William, Patrol Acct, French and Indian War   39

Index

Hines
    Thomas, soldier in 3rd Virginia Continental Rgt — 56
    Thomas, soldier in Virginia Continental Line, petition granted for support of his wife and child, February 1779 Court — 65
    Thomas, as prvt, Captain John Peyton's Company, 3rd Virginia Continental Rgt, Revolutionary War — 65, note 13

Hite
    Abraham, proved Benjamin Bullitt decd service and death as ensign, Virginia Rgt, April 1757, French and Indian War — 173

Hixon
    William, Ensign, 89th Rgt, 1805, resignation of — 116

Hoard, Hord
    Thomas, Corporal, Prince William Militia, militia claim for service, French and Indian War — 185

Hodges
    Samuel, Patrol Acct, 1813, assigned to Mary Ann Cave — 119

Hoff
    Cornelius, Corporal, 89th Rgt, Virginia Militia, War of 1812 Roster — 218

    Joshua, Corporal, Captain Benjamin Tyler's Company Muster Roll, 89th Rgt, Virginia Militia, War of 1812 — 215

    Thomas, Prvt, Captain Benjamin Tyler's Company Muster Roll, 89th Rgt, Virginia Militia, War of 1812 — 216

Hogg
    Peter, Captain, Virginia Rgt, French and Indian War — 176

Holifield
    Daniel, Soldier, 3rd Virginia Continental Rgt, Revolutionary War — 56
    Daniel decd, 3rd Virginia soldier who died in Revolutionary War; husband of Ruth Holifield, July 1778 — 63

    Ruth, wid/o Daniel Holifield decd, soldier in 3rd Virginia, Petition for relief for support of herself and child granted, July 1778 — 63, 142

Holliday
    James, 3rd Virginia Continental Rgt, Revolutionary War — 56
    James, 3rd Virginia veteran from Prince William who applied for 1818 need-base pension — 139

    John, PSC, Revolutionary War — 86

    Zacheus, Prvt, Captain Joseph R. Gilbert's Company Muster Roll, 36th Rgt, Virginia Militia, War of 1812 — 198

Holmer
    Christian, Field Officer, 1st Continental Artillery, Revolutionary War — 60

Index

Holmes, Hoomes
    Elizabeth, 2 PSCs, Revolutionary War   85, 86

    Peter, 1st Lt, 36th Rgt, Virginia Militia, in Camp Equipage Papers, May 1815   220
        From Fauquier County Court Clerks Loose Papers
    Peter, Lt, 36th Rgt, Virginia Militia, 1812   109
    Peter, as resident of Fauquier County in 1810   109, note 80

    Thomas, Patrol Acct, French and Indian War   39

    Thomas, PSC, Revolutionary War   79

    Thomas, Prvt, Captain Alexander Howison's Company Muster Roll, 36th Rgt,   201
        Virginia Militia, War of 1812
    Thomas, Prvt, Captain Joseph Smith's Company Muster Roll, 36th Rgt,   205
        Virginia Militia, War of 1812

Hooe
    Bernard, captain, Prince William Militia, July 1778 Court, Revolutionary War   63
    Bernard, receipts as collector for class 21, July 1781 Court, Revolutionary War   75
    Bernard, 3 PSCs, Revolutionary War   80, 85

    Howson, Oath as captain, Prince William Militia, September 1755 Court,   37
        French and Indian War
    Howson, captain, Prince William Militia, July 1762 Court, French and Indian War   41
    Howson Sr, PSC, Revolutionary War   85

    Howson, Lt, 89th Rgt, Virginia Militia, War of 1812 Roster   217

    John, Oath as Lt, Prince William Militia, September 1755 Court, French and Indian War   37
    John, PSC, Revolutionary War   82

    John, Prvt, 89th Rgt, Virginia Militia, War of 1812 Roster   218

Hope
    James, Prvt, Captain Alexander Howison's Company Muster Roll, 36th Rgt,   203
        Virginia Militia, War of 1812

    William, Prvt, Captain Alexander Howison's Company Muster Roll, 36th Rgt,   203
        Virginia Militia, War of 1812

Hopper
    Moses, soldier, Prince William Militia, deserted June 1757 and never returned to duty,   184
        French and Indian War

    Rawleigh, soldier, Prince William Militia, deserted June 1757 and never returned to duty,   184
        French and Indian War

Hopwood
    James, Prvt, Captain Alexander Howison's Company Muster Roll, 36th Rgt,   201
        Virginia Militia, War of 1812

Index

Horton
    Craven, Court ordered Craven Horton and William Brook to sell property lately belonging to Thomas Love and divide proceeds among his heirs, May 1804 Court   114

    Gavin, Prvt, 89th Rgt, Virginia Militia, War of 1812 Roster   218

    Snowden, PSC, Revolutionary War   83

Howard
    Hawkins, Prvt, 89th Rgt, Virginia Militia, War of 1812 Roster   218

Howison
    Alexander, Captain, 36th Rgt, Virginia Militia, Muster Rolls   111
    Alexander, as resident of Prince William in 1810   111, note 97
    Alexander, Captain, 36th Rgt, Virginia Militia, 1812 Muster Rolls, 1813 and 1814   199–203
    Alexander, Captain, 36th Rgt, Virginia Militia, War of 1812   111, 199, 219

    Robert, Lt, 36th Rgt, Virginia Militia, 1805   115

    Stephen [Steven], 2nd Lt, Captain Charles Lee's Company, Prince William Militia, August 1779 Court, Revolutionary War   66
    Stephen, oath as Prince William Militia Officer, September 1779 Court, Revolutionary War   67
    Stephen, security for John Sidebottom's appearance before the Grand Jury, September 1780 Court   71
    Stephen, as Lt in Prince William Militia in 1779   71, note 42
    Stephen, PSC, Revolutionary War   86
    Stephen, Jr. 2 patrol accts, 1805   116
    Stephen Jr   116, note 14

Huber
    George, Sgt, Captain Joseph R. Gilbert's Company Muster Roll, 36th Rgt, Virginia Militia, War of 1812   197

Huff
    Thomas, Prvt, Captain Alexander Howison's Company Muster Roll, 36th Rgt, Virginia Militia, War of 1812   203

Hughlett, Hulett, Hulet
    Hannah, d/o William Hughlet decd, soldier in Virginia Continental Line, certified as his heir at law, August 1835 Court   156

    William decd, soldier Virginia Continental Line, intestate death certified   156

Hull
    John G, Attorney appointed by Spencer Anderson, to collect arrears due in his pension September 1834   134

Hume
    Alexander, security for John Sidebottom's appearance before Grand Jury, September 1780 Court   71

Humphries (?) (may be **Humberfiled, Umberfield?**)
    Eliphalet, Prvt, 36th Rgt, Virginia Militia, War of 1812 Roster   210

Hungerford
    John, Brigadier General, Virginia Militia, War of 1812   219

Index

Hunting Path, Shenandoah	6, 9, 14

Hurley
Cornelius, veteran from Prince William who applied for a pension for 3rd Virginia service — 56, note 48

Hutchinson,
John, Captain, 89th Rgt, Virginia Militia, resignation of, September 1805 Court — 116

Robert, PSC, Revolutionary War — 85

Thomas, applied for 1818 Pension — 139

Hutchison
Thomas, Sgt, Captain Thomas Winder Ewell, 1 VSR, — 61
Thomas, decd, Sgt, Captain Thomas Ewell, 1 VSR, intestate death certified, December 1833 Court — 153

George, Patrol Acct, 1813 — 119

Thompson, s/o Thomas Hutchison decd, Sgt, Captain Ewell, 1 VSR, certified as heir at law, December 1833 Court — 153

William, Patrol Acct 1813, assigned to Mary Ann Cave — 119
William, as Patroller and Prvt, 36th Rgt, Virginia Militia, War of 1812 — 196

Independent Militia Companies, Virginia, creation of — 51

Indians
   Chiefs — 16
   Half King (aka Tanacharison) — 20–24
   Iroquois Confederacy — 10–11, 14, 16, 24
   Scarouady, Oneida Indian — 24
   Tribes — 4, 6–7, 10, 12, 15–16, 20, 24, 33

Istobe
William, soldier, Captain John Ashby's Company of Rangers, French and Indian War — 177
William, soldier, Captain John Ashby's Ranger Company, Petition granted for pay for 2 Months at time of his capture and imprisonment by French at Quebec, French and Indian War — 177

Jackson
Forysthe, Prvt, 89th Rgt, Virginia Militia, War of 1812 Roster — 218

Francis, s/o Frank, PSC, Revolutionary War — 82

Francis Jr, PSC, Revolutionary War — 82

Francis, Captain, 36th Rgt, Virginia Militia, September and October 1804 — 113–114

George, Lt, 2nd Battn, 36th Rgt, Virginia Militia, 1804, resignation of — 113

George W, Captain, 36th Rgt, Virginia Militia, War of 1812 — 219
George W, Captain, 36th Rgt, stationed at Ellicott Mills, War of 1812 — 218

Grace, certified as heir at law to Captain Jesse Evans decd, August 1835 Court — 156

Index

Jackson (Cont.)
    John F, Prvt, 36th Rgt, Virginia Militia, War of 1812 Roster   210
    John Jr, Prvt, Captain Benjamin Tyler's Company Muster Roll, 89th Rgt,   216
        Virginia Militia, War of 1812

    Samuel, PSC, Revolutionary War, assigned to George Purcell,   81
    Samuel Jr, PSC, Revolutionary War   84

    Samuel, s/o Sam, appointed guardian to Richard Calvert, orphan of Reuben Calvert decd,   88
        September 1782 Court
    Samuel, s/o Sam, appointed guardian to Thomas Calvert, orphan of Reuben Calvert decd,   88
        September 1782 Court

Jacobs
    Fontine, Prvt, 36th Rgt, Virginia Militia, War of 1812 Roster   210

James
    —— Mr, Patrol Acct, 1805   117

    John, Oath as Prince William Militia officer, August 1755 Court, French and Indian War   37

    John, attended Shenandoah Court to give evidence against Joseph Sidebottom,   70
        July 1780 Court

Jameson
    David, PSC, Revolutionary War   79

    Enoch, Lt, 2nd Battn, 36th Rgt, 1804, Resignation of   113

    George, Sgt, 36th Rgt, Virginia Militia, War of 1812 Roster   207
    George, Prvt, 36th Rgt, Virginia Militia, War of 1812 Roster   210

    Townsend, 36th Rgt, Virginia Militia, War of 1812 Roster   219

Janney, Janny
    Jacob, Prvt, Captain Alexander Howison's Company Muster Roll, 36th Rgt,   201
        Virginia Militia, War of 1812

    Samuel H, Justice of the Peace, who certified Dekeandra Mattingly's Pension Declaration,   157
        October 1838 Court

Jansen
    Benjamin G, s/o George and Elizabeth (Bowne) Jansen, certified as heir at law to   159
        Captain Thomas Bowne, decd of Virginia Continental Line, March 1839 Court

    Elizabeth (Bowne), d/o Captain Thomas Bowne decd, of Virginia Continental Line,   159
        Intestate death in 1824 with heirs certified, March 1839 Court
    Elizabeth (Bowne), d/o Captain Thomas Bowne decd, Captain Virginia Continental   159
        Line, and wife of George Jansen of New York City, March 1839

    George, husband of Elizabeth (Bowne) Jansen, death in 1800 certified, March 1839   159
        Court

Index

Jansen (Cont.)
    Helen M, d/o George and Elizabeth (Bowne) Jansen, certified as heir at law to Captain   159
        Thomas Bowne, decd, Virginia Continental Line, March 1839 Court

    Thomas Bowne, s/o George and Elizabeth (Bowne) Jansen, certified his death occurred   159
        in August 1838, intestate, unmarried and without issue, March 1839 Court

Jefferson
    Peter, Virginia surveyor   19

Jeffreys, Jeffries
    Asa, Prvt, 36th Rgt, Virginia Militia, War of 1812 Roster   210

    George, Corporal, 36th Rgt, Virginia Militia, War of 1812 Roster   207

    Moses, PSC, Revolutionary War   85

    Pleasant, Prvt, Captain Benjamin Tyler's Company Muster Roll, 89th Rgt,   216
        Virginia Militia, War of 1812

Jenkins
    Elisha, Ensign, 89th Rgt, 1804–1806   111
    Elisha, as resident of Prince William in 1810   111, note 113

    Robert, Sea Captain, in War of Jenkins Ear   11

Jennings
    Augustine, Oath as Militia Officer, July 1753 Court, French and Indian War   35
    Augustine, Oath as Militia Officer, August 1756 Court, French and Indian War   39

    Edmund, a representative from Virginia at Treaty of Lancaster, 1774   12

Jennings (Cont.)
    William, Soldier, Prince William Militia, militia claim for service, French and Indian War   185

Jett
    Burkett, Prvt, 36th Rgt, Virginia Militia, War of 1812 Roster   210

Jett (Cont.)
    Peter, Ensign, 2nd Battn, 36th Rgt, Virginia Militia, 1804   113
    Peter, Prvt, 36th Rgt, Virginia Militia, War of 1812 Roster   210

Jewell
    Benson, Patrol Acct, 1813, assigned to Benoni Harrison   119
    Benson, 1813 Patroller and Prvt, 36th Rgt, Virginia Militia, War of 1812   196
    Benson, Prvt, 36th Rgt, Virginia Militia, War of 1812 Roster   210

    Fielding, Prvt, Captain Alexander Howison's Company Muster Roll, 36th Rgt,   201
        Virginia Militia, War of 1812
    Fielding, Prvt, 36th Rgt, Virginia Militia, War of 1812 Roster   210

Johnson (See also Johnston)
    Allison, Prvt, 36th Rgt, Virginia Militia, War of 1812 Roster   210

    Dennis M, Prvt, 89th Rgt, Virginia Militia, War of 1812 Roster   218

Index

Johnson (See also Johnston) (Cont.)
    William, Captain, Prince William Minute Battalion, 1775   53
    William, Captain, 11th Virginia Continental Rgt, Revolutionary War   57

Johnston (See also Johnson)
    Allison, Corporal, Captain Alexander Howison's Company Muster Roll, 36th Rgt,   200
        Virginia Militia, War of 1812
    Allison, Prvt, Captain John Linton's Company Muster Roll, Cavalry, 36th Rgt,   204
        Virginia Militia, War of 1812

    Davis, certified as heir at law to Francis Johnston, decd, a revolutionary war soldier,   162
        September 1843 Court

    Francis, decd, a Revolutionary War soldier, heirs at law certified, September 1843 Court   162

    Francis, Captain, 36th Rgt, Virginia Militia, 1806, removed from county   162

    George, certified as heir at law to Francis Johnston, decd, a Revolutionary War soldier,   162
        September 1843 Court

    Moses, soldier in Captain David Bell's Company, Virginia Regiment, French and Indian War   177

    Richard, Prvt, Captain Alexander Howison's Company Muster Roll, 36th Rgt,   201
        Virginia Militia, War of 1812
    Richard, Prvt, 36th Rgt, Virginia Militia, War of 1812 Roster   210
    Ruff, 2 PSCs, Revolutionary War   85

    Thomas, Prvt, Captain Joseph R. Gilbert's Company Muster Roll, 36th Rgt,   198
        Virginia Militia, War of 1812
    Thomas, Prvt, 36th Rgt, Virginia Militia, War of 1812 Roster   210

    William, Prvt, 36th Rgt, Virginia Militia, War of 1812 Roster   210

Jones
    Alexander, Prvt, Captain Thomas W. Ewell's Company, 1 VSR   61
    Alexander, as wounded soldier, May 1783 Court, Revolutionary War   89

    Benjamin, PSC, Revolutionary War   89

    Daniel, Prvt, 36th Rgt, Virginia Militia, War of 1812 Roster   210

    Elizabeth (Carr), d/o John Carr, U.S. Pensioner at time of his death in September 1837,   163
        April 1850 Court

    Fielding, Prvt, 36th Rgt, Virginia Militia, War of 1812 Roster   210

    Gustavus, Prvt, 36th Rgt, Virginia Militia, War of 1812 Roster   210

    John, Prvt, 36th Rgt, Virginia Militia, War of 1812 Roster   210

    Solomon, Soldier in Captain Thomas Waggener's Company, Virginia Rgt, French and   178
        Indian War
    Solomon, 2 PSCs, Revolutionary War   78

Index

Jones (Cont.)
    Starling, Prvt, 36th Rgt, Virginia Militia, War of 1812 Roster   210

    Thomas, Prvt, 36th Rgt, Virginia Militia, War of 1812 Roster   211

Jordan, Jourdan
    James, Corporal, Captain Alexander Howison's Company Muster Roll, 36th Rgt,   200
        Virginia Militia, War of 1812
    James, Corporal, Prvt, 36th Rgt, Virginia Militia, War of 1812 Roster   207
    James, Prvt, Captain Joseph R. Gilbert's Company Muster Roll, 36th Rgt,   198
        Virginia Militia, War of 1812
    James, Prvt, Captain John Merchant's Company Muster Roll, 89th Rgt,   215
        Virginia Militia, War of 1812

Jumonville Glen   17, 21–23, 27

Keach
    James, Prvt, Captain Alexander Howison's Company Muster Roll, 36th Rgt,   203
        Virginia Militia, War of 1812
    James, Prvt, 36th Rgt, Virginia Militia, War of 1812 Roster   211
    James, Prvt, 89th Rgt, Virginia Militia, War of 1812 Roster   218

Keith
    Alexander, 3 PSCs, Revolutionary War   84, notes 90, 87

    James, Prvt, 36th Rgt, Virginia Militia, War of 1812 Roster   211

Kelly
    Henry, Soldier Prince William Militia, deserted June 1757; paid for the time he served,   184
        by legislature in September 1758, French and Indian War

    William, Soldier Prince William Militia, deserted June 1757; paid for the time he served,   184
        by legislature, in September 1758, French and Indian War

Kembler (?)
    Moses, 89th Rgt, Virginia Militia, War of 1812 Roster   218

Kemper
    Henry, Trooper, Prince William Militia, militia claim for service, French and Indian War   185

    Spencer, 36th Rgt, Virginia Militia, War of 1812 Roster   211

    William, Lt, 36th Rgt, Virginia Militia, 1812   109
    William, 36th Rgt, Virginia Militia, War of 1812 Roster   206

Kendall
    Charles, Prvt, 36th Rgt, Virginia Militia, War of 1812 Roster   211

    Francis, Soldier, 3rd Virginia Continental Rgt, Revolutionary War   56
    Francis, Revolutionary War veteran from Prince William who applied for 1818 Pension   139

Kennedy
    John, 36th Rgt, Virginia Militia, War of 1812 Roster   211

Index

Kenner
    George Turberville, Oath as Militia Officer, May 1756 Court, French and Indian War   38

    George, Corporal, Prince William Militia, militia claim for service, French and Indian War   38, note 15, 185

    Howson, commission and oath as Captain, Prince William Militia, French and Indian War   35
    Howson, Captain, Prince William Militia, excuse accepted by Court for not attending Council of War, French and Indian War   39

Kenny
    John, 36th Rgt, Virginia Militia, War of 1812 Roster   210

Kerr
    John, Sgt, 36th Rgt, Virginia Militia, War of 1812 Roster   207

Key
    Francis Scott, Composer Star Spangled Banner at Bombardment of Fort McHenry, War of 1812   108

Keys, Kees
    — [unnamed], Paymaster Acct, 36th Rgt, Virginia Militia, 1806   122

    George, 1813 Patrol Acct, assigned to William S. Colquhoun   119
    George, 1813 Patroller and Prvt, 36th Rgt, Virginia Militia, War of 1812   196
    George, Prvt, Captain Alexander Howison's Company Muster Roll, 36th Rgt, Virginia Militia, War of 1812   202
    George, Prvt, 36th Rgt, Virginia Militia, War of 1812 Roster   210
    George, Prvt, Captain John Merchant's Company Muster Roll, 89th Rgt, Virginia Militia, War of 1812   215

    James, Prvt, Captain Alexander Howison's Company Muster Roll, 36th Rgt, Virginia Militia, War of 1812   201
    James, Prvt, 36th Rgt, Virginia Militia, War of 1812 Roster   210
    James, Captain John Merchant's Company Muster Roll, 89th Rgt, Virginia Militia, War of 1812   215

    John, Prvt, Captain Joseph R. Gilbert's Company Muster Roll, 36th Rgt, Virginia Militia, War of 1812   199

    Robert, in Paymaster Acct, 36th Rgt, Virginia Militia, 1806   122
    Robert, Patrol Acct 1813, assigned to William S. Colquhoun   119
    Robert, Prvt, Captain Joseph R. Gilbert's Company Muster Roll, 36th Rgt, Virginia Militia, War of 1812   198
    Ro[bert], in Paymaster's Acct, 36th Rgt, Virginia Militia, 1806   122

    Sandy, Prvt, Captain Joseph Smith's Company Muster Roll, 36th Rgt, Virginia Militia, War of 1812   205

    Thomas, Patrol Acct 1813, assigned to William S. Colquhoun   119
    Thomas, Patrol Acct 1813, assigned to Benoni Harrison   120

Index

Kincaid, Kincade
    Archibald, Prvt, 36th Rgt, Virginia Militia, War of 1812 Roster   210

    John L, Sgt, 36th Rgt, Virginia Militia, War of 1812 Roster   207

    Thomas, Prvt, 36th Rgt, Virginia Militia, War of 1812 Roster   210

Kincheloe (see also Kinchelow)
    Cornelius, PSC, Revolutionary War   83

    Daniel, Captain, Prince William Militia, May 1762 Court, French and Indian War   41

    Daniel, Lt, 89th Rgt, Virginia Militia, 1804–1806   111
    Daniel, Ensign, Lt, 89th Rgt, Virginia Militia, 1805   116

    Daniel, Prvt, 36th Rgt, Virginia Militia, War of 1812 Roster   210

    John, Captain, 89th Rgt, Virginia Militia, 1804–1806   111
    John, Lt, Captain, 89th Rgt, Virginia Militia, 1805   115–116
    John, Captain, 89th Rgt, Virginia Militia, 1813, resignation of   121

    Robert, Prvt, 36th Rgt, Virginia Militia, War of 1812 Roster   210

    William, Captain, 89th Rgt, Virginia Militia, 1804–1806   111
    William, Lt, Captain, 89th Rgt, Virginia Militia, 1805   115–116

    John, Prvt, Captain Benjamin Tyler's Company Muster Roll, 89th Rgt, Virginia Militia, War of 1812   216

King
    Benjamin, Captain Benjamin Tyler's Company Muster Roll, 89th Rgt, Virginia Militia, War of 1812   216

    Charles W, Prvt, Captain Benjamin Tyler's Company Muster Roll, 89th Rgt, Virginia Militia, War of 1812   216

    Daniel, as assignee of James Smith's 1813 Patrol Acct   119
    Daniel, ass assignee of John Webster's 1813 Patrol Acct   119
    Daniel, Patrol Acct, 1813, assigned to Benoni Harrison   120
    Daniel, 1813 Patroller and Prvt, 36th Rgt, Virginia Militia, War of 1812   196
    Daniel, Prvt, 36th Rgt, Virginia Militia, War of 1812 Roster   210

    Elias, Prvt, Captain John Linton's Company Muster Roll, Cavalry, 36th Rgt, Virginia Militia, War of 1812   204
    Elias, 36th Rgt, Virginia Militia, War of 1812 Roster   210

    Elias Jr, Prvt, 36th Rgt, Virginia Militia, War of 1812 Roster   210

    George, Soldier, 3rd Virginia, Revolutionary War   56
    George, PSC, Revolutionary War   77

    George, Prvt, 36th Rgt, Virginia Militia, War of 1812 Roster   210

    John, 3rd Virginia Continental Rgt, Revolutionary War   56

Index

King (Cont.)
John, s/o Samuel King, in Continental Army, Revolutionary War	64
John, disabled veteran, May 1783 Court, Revolutionary War	89
John, Revolutionary War soldier who applied for a disability pension	144
John, as Revolutionary War soldier who received a state disability pension	144, note 83
John, Prvt, Captain Alexander Howison's Company Muster Roll, 36th Rgt, Virginia Militia, War of 1812	203
John Jr, Prvt, Captain Benjamin Tyler's Company Muster Roll, 89th Rgt, Virginia Militia, War of 1812	216
John, Prvt, 89th Rgt, Virginia Militia, War of 1812 Roster	218
John Sr, Captain Benjamin Tyler's Company Muster Roll, 89th Rgt, Virginia Militia, War of 1812	216
Robert, Colonel, a Maryland representative to Treaty of Lancaster, 1744	12
Samuel, as father of two sons in Continental Army, relief granted, November 1778 Court, Revolutionary War	64
William, as veteran from Prince William who applied for an 1818 Pension	139
William, Prvt, 36th Rgt, Virginia Militia, War of 1812 Roster	210
William, Prvt, Captain John Merchant's Company Muster Roll, 89th Rgt, Virginia Militia, War of 1812	215
William W, Prvt, 89th Rgt, Virginia Militia, War of 1812 Roster	215

King George County, Virginia	219
King George's War	13–14, 16

Kinsey
Solomon, Prvt, 36th Rgt, Virginia Militia, War of 1812 Roster	210

Kirkpatrick
Hugh, Prvt, 36th Rgt, Virginia Militia, War of 1812 Roster	210
John, Prvt, Captain Benjamin Tyler's Company Muster Roll, 89th Rgt, Virginia Militia, War of 1812	216
Thomas, Prvt, 36th Rgt, Virginia Militia, War of 1812 Roster	210
Thomas, Prvt, Captain Benjamin Tyler's Company Muster Roll, 89th Rgt, Virginia Militia, War of 1812	216

Klipstine, Klepstine
Philip, Colonel, 89th Rgt, Virginia Militia, War of 1812	112
Philip, Colonel, 89th Rgt, Virginia Militia, War of 1812 Roster	217

Knox
Henry, helped draw up plan to enlarge artillery after loss of Fort Washington in November 1776, Revolutionary War	60

Index

Koon
    Michael, Prvt, Captain Alexander Howison's Company Muster Roll, 36th Rgt,   201
        Virginia Militia, War of 1812
    Michael, Prvt, 36th Rgt, Virginia Militia, War of 1812 Roster   210

Laid
    William, Patrol Acct 1813, assigned to Mary Ann Cave   119

Lakin
    Benjamin V, Provost General in Major Townsend Dade's Court martial proceedings,   219
        November 1807, from Fauquier County Clerks Loose Papers

Lancaster, Pennsylvania   12

Lancaster, Treaty of, 1744   12, 14, 16

Landrum
    William, PSC, Revolutionary War   77

Landsdown (See also Lansdown, Lansdowne)
    John, Prvt, Captain Joseph R. Gilbert's Company Muster Roll, 36th Rgt,   199
        Virginia Militia, War of 1812

Langfitt (See also Langfelt)
    Henry, Prvt, Captain Alexander Howison's Company Muster Roll, 36th Rgt,   203
        Virginia Militia, War of 1812
    Henry, Prvt, 36th Rgt, Virginia Militia, War of 1812 Roster   210

    Philip, Ensign, 36th Rgt, Virginia Militia, 1812,   110
    Philip, Ensign, 36th Rgt, Virginia Militia, 1813   121
Langfitt (Cont.)
    Philip, Ensign, Captain Alexander Howison's Company Muster Roll, 36th Rgt,   206
        Virginia Militia, War of 1812
    Philip, Ensign, 36th Rgt, Virginia Militia, War of 1812 Roster   206

Langfelt (See also Langfitt)
    Henry, Prvt, Captain Benjamin Tyler's Company Muster Roll, 89th Rgt,   216
        Virginia Militia, War of 1812

Lansdown, Lansdowne (See also Landsdown)
    George, Ensign, 36th Rgt, Virginia Militia, 1812, 1813   110, 119
    George, Ensign, Captain Joseph Smith's Company Muster Roll, 36th Rgt,   204
        Virginia Militia, War of 1812
    George, Ensign, 36th Rgt, Virginia Militia, War of 1812 Roster   206

    John, Prvt, 36th Rgt, Virginia Militia, War of 1812 Roster   210

Lansford
    William, Prvt, 36th Rgt, Virginia Militia, War of 1812 Roster   210

Larkin, Learkin
    Daniel, Ensign, 36th Rgt, Virginia Militia, War of 1812 Roster   206
    Daniel, Prvt, Captain Benjamin Tyler's Company Muster Roll, 89th Rgt,   216
        Virginia Militia, War of 1812

Index

Larkin, Learkin (Cont.)
   William, Prvt, Captain Alexander Howison's Company Muster Roll, 36th Rgt,   203
      Virginia Militia, War of 1812

Lary
   John, Revolutionary War veteran from Prince William who applied for an 1818 Pension   139

Latham
   Daniel, Prvt, 36th Rgt, Virginia Militia, War of 1812 Roster   210

   James, Prvt, 36th Rgt, Virginia Militia, War of 1812 Roster   210

   John, Prvt, 36th Rgt, Virginia Militia, War of 1812 Roster   210

   John, Corporal, 89th Rgt, Virginia Militia, War of 1812 Roster   217

   Jonathan, PSC, Revolutionary War   81

Lattin
   Thomas, Soldier, Captain George Mercer's Company, Virginia Rgt, French and Indian War   178

Lawrence
   Edward, Soldier, Prince William Militia, deserted June 1757, paid for time served,   184
      by legislature in September 1758, French and Indian War

   Peter, Soldier, Prince William Militia, deserted June 1757 paid for time served,   184
      By legislature in September 1758, French and Indian War

Laws, Virginia
   Act to Protect against French encroachment, 1754   18–19

   Military, 1676, 1679, 1680, 1682   4–5

   Militia Acts, 1680, 1682   5
   Militia Act, 101   7
   Militia Act, 1705   8–9
   Militia Acts, 1734, 1740, 1748   11, 13

Lawson
   Archibald, Prvt, Captain Joseph R. Gilbert's Company Muster Roll, 36th Rgt,   199
      Virginia Militia, War of 1812
   Archibald, Prvt, Captain John Merchant's Company Muster Roll, 89th Rgt,   215
      Virginia Militia, War of 1812

   Robert, Receipt for beef as collector, Class 31, July 1781 Court, Revolutionary War   76
   Robert, PSC, Revolutionary War   86

   Thomas, Acct produced to Court for supplies and relief furnished soldier's wives and   70
      children, June 1780 Court, Revolutionary War
   Thomas, Receipts produced for beef and clothing as collector for Class, 32, 33, 34,   76
      July 1781 Court, Revolutionary War
   Thomas, 2 PSCs, Revolutionary War   86

Index

Lawson (Cont.)
    Thomas, Patrol Acct, 1813 — 119
    Thomas, 1813 Patroller and Prvt, 36th Rgt, Virginia Militia, War of 1812 — 196
    Thomas, Prvt, Captain Joseph R. Gilbert's Company Muster Roll, 36th Rgt, Virginia Militia, War of 1812 — 199
    Thomas, Prvt, Sgt, 36th Rgt, Virginia Militia, War of 1812 Roster — 207, 210

Le Mercier, — French Captain, French and Indian War — 22, 26

Leach, (See also Leitch)
    Andrew, Captain 3rd Virginia Continental Rgt, Revolutionary War — 156

    George, Prvt, 36th Rgt, Virginia Militia, War of 1812 Roster — 210

    Thornton K, Prvt, 36th Rgt, Virginia Militia, War of 1812 Roster — 210

    William, 2 PSCs, Revolutionary War — 78, 88

Leachman
    Leonard, Soldier, Prince William Militia, Petition for pay for service, November 1759, French and Indian War — 178
    Leonard, Soldier Prince William Militia, Petition allowed for pay for service, March 1761, French and Indian War — 178

Ledman (?)
    George, 36th Rgt, Virginia Militia, War of 1812 Roster — 210

Lee
    Charles, Captain, Prince William Militia, May 1778 Court, Revolutionary War — 63
    Charles, Captain, Prince William Militia, August 1779 Court, Revolutionary War — 66
    Charles, former Captain, Prince William Militia, May 1780 Court, Revolutionary War — 69

    Charles, exempt from taxes on Negroes Beck, Yellow Moll, and Pickett, June 1805 Court — 115

    David, 3 PSCs, Revolutionary War — 77, 87

    Hancock, Prvt, Sgt, 36th Rgt, Virginia Militia, War of 1812 Roster — 207, 210

    Henry, Oath as County Lt, Prince William Militia, July 1755 Court, French and Indian War — 36
    Henry, Oath certified for receipt for money spent on militia, March 1756 Court, French and Indian War — 37
    Henry, militia claim and House of Delegates service — 37, note 10
    Henry, Colonel, Prince William Militia, French and Indian War, in correspondence from Colonel George Washington to Francis Fauquier, June 1758 — 179, 185
    Henry, Colonel, Prince William Militia, French and Indian War — 180–181
    Henry, Prince William Militia Accts and Schedules, October 1765, French and Indian War — 180
    Henry, Colonel, Prince William Militia, French and Indian War, Biography of — 179–180

    Henry, Captain, Prince William Minute Battalion, 1775 — 54 and note 27
    Henry, Captain, 1st Continental Dragoons, June 1776 — 54, 59 and note 67
    Henry, Colonel, Lee's Legion — 58–59, 94
    Henry, receipts for beef and clothing as collector for Class 29, August 1781 Court, Revolutionary War — 76

Index

Lee (Cont.)

Henry, 2 PSCs, Revolutionary War	57, note 57, 77
Jane, if living, d/o John Wright decd and heir at law to John Wright decd, Revolutionary War soldier, death certified as intestate, August 1835 Court	156
Jane, if living, d/o John Wright decd and heir at law to William Wright decd, Revolutionary War soldier, death certified as intestate, August 1835	156
Jeremiah, Prvt, 89th Rgt, Virginia Militia, War of 1812 Roster	218
John, Lt, Captain, 89th Rgt, Virginia Militia, 1813	121
John, oath as Captain, 89th Rgt, Virginia Militia, 1813	121
John Jr, Ensign, 89th Rgt, Virginia Militia, 1813	121
P.T. T [should be P. R. F, Philip Richard Francis), Captain 3rd Virginia Continental Rgt, Revolutionary War	158, and note 32
Philip Richard Francis, Captain, 3rd Virginia Continental Rgt, Revolutionary War	51, 55–56, note 43, 61 and note 10, 132, 139
Richard, Prvt, Captain Alexander Howison's Company Muster Roll, 36th Rgt, Virginia Militia, War of 1812	202
Richard, Prvt, Captain Richard Weedon's Company Muster Roll, 36th Rgt, Virginia Militia, War of 1812	206
Stephen, Surveyor of Road from Fauquier line to bridge on Slatey Run, June 1767 Court	43
Stephen, Receipts for beef and clothing as collector, Class 17, July 1781 Court, Revolutionary War	75
Stephen, PSC, Revolutionary War	84
Thomas, a representative from Virginia at Treaty of Lancaster, with Iroquois, 1744	12
Thomas Sr, Colonel 89th Rgt, Virginia Militia, 1804–1806	111
Thomas Sr, Colonel, 89th Rgt, Virginia Militia, death of	111, 117

Lee's Legion	58–59

Leitch (See also Leach)

Andrew, Captain, 3rd Virginia Continental Rgt, Revolutionary War	53
Andrew, Captain, 3rd Virginia Continental Rgt, Revolutionary War, death of	56, note 42
Andrew, decd, Inventory and appraisement	68
Andrew, decd	139

Lennox (See also Lenox)

Michael, Prvt, Captain Alexander Howison's Company Muster Roll, 36th Rgt, Virginia Militia, War of 1812	202
Michael, Prvt, 36th Rgt, Virginia Militia, War of 1812 Roster	210

Lenox (See also Lennox)

Charles, Revolutionary War service in 3rd Virginia Continental Rgt,	56
Charles, Court appearance to show wound suffered as soldier in Revolutionary War, August 1779 Court, May 1783 Court	66, 89

Index

Lenox (See also Lennox) (Cont.)
   Charles, as Prvt, Captain John Peyton's Company, 3rd Virginia Continental Rgt,   66, note 19
      Revolutionary War
   Charles, provided disability pension for life, August 1779 Court,   66–67
   Charles, Recognizance for appearance in Court to answer charge of assault on   71
      Lewis Reno, September 1780 Court
   Charles, Indictment for riot, November 1780 Court   73, 74
   Charles, Revolutionary War veteran who applied for a disability pension   139, 142, 144

Leslie
   George W, Prvt, 36th Rgt, Virginia Militia, War of 1812 Roster   210

Lewis
   Andrew, Captain, arrival at Fort Necessity, from Alexandria, June 1754,   24
      French and Indian War
   Andrew, Major, Virginia Rgt, French and Indian War   174, 176, 185

   Mary, as Executrix with David Blackwell as Executor, Zachariah Lewis Estate, summoned   114
      To Court to give counter security for administration of estate, April 1805 Court

   William, Ensign 89th Rgt, Virginia Militia, 1804–1806   111
   William, as resident of Prince William in 1810   111, note 112
   William, Ensign, 89th Rgt, Virginia Militia, 1805   116

   Zachariah decd, on motion of Moses Moss, Court ordered Mary Lewis and David Blackwell   114
      to give counter security for administration of his estate, April 1805 Court

Limbrick
   John, Prvt, 36th Rgt, Virginia Militia, War of 1812 Roster   210

Lindsay (See also Lyndsey)
   George, Captain, 36th Rgt, Virginia Militia, 1805   115

Linebough
   Joseph B, Prvt, Captain Joseph R. Gilbert's Company Muster Roll, 36th Rgt,   199
      Virginia Militia, War of 1812
   Joseph B, Prvt, 36th Rgt, Virginia Militia, War of 1812 Roster   210

Linton
   John, Oath as Captain Prince William Militia, June 1778 Court, Revolutionary War   63
   [John], Captain, Prince William Militia, February 1779 Court, Revolutionary War   65
   John, Captain, Prince William Militia, Resignation of, July 1779 Court,   66
      Revolutionary War
   John, in Grayson's Additional Continental Rgt   58

   John, Captain, 36th Rgt, Virginia Militia, 1812   109
   John, Captain, Cavalry, 36th Rgt, Virginia Militia, Muster Rolls   110–111, 203–204
   John, Captain, Cavalry, 36th Rgt, Virginia Militia, War of 1812   203, 219
   John, Captain, 36th Rgt, Virginia Militia, War of 1812 Roster   206

   Sally, as w/o Henry Taliaferro, death before 1796 certified, July 1833 Court   151–152

   William, Lt, Captain Linton's Company, Prince William Militia, July 1778 Court,   63
      Revolutionary War

Index

Linton (Cont.)
 William, 2nd Lt, Captain Brent's Company, Prince William Militia, February 1779 Court,   65
  Revolutionary War
 William, as Cadet, Ensign, Grayson's Additional Continental Rgt, 1777–1778   58, 65, note 11
 William, Judgment against, as collector for Class 20, May 1783 Court,   91
  Revolutionary War

 William Jr, Ensign, Captain William Brown's Company, Prince William Militia,   77
  March 1782 Court, Revolutionary War

Lithgow
 Alexander, Captain Prince William Militia, replaced Reginald Graham, decd,   77
  March 1782, Revolutionary War
 Alexander, PSC, Revolutionary War   80
 Alexander, one of three ordered to set apart dower of Mary Graham, wid/o Reginald   88
  Graham decd, September 1782 Court
 Alexander, Oath as Justice of Peace and Justice of Oyer and Terminer, March 1783 Court,   89

Little
 Robert, Captain, 89th Rgt, Virginia Militia, 1804–1806   111, 116

Little Meadows, French and Indian War   29–30

Lloyd
 John, Prvt, 36th Rgt, Virginia Militia, War of 1812 Roster   210

 Joseph A, Prvt, 36th Rgt, Virginia Militia, War of 1812 Roster   210

Lockard, Lockhart, Lockett
 Archibald, Soldier, Captain George Mercer's Company, 1st Virginia Rgt,   180
  French and Indian War
 Archibald, proved right to 50 acres bounty land in Kentucky in February 1788 for   180
  Service in 1st Virginia Rgt, French and Indian War; assigned warrant

Lofland
 Lucy (Moore), d/o Hannah Moore, heir at law to Captain Thomas Ransdell, decd, Virginia   161
  Continental line, September 1843 Court

Logstown, Treaty of, 1752   15

Lomax
 Lunsford, a Commissioner ratifying Treaty of Logstown, 1752   15

Long
 Francis, as assignee of John Askins, received bounty land warrant for Askins's service in   170
  French and Indian War, while living in Augusta County, Virginia

Lord
 Judah, Prvt, Sgt, 36th Rgt, Virginia Militia, War of 1812 Roster   207, 210
 Judah, Sgt, Captain Joseph R. Gilbert's Company Muster Roll, 36th Rgt,   197
  Virginia Militia, War of 1812

Loudoun County Virginia Militia   83

Index

Love
Charles, PSC, Revolutionary War	85
John, summoned to Court to shew cause why Thomas Love's lands should not be sold April 1805 Court	114
Lucinda, summoned to Court to shew cause why Thomas Love's lands should not be sold April 1805 Court	114
Philip, summoned to Court to shew cause why Thomas Love's lands should not be sold April 1805 Court	114
Philip, as administrator of Thomas Love, decd, May 1805 Court	114, 115
Philip, Patrol Acct, 1805	116
Samuel, as Sgt, 3rd Virginia Continental Rgt, Revolutionary War	63, note 2; 66, note 16; 139
Samuel, 2nd Lt, Captain Linton's Company, Prince William Militia, July 1778 Revolutionary War	63
Samuel, 1st Lt, Prince William Militia, July 1779 Court, Revolutionary War	66
Samuel, 2 PSCs, Revolutionary War	78,
Samuel Sr, PSC, Revolutionary War	86
Samuel, summoned to Court to shew cause why Thomas Love's lands should not be sold April 1805 Court	114
Thomas, PSC, Revolutionary War	88
Thomas, decd, Administration of Estate granted Philip Love, April 1805 Court	114
Thomas, on Philip Love's motion, Jesse Barron summoned to court to settle his guardian Acct, May 1804 Court	115
William, former Ensign, 89th Rgt, Virginia Militia, 1805, removed from County, Replaced by James Rose Jr, May 1805 Court	116

Loveless
Francis, certified as heir at law to William Wright, decd, soldier in Northwest Army of Revolution, August 1835 Court	156

Low, (See also Lowe)
John, Soldier Prince William Militia, militia claim for service, French and Indian War	185
William, 3 lives lease in Prince William, to James Evans, wife Mary and son Joseph Evans, November 1740	176

Lowe (See also Low)
John, Revolutionary War Pension, February 1839 Court	135, 159
John, as Prvt, Captain Thomas's Company, 3rd Maryland Continental Line, Revolutionary War	159, note 34
John, U.S. Pensioner at time of his death; death in June 1843 leaving no widow or children certified, September 1843 Court	162
John, Pension File S 8859, Revolutionary War	162, See note 45

Index

Lowry
    Francis, husband of Susan (Chapman) Lowy, d/o Carr and Sarah (Thornton) Chapman,   157
        December 1836 Court
    Francis, entitled to 1/3 of another ninth of Captain Thomas W. Ewell's estate   157–158
        December 1836 Court

    Susan (Chapman), w/o Francis Lowry of Fredericksburg, and d/o Carr and Sarah   157
        (Thornton) Chapman, December 1836 Court
    Susan (Chapman), w/o Francis Lowry, appointment of daughter Sarah (Lowry) Southard   158
        as her executrix, December 1836 Court

Lucas
    Anthony, PSC, Revolutionary War   85

Luckett
    Richard, Prvt, 36th Rgt, Virginia Militia, War of 1812 Roster   211
Lunceford
    Benjamin, Prvt, 36th Rgt, Virginia Militia, War of 1812 Roster   211
Lunebough
    Joseph B, Sgt, Captain Alexander Howison's Company, 36th Rgt, Virginia Militia   199
        War of 1812
Luttrell, Luttrel
    John, Trooper, Prince William Militia, militia claim for service   185

    Robert, 3PSCs, Revolutionary War   80, 85

    Samuel, Soldier Prince William Militia, deserted June 1757, and never returned to duty,   184
        French and Indian War

    Simon, Prvt, 36th Rgt, Virginia Militia, War of 1812 Roster   211

Lyder (?)
    Lewis, Prvt, 36th Rgt, Virginia Militia, War of 1812 Roster   211

Lyndsey (See also Lindsey)
    William, PSC, Revolutionary War   84

Lynn, Lynne
    Benson, Patrol Acct, 1813, assigned to Joseph R. Lynn   120

    John, PSC, Revolutionary War   81
    John, Judgment against, as collector, Class 23, June 1783 Court, Revolutionary War   92

    John, Sgt, Captain Alexander Howison's Company, 36th Rgt, Virginia Militia   200
        War of 1812
    John, Sgt, Prvt, 36th Rgt, Virginia Militia, War of 1812 Roster   207, 211

    Joseph, Ensign, 2nd Battn, 36th Rgt, Virginia Militia, 1804   113
    Joseph R, Captain, 36th Rgt, Virginia Militia, 1812   109, and note 69, 219
    Joseph R, Patrol Acct 1813, as assignee of Benson Lynn   120
    Joseph R, Patrol Acct 1813, as assignee of Bernard Botts   120
    Joseph R, Patrol Acct 1813, as assignee of Charles Reno   120
    Joseph R, Patrol Acct 1813, as assignee of James Norman   120
    Joseph R, 1813 patroller and Captain, 36th Rgt, Virginia Militia, War of 1812   196

Index

Lynn, Lynne (Cont.)
    Joseph R, Captain, 36th Rgt, Virginia Militia, Muster Roll   206
    Joseph R, Captain, 36th Rgt, stationed at Fredericksburg, August– September 1814,   219
        War of 1812
    Joseph R, Captain, 36th Rgt, stationed at Mattox Bridge, Virginia, August–September 1814,   219
        War of 1812

    Malinda (Thomas), w/o Leroy W. Lynn, and heir at law to J. Bullitt, Colonel,   164
        Virginia Continental Line, February 1854 Court

    Michael, Soldier Prince William Militia, petition for relief from wounds suffered in   180–181
        engagement with Indians, French and Indian War
    Michael, PSC, Revolutionary War   85

    Moses, Prvt, 36th Rgt, Virginia Militia, War of 1812 Roster   211

    William, 2 PSCs, Revolutionary War   79

Lyon
    Robert, Prvt, 36th Rgt, Virginia Militia, War of 1812 Roster   211

MacAboy, McAboy, Muccaboy
    James, Prvt, Captain John Linton's Company Muster Roll, Cavalry, 36th Rgt,   204
        Virginia Militia, War of 1812
    James, 36th Rgt, Virginia Militia, War of 1812 Roster   211

    Thomas, proved service in 47th British Rgt of Foot, March 1780, discharged as unfit   181
        for duty by Colonel William Russell, French and Indian War

    Thomas, Prvt, 89th Rgt, Virginia Militia, War of 1812 Roster   218

Mack
    William, Prvt, 36th Rgt, Virginia Militia, War of 1812 Roster   211

MacKay
    James, British commissioned Captain whose troops were with Washington's at Fort   24–26
        Fort Necessity, French and Indian War

MacMillon, MacMillion, M'Millon, Maxmillion (See also McMillon, McMillion)
    John, Ensign, Captain Lewis Reno's Company, Prince William Militia, July 1763 Court,   42
        French and Indian War
    John, as trooper, Prince William Militia, militia claim for service, July 1756,   42, note 23; 80, note 71
        French and Indian War
    John, Oath as Prince William Militia officer, September 1767 Court   43

Madden, Maddin
    Scarlett, Commission and oath as Captain, Prince William Militia, January 1762 Court,   40
        French and Indian War
    Scarlett, security for Charles Lenox's appearance in Court on charge of assault on   71
        Lewis Reno, September 1780 Court

Maddox, Maddux, Mattox
    Alexander, Prvt, Captain Thomas Winder Ewell's Company, 1 VSR, Revolutionary War   61

Index

Maddox, Maddux, Mattox (Cont.)

    Alexander, Prvt, Captain Thomas Winder Ewell's Company, 1 VSR, death intestate and heir at law certified, June 1835 Court   155

    George, Prvt, Captain Joseph R. Gilbert's Company Muster Roll, 36th Rgt, Virginia Militia War of 1812   199

    George, Prvt, Captain Alexander Howison's Company Muster Roll, 36th Rgt, Virginia Militia, War of 1812   202

    George, Prvt, Captain Richard Weedon's Company Muster Roll, 36th Rgt, Virginia Militia, War of 1812   206

    George, Prvt, 36^h Rgt, Virginia Militia, War of 1812 Roster   211

    James, s/o Elizabeth Gray, and heir at law to Captain Thomas Ransdell, decd, officer, Virginia Continental Line, September 1843 Court   161

    Margaret E (Gray), d/o Elizabeth Gray and heir at law to Captain Thomas Ransdell, decd, officer, Virginia Continental Line, September 1843 Court   161

    Nat W, s/o Elizabeth Gray and heir at law to Captain Thomas Ransdell, decd, officer, Virginia Continental Line, September 1843 Court   161

    Walter, Prvt, Captain Alexander Howison's Company Muster Roll, 36th Rgt, Virginia Militia, War of 1812   202

    Walter, Prvt, 36th Rgt, Virginia Militia, War of 1812 Roster   211

    William, Prvt, 89th Rgt, Virginia Militia, War of 1812 Roster   218

Madison

    Dolly, w/o James Madison, War of 1812   104, 106

    James, 4th President of United States, War of 1812   101, 104
    James, arrival at Bladensburg, just before battle, War of 1812   106

    William, Brigadier General, Virginia Militia, War of 1812   219

Mahew

    Susannah, CW Indenture to John Crook, October 1778 Court   64

Mallory

    Solomon W, Prvt, 36th Rgt, Virginia Militia, War of 1812 Roster   211

Manuel

    Allen, Prvt, 36th Rgt, Virginia Militia, War of 1812 Roster   211

    John, Prvt, 36th Rgt, Virginia Militia, War of 1812 Roster   211
    John, Prvt, 89th Rgt, Virginia Militia, War of 1812 Roster   218

Margarum, Marjorum

    Henry, PSC, Revolutionary War   83– 84, note 87
    Henry, Captain, Artillery, Colonel Wadsworth Rgt, Revolutionary War   132

Margerum & Moore

    As assignee of George Hill's PSC, March 1782 Court, Revolutionary War   82

Index

Markham
    John, Solider, Prince William Militia; petition for pay as corporal with service in   186
        Prince William Militia, left off militia List, claim allowed by colonial legislature,
        September 1758, French and Indian War

Marlborough, Maryland,   British face resistance at, after landing, War of 1812   106

Marr
    John, Ensign, 36th Rgt, Virginia Militia, 1812   110
    John, Ensign, 36th Rgt, Virginia Militia, War of 1812 Roster   206

Marsh, The Great North   10

Marshall
    Benjamin, Ensign, Lt, 89th Rgt, Virginia Militia, 1813   121

    Jacob, Judgment against as collector for Class 42, May 1783 Court,   92
        Revolutionary War

    Richard, Trooper, Prince William Militia, militia claim for service   185
        French and Indian War

    Thomas, Trooper, Prince William Militia, militia claim for service,   185
        French and Indian War
    Thomas, Colonel, 3rd Virginia Continental Rgt, in Spencer Anderson's 1819   132
        Pension Declaration

    William, security for John Sidebottom's appearance in court to answer charge of   74
        Receiving stolen goods, November 1780 Court, Revolutionary War
Martin
    Clane, Patrol Acct, 1805   117

    Eveline H, heir of John Ransdell and heir at law to Captain Thomas Ransdell, decd,   161
        officer, Virginia Continental Line, September 1843 Court

    Felicia, heir of John Ransdell and heir at law to Captain Thomas Ransdell, decd,   161
        officer, Virginia Continental Line, September 1843 Court

    John, Patrol Acct, French and Indian War   39

    Joseph, heir of John Ransdell and heir at law to Captain Thomas Ransdell, decd,   161
        officer, Virginia Continental Line, September 1843 Court

    Maria, heir of John Ransdell and heir at law to Captain Thomas Ransdell, decd,   161
        officer, Virginia Continental Line, September 1843 Court

    Nancy, heir of John Ransdell and heir at law to Captain Thomas Ransdell, decd,   161
        officer, Virginia Continental Line, September 1843 Court

    William, discharged from paying taxes, March 1782 Court   87

    William C, Prvt, 36th Rgt, Virginia Militia, War of 1812 Roster   211
    William, Corporal, Captain John Merchant's Company Muster Roll, 89th Rgt,   214
        Virginia Militia, War of 1812

Index

Martindale
 Olivia (Ewell), d/o James Ewell decd, certified as heir at law to Colonel Jesse   157
  Ewell, decd, September 1835 Court

Marvel
 Henry, Musician, 36th Rgt, Virginia Militia, War of 1812 Roster   207

Mason
 George, Colonel, to provide supplies for garrison at Neabsco, near the Occoquan, in   5
  Stafford County, November 1679

 George, Colonel, PSC, Revolutionary War   93

 James, Prvt, Captain Alexander Howison's Company Muster Roll, 36th Rgt,   203
  Virginia Militia, War of 1812
 James, Prvt, 36th Rgt, Virginia Militia, War of 1812 Roster   211

 Nelson, Prvt, 36th Rgt, Virginia Militia, War of 1812 Roster   211

 Mason, Prvt, 89th Rgt, Virginia Militia, War of 1812 Roster   218

 Thomas, Prvt, Captain Benjamin Tyler's Company Muster Roll, 89th Rgt,   216
  Virginia Militia, War of 1812

 Thompson, General, in Major Townsend Dade's Court martial proceedings,   219
  November 1807, from Fauquier County Clerks Loose Papers

Massey
 John, Cornet, Paymaster, 1st Continental Dragoons, Revolutionary War   59
 John, as Cornet, Revolutionary War, military land to go to John H and   154
  William D Massey, orphans of Henry Massey, December 1834 Court

 John H, orphan of Henry Massey decd, selected Robert Massey as his guardian,   154
  December 1834 Court
 John H, orphan of Henry Massey decd, entitled to land scrip instead of warrants for   154
  Service of John Massey, a cornet in Revolutionary War

 Robert, chosen by John H and William D Massey, orphans of Henry Massey as their   154
  Guardians, December 1834 Court
 Robert, authorized by Court to sell military land scrip for the benefit of William D and   59, 154
  John H Massey, orphans of Henry Massey

 Thomas, bond given to appear as witness against John Sidebottom indicted for receiving   74
  and purchasing stolen goods, November 1780 Court

 William D, orphan of Henry Massey decd, selected Robert Massey as his guardian,   154
  December 1834 Court
 William D, orphan of Henry Massey decd, entitled to land scrip instead of warrants for   154
  Service of John Massey, a cornet in Revolutionary War

Masters
 Gerrard, Patrol Acct, French and Indian War   39

Index

Matthews
 Griffith, Trooper, Prince William Militia, militia claim for service, French and Indian War   185

 Norman, PSC, Revolutionary War   77

 Richard, Trooper, Prince William Militia, militia claim for service, French and Indian War   185

 Thomas, Patrol Acct, French and Indian War   39

Mattingly
 Dekandra, Revolutionary War Pension Declaration for pension for services of decd husband, John Mattingly, October 1838 Court   137, 158

 John, as soldier in the Revolution, service revealed, October 1838 Court   158, note 31

 John, as soldier in Captain Charles Gallahue's Company, 11th Virginia Continental Line, Revolutionary War   57, note 57

 John, certified as U. S. Pensioner at his death in February 1824, leaving widow Dekandra Mattingly, July 1840 Court   160

Mattox Bridge, Virginia,
 Captain John Brawner, 89th Rgt, marched to, August 1814   219

 Captain Joseph Lynn's Company, 36th Rgt, stationed at, August–September 1814   219

Mauck
 William, Prvt, Captain John Merchant's Company Muster Roll, 89th Rgt, Virginia Militia, War of 1812   206

McBee
 William, Prvt, 36th Rgt, Virginia Militia, War of 1812 Roster   211

McCaughan
 Charles, Ensign, Lt, Infantry 36th Rgt, 1804   113

McClanaham, McClanahan, McClenaham
 Charles, Corporal, 89th Rgt, Virginia Militia, War of 1812 Roster   217

 Thomas, Oath as Captain, Prince William Militia, May 1757 Court, French and Indian War   40
 Thomas, Captain, Prince William Militia, militia acct, French and Indian War   180
 Thomas, Captain, Virginia Rgt, French and Indian War   181
 Thomas, Captain, Virginia Rgt, in schedule attached to October 1765 Prince William Militia Acct, French and Indian War   181
 Thomas, Captain, Virginia Rgt, issued six bounty land warrants for 50 acres each as assignee of five soldiers for their service in French and Indian War   181
 Thomas, Captain, Virginia Regiment, petition to colonial legislature in September 1758 for payment of horse lost on an express to Henry Lee   181

 Thomas, Trumpeter, 89th Rgt, Virginia Militia, War of 1812 Roster   217

 William, Prvt, 36th Rgt, Virginia Militia, War of 1812 Roster   211

McClenachan
 Alexander, Captain, Virginia Rgt, French and Indian War   170

Index

McCormick
    Edmund, Corporal, 36th Rgt, Virginia Militia, War of 1812 Roster   207

    George, as Captain, 13th Virginia Continental Rgt, Revolutionary War   152, note 9

McCoy
    Benjamin, Prvt, 36th Rgt, Virginia Militia, War of 1812 Roster   211

McCuin (See also McCune, McEwen)
    Alexander, Prvt, 36th Rgt, Virginia Militia, War of 1812 Roster   211

    Elias, Prvt, 36th Rgt, Virginia Militia, War of 1812 Roster   211

McCune (See also McCuin, McEwen)
    Patrick, Soldier, Captain Thomas Winder Ewell's Company, 1st VSR   61
    Patrick, Revolutionary War service and pension file   160, note 38

McDaniel
    James, Prvt, Captain Richard Weedon's Company Muster Roll, 36th Rgt,   206
        Virginia Militia, War of 1812
    James, Prvt, 36th Rgt, Virginia Militia, War of 1812 Roster   211

McDonald
    Theodosius, Prvt, 36th Rgt, Virginia Militia, War of 1812 Roster   211

McEwen, McEwin (See also McCune, McCuin, McEwing)
    Alexander, Prvt, 89th Rgt, Virginia Militia, War of 1812 Roster   218

    Mary, certified by Court as d/o Patrick McEwin decd; his death also certified as having   160
        taken place in February 1840, January 1841 Court
    Mary, certified by Court as d/o Patrick McEwin decd; his death also certified as having   160
        taken place in February 1841, leaving two children Mary and William McEwin,
        March 1841 Court

McEwen, McEwin (See also McCune, McCuin, McEwing) (Cont.)
    Patrick, as Prvt, Captain Thomas Ewell's Company, 1st VSR, and pension file   160, note 38
    Patrick, decd, certified by Court as pensioner of U. S. at time of his death in February 1840,   160
        leaving two children, Mary and William McEwin, January 1841 Court
    Patrick, decd, certified by Court a pensioner of U. S. at time of his death in February 1841,   160
        leaving two children, Mary and William McEwin, March 1841 Court

    William, certified by Court as s/o Patrick McEwin decd; Patrick's death certified as having   160
        Taken place in February 1840, January 1841 Court
    William, certified by Court as s/o Patrick McEwin decd; Patrick's death certified as having   160
        Taken place in February 1841, March 1841 Court

McEwing (See also McEwen, McEwin, McCune, McCuin)
    Patrick, affidavit in Elijah Green's Pension Papers for service in 1 VSR   190

McGinnis
    Elizabeth, w/o Peter McGinnis, a soldier in the Continental Army, allowed corn and   72
        pork for support of herself and her two small children, September 1780 Court,
        Revolutionary War

Index

McGinnis (Cont.)
    Peter, soldier in Continental Army   72
    Peter, as Prvt, Captain Thomas Will's Company, 11th, 11th and 15th Virginia Continental Rgt, Revolutionary War   72, note 43

McGuin
    Timothy, Prvt, 36th Rgt, Virginia Militia, War of 1812 Roster   211

McInteer
    William, Lt, 36th Rgt, Virginia Militia, 1812   109
    William, Lt, 36th Rgt, Virginia Militia, War of 1812 Roster   206

McIntosh
    John decd, former Ensign, 36th Rgt, Virginia Militia, 1813   118

    William, as Prvt, Captain Thomas Winder Ewell's Company, 1 VSR   61; 153, note 12
    William, decd, Prvt Captain Thomas Ewell's Company, 1VSR, death certified as Intestate; Court certified Elizabeth Hamil, wid/o John Hamil decd as heir at law, December 1833 Court   153

McJoy
    Travers, in Paymaster's Acct, 36th Rgt, Virginia Militia, 1805   122

McKenzie
    Robert, Captain, Virginia Rgt, French and Indian War   169

McKillup
    Hugh, PSC, Revolutionary War   83

McLean
    Daniel, Prvt, 36th Rgt, Virginia Militia, War of 1812 Roster   211

McLennan
    James, Sgt, 36th Rgt, Virginia Militia, War of 1812 Roster   207

McMahan, McMahon
    Mary, appearance bond to appear before grand jury, to answer complaint against her, September 1780 Court   72
    Maryann, Commonwealth cause against for riot, November 1780 Court   73
    Mary Ann, Commonwealth cause against for riot, she pleaded not guilty, November 1780 Court   73

    Roger, bond for Mary McMahon's appearance in Court to answer charge of riot   73
    Roger, as former Prvt, Captain Charles Gallahue's Company, 11th and 15th Virginia Continental Rgt, Revolutionary War   57; 73, note 44

    Margaret, Commonwealth Cause against her and other for riot; she pleaded not guilty, November 1780 Court   73
    Margaret, appearance bond to appear in Court to answer charge of riot, November 1780 Court   73

Index

McMillan, McMillon, McMillion, Maxmillion (See also Macmillon)
   John, Ensign, Captain Lewis Reno's Company, Prince William Militia, July 1763 Court   42
      French and Indian War

   John, as Trooper, Prince William Militia, militia claim for service,   80, note 71; 185
      French and Indian War
   John, 3 PSCs, Revolutionary War   80, 87

   Seth, PSC, Revolutionary War   80

McMorris
   Thomas, Prvt, 36th Rgt, Virginia Militia, War of 1812 Roster   211

McPherson
   Peter C, Prvt, 36th Rgt, Virginia Militia, War of 1812 Roster   211

McQueen
   Thomas, Prvt, Captain Alexander Howison's Company Muster Roll, 36th Rgt,   202
      Virginia Militia, War of 1812

McRae
   John, in Major Townsend Dade's Court martial proceedings, November 1807,   219
      From Fauquier County Clerks Loose Papers

Melton
   Richard, PSC, Revolutionary War   80

   William, PSC, Revolutionary War   81

Meng
   Charles, as Magistrate, Prince William, in Sarah Florance's pension papers,   158
      December 18383 Court

Mercer
   C. J, Member of House of Representatives, received Elijah Green's Pension Certificate,   191
      Pension to commence in August 1831

   George, Captain, Virginia Rgt, French and Indian War   170-171, 173–174, 183, 187

   Hugh, Colonel, 3rd Virginia Continental Rgt, Revolutionary War   55

   John, Proprietor of Ohio Company, 1747   12

Merchant
   James, Prvt, Captain Joseph R. Gilbert's Company Muster Roll, 36th Rgt,   199
      Virginia Militia, War of 1812
   James, 2nd Corporal, Captain John Merchant's Company Muster Roll, 89th Rgt,   214
      Virginia Militia, War of 1812
   James, Corporal, 36th Rgt, Virginia Militia, War of 1812 Roster   207

   John, Captain, 36th Rgt, Virginia Militia, 1812   109
   John, Captain, 36th Rgt, Virginia Militia, 1813   118
   John, Lt, Captain, 36th Rgt, Virginia Militia, War of 1812 Roster   206
   John, Captain, 89th Rgt, Virginia Militia, 1814   112
   John, Captain, 89th Rgt, Virginia Militia, War of 1812, Muster Rolls   214–215

Index

Merchant (Cont.)
    John, Captain, 89th Rgt, Virginia Militia, company served August and September 1814,   112, 219
        War of 1812

Metcalf
    Robert, Prvt, 36th Rgt, Virginia Militia, War of 1812 Roster   211

Milburn
    Timothy, Prvt, 36th Rgt, Virginia Militia, War of 1812 Roster   211

Militia Acts, U.S.   98, 101

Military Establishment, Amerian, 1798–1814   97–98

Militia Acts, Virginia   98–101

Miller
    John I, Prvt, 36th Rgt, Virginia Militia, War of 1812 Roster   211

    Robert, Sgt, 36th Rgt, Virginia Militia, War of 1812 Roster   207

    Simon, Oath as Prince William Militia Officer, May 1757 Court, French and Indian War   40

Mills
    Elizabeth (Garner), w/o John Dyson Mills, and d/o William Garner, a Revolutionary War   153
        Soldier, certified as his her at law, December 1833 Court

    George, as soldier, Prince William Militia in Revolutionary War,   137, 158, note 30
    George, decd, certified as Revolutionary Pensioner at time of his death, August 1838 Court   158
    George, decd, certified as U. S. Pensioner at time of death in 1838, leaving widow   163
        Lydia and three children, August 1853   163

    John D, Prvt, 36th Rgt, Virginia Militia, War of 1812 Roster   211
    John D, s/o George and Lydia Mills, father was U. S. Pensioner; John was 67 in July, 1853   163

    Lydia, wid/o George Mills, Pension Application, August 1838 Court   137
    Lydia, wid/o George Mills, Revolutionary Pensioner at time of his death; Court certified   158
        marriage previous to 1794, August 1838 Court
    Lydia, decd, wid/o George Mills, death "some years after her husband," certified; she left   163
        3 children, John D, 67; Caty Russell, 64; and Ann Woodyard, 58, August 1853 Court

    Martin, Patrol Acct, 1813   120
    Martin, 1813 Patroller and Prvt, 36th Rgt, Virginia Militia, War of 1812   196

    Ignatius, Prvt, 36th Rgt, Virginia Militia, War of 1812 Roster   211
    Ignatius, Prvt, Captain John Merchant's Company Muster Roll, 89th Rgt,   215
        Virginia Militia, War of 1812

Milstead
    Ignatius, Prvt,
    Ignatius, Prvt, Captain Alexander Howison's Company Muster Roll, 36th Rgt,   202
        Virginia Militia, War of 1812
    Ignatius, Prvt, Captain Richard Weedon's Company Muster Roll, 36th Rgt,   206
        Virginia Militia, War of 1812

Index

Milstead (Cont.)
    Ignatius, Prvt, 36th Rgt, Virginia Militia, War of 1812 Roster   211
    Ignatius, Prvt, Captain John Merchant's Company Muster Roll, 89th Rgt,   215
        Virginia Militia, War of 1812

    Isaac, Patrol Acct, 1805   116
    Isaac, Prvt, 36th Rgt, Virginia Militia, War of 1812 Roster   211

    John Jr, Prvt, Captain Benjamin Tyler's Company Muster Roll, 89th Rgt,   216
        Virginia Militia, War of 1812

    Samuel, Prvt, 36th Rgt, Virginia Militia, War of 1812 Roster   211

Minitree
    Jacob, 2 PSCs, Revolutionary War   81

Minute Battalions
    Military Districts   54
    Prince William   53–54

Mitchell
    Edward, Prvt, Captain Richard Weedon's Company Muster Roll, 36th Rgt,   206
        Virginia Militia, War of 1812
    Edward, Prvt, 36th Rgt, Virginia Militia, War of 1812 Roster   211

    Ignatius, PSC, Revolutionary War   80

    Ignatius, Sgt, Captain Richard Weedon's Company Muster Roll, 36th Rgt,   205
        Virginia Militia, War of 1812
    Ignatius, Sgt, Prvt, 36th Rgt, Virginia Militia, War of 1812 Roster   207, 211

    James, certified as heir at law to William Mitchell, decd, a soldier in Captain   155
        Triplett's Company, Grayson's Additional Continental Rgt, April 1835 Court

    Samuel, Patrol Acct 1813, assigned to Benoni Harrison   119
    Samuel, Prvt, 36th Rgt, Virginia Militia, War of 1812 Roster   211

    William, PSC, Revolutionary War   85
    William, as Prvt, Captain Thomas Triplett's Company, Grayson's Additional   58, note 64
        Continental Rgt, Revolutionary War
    William, decd, Prvt, Captain Thomas Triplett's Company, death intestate and   155
        without issue certified, April 1835 Court
    William decd, soldier in Captain Thomas Triplett's Company, heirs at law certified,   155
        as Catharine Williams and James Mitchell, April 1835 Court

Molair
    Thomas, Corporal, Captain Alexander Howison's Company Muster Roll, 36th Rgt,   207
        Virginia Militia, War of 1812
    Thomas, Corporal, Prvt, 36th Rgt, Virginia Militia, War of 1812 Roster   211

Monceau, — (Canadian militiamen who took the news of Jumonville Glen back to French   21

Index

Moncure
    Thomas, Attorney in fact for heirs at law of Elijah Green; he collected arrears in pension   192
    Due them from September 4, 1832 to January 15, 1833 when Green died

Monday, Munday
    Robert, Prvt, 36th Rgt, Virginia Militia, War of 1812 Roster   211

    William, 2 PSCs, Revolutionary War   82

Money
    Catharine (Dickinson), d/o John Sr and Pricey Dickinson and heir at law to John   160
    Dickinson the Elder, a Revolutionary War soldier, August 1841 Court

Monroe
    James, Secretary of State under President James Madison   106, 108

Montgomerie (See also Montgomery)
    Francis, Captain 89th Rgt, Virginia Militia, 1805, resignation of   115

    Thomas, Sgt Major, 36th Rgt, Virginia Militia, War of 1812 Roster   207

    William, PSC, Revolutionary War   85

Montgomery (See also Montgomerie)
    John, Prvt, 36th Rgt, Virginia Militia, War of 1812 Roster   211

    P, QM Sgt, 89th Rgt, Virginia Militia, War of 1812 Roster   217

    Thomas, Prvt, Captain Joseph R. Gilbert's Company Muster Roll, 36th Rgt,   199
    Virginia Militia, War of 1812
    Thomas, Prvt, Captain Joseph R. Gilbert's Company Muster Roll, 36th Rgt,   199
    Virginia Militia, War of 1812
    Thomas, Sgt Major, 36th Rgt, Virginia Militia, War of 1812   197
    Thomas, Sgt Major, 36th Rgt, Virginia Militia, War of 1812 Roster   207

Moor, Moore
    Charles C, s/o Hannah Moore and heir at law to Captain Thomas Ransdell, decd,   161
    officer, Virginia Continental Line, September 1843 Court

    Daniel, 2 PSCs, Revolutionary War   81–82

    David, Corporal, Captain Joseph R. Gilbert's Company, 36th Rgt, Virginia Militia,   197
    War of 1812
    David, Corporal, 36th Rgt, Virginia Militia, War of 1812 Roster   207

    Hannah, sister and heir at law to Captain Thomas Ransdell, decd, officer,   161
    Virginia Continental Line, September 1843 Court

    Hannah J, d/o Hannah Moore and heir at law to Captain Thomas Ransdell, decd, officer,   161
    Virginia Continental Line, September 1843 Court

    Jesse, CW Indenture of Martin Wingate, s/o Betty and Henry Wingate to Jesse Moore,   43
    June 1769 Court

Index

Moor, Moore (Cont.)
 John, Sgt, 89th Rgt, Virginia Militia, War of 1812 Roster   217

 John W, s/o Hannah More and heir at law to Captain Thomas Ransdell decd, officer   161
  Virginia Continental Line, September 1843 Court

 Margaret, Commonwealth Cause against, for assault on Lewis Reno   71
 Margaret, Commonwealth Cause against, for riot, November 1780 Court   73–74

 Samuel R, s/o Hannah Moore and heir at law to Captain Thomas Ransdell, officer,   161
  Virginia Continental Line, September 1843 Court

 Thomas, Prvt, 36th Rgt, Virginia Militia, War of 1812 Roster   211

 William, Patrol Acct, French and Indian War   40

 William, Patrol Acct 1813, assigned to Mary Ann Cave   119
 William, 1813 Patroller and Prvt, 36th Rgt, Virginia Militia, War of 1812   196
 William, Prvt, Captain Joseph R. Gilbert's Company Muster Roll, 36th Rgt,   199
  Virginia Militia, War of 1812
 William, Prvt, Captain Richard Weedon's Company Muster Roll, 36th Rgt,   206
  Virginia Militia, War of 1812
 William, Prvt, 36th Rgt, Virginia Militia, War of 1812 Roster   212
 William, Prvt, Captain John Merchant's Company Muster Roll, 89th Rgt,   215
  Virginia Militia, War of 1812

 William F, Prvt, Captain Joseph Smith's Company Muster Roll, 36th Rgt,   205
  Virginia Militia, War of 1812

Moredock
 Martin, Prvt, Captain Benjamin Tyler's Company Muster Roll, 89th Rgt,   216
  Virginia Militia, War of 1812

Morehead
 James W, 89th Rgt, Virginia Militia, War of 1812 Roster   218

Morgan
 Daniel, General, American Forces, Revolutionary War   79, and note 65, 79, 83, 133

 John, Soldier, Prince William Militia, Petition to colonial legislature for pay for service,   186
  May 1757, French and Indian War

Morris
 Stephen, Trooper, Prince William Militia, militia claim for service, French and Indian War   185

Morton
 Thomas, 36th Rgt, Virginia Militia, War of 1812 Roster   212

Moseby
 Robert, receipts for clothes and beef as collector for Class 26, July 1781 Court,   76
  Revolutionary War

Mosely
 Robert, PSC, Revolutionary War   84

314

Index

Moss
    Keland, Prvt, 36th Rgt, Virginia Militia, War of 1812 Roster   212

    Moses, receipts for clothes and beef, as collector, Class 18, July 1781 Court,   76
        Revolutionary War
    Moses, PSC, Revolutionary War   81

    Vester, as witness against John Sidebottom, for threatening his and Lewis Reno's lives,   70
        July 1780 Court
    Vester, Bond to appear as witness against John Sidebottom who was indicted for   72, 74
        Receiving and purchasing stolen goods, November 1780 Court
    Vester, PSC, Revolutionary War   85
    Vester, defendant in suit adversus Valentine Peyton, suit abates, plaintiff dead,   88
        September 1782 Court
    Vester, soldier, 3rd Virginia Continental Rgt, spent entire enlistment "sick in Virginia,"   70, note 34; 139
        Revolutionary War

Munk
    John, Soldier, Prince William Militia, Petition to colonial legislature for pay, May 1757,   186
        French and Indian War

Murphy
    Hedgeman, Patrol Acct, 1805   117

    Isaac, Prvt, Captain Joseph R. Gilbert's Company Muster Roll, 36th Rgt,   199
        Virginia Militia, War of 1812
    Isaac, Prvt, Captain Joseph Smith's Company Muster Roll, 36th Rgt,   205
        Virginia Militia, War of 1812
    Isaac, Prvt, 36th Rgt, Virginia Militia, War of 1812 Roster   212
    Leander, Soldier, Captain Gallahue's Company, 11th Virginia Continental Rgt,   57
        Revolutionary War
    Leander (aka Leonard), certified by Court that he was entitled to bounty lands for   68–69
        service in Revolutionary War, May 1780 Court
    Leander (aka Leonard), as Prvt, Captain Gallahue's Company, 11th Virginia Continental   68, note 28
        Rgt, Revolutionary War

    William, granted pay for Thomas Lawson as collector for class 32, 33, 34, July 1781 Court,   76
        Revolutionary War

    William, Prvt, Captain John Merchant's Company Muster Roll, 89th Rgt,   215
        Virginia Militia, War of 1812

Murray
    John, CW Indenture of William Gunyon, s/o John Gunyon decd, a Revolutionary War   74
        soldier, to him, April 1781 Court

    John, Trooper, Prince William Militia, militia claim for service, French and Indian War   185
    John, Trooper, Prince William Militia, Petition to legislature for service as blacksmith,   186
        September 1757; Petition rejected
    John, 2 PSCs, Revolutionary War   80
    John, as Trooper, Prince William Militia, petition for pay as blacksmith, rejected   80, note 70
        by colonial legislature, French and Indian War

Index

Muschett
Frederick, Prvt, 36th Rgt, Virginia Militia, War of 1812 Roster — 212

John M, Captain, Major, 36th Rgt, Virginia Militia, 1804 — 113

Muse
George, American Major, French and Indian War — 24

Nalley, Nalle, Nally
Charles D, Prvt, 89th Rgt, Virginia Militia, War of 1812 Roster — 218

Nantucket, Response to British Raids, War of 1812 — 104

Nash
John, Patrol Acct, 1805 — 116

Neal
Benjamin, Soldier, Prince William Militia, deserted June 1757, pay allowed for time served by legislature, September 1758, French and Indian War — 184

Joseph, Soldier, Prince William Militia, militia claim for service, French and Indian War — 185

George, oath as Prince William Militia officer, May 1753 Court, French and Indian War — 35

Negroes
  Beck, belonging to Charles Lee, levy free — 115

  Boy, unnamed, in Paymaster Acct, 36th Rgt, Virginia Militia, 1805 — 122

  Moses, in Paymaster Acct, 36th Rgt, Virginia Militia, 1806 — 122

  Picket, belonging to Charles Lee, levy free — 115

  Unnamed, in Paymaster Acct, 36th Rgt, Virginia Militia, 1806 — 122

  Yellow Moll, belonging to Charles Lee, levy free — 115

Neile
Charles, PSC, Revolutionary War — 77

Nelson
Thomas, Proprietor of Ohio Company, 1747 — 12

— [Thomas], General, PSC, Revolutionary War — 78
— [Thomas], General, orders for impressments of horses in Francis Floyd's PSC, Revolutionary War — 79
— [Thomas], General, Revolutionary War service detailed — 79, note 66

Thomas, Prvt, Captain Alexander Howison's Company Muster Roll, 36th Rgt, Virginia Militia, War of 1812 — 202
Thomas, Prvt, 36th Rgt, Virginia Militia, War of 1812 Roster — 212
Thomas, Prvt, Captain John Merchant's Company Muster Roll, 89th Rgt, Virginia Militia, War of 1812 — 215

Index

Nelson (Cont.)
    William, Revolutionary War veteran from Prince William who applied for Pension for Revolutionary War services   139

    William, Lt, 36th Rgt, Virginia Militia, 1812   109
    William, as resident of Prince William in 1810   110, note 82
    William, 1st Lt, 36th Rgt, Virginia Militia, War of 1812 Roster   206

Nevil, Nevill (See also Neavill)
    Gabriel, Soldier, Captain George Mercer's Company, French and Indian War   181

    Henry, Soldier, Captain George Mercer's Company, French and Indian War   182
    Henry, proved right to bounty land for service in French and Indian War, In Rockbridge County, Virginia, September 1779.   182

    Joseph, Oath as Prince William Militia officer, March 1755 Court, French and Indian War   36

    Joseph, Trooper, Prince William Militia, militia claim for service, French and Indian War   36, note 3; 185

    Robert, Trooper, Prince William Militia, militia claim for service   185

New Grenada, Porto Bello American capture of   11

Newman
    Albert, Prvt, Captain Benjamin Tyler's Company Muster Roll, 89th Rgt, Virginia Militia, War of 1812   216

    Burkett, Prvt, Captain Benjamin Tyler's Company Muster Roll, 89th Rgt, Virginia Militia, War of 1812   216

    George, Soldier, Lee's Legion   59
    George decd, soldier, Colonel Henry Lee's Legion, died in service; John Posey Newman certified as heir at law, May 1784 Court   94

    John, Judgment against, as collector for class 12, May 1783 Court   90

    John Posey, certified as heir at law to George Newman decd, soldier in Colonel Henry Lee's Legion who died in the service, May 1784 Court   94

    Thomas, Judgment against, as collector for class 22, May 1783 Court   91

    Thomas J, Prvt, Captain John Linton's Company Muster Roll, Cavalry, 36th Rgt, Virginia Militia, War of 1812   204

Nichols
    Hannah S. (Gray), d/o Elizabeth Gray, and heir at law to Captain Thomas Ransdell, officer Virginia Continental Line, September 1843 Court   161

Nimms
    William, Proprietor of Ohio Company, 1747   12

Nixon
    Andrew, Captain, 1st Continental Dragoons   59
    Andrew, decd, Revolutionary War service detailed   161, note 40

Index

Nixon (Cont.)

    Andrew, decd, service as a Captain in Continental Line and death in 1790 intestate, without issue certified; nearest collateral heir at law was Daniel A. Nixon, October 1841 Court   161

    Daniel A, certified as heir at law to Captain Andrew Nixon, officer in Virginia Continental Line, October 1841 Court   161

Ninth (9th) Virginia Continental Rgt, Capture at Germantown, October 1777   61

Norfolk,
    British plan of attack, War of 1812   104
    British Raid on   104
    Militia response   104

Norman

    Clement, Appearance on 1751 List of Taxpayers, Elk Run and vicinity   181
    Clement, Plaintiff in Court suit against Jonathan Gibson, Judgment for plaintiff, March 1756 Court   38
    Clement, as Trooper, Prince William Militia, militia claim for service, French and Indian War   38, note 13; 185
    Clement, Trooper Prince William Militia, reimbursed by legislature for paying Doctor for attending his son, who was shot and died in service, March 1760, French and Indian War   182
    Clement, allowed pay in tobacco in 1796 for service as a trooper, French and Indian War   182

    Daniel, Prvt, 89th Rgt, Virginia Militia, War of 1812 Roster   218

    Edward, Patrol Acct, 1813   120
    Edward, 1813 Patroller and Prvt, 36th Rgt, Virginia Militia, War of 1812   196
    Edward, Prvt, Captain Joseph Smith's Company Muster Roll, 36th Rgt, Virginia Militia, War of 1812   205
    Edward, Prvt, 36th Rgt, Virginia Militia, War of 1812 Roster   212

    George, Prvt, Captain Alexander Howison's Company Muster Roll, 36th Rgt, Virginia Militia, War of 1812   202
    George, Sgt, Captain John Linton's Company Muster Roll, Cavalry, 36th Rgt, Virginia Militia, War of 1812   203
    George, Prvt, Sgt, 36th Rgt, Virginia Militia, War of 1812 Roster   207, 212

    James, Patrol Acct 1813, assigned to Joseph R. Lynn   120
    James 1813 Patroller and Prvt, 36th Rgt, War of 1812   196
    James, Prvt, 36th Rgt, Virginia Militia, War of 1812 Roster   212

    Thomas, PSC, Revolutionary War   86

    William, Patrol Acct, 1805   117

North Point, Battle of, War of 1812   108

Northern Neck, Virginia, Prince William Militia called out to assist in defense of, Summer of 1814, War of 1812   219

Index

Norvell (See also Norville)
   Peyton, Fife Major, 36th Rgt, Virginia Militia, War of 1812   197
   Peyton, Surgeon's Mate, 36th Rgt, Virginia Militia, War of 1812   197

   Washington H, Affidavit in John Lowe's Revolutionary War pension papers,   159
      February 1839 Court

Norville (See also Norvell)
   Peyton, Sgt Major, Forage Master, 36th Rgt, Virginia Militia War of 1812 Roster   207

Obannion, (See also Obannon)
   Elias, Captain, 89th Rgt, Virginia Militia, 1804–1806   111
   Elias, as resident of Prince William in 1810   111, note 107

Obannon (See also Obannion)
   Alexander, Corporal, 36th Rgt, Virginia Militia, War of 1812 Roster   207

   Elias, Captain, 2nd Battn, 89th Rgt, Virginia Militia, 1806   117

   John, Captain, in Major Townsend Dade's Court martial proceedings, November 1807   219
      From Fauquier County Clerks Loose Papers

   William, Captain, 36th Rgt, Virginia Militia, 1812   109
   William, as resident of Fauquier County in 1810   109, note 71
   William, Captain, 36th Rgt, Virginia Militia, War of 1812 Roster   206
   William, Captain, 36th Rgt, Virginia Militia, receipt for Camp Equipment, May 1815   220
      From Fauquier County Clerks Loose Papers

OCain
   Thornton, Prvt, 36th Rgt, Virginia Militia, War of 1812 Roster   212

Oden
   Lewis, Soldier, Prince William Militia, militia claim for service, French and Indian War   185

Ogden
   Charles, Prvt, 36th Rgt, Virginia Militia, War of 1812 Roster   212

Ohio Company   12–15, 34

Ohio Valley   15

Oliver
   Heaven (?) Prvt 36th Rgt, Virginia Militia, War of 1812 Roster   211

   Leonard, Prvt, 89th Rgt, Virginia Militia, War of 1812 Roster   218

ONeal
   Edward, Soldier, Prince William Militia, militia claim for service, French and Indian War   185

Orchard
   Anthony, Soldier Prince William Militia, deserted in June 1757, pay allowed by legislature   184
      for time served, September 1758, French and Indian War

Index

ORear
    Daniel, Pension Declaration noted in Prince William Court Minutes, April 1846 Court   135
    Daniel, Revolutionary War Pension Declaration, August 1846 Court   162
    Daniel, Pension File S 7376   162, in note 46

    Enoch, as Major, 36th Rgt's commanding officer, May 1809, War of 1812   212, 219
    Enoch, Major, 36th Rgt, took charge of Captain John Brawner's Company and marched   219
        To Round Hill Church, War of 1812

    John, PSC, Revolutionary War   85

    — [unnamed], in Paymaster's Acct, 36th Rgt, Virginia Militia, 1806   122

Orme
    William, Aide de Camp to Major General Edward Braddock, French and Indian War   29

Orphans, Prince William Soldiers
    To be bound out by Churchwardens if widows are unable to support   69

Overall
    Nathaniel, Oath as Prince William Militia officer, May 1756 Court, French and Indian War   38
    Nathaniel, as trooper, militia claim for service   38, note 14; 185
    Nathaniel, Patrol Acct, French and Indian War   39
    Nathaniel, Presentment against, for living in adultery with Charity Higgins   41

    Robert, Captain, Prince William Militia, to replace William Brent, who resigned,   92
        June 1783 Court, Revolutionary War

Owens
    Eliza, certified as heir at law to George Stubblefield, decd, Ensign in Virginia Continental   162
        Line, September 1843 Court

Owens (Cont.)
    Josiah, Prvt, 36th Rgt, Virginia Militia, War of 1812 Roster   211

Page
    Mann, PSC, Revolutionary War   87

    Thomas, Paymaster Acct, 36th Rgt, Virginia Militia, 1805–1807   121–123

Pair
    William, Prvt, 36th Rgt, Virginia Militia, War of 1812 Roster   211

Palmer
    Joseph, Prvt, 36th Rgt, Virginia Militia, War of 1812 Roster   211

Parker
    Richard, Colonel, Virginia Militia, War of 1812   219

    William S, Prvt, Captain Alexander Howison's Company Muster Roll, 36th Rgt,   200
        Virginia Militia, War of 1812

Parmer
    Thomas, Prvt, 36th Rgt, Virginia Militia, War of 1812 Roster   211

Index

Parr
    William, Prvt, 36th Rgt, Virginia Militia, War of 1812 Roster   211

Parsons
    David, Soldier, Prince William Militia, militia claim for service, French and Indian War   185
    David, Soldier, Prince William Militia, petition to legislature for pay for service, May 1756, French and Indian War   186

Patent Office, District of Columbia, saved from destruction by British by William Thornton, War of 1812   108

Patrols, Slaves, Explanation of   195–196

Patterson (See also Pattison)
    Jesse, Patrol Acct, 1813, assigned to Benoni Harrison   120

    John, Prvt, Captain Alexander Howison's Company Muster Roll, 36th Rgt, Virginia Militia, War of 1812   202

    William, Prvt, Captain John Linton's Company Muster Roll, Cavalry, 36th Rgt, Virginia Militia, War of 1812   204
    William, Prvt, Captain Joseph R. Gilbert's Company Muster Roll, 36th Rgt, Virginia Militia, War of 1812   199

    William Jr, Prvt, Captain Alexander Howison's Company Muster Roll, 36th Rgt, Virginia Militia, War of 1812   202

    William Sr, Prvt, Captain Alexander Howison's Company Muster Roll, 36th Rgt, Virginia Militia, War of 1812   202

Pattison (See also Patterson)
    Aaron, Prvt, 36th Rgt, Virginia Militia, War of 1812 Roster   211

    Alexander, Prvt, 36th Rgt, Virginia Militia, War of 1812 Roster   211
    Alexander, Prvt, Captain John Merchant's Company Muster Roll, 89th Rgt, Virginia Militia, War of 1812   215

    John, Prvt, Captain John Merchant's Company Muster Roll, 89th Rgt, Virginia Militia, War of 1812   215

    John Jr, Prvt, 36th Rgt, Virginia Militia, War of 1812 Roster   211

    William Jr, Prvt, 36th Rgt, Virginia Militia, War of 1812 Roster   211

    William Sr, Prvt, 36th Rgt, Virginia Militia, War of 1812 Roster   211

Patton
    James, Commissioner ratifying Treaty of Logstown, 1752   16

    Larkin, Prvt, 36th Rgt, Virginia Militia, War of 1812 Roster   211

Patuxent River, British operations of, in War of 1812   104

Index

Payne
    Benjamin, Prvt, 36th Rgt, Virginia Militia, War of 1812 Roster   211

    Henry, Ensign, Lt, 89th Rgt, Virginia Militia, 1813   121
    H. R, Lt, Captain Benjamin Tyler's Company Muster Roll, 89th Rgt,   215
        Virginia Militia, War of 1812

    John, Prvt, 36th Rgt, Virginia Militia, War of 1812 Roster   211
    John, Prvt, Captain John Merchant's Company Muster Roll, 89th Rgt,   215
        Virginia Militia, War of 1812

    Lewis, Prvt, 36th Rgt, Virginia Militia, War of 1812 Roster   211

    Richard, Prvt, Captain Alexander Howison's Company Muster Roll, 36th Rgt,   203
        Virginia Militia, War of 1812
    Richard, Prvt, 36th Rgt, Virginia Militia, War of 1812 Roster   211

    Sanford, Prvt, 36th Rgt, Virginia Militia, War of 1812 Roster   211

    Travis, Prvt, Captain Alexander Howison's Company Muster Roll, 36th Rgt,   202
        Virginia Militia, War of 1812
    Travis, Prvt, 36th Rgt, Virginia Militia, War of 1812 Roster   211
    Travis, Prvt, Captain John Merchant's Company Muster Roll, 89th Rgt,   215
        Virginia Militia, War of 1812

    William, Levy free, October 1805   116
    William, as possible Captain, 1 VSR, Revolutionary War   116, note 13

    William, Prvt, 36th Rgt, Virginia Militia, War of 1812 Roster   211

Peachy
    Samuel, Captain, Prince William Militia, Resignation of, May 1778 Court,   63
        Revolutionary War

Peak, Peake
    Craven, Prvt, 36th Rgt, Virginia Militia, War of 1812 Roster   211

    James, Oath as Ensign, Captain Charles Lee's Company, Prince William Militia,   66
        July 1779 Court, Revolutionary War

    Lloyd, Prvt, 36th Rgt, Virginia Militia, War of 1812 Roster   211

    William, Trooper, Prince William Militia, militia claim for service, French and Indian War   185

Pearl
    George, recruiting officer, Revolutionary War, proved service of Hugh Davis   94

Pearsall
    Job, owned plantation where Fort Pearsall was built in 1756, French and Indian War   184

    John, owned plantation where Fort Pearsall was built in 1756, French and Indian War   184

Index

Pearson, Person (See also Pierson)
    Asa, Prvt, 36th Rgt, Virginia Militia, War of 1812 Roster   211

    Cumberland, Prvt, Captain Joseph Smith's Company Muster Roll, 36th Rgt,   205
        Virginia Militia, War of 1812
    Cumberland, Prvt, 36th Rgt, Virginia Militia, War of 1812 Roster   211

    George, Prvt, Captain Joseph Smith's Company Muster Roll, 36th Rgt,   205
        Virginia Militia, War of 1812
    George, Prvt, 36th Rgt, Virginia Militia, War of 1812 Roster   211

    John, Prvt, 36th Rgt, Virginia Militia, War of 1812 Roster   211

    Thomas, Prvt, Captain Alexander Howison's Company Muster Roll, 36th Rgt,   202
        Virginia Militia, War of 1812
    Thomas, Prvt, 36th Rgt, Virginia Militia, War of 1812 Roster   211

    Watson, Captain Joseph Smith's Company Muster Roll, 36th Rgt,   205
        Virginia Militia, War of 1812
    Watson, Prvt, 36th Rgt, Virginia Militia, War of 1812 Roster   211

    Whittington, Prvt, 36th Rgt, Virginia Militia, War of 1812 Roster   211

    William, Prvt, 36th Rgt, Virginia Militia, War of 1812 Roster   211

Pell
    Richard, Prvt, Captain Alexander Howison's Company Muster Roll, 36th Rgt,   202
        Virginia Militia, War of 1812
    Richard, Prvt, 36th Rgt, Virginia Militia, War of 1812 Roster   211

Penquite
    Abraham, Sgt, 89th Rgt, Virginia Militia, War of 1812 Roster   217

    John, Prvt, 36th Rgt, Virginia Militia, War of 1812 Roster   211

Pension Acts, Congressional
    Congressional, for disability   130
    Congressional, Consolidated Pension Act, April 1806   130–131
    Congressional, War of 1812 Pensions   131
    Congressional, War of 1812 relief for widows and orphans   136
    Congressional, Need-based for Continental Line soldiers, 1818   131–133
    Congressional, Need-based for Continental Line soldiers, 1823   134
    Congressional, for Officers and Soldiers, Revolutionary War, 1828   136–137
    Congressional, for General Service, Revolutionary War, June 1832   134–135
    Congressional, Indian War acts for relief of widows and orphans,   136
    Congressional, for Revolutionary War widows and Orphans, 1836   137
    Congressional, for Revolutionary War widows and orphans, 1838–1848   137–138
    Congressional, Pension Act of 1848 and 1853   150
    Congressional, Act of 1853 for relief of widows and orphans   150

Pension Acts, Continental Congress Legislation   128–130
    Continental, National Pension Act, August 1776   128
    Continental, for Officers and Supernumeraries, 1778–1780   129

Index

Pension Acts, Continental Congress Legislation (Cont.)	
Continental, Revolutionary War Legislation for relief of officers, widows and orphans, 1778–1780	135–136
Continental, Disability, April 1782	129
Continental, Commutation Act, March 1783	129
Continental, Disabled Veterans Pension Act, June 1785	129–130
Continental, Invalid, April 1782	129
Pension Acts, Virginia	141–142
Virginia, Pension Act, October 1782	143–144
Virginia, Pension Act, October 1784	144
Virginia, Pension Acts to extend and amend relief, 1784–1786	144–145
Virginia, Pension Act, October 1785	145–146
Virginia, Pension Act, October 1786	146

Petty

Eli, Prvt, 36th Rgt, Virginia Militia, War of 1812 Roster	211
Hough, Prvt, 36th Rgt, Virginia Militia, War of 1812 Roster	211
Hugh, Prvt, Captain Alexander Howison's Company Muster Roll, 36th Rgt, Virginia Militia, War of 1812	202
Hugh, Prvt, Captain John Merchant's Company Muster Roll, 89th Rgt, Virginia Militia, War of 1812	215
Jesse, Patrol Acct, 1805	116
Joseph, PSC, Revolutionary War	81
Travis, Prvt, 89th Rgt, Virginia Militia, War of 1812 Roster	218
William, Prvt, 89th Rgt, Virginia Militia, War of 1812 Roster	218

Peyton

Burr, Judgment against, as collector, class 11, May 1783 Court, Revolutionary War	90
George decd, as Ensign, 3rd Virginia Continental Rgt, Revolutionary War	56
George decd, right to bounty land for Revolutionary War service claimed by heir at law Valentine Peyton, August 1783 Court	93
George decd, Revolutionary War service detailed	93, note 104
George decd, death in 1777 while in Continental service certified by Court, August 1783	93, 149
Henry, Oath as Prince William Militia officer, June 1753, French and Indian War	35
Henry, Lt Colonel, Prince William Militia, French and Indian War	50
Henry, decd, Inventory and appraisement ordered by Court, August 1781 Court	76
Henry decd, Estate, Judgment against by Evan Williams, Bursar Prince William, for fines imposed by Court martials and placed in Peyton's hands for collection, May 1783 Court	89
Henry, Lt Colonel, Prince William Militia, French and Indian War, biography of	182–183
Henry, Correspondence with Colonel George Washington, May and June 1756 and June 1757	183
John, Captain, 3rd Virginia Continental Rgt, Revolutionary War	56
John H, Captain, Cavalry, 36th Rgt, Virginia Militia, 1805	116

Index

Peyton (Cont.)

Margaret, Mrs, PSC, Revolutionary War	82
Robert, orphan of Valentine Peyton, decd, chose Benjamin Rush as his guardian, November, 1762 Court	42
Robert, as Ensign, Lt, Captain John Peyton's Company, 3rd Virginia Continental Rgt, Revolutionary War	42, note 21
Robert decd, death in 1777 and heirs at law certified, August 1783 Court	93, 149
Robert decd, Revolutionary War service detailed	93, note 105
Seth, PSC, Revolutionary War	87
Timothy, administration of Valentine Peyton decd estate granted to him, September 1782 Court	87
Valentine Peyton, decd, his orphan Robert Peyton chose Benjamin Rush as his Guardian, November 1762 Court	42
Valentine, as Captain, 3rd Virginia Continental Rgt, Revolutionary War, died at Siege of Charleston, June 1780	56; 87, note 93
Valentine, as officer, 3rd Virginia Continental Rgt, Revolutionary War	139
Valentine decd, Administration of estate granted to Timothy Peyton, September 1782 Court	86
Valentine, Plaintiff in Court suit versus Vester Moss; suit abates, Plaintiff dead, September 1782 Court	88
Valentine, Order to by Court to appraise and inventory estate of Henry Peyton decd, August 1781 Court	76
Valentine, as former 1st Lt, Captain John Peyton's Company, 3rd Virginia Continental Regiment, Revolutionary War	76, note 54
Valentine, PSC, Revolutionary War	87
Valentine, Judgment against, as collector, class 13, May 1783 Court	90
Valentine, Oath as Justice of Peace and Justice of Court of Oyer and Terminer, May 1783 Court	92
Valentine, certified as heir at law to George Peyton, decd, Ensign, 3rd Virginia Continental Rgt, Revolutionary War, August 1783 Court	93
Valentine, claimed bounty land rights of George Peyton decd, as Ensign, 3rd Virginia Continental Rgt, Revolutionary War, August 1783 Court	93
Valentine, certified as heir at law to Robert Peyton decd, Lt, 3rd Virginia Continental Rgt, Revolutionary War, August 1783 Court	93
Valentine, claimed bounty land rights of Robert Peyton decd, as Lt, 3rd Virginia Continental Rgt, Revolutionary War, August 1783 Court	93
Valentine, as officer (Lt), 3rd Virginia Continental Rgt, Revolutionary War	139

Philbrick

Patton, Patrol Acct, 1813	119

Phillips, Phillip

John S, Prvt, 36th Rgt, Virginia Militia, War of 1812 Roster	211
Silem (?), Corporal, 36th Rgt, Virginia Militia, War of 1812 Roster	207

Index

Phillips, Phillip (Cont.)
    William, Prvt, Captain Alexander Howison's Company Muster Roll, 36th Rgt,   200
        Virginia Militia, War of 1812
    William, Corporal, Prvt, 36th Rgt, Virginia Militia, War of 1812 Roster   207, 211
    William, Prvt, Captain Joseph R. Gilbert's Company Muster Roll, 36th Rgt,   199
        Virginia Militia, War of 1812
    William, Prvt, Captain John Merchant's Company Muster Roll, 89th Rgt,   215
        Virginia Militia, War of 1812

Pickens
    Andrew, General, led expedition against Cherokees, Revolutionary War   59

Pierce
    Gavin/Garvan, Patrol Acct, French and Indian War   39

    Jacob, Garoon, PSC, Revolutionary War   79

    Peter, Trooper, Prince William Militia, militia claim for service, French and Indian War   185

Pierson (See also Pearson)
    Ace (Asa?) Prvt, Captain John Merchant's Company Muster Roll, 89th Rgt,   215
        Virginia Militia, War of 1812

    George, Prvt, Captain John Merchant's Company Muster Roll, 89th Rgt,   215
        Virginia Militia, War of 1812

    William, Prvt, Captain Alexander Howison's Company Muster Roll, 36th Rgt,   202
        Virginia Militia, War of 1812

Pilcher
    Jesse, Prvt, Captain Alexander Howison's Company Muster Roll, 36th Rgt,   202
        Virginia Militia, War of 1812
Pilcher (Cont.)
    Jesse, Prvt, 36th Rgt, Virginia Militia, War of 1812 Roster   211

    John, Patrol Acct, 1805   116
    John, 1805 Patroller and Prvt, 36th Rgt, Virginia Militia, War of 1812   196
    John, 36th Rgt, Virginia Militia, War of 1812 Roster   212

    Moses, Patrol Acct 1813, assigned to Mary Ann Cave   119
    Moses, 1813 Patroller and Prvt, 36th Rgt, Virginia Militia, War of 1812   196
    Moses, Prvt, 36th Rgt, Virginia Militia, War of 1812 Roster   212
Pinson
    Cumberland, Prvt, Captain Alexander Howison's Company Muster Roll, 36th Rgt,   202
        Virginia Militia, War of 1812

    John, Prvt, Captain Alexander Howison's Company Muster Roll, 36th Rgt,   202
        Virginia Militia, War of 1812

Plant
    John, Prvt, 36th Rgt, Virginia Militia, War of 1812 Roster   212

Index

Pope
Humphrey, Prvt, 36th Rgt, Virginia Militia, War of 1812 Roster — 212

John, Corporal, Captain George Mercer's Company, Virginia Rgt, French and Indian War — 183, 79, note 67

John, as collector of hats and overalls, class 38, July 1781 Court, Revolutionary War — 76
John, PSC, Revolutionary War — 79

John, Prvt, 36th Rgt, Virginia Militia, War of 1812 Roster — 212

Porter
Samuel, Corporal, Prince William Militia, militia claim for service — 185

Posey
Ashford, Prvt, 36th Rgt, Virginia Militia, War of 1812 Roster — 212
Ashford, Prvt, Captain John Merchant's Company Muster Roll, 89th Rgt, Virginia Militia, War of 1812 — 215

Potes (?)
Valentine, Sgt, 36th Rgt, Virginia Militia, War of 1812 Roster — 207

Powell
John, Revolutionary War Pension Declaration, 1818 — 133

John, Prvt, 89th Rgt, Virginia Militia, War of 1812 Roster — 218

Levin, Major, Replaced John Quarles as commanding officer of Prince William Minute Battalion, March 1776, Revolutionary War — 54

Lucy, heir of John Ransdell decd and certified as heir at law to Captain Thomas Ransdell, officer, Virginia Continental Line, September 1843 Court — 161

William, Ordered by Court to appraise and inventory estate of Valentine Peyton, decd, September 1782 Court — 88

Powers
Mary S. (Jensen), d/o George and Elizabeth (Bowne) Jansen, certified as heir at law to Thomas Bowne decd, Captain, Continental Line, March 1839 Court — 159

Priest
John, Soldier, Prince William Militia, deserted June 1757; pay allowed by legislature for time served, September 1758 — 184

Primm
William, Prvt, 36th Rgt, Virginia Militia, War of 1812 Roster — 212

Prince William County
Independent Company, — 51

Militia, in French and Indian War — 49, 184
Militia, Incident in May 1756, French and Indian War — 179
Militia, French and Indian War, Problems with — 183
Militia Claims, French and Indian War — 185–186
Militia Petitions, French and Indian War — 186

Index

Prince William County (Cont.)
    Militia, in Revolutionary War PSCs   86
    Militia, Patrols 1804–1806   195–196
    Militia, called out to assist in defense of Northern Neck, summer of 1814   219

Prince William County Court
    Furnishing clothing and other articles for Revolutionary War soldiers by classes   75–77
    Furnishing clothing etc by classes, explanation   75, note 49

Pritchett
    Lewis, Patrol Acct, French and Indian War   39

Prosser
    John H, Lt, 36th Rgt, Virginia Militia, War of 1812 Roster   206

Purcell
    Charles, summoned to Court to shew why he should not be removed as a Constable October 1804 Court   113

    George, as Ensign Captain George McCormick's Company, 11th and 13th Virginia Continental Rgt, Revolutionary War   58; 73, note 46
    George, as security for John Sidebottom's appearance in Court on charge of riot, November 1780 Court   73
    George, as security for John Sidebottom's appearance in Court on charge of buying and receiving stolen goods, November 1780 Court   74
    George, as assignee of Samuel Jackson's PSC, Revolutionary War   82
    George, Revolutionary War service and Pension application detailed   82, note 79

    Hugh, Prvt, 36th Rgt, Virginia Militia, War of 1812 Roster   212

    Samuel, Prvt, 89th Rgt, Virginia Militia, War of 1812 Roster   218

    William, Soldier, Prince William Militia, petition to legislature for payment as an Express rider; Petition allowed, November 1762, French and Indian War   186

Purnell
    Barnaby, Prvt, 36th Rgt, Virginia Militia, War of 1812 Roster   212

    Francis, Corporal, Captain Joseph R. Gilbert's Company Muster Roll, 36th Rgt, Virginia Militia, War of 1812   197
    Francis, Corporal, Prvt, 36th Rgt, Virginia Militia, War of 1812 Roster   208, 212

    William, Fife Major, 36th Rgt, Virginia Militia, 1812   110, 196
    William, in Paymaster Acct, 36th Rgt, Virginia Militia, 1806–1807   122
    William, Prvt, Captain Alexander Howison's Company Muster Roll, 36th Rgt, Virginia Militia, War of 1812   202
    William, Musician, Fife Major, 36th Rgt, Virginia Militia, War of 1812 Roster   207

Quarles
    John, Colonel, Replaced William Grayson, Prince William Minute Battalion, Revolutionary War   54

Queen Ann's War   7–8

Index

Quisenberry
   George, Prvt, 36th Rgt, Virginia Militia, War of 1812 Roster — 212

   John, Prvt, 36th Rgt, Virginia Militia, War of 1812 Roster — 212

Ragans
   John, Prvt, 36th Rgt, Virginia Militia, War of 1812 Roster — 212

Rakestraw
   Joseph, Corporal, 36th Rgt, Virginia Militia, War of 1812 Roster — 208

Ralls
   Alexander P, Prvt, Captain Joseph R. Gilbert's Company Muster Roll, 36th Rgt, Virginia Militia, War of 1812 — 199

   Alexander P, Prvt, 36th Rgt, Virginia Militia, War of 1812 Roster — 212

   Charles, Prvt, 36th Rgt, Virginia Militia, War of 1812 Roster — 212

Ramey, Ramie
   Cada, soldier in Continental Army, Revolutionary War — 67

   David, Prvt, Captain Alexander Howison's Company Muster Roll, 36th Rgt, Virginia Militia, War of 1812 — 203

   David, Prvt, 36th Rgt, Virginia Militia, War of 1812 Roster — 212
   David, Prvt, Captain Benjamin Tyler's Company Muster Roll, 89th Rgt, Virginia Militia, War of 1812 — 216

   Thomas, PSC, Revolutionary War — 87

Randall
   Augustus, Prvt, 36th Rgt, Virginia Militia, War of 1812 Roster — 212

Randolph
   Ann, Commonwealth cause against, for assault on Lewis Reno, September 1780 Court — 71
   Ann, Commonwealth cause against, for riot, November 1780 Court — 73–74

   John, 2 Patrol Accts, French and Indian War — 37, 39

   John, as Soldier, Captain John Peyton's Company, 3rd Virginia Continental Rgt, Revolutionary War — 70, note 35

   John, bond for John Sidebottom's good behavior, July 1780 Court — 70
   John, as probable husband of Ann Randolph, a former 3rd Virginia soldier in Captain John Peyton's 3rd Virginia Continental Rgt, Revolutionary War — 56; 71, note 38
   John, 2 PSCs — 82
   John, Commonwealth Cause against, Prosecution discontinued, July 1783 Court — 93

   — [unnamed], in Paymasters Acct, 36th Rgt, Virginia Militia, 1805 — 122

Ransdell, Randall
   Agnes, d/o Chilton Ransdell, certified as heir at law to Thomas Ransdell decd, Captain, Virginia Continental Line, September 1843 Court — 161

   Benjamin T, heir of John Ransdell decd and certified as heir at law to Thomas Ransdell, decd, Captain, Virginia Continental Line, September 1843 Court — 161

Index

Ransdell, Ransdall (Cont.)
    Chilton, brother to Thomas Ransdell and certified as heir at law to Thomas Ransdell,   161
        decd, Captain, Virginia Continental Line, September 1843 Court

    Horace, s/o Chilton Ransdell and certified as heir at law to Thomas Ransdell decd ,   161
        Captain, Virginia Continental Line, September 1843 Court

    John, brother and heir at law to Thomas Ransdell decd, Captain, Virginia Continental   161
        Line, September 1843 Court

    John, s/o Captain Thomas Ransdell decd, Virginia Continental Line, death intestate,   161
        without issue, certified, September 1843 Court

    John, as only s/o Stephen Ransdell, September 1843 Court   161

    John C, heir of John Ransdell decd and certified as heir at law to Thomas Ransdell decd,   161
        Captain, Virginia Continental Line, September 1843 Court

    John M, s/o Chilton Ransdell and certified as heir at law to Thomas Ransdell, decd,   161
        Captain, Virginia Continental Line, September 1843 Court

    Maria, d/o Captain Thomas Ransdell, Virginia Continental Line, death intestate and   161
        without issue certified, September 1843 Court

    Thomas, as Lt, Captain, 11th Virginia Continental Rgt, Revolutionary War,   58; 161, note 41
    Thomas, Captain, Virginia Continental Line, death in 1796 certified,   161
        September 1843 Court

    Thomas J, heir of John Ransdell and certified as heir at law to Thomas Ransdell, decd,   161
        Captain, Virginia Continental Line, September 1843 Court

    Ursula, d/o Chilton Ransdell and certified as heir at law to Thomas Ransdell, decd,   161
        Captain, Virginia Continental Line, September 1843 Court

    William, Prvt, 36th Rgt, Virginia Militia, War of 1812 Roster   212

    William H, heir of John Ransdell and certified as heir at law to Thomas Ransdell, decd,   161
        Captain, Virginia Continental Line, September 1843 Court

Ratcliffe
    Zephaniah, PSC, Revolutionary War   85

Rawlins
    R, in Paymaster Acct, 36th Rgt, Virginia Militia, 1806   122

Read (See also Reed, Reid)
    Peyton, Patrol Acct, 1813   120
    Peyton, 1813 Patroller and Prvt, 36th Rgt, Virginia Militia, War of 1812   196

Reardon
    William T, Ensign, Lt, 2nd Battn, 36th Rgt, Virginia Militia, 1804   113

Rector
    Lewis, Prvt, 36th Rgt, Virginia Militia, War of 1812 Roster   212

Index

Redman
John, Judgment against, as collector, class 14, May 1783 Court — 90–91

Reed (See also Read, Reid)
Andrew, Prvt, 36th Rgt, Virginia Militia, War of 1812 Roster — 212

Thomas, Prvt, 36th Rgt, Virginia Militia, War of 1812 Roster — 212
William, Prvt, 89th Rgt, Virginia Militia, War of 1812 Roster — 218

Reeve, Reeves
Asa, 2 PSCs, Revolutionary War — 82, 87

Benjamin, Appointed Constable, in district of 1st Battn, 89th Rgt, June 1805 Court — 115

George, Patrol Acct, French and Indian War — 39

James, Prvt, 36th Rgt, Virginia Militia, War of 1812 Roster — 212

Reuben, 2 Patrol Accts, French and Indian War — 37, 39

William, Ensign, Captain Linton's Company, Prince William Militia, February 1779 Court, Revolutionary War — 65
William, Lt, Prince William Militia, July 1779 Court, Revolutionary War — 66

Reid (See also Read, Reed)
Peyton, Prvt, Captain Joseph R. Gilbert's Company Muster Roll, 36th Rgt, Virginia Militia, War of 1812 — 199
Peyton, Prvt, 36th Rgt, Virginia Militia, War of 1812 Roster — 212

William, Prvt, 36th Rgt, Virginia Militia, War of 1812 Roster — 212

Renno, Rennoe, Reno
Charles, Patrol Acct, 1813, assigned to Joseph R. Lynn — 120
Charles, 1813 Patroller and Sgt, Prvt, 36th Rgt, Virginia Militia, War of 1812 — 196
Charles, Sgt, Captain Alexander Howison's Company Muster Roll, 36th Rgt, Virginia Militia, War of 1812 — 199
Charles, Prvt, Sgt, 89th Rgt, Virginia Militia, War of 1812 Roster — 207, 218

David, PSC, Revolutionary War — 81

Eli, Prvt, 89th Rgt, Virginia Militia, War of 1812 Roster — 218

Enoch, PSC, Revolutionary War — 78

Enoch, Lt Colonel, 36th Rgt, Virginia Militia, War of 1812 — 108, 196
Enoch, Colonel, 36th Rgt, Virginia Militia, 1804 — 113, 219
Enoch, Colonel, in Paymaster Acct, 36th Rgt, Virginia Militia, 1806 — 122, 219
Enoch, Lt Colonel, Colonel, 36th Rgt, Virginia Militia, War of 1812 Roster — 206
Enoch, as resident of Prince William in 1810 and 1820 — 108, notes 61 and 62

Francis, Patrol Acct, French and Indian War — 39
Francis, PSC, Revolutionary War — 78

Index

Renno, Rennoe, Reno (Cont.)
   George, Prvt, Captain Alexander Howison's Company Muster Roll, 36th Rgt,   202
      Virginia Militia, War of 1812
   George, Prvt, 36th Rgt, Virginia Militia, War of 1812 Roster   212
   George, Prvt, Captain John Merchant's Company Muster Roll, 89th Rgt,   215
      Virginia Militia, War of 1812

   George, in Major Townsend Dade's Court martial proceedings, November 1807,   219
      From Fauquier County Clerks Loose Papers

   George Jr, Prvt, Captain Joseph Smith's Company Muster Roll, 36th Rgt,   205
      Virginia Militia, War of 1812

   George Sr, Prvt, Captain Joseph Smith's Company Muster Roll, 36th Rgt,   205
      Virginia Militia, War of 1812

   Lewis, Patrol Acct, French and Indian War   39
   Lewis, Corporal, Prince William Militia, militia claim for service, French and Indian War   185

   Lewis, Captain, Prince William Militia, June 1763 Court, French and Indian War   42
   Lewis, to allot tithes on road from Fauquier line to Slatey Run, where Stephen Lee is   43
      Surveyor, June 1767 Court

   Lewis, brought charges of assault and riot against Catherine Davis, John Sidebottom,   71
      Anne Randolph, Margaret Moore, Marianne McMahan, and Charles Lenox,
      September 1780
   Lewis, appearance bond as witness against Catharine Davis, John Sidebottom, Anne   73
      Randolph, Margaret Moore, Marianne McMahan, and Charles Lenox,
      November 1780 Court
   Lewis, PSC, Revolutionary War   83

   Lewis, Jr, oath as 2nd Lt, Captain John Hedges Company, Prince William Militia,   63
      July 1778 Court, Revolutionary War
   Lewis, life threatened by John Sidebottom, July 1780 Court   70

   Madden, Prvt, Captain Alexander Howison's Company Muster Roll, 36th Rgt,   202
      Virginia Militia, War of 1812

   Madden, Prvt, Captain Joseph Smith's Company Muster Roll, 36th Rgt,   205
      Virginia Militia, War of 1812
   Madden, Prvt, 36th Rgt, Virginia Militia, War of 1812 Roster   212
   Madden, Prvt, Captain John Merchant's Company Muster Roll, 89th Rgt,   215
      Virginia Militia, War of 1812

   Margaret, alias Weeks, Indicted for assault on Catharine Davis, November 1780 Court   74

   Molly, certified as niece and heir at law to William Wright, decd, soldier in   156
      North West Army of the Revolution, August 1835 Court

   Sibi, alias Weeks, indicted for assault on Catharine Davis, November 1780 Court   74
   Sibi, alias Weeks, Commonwealth Cause on indictment for assault on Catharine Davis,   93
      Prosecution discontinued, June 1783 Court

Index

Renno, Rennoe, Reno (Cont.)
   Strother, Ensign, 89th Rgt, 1805, Resignation of   116

   Strother, Prvt, Captain Benjamin Tyler's Company Muster Roll, 89th Rgt,   216
      Virginia Militia, War of 1812

   — [unnamed], in Paymaster's Acct, 36th Rgt, Virginia Militia, 1805   122

   William, Ensign, 36th Rgt, Virginia Militia, 1813   120

   William, Prvt, Captain Joseph R. Gilbert's Company Muster Roll, 36th Rgt,   199
      Virginia Militia, War of 1812

Rice
   John, Soldier, Prince William Militia, militia claim for service, French and Indian War   185

Richardson
   Henry W, Sgt, 36th Rgt, Virginia Militia, War of 1812 Roster   207

   William, Prvt, 36th Rgt, Virginia Militia, War of 1812 Roster   212

Richmond
   Braddock, Ensign, 2nd Battn, 36th Rgt, Virginia Militia, 1804, resignation of   113

Riley
   Edward, Prvt, 36th Rgt, Virginia Militia, War of 1812 Roster   212

   William, Prvt, Captain Alexander Howison's Company Muster Roll, 36th Rgt,   203
      Virginia Militia, War of 1812

   William, Prvt, 36th Rgt, Virginia Militia, War of 1812 Roster   212

   William, Prvt, 89th Rgt, Virginia Militia, War of 1812 Roster   218

Ring
   Cordelia (Ewell), d/o James Ewell, decd; certified as heir at law to Colonel Jesse Ewell,   157
      Decd, September 1835 Court

Ringo, Ringoe
   Peter, PSC, Revolutionary War   77

Rison
   James, Prvt, Captain Alexander Howison's Company Muster Roll, 36th Rgt,   202
      Virginia Militia, War of 1812
   James, Prvt, 36th Rgt, Virginia Militia, War of 1812 Roster   212

   William, Prvt, 36th Rgt, Virginia Militia, War of 1812 Roster   212

Roach
   George, Patrol Acct, 1805   116

   James, PSC, Revolutionary War   81

Index

Roach (Cont.)
  James, Prvt, Captain Alexander Howison's Company Muster Roll, 36th Rgt,   203
    Virginia Militia, War of 1812
  James, Prvt, 36th Rgt, Virginia Militia, War of 1812 Roster   212

  Robert, Prvt, 36th Rgt, Virginia Militia, War of 1812 Roster   212

  William, Prvt, 89th Rgt, Virginia Militia, War of 1812 Roster   218

Robertson (See also Robinson)
  Arthur J, Prvt, 36th Rgt, Virginia Militia, War of 1812 Roster   212

  Arthur S, Prvt, Captain Joseph R. Gilbert's Company Muster Roll, 36th Rgt,   199
    Virginia Militia, War of 1812
  Arthur S, Prvt, 36th Rgt, Virginia Militia, War of 1812 Roster   212
  Arthur S, Prvt, Captain John Merchant's Company Muster Roll, 89th Rgt,   215
    Virginia Militia, War of 1812

  George, certified by Court as U. S. Pension at time of his death in November 1841,   163
    leaving widow Priscilla Robertson surviving him, February 1849 Court
  George, as War of 1812 prvt, 36th Rgt, Virginia Militia   163, note 48

  John, Soldier, Prince William Militia, deserted June 1757 and never returned to duty,   184
    French and Indian War

  Martin, Prvt, Captain Alexander Howison's Company Muster Roll, 36th Rgt,   203
    Virginia Militia, War of 1812

  Priscilla, wid/o George Robertson, a U.S. Pensioner at time of his death in   163
    November 1841, February 1849 Court

Robey, Roby
  William, Prvt, Captain Alexander Howison's Company Muster Roll, 36th Rgt,   202
    Virginia Militia, War of 1812
  William, Prvt, 36th Rgt, Virginia Militia, War of 1812 Roster   212

Robinson (See also Robertson)
  Arthur S, Prvt, Captain Alexander Howison's Company Muster Roll, 36th Rgt,   202
    Virginia Militia, War of 1812

  Daniel, Soldier, Lt Colonel Adam Stephen's Company, Virginia Rgt, French and Indian War   186

  George, Patrol Acct, 1806   177

  Martin, Prvt, 36th Rgt, Virginia Militia, War of 1812 Roster   212

Rockinbaugh
  George, Prvt, 36th Rgt, Virginia Militia, War of 1812 Roster   212

Roe
  James P, Corporal, 36th Rgt, Virginia Militia, War of 1812 Roster   208

Index

Rogers
    Henry, Prvt, 36th Rgt, Virginia Militia, War of 1812 Roster   213

    Reuben, Ensign, 36th Rgt, Virginia Militia, War of 1812 Roster   206

    William, appointed Ensign, 89th Rgt, Virginia Militia, 1805, refused to act   116

Roles (See also Ralls, Rolls)
    John, Prvt, Captain John Merchant's Company Muster Roll, 89th Rgt,   215
    Virginia Militia, War of 1812

Rollings, Rollins
    Henry, Prvt, 89th Rgt, Virginia Militia, War of 1812 Roster   218

    John, Prvt, 89th Rgt, Virginia Militia, War of 1812 Roster   218

    William, Prvt, Captain Benjamin Tyler's Company Muster Roll, 89th Rgt,   216
    Virginia Militia, War of 1812

Rollow (?)
    Russell, Prvt, 36th Rgt, Virginia Militia, War of 1812 Roster   213

Rolls (See also Roles, Ralls)
    Jacob, Prvt, Captain Alexander Howison's Company Muster Roll, 36th Rgt,   202
    Virginia Militia, War of 1812
    Jacob, as husband of Sally (Green), who was an heir at law to Elijah Green decd, a   192
    U. S. Pension when he died in January 1832

    John, 2 Patrol Accts, 1805   117
    John, as Prvt, 36th Rgt, Virginia Militia, War of 1812   117, note 17
    John, Prvt, 36th Rgt, Virginia Militia, War of 1812 Roster   213

    Sally (Green), w/o Jacob Rolls and d/o Elijah Green decd, a U. S. Pensioner at his death;   153–154
    Certified as heir at law to Elijah, October 1834
    Sally (Green), as d/o Elijah Green in his pension file   189
    Sally (Green), certified as heir at law to Elijah Green decd, a soldier in Captain Thomas   192
    Ewell's Company, 1 VSR, Revolutionary War, December 1833 Court and February
    1835 Court
    Sally (Green), and husband Jacob Rolls, appointed Thomas G. Moncure as their attorney to   192
    collect arrears in pension due Elijah Green from September 4, 1832 until his death
    January 15, 1833.
    Sally (Green), d/o Elijah Green decd, certified as heir at law by William S. Colquhoun,   193
    August 1836 in a separate certificate

Rookard
    William, PSC, Revolutionary War   82

Rose
    Daniel, Ensign, Lt, 89th Rgt, Virginia Militia, 1805   116
    Daniel, Lt, 89th Rgt, Virginia Militia, 1804–1806   111
    Daniel, as resident of Prince William in 1810   111, note 111
    Daniel, appointed Constable in district of 2nd Battn, 89th Rgt, June 1805 Court   115

    George, Soldier Prince William Militia, militia claim for service, French and Indian War   185

Index

Rose (Cont.)
    Isaac, Prvt, 36th Rgt, Virginia Militia, War of 1812 Roster   213

    James Jr, Ensign, 89th Rgt, Virginia Militia, 1804–1806   111, 116

Ross
    John, Ensign, Captain Brent's Company, Prince William Militia, February 1779, Revolutionary War   65

    John, decd, Virginia Continental soldier, death certified as intestate, September 1834 Court   154
    John, decd, Virginia Continental soldier, heir at law certified by Court as John S. Ross, September 1834 Court   154

    John, Ensign, 36th Rgt, Virginia Militia, War of 1812 Roster   206

    John, Prvt, 89th Rgt, Virginia Militia, War of 1812 Roster   218

    John S, certified as heir at law to John and William Ross, Virginia Continental soldiers, during Revolutionary War, September 1834 Court   154

    Robert, British Brigadier Major General, War of 1812   105, 108

    William, PSC, Revolutionary War   85

    William, decd, Virginia Continental soldier, death certified as intestate, September 1834 Court   154
    William, decd, Virginia Continental soldier, heir at law certified by Court as John S. Ross, September 1834 Court   154

Roy
    Richard, in Major Townsend Dade's Court martial proceedings, November 1807, From Fauquier County Clerks Loose Papers   219

Rush
    Benjamin, Bond for guardianship of Robert Peyton, orphan of Valentine Peyton, November 1762 Court, French and Indian War   42

Rush (Cont.)
    Richard, Attorney General under President Madison, during War of 1812   108

Russell
    Caty (Mills), d/o George and Lydia Mills, her father was a U. S. Pensioner; she was 63 years old in August 1853   163

Rust
    Jeremiah, Prvt, 36th Rgt, Virginia Militia, War of 1812 Roster   213

Rye
    Jacob, Prvt, 36th Rgt, Virginia Militia, War of 1812 Roster   213

Ryme, Rymes
    William, Prvt, 36th Rgt, Virginia Militia, War of 1812 Roster   213
    William, Prvt, Captain John Merchant's Company Muster Roll, 89th Rgt, Virginia Militia, War of 1812   215

Index

Sale
    Andrew, Sgt, 36th Rgt, Virginia Militia, War of 1812 Roster   207

Sanders (See also Saunders)
    Wesley, Prvt, 36th Rgt, Virginia Militia, War of 1812 Roster   213

Sandford
    Thomas, 1st Lt, Captain William Brown's Company, Prince William Militia, March 1782 Court, Revolutionary War   77
    Thomas, Order by Court to appraise estate of Valentine Peyton decd, September 1782 Court, Revolutionary War   88
    Thomas, Judgment against, as collector for class 18, May 1783 Court, Revolutionary War   90

    William, PSC, Revolutionary War   77

Sanger
    Philip, 2 PSCs, Revolutionary War, assigned to William Carr   86

Saunders (See also Sanders)
    John L, Prvt, 36th Rgt, Virginia Militia, War of 1812 Roster   213

    Presley, Prvt, 36th Rgt, Virginia Militia, War of 1812 Roster   213

    William B, Ensign, 89th Rgt, Virginia Militia, 1804–1806   111, 116

    William S, Prvt, 89th Rgt, Virginia Militia, War of 1812 Roster   218

Scanland
    Benjamin, summoned to Court to answer complaint by William Grayson for Impressing more beeves than required, March 1782 Court, Revolutionary War   78

Scott
    George, Prvt, Captain Joseph R. Gilbert's Company Muster Roll, 36th Rgt, Virginia Militia, War of 1812   199
    George, Prvt, 36th Rgt, Virginia Militia, War of 1812 Roster   213
    James, Reverend, 2 PSCs, Revolutionary War   80, 85

    James, Prvt, Captain Alexander Howison's Company Muster Roll, 36th Rgt, Virginia Militia, War of 1812   202
    James, Prvt, 36th Rgt, Virginia Militia, War of 1812 Roster   213

    John, Prvt, Corporal, Captain Henry Woodward's Company, Virginia Militia, French and Indian War   186–187

    Levi, Ensign, 36th Rgt, Virginia Militia, 1804   113
    Levi, in Major Townsend Dade's Court martial proceedings, November 1807, From Fauquier County Clerks Loose Papers   219

    Sarah E, heir of John Ransdell and heir at law to Thomas Ransdell decd,, Captain, Virginia Continental Line, September 1843 Court   161

    William, security for appearance of Mary McMahon before grand jury, on charge of assault and riot   72

Index

Scott (Cont.)
William, PSC for Fairfax Militia, Revolutionary War 84

Winfield, American General, War of 1812 108

Seale, Seal
Anthony, Oath as Prince William Militia Officer, May 1753 Court, French and Indian War 35
Anthony, as Captain, in County Levy, November 1756 Court, French and Indian War 39
Anthony, 3 PSCs, Revolutionary War 78, 83
Anthony as Prince William Militia Officer, French and Indian War 78, note 63

Anthony Jr, PSC, Revolutionary War 79

John, PSC, Revolutionary War 79

Seaton
George, Soldier, Captain George Mercer's Company, Virginia Rgt, French and Indian War 187

Selecman
William, Prvt, 36th Rgt, Virginia Militia, War of 1812 Roster 213

Settle (See also Suttle)
Fanny, d/o John Wright decd and heir at law to John Wright decd, a Revolutionary War whose death as intestate was certified by Court, August 1835 Court 156
Fanny, d/o John Wright decd and certified as heir at law to Richard Wright, decd, whose death as intestate was certified by Court, August 1835 Court 156

William, Solider, Prince William Militia, militia claim for service, French and Indian War 185

Severo
John, Surgeon, 89th Rgt, Virginia Militia, War of 1812 Roster 217

Shackleford, Shackelford
Robert, Prvt, 36th Rgt, Virginia Militia, War of 1812 Roster 213

Shaw
Charles, Prvt, Captain Alexander Howison's Company Muster Roll, 36th Rgt, Virginia Militia, War of 1812 202
Charles, Prvt, 36th Rgt, Virginia Militia, War of 1812 Roster 212

Jarvis, Sgt, 89th Rgt, Virginia Militia, War of 1812 Roster 217

Stephen, Patrol Acct, 1805 116

Shelton
James, PSC, Revolutionary War 84

Shilkett
James, Prvt, 36th Rgt, Virginia Militia, War of 1812 Roster 212

Shirley
George, Prvt, 89th Rgt, Virginia Militia, War of 1812 Roster 218

Thomas, Soldier, Prince William Militia, militia claim for service 185

Index

Shirley (Cont.)
    William, of New York, ordered by General Braddock to capture French fort at Niagara,   28
        French and Indian War

Shortridge
    Mary, certified as heir at law to George Stubblefield decd, an Ensign in Virginia   162
        Continental Line, September 1843

Shumake
    Joshua, Soldier, Prince William Militia, deserted June 1757, and never returned to duty,   184
        French and Indian War

Sidebottom, Sidebotham
    Charles, security for John Sidebottom's good behaviour, July 1780 Court   70

    John, Corporal, Captain Charles West, 3rd Virginia Continental Rgt, Revolutionary War   56
    John, Corporal, 3rd Virginia, as probable son of Mary Sidebottom, November 1778 Court   64, see note 10
    John, charged with threatening lives of Lewis Reno and Vester Moss, July 1780 Court   70
    John, as Corporal, Captain Charles West, 3rd Virginia Continental Rgt, Revolutionary War   70, see note 33
    John, appearance bond before Grand Jury for threatening lives of Lewis Reno and   71–72
        Vester Moss, September 1780 Court
    John, Indictment for purchasing and receiving stolen goods, November 1780 Court   72–74
    John, PSC, Revolutionary War   81
    John, 2 Commonwealth Causes against, discontinued, June 1783 Court   92
    John, as Prince William veteran who filed a federal pension   139

    Joseph, as probable son of Mary Sidebottom, November 1778 Court,   64, see note 10
    Joseph, Commonwealth cause against, for passing forged money, found not guilty,   65–66
        June 1779 Court
    Joseph, as Prvt, Captain Charles West's Company, 3rd Virginia Continental Rgt,   65, note 14
        Revolutionary War
    Joseph, Commonwealth Presentment against, (unspecified), October 1779 Court   67
    Joseph, in jail in Shenandoah as "a notorious horse thief," broke out before trial,   67–68
        July 1780 Court
    Joseph, as Prince William veteran who filed a federal pension   139
    Mary, granted support due to her sons being in the Continental Army, November 1778   64, 143
        Court, Revolutionary War

    Nancy, certified as heir at law to Elias Wingate, decd, a soldier in the Virginia State   162
        Artillery, Revolutionary War, September 1843 Court

    Wilford D, Prvt, Captain Joseph R. Gilbert's Company Muster Roll, 36th Rgt,   199
        Virginia Militia, War of 1812
    Wilford, Prvt, 36th Rgt, Virginia Militia, War of 1812 Roster   212
    Wilford, Prvt, 89th Rgt, Virginia Militia, War of 1812 Roster   218

    William, PSC, Revolutionary War   82

Sifle, Stifle
    Frederick, Prvt, 36th Rgt, Virginia Militia, War of 1812 Roster   212

Silvey
    Isaac, Prvt, 36th Rgt, Virginia Militia, War of 1812 Roster   212

Index

Simms
    Charles, Major 12th Virginia Continental Rgt, Revolutionary War — 57, note 60
    Charles, Lt Colonel, transferred to 2nd Virginia, September 1778 — 57, note 61; 68, note 23
    Charles, Certificate for lands presented to Court, April 1780 Court — 68
    Charles, as Major, 12th Virginia, Lt Colonel, 6th Virginia Continental Rgt, Revolutionary War — 68, note 23

    John, Oath as Lt, in Captain Lewis Reno's Company, Prince William Militia, June 1763, French and Indian War — 42
    John, Oath as Prince William Militia officer, August 1767 Court, French and Indian War — 43

    Presley, Prvt, 36th Rgt, Virginia Militia, War of 1812 Roster — 212

Simpson
    Francis, Corporal, 36th Rgt, Virginia Militia, War of 1812 Roster — 208

    Rhodham, Prvt, 36th Rgt, Virginia Militia, War of 1812 Roster — 212

    William, Prvt, 89th Rgt, Virginia Militia, War of 1812 Roster — 218

Sinclair
    Alexander, Prvt, 36th Rgt, Virginia Militia, War of 1812 Roster — 212

    Jesse, Prvt, 36th Rgt, Virginia Militia, War of 1812 Roster — 212

Sincock, Sincox
    James, Prvt, Captain Joseph R. Gilbert's Company Muster Roll, 36th Rgt, Virginia Militia, War of 1812 — 199

    Jesse, Prvt, Captain Alexander Howison's Company Muster Roll, 36th Rgt, Virginia Militia, War of 1812 — 202

Singleton
    Stanley, Trooper, Prince William Militia, militia claim for service, French and Indian War — 185

Sisson
    Marmaduke, Prvt, 36th Rgt, Virginia Militia, War of 1812 Roster — 212

Skinker
    William, Receipts as collector, class 10, July 1781 Court, Revolutionary War — 75
    William, 4 PSCs, Revolutionary War — 75, 78–79, 87–88

Skinner
    Phineas, Prvt, 36th Rgt, Virginia Militia, War of 1812 Roster — 212

Slade
    Amy (Ewell), d/o Bertrand Ewell, certified as heir at law to Colonel Jesse Ewell, decd, September 1835 Court — 157

Slaughter
    Stanton, in Major Townsend Dade's Court martial proceedings, November 1807 From Fauquier County Clerks Loose Papers — 219

Index

Slaughter (Cont.)
    Thomas, Petition to legislature for expenses in settling militia accts for pay and provisions for Prince William Militia and for damages done in Prince William, March 1761 — 183

Smallwood
    George, Patrol Acct, 1813, assigned to William S. Colquhoun — 119
    George, Patrol Acct, 1813, assigned to Benoni Harrison — 120
    George, 1813 Patroller and Prvt, 36th Rgt, Virginia Militia, War of 1812 — 196
    George, Prvt, 36th Rgt, Virginia Militia, War of 1812 Roster — 212

Smith
    Austin, Colonel, Virginia Militia, War of 1812 — 219

    Charles, Trooper, Prince William Militia, militia claim for service, French and Indian War — 185

    Francis, Ensign, 36th Rgt, Virginia Militia, War of 1812 Roster — 206

    George, QM, 36th Rgt, Virginia Militia, War of 1812 — 196
    George, QM, 36th Rgt, Virginia Militia, War of 1812 Roster — 207

    Harris, Prvt, 36th Rgt, Virginia Militia, War of 1812 Roster — 212

    Isaac, Ensign, Prince William Militia, July 1779 Court, Revolutionary War — 66

    James, Patrol Acct 1813, assigned to James Smith — 119
    James, Patrol Acct 1813, assigned to Benoni Harrison — 120
    James, 1813 Patroller and Prvt, 36th Rgt, Virginia Militia, War of 1812 — 196
    James, Prvt, Captain Joseph R. Gilbert's Company Muster Roll, 36th Rgt, Virginia Militia, War of 1812 — 199
    James, Prvt, 36th Rgt, Virginia Militia, War of 1812 Roster — 212
    James, Prvt, Captain John Merchant's Company Muster Roll, 89^{h} Rgt, Virginia Militia, War of 1812 — 215

    John, PSC, Revolutionary War — 86

    John, Prvt, Captain Alexander Howison's Company Muster Roll, 36th Rgt, Virginia Militia, War of 1812 — 202
    John, Prvt, 36th Rgt, Virginia Militia, War of 1812 Roster — 212
    John, Prvt, Captain John Merchant's Company Muster Roll, 89^{h} Rgt, Virginia Militia, War of 1812 — 215

    Joseph, in Major Townsend Dade's Court martial proceedings, November 1807, From Fauquier County Clerks Loose Papers — 219
    Joseph, Captain, 36th Rgt, Virginia Militia, War of 1812 — 109, 111, 204, 219
    Joseph, Captain, 36th Rgt, Virginia Militia, September 1813 Court, War of 1812 — 120
    Joseph, Captain, 36th Rgt, Virginia Militia, called up on Regimental Orders, August 14, 1814, War of 1812 — 204
    Joseph, Captain, 36th Rgt, Virginia Militia, War of 1812 Roster — 206

    Mourning, Prvt, 36th Rgt, Virginia Militia, War of 1812 Roster — 212

    Richard, Interpreter to Indians at Fort Chiswell, advanced money by Thomas Bullitt, French and Indian War — 174

Index

Smith (Cont.)
    Robert, Soldier, 1st Virginia Rgt, who died in French and Indian War; heir at law William   187
        Smith certified by Fauquier County Court, March 1780

    Thomas, Patrol Acct, French and Indian War   39

    Thomas A, Ensign, 36th Rgt, Virginia Militia, September 1804 Court   113

    Thomas A, Prvt, 89th Rgt, Virginia Militia, War of 1812 Roster   218

    Townly, Prvt, Captain Alexander Howison's Company Muster Roll, 36th Rgt,   202
        Virginia Militia, War of 1812
    Townly, Prvt, 36th Rgt, Virginia Militia, War of 1812 Roster   212

    William, Corporal, Major Andrew Lewis's Company, Virginia Rgt, French and Indian War   187
    William, produced certificate of service from General Stephen proving French and Indian   187
        War service, March 1780 Fauquier County Court
    William, proved right to bounty land for service in French and Indian War, while living in   187
        Fauquier County, March 1780
    William, certified as heir at law to Robert Smith, in March 1780 in Fauquier County   187
        Court; Robert was soldier in 1st Virginia Rgt, French and Indian War

    William, Patrol Acct 1813, assigned to Benoni Harrison   120
    William, Prvt, Captain Richard Weedon's Company Muster Roll, 36th Rgt,   206
        Virginia Militia, War of 1812
    William, Prvt, 36th Rgt, Virginia Militia, War of 1812 Roster   212

Smithers
    Westward, Prvt, Captain Benjamin Tyler's Company Muster Roll, 89th Rgt,   216
        Virginia Militia, War of 1812

    William, Prvt, Captain Joseph R. Gilbert's Company Muster Roll, 36th Rgt,   199
        Virginia Militia, War of 1812

Smoot, Smoote
    George, Prvt, 36th Rgt, Virginia Militia, War of 1812 Roster   212

    Henry M, Sgt, Captain Joseph R. Gilbert's Company Muster Roll, 36th Rgt,   197
        Virginia Militia, War of 1812
    Henry, Sgt, 36th Rgt, Virginia Militia, War of 1812 Roster   207

    Henry, Prvt, 89th Rgt, Virginia Militia, War of 1812 Roster   218

    Matthew H, Prvt, 36th Rgt, Virginia Militia, War of 1812 Roster   212

Snelling
    William, Prvt, 36th Rgt, Virginia Militia, War of 1812 Roster   212

Snipe
    William, Prvt, 36th Rgt, Virginia Militia, War of 1812 Roster   212

Sorrel
    Alexander, Prvt, 36th Rgt, Virginia Militia, War of 1812 Roster   212

Index

Southard (See also Suthard)
   Sarah (Lowry), d/o Francis and Susan (Chapman) Lowry, entitled to 1/9th part of   158
   Captain Thomas W. Ewell decd estate under her mother's will for life

Sowden
   Allen, Captain 2nd Battn, 36th Rgt, Virginia Militia, September 1804 Court   113
   Allen, Captain, 36th Rgt, Virginia Militia, replaced as Captain, removed from   115
   County, September 1805 Court

Sparks
   James, Patrol Acct, 1805   116

Speak
   Richard, Prvt, 36th Rgt, Virginia Militia, War of 1812 Roster   212

Spence
   John, Surgeon, 36th Rgt, Virginia Militia, War of 1812   110, 196
   John, as resident of Prince William, 1810   110, note 88
   John, Surgeon, 36th Rgt, Virginia Militia, War of 1812 Roster   207

Spillman
   Jacob, Corporal, Prince William Militia, militia claim for service, French and Indian War   196

Spindle
   Thomas, Major, in Major Townsend Dade's Court martial proceedings, November 1807   219
   From Fauquier County Clerks Loose Papers

Spinks
   Raleigh, Prvt, Captain Alexander Howison's Company Muster Roll, 36th Rgt,   202
   Virginia Militia, War of 1812

Splane, Splawn
   William, Oath taken to number of days Prince William Militia was on frontier duty,   37
   March 1756 Court, French and Indian War
   William, as Lt, Prince William Militia, militia claim for service   37, note 9; 185

Spotswood
   Robert, Captain, Virginia Rgt, French and Indian War   172

Stark
   James PSC, Revolutionary War   87

Steel
   John, PSC, Revolutionary War   82

Stephen
   Adam, Lt Colonel, Colonel, 1st Virginia Rgt, French and Indian War   176, 186
   Adam, General, his certificate proved service of William Smith in French and Indian War,   187
   and death of Robert Smith, also in French and Indian War, March 1780 in Fauquier
   County Court

Stewart
   Daniel, Patrol Acct, French and Indian War   39

Index

Stisle
   John, PSC, Revolutionary War   85

Stobo
   Robert, Captain, Virginia Rgt, French and Indian War   24, 27

Stoke
   John C, Prvt, Captain John Linton's Company Muster Roll, Cavalry, 36th Rgt, Virginia Militia, War of 1812   204

Stone
   Barton S, Captain, 36th Rgt, Virginia Militia, War of 1812   109
   Barton S, as resident of Stafford, 1810   109, note 73
   Barton S, Captain, 36th Rgt, Virginia Militia, War of 1812 Roster   206

   John C, Prvt, Captain John Linton's Company Muster Roll, Cavalry, 36th Rgt, Virginia Militia, War of 1812   204
   John C, Prvt, 36th Rgt, Virginia Militia, War of 1812 Roster   212

   Joseph, PSC, Revolutionary War   85

   Lemuel, Prvt, Captain Joseph R. Gilbert's Company Muster Roll, 36th Rgt, Virginia Militia, War of 1812   199
   Lemuel, Sgt, Captain John Linton's Company Muster Roll, Cavalry, 36th Rgt, Virginia Militia, War of 1812   203
   Lemuel, Prvt, Sgt, 36th Rgt, Virginia Militia, War of 1812 Roster   207, 212

   Spilsby, 2 PSCs, Revolutionary War   85

   Thomas, PSC, Revolutionary War   83

Stonell
   Richard, PSC, Revolutionary War, assigned to Christian Bower   84

Stonington, Connecticut, British raid on, War of 1812   104

Stribling
   Francis, Oath as Lt, Prince William Militia, August 1755 Court, French and Indian War   37

   Samuel, Veteran from Prince William who applied for a federal pension   139

   Thomas, Oath as Lt, Prince William Militia, February 1762 Court, French and Indian War   41

Strickley
   John, General, Maryland Militia, War of 1812   108

Stroke, Storke
   John Jr, Prvt, Captain Joseph R. Gilbert's Company Muster Roll, 36th Rgt, Virginia Militia, War of 1812   199

Strother, Strawther
   Larkin, Prvt, Captain Alexander Howison's Company Muster Roll, 36th Rgt, Virginia Militia, War of 1812   202

Index

Stubblefield
    Benjamin, decd heir at law to George Stubblefield, Ensign, Virginia Continental Line,   162
        Revolutionary War; Benjamin's death certified in 1795 with heirs, September 1843 Court
    Benjamin, received bounty land warrant for George's service in Revolutionary War   162, note 42

    Carter, certified as heir at law to George Stubblefield, decd, Ensign, Virginia Continental   162
        Line, Revolutionary War

    George, decd, Ensign, Virginia Continental Line, Revolutionary War; heir at law certified   162
        As Benjamin Stubblefield, decd, September 1843 Court

    Robert, certified as heir at law to George Stubblefield, decd, Ensign, Virginia Continental   162
        Line, Revolutionary War, September 1843 Court

Sullivan
    Owen, Major, in Major Townsend Dade's Court martial proceedings, November 1807,   219
        From Fauquier County Clerks Loose Papers

Summons
    William B, former Ensign, 36th Rgt, Virginia Rgt, 1813, removed from County   118

Suthard (See also Southard)
    Lawrence, PSC, Revolutionary War   83

Suttle (See also Settle)
    Henry Sr, Prvt, 36th Rgt, Virginia Militia, War of 1812 Roster   212

    Isaac, Soldier, Prince William Militia, deserted June 1757 and never returned to duty,   184
        French and Indian War

Suttle (See also Settle)
    James, Prvt, Captain Benjamin Tyler's Company Muster Roll, 89th Rgt,   216
        Virginia Militia, War of 1812

    Martin, Soldier, Prince William Militia, militia claim for service, French and Indian War   185

    Strother, 2 PSCs, Revolutionary War   81
    Strother, as Prvt, Colonel Steven Moylan's 4th Rgt, Light Dragoons,   60; 81, note 76
        Revolutionary War

    William, Soldier Prince William Militia, militia claim for service, French and Indian War   185

Swarts, Swartz
    Thornton, Prvt, 36th Rgt, Virginia Militia, War of 1812 Roster   213

Talbott
    William, certified as heir at law to William Hickman decd, who held sundry military   161
        warrants, October 1841 Court

Taliaferro
    Henry, as guardian of infant daughter Helen, by wife Mary Ann (Tyler) Taliaferro, his   152
        motion to sell military land warrant, July 1833 Court

Index

Taliaferro (Cont.)
    Henry, his motion to sell military warrant of Nathaniel Tyler, assignee of Lt John   152
        Tyler decd, for benefit of infant daughter Helen

Tansil
    George, Patrol Acct 1813, assigned to Benoni Harrison   120
    George, 1813 Patroller and Prvt, 36th Rgt, Virginia Militia, War of 1812   196
    George, Prvt, 36th Rgt, Virginia Militia, War of 1812 Roster   213

    William, Patrol Acct 1813, assigned to Benoni Harrison   120
    William, 1813 Patroller and Prvt, 36th Rgt, Virginia Militia, War of 1812   196
    William, Prvt, 36th Rgt, Virginia Militia, War of 1812 Roster   213

Tarlton
    Moses, in Paymaster Acct, 36th Regt, Virginia Militia, 1806–1807   122

Tarte
    Alexander, 2 PSCs, Revolutionary War   82

Tasker
    Henry, Prvt, Captain Joseph R. Gilbert's Company Muster Roll, 36th Rgt,   199
        Virginia Militia, War of 1812
    Henry, Prvt, Captain Alexander Howison's Company Muster Roll, 36th Rgt,   202
        Virginia Militia, War of 1812
    Henry, Prvt, 36th Rgt, Virginia Militia, War of 1812 Roster   213
    Henry, Prvt, Captain John Merchant's Company Muster Roll, 89th Rgt,   215
        Virginia Militia, War of 1812

Taylor
    Bailey, Corporal, 36th Rgt, Virginia Militia, War of 1812 Roster   208

    Francis, Prvt, 89th Rgt, Virginia Militia, War of 1812 Roster   218

    Joseph, Soldier, Prince William Militia, deserted June 1757 and never returned to duty,   184
        French and Indian War

    Mary, certified as heir at law to William Hickman, decd, holder of sundry military warrants,   161
        October 1841 Court

    Pendleton, Prvt, 36th Rgt, Virginia Militia, War of 1812 Roster   213

    Richard , Lt of Horse, Prince William Militia, militia claim for service,   185
        French and Indian War

    Robert B, General, in charge of defense of Norfolk, War of 1812; called out 700 militia for   103
        defense of city, War of 1812

Teagle
    Joseph, Prvt, 36th Rgt, Virginia Militia, War of 1812 Roster   213

Tebbs (See also **Tibbs**)
    Foushee, Oath as Captain, Prince William Militia, August 1755 Court,   37
        French and Indian War
    Foushee, militia claim for service, French and Indian War   37, note 5

Index

Tebbs (See also Tibbs) (Cont.)
    Foushee, Oath as Captain of Horse, Prince William Militia, August 1756 Court, — 39
        French and Indian War

    James, Oath as Captain, Prince William Militia, February 1762 Court, — 40
        French and Indian War
    James, Captain, Prince William Militia, May 1762 Court, French and Indian War — 41

    Thomas, Prvt, Captain Alexander Howison's Company Muster Roll, 36th Rgt, — 202
        Virginia Militia, War of 1812

    Thomas F, Corporal, Surgeon's Mate, 36th Rgt, Virginia Militia, War of 1812 — 110
    Thomas, QM Sgt, 36th Rgt, Virginia Militia, War of 1812 — 196
    Thomas F, Sgt, Captain Joseph R. Gilbert's Company Muster Roll, 36th Rgt, — 197
        Transferred to Staff, August 1814, Virginia Militia, War of 1812
    Thomas F, Corporal, Surgeon's Mate, 36th Rgt, Virginia Militia, War of 1812 Roster — 207–208

    — [unnamed], Major, to allot and divide tithes [for a road?] under Warren and Bland, — 42
        June 1767 Court

    William, Captain, Prince William Militia, French and Indian War — 180
    William, Captain, to allot and divide tithes to work under Warren and Bland, — 42
        June 1767 Court

    William, Captain, PSC, Revolutionary War — 80

    William H, Prvt, Captain John Linton's Company Muster Roll, Cavalry, 36th Rgt, — 204
        Virginia Militia, War of 1812
    William H, Prvt, 36th Rgt, Virginia Militia, War of 1812 Roster — 213

Tibbs (See also Tebbs)
    Thomas F, Prvt, Captain Joseph R. Gilbert's Company Muster Roll, 36th Rgt, — 199
        Virginia Militia, War of 1812

Templeman
    Ephraim, Sgt, 36th Rgt, Virginia Militia, War of 1812 Roster — 207

Tennell
    Benjamin, PSC, Revolutionary War — 77
    Benjamin, as Sgt, Captain Philip R. F. Lee's Company, 3rd Virginia Continental Rgt, — 77, note 56
        Revolutionary War
    Benjamin, 2nd Lt, Captain William Brown's Company, Prince William Militia, — 77
        March 1782 Court, Revolutionary War

Tennille
    James D, as Magistrate, Prince William, Certificate for Lucy Fortune's Pension, — 159
        July 1839 Court

Tenth (10th) Virginia Continental Rgt — 56–57

Tharp, Tharpe
    James, Prvt, 36th Rgt, Virginia Militia, War of 1812 Roster — 213

    Mark, PSC, Revolutionary War — 84

Index

Thirteenth (13th) Virginia Continental Rgt	58

Thomas

Benjamin, as security on good behavior recognizance for George Thomas, September 1779 Court	67
Charles, Prvt, Captain Joseph R. Gilbert's Company Muster Roll, 36th Rgt, Virginia Militia, War of 1812	199
Charles, Prvt, 36th Rgt, Virginia Militia, War of 1812 Roster	213
Evan, as veteran from Prince William who applied for a federal pension	139
George, Lt Governor of Pennsylvania	12
George, Commonwealth cause against, for advising a soldier to desert and fleecing him in an illegal card game, September 1779 Court	67
James, Patrol Acct 1813, assigned to Benoni Harrison	120
John, Soldier, Prince William Militia, deserted June 1757 and never returned to duty, French and Indian War	184
John W, certified as heir at law to J. Bullitt, Colonel, Virginia Continental Line, now of legal age, February 1854 Court	164
Newton F, certified as heir at law to J. Bullitt, Colonel, Virginia Continental Line February 1854 Court	164
Philip, Representative from Maryland at Treaty of Lancaster, 1744	12

Thomason

John, as veteran from Prince William who applied for a pension	139

Thompson

Edward, Prvt, Captain Thomas Waggener's Company, Virginia Rgt, French and Indian War	187–188
John, Prvt, 36th Rgt, Virginia Militia, War of 1812 Roster	213
Vincent, Prvt, 36th Rgt, Virginia Militia, War of 1812 Roster	213
William, Lt, 36th Rgt, 1812	109
William, Lt, Paymaster, 36th Rgt, Virginia Militia, War of 1812 Roster	206

Thorn

John, ordered by Court to divide estate of Reuben Calvert decd between widow and Orphans and to set apart widow's dower, September 1782 Court	88

Thornton

Ann, d/o Thomas and Mary Ann (Ewell) Thornton, December 1836 Court	157
Mary Ann (Ewell), w/o Thomas Thornton and sister to Captain Thomas W. Ewell, Revolutionary War officer, December 1836 Court	157
Mary Ann (Ewell), inherited husband's estate by his will, December 1836 Court	157

Index

Thornton (Cont.)
    Mary Ann (Ewell) decd, w/o Thomas Thornton; her property left to daughter   157
        Susan (Thornton) Chapman as life estate and then to grand daughter
        Susan (Chapman) Lowry, December 1836 Court

    Thomas, Surgeon's Mate, Surgeon, 36th Rgt, Virginia Militia, War of 1812   110, 196
    Thomas, as resident, Prince William in 1810   110, note 89
    Thomas, Surgeon, 36th Rgt, Virginia Militia, War of 1812 Roster   207
    Thomas, s/o Thomas and Mary Ann (Ewell) Thornton and heir at law to Captain   157
        Thomas W. Ewell, Revolutionary War officer, December 1836 Court

    William, as Proprietor of Ohio Company, 1747   12
    William, prevented destruction of Patent Office by British, War of 1812   108
    William, and wife Mary sold 50 acres in Prince William to John Frogg, June 1740   177

Thruston
    Charles M, as assignee of Francis Austin, Sgt in 1st Virginia Rgt, bounty land warrant for   172
        200 acres

Thumb Run, Fort on; Charles Duncan appointed Surveyor of Road from Fort on Thumb Run to   40
    Meet lower road on Carter's Run, March 1757 Court

Thurman
    Edmond, Prvt, Captain Benjamin Tyler's Company Muster Roll, 89th Rgt,   216
        Virginia Militia, War of 1812

    Robert, Corporal, Captain Benjamin Tyler's Company Muster Roll, 89th Rgt,   216
        Virginia Militia, War of 1812

    Thomas, Prvt, 89th Rgt, Virginia Militia, War of 1812 Roster   218

    William, as veteran from Prince William who applied for a pension   139

    William, Corporal, 89th Rgt, Virginia Militia, War of 1812 Roster   217

Timberlake
    John, Prvt, 36th Rgt, Virginia Militia, War of 1812 Roster   213

Tippett
    John, Ensign, 36th Rgt, Virginia Militia, 1812   110
    John, Ensign, 36th Rgt, Virginia Militia, War of 1812 Roster   207

Tomlin
    Thomas, Prvt, Captain Joseph R. Gilbert's Company Muster Roll, 36th Rgt,   199
        Virginia Militia, War of 1812
    Thomas, Prvt, 36th Rgt, Virginia Militia, War of 1812 Roster   213

Tracey
    Bayliss, Prvt, 36th Rgt, Virginia Militia, War of 1812 Roster   213

Treaty of Albany   10

Index

Trialor
    Peter, as security on guardian bond of Robert Massey for William D and John H. Massey, 154
        orphans of Henry Massey decd, December 1834 Court

Triplet, Triplett
    Francis, Solider, Prince William Militia, petitioned legislature for expenses incurred from 186
        wound in his arm in June 1756; claim allowed

    Francis, as part of Francis Floyd's PSC for horse impressed by Nemenus Bullitt under 79
        Francis Triplett's direction, to impress horses for use of General Morgan,
        March 1782 Court, Revolutionary War
    Francis, as Adjutant, Captain, Major in Fauquier Militia, he fought at Cowpens in 79, note 64
        In December 1781 and went on to be a Colonel in General Morgan's State Troops.

    James, Captain, Prince William Militia, resignation of, April 1781 Court, Revolutionary War 74
    James, PSC, Revolutionary War 79

    Thomas, as Captain of company in which Edward Williams was a member, 155
        April 1835 Court
    Thomas, as Captain, Grayson's Additional Continental Rgt, Revolutionary War 58; 155, note 19

Trone
    Peter, Prvt, Captain Alexander Howison's Company Muster Roll, 36th Rgt, 202
        Virginia Militia, War of 1812
    Peter, Prvt, Captain John Linton's Company Muster Roll, Cavalry, 36th Rgt, 204
        Virginia Militia, War of 1812
    Peter, Prvt, 36th Rgt, Virginia Militia, War of 1812 Roster 213

Truman
    Smallwood, Prvt, Captain John Merchant's Company Muster Roll, 89th Rgt, 215
        Virginia Militia, War of 1812

Tullos
    Joshua, Patrol Acct, French and Indian War 39

Turley
    Sampson, Prvt, 36th Rgt, Virginia Militia, War of 1812 Roster 213

Turner
    Henry, Prvt, 36th Rgt, Virginia Militia, War of 1812 Roster 213

    John, Prvt, 36th Rgt, Virginia Militia, War of 1812 Roster 213

    Levi, Prvt, 36th Rgt, Virginia Militia, War of 1812 Roster 213
    Levi, Prvt, 89th Rgt, Virginia Militia, War of 1812 Roster 218

    Thomas, in Paymaster Acct, 36th Rgt, Virginia Militia, 1805–1806 122
    Thomas, Prvt, Captain John Linton's Company Muster Roll, Cavalry, 36th Rgt, 204
        Virginia Militia, War of 1812
    Thomas, Prvt, 36th Rgt, Virginia Militia, War of 1812 Roster 213

    William, Soldier, Prince William Militia, petition to legislature for pay for service, 186
        May 1757, French and Indian War

Index

Turner (Cont.)
    Willis, Prvt, Captain Joseph Smith's Company Muster Roll, 36th Rgt,   205
        Virginia Militia, War of 1812

Twelfth (12th) Virginia Continental Rgt   57–58

Twentyman
    John, Soldier, Prince William Militia, petition to legislature for pay for service, May 1757   186
        French and Indian War

Tyler
    Alice, certified as heir at law to Henry Tyler, decd, a reputed Midshipman, in VSN,   154
        Revolutionary War, September 1834 Court

    Benjamin, Captain, 89th Rgt, Virginia Militia, Muster Rolls   112, 215–217
    Benjamin, Captain, 89th Rgt, Virginia Militia, War of 1812   219

    Charles, heir to John Tyler decd, Ensign 3rd Virginia Continental Rgt, July 1833 Court   151

    George G, heir to John Tyler decd, Ensign 3rd Virginia Continental Rgt, July 1833 Court   151

    Gustavus B, Prvt, 89th Rgt, Virginia Militia, War of 1812 Roster   218

    Henry, as Midshipman, VSN   62
    Henry decd, late Midshipman, VSN, Court certified as Heirs, Alice P. Tyler, and Mary   154
        Ann Beard, September 1834 Court
    Henry decd, death certified as testate with will filed in Prince William,   154
        September 1834 Court

    Henry B, on his motion, heirs of John Tyler decd, a Lt in Continental Line, "be spread   152
        on the records of this Court," July 1833 Court

    John, Lt, Captain James Tebb's Company, Prince William Militia, May 1762 Court   41
        French and Indian War
    John, as security for Benjamin Rush's guardian bond for Robert Peyton, orphan of   42
        Valentine Peyton decd, November 1762 Court

    John, PSC, Revolutionary War   83
    John, as Lt, 3rd Virginia Continental Rgt, commissioned February 1776, resigned,   83, note 82
        August 1776, Revolutionary War

    John, 3rd Virginia Continental Rgt officer from Prince William, Revolutionary War   40, note 20, 139
    John, as heir to John Tyler decd, Ensign 3rd Virginia Continental Rgt, July 1833 Court   151
    John decd, Court certified death previous to 1796, July 1833   151
    John decd, as Ensign, 3rd Virginia Continental Rgt, death in January 1777,   151, note 4

    Joseph, PSC, Revolutionary War   83

    Joseph, Prvt, Captain Alexander Howison's Company Muster Roll, 36th Rgt,   202
        Virginia Militia, War of 1812
    Joseph, Prvt, 36th Rgt, Virginia Militia, War of 1812 Roster   213
    Joseph, Sgt, Captain Benjamin Tyler's Company Muster Roll, 89th Rgt,   215
        Virginia Militia, War of 1812

Index

Tyler (Cont.)
    Nathaniel, as brother and heir at law to John Tyler, decd, July 1833 Court   151–152
    Nathaniel decd, issued bounty land warrants in July 1784 for John Tyler decd   152
        Service as Lt in Continental Line for three years, to be sold, July 1833 Court
    Nathaniel, as sister to Sally (Tyler) Linton, an heir at law to John Tyler decd   152

    Richard B, Prvt, 89th Rgt, Virginia Militia, War of 1812 Roster   218

    William, Major, Colonel, 89th Rgt, 1804–1806   111, 117
    William, as resident of Prince William in 1810   111, note 102
    William, Colonel, in Major Townsend Dade's Court martial proceedings, November 1807   219
        From Fauquier County Clerks Loose Papers

Umberfield
    Eliphalet, Prvt, Captain John Merchant's Company Muster Roll, 89th Rgt,   215
        Virginia Militia, War of 1812

    Elistett, Prvt, Captain Joseph R. Gilbert's Company Muster Roll, 36th Rgt,   199
        Virginia Militia, War of 1812

Utterback
    Elias, Sgt, 36th Rgt, Virginia Militia, War of 1812 Roster   207

Valley, Elk Run   10

Van Ness, John, Major General, District of Columbia Militia, War of 1812   104–105

Veale
    Bond, Patrol Acct, French and Indian War   37

Vernon, Edward, British Admiral, led Carthagena Expedition   11

Virginia
    Act, 1807 for distribution of arm to militia   101
    Continental Rgts
        1st Virginia   55, 133
        2nd Virginia   55
        3rd Virginia   55-56; 132
        9th Virginia   60
        10th Virginia   56–57
        11th Virginia   57
        12th Virginia   57–58
        13th Virginia   58

    Conventions, Revolutionary War   50
        2nd Virginia Convention
            Revamps military establishment in Virginia   51–52, 55
        3rd Virginia Convention
            Created three tier system in military: two Virginia Rgts, and fifteen   52–53
                Minute Battalions, and a militia
    Council   6

    Counties   3–5, 9–12, 14, 33

Index

Virginia (Cont.)
    Militia, War of 1812,
        Prince William Rgts   219
        Prince William Rgts, in 5th Brigade, 2nd Division   219

    Militia, War of 1812
        36th Rgt, Virginia Militia, Paymaster Acct 1805–1807   108
        36th Rgt, Virginia Militia, War of 1812, Field and Staff Muster Rolls, 1813–1814   196
        36th Rgt, Virginia Militia, War of 1812, Rosters   206–213
        36th Rgt, Virginia Militia, Captain Joseph R. Gilbert's Company Muster Rolls, 1813, 1814   197–199
        36th Rgt, Virginia Militia, Captain Alexander Howison's Company Muster Rolls, 1813, 1814   199–203
        36th Rgt, Virginia Militia, Captain John Linton's Company Muster Rolls, Cavalry, 1813, 1814   203–204
        36th Rgt, Virginia Militia, Captain Joseph Smith's Company Muster Rolls, 1813   204–205
        36th Rgt, Virginia Militia, Captain Richard Weadon's Company Muster Rolls, 1814 1814   205–206

        89th Rgt, Virginia Militia, 1804–1806   111
        89th Rgt, Virginia Militia, 1812–1814   112
        89th Rgt, Virginia Militia, Captain John Merchant's Company Muster Rolls, 1814   214–215
        89th Rgt, Virginia Militia, Captain Benjamin Tyler's Company Muster Rolls, 1814   214–217
        89th Rgt, Virginia Militia, War of 1812 Roster   217–218

    Militia Acts
        Act of 1803   98–100

        Act of 1808   101

    Militia, Court martial of Major Townsend Dade, 2nd Battn, 36th Rgt, November 1807   219–220

    Virginia Regiment, French and Indian War   33

    Virginia State Navy (VSN), Revolutionary War   62

    Virginia State Regiments and Troops, Revolutionary War   60–61
        1st VSR   60
        2nd VSR   60
        3rd VSR   60
        Virginia Troops, Illinois Regiment   61–62

Vowles
    James, Prvt, 36th Rgt, Virginia Militia, War of 1812 Roster   213

Waddell
    James, Prvt, 36th Rgt, Virginia Militia, War of 1812 Roster   213

Wade
    Thomas, Prvt, 36th Rgt, Virginia Militia, War of 1812 Roster   213

Wadsworth
    —, Colonel, in John Bell's 1818 Pension Papers   132

Index

Waggener
   Thomas, Captain, Virginia Rgt, French and Indian War   170–173, 175, 177–178, 188

Walker
   Caleb, Prvt, 36th Rgt, Virginia Militia, War of 1812 Roster   213

   William, Prvt, 36th Rgt, Virginia Militia, War of 1812 Roster   213

Waller
   George, Lt, 36th Rgt, Virginia Militia, 1812   109
   George, Lt, 36th Rgt, Virginia Militia, War of 1812 Roster   206

Walter, Walters
   Thomas, Prvt, 36th Rgt, Virginia Militia, War of 1812 Roster   213

   Warden, Prvt, Captain John Linton's Company Muster Roll, Cavalry, 36th Rgt, Virginia Militia, War of 1812   204

War of 1812   101–105
   Prince William Militia Rgts in   108–112

War of Jenkins Ear, 1739–1742   11–12

Ward
   Charles, Soldier, Prince William Militia, deserted June 1757; pay allowed for his time of duty by legislature, September 1758, French and Indian War   184

Warder
   Walter, Prvt, 36th Rgt, Virginia Militia, War of 1812 Roster   213

Wardie
   John, Prvt, 36th Rgt, Virginia Militia, War of 1812 Roster   213

Ware
   Gustavus M, 1st Sgt, 36th Rgt, Virginia Militia, War of 1812 Roster   207

   John, late Lt, 36th Rgt, Virginia Militia, 1805, decd   115

   Nicholas, PSC, Revolutionary War   81

Waring
   Thomas, Prvt, Captain Benjamin Tyler's Company Muster Roll, 89th Rgt, Virginia Militia, War of 1812   217

Warren
   Robert, Oath as 1st Lt, Captain John Linton's Company, Prince William Militia, July 1778 Court, Revolutionary War   63
   Robert, as Captain, Prince William Militia, replaced Captain John Linton, who resigned, July 1779 Court, Revolutionary War   66
   Robert, PSC, Revolutionary War   76
   Robert, as Lt and Captain, Prince William Militia, Revolutionary War   76, note 55
   Robert, Judgment against, as collector, class 7, May 1783 Court   90

Index

Washington
    Augustine Jr, Proprietor of Ohio Company, 1747   12

    Eupham M, wid/o Colonel John M. Washington, Pension Declaration for March 1854   164–165
        relief of U. S. Troops who drowned on Steamship *San Francisco*, December 1854 Court
    Eupham M, wid/o John M. Washington, as certified on Court Record, March 1855 Court   165

    George, Major, French and Indian War   18
    George, as Aide de Camp to Major General Edward Braddock, French and Indian War   32
    George, Lt Colonel, Virginia Rgt, French and Indian War   19–20, 23, 25, 28–29
    George, Colonel, Virginia Rgt, French and Indian War   33, 48, 50–51, 170–171, 182–183
    George, Colonel, Virginia Rgt, correspondence with Colonel Henry Lee, Prince William   179
        Militia, July 1757, French and Indian War
    George, Colonel, Virginia Rgt, correspondence with Lt Colonel Henry Peyton,   182–183
        Prince William Militia, May 1756, June 1756, June 1757, French and Indian War
    George, Colonel, Virginia Rgt, correspondence with Governor Dinwiddie re behavior of   184
        Prince William Militia, June 1757
    George, Colonel, Virginia Rgt, complains of Prince William Militia negligence in care of   184
        ammunition, French and Indian War
    George, Colonel, Virginia Rgt, correspondence in June 1758 with Francis Fauquier re   184–185
        Prince William Militia
    George, letter to Prince William Independent Militia Company, 1775   51
    George, General, appointed Commander in Chief, Continental Forces, Revolutionary War   51, 60

    H. W. M, s/o John M. and Eupham M. Washington, Court certified he was of legal age,   165
        November 1855 Court

    John M, decd, a brevet Colonel in U.S. Army, death certified in December 1853 on   164–165
        Steamship *San Francisco*, December 1854 Court
    John M, his Army record detailed   164, note 53

    Lawrence, Proprietor of Ohio Company, 1747   12

    Stark, Prvt, 89th Rgt, Virginia Militia, War of 1812 Roster   218

    Washington John, Captain, Major, 89th Rgt, Virginia Militia, 1804–1806   111, 117
    Washington J, as resident of Prince William in 1810   117, note 104

    W. L, Major, as commanding officer, 89th Rgt, Virginia Militia, 1805   219
    William T, s/o John M and Eupham M. Washington, Court certified as being of legal   165
        age, November 1855 Court

Washington, DC, Burning of, War of 1812   107–108

Waters
    Alexander H, certified as heir at law to Lt John Galloway decd, an officer in Virginia   154
        Continental Line, Revolutionary War, September 1834 Court

    John, security for Catharine Davis's appearance in court on charge of riot, November   73
        1780 Court

    Letitia, heir of John Ransdell and certified as heir at law to Captain Thomas Ransdell decd,   161
        Virginia Continental Line, September 1843 Court

Index

Waters (Cont.)
 William, Patrol Acct, French and Indian War   39

Watson
 James, Prvt, Captain Joseph R. Gilbert's Company Muster Roll, 36th Rgt, Virginia Militia, War of 1812   199
 James, Prvt, 36th Rgt, Virginia Militia, War of 1812 Roster   213

Watts
 Thomas, Prvt, 36th Rgt, Virginia Militia, War of 1812 Roster   213

Way
 John, Prvt, 36th Rgt, Virginia Militia, War of 1812 Roster   213

Wayne, Anthony, American General, Revolutionary War, Indian Wars   59, 83

Weadon, Weedon
 George, Colonel, 3rd Virginia Continental Rgt, Revolutionary War   55

 George, former Lt, 36th Rgt, Virginia Militia, 1813, removed from County   119

 Richard, Ensign, 36th Rgt, Virginia Militia, 1806   117
 Richard, as resident of Prince William in 1810   117,
 Richard, Captain, 36th Rgt, Virginia Militia, 1812   109, 219
 Richard, as resident of Loudoun in 1810   109, note 74
 Richard, Captain, 36th Rgt, Virginia Militia, Muster Rolls   111, 205–206
 Richard, Captain, 36th Rgt, Virginia Militia, War of 1812 Roster   206

Weaver
 Henry, Prvt, 36th Rgt, Virginia Militia, War of 1812 Roster   213

Webster
 Henry, Prvt, Captain Joseph Smith's Company Muster Roll, 36th Rgt, Virginia Militia, War of 1812   205
 Henry, Prvt, Sgt, 36th Rgt, Virginia Militia, War of 1812 Roster   207, 213

 John, Patrol Acct 1813, assigned to Daniel King   119
 John, 1813 Patroller and Prvt, 36th Rgt, Virginia Militia, War of 1812   196
 John, Sgt, Captain Alexander Howison's Company Muster Roll, 36th Rgt, Virginia Militia, War of 1812   200
 John, Sgt, Captain Joseph Smith's Company Muster Roll, 36th Rgt, Virginia Militia, War of 1812   204

 William, Prvt, 36th Rgt, Virginia Militia, War of 1812 Roster   213

Weeks
 Sibi, alias Reno, Commonwealth Cause against, for assault on Catharine Davis, November 1780   74
 Sibi, alias Reno, Commonwealth Cause against, discontinued, June 1783 Court   93

 William, Prvt, 36th Rgt, Virginia Militia, War of 1812 Roster   213

Index

Weems
Fanny (Ewell), certified as heir at law to Colonel Jesse Ewell decd, September 1835 Court   157

Jesse, on his motion, Captain Thomas W. Ewell's Revolutionary War service proved, February 1834 Court   153–154

Jesse E, Prince William clergy man, in Elijah Green's Pension Papers   159–160

Welch, Welsh
Benjamin, Prvt, 89th Rgt, Virginia Militia, War of 1812 Roster   218

Joseph, Trooper, Prince William Militia, militia claim for service   185

Joseph, Prvt, 36th Rgt, Virginia Militia, War of 1812 Roster   213

Joshua, Soldier, Prince William Militia, petition to legislature for pay for service, May 1757, French and Indian War   188

Randolph, Prvt, Captain Alexander Howison's Company Muster Roll, 36th Rgt, Virginia Militia, War of 1812   203

Randolph, Prvt, 36th Rgt, Virginia Militia, War of 1812 Roster   213

Randolph, Prvt, Captain Benjamin Tyler's Company Muster Roll, 89th Rgt, Virginia Militia, War of 1812   217

Wells
Caty, PSC, Revolutionary War   85

Joshua, Soldier, Captain Joshua Lewis's 7th Company, Virginia Rgt, French and Indian War   186

West
Thomas, Prvt, Captain Alexander Howison's Company Muster Roll, 36th Rgt, Virginia Militia, War of 1812   203

Thomas, Prvt, 36th Rgt, Virginia Militia, War of 1812 Roster   213

Weston
John, in Paymaster's Acct, 36th Rgt, Virginia Militia, 1806   122

Whalley
William, Corporal, Prince William Militia, militia claim for service   185

Wharton
Isaac, Prvt, 36th Rgt, Virginia Militia, War of 1812 Roster   213

Wheatley
Lawson, Prvt, 36th Rgt, Virginia Militia, War of 1812 Roster   213

White
George, Prvt, Captain Gallahue's Company, 11th Virginia   57; 69, note 29

George, certified by Court that he was entitled to bounty land as a Prvt, in the Virginia Continental Line, April 1780 Court   69

George, Prvt 36th Rgt, Virginia Militia, War of 1812 Roster   213

George Sr, Prvt, 36th Rgt, Virginia Militia, War of 1812 Roster   213

Index

White (Cont.)
    James, PSC, Revolutionary War   87

    James, Prvt, 36th Rgt, Virginia Militia, War of 1812 Roster   213

    John, Prvt, 36th Rgt, Virginia Militia, War of 1812 Roster   213
    Thomas, Sgt, 1st VSR, Revolutionary War   55
    Thomas, Sgt, Lt, 1st VSR, Revolutionary War, service proved, July 1833 Court   151
    Thomas, further Revolutionary War service detailed   151, note 3
    Thomas, Sgt, Lt, 1st VSR, Revolutionary War, certified by Court that he returned to Prince William after close of war and then removed to southern Virginia   151

    Thomas, Captain, in Major Townsend Dade's Court martial proceedings, November 1807 From Fauquier County Clerks Loose Papers   219

Whitfield
    Edward, Prvt, Captain Thomas W. Ewell's Company, 1st VSR   61
    Edward decd, certified by Court that he died in service and his mother Elizabeth was his heir at law, March 1784 Court   93

    Elizabeth, wid/o John Whitfield decd, certified as heir at law to her son Edward, who died in Revolutionary War   93

    John decd, his widow Elizabeth was mother and heir at law to son Edward Whitfield who died in Revolutionary War   93

Whiting
    George, former Lt, 89th Rgt, Virginia Militia, resignation of, September 1805 Court   116

    Matthew, Lt, 3rd Virginia Continental Rgt, Revolutionary War   56; 75, note 52
    Matthew, Receipts for clothes as collector, class 11, July 1781 Court, Revolutionary War   75
    Matthew, PSC, Revolutionary War   78

Whitledge
    John, Captain, Prince William Militia, Revolutionary War   63
    John, former Captain, Prince William Militia, March 1779 Court   65

    William Jr, PSC, Revolutionary War   83

Wiatt
    Conquest, PSC, Revolutionary War   78

    James, 3 PSCs, Revolutionary War   78–79

    William Edward, PSC, Revolutionary War   83

    William, PSC, Revolutionary War   87

Wickliffe
    David, veteran from Prince William, who served in 3rd Virginia Continental Rgt, Revolutionary War, who applied for a pension   139

    Isaac, Captain, Prince William Militia, March 1779 Court, Revolutionary War   65, 76, note 53

Index

Wickliffe
    Isaac, Receipts for clothes and beef as collector, class 39, July 1781 Court, Revolutionary War   76
    Isaac, oath as deputy Sheriff, November 1782 Court   88

    Nathaniel, PSC, Revolutionary War   87
    Nathaniel, certified as heir at law to Robert Wickliffe decd, October 1783 Court   93

Wickliffe (Cont.)
    Robert decd, of Westmoreland, Pennsylvania; Court certified heir at law as Nathaniel Wickliffe, October 1783 Court   93

Widows and Families,
    Support for, during War   142–143

    Relief for officers and soldiers of army and navy raised by Acts of General Assembly, October 1778   143

    Support for, repealed in favor of indigency, October 1779   143

    Allowances provided for, by legislation, May 1782   144

Wigginton
    Benjamin, 2 PSCs, Revolutionary War   85, 87

Willingham
    George, Prvt, 36th Rgt, Virginia Militia, War of 1812 Roster   213

Wilcocks, Wilcox
    John, as Soldier, Captain George Mercer's Company, Virginia Rgt, French and Indian War   80, note 75
    John PSC, Revolutionary War   80

Willet, Willett
    David, Prvt, Captain Alexander Howison's Company Muster Roll, 36th Rgt, Virginia Militia, War of 1812 as substitute for John Willett   203
    David, Prvt, 36th Rgt, Virginia Militia, War of 1812 Roster   213

    John, Prvt, 36th Rgt, Virginia Militia, War of 1812 Roster   213

Williams
    — Mrs, PSC, Revolutionary War   81

    Catharine, certified as heir at law to Edward Williams decd, a solider in Captain Thomas Triplett's Company; Edward Williams death as intestate and without issue certified, April 1835 Court   155

    Edward decd, as Sgt, Captain Thomas Triplett's Company, Grayson's Additional Continental Rgt, Revolutionary War; he died in service   58, 155, note 18
    Edward decd, a Revolutionary War soldier in Grayson's Additional Continental Rgt, death certified as intestate and without issue; sole heir at law certified as Catharine Williams, April 1835 Court   155

    Evan, Money from Richard Graham, collector for class 30, assigned to him, July 1781 Court   75
    Evan, for Mrs Rawlings, PSC, Revolutionary War   81

Index

Williams (Cont.)
    Evan, order by Court to set apart dower for Mary Graham, wid/o Reginald Graham decd, September 1782 Court   88
    Evan, as Bursar of Prince William Militia, on his motion, judgment granted against estate of Henry Peyton decd, for collection of Court martial fines, May 1783 Court   89

    George, former Captain, 36th Rgt, Virginia Militia, 1804, resignation of   113

    John, in Major Townsend Dade's Court martial proceedings, November 1807, From Fauquier County Clerks Loose Papers   219
    John, Clerk of Prince William Court, October 1838   158
    John W, Justice, Prince William, correspondence with William S. Colquhoun regarding Elijah Green's Pension, June 1831   190
    John W, acting clerk, Prince William Court, correspondence with Pension Agency, regarding Elijah Green's Pension, June 1832   191–192

    Sarah, PSC, Revolutionary War   85

    Thomas, Prvt, 36th Rgt, Virginia Militia, War of 1812 Roster   213

    William C, Sgt, Captain Joseph R. Gilbert's Company Muster Roll, 36th Rgt, Virginia Militia, War of 1812   197
    William C, Sgt, Captain John Linton's Company Muster Roll, Cavalry, 36th Rgt, Virginia Militia, War of 1812   203
    William C, Prvt, Sgt, 36th Rgt, Virginia Militia, War of 1812 Roster   207, 213

Willis, Williss
    John, PSC, Revolutionary War   83

    John, in Major Townsend Dade's Court martial proceedings, November 1807 From Fauquier County Clerks Loose Papers   219

Wilson
    Benjamin, Trooper, Prince William Militia, militia claim for service   185

    Jacob, Prvt, 36th Rgt, Virginia Militia, War of 1812 Roster   213
    Jacob, Prvt, 89th Rgt, Virginia Militia, War of 1812 Roster   218

Winder
    Levi, Governor of Maryland, War of 1812   104

    William, Brigadier of new military command for D. C, Maryland, and Northern Virginia, War of 1812   104
    William, Brigadier General, Militia, War of 1812   105–106
    William, Brigadier General, Militia, War of 1812, Court martial of   107–108

Windsor
    Thomas, Prvt, 36th Rgt, Virginia Militia, War of 1812 Roster   213
    Thomas, Prvt, 89th Rgt, Virginia Militia, War of 1812 Roster   218

    William, Prvt, 36th Rgt, Virginia Militia, War of 1812 Roster   213

Wine
    George, Prvt, 36th Rgt, Virginia Militia, War of 1812 Roster   213

Index

Winekoop, Winechoof
    Philip, Prvt, Captain Alexander Howison's Company Muster Roll, 36th Rgt,   203
        Virginia Militia, War of 1812
    Philip, Prvt, Captain Benjamin Tyler's Company Muster Roll, 89th Rgt,   217
        Virginia Militia, War of 1812

Wingate
    Betty, w/o Henry, her son Martin bound out by CW Indenture to Jesse Moore,   43
        June 1769 Court

    Elias decd, Revolutionary War soldier in Virginia State Artillery, heirs certified   162
        as Nancy Sidebottom and Sarah Anderson, September 1843 Court
    Elias decd, as corporal, Captain John Danbridge's Company, 1st Continental   162, note 43
        Rgt of Artillery, June 1778

    Henry, his son Martin bound out by CW Indenture to Jesse Moore,   43
        June 1769 Court

    Martin, as s/o Henry and Betty Wingate, bound out by CW Indenture to Jesse Moore   43
        June 1769 Court

Winn, Winne
    Zachariah, Prvt, Captain Alexander Howison's Company Muster Roll, 36th Rgt,   203
        Virginia Militia, War of 1812
    Zachariah, Prvt, 36th Rgt, Virginia Militia, War of 1812 Roster   213

Wood
    Benjamin, PSC, Revolutionary War   85

    Elijah, Affidavit for Spencer Anderson's 1818 Pension Declaration   132
    Elijah, as soldier, Captain Philip Richard Francis Lee's Company, 3rd Virginia Continental   132
        Rgt, Revolutionary War

    Elijah, Prvt, 36th Rgt, Virginia Militia, War of 1812 Roster   213

    Hezekiah, Prvt, 36th Rgt, Virginia Militia, War of 1812 Roster   213

Woodrop
    James, Proprietor of Ohio Company, 1747   12

Woods
    James, Patrol Acct, 1806   117

Woodward
    George, Prvt, Captain Alexander Howison's Company Muster Roll, 36th Rgt,   203
        Virginia Militia, War of 1812
    George, 36th Rgt, Virginia Militia, War of 1812 Roster   213

    Henry, Captain, Virginia Rgt, French and Indian War   186

    Jabaz, Prvt, 36th Rgt, Virginia Militia, War of 1812 Roster   213

Index

Joseph, Prvt, 36th Rgt, Virginia Militia, War of 1812 Roster 213

Woodyard
Ann, d/o George and Lydia Mills, her hater was U. S. Pensioner, certified by Court that she 163
was 58 years old in July 1853

George, Prvt, Captain Benjamin Tyler's Company Muster Roll, 89th Rgt, 217
Virginia Militia, War of 1812

Jesse, Prvt, Captain Benjamin Tyler's Company Muster Roll, 89th Rgt, 217
Virginia Militia, War of 1812

John, Prvt, Captain Benjamin Tyler's Company Muster Roll, 89th Rgt, 217
Virginia Militia, War of 1812

Wright
John, Lt, Virginia Rgt, French and Indian War 175
— [John?]Lt, Captain Joshua Lewis's Company, Virginia Rgt, French and Indian War 188

John B, Prvt, 36th Rgt, Virginia Militia, War of 1812 Roster 213

John, s/o John Wright decd, certified as heir at law to John Wright decd, a soldier 156
in Revolutionary War, August 1835 Court
John, s/o John Wright decd, certified as heir at law to Richard Wright, a soldier in 156
Revolutionary War, August 1835 Court

John, s/o John Wright decd, certified as heir at law to William Wright, decd, a soldier 156
in Northwest Army of the Revolution, August 1835 Court

Lucy W, d/o John Wright decd, certified as heir at law to John Wright decd, a soldier in 156
Revolutionary War, August 1835 Court
Lucy W, d/o John Wright decd, certified as heir at law to Richard Wright, a soldier in 156
Revolutionary War, August, 1835 Court
Lucy W, d/o John Wright decd, certified as heir at law to William Wright, a soldier in 156
Northwest Army of the Revolution, August 1835 Court

Mary, d/o John Wright decd, certified as heir at law to John Wright decd, a soldier in 156
Revolutionary War, August 1835 Court
Mary, d/o John Wright decd, certified as heir at law to Richard Wright, a soldier in 156
Revolutionary War, August, 1835 Court
Mary d/o John Wright decd, certified as heir at law to William Wright, decd, a soldier 156
in Northwest Army of the Revolution, August 1835 Court

Thomas B, s/o John Wright decd, certified as heir at law to John Wright decd, a soldier 156
in Revolutionary War, August 1835 Court
Thomas B, s/o John Wright decd, certified as heir at law to Richard Wright, a soldier in 156
Revolutionary War, August 1835 Court
Thomas B, s/o John Wright decd, certified as heir at law to William Wright, decd, a soldier 156
in Northwest Army of the Revolution, August 1835 Court

William, as Soldier, Clark's Illinois Rgt of State Troops, Revolutionary War 62, note 83; 156, note 24
William decd, Soldier, Northwest Army of the Revolution, who died intestate, heirs at law 156
certified by Court, August 1835 Court

Index

William, s/o John Wright decd, certified as heir at law to John Wright decd, a soldier in Revolutionary War, August 1835 Court	156

Wright (Cont.)
William, s/o John Wright decd, certified as heir at law to Richard Wright, a soldier in Revolutionary War, August 1835 Court	156
William, s/o John Wright decd, certified as heir at law to William Wright, decd, a soldier in Northwest Army of the Revolution, August 1835 Court	156

Wyatt
Vincent, Prvt, 36th Rgt, Virginia Militia, War of 1812 Roster	213

Wyckoff, Wikcoff
Abraham, Drummer, 36th Rgt, Virginia Militia, 1812	110
Abraham, Drummer, 36th Rgt, Virginia Militia, War of 1812 Roster	213

Yates
David, Prvt, 36th Rgt, Virginia Militia, War of 1812 Roster	213

Yorktown, Battle at,	133

Young
Ezekiel, Soldier, Captain Thomas Waggener's Company, Virginia Rgt, French and Indian War	188
Nicholas, Prvt, Captain Joseph R. Gilbert's Company Muster Roll, 36th Rgt, Virginia Militia, War of 1812	199
Nicholas, Prvt, 36th Rgt, Virginia Militia, War of 1812 Roster	211
Richard, as Deputy Quartermaster General, his PSC, Revolutionary War	86

Index

BIBLIOGRAPHY

Derivative Sources

Alcock, John P. *Fauquier Families 1759–1799*. Athens: Iberian Publishing Company, 1994.
Anderson, Fred. *The War That Made America: A Short History of the French and Indian War*. New York: Penguin, 2005.
Axelrod, Alan. *Blooding at Great Meadows: Young George Washington and the Battle that Shaped the Man*. Philadelphia: Running Press, 2007.
Benn, Carl. *The War of 1812*. Oxford: Osprey Publishing Company, 2002.
Black, Henry Campbell. *Black's Law Dictionary*. St Paul: West Publishing Company, 1990.
Boatner, Mark M. *Encyclopedia of the American Revolution*. Mechanicsburg: Stackpole Books, 1996.
Borneman, Walter R. *The French & Indian War: Deciding the Fate of America*. New York: Harper Collins, 2006.
—. *1812: The War that Forged a Nation*. New York: Harper Collins, 2004.
Butler, Stuart Lee. *A Guide to Virginia Militia Units in the War of 1812*. Athens: Iberian Publishing Company, 1988.
Cecere, Michael. *The Behaved Like Soldiers: Captain John Chilton and the Third Virginia Regiment. 1775–1778*, Bowie: Heritage Books, 2003.
Drake, Paul. *What Did They Mean By That? A Dictionary of Historical Terms for Genealogists*. Bowie: Heritage Books, 1994.
Everton, George. *The Handy Book for Genealogists*. 8th Edition. Logan: Everton Publishers, 1991.
Fauquier County Bicentennial Committee, *Fauquier County, Virginia 1759–1959*. Warrenton: Virginia Publishing, 1959.
Fairfax, Harrison. *Landmarks of Old Prince William*, 1924, Reprint, Baltimore: Gateway Press, 1987.
Fowler, William M. Jr. *Empires at War: The French and Indian War and the Struggle for North America, 1754–1763*. New York: Walker and Company, 2005.
Gott, John K. and T. Triplett Russell, *Fauquier County in the Revolution*. Warrenton: Warrenton Printing and Publishing Company, 1977.
Hadden, Sally E. *Slaves Patrols: Law and Violence in Virginia and the Carolinas*. Cambridge: Harvard University Press, 2001.
Hickey, Donald R. *The War of 1812: A Forgotten Conflict*. Chicago: University of Illinois Press, 1995.
Jones, Mary Steven, editor. *An 18th Century Perspective: Culpeper County, Virginia*. Culpeper: Culpeper Historical Society, 1976.
Langguth, A. J. *Union 1812: The Americans Who Fought the Second War of Independence*. New York: Simon and Shuster, 2006.
Millett, Arthur and Peter Maslowski. *For the Common Defense: A Military History of the United State of America*. New York: The Free Press, 1994.
Minis, M. Lee. *The First Virginia Regiment of Foot, 1775–1778*. Westminster: Willow Bend Books, 1998.
Peters, Joan W. *The Tax Man Cometh: Land and Property in Colonial Fauquier County, Virginia 1759–1782*. Westminster: Willow Bend Books, 1999.
—. *Being of Sound Mind ... An Index to the Probate Records in the Fauquier County, Virginia Loose Papers and Superior and Circuit Court Records, 1759–1919*. Westminster: Willow Bend Books, 2001.
—. *The Third Virginia Regiment of Foot, Continental Line 1775–1778: With Drums Beating and Flags Flying*. Westminster: Willow Bend Books, 2009.
Peterson, Harold L. *The Book of the Continental Soldier*. Harrisburg: The Stackpole Company, 1968.
Sanchez-Saavedra, E. M. *A Guide to Virginia Military Organizations in the American Revolution, 1774–1787*. Richmond: Virginia State Library, 1978.
Sheppard, Ruth, editor. *Empires Collide: The French and Indian War 1754–1763*. UK: Osprey Publishing, 2006.
Torrence, Clayton. *Virginia Wills and Administrations, 1632–1800*. 1930, Reprint, Baltimore: Genealogical Publishing Company, 2000.
Ward, Matthew. *Breaking the Backcountry: The Seven Years War in Virginia and Pennsylvania, 1754–1765*. Pittsburg: University of Pittsburg Press, 2003.
Webster's *New World Dictionary of the American Language, College Edition*. New York: World Publishing Company, 1953.

Webster's *New World Dictionary, 2nd College Edition*. New York: World Publishing Company, 1972.

Journals and Periodicals

Stanard, W. G., editor. "The American Regiment in the Carthagena Expedition." *The Virginia Magazine of History and Biography*, XXX, January 1922. Richmond, Virginia.
Hiatt, Marty, editor. "Prince William County Court Order Books 1778–1785," *Northern Virginia Genealogy*, 7 (2002).

Microfilm of Original Sources

Library of Virginia, *Prince William Court Minute Books 1752–1856*, MR 25–27, 88. Richmond, Virginia.
—. *Prince William County Deed Book 1805–1807*. MR 8. Richmond, Virginia.
National Archives and Records Administration, *Compiled Service Records of Soldiers who served in the American Army during the Revolutionary War*. Record Group 93. NARA, Washington, D.C.
    Grayson's Additional Continental Regiment, Compiled Service Records, M 881 MR 73–76.
    The 3rd Virginia Regiment, MR 951–956.
    The 3rd and 4th Virginia Regiments, MR 957–970.
    The 11th Virginia Regiment, MR 1072–1073
National Archives and Records Administration, *Revolutionary War Pension and Bounty Land Warrant Application Files*, 1800–1900. Record Groups 15, 49, and 217. NARA, Washington, D.C. Representative examples follow:
    Joseph Sidebotham's Pension File W 8727, M 804 MR 2183
    Leander Murphy's Pension File S 11126, M 804 MR 1794
    James Alverson's Pension File W 8236, M 804 MR 48.

Online Sources

Ancestry.com. *Index to the Compiled Service Records for Volunteer Soldiers Who Served During the War of 1812*. M 602. http:;searcancestry.com (aka *War of 1812 Service Records*.)
"Black Loyalists." http://www.collections.ic.gc.ca.
Footnote.com, *Revolutionary War Service Records*. M 881. http://www.footnote.com. Representative examples follow:
    Garner Fortune's compiled service records, 1st Virginia State Regiment.
    William Wright's compiled service records, Clark's Illinois Regiment of Virginia State Troops.
    Zachariah Crook's compiled service records, 3rd Virginia Regiment.
    Leander Murphey's compiled service records, 7th Virginia Regiment.
    George White's compiled service records, 11th, 15th and 7th Virginia Regiments.
    Richard Bradley's compiled service records, 2nd Virginia Regiment.
    Peter McGinnis's compiled service records, 11th Virginia Regiment and 11th and 15th Virginia Regiments.
    George Purcell's compiled service records, 13th Virginia Regiment.
    Alexander Jones's compiled service records, 1st Virginia State Regiment.
    John Bristoe's compiled service records, Continental Troops: Lee's Legion.

— *Revolutionary War Pension Files*, M 804. http://www.footnote.com. Representative examples follow:
    Thomas Arrington's Pension File R 269, M 804.
    David Blackwell's Pension File W 9358, M804.
    Garner's Fortune's Pension File W 24233, M 804.
    George Mill's Pension File W 7449, M 804.
    John Sydebothom's Pension File W 8775, M 804
    George White's Pension File R 11413, M 804.
    Alexander Jones's Pension File S 34939, M 804.
Hedges, Robert, editor. *The Encyclopedia of Dumfries, Virginia 1740–1759*. http://www.ecsd.com.
Hening, William Waller. *Hening's Statutes at Large*. http://vagenweb.org/hening.

"Journals of Continental Congress," *A Century of Lawmaking for a New Nation: U. S. Congressional Documents and Debates, 1774–1875. Library of Congress.* http://www.loc.gov.
Historic Prince William. "Burgesses of Prince William County." http://www.historicprincewilliam.org.
Mayo, Sandra. "Fairfax and Prince William Counties in the French and Indian War," *Northern Virginia Heritage,* IX, February 1987. http://www.historic.princewilliam.org.
National Park Service, "Fort Necessity National Battlefield—Prelude to War." http://www.nps.gov.
"Ohio Historical Society, "King George's War." http://www.ohiohistorycentral.org.
"Powhatan Indian Tribe History." http://www.accessgenealogy.com.
University of Nebraska. "Early Recognized Treaties with the American Indian Nations." http://earlytreaties.unl.edu.treaty.
    Ratified Treaty #1 The Great Treaty of 1722.
    Ratified Treaty # 3 A Treaty Held at the Town Of Lancaster... June 1744.
    Ratified Treaty # 4 The Treaty of Logstown, 1752.
University of Virginia, "The Logstown Treaty," *Papers of Walker and Page Families, 1742–1886.* Accession Number 3098, Special Collections, University of Virginia Library, Charlottesville, Virginia. http://www.vcdh.virginia.edu.
"Virginia County Formation Maps, [Maps for] 1720, 1728, 1730, 1731, 1732, 1734, and 1735." http://www.family history101.com.
"Virginia Gazette." *Colonial Williamsburg Foundation.* http://research.history.org. Representative examples follow:
    "Proceedings of the 2nd Virginia Convention," March 30, 1775
    "Minute Men of Prince William arrive in Williamsburg," December 29, 1775.
    "Resignations in Prince William Minute Battalion," March 22, 1776
Wikipedia, the free encyclopedia, http://en.wikipedia.org.
    Articles on "Battle of Cartagena de Indias," "Fort Duquesne," "Fort LeBoeuf," "Fort Machault," " Fort Pearsall," "Fort Presque Isle," "Logstown," "Nathaniel Bacon (diplomat)," "Richard Henry Lee," "Tanacharison," "The Ohio Company," "Thomas Bullitt," "Thomas Lee (Virginia Colonist)," "William Grayson," and "Wills Creek."

Original Sources

Auditor's Rolls, Richmond. *Virginia Militia in the War of 1812.* 2 volumes. 1851, Reprint, Baltimore: Genealogical Publishing Company, 2001.
Bockstruck, Lloyd deWitt. *Bounty and Donation Land Grants in British Colonial America.* Baltimore: Genealogical Publishing Company, 2007.
—. *Virginia's Colonial Soldiers.* Baltimore: Genealogical Publishing Company, 1998.
—. *Revolutionary War Bounty Land Grants Awarded By State Governments, 1996.*
Brumbaugh, Gauis Marcus. *Revolutionary War Records: Virginia.* 1936, Reprint, Baltimore: Genealogical Publishing Company, 1995.
Burgess, Louis A. *Virginia Soldiers of 1776.* 3 Volumes. 1927, Reprint, Baltimore: Clearfield Publishing Company, 2004.
Bentley, Elizabeth Petty. *Index to the 1810 Census of Virginia.* Baltimore: Genealogical Publishing Company, 1980.
Clark, Murtie June. *Colonial Soldiers of the South 1732–1774.* Baltimore: Genealogical Publishing Company, 1999.
Eckenrode, Hamilton J. *Virginia Soldiers of the American Revolution.* 2 Volumes. 1913, Reprint, Richmond: Virginia State Library and Archives, 1989.
Felldin, Jeanne Robey. *Index to the 1820 Census of Virginia.* Baltimore: Genealogical Publishing Company, 1981.
Heitman, Francis B. *Historical Register of Officers of the Continental Army during the War of the Revolution, April, 1775 to December, 1783.* 2 Volumes. 1914, Reprint, Baltimore: Clearfield Company, 2003.
—. Historical *Register and Dictionary of the United States Army, 1789–1903.* 1903, Reprint, Baltimore: Genealogical Publishing Company, 1994.
Hopkins, William Lindsey. *Virginia Revolutionary War Land Grant Claims 1783–1850 (Rejected).* Richmond: William L. Hopkins, 1988.

Journals of Continental Congress, 1774–1789. Washington: Government Printing Office, 1906.

McIlwaine, H. R. ed, *Journals of the House of Burgesses of Virginia 1752–1755, 1756–1758*. 1909, Reprint, Bowie: Heritage Press, 1995.

National Archives Trust Fund Board, *Military Service Records: A Select Catalog of National Archives Microfilm Publications*. Washington: National Archives and Service Administration, 1985.

Pierce, Alycon Trubey. *Selected Final Pension Payment Vouchers, Virginia, 1818–1864*. 2 Volumes. Athens: Iberian Publishing Company, 1996.

Peters, Joan W. *Military Records, Patriotic Service & Public Service Claims, 1759–1784*. Westminster: Willow Bend Books, 1999.

— . *Neglected and Forgotten: Fauquier County, Virginia, French and Indian War, Revolutionary War, and War of 1812 Veterans from the Military Records Series of the Fauquier County Clerks Loose Papers, 1759–1825*. Westminster: Willow Bend Books, 2004.

— . *Military Records, Certificates of Service, Discharges, Heirs, & Pension Declarations and Schedules from the Fauquier County Virginia Court Minute Books 1784–1840*. Westminster: Heritage Books, 2007.

Rose, Christine. *Military Pension Laws, 1776–1858*. San Jose: Rose Family Association, 2001.

Saffell, W. T. R. *Records of the Revolutionary War*

Shepherd, Samuel. *Statutes at Large of Virginia from October 1792 to December 1806*. 3 Volumes. 1835, Reprint, New York: AMS Press, 1970.

Virginia Genealogical Society, *Virginia State Revolutionary War Pensions*. 1982, Reprint, Greenville: Southern Historical Press, 1992.

"Letters of David Griffith &c" David Griffith Papers, 1776–1778. Virginia Historical Society, Richmond.

Virginia Military Records from the Virginia Magazine of History and Biography, the William and Mary College Quarterly, and Tyler's Quarterly. 1983, Reprint, Baltimore: Clearfield, 2007.

Other Heritage Books by Joan W. Peters:

Abstracts of Fauquier County, Virginia Birth Records, 1853-1896

Being of Sound Mind: An Index to the Probate Records in Fauquier County Virginia's Clerks Loose Papers and Superior and Circuit Court Papers, 1759-1919

Fauquier County, Virginia's Clerk's Loose Papers: A Guide to the Records, 1759-1919

Military Records, Certificates of Service, Discharge, Heirs, and Pensions Declarations and Schedules from the Fauquier County, Virginia Court Minute Books, 1784-1840

Military Records, Patriotic Service, and Public Service Claims from the Fauquier County, Virginia Court Minute Books, 1759-1784

Military Records, Pension Applications, Heirs at Law and Civil War Military Records from the Fauquier County, Virginia Court Minute Books, 1840-1904

Neglected and Forgotten: Fauquier County, Virginia French and Indian War, Revolutionary War and War of 1812 Veterans

Prince William County, Virginia General Index to Wills, 1734-1951

Prince William County, Virginia Patriots and Pensioners, 1752-1856 Military Records from the Prince William County, Virginia Minute and Order Books and Other Source Records

The Tax Man Cometh—Land and Property in Colonial Fauquier County, Virginia: Tax Lists from the Fauquier County Court Clerk's Loose Papers, 1759-1782

The Third Virginia Regiment of Foot, 1776-1778, with Flags Flying and Drums Beating Volume One: A History

The Third Virginia Regiment of Foot, 1776-1778, with Flags Flying and Drums Beating Volume Two: Biographies

www.ingramcontent.com/pod-product-compliance
Lightning Source LLC
Chambersburg PA
CBHW051626230426
43669CB00013B/2197